The Cambridge History of American Theatre
Volume Two

The Cambridge History of American Theatre is an authoritative and wide-ranging history of American theatre in all its dimensions, from theatre building to play-writing, directors, performers, and designers. Engaging the theatre as a performance art, a cultural institution, and a fact of American social and political life, the History recognizes changing styles of presentation and performance, and addresses the economic context that conditions the drama presented. The History approaches its subject with a full awareness of relevant developments in literary criticism, cultural analysis, and performance theory. At the same time, it is designed to be an accessible, challenging narrative. All volumes include an extensive overview and timeline, followed by chapters on specific aspects of theatre.

Volume Two begins in the post–Civil War period and traces the development of American theatre up to 1945. It discusses the role of vaudeville, European influences, the rise of the Little Theatre movement, changing audiences, modernism, the Federal Theatre movement, major actors and the rise of the star system, and the achievements of notable playwrights.

The Cambridge History
of American Theatre

Volume Two:
1870–1945

Edited by

Don B. Wilmeth
Brown University

Christopher Bigsby
University of East Anglia

 **CAMBRIDGE**
UNIVERSITY PRESS

PUBLISHED BY THE PRESS SYNDICATE OF THE UNIVERSITY OF CAMBRIDGE
The Pitt Building, Trumpington Street, Cambridge CB2 1RP, United Kingdom

CAMBRIDGE UNIVERSITY PRESS
The Edinburgh Building, Cambridge CB2 2RU, UK   http: //www.cup.cam.ac.uk
40 West 20th Street, New York, NY 10011-4211, USA   http: //www.cup.org
10 Stamford Road, Oakleigh, Melbourne 3166, Australia

First published 1999

Printed in the United States of America

Typeset in ITC Cheltenham Book in QuarkXPress [G&H]

Library of Congress Cataloging-in-Publication Data

The Cambridge history of American theatre / edited by Don B. Wilmeth,
    Christopher Bigsby.
        p.   cm.
    Includes bibliographical references and index.
    Contents: v. 1. Beginnings to 1870   v. 2. 1870–1945
    ISBN 0-521-65179-4 (hc)
    1. Theatre – United States – History. 2. American drama – History
and criticism. I. Wilmeth, Don B. II. Bigsby, C. W. E.
PN2221.C37   1998
792'.0973 – dc21   97-12097
                                                                        CIP

*A catalog record for this book is available from
the British Library*

ISBN 0 521 65179 4 hardback

*To the memory of Warren Kliewer (1931–1998),
artist, scholar, and friend*

Contents

List of Illustrations

Contributors

The Editors

CHRISTOPHER BIGSBY is Professor of American Studies at the University of East Anglia in Norwich, England, and has published more than twenty books on British and American culture, including *Confrontation and Commitment: A Study of Contemporary American Drama 1959–1966* (1967); *The Black American Writer,* two volumes (1969); *The Second Black Renaissance* (1980); *Joe Orton* (1982); *A Critical Introduction to Twentieth Century American Drama,* three volumes (1982–85); *David Mamet* (1985); and *Modern American Drama 1940–1990* (1992). He is the editor of *Contemporary English Drama (1991); Arthur Miller and Company* (1990); *The Portable Arthur Miller* (1995); and *The Cambridge Companion to Arthur Miller* (1997). He is also the author of radio and television plays and of three novels: *Hester* (1994), *Pearl* (1995), and *Still Lives* (1996).

DON B. WILMETH is Asa Messer Professor and Professor of Theatre and English and Honorary Curator of the H. Adrian Smith Collection of Conjuring Books and Magicana at Brown University, Providence, Rhode Island. He is the author, editor, or co-editor of more than a dozen books, including *The American Stage to World War I: A Guide to Information Sources* (1978), the award-winning *George Frederick Cooke: Machiavel of the Stage* (1980), *American and English Popular Entertainment* (1980), *The Language of American Popular Entertainment* (1981), *Variety Entertainment and Outdoor Amusements* (1982), the *Cambridge Guide to American Theatre* (co-editor 1993 edition with Tice L. Miller; editor 1996 paperback edition), and *Staging the Nation: Plays from the American Theatre 1787–1909* (1998). With Rosemary Cullen he has co-edited plays by Augustin Daly and William Gillette, and currently he edits for Cambridge a series, Studies in American Theatre and Drama. He is a frequent contributor to reference works and sits on editorial boards of six journals. A past Guggenheim Fellow and president of the American Society for Theatre Research, he was Dean of the College of Fellows of the American Theatre, 1996–98.

The Contributors

JONATHAN CURLEY, a graduate of Brown University, is a former Fulbright recipient to Ireland and currently a doctoral student in English at New York University.

MARK FEARNOW is Associate Professor of Theatre Arts at Penn State University and author of *Clare Booth Luce: A Research and Production Sourcebook* (1995) and *The American Stage and the Great Depression: A Cultural History of the Grotesque* (1997).

JOHN W. FRICK, a member of the theatre faculty at the University of Virginia, is the author of *New York's First Theatrical Center: The Rialto of Union Square* (1985), is co-editor of *The Directory of Historic American Theatres* (1987) and *Theatrical Directors: A Biographical Dictionary* (1994), and is currently working on a book on the theatre and temperance reform in nineteenth-century America. Editor of *Theatre Symposium,* he has published in numerous journals and reference works and has directed over sixty productions in academic and professional theatre.

MARY C. HENDERSON has had a multifaceted career as Curator of the Theatre Collection of the Museum of the City of New York, as Adjunct Professor of Graduate Drama at New York University's Tisch School of the Arts, and currently as a freelance writer of books about the theatre. She is well known for *The City and the Theater* (1973) and *Theater in America* (new edition, 1996), has completed a biography of designer Jo Mielziner, and has written a history of the New Amsterdam Theatre for Hyperion.

WARREN KLIEWER was the founder and producing Artistic Director of the East Lynn Company, a professional, not-for-profit organization dedicated to the performance, study, and preservation of America's theatrical heritage. The company has produced (and he directed) revivals of works by such playwrights as Samuel Low, David Belasco, Steele MacKaye, Bronson Howard, William Dean Howells, Nathaniel Parker Willis, George Middleton, and Dion Boucicault, among others. Mr. Kliewer published essays in various journals and serials and was writing a history of American acting at the time of his death.

BROOKS McNAMARA, a pioneer in the serious study of popular entertainment, is Professor of Performance Studies at New York University and Director of the Shubert Archives. His publishing credits are extensive and include the following books: *The American Playhouse in the Eighteenth Century* (1969), *Step Right Up* (1976; revised 1995), *The Shuberts of Broadway* (1990), and *Day of Jubilee: The Great Age of the Public Celebration in New York City, 1788–1909* (1997). He has edited or co-edited *Theatre, Spaces, Environments, American Popular Enter-*

tainments, The Drama Review: Thirty Years of Commentary on the Avant-Garde, Plays from the Contemporary American Theatre, and *Inside the Minstrel Mask.* In 1990 he was elected to the College of Fellows of the American Theatre and in 1997 was honored by the American Society for Theatre Research for lifetime achievement.

TICE L. MILLER is Professor of Theatre at the University of Nebraska–Lincoln where he has served as chair, graduate chair, and head of the Ph.D. program in theatre. Author of *Bohemians and Critics* (1981), he has co-edited the *Cambridge Guide to American Theatre* (1993; revised 1996) and, with Ron Engle, *The American Stage* (1993). He has also served on the editorial advisory board for the *Cambridge Guide to Theatre,* as associate editor and contributor to *Shakespeare around the Globe,* and, since its founding, on the editorial board of *Theatre History Studies.*

BRENDA MURPHY is Professor of English at the University of Connecticut and the author of *American Realism and American Drama, 1880–1940* (1987), *A Realist in the American Theatre: Selected Drama Criticism of William Dean Howells* (1992), *Tennessee Williams and Elia Kazan: A Collaboration in the Theatre* (1992), and *Miller: Death of a Salesman* (1995). Two recent books are *Cambridge Companion to American Women Playwrights* and *Called to Testify: The Un-American Activities Committee on Stage, Film, and Television.*

THOMAS POSTLEWAIT, Professor of Theatre at Ohio State University, is co-editor of *Interpreting the Theatrical Past* and series editor for "Studies in Theatre History and Culture" (University of Iowa Press). He publishes regularly on American and British theatre. Forthcoming are *An Introduction to Theatre Historiography* and an edition of the letters of Bernard Shaw and William Archer. He has served as President of the American Society for Theatre Research (1994–97).

THOMAS RIIS, Professor of Musicology and Director of the American Music Research Center at the University of Colorado–Boulder, has taught music history and directed the early-music performing ensembles at the National Music Camp (Interlochen, Michigan) and at the University of Georgia. Senior Fellow at Brooklyn College's Institute for Studies in American Music in 1987, he has published three monographs on the history of African American musical theatre, including the prize-winning *Just Before Jazz: Black Musical Theater in New York, 1890–1915* (1989).

RONALD WAINSCOTT is the Director of Graduate Studies in the Department of Theatre and Drama at Indiana University and author of two books: *Staging O'Neill: The Experimental Years, 1920–1934* (1988) and *The Emergence of the Modern American Theater, 1914–1929* (1997), both published by Yale University Press. He has also written numerous articles and entries in professional journals and books, including *The American Stage* and the *Cambridge Guide to American Theatre*.

DANIEL J. WATERMEIER is Professor of Theatre and English at the University of Toledo. He is the editor or co-editor of *Between Actor and Critic: Letters of Edwin Booth and William Winter* (1971), *Shakespeare Around the Globe* (1986), *Edwin Booth's Performances* (1990), and *Shakespeare Companies and Festivals* (1995). A contributor to numerous books and journals and a recipient of Guggenheim and Folger Shakespeare Library fellowships, Watermeier is completing two projects: *History of Theatre in North America* (with Felicia Londré) and *Edwin Booth on the Gilded Stage* (Cambridge Studies in American Theatre and Drama).

Preface and Acknowledgments

The study of American theatre and drama has never established itself securely in academe. Histories of American literature have regularly assigned the most marginal of roles to its accomplishments, as Susan Harris Smith has recently illustrated (see Bibliography). Too few universities teach its development over the centuries or consider its role in a developing social, political, and cultural world.

It is as though American theatre came into existence as a sudden grace with Eugene O'Neill and his suitcase of plays its only begetter. As was demonstrated in Volume One of this study, it has a history going back to the first encounter of Europeans with what, to them, was a new continent and, in the form of Native American rituals and ceremonies, a prehistory.

The theatre, the most public of the arts, has always been a sensitive gauge of social pressures and public issues; the actor has been a central icon of a society that, from its inception, has seen itself as performing, on a national stage, a destiny of international significance. For students of drama, of theatre, of literature, of cultural experience, and of political development, the theatre should be a central subject of study.

For the purposes of this History we have chosen to use the word "theatre" to include all aspects of the dramatic experience, including major popular and paratheatrical forms. Contributors were asked to address particular aspects of that experience – whether it be theatre architecture, stage design, acting, playwriting, directing, and so forth – but they were also invited to stress the wider context of those subjects. Indeed, they were encouraged to engage the context within which theatre itself operates. Hence, we have set out to produce a history that is authoritative and wide-ranging, that offers a critical insight into plays and playwrights, but that also engages the theatre as a performance art, a cultural institution, and a fact of American social and political life. We have sought to recognize changing styles of presentation and performance and to address the economic context that conditions the drama presented. This may lead, on occasion, to a certain recrossing of tracks as, for example, a chapter on playwrights invokes the career of particular actors, and a chapter on actors describes the plays in which they appeared, but this is both inevitable and desirable, stressing, as it does, the interdependence of all aspects of the craft of theatre making.

The theatre has reflected the diversity of America and the special circumstances in which it has operated in an expanding country moving toward a sense of national identity. The history of the American stage and the making of America have been co-terminous, often self-consciously so, and to that end each volume of this history begins with a timeline followed by a wide-ranging essay that attempts to locate the theatre in the context of a developing society. Both timeline and overview also allow individual authors to avoid any urge to offer inclusiveness and to provide, when appropriate, more detailed coverage of important individuals or events, enabling, for example, Tom Postlewait to offer a unique perspective in his introductory chapter and Brenda Murphy in Chapter 3 to provide a lengthy section on Eugene O'Neill.

The History could have run to many more volumes, but the economics of publication finally determined its length (and the number of illustrations allowed, which in this volume led to much frustration because of necessary iconographic omissions). The precise division between the three volumes and the strategies involved in structuring this History, however (especially because from the outset it was agreed that this would be a collective history), was a matter of serious debate, a debate in which the editors were assisted by others in meetings that took place at Brown University, in the United States, and at York University in Canada. It is proper, in fact, to pause here and, as we did in Volume One, gratefully acknowledge the financial assistance for the Brown meeting of Brown University, its special collections, and Cambridge University Press. For the York meeting we are indebted to Christopher Innes, who served as an adviser to the editors, and to the Social Sciences and Humanities Research Council of Canada, who helped fund the expenses. In Providence we were able to gather a notable group of experts: Arnold Aronson, the late Frances Bzowski, T. Susan Chang, Rosemary Cullen, Spencer Golub, James V. Hatch, the late Warren Kliewer, Brooks McNamara, Brenda Murphy, Tom Postlewait, Vera Mowry Roberts, Matthew Roudané, David Savran, Ronn Smith, Susan Harris Smith, and Sarah Stanton. In Canada the editors were joined by Innes and the authors of overview essays (Aronson, Postlewait, and Bruce McConachie). We are indebted to these experts for their thoughtful and challenging ideas and recommendations.

Ultimately, of course, the editors accept responsibility for the present format, but without the preliminary discussions we would have doubtlessly floundered. In the final analysis, the fact that we have chosen roughly 1870 and 1945 as defining chronological parameters is, in part, an expression of our desire to relate the theatre to a wider public history but in part also a recognition of certain developments internal to theatre itself. Any such divisions have an element of the arbitrary, however, chronological periods doing damage to the continuity of individual careers and stylistic modes. Nevertheless, division there must be, and those we have chosen seem more cogent than any of the others we considered, despite our strong suspicion that any periodization can be misleading. In truth, Volume One extends to the post–Civil War period, and this volume, in order to establish some sense of continuity, dovetails the time frame of that volume (as Postlewait explains in his overview).

The organization of the three volumes does, however, still reveal a bias in favor of the modern, a bias this preface began by deploring. Yet it does not presume that theatrical history began with O'Neill but simply recognizes that the story of the American theatre is one of a momentum that has gathered pace with time, while acknowledging the rich heritage and accomplishments of American theatre during its earlier periods.

As implied above, the History does not offer itself as encyclopedic. Given restrictions of space, this could never have been an objective, nor was such a strategy deemed appropriate. Those wishing to research details not found in these pages should consult the *Cambridge Guide to American Theatre* (1993, 1996), edited by Wilmeth and Miller, and *Theatre in the United States: A Documentary History* (Vol. I, 1750–1915), edited by Witham (Vol. II is well under way). Both volumes were published by Cambridge, and this History was planned with those texts in mind as complementary to this effort. The reader will, however, find detailed bibliographies of further reading at the end of each chapter.

What the History does aim to do is tell the story of the birth and growth, on the American continent, of a form that, the Puritans notwithstanding, in river-front towns, in mining settlements, in the growing cities of a colony that in time became a country, proved as necessary to life as anything else originally imported from Europe but then turned to serve the purposes of a new society reaching toward a definition of itself.

A nation is constructed of more than a set of principles enforced by a common will. It builds itself out of more than contradictions denied by rhetoric or shared experience. The theatre played its part in shaping the society it served, as later it would reflect the diversity that was always at odds with a supposed homogeneity. Inevitably derivative, in time it accommodated itself to the New World, and, in creating new forms, in identifying and staging new concerns, was itself a part of the process it observed and dramatized.

Theatre is international. Today, an American play is as likely to open in London as in New York and to find its primary audience outside the country of its birth. Despite the restrictions imposed by Actors' Equity, actors move between countries, as do directors and designers. Film and television carry drama across national frontiers. Yet, the American playwright still addresses realities, myths, and concerns born out of national experiences; the American theatre still stages the private and public anxieties of a people who are what they are because of history. The accomplishments of the American theatre are clear. This is an account of those accomplishments as it is, in part, of that history.

Finally, we are extremely grateful for financial support from our institutions – Brown University and the University of East Anglia – and we are pleased to acknowledge the editorial assistance of Diana Beck, funded by the Brown Graduate School, who made many of our chores less arduous in the preparation of this volume. The initial idea for this history came from Cambridge editors Sarah Stanton and Victoria Cooper, who not only brought the editors together but have also been a constant source of support and encouragement; Anne Sanow in the New York office of Cambridge University Press helped to shepherd this volume through its various stages; and Françoise Bartlett and her colleagues have served us well in the production process. The eleven authors of chapters in this volume are clearly indebted to the scholarship of those who have gone before, as well as to colleagues still active in the field. The specific debts of each author are suggested in notes and, most significantly, in the bibliographic essays that conclude each chapter. Credits for illustrations are indicated with each photograph, though we are equally grateful to individual authors who furnished or suggested illustrations and to the staffs of the collections identified who helped to locate or furnish illustrations.

Introduction

Christopher Bigsby and Don B. Wilmeth

For theatre historian Arthur Hornblow, writing in 1919, American drama had virtually ceased to exist by 1870. In its place, he insisted, had come foreign imports, a characteristic lament of American critics from the eighteenth to the twenty-first century. Nor, according to Henry James, did the theatre have a direct and organic relationship to American society in the way that, for example, the novel did. It was the source of distraction, entertainment, and amusement but not of a cogent engagement with the values and experiences of a nation in other respects so concerned with its own exceptionalism. Writing in 1875, he remarked that

> If one held the belief that there is a very intimate relation between the stage, as it stands in this country, and the general cause of American civilization, it would be more than our privilege, it would be our duty . . . to keep an attentive eye upon the theatres. . . . But except at the Fifth Avenue Theatre, [the public] does not go with the expectation of seeing the mirror held up to nature as it knows nature – of seeing a reflection of its actual, local, immediate physiognomy. The mirror, as the theatres show it, has the image already stamped upon it – an Irish image, a French image, an English image . . . !" (Quoted in Moses and Brown, 122)

To James's mind, the fault lay in large part with audiences who seemed to show little interest in work of subtlety, of aesthetic or social value. The public at large, he insisted, "is very ignorant." And as far as he was concerned, it was likely to remain such if the native theatre chose to refuse any engagement with the realities of a country emerging from a civil war and encountering the reality of modernity.

Just over a decade later, William Dean Howells, like James a frustrated playwright, was equally despairing: "[W]e are talking now about the American drama, or non drama; for, in spite of theatres lavishly complete in staging, and with all the sanitary arrangements exemplary – the air changed every fifteen minutes, and artificially refrigerated in the summer – we still have no drama" (quoted in Moses and Brown, 132–33). It may have been a familiar complaint but it remained true that whereas the American writer had adapted the novel to a new environment, producing superior work that even at the time was acknowledged to engage anxieties about national identity, the relationship of the individual to his society, and the tensions and ambiguities of an expanding country, the theatre seemed very much the poor relation.

1

Poetry had its Emerson, Whitman, Longfellow, Whittier, and Lowell, and Cooper, Irving, Hawthorne, Melville, and Thoreau explored aspects of their own society through prose, looking for a central metaphor to capture the essence of a new world of fact and imagination. But for the most part all the theatre could boast, besides foreign imports, translations and adaptations, was melodrama.

It is, however, worth asking ourselves exactly what Europe had to offer at this time. For there, too, poetry and the novel flourished while drama, until comparatively late in the century, played a far from dominant role. Ibsen's career did not begin until the mid-1860s, Strindberg's and Chekhov's until the 1870s.

The truth is that it was not only Americans who lamented the state of their drama. Shelley saw its decline as a mark of "the corruption of manners" and "an extinction of the energies which sustain the soul of social life" (quoted in Steiner, 109). Until the final decades of the century what mattered was less the play than the player. This was a theatre dominated by spectacle and by the actor, a romantic figure. It was not for nothing that Lord Byron admired Edmund Kean, who appeared in his play *Sardanapulus,* or that William Macready maintained Byron's *Werner* as a regular part of his repertoire. The actor was an embodiment of a certain romantic posturing just as, later, he could be seen as an aspect of bourgeois individualism and an icon of success. And the actor was fully aware of his or her centrality and frequently behaved accordingly. The French were perhaps not wrong when they called star actors, *monstres sacrés.*

The argument that the heyday of drama corresponds with periods of national energy, which seems persuasive when applied to the Spanish, English, and French theatres of the seventeenth century, would seem to suggest that nineteenth-century America should have generated a drama commensurate with the energy unleashed by settlement and appropriation. It did not, although the level of theatrical activity greatly expanded. (One might, however, plausibly argue that what Henry Luce called "the American century," that is, the twentieth century, did.) What dominated was melodrama, a form that, through the gothic novel, already had a purchase on the American sensibility. Indeed, viewed in one way, melodrama can be seen as an aspect of the romance, itself a central dimension of nineteenth-century prose, with its fondness for heightened effects and scenes of emotional intensity.

Melodrama, though, was not an American invention. Its origins lie in France, where it was born out of a democratic spirit. The playwright René Pixérécourt wrote, he explained, for those who could not read. He staged the collision between good and evil in such a way that the moral universe was presented purged of ambiguity. Melodrama was a dramatic form that purported to peel off social deceits and expose the polarities of human nature. The very broadness of its appeal was its philosophic and financial justification. Perhaps that accounts for the enthusiasm with which the form was embraced by American audiences. It is democratic in its assertion of the moral superiority of the powerless. Melodrama implies, finally, that it is possible to tell the counterfeit from the real and that the illiterate playgoer can understand the text as clearly as anyone. This became important in an immigrant society, such as America.

Melodrama offers a heightened world in which emotions are amplified, gestures exaggerated, social roles polarized, and moral qualities distilled into their pure essence. Its characters exist through their emotions, reducing complex experiences to simple conflicts. Virtue and vice are spun off in pure form. The confusing and deceptive surfaces of experiences are scoured away to expose the truth of human nature, itself reassuringly unchanging in a changing world.

Melodrama exists in and through a theatricalized environment in which verbal and physical gestures are conventionalized. It can seem conservative in its implicit defense of normative values, in pieties paraded as the logic of experience, in social roles regarded as archetypal functions. The vulnerable heroine, cast out in the snow by a vengeful landlord, pursued by a rich man attracted by her virtue, tempted by drink, drugs or prostitution, is, admittedly, a theatrical construct, but she hints at a vulnerability that is real enough. Such was the drama of a society in which the crude forces of money, social power, and sexual inequity were as much defining qualities as were expanding frontiers and growing cities. Yet if conservative in one sense – in that it celebrated received values – melodrama nonetheless reflected a widespread and democratic suspicion of those who exercised undue power: the landlord, the businessman, the domestic tyrant. So, melodrama could be seen as dramatizing opposing impulses in the culture. It acknowledged the potential collapse of social form but stressed the virtue of continuity. Like the gothic, it was a natural product of a period of change and yet was self-consciously archaic. In a sense, what could have been better suited to an increasingly polyglot and immigrant society, aware of the danger of dissolution as well as the necessity for transformation, nostalgic for the fixities that had been relinquished, yet conscious of the inequities of the New World no less than of the Old?

What melodrama did was insist that the essential life was domestic, the perfect social unit a marriage, and hence that any challenge to such a union carried with it the threat of a greater collapse of order – and this at a time when America had so recently faced the violence of political dissolution. Western melodramas, meanwhile, reflected a situation in which everything was indeed reduced to essentials, social niceties being displaced by other exigencies. Like the Hollywood Western they in part spawned, melodramas had more distant and mythical roots, staging, as they did, a morality tale in which a damaged society is restored to itself through the action of a hero. But here was drama that satisfied both the East's fascination with the West and that desire for drama commensurate with the country, so often expressed throughout the nineteenth century. Melodrama, then, was more adaptable and more expressive of a changing world than may at first have been apparent.

In 1870, America was five years removed from the Civil War, a war that marked, as clearly as anything else, the loss of a particular notion of American innocence. The City on the Hill was stained with blood. The dark side of technology, exposed by that war, had hinted at a future alternative to that compounded out of spiritual quest wedded to material dream. The assassination of a president who had proposed a version of brotherhood that would, at least retrospectively, validate a national rhetoric of freedom and equality, seemed to imply that there was to be no move back toward Eden, no prospect of a New Jerusalem. And, indeed, America was changing. Though it would be twenty years before the frontier was declared closed, the city was already a central fact of American experience, as the rhythms of technology began to replace those of a natural world increasingly seen as a simple resource to fuel those population centers in which the individual could no longer credibly lay claim to iconic status.

The link between land and democracy, between the isolate existential self and society, was broken. Literature, in the forms of the naturalistic novel and the melodramatic play, increasingly offered a pathological account of social process and human development. The American hero, standing out against the flaming skies of the prairie or the lowering mists of the ocean, morally intact, exemplary, gave way to the self as an expression of determinism, as product of an environment that was man-made but not made for man. For a society that had invested so much in the future the modern came, at first, as a shock, a shock that would be registered in the moral dislocations of melodrama or the disturbing realities of works that did little more than document a threatening urban environment or, occasionally, a bleak rural version of a Darwinian struggle, for these works could not yet be accommodated to the rhetoric of American liberal values. Thus Clyde Fitch and James A. Hearne confronted America with an image of itself at odds with its expansive myths. And for his part, David Belasco lovingly re-created the tactile facticity of ordinary life rendered extraordinary only by its presentation on a stage. Previously two-dimensional scenery had offered a correlative for characters and language themselves self-consciously theatrical and hence removed from the business of daily experience.

The same documentary impulse was strong in the naturalistic novel and for good reasons. If the individual was in part a product of his or her environment, then the re-creation of that environment was a vital part of the character presented. And what was true of the novel was true, too, of the theatre. It was an impulse that would lead from Clyde Fitch's *The City* (1909) to Elmer Rice's *Street Scene* (1929) and Sidney Kingsley's *Dead End* (1935). And it is worth reminding ourselves that the naturalistic presentation of character, event, and setting was in itself a first response to the modern, even if it eventually gave way to a more radical revisioning of experience. As influences on the American avant-garde, André Antoines's Théâtre Libre (1887) and Otto Brahm's Freie Bühne (1889), in Paris and Berlin, respectively, were both, in fact, dedicated to naturalism, just as Bernard Shaw, Granville Barker, and John Galsworthy were, on the whole, writers of realism, and the Moscow Art Theatre, in turn, was dedicated to the realism of Chekhov.

Perhaps the greatest shock to a somewhat self-satisfied theatre came from outside the country in the form first of the work of Henrik Ibsen and then that of his enthusiastic proponent, George Bernard Shaw. At first what was seen as Ibsen's relentless pessimism, so much at odds with American values, was softened by judicious rewriting. Thus, *A Doll's House* opened, in 1883, as *Thora,* with a conventional, if unconvincing, happy ending. America's moralists were not fooled. They recognized the contagion of pessimism when they saw it and, to a remarkable degree, it was the language of pathology they deployed to welcome the new realistic and socially engaged drama. For critic William Winter, "Ibsen is not a dramatist, in the true sense of that word, and Ibsenism, which is rank, deadly pessimism, is a disease, injurious alike to the Stage and to the Public, – in so far as it affects them at all, – and therefore an evil to be deprecated" (quoted in Moses and Brown, 94). To his mind, Ibsen and his followers had "altogether mistaken the province of the Theatre in choosing it as the fit medium for the expression of sociological views, views, moreover, which, once adopted, would disrupt society." Since when, he inquired, "did the Theatre become a proper place for a clinic of horror and the vivisection of moral ailments?" (the word "vivisection" perhaps being a conscious reference to Zola, who at a lecture had called for the writer to be as cold as a vivisectionist). The actress Mrs. Fiske was denounced for forsaking her normal repertory in favor of this dour Scandinavian when she possessed "a good repertory of old plays," and had previously exhibited "judgement and taste" in choosing new ones (Winter, quoted in Moses and Brown, 95–96).

Bernard Shaw was predictably welcomed in much the same way. The *Sun* newspaper characterized his work as "a dramatized stench," and the *New York Herald* contented itself with observing, of *Mrs Warren's Profession*, that "the play is morally rotten." Even with certain lines excised, "there was a superabundance of foulness left." It "glorifies debauchery," readers were told,

"It besmirches the sacredness of a clergyman's calling" (Moses and Brown, 163, 166). Arnold Daly, who staged the play in 1905, was forced to offer a defense reminiscent of that made by those who confronted American Puritanism more than a hundred years earlier. It was, he claimed, not so much an entertainment as a dramatic sermon and an exposé of a social condition and evident evil.

When this European influence showed signs of contaminating American drama itself, critics denounced this as well. Langdon Mitchell's *The New York Idea* (1906) was greeted by James Metcalf, of *Life,* as a baleful influence on "unsophisticated minds," and its mockery of fashion, he insisted, risked stirring up anarchy. James A. Herne's *Margaret Fleming* (1891) was similarly indicted for portraying life as "sordid and mean" and for its effect on sensitive minds, which was presumed to be "depressing." It would, readers were told, "be a stupid and useless thing if such plays as *Margaret Fleming* were to prevail" (Moses and Brown, 143).

It is easy to mock such assaults on those we now regard as laying the foundations of modern drama, but the attacks tell us something both of the state of theatre and its presumed function in a society itself undergoing radical change. For in many ways the old virtues were under assault, and writers and critics were fully aware of this.

Though presented and defended by its proponents as the ultimate triumph of individualism, the spectacular growth of combinations, trusts, and monopolies, as capitalism organized itself to exploit newly discovered resources, low-cost labor, and the mechanical organization of work, was further evidence of the collapse of that Jeffersonianism ideal that had turned on an endlessly replicated yeoman ideal. It was a growth that affected the theatre no less than the oil and steel industries as the benefits of scale and the power of monopoly capitalism, along with the manifest virtues of rational organization, were employed to turn the loose system of discrete companies, scattered throughout the country, into a powerful and efficient theatrical circuit. The newly formed Syndicate had the virtue of perceiving a national market and organizing itself accordingly. It had the vice of creating a monopoly that shifted power from the actors and managers of individual theatres to those at the center of the new system.

The author and critic Sheldon Cheney saw the Syndicate as destroying the repertory system, consolidating the power of New York, undermining experimentation, and weakening all aspects of theatre, from writing to acting and direction. The playwright, in particular, was now required to produce work that could find a ready audience around the entire country. In other words, theatre was at risk of becoming part of a system of commercial production that thrived on a standardized product. The Syndicate thus had a certain symbolic force as well as a practical reality. That was certainly how theatre historian Arthur Hornblow saw it: "[T]he triumph of the Syndicate meant the end of honest competition, the degradation of the art of acting, the lowering of the standards of drama, the subjugation of the playwright and the actor to the capricious whims and sordid necessities of a few men who set themselves up as despots" (320).

Scarcely equivocal, such a statement tells us as much about the new enthusiasms of early-twentieth-century criticism as it does of the realities of the Syndicate era, for Hornblow was writing at a time when commitment to a new theatre, drawing on European models but reanimating a domestic drama, was at its height. In fact the virtue of "honest competition" had often concealed dismaying disorganization and exploitation, and the supposedly elevated art of acting and the implicit high standards of drama had not always been apparent. Indeed, Hornblow himself, in the very same study, lamented aspects of both. However, the Syndicate was a reminder that the theatre was a business subject to the same forces that were then in the process of transforming America.

The Syndicate was challenged by the Shubert brothers, and though they were at first welcomed on the democratic grounds that they were "of humble origin" and the pragmatic grounds that they challenged a monopoly, all they succeeded in doing was creating a duopoly with too many competing theatres to sustain high standards. Hornblow saw this development in apocalyptic terms as the surrender of art to Caesarism, but, then, apocalypse was in the air, as attested Oswald Spengler's hugely influential study *The Decline of the West,* whose thesis was that the nadir of the historical cycle was marked by the dominance of money and power and the subordination of art. But for Hornblow, beginning with the last decade of the nineteenth century,

> the theatre in America already showed signs of a marked and steady decline. . . . The making of money became the one and only aim of every effort. Of the great actors, not one remained. The stage was engulfed in a wave of commercialism that gradually destroyed the art of acting, elevated mediocrities to the dignity of stars, turned playwrights into hacks, misled and vitiated public taste, and the drama, from an art, became a business. (318–19)

Each generation of theatregoers in America thus lamented a decline from a golden age that had in turn been unfavorably compared to previous ages by a succession of critics convinced that they lived at a time uniquely inimical to the production of distinguished drama.

One actress who fell foul of the battle between the Shuberts and the Syndicate was Sarah Bernhardt. Her farewell tour of 1905 was to be produced by the Shuberts. She was, accordingly, banned from all Syndicate theatres, a move that forced her, on occasion, to perform in such venues as a skating rink and a swimming pool–auditorium. For some of the tour, however, the problem was solved by the construction of a huge tent, seating six thousand people, in which, as Stephen M. Archer has indicated, "no one past the tenth row could hear a word, and those who could hear did not understand French."[1] Like audiences at a pop concert, people went not to hear but to be there. Theatre was an event, and the stars icons, images of celebrity, in a society that supposedly despised social distinctions but in fact canonized the successful. In Kansas City Bernhardt played to an audience of more than six and a half thousand. On occasion, as Archer points out, she would abuse her audiences for their ignorance but, because she did so in a language they did not understand, was rewarded with wild applause. The 206 performances grossed a million dollars, and this for an oversized actress in her sixties, portraying a young consumptive woman (the play was *Camille*) while speaking a language that meant nothing to those who watched, sometimes from a distance of more than a hundred and fifty feet.

The constituent identity of Americans was and remains, in some sense, problematic. Indeed, it is the provisional nature of that identity that unlocks the social energy of a country whose definition is endlessly debated and deferred, if confidently asserted. Each wave of immigrants brought with it a taste for its own cultural expressions as well as for its own food and social customs. Thus, plays were performed in Yiddish, German, and Italian, languages equally to be heard on the street and in the factory. The editor and drama critic Norman Hapgood even suggested that German-language theatre represented America's primary claim to high achievement in drama. Yet there was a counterimpulse, a desire to plunge into the new linguistic and social world, to embrace its prejudices, its values, and its symbolic forms. If people could cling to the reassurances of the familiar in ethnic theatres, they could also come together as Americans to share experiences that, as with the performances of Sarah Bernhardt, might not be wholly understood but that communicated on more levels than the merely linguistic. Thus they watched minstrel shows, visited circuses, vaudeville, and burlesque, and explored the paratheatrical world of Barnum and Bailey. In doing so they bought into a classless and, it should be said, a racist and sexist society that democratized art and thumbed its nose at convention but that managed, in the process, to conform to myths of America's good-natured and essentially adolescent spirit.

As far as serious drama was concerned, however, this exuberant confidence was lacking, or at least seemed to be to those who charted its accomplishments or, more frequently, insisted on its failures, and by now it must be apparent that the history of American theatre is in some degree a history of jeremiads by its critics. Somehow, to their eyes, it never seemed to live up to its possibilities. It either shamelessly copied feeble European models or fell so far short of classical theatre as to mock its own pretensions. Yet not only was European theatre itself frequently overrated, and the native product correspondingly denigrated, but American drama was itself changing. Hornblow acknowledged the rise of playwrights such as Clyde Fitch and Augustus Thomas but suggested that they could do little in the face of the evils identified. William Winter, in 1908, likewise insisted that theatre had fallen into the clutches of sordid, money-grubbing tradesmen, who degraded it into a "bazaar" and captured it for "the Amusement Business."

But Hornblow and Winter were in recoil from something more than the theatre's embrace of Mammon (into whose grasp most people involved in it had been rushing with every sign of enthusiasm for centuries). They were reacting against the world identified by Mark Twain in *The Gilded Age.* They were reacting, in other words, against a betrayal of values that went far beyond the supposed corruption of the theatre. They were also evidencing a dislike for the taste of the new mass public, which showed a predilection for the kind of large-scale spectacles that Spengler was to see as evidence of the degraded taste of a jaded society. In 1879 David Belasco staged Salmi Morse's *Passion Play* at San Francisco's Grand Opera House, with James O'Neill as Christ, together with a cast of four hundred actors and two hundred singers. The Massacre of the Innocents alone required a hundred women and babies and a flock of real sheep. Members of the audience, reportedly, fainted at the sight of O'Neill dragged off to crucifixion while, more alarmingly, and beyond the doors of the theatre, Jews were attacked in the street as Christ killers. Cecil B. DeMille was not far away.

The fact is, however, that spectacle offered a scale commensurate with a nation still in awe of its own potential, still celebrating a redefined sense of size, distance, and possibility. The technology of theatre mirrored that of a society prepared to amaze itself with inventions, innovations, and novelties. Theatres were to be large because, in America, size meant significance. It was theatre's claim to its own importance. When the New Theatre opened in New York in 1909 it seated twenty-five hundred people. The actors were all but inaudible, but how could anyone doubt that the theatre should be seen as part of a modern world of which New York was emerging as a central symbol, a city that celebrated its skyscrapers as an image of the new. And, indeed, that skyline was synonymous with futurity for more than its own citizenry. European modernists, too, responded to its implied suggestion that art and architecture could not only define the space within which people lived their lives but make those lives products of a new sense of expanding possibility.

Meanwhile, the cinema brought another sense of scale to drama, project-ing its images onto a screen so large as to dominate the sensibility of those who watched. Predictably, Hornblow saw this new art as appropriating the theatre's buildings, seducing its actors, and buying up its playwrights. Beyond that, he saw it as appealing to the "sensual and the vicious," thus ini-tiating a debate that was to accompany the development of American cinema throughout the twentieth century.

Yet in another sense modernism was a reaction against the large scale. The diminutive in the so-called Little Theatre movement (small, often amateur theatres playing brief plays) was an aesthetic statement no less than an admission of financial stringency. The scale was in some sense a guarantee of authenticity. Even the preferred dramas were small scale – one-act plays, by definition unprofitable for Broadway to stage. In the context of a commercial imperative, for which the theatrical was synonymous with the elaborate, the rhetorical, the factitious, the amateur actor, appearing in a small theatre to perform plays whose purpose seemed to lie in poetic truth or psychological reality, offered a new account of drama's potential.

These were theatres that did not aim to reach large audiences. Broad effects did not interest them. The poetic drama, the social play, and the experimental work attracted actors drawn to the theatre not as a profession but as an extension of their aesthetic, social, and political commitments. Such people were committed to acting but not as a means to commercial suc-cess. Indeed, when George Cram Cook, co-founder of the Provincetown Play-ers, realized that the group was achieving a genuine popular following, he began to suspect that their work might be tainted and withdrew to Greece, there to revivify classical drama with its organic connection to the commu-nity and its roots in myth. Indeed, it was precisely the trappings of commer-cial theatre, itself part of a suspect social system, that he despised and rejected (and Cook, like many of those who founded and sustained such the-atres, was a radical in more than an aesthetic sense). So it was that a decrepit wharf in Provincetown, a small brownstone on MacDougal Street in New York, or its equivalent elsewhere across the nation, was to be the site of theatre offering a poetic vision, self-consciously expressing, or even satirizing, the new, celebrating the subversive, elevating the New Women, the New Negro, the socially marginal to center stage.

Perhaps the greatest proponent of the Little Theatre movement was Mau-rice Browne, whose Little Theatre in Chicago (which lasted only five years) employed both amateur and professional actors. Seating a mere ninety-nine people, it was well named. Its repertoire was heavily European, with plays by Yeats, Schnitzler, Strindberg, Shaw, and Dunsany. Soon, however, such the-atres began to generate their own plays, the Washington Square Players and the Provincetown Players, in particular, looking to stage the works of emerging American playwrights, often those who, if they had any reputation at all, had made their mark in other fields: the novel, poetry, journalism. Thirty-eight of the Washington Square Players' sixty-two productions were by American authors. By 1917 there were in excess of fifty Little Theatres in America and this, in itself, increased pressure for the emergence of American plays that would be published either under the imprint of Samuel French or the influential Drama League.

Yet even this movement had its roots in Europe, in André Antoine's Théâtre Libre and Strindberg's 161-seat Intimate Theatre in Stockholm, for which he wrote a series of Chamber Plays. But if its origin, and, indeed, initially, its repertoire, lay overseas, it soon found American champions for whom it marked an approach to drama that accorded it a more central position in the avant-garde, granted it a seriousness that would bring a Nobel Prize to one of its major authors within two decades (Eugene O'Neill received the honor in 1936) and would attract the kind of talents that would lift this apparently derivative and marginalized art to a central position in world theatre.

The changes in theatre did not take place in a vacuum. Change was celebrated or denounced in all aspects of life. The turn of the century had acted as a slingshot, hurling Americans into a new era in which it genuinely became their manifest destiny to take possession of "the American century." There was some doubt as to the precise date when change came about. Floyd Dell, editor of *The Masses* and *The Liberator,* whose very titles hinted at the imperative for change, identified 1912 as a key year, marking, as it did, in Chicago, the founding of Harriet Monro's *Poetry* magazine, the birth of the Little Theatre, and an outbreak of suffragist activity. Others might have picked 1913, the year in which the Armory Show brought European modernism to New York. Whatever the year, there was a sense that America was struggling to give birth to something new. As Hornblow said in his *History,* "the American theatre awaits a modern Moses to lead the way out of captivity" (350). A modern Moses duly appeared, carrying a suitcase of plays and determined to turn his back on the theatre of his elders, particularly that typified by his own father. The man was Eugene O'Neill. The two attending midwives were George Cram Cook and his artistically talented wife, Susan Glaspell, who together founded the Provincetown Players.

Yet, as Susan Harris Smith has shown, the groundwork for this new theatre had been prepared earlier. The American Drama Society was founded in 1909 and the MacDowell Club and the Drama League in 1910. The Drama League claimed a membership of one hundred thousand by 1915 and was dedicated to distributing books and encouraging productions, albeit those that conformed to its desire to see "clean, wholesome, clever, worthwhile drama"

(Smith, 84). The teaching of American drama also began to find its way into academe, most famously through the work of George Pierce Baker, first at Harvard and then Yale. An audience at last was beginning to emerge.

There was something almost puritanical about the advocates of the new theatre. Certainly Cheney's characterization of the standard New York audience, although not without a certain truth, also smacks of something more than mere condescension. It consisted, he asserted, of the

> half-educated product of our stereotyped grade schools; the newly rich; the sentimental ladies; the merely restless-minded with no other resources or amusement . . . further vulgarized by a constant stream of travelers on holiday, convention delegates temporarily freed from home restraints, out-of-town buyers being jovially entertained by local salesmen, rich provincials wanting something startling to talk about when they return home. (Cheney, *Art Theater*, 22)

The new theatre, he need hardly say, was not for them but for the intelligentsia, for an aspiring middle class, indeed, in some essential way, for those who produced it (quite literally so, insofar as the Provincetown Players were at first concerned). In revulsion from the slick professionalism of Broadway, it embraced, or at least evidenced, a certain amateurism (the Irish Players, too, were a blend of the amateur and the professional, as was the Moscow Art Theatre). In reaction against commercialism it sometimes took a perverse pride in fiscal irresponsibility. Successful plays were often dropped after short runs in deference to the repertory principle.

The new theatre was in part inspired by the work of Gordon Craig (son of actress Ellen Terry), and Konstantin Stanislavsky, who himself took Craig to Moscow to design his production of *Hamlet* (and who also visited New York). In part it was influenced by director-entrepreneur Max Reinhardt, whose work for the Deutsches Theater showed a commitment to art theatre wedded (a little too completely for Sheldon Cheney's taste) to commercial flair, and in part by Jacques Copeau (himself influenced by Craig and Adolphe Appia as well as the Irish Players), whose Paris-based Théâtre du Vieux-Colombier was, perhaps ironically, itself modeled in part on New York's Garrick Theatre. All of which underlines the extent to which this new movement was international; the extent, too, to which America was increasingly a part of these wider developments in theatre.

Copeau, who operated a repertory group, took his company to New York (1917–19) and discovered fertile ground. The novelist Waldo Frank's response to the visit was to hail the company for moving "outside the vicious circle of material competition and material success" and revolting against "all those artistic hindrances and falsities that come with a great financial burden" (quoted in Cheney, *Art Theater*, 57). Copeau's action in taking his company to the country for the summer to develop their acting skills and explore texts was later adopted by the Group Theatre, spun off from the Theatre Guild, itself created in 1919 by several people associated with the Washington Square Players.

Continued exposure to European theatre, perhaps especially, though not exclusively, through the Washington Square Players and subsequently the Theatre Guild, played its part in inspiring American playwrights to experiment; and it is certainly hard to think of a more eclectic playwright than Eugene O'Neill, whose own career showed the influence of everything from the Irish Players, who visited America in 1911, to the work of the expressionists. It is equally true, however, that European acting styles also had their impact, with Stanislavsky's system entering the national bloodstream via Richard Boleslavsky (who established the Laboratory Theater in New York), Maria Ouspenskaya, and Lee Strasberg, whereas approaches to directing and design were influenced by the work of Gordon Craig and Jacques Copeau. However great those influences, the effect was to produce a theatre that was increasingly self-confident, reshaping and redefining the nature of American theatrical experience. Not that everyone welcomed this new direction.

David Belasco, who was associated with a new realism in production, was hostile to the experimental groups: "This so-called new art of the theater is but a flash in the pan of inexperience," he insisted. "It is the cubism of the theater – the wail of the incompetent and degenerate. . . . The whole thing merely shows an ignorance and a diseased and depraved understanding and appreciation of any art at all" (quoted in Cheney, *Art Theater,* 6).

By contrast, writing in 1917, Sheldon Cheney, founder of *Theatre Arts* magazine, and student to George Pierce Baker at Harvard, confessed to the conviction that in the activities of the Little Theatre movement "lay the only real promise of a better dramatic art in this country. Because their roots were in native soil, I felt that here were beginnings of true community theaters – which collectively would be our ultimate national theater" (4–5). Yet even Cheney, whose books, *The New Movement in Theater* (1914) and *The Art Theater* (1916; revised 1925), were key texts, admitted that "we have not in America a single important professional acting company, permanently organized and permanently housed, under the leadership of a recognized artist-director" (Cheney, *Art Theater,* 10).

The so-called art theatre, which Cheney defined as "a place where the arts of the theatre are creatively practiced, free alike from the will of the businessman, from the demands of movie-minded audiences, and from the fetters of superstitious traditionalism" in which "the several contributive arts of the playwright, the actor and the designer" were "brought together in a union, a synthesis" (Cheney, *Art Theater,* 15), had no history in America. The weak link in all these new American "art theatres" was, indeed, the acting. The commitment to amateurism, often a deliberate gesture toward authenticity, frequently marred otherwise interesting work. Some of these theatres declared a commitment to American writing; others, such as the Theatre Guild, were criticized for failing to do so. Only six of the Theatre Guild's first thirty-eight productions were by American authors. Nonetheless there was a certain hubris on the part of those who saw themselves as pioneers or spokespersons for the new. Thus Cheney remarked in 1925 that "theatrical leadership of the English-speaking world has now shifted to New York" (Cheney, *Art Theater,* 61). His case essentially rested on the achievements of the Neighborhood Playhouse, which, as its name implies, was particularly interested in addressing the concerns of its own community on the Jewish East Side, and on the Provincetown Playhouse. The list of plays that he thought particularly worthy, and that justified his confidence, today looks decidedly odd. It includes Percy MacKaye's *The Scarecrow,* Mrs. Marks's *The Piper,* Charles Kenyon's *Kindling,* and Augustus Thomas's *As a Man Thinks.* Only O'Neill's *Beyond the Horizon* seems unchallengeable. He did, however, identify, in a list of emerging talents, Susan Glaspell, Sidney Howard, and John Howard Lawson.

Where the American theatre did seem to excell was in all aspects of design, with such talents as Robert Edmond Jones, Norman Bel Geddes, Mordecai Gorelik, and Jo Mielziner, all of whom reacted against both the artifice of the nineteenth century and the literalism of David Belasco's stagecraft.

World War I was not an experience shared by many Americans. Nonetheless, the number of writers who made it their business to disillusion themselves in Europe, as ambulance drivers rather than combatants, was a long one. Those who failed to make it into the trenches – like F. Scott Fitzgerald – deeply regretted it. Hemingway told him that death in war offered a central truth about human experience, to be observed unblinkingly, and Fitzgerald was gullible enough to believe him. The irony was that a war which, from an official American point of view, was fought to sustain liberal principles was seen by many writers as marking the impotence of those principles in the face of an implacable world. Social realities were seen as a clue to metaphysical truths. Old notions of an integral self, socially and morally secure, already under assault from deterministic theories and the realities of modernity, now fractured on the patent absurdities of trench warfare.

The result was an ironic literature. Pound, Eliot, Hemingway, Cummings, and Fitzgerald described a world in which all gods were dead, language was denatured, and order inverted. They created works in which sexuality was distorted, the imagination suspect, and character parodic. And when consumerism offered itself as a new value, a religion whose text was a mix of *Mark, the Match Boy* and bland advertisements, Sinclair Lewis was on hand to expose its vacuity. Seen in this way, America's possibilities were closing down. And what was true of poetry and the novel was also true, to some degree, of drama.

Maxwell Anderson and Laurence Stallings's *What Price Glory* (1924) reflected Hemingway's sense of the antitragic nature of warfare, its betrayal of the principles in whose name it was waged, although, like Hemingway's work, it was not without a sentimentality of its own. Meanwhile, O'Neill was on hand to mock America with its substitution of material for spiritual satisfaction, its class divisions, racism, and worship of the machine. Elmer Rice's *The Adding Machine* (1923) and *Street Scene* (1929) saw the individual as manipulated and coerced by the forces of modernity as well as by capitalism, which is seen as its agent. Unlike O'Neill, however, Rice was a satirist whose assaults on the modern world were launched in the name of familiar American pieties.

But the breakup of American values, occasioned not only or even primarily by war, released an energy that was reflected in the theatre as readily as in other genres. The modern itself seemed both seductive and threatening at the same time, the machine appearing as both an image of human oppression and the source of kinetic energy. The new social role of women and the emergence of African Americans (following the Great Migration, which saw millions move north and into the great urban centers) were facts acknowledged by the theatre. From the sentimental heroines of melodrama women became the protagonists of plays that explored equally their marginalization and their new sense of self-awareness. Susan Glaspell's *Trifles* was thus simultaneously an account of the acuity and the social powerlessness of women, and *The Verge* dramatized the cost of a woman's struggle to transcend her social roles. African Americans, previously required to act out stereotypical roles in the self-mocking antics of minstrelsy, now found themselves central characters in plays by America's leading white playwright as well as in a few works by black authors. As with Eugene O'Neill's black characters in *The Emperor Jones* (1920) and *All God's Chillun Got Wings* (1923), paying the price of challenging American values was often madness, as though the psyche could not stand the pressure of resisting the weight of convention and prejudice. The fate of the young woman at the center of Sophie Treadwell's *Machinal* (1928) is scarcely better, as she is victimized and destroyed.

The theatre, no less than the other arts, thus bore the marks of the intellectual, social, and political interests of the day. And everywhere a profound ambivalence reigned. Women were celebrated, even in extremis, in the work of Susan Glaspell, Zoë Akins, and Sophie Treadwell, and condescended to by

Philip Barry in comedies in which they were granted wit and social poise but largely relegated to a supportive role. The African American may have been licensed to star in his own drama, but Thomas Dixon's prewar *The Clansman* had acquired iconic status through the 1915 movie *The Birth of a Nation.* Psychology was mocked by Susan Glaspell and George Cram Cook, and embraced, somewhat uncritically, by Eugene O'Neill.

Those groups that had been founded before the war now reconstituted themselves. Most significantly, the Washington Square Players were reborn as the Theatre Guild, named for its association with the craftsmanship and the communalism of the medieval trade guilds. The amateur status preferred and proclaimed by such groups and the one-act plays they performed Off Broadway were to be abandoned in favor of professionally produced full-length works on Broadway. Still a conduit for European plays – Shaw's realism, Kaiser's expressionism – the Guild also staged powerful American plays: Elmer Rice's *The Adding Machine,* John Howard Lawson's *Processional* (1925), Sidney Howard's *They Knew What They Wanted* (1924), Maxwell Anderson's *Elizabeth the Queen* (1930), S. N. Behrman's *Biography* (1931), and Robert Sherwood's *Idiot's Delight* (1936), along with a number of plays by Eugene O'Neill. In time, however, the Theatre Guild's idealism gave ground to practicality, and it began to resemble the Broadway ethos against which it was in revolt, producing not only a comedy such as *The Philadelphia Story* but also popular musicals, including *Oklahoma!,* a process perhaps only seen as compromise by those who failed to recognize the achievements of such works.

From its first production in 1919 the Theatre Guild became for nearly two decades the single most important producing organization in the United States. Its intention was to stage plays unlikely to find a home in the commercial theatre and to establish its own actors. It had the inestimable benefit of having Eugene O'Neill as its principal author, though it was not until 1928 that it produced one of his plays. The Guild also presented a number of works by Bernard Shaw. Indeed, it produced fifteen of his plays between 1919 and 1935; in 1925 four of its nine productions were of his plays.

But this was not an experimental theatre. Nor was it established to foster American drama. Indeed, there were those who found its autocratic attitude hostile to the writer and to the American writer in particular. As a result, disgruntled dramatists formed The Playwrights Theatre, and directors and actors, keen to develop their skills, broke away to form the Group Theatre, its founders originally a part of the Theatre Guild but soon to form a producing company in its own right.

The Group Theatre was born not merely out of the Theatre Guild but also out of Harold Clurman's experience in France, with Jacques Copeau, and, in America, as an actor with the Provincetown Players and the Guild and as a student of Boleslavsky and Ouspenskaya at the American Laboratory Theatre. Together with Stella Adler, Lee Strasberg, and Cheryl Crawford, Clurman gathered together a group of Guild actors and withdrew to a summer home to explore the text of Paul Green's *The House of Connelly.* More important was their purpose to hone their craft as directors and actors. They produced Green's play in 1931 and broke away from the Guild to form a separate company the following year.

The Group Theatre had no particular social or political agenda at first, but, as the decade progressed, the context in which it worked served to radicalize its repertoire and led a number of its members to believe that theatre could play a central role in transforming the world it set out to engage. However, when producing on Broadway, the Group's members kept too close an eye on box office receipts for Clurman's taste. Redemption appeared to come with the emergence, from the company's own ranks, of a radical playwright, Clifford Odets. Of its five productions in 1935 four were of his plays, and three more followed before the Group collapsed in 1941.

Odets was the poet of a middle-class America cut off from faith in the ideals that had once given it purpose and direction. Ostensibly a radical, what he seems to have yearned for was the restoration of a lost communalism, a sense of spiritual transcendence glimpsed less through characters who serve an ideological purpose than through a language whose poetic arias hint at a level of experience denied by simple materialism. America was to be restored to itself. With *Waiting for Lefty* (1935) his radicalism seems to have been displaced onto style, but in fact that play is an exception. For stylistic innovation it is necessary to look elsewhere, and perhaps especially to the Playwrights' Theatre.

The Group Theatre collapsed in part because of a series of internal disagreements about its objectives and in part because Hollywood beckoned its leading figures. In many ways the film industry was an embodiment of those things they had revolted against – a capitalist enterprise dedicated to distracting its audience from the reality of their lives. But it paid well. Odets earned forty times more as a screenwriter than a Group Theatre actor received. Harold Clurman, meanwhile, took pleasure in the fact that his Hollywood stint gave him time to write a history of the Group Theatre and sufficient money to pay off its debts.

In the 1930s, of course, theatre was very self-consciously seen by some as a means of exploring the workings of society and as a model for that cooperative endeavor needed to redeem a country whose myth of individual enterprise and initiative had come close to destroying it. That perspective had been anticipated and, indeed, in part inspired by the work of Charles Klein, who had turned from writing melodramas to creating social plays that paralleled the novels of Sinclair Lewis and the journalism of Ida Tarbell, who had exposed the working of the Standard Oil Company. American drama had often chosen to engage contemporary issues, but Klein marked the beginnings of a more direct assault on social ills that reflected at first Progressive and then radical thought. Political drama, in other words, was not born with the Great Depression, even if it undoubtedly came into its own in that political ferment.

If Klein was a Progressive, Mike Gold, whose first plays were performed by the Provincetown Players, was a radical, tracing his commitment and approach on the one hand to Walt Whitman – democratic, inclusive, and aesthetically innovative – and on the other to Russia, which placed art in the vanguard of change. Typically, Gold's was a radicalism that blended a belief in new structures and forms – social and artistic – with nostalgia for a lost organicism, a communal spirit destroyed not by modernity but by capitalism. Theatre was to be regenerated from without, not from within. It had to express the vigor and energy of class revolt and the power of a technology that spoke of new possibilities. It substituted a melodrama of social revolt for a melodrama of bourgeois sensibility. In Meyerhold, Gold saw the human body suddenly released, theatre offering a paradigm of that liberation of spirit and body he believed to be the logic of history.

With John Dos Passos, John Howard Lawson, Em Jo Basshe, and Francis Edward Faragh, Gold founded the New Playwrights Theatre in 1926, funded, perhaps paradoxically, by a banker. The attitude to the working class of this supposedly worker's theatre and others like it was naive and condescending. John Dos Passos talked of hammering truths into the heads of a putative working-class audience without explaining either to himself or others how such an audience was to be attracted to such a dubious educational experience. John Howard Lawson later identified such authorial presumption as a central problem. Nonetheless, their plays were remarkably adventurous, using futurist, expressionist, and constructivist elements, and deploying music, masks, pantomime, and fantasy. This was no agit-prop drama, though it did incorporate the stereotypes and representative figures of that mode of theatre. Like so many other radical groups, however, the New Playwrights Theatre had little discernible political or theatrical impact.

The fact was that political theatre had shallow historical and political roots in America. This was, after all, the place to which immigrants had come to escape politics. Just as the pose of world-weary disillusionment, adopted by so many American writers and intellectuals, which in Europe could be seen as a logical response to mass slaughter and betrayed values, was not shared by a population for which the American promise was the essence of national purpose, so the political revolts of revolutionary Russia had little meaning in an America in which everyone aspired to the status of the bourgeoisie and had no wish to revolt against a system they had chosen rather than inherited. African Americans, meanwhile, discovering their political, economic, and cultural strength in America's urban centers, responded not with disillusionment but with optimism in the twenties and even into the thirties, despite their own particular hardships. The New Deal, in particular, was for many a liberating force. The Depression did radicalize America but more in the sense that socialism repackaged as Americanism became the state religion.

A number of radical theatre groups were formed, many of which, once again, looked to Europe for their models. Most, however, were short-lived. Some opted for agit-prop sketches to "cheer up strikers," others for a sturdy realism. Still others bridged the gulf. Clifford Odets's *Waiting for Lefty,* a product of the New Theatre League and winner of the *New Theatre* and *New Masses* award for a revolutionary play, was one such middle-ground work, a play swiftly picked up by the Group Theatre, whose actors had appeared in the original production. However, despite its success, it did not signal a general triumph for radical drama.

Left-wing theatre was in part, and ironically, subverted by the New Deal, whose policies were practical and did not rely on myths of working-class solidarity recycled by middle-class authors or on the need for a revolution. The Declaration of Independence, notwithstanding, revolution has, as Lenin acknowledged, never been a preferred option in a country that persists in congratulating itself on a system it believes the envy of the world. Left-wing theatre was undermined, too, by the very success of a major theatrical enterprise sponsored by the federal government – the Federal Theatre, well funded, cogently organized, and theatrically innovative.

In *Theatre Arts* magazine, in 1919, Walter Eaton called for a national theatre. He was not looking for a building but for a means by which people might share in drama in the same way they could in a newly published novel. His suggestion was for the simultaneous production of new American plays of general interest in as many communities as possible. Writing in 1997, Susan Harris Smith dismissed such a thought as utopian, but the truth is that Eaton's dream became a reality. However, a utopian organization was required to bring it about. On 27 October 1936, Sinclair Lewis's *It Can't Happen Here* opened in twenty-one cities at once. The organization responsible only flourished for a brief four years, but in that time it had a remarkable impact not merely on playwriting, though Arthur Miller submitted a play to the company and Tennessee Williams tried to join it, but on acting, directing, and stage design. More important, perhaps, it provided evidence that theatre need not be remote from the lives of those who had previously shunned it as elitist. Had this product of Roosevelt's Works Progress Administration been no more than an institution based in Washington or New York, producing plays from the national and international repertoire, it would have been no more than a footnote in American theatrical history. As it was, not merely were productions staged across the country but the Negro Unit, itself an innovation, employed 851 people, thereby fostering talents that would sustain African American theatre in the decades to come.

Entry to Federal Theatre productions cost anywhere from ten cents to a dollar and ten cents (with some free seats). The theatre operated anywhere that could be transformed into a performance space. In its brief existence it attracted over thirty million people to work, which ranged from circus, vaudeville, and puppet productions to the Living Newspapers, an innovatory documentary form that had its origins in revolutionary Russia. Sixty-five percent of Federal Theatre audiences had never been to the theatre before. The Living Newspapers, which dramatized contemporary events, were researched by teams of journalists and shaped by writers. They were designed to employ as many people as possible, since theirs was a relief organization, and the effect of this was to create something of an epic theatre, one, moreover, that, whatever the ostensible subject of the plays, was itself a paradigm of that mutually supportive society its politically committed creators wished to advocate. The Living Newspaper production of *Power* in Seattle lists eighty-one actors, together with twenty-eight further personnel (Engle and Miller, 203). Here, if ever, was an American theatre engaging American subjects for the benefit of a representative American audience.

The Living Newspaper productions were stylistically eclectic and often ideologically simplistic. They used movie clips, slides, music, and documentary recordings in engaging issues of the moment and in doing so attracted sizable audiences. The most successful production, *One Third of a Nation,* ran for ten months in New York City and was seen by well over two hundred thousand people there.

The Federal Theatre also had a radio division, and radio drama flourished in America until television effectively killed it (Mercury Theatre's productions, directed by Orson Welles, included not only the infamous *War of the Worlds* but also a script by a young man from the University of Michigan, Arthur Miller).

One notable achievement of the Federal Theatre lay in the Negro Unit, but it did not pioneer in this area. Ridgely Torrence, a white man, staged plays that featured the African American, as did Eugene O'Neill, Marc Connelly,

Paul Green, Charles MacArthur, Edward Sheldon, Mike Gold, and DuBose and Dorothy Hayward. Meanwhile, such black theatre companies as the Howard Players, the Negro Playwrights' Company, the Harlem Experimental Theatre, Negro Art Theatre, the Rose McClendon Players, and the American Negro Theatre staged plays by black Americans. The single most significant writer was Langston Hughes, whose *Don't You Want to Be Free* ran for a year and whose *Mulatto,* a racial melodrama, ran successfully on Broadway and, together with Theodore Ward's *Big White Fog,* a Federal Theatre production, was the outstanding black-authored play to be staged before World War II. Also significant, however, were two other Negro Unit productions, the "voodoo" *Macbeth* and the *Swing Mikado* (1938), the latter seen by a quarter of a million people in the first five months of its run, before its transfer to Broadway.

The Federal Theatre made theatre itself seem a central experience of American life, with an organic relationship to the society that produced and watched it. Few of its plays can withstand critical analysis, but they were not offered in that spirit. Born out of social needs, it was a theatre that chose to address those needs. The Federal Theatre was at antipodes to those Little Theatres on which many had placed their hopes for a revivified drama. It was Whitmanesque in its inclusiveness, democratic in its spirit, irresponsibly direct in its methods and its appeal. It was killed by those who recognized its social agenda and who thought they discerned its subversive intent. It could not survive the hostility it provoked in those who thereby acknowledged what they would never previously have suspected: the power of theatre to engage public issues and address an audience far beyond those drawn to Broadway entertainments or Little Theatre aestheticism.

The Federal Theatre gave three hundred plays or adaptations their first U.S. productions. It is true that the theatre's national impact was not as great as its own publicity suggested (nearly 50 percent of all expenditure was in New York City, and 81 percent in New York City, Massachusetts, Illinois, and California combined[2]), but it remains the greatest theatrical experiment ever conducted in the United States and the most successful in the attempt to broaden the base of audiences.

The Depression may have given life to radical drama and been responsible for the innovations of the Federal Theatre, but it was anything but good news to the American theatre at large or to the public it served and whose support it needed. In 1929 there were 225 productions on Broadway, sixty companies were on tour, and amateur theatre thrived. Those figures shrank rapidly. By 1932 there were fourteen thousand movie houses with a weekly attendance of seventy million, though this marked a decline in figures from the mid-1920s. Theatres closed or converted to the now dominant medium of cinema. In 1931 Loews had staged vaudevilles in thirty-six theatres. In 1932 the number was twelve. A year later the figure was three. Repertory companies died; road companies ceased traveling. By 1933 half of New York's theatres were closed.

Yet, for all this, American drama flourished. The comedies of S. N. Behrman and Philip Barry, the moral melodramas of Robert Sherwood, Maxwell Anderson, and Lillian Hellman, the sentimentalities of William Saroyan and Thornton Wilder, the musicals of George and Ira Gershwin, Richard Rodgers and Lorenz Hart, Jerome Kern and Oscar Hammerstein II more than justified what had once seemed the irresponsible optimism of Sheldon Cheney in proposing that America had now claimed leadership in the English-speaking world.

With the war approaching, however, the mood of this theatre began to change. A new cause for national solidarity appeared that commanded the loyalty of writers as powerfully as had the radical politics of the previous decade. Robert Sherwood and Maxwell Anderson abandoned their pacifism in favor of a new commitment. Sherwood demonstrated his new values in *Abe Lincoln in Illinois* (1938) and *There Shall Be No Night* (1940), and Maxwell Anderson dramatized his shift from the early pacifism of *What Price Glory* (1924) with *Key Largo* (1939). Lillian Hellman lent her weight to the cause of global war with *Watch on the Rhine* (1941).

A key period in American drama was coming to an end. But already those who were to prove the backbone of the theatre in the postwar period were at work. The directors who founded the Theatre Guild would train some of the principal actors to dominate theatre and film from the 1940s until the end of the century. Elia Kazan, a product of the Group Theatre, would stage some of the most significant plays of the postwar era, working with a designer, Jo Mielziner, whose roots lay securely in the art theatre of the prewar world. Eugene O'Neill, silent since his Nobel Prize in 1936, was at work on the plays that would determine his reputation, and Arthur Miller and Tennessee Williams were already a part of the theatre that they would command for so many decades.

The American theatre, so long condescended to by its own critics no less than those abroad, was now, and would remain, an inspiration to people in other countries, whose own theatre was thereby liberated by the vernacular energy, the social engagement, the sexual power, the melodramatic violence, the democratic drive of drama that no longer felt the need to apologize for its eclecticism any more than for its concerns with the myths, the values, the fantasies of the country that produced it. America would continue to learn from the world, theatre having its own history abroad and its own international community. But without doubt the world did now and would hereafter learn from America.

Notes

1 In Engle and Miller, 163.
2 See W. McDonald, 282.

Timeline: Post–Civil War to 1945

Compiled by Don B. Wilmeth and Jonathan Curley

This chronological chart by years (only major events are ordered chronologically within each year) provides a quick overview of selective events during the time period covered by this volume. More important, the inclusion of factual details here allows authors of individual chapters freedom to approach their topics with greater flexibility and without the constraints of a traditional chronological, encyclopedic history. Briefly noted in the timeline are the following: in column one, major theatrical events in the his-tory of the American theatre; in column two, other U.S. cultural and historical events of significance, or representative data; and in column three, key historical and cultural events from other parts of the world, included in order to provide points of reference in a wider context. Unless otherwise indicated, specific theatrical events in column one occurred in New York City and dates refer to production.

DATES	THEATRE EVENTS IN AMERICA	SELECTED HISTORICAL/CULTURAL EVENTS IN AMERICA	SELECTED HISTORICAL/CULTURAL EVENTS THROUGHOUT THE WORLD
1870s	Word "vaudeville" established (by either M. B. Leavitt or H. J. Sargent).		
	Irish and Jewish comic characters integrated into minstrel shows, which reach their peak of popularity.		
	Early western vaudeville circuit develops.		
1870	*Saratoga* (21 Dec.) by Bronson Howard, often credited as the first professional American playwright to earn his living entirely by writing plays.	First blacks elected to Congress. Fourteenth Amendment, ensuring citizenship to former slaves and prohibiting Confederates from holding public office, ratified.	Franco–Prussian War; Siege of Paris. Abdication of Napoleon III.
	Augustin Daly's first major success, *Frou-Frou*, adapted from French play by Meilhac and Halevy, opens 15 February.	Atlantic Refining Co. incorporates.	Unification of Italy.

24

Clara Morris joins Daly's company; leaves in 1873.

Mme Rentz's Female Minstrels (renamed Rentz–Santley Novelty and Burlesque Company), created by Michael B. Leavitt, is credited as first American burlesque show.

J. J. McCloskey's *Across the Continent* premieres at the Park Theatre, Brooklyn, on 28 November. One of the dramatic successes of the nineteenth century; used as a vehicle for star Oliver Doud Byron and features an elaborate climactic Indian battle.

"Colonel" T. Allston Brown's (1836–1918) *History of the American Stage.*

Kate Claxton ("the American Sarah Bernhardt") begins acting with Charlotte Crabtree.

Drama critic L. Clarke Davis becomes editor of *The Philadelphia Inquirer.*

T. B. De Walden's successful version of *Kit, The Arkansas Traveler,* vehicle for F. S. Chanfrau.

London-born actor Charles Fechter (1824–79) has U.S. debut.

Former actress and playwright Olive Logan publishes book *Before the Footlights and Behind the Scenes.*

Standard Oil of Ohio incorporates, with John D. Rockefeller as president.

Railway track mileage exceeds 53,000 miles nationally.

U. S. Grant attempts to annex Santo Domingo and Dominican Republic; blocked by Senate.

First headquarters established for Weather Bureau.

Celluloid introduced for manufacture of dentures, billiard balls, and shirt collars.

Northern "carpetbaggers" and white Southern "scalawags" join the Republican Party to carry out the congressional reconstruction program in the South.

J. Q. A. Ward sculpts "Shakespeare" in Central Park.

Boardwalk in Atlantic City, New Jersey, first in the United States, completed.

Cartoon using the donkey as a symbol of the Democratic Party is printed for the first time in *Harper's Weekly.*

Premiere (26 June) of Wagner's *The Valkyrie* in Munich.

French writer Jules Verne's *Twenty Thousand Leagues Under the Sea* published.

Charles Dickens's *Edwin Drood.*

Pierre-Auguste Renoir's *Odalisque* completed.

Paul Cézanne completes *Snow at Estaque.*

First Vatican Council pronounces the doctrine of papal infallibility.

Swede N. A. Nordenskjold explores the interior of Greenland.

English warship *Captain* sinks off Finistère, France; 472 people are lost.

T. H. Huxley's "Theory of Biogenesis."

DATES	THEATRE EVENTS IN AMERICA	SELECTED HISTORICAL/CULTURAL EVENTS IN AMERICA	SELECTED HISTORICAL/CULTURAL EVENTS THROUGHOUT THE WORLD
1870	Merced Theatre in Los Angeles opens.	General Robert E. Lee (b. 1807) dies.	
	Lew Johnson's Minstrels give their first performance at Fort Wayne, Indiana.	Rollerskating spreads across the country.	
1871	Augustin Daly's *Horizon* premieres 21 March at New York Olympic Theatre; in September his *Divorce* runs a record 200 consecutive performances.	Oleomargarine first produced.	Verdi's *Aida*, to celebrate the opening of the Suez Canal, is finished.
	The first Union Square Theatre built.	In "Legal Tender Case" (Second), Supreme Court decides Legal Tender acts of 1862 and 1863, which fall within federal government's powers to meet emergencies.	Wilhelm I declared German Kaiser at Versailles.
	H. J. Sargent's Great Vaudeville Co. plays Louisville (considered by some first documented use of term "vaudeville.")	Great Chicago Fire, one of the worst in U.S. history, destroys much of the city.	Russian Nikolay Przhevalsky explores central Asia (1871–88), locating and describing major geological features and collecting animals and plants.
	P. T. Barnum heads his last circus, actually organized by W. C. Coup, who is responsible for creating the modern traveling circus.	U.S. federal prison system created.	Welsh journalist Henry Stanley, on assignment for a New York newspaper, searches for and finds explorer David Livingstone, greeting him with the famous "Dr. Livingstone, I presume?"
		Carbon black first produced from natural gas.	British Columbia becomes Canadian province.
			Rome becomes capital of Italy.
		"Boss" William Marcy Tweed of New York's Tammany Hall is indicted on charges of corruption.	Commune of Paris: Radical workers revolt against new government and humiliating peace terms it accepted in Franco–Prussian War; 17,000 rebels are killed before revolt is quashed.

1872

White Star Line's *S.S. Oceanic*, first modern luxury liner, is launched.

Feudalism abolished in Japan.

Fyodor Dostoyevsky's *The Possessed*.

Arthur Rimbaud's *The Drunken Boat*.

Charles Darwin's *The Descent of Man and Selection in Relation to Sex*.

British actor Henry Irving joins Lyceum Theatre, appearing for the first time in *The Bells*.

English explorer Verney Cameron commands Royal Geographic Society expedition to locate Livingstone; encounters servants bearing his body, explores further, and becomes first European to cross equatorial Africa from coast to coast.

Lewis Carroll's *Through the Looking Glass*.

Arthur Rimbaud's *Une Saison en enfer*.

Claude Monet's *Basin at Argenteuil* and *Impression: Fog*.

Friedrich Nietzsche's *The Birth of Tragedy*.

Square-bottomed grocery bag (and machine to make it) are patented.

Arbor Day first celebrated, in Nebraska, as a day for planting trees.

Boston hit by a fire that burns almost 1,000 buildings.

Anthony Comstock forms Committee for the Suppression of Vice.

Ulysses S. Grant reelected president.

The Credit Mobilier Scandal, in which prominent Republicans accepted bribes in the form of stock in the construction company that built the Union Pacific Railroad.

Tony Pastor separates the saloon from the theatre in his variety house.

Frank Mayo appears in Frank Murdoch's *Davy Crockett*; plays role for almost quarter of a century.

With *Monaldi*, Steele MacKaye makes professional debut as actor, playwright, and manager.

A. M. Palmer begins quarter-of-century career as prominent New York producer.

English actress Adelaide Neilson makes first of two tours.

Founding of Callender's Original Georgia Minstrels, a black troupe.

DATES	THEATRE EVENTS IN AMERICA	SELECTED HISTORICAL/CULTURAL EVENTS IN AMERICA	SELECTED HISTORICAL/CULTURAL EVENTS THROUGHOUT THE WORLD
1872	Germania Theatre Company, New York German-speaking troupe, organized (lasts until 1883).		
1873	Noted Italian actor Tommaso Salvini tours the country with *Othello* and other plays (first of five tours).	Major business recession following the failure of Jay Cooke and Co. investment-banking house (ends in 1878).	Indian Army officer Peter Egerton Warburton is first man to cross Australia from central Alice Springs to western coast, a journey that exceeds 2,000 miles.
	Washington, D.C.'s National Theatre (the fourth) reopens on 1 December after fire destroyed most of the structure in January.	Continuous-ignition combustion is invented.	Stanley returns to Africa; later proves Lake Victoria is Nile source.
	Augustin Daly's *Roughing It*.	Remington Company begins manufacturing modern typewriter.	Railroad is completed between Veracruz and Mexico City.
	T. B. De Walden's adaptation of James Fenimore Cooper's *The Deerslayer, The Life and Death of Natty Bumpo*, is produced.		Canada suffers prolonged economic depression (1873–76).
	First documented comic sketch seen on the vaudeville stage (John and Maggie Fielding).	First public school kindergarten established in Missouri.	Onset of Second Carlist War leads to reestablishment of monarchy in Spain, after a republic briefly emerges.
	William F. "Buffalo Bill" Cody forms the "Buffalo Bill Combination," a traveling theatrical troupe, with Texas Jack Omohundro and "Wild Bill" Hickok.	First cable car is put to use in San Francisco.	Jules Verne's *Around the World in Eighty Days*.
	W. C. Coup adds a second ring to the Barnum circus.	Mark Twain and C. D. Warner, *The Gilded Age*.	Tolstoy's *Anna Karenina* begun (completed 1876).
	Edwin Booth loses his theatre after bankruptcy.		British actor William C. Macready dies.
	First Polish play in Chicago, Theofilia		

1874

Preface to Emile Zola's *Thérèse Raquin* (adapted from his novel) becomes battle-cry for naturalism.

Modest Mussorgsky's opera *Boris Godunov*.

Mexican government suppresses religious orders.

Thomas Hardy's *Far from the Madding Crowd*.

Paul Verlaine's *Romances sans paroles*.

First Impressionist exhibition (Paris).

Artist Dante Gabriel Rossetti's *Proserpine*.

Sculptor Pierre-Auguste Renoir's *Dancer*.

Benjamin Disraeli becomes prime minister of England for a second time.

Johann Strauss II's operetta *Die Fledermaus* premieres in Vienna.

Michigan Supreme Court upholds taxes for public high schools.

Philadelphia opens the first American public zoo.

The Chautauqua Movement for adult education begins.

The Women's Christian Temperance Union is formed in Cleveland, Ohio.

Cartoonist Thomas Nast establishes the elephant as a symbol of the Republican Party in *Harper's Weekly*.

Samolinska's *The Emancipation of Women*.

DeBar's Grand Opera House opens in St. Louis; Macauley's opens in Louisville.

Augustin Daly opens New Fifth Avenue Theatre (Broadway and 28th St.) 3 December after Fifth Avenue Theatre burns.

Edward E. Rice and J. C. Goodwin's *Evangeline* (produced by Maurice Grau); the first show billed as "musical comedy," it is also the first to feature an original score with popular music, language, and dance.

Kate Claxton appears in *The Two Orphans*, in which she then tours for years.

Dion Boucicault's *The Shaughraun* at Wallack's Theatre; earns half a million dollars in the United States.

Polish star Mme Janauschek opens the fall season with Schiller's *Mary Stuart* at the National Theatre.

Oldest surviving theatrical club, The Lambs, is formed.

Daly's produces *Love's Labour's Lost* for first time in New York.

DATES	THEATRE EVENTS IN AMERICA	SELECTED HISTORICAL/CULTURAL EVENTS IN AMERICA	SELECTED HISTORICAL/CULTURAL EVENTS THROUGHOUT THE WORLD
1874			Paris Opera House completed.
			German Meiningen Players tour world (last time in 1890).
1875	Machinery built to handle complex stagecraft and sets.	Pennsylvania Coal Miners Strike is led by the Molly Maguires, a secret and violent organization of Irish American workers.	British Royal College of Surgeons admits women.
	Armbruster Scenic Studios founded in Columbus, Ohio.		
	Directors begin to appear, taking the places of actors who staged plays while also acting.	Congress passes the Specie Resumption Act, providing for the resumption of specie payments.	Gerard Manley Hopkins's *The Wreck of Deutschland.*
	The Kiralfy brothers produce the lavish *Around the World in Eighty Days.*	Congress passes Civil Rights Act, guaranteeing blacks equal rights in public places and the right to serve on juries.	Charles Stewart Parnell is elected to the British Parliament and begins movement for Irish independence.
	Trade paper *The Dramatic News* is established.	R. J. Reynolds organizes as tobacco company.	Georges Bizet's *Carmen* premieres.
	Tony Pastor moves his variety show from the Bowery uptown to the central show business area on Broadway; likely eliminates consumption of alcoholic beverages in his venue.	Mary Baker Eddy's *Science and Health.*	Kuang Hsu becomes Emperor of China.
	Nate Salsbury organizes Salsbury's Troubadours (*The Brook* influences early musical comedy).		
	James Bland, "The Negro Stephen Foster," enters black minstrelsy; publishes his first songs, "Morning by the Bright Light" and "Carry Me Back to Old Virginny."		Gilbert and Sullivan's *Trial by Jury.*
	Daly produces his play *Pique*; John Drew joins Daly's company.		

1876

Benjamin E. Woolfe's *The Mighty Dollar*, with W. J. Florence as a congressman; congressman established as an American stage type.

Mary Anderson debuts as Juliet at Macauley's Theatre in Louisville, Kentucky.

William F. "Buffalo Bill" Cody produces and stars in dramatization of the War Bonnet battle, *The Red Right Hand; or, Buffalo Bill's First Scalp for Custer.*

Bret Harte's *Two Men of Sandy Bar* written for actor Stuart Robson.

Nearly 100 companies are on the road for the 1876–77 season.

The Grand Opera House opens in San Francisco, as does Baldwin's Academy of Music.

Denman Thompson begins twenty-four-year career as Uncle Joshua in *The Old Homestead,* a play glorifying rural life (revised 1886).

During a performance of *The Two Orphans* at the National Theatre, a fight breaks out. Panic sets in when audience members think they hear "Fire, Fire, Fire!" instead of "Fight, Fight, Fight!"

Goodspeed Opera House built in East Haddam, Connecticut.

First U.S. reformatory for young offenders opens in Elmira, New York.

Intercollegiate Football Association is formed by Harvard, Yale, Princeton, Rutgers, and Columbia.

At Little Bighorn (25 June) General George A. Custer and all 264 troops of his Seventh Cavalry are killed by Indians led by Sitting Bull.

Telephone patented by Alexander Graham Bell.

Mark Twain's *The Adventures of Tom Sawyer.*

National baseball league founded.

Amilcare Ponchielli's *La Gioconda.*

Englishman Charles Montagu Doughty explores Arabia (1876–78); *Travels in Arabia* is his published account.

Porfirio Diaz, rebel leader in earlier period of unrest, takes up new rebellion against Mexican government.

Poet Stéphane Mallarmé's *The Afternoon of a Faun.*

Famine in India lasts two years and kills about 5 million people.

DATES	THEATRE EVENTS IN AMERICA	SELECTED HISTORICAL/CULTURAL EVENTS IN AMERICA	SELECTED HISTORICAL/CULTURAL EVENTS THROUGHOUT THE WORLD
1876	Augustin Daly's *Pique* helps establish Fanny Davenport as a serious actress and two years later becomes Ada Rehan's first vehicle with Daly.		
	Broad Street Theatre opens in Philadelphia.	World Exhibition in Philadelphia.	Bayreuth (Germany) Festspielhaus opens with first complete production of Wagner's *The Ring*.
	Central City Opera House built in Colorado mining town.		
	Mrs. John Drew at Philadelphia's Arch Street Theatre drops stock in favor of combination house.		
1877	The Lambs Club is incorporated in New York.	Rutherford B. Hayes is inaugurated nineteenth president.	Henrik Ibsen's *Pillars of Society*.
	Mark Twain and Bret Harte collaborate on *Ah Sin* for actor Charles Parsloe.	Thomas Alva Edison invents phonograph.	Women doctors are allowed to practice in England.
	Black performers Anna and Emma Hyers tour in musical *Out of Bondage*.	Louis Henry Morgan's *Ancient Society* introduces stage theory of social evolution.	
	Joaquin Miller's *The Danites; or, The Heart of the Sierras* performed in revised version by McKee Rankin for several years.	*Washington Post* founded by Melville Stone.	
	William Dean Howells's *A Counterfeit Presentment* acted by Lawrence Barrett.	Post–Civil War Reconstruction officially ends with the withdrawal of federal troops from the South.	Britain annexes the Transvaal and Walvis Bay on the coast of Southwest Africa. War breaks out between the British and the Kaffirs.
	Footlights Club of Jamaica, Massachusetts, an amateur company, founded.	Violent strikes rock nation's railroads.	

1878

Helena Modjeska's U.S. debut in *Adrienne LeCouvreur*.	The first intercity telephone lines begin operation.	Konstantin Stanislavski organizes his first amateur group, the Alexeyev Circle, producing operettas, farces, and melodramas.
Stuart Robson and W. H. Crane become successful comic acting team, continuing to 1889.	The first bicycle factory opens.	Four great African rivers – Niger, Nile, Congo, and Zambezi – have been explored and their courses determined by this date.
	The Nez Perce Indians, led by Chief Joseph, fight U.S. forces and retreat across 1,600 miles of Washington, Oregon, Idaho, and Montana. Forced to surrender, Joseph's tribe is sent to a reservation in Indian Territory.	Brahms composes Symphony no. 2, op. 75.
	Henry James's *The American*.	Gilbert and Sullivan's *H.M.S. Pinafore* premieres in London.
"Buffalo Bill" Cody employs reservation Indians as actors in stage melodramas for the first time.	Indian-manned police forces established by government for reservation supervision.	Antisocialist laws passed in Germany.
Gilbert and Sullivan's work established in New York with successful *H.M.S. Pinafore* production (*Trial by Jury* in 1875 closed soon after its opening).	Southern herd of buffalo nears extinction.	Scottish explorer Joseph Thomson journeys to eastern-central Africa with Royal Geographic Society expedition, traveling to Lake Nyasa and Lake Tanganyika, and discovers Lake Rukwa.
Bronson Howard's *The Banker's Daughter* produced at Union Square (an 1886 lecture, published in 1914, details evolution of play).	Tiffany glass factory established.	Swedish explorer Nils Nordenskjold becomes first man to sail through Northeast Passage to the Bering Strait.
The Murray-Cartland Co. (known also as The Great Metropolitan Theatre Co.), a Minneapolis stock company, founded.	The Edison Electric Light Co. opens.	Thomas Hardy's *The Return of the Native*.
J. H. Haverly's "United Mastodan Minstrels" expand size and spectacle of minstrel shows to be more competitive.	Thomas Alva Edison patents the phonograph.	

DATES	THEATRE EVENTS IN AMERICA	SELECTED HISTORICAL/CULTURAL EVENTS IN AMERICA	SELECTED HISTORICAL/CULTURAL EVENTS THROUGHOUT THE WORLD
1878	Burt and Leon become the first variety team to present a Jewish comic routine in the East.	Yellow fever epidemic kills about 14,000 in the southern United States.	Johannes Brahms's Violin Concerto in D minor.
	Sam Lucas becomes the first black star in the title role of *Uncle Tom's Cabin*.	Birth of Rachel Crothers.	War breaks out between Britain and Afghanistan.
	Bartley Campbell's *The Lower Million*, a dramatization of the great riot of 1877, is produced.		Actress Ellen Terry joins Irving's company at London's Lyceum.
	A. B. French operates first of five showboats (to 1901).		
	James A. Bailey's circus emerges as a major rival to Barnum.		
1879	Edward Harrigan with Tony Hart open their ethnic *The Mulligan Guard* (music by David Braham), a musical play, in New York, the first of many.	"Buffalo Bill" Cody's *The Life of Hon. William F. Cody, Known as Buffalo Bill, the Famous Hunter, Scout and Guide: An Auto-biography*.	First successful electric locomotive demonstrated in Berlin.
	Bartley Campbell's mining camp melodrama *My Partner* becomes vehicle for Louis Aldrich and Charles Parsloe.	Scott Paper Co. established.	Henrik Ibsen's *A Doll's House* premieres in Copenhagen.
	The Boston Ideal Opera Co., a comic opera company, is founded by Henry Clay Barnabee.	First U.S. automobile patent granted to George B. Selden.	Tchaikovsky's *Eugene Onegin* premieres in Moscow.
	Neil Burgess becomes star in dame role touring in *The Widow Bedott Papers*.	Edison demonstrates incandescent light bulb; obtains patent following year.	Dostoyevsky's *The Brothers Karamazov*.
	Daly opens Daly's Theatre (formerly Wood's Museum) at 30th and Broadway; remains there for 20 years.	The first floating Ivory Soap is marketed.	George Meredith's *The Egoist*.
		Henry James's novelette *Daisy Miller*.	

34

1880

James Bland introduces his song "In the Evening by the Moonlight" with Callender's Original Georgia Minstrels and writes "Oh Dem Golden Slippers."

Dramatic Mirror founded as *New York Mirror*.

German-speaking theatre, the Thalia, opens in New York City under Gustav Amberg, Heinrich Conried, and Mathilde Cottrelly.

Opening 12 February of Steele MacKaye's Madison Square Theatre, which featured two stages raised and lowered into place by an elevator mechanism.

U.S. debut (8 Nov.) of actress Sarah Bernhardt (brought by Henry Abbey) at Booth's Theatre in *Adrienne LeCouvreur*.

Steele MacKaye's *Hazel Kirke* with Effie Ellsler begins 486-performance run at the Madison Square.

P. T. Barnum joins up with James A. Bailey to found the Barnum and Bailey Circus.

Mary Baker Eddy charters the Church of Christ Scientist in Boston.

An uprising of the Ute Indians is suppressed. By a treaty in 1880, the Utes are moved from Colorado and Utah.

Richard Henry Pratt founds the Carlisle Indian School in Pennsylvania, one of the most successful schools for Indians.

Radcliffe College established in Cambridge, Massachusetts.

Frank W. Woolworth opens his first successful 5-and-10-cent store in Lancaster, Pennsylvania.

"Uncle Remus" stories begun by Atlanta journalist Joel Chandler Harris.

The Northern Pacific Railroad is completed.

In this period, U.S. railroad building boom peaks. Over 70,000 miles of track are laid in this decade.

George Eastman establishes business that will later be incorporated as Eastman Kodak Co.

First appearance of canned fruits and meats on store shelves.

First wireless telephone message transmitted 3 June by Bell.

Zulus defeat the British at Isandhlwana, but are defeated at Ulundi, South Africa. Peace is made with the Zulu chiefs.

War of the Pacific, over mineral-rich Atcama Desert, between Chile and Bolivia, with Peru declaring war on both nations.

Austro–German alliance signed in October.

Gilbert and Sullivan's *The Pirates of Penzance.*

Rapid industrialization of Germany and a more active policy of colonization through 1880s.

France expands colonial empire into Africa and Indochina.

First steam-powered plant for generating electricity is built in London.

DATES	THEATRE EVENTS IN AMERICA	SELECTED HISTORICAL/CULTURAL EVENTS IN AMERICA	SELECTED HISTORICAL/CULTURAL EVENTS THROUGHOUT THE WORLD
1880	The Societa Filodrammatico Italiana di New York performs *Maria Giovanni* at the Dramatic Hall. It is considered the first native Italian American dramatic performance.	National Baptist Convention of America established to reorganize the growing number of black Baptist churches formed by free slaves after Civil War.	M. Kalokairinos, excavating at Knossos on Crete, discovers wall of legendary labyrinth at palace of King Minos.
	Miner and Canary form the nucleus of the first Eastern vaudeville circuit, offering sixteen weeks of work for performers.	Andrew Carnegie begins establishing libraries.	Rodin's sculpture *The Thinker*.
	Daly begins series starring "Big Four": Ada Rehan, John Drew, Mrs. Gilbert, and James Lewis.	New York streets first lit by electricity.	
	Lillian Russell billed as "the English Ballad Singer" by Tony Pastor.	New York's Metropolitan Museum of Art moves into Central Park building.	
1881	Tony Pastor's Fourteenth Street Theatre opens, considered by some the birthplace of true vaudeville.	Helen Hunt Jackson's indictment of U.S. Indian policy, *A Century of Dishonor*.	Ibsen's *Ghosts*.
	Pastor attracts women to his "high class" clean variety shows by giving away sewing kits and dress patterns.	Sitting Bull returns to United States from Canada; military breaks promise of pardon and imprisons him.	Alexander III begins reign as Russian czar.
	Third ring added to Barnum and Bailey Circus.	James A. Garfield inaugurated president, but is assassinated in September. Chester A. Arthur succeeds him.	First electric streetcar system is built in Berlin.
	George Jessop's *Sam'l of Posen*.	First halftone photographs appear in newspapers (first in *New York Daily Graphic* on 4 March).	First true cabaret, Chat Noir, founded in Paris by Rodolphe Salis.
	Hanlon–Lee spectacular acrobatic comedy *Le Voyage en Suisse*.	Labor leader Samuel Gompers founds Federation of Organized Trades and Labor Unions.	Artist Edouard Manet's *Springtime*.
	Wallack's Theatre renamed the Star.		Birth of Pablo Picasso.

1882	Booker T. Washington founds the Tuskegee Institute to promote industrial and agricultural education.	Ibsen's *An Enemy of the People.*
David Belasco becomes manager of Madison Square.	Exxon incorporates as Standard Oil Co. of New Jersey.	Jose Marti's *Ismaelillo.*
Actors' Fund of America founded to assist aged and needy actors.	John L. Sullivan becomes American heavyweight boxing champion.	French clinician Jean-Martin Charcot opens Europe's foremost neurological clinic of the time.
Avrom Goldfadn's *Koldunye; or, The Witch* staged, sounding the arrival of Yiddish theatre in the United States.	Chinese Exclusion Act, which bars Chinese Immigration (on the books for ten years).	German bacteriologist Robert Koch links germ with disease for first time by identifying tuberculosis bacterium.
The Ringling Brothers field their Classic and Comic Concert Company, a small Wisconsin variety show.	Mark Twain's *The Prince and the Pauper.*	Fenians seeking Irish independence from England murder British secretary and undersecretary in Phoenix Park, Dublin.
The Casino Theatre opened by Rudolph Aronson in New York; the first theatre building to include a roof garden in its design. The performance of Prince Methusalem on 7 July 1883 officially opens the roof garden to theatre patrons.		Paul Verlaine's *Art poétique.*
"Buffalo Bill" Cody organizes a precursor of Wild West exhibition, "Old Glory Blowout" (4th of July celebration) in North Platte, Nebraska.		Claude Monet completes his last major painting, *A Bar at the Folies Bergères.*
Third Wallack's Theatre opens at Broadway and 30th St.		Founding of Deutches Theater in Berlin.
Lillie Langtry's U.S. debut.		
1883		
B. F. Keith, future vaudeville king, opens dime museum in Boston with "Baby Alice," a premature black baby, as featured attraction.	Sitting Bull participates in last traditional buffalo hunt of the Sioux; the northern herd is now extinct.	Friedrich Nietzsche's *Thus Spake Zarathustra* begun (completed 1892).

DATES	THEATRE EVENTS IN AMERICA	SELECTED HISTORICAL/CULTURAL EVENTS IN AMERICA	SELECTED HISTORICAL/CULTURAL EVENTS THROUGHOUT THE WORLD
1883	First Wild West exhibition seen in Omaha, Nebraska.	Mobil Oil Corp. incorporates as Standard Oil Co. of New York.	Guy de Maupassant's *Une Vie.*
	First Ibsen production in New York, a commercial failure, is an adaptation by Helena Modjeska of *A Doll's House,* called *Thora.*	Brooklyn Bridge built over New York's East River.	Robert Louis Stevenson's *Treasure Island.*
	Lawrence Barrett successfully revives G. H. Boker's *Francesca da Rimini.*		
	Abbey brings English actors Henry Irving and Ellen Terry and the Lyceum Company to the United States for the first of eight tours.		Howard Pyle writes and illustrates *The Merry Adventures of Robin Hood.*
	Bronson Howard's *Young Mrs. Winthrop.*		Royal College of Music, London, is founded.
	Richard Mansfield appears in *A Parisian Romance.*		
	James O'Neill first appears in *The Count of Monte Cristo.*		
	Cordelia's Aspirations, the last of the "Mulligan Guard" series by Edward Harrigan, runs 176 performances.		
	William Warren Jr. retires from Boston Museum.		
1884	Augustin Daly tours his company to London – the first American to do so.	Soda-works plant opens in Onondaga salt region of New York.	Society of Authors founded in England to address fair contract procedures and royalty payments.
	A. M. Palmer becomes manager of the Madison Square Theatre.		Oxford University admits women (but not as full-time students until 1920).

Steele MacKaye builds the Lyceum Theatre.

The Astor Place Company of Colored Tragedians debuts with a Shakespeare repertoire.

The American Academy of Dramatic Arts is founded as the Lyceum Theatre School of Acting.

Robert Boodey Cavely's "Indian plays" produced: *King Philip, The Last of a Nation, Miantonimoh,* and *The Regicides.*

Musical folk play *The People of Varmland,* most popular Swedish play in the United States (into 1920s).

William Gill's musical burlesque *Adonis* makes matinee idol of Henry E. Dixey.

Magician Harry Kellar sets record of 323 consecutive performances at Philadelphia's Egyptian Hall.

Founding of the Astor Place Company of Colored Tragedians under J. A. Arneaux.

Ringling brothers stage their first circus in Baraboo, Wisconsin.

Los Angeles's Grand Opera House built.

First modern metal-frame skyscraper, Chicago's ten-story Home Insurance Building, designed by U.S. architect William Jenney.

Moses Fleetwood Walker, first black major-league player, signs with American Association.

Inventor Hiram Maxim invents recoil-operated Maxim machine gun, first successful automatic machine gun.

The first baseball World Series is held.

Independent Republicans, called "Mugwumps," walk out of Republican National Convention, refusing to support Republican presidential nominee James G. Blaine, who they feel is corrupt, and backing the Democratic candidate.

Artist Winslow Homer's *The Life Line.*

Early, mechanical scanner type of television patented in Germany.

Steam engine developed by British inventor Charles Parsons.

French invent smokeless gunpowder.

Henrik Ibsen's *The Wild Duck.*

The first volume of the Oxford English Dictionary is published.

DATES	THEATRE EVENTS IN AMERICA	SELECTED HISTORICAL/CULTURAL EVENTS IN AMERICA	SELECTED HISTORICAL/CULTURAL EVENTS THROUGHOUT THE WORLD
1885	Edward F. Albee joins B. F. Keith; they present in Boston a condensed version of *The Mikado*, five times a day, with variety acts between, thus forming the first continuous-performance venue.	Grover Cleveland inaugurated twenty-second president. Mark Twain's *Huckleberry Finn*.	First trans-Canadian railway, Canadian Pacific Railway, completed.
	First of four Alcazar Theatres opens in San Francisco.	American Telephone & Telegraph incorporates.	International conference in Berlin calls for end of slave trade that supplies African slaves to Middle Eastern countries.
	Fifth Washington, D.C., National Theatre built; same structure stands today.	George Eastman develops first successful chemically treated photographic film.	Edgar Degas's *Woman Bathing*. Paul Cézanne's *Group of Bathers*.
	Annie Oakley ("Little Sure Shot") joins Cody's show; remains (except for 1888) until 1901.	William Dean Howells's *The Rise of Silas Lapham*. The Cuban Giants, first black professional team, is formed on Long Island, New York.	Symbolist drama develops in France. Louis Pasteur administers first inoculation for rabies. Khartoum, victory for Sudanese rebels over British colonial governor-general; rebels kill Gordon and his entire garrison.
1886	William Gillette's *Held by the Enemy*, his first Civil War play.	In Haymarket Square riot, anarchist bomb and police gunfire kill eleven during Chicago labor demonstration.	First oil tanker, *Gluckhauf*, built in Great Britain.
	Denman Thompson's *The Old Homestead* premieres in a revised full-length version at the Boston Museum.	Statue of Liberty, gift from France, unveiled in New York.	Karl Benz patents vehicle powered by gasoline engine.
	Richard Mansfield in *Prince Karl*.	Westinghouse Electric Corp. incorporates. American Federation of Labor (AF of L) founded in Ohio.	Robert Louis Stevenson's *Kidnapped* and *The Strange Case of Dr. Jekyll and Mr. Hyde*. Vincent Van Gogh's *Self-Portrait*. Georges Seurat's *Sunday Afternoon on the Island of La Grande Jatte*.

1887

Bronson Howard's *The Henrietta* portrays high finance and romantic treachery on Wall Street.

Joaquin Miller's *The Danites in the Sierras.*

The Bostonians succeeds the Boston Ideal Opera Co.

Steele MacKaye directs his play *Paul Kauvar,* demonstrating skill in staging crowd scenes.

B. F. Keith and E. F. Albee present their first complete variety shows.

The Hungarian Amateur Theatrical Society of New York is established and opens with a presentation of Gergely Csiky's *A Sarga Cskio (The Yellow Colt).*

Edwin Booth (with Lawrence Barretts) begins two-year tour.

Second Broadway Theatre opens (at 41st Street).

Lyceum Theatre school and stock company under control of Daniel Frohman until 1902. E. A. Sothern engaged as romantic leading man.

Coca-Cola and Dr. Pepper are introduced.

Tailless dinner jackets debut in Tuxedo Park, New York.

John Singer Sargent's painting *Carnation, Lily, Lily, Rose.*

Johnson and Johnson incorporates in New Jersey.

Interstate Commerce Act.

Congress passes Dawes Allotment Act, dividing reservation lands on basis of 160 acres per head of family.

Auguste Rodin's *The Kiss.*

Marx's *Das Kapital* published in English.

First battery-powered submarine developed in France.

Monotype typesetting machine invented.

Ibsen's *Rosmersholm* performed in Oslo.

A. Conan Doyle's *A Study in Scarlet* published.

Celluloid roll film developed, making motion-picture photography possible.

August Strindberg's *The Father.*

DATES	THEATRE EVENTS IN AMERICA	SELECTED HISTORICAL/CULTURAL EVENTS IN AMERICA	SELECTED HISTORICAL/CULTURAL EVENTS THROUGHOUT THE WORLD
1888	Augustin Daly produces *The Taming of the Shrew* at Stratford-upon-Avon in the Shakespeare Memorial Theatre.	Adding machine patented by William Burroughs.	Stanley discovers Ruwenzori Mountain Range, which proves to be the Mountains of the Moon mentioned by Ptolemy in second century.
	Wallack's old theatre (later renamed Palmer's) opens.	Eastman Kodak introduces portable twenty-five-dollar camera.	German physicist produces and detects radio waves over short distances.
	Edwin Booth founds the best-known U.S. theatrical club, The Players, at 16 Gramercy Park in New York City.	First ballpoint pen patented by American inventor.	Scot John Dunlop invents pneumatic tire.
	Imre Kiralfy stages *The Fall of Rome* outdoors on Staten Island, New York, with a cast of 2,000.	Composer and bandmaster John Philip Sousa writes military march "Semper Fidelis" for the Marines.	Gramaphone invented.
	The skirt dance, popularized by performers at the Gaiety Theatre in London, is introduced by them to New York.		Vincent Van Gogh's painting *Sunflowers*.
	Polite vaudeville introduced to the West Coast by John Cordray in Seattle.		
	"Casey at Bat," a popular ballad by Ernest Lawrence Thayer, publicly recited for the first time by actor DeWolf Hopper.		
	Maurice Barrymore stars in *Captain Swift*.		
	Gustav Amberg opens Amberg Theatre (later Irving Place).		
1889	Charles Frohman's first great success as New York manager with Bronson Howard's *Shenandoah*.	Benjamin Harrison inaugurated twenty-third president.	General Georges Boulanger unsuccessfully tries to seize power and establish dictatorship in France.
	The first Lithuanian American production, Anatanas Turskis's *Be Sumnenes* (*Without*	Dow Jones begins daily newspaper, *The Wall Street Journal*.	Eiffel Tower built in downtown Paris for Universal Exposition of 1889.

DATES	THEATRE EVENTS IN AMERICA	SELECTED HISTORICAL/CULTURAL EVENTS IN AMERICA	SELECTED HISTORICAL/CULTURAL EVENTS THROUGHOUT THE WORLD
1890	David Belasco and Henry C. DeMille's *Men and Women.*	Electric chair is used for death penalty in United States for the first time.	
	Charles Hoyt's *A Texas Steer.*	Wyoming is the first state to include women as voters.	Henrik Ibsen's *Hedda Gabler.*
	Clyde Fitch's *Beau Brummell* stars Richard Mansfield.	Women's baseball team is organized.	
	The Edward Harrigan Theatre opens (later renamed Garrick) on West 34th Street.	Sherman Antitrust Act passed.	
	Actor-manager Dion Boucicault dies.	The Ghost Dance, a religious movement originating with the Paiute prophet Wovoka, reaches Sioux. It promises the disappearance of the white man and the return of the buffalo.	Scottish anthropologist Sir James George Frazer's *The Golden Bough.*
		Sitting Bull shot and killed by Indian police attempting to arrest him.	
	Creole Show, popular black musical burlesque, produced by Sam Jack, opens; tour takes it to Chicago's World Fair.	More than 300 Sioux massacred at Wounded Knee on 29 December by the U.S. Seventh Cavalry.	
		Educational testing begun in some U.S. schools.	
		Ellis Island opens for the processing of newly arrived immigrants.	
1891	Augustus Thomas's *Alabama.*	The zipper is patented.	First international copyright law takes effect.
	Sinbad the Sailor, followed next season by *Ali Baba,* both with Eddie Foy.	Carnegie Hall opens on West 57th Street.	J. T. Grein founds The Independent Theatre Society in London.

Edwin Booth and Lotta Crabtree retire.

Imre Kiralfy combines with Barnum and Bailey to stage the massive *Columbus and the Discovery of America*.

Bostonians premiere Reginald De Koven and Harry Smith's *Robin Hood*, the most popular American comic opera of the era.

Pioneer clown Dan Rice begins last appearances (final in 1892).

Lee Lash [Scenery] Studio founded in San Francisco; 1898 settles in New York City for next thirty years.

Broadway tryout system pioneers at the Boston Theatre with Charles Hoyt's *A Trip to Chinatown*, a musical trifle with 657 consecutive performances in New York; run thought to be the longest in the nineteenth century.

1892 James A. Herne's *Shore Acres*, his most successful play, premieres in Chicago.

Christopher Colombus, by M. M. A. Hartnedy, opens.

Yiddish actor Jacob Adler stars in Jacob Gordin's *The Jewish King Lear*.

Physical-education teacher James Naismith invents basketball for his students in YMCA training school in Springfield, Massachusetts.

Coca-Cola Co. is established in Georgia. General Electric incorporates.

Homestead Strike by Pennsylvania steelworkers erupts in violence.

First gasoline-powered tractor built in Iowa.

The first Ferris Wheel is built for the Chicago World's Fair.

Thomas Hardy's *Tess of the d'Urbervilles*.

Oscar Wilde's *The Picture of Dorian Gray*, his only novel.

Music mass-produced on records for first time.

A. Conan Doyle's *The Adventures of Sherlock Holmes*.

Oscar Wilde's *Lady Windermere's Fan*.

Henri de Toulouse-Lautrec's *At the Moulin Rouge*.

DATES	THEATRE EVENTS IN AMERICA	SELECTED HISTORICAL/CULTURAL EVENTS IN AMERICA	SELECTED HISTORICAL/CULTURAL EVENTS THROUGHOUT THE WORLD
1892		James J. "Gentleman Jim" Corbett knocks out John L. Sullivan in New Orleans, Louisiana, to become first boxing heavyweight champion under Marquis of Queensberry's rules.	Tchaikovsky's ballet *The Nutcracker Suite*.
1893	Steele MacKaye's colossal theatre experiment, the Spectatorium, fails in Chicago.	Grover Cleveland again elected president.	Swede Sven Hedin explores deserts of central Asia, Tibetan Plateau, and Himalayas (until 1938).
	Wild West show opens next to the World's Columbian Exposition in Chicago.	Business recession (1893–97); nearly 500 banks and 15,000 commercial firms fail.	New Zealand is first nation to give vote to women.
	Eleonora Duse appears in New York as Camille and begins first of four tours (last in 1924).	First practical American automobile built by businessmen Charles and Frank Duryea.	Kinetoscope (peep show) for showing early moving pictures to single viewer patented.
	Augustus Thomas's *In Mizzoura* vehicle for actor Nat Goodwin.		Art Nouveau in Europe.
			Verdi's last opera, *Falstaff*.
	Charles Frohman's Empire Theatre opens; becomes a "star factory."	Kellogg Company develops new cereal, shredded wheat (introduces corn flakes in 1906).	Oscar Wilde's *A Woman of No Importance* and *Salomé*.
	French's American Theatre opens on West 42nd Street.		
	Formation of the National Alliance of Theatrical and Stage Employees.	Cracker Jacks first sold in Chicago.	Artist Edvard Munch's *The Scream*.
	David Belasco and Franklin Fyles's *The Girl I Left Behind Me* produced by C. Frohman.	Black Maria, early film studio, built at Edison's New Jersey laboratory.	Arthur Wing Pinero's *The Second Mrs. Tanqueray*.
	"Little Egypt" (or similar peformer; may not have actually been her) tittilates visitors at the Chicago World's Fair with her "cootch" dance.	Henry Ford road-tests his first automobile.	Bernard Shaw's *Mrs Warren's Profession* is banned in England until 1924.

1894			
Ziegfeld enters show business by promoting strongman Eugen Sandow into a show business attraction at the Chicago World's Fair.	Edward McDowell's opera *Hamlet and Ophelia* in Boston.		Poet Paul Claudel's "L'Echange."
Bert Williams and George Walker form their black vaudeville act.	Lizzie Borden on trial in Fall River, Massachusetts.		Englebert Humperdink's opera *Hansel and Gretel.*
Charles Townsend's *The Golden Gulch,* an unflattering portrait of Native Americans in three acts.			Aubrey Beardsley illustrates a new edition of Sir Thomas Malory's *Morte d'Arthur* (1485).
First critic expressly for vaudeville, "Chicot," begins long career.			
Depression closes many western theatres.			
Augustin Daly opens Daly's Theatre in London.	Treaty with China calls for end to immigration of Chinese laborers in United States.		French army officer Alfred Dreyfus wrongly accused of treason charges in the Dreyfus Affair.
Richard Mansfield introduces Bernard Shaw to the United States, appearing as Bluntschli in *Arms and the Man,* written the same year.	Coxey's Army, a group of 400 unemployed demonstrators led by Jacob Coxey, march unsuccessfully to Washington, D.C., demanding federal help.		First skeletal remains of *Homo erectus* discovered at Java.
Mrs. Minnie Maddern Fiske stars as Nora in Ibsen's *A Doll's House,* bringing his work to the U.S. stage successfully for the first time.	Pullman Strike begins in Chicago; ended by federal troops.		Sino-Japanese War between Japan and China for control of Korea (continues 1895).
Keith builds the Boston Colonial, considered by some the first venue exclusively for vaudeville.			
Boston Museum stock company disbands.	Painter Mary Cassatt's *La Toilette.*		W. B. Yeats's play *The Land of Heart's Desire* in London.
Victor Herbert's first Comic Opera, *Prince Ananias.*			

DATES	THEATRE EVENTS IN AMERICA	SELECTED HISTORICAL/CULTURAL EVENTS IN AMERICA	SELECTED HISTORICAL/CULTURAL EVENTS THROUGHOUT THE WORLD
1894	George Lederer's *The Passing Show*, considered the first successful revue ("review" used at first) in the United States.	First Hershey bar is sold.	
	Joe Weber and Lew Fields, the most famous double Dutch (German) act in vaudeville during the 1880s and early 1890s play their first legitimate theatre engagements.	Boston Nationals outfielder Hugh Duffy slugs season batting average of .438, highest yet on record in major leagues.	Aubrey Beardsley illustrates an English version of Wilde's *Salomé.*
	The foremost British male impersonator, Vesta Tilley, makes her first trip to the United States.	Development of the Kinetoscope Private Viewer.	Emile Zola's *Les Trois Villes.*
	Billboard, theatre trade paper, begins publication.	Sears Roebuck mail-order service begins.	
	Nudity in form of poses plastiques given veneer of culture in Eduard Kilyani's *1492.*		
	New York's Proctor Pleasure Palace opens.		
1895	David Belasco's Civil War melodrama *The Heart of Maryland.*	First U.S. automobile company founded by Charles Duryea.	First commercially successful movie projector developed in France.
	Nate Salsbury's *Black America*, the epitome of the black minstrel show.	Stephen Crane's *The Red Badge of Courage.*	Oscar Wilde's *The Importance of Being Earnest.* This same year, Wilde is imprisoned for a sex scandal involving his young friend and sometime lover, Lord Alfred Douglas.
	First films seen as vaudeville (most often used as "chasers," or dumb acts at end of bills).	"The Yellow Kid," the first comic-strip character, debuts in the *New York World.*	William Roentgen uses x-rays to photograph bones and internal organs of patients for first time.

1896	E. H. Sothern stars in *The Prisoner of Zenda*.	Painter John Singer Sargent's *Mountain Fire*.	Revolution of 1895 in Ecuador.
	Steele MacKaye's Scenitorium in Chicago.	First pizzeria opens in New York City.	Italy mounts failed invasion of Ethiopia.
	John W. Isham adds story line to olio specialties in *The Octoroons*, an all-black show.	King C. Gillette develops the safety razor.	Thomas Hardy's *Jude the Obscure*.
	William Gillette's Civil War spy melodrama, *Secret Service*, premieres in Philadelphia.		H. G. Wells's *The Time Machine*.
	May Irwin stars in *The Widow Jones*.		First full performance of Tchaikovsky's *Swan Lake* in St. Petersburg.
	Oscar Hammerstein I's Olympia (theatre and music hall) launches Broadway district in Times Square [Longacre] area.		Kiel Canal, originally Kaiser Wilhelm Canal, connects North and Baltic seas.
	Harry Houdini gains prominence as escapologist.		U.S. President McKinley tries to arbitrate a border dispute between Britain and Venezuela in British Guiana.
	Twin City Scenic Studio opens in Minneapolis–St. Paul (last studio closed in Detroit, 1937).		
	Theatrical Syndicate organized under the leadership of Klaw and Erlanger (with four others).	In *Plessy v. Ferguson*, U.S. Supreme Court upholds separate accommodations for races on railroads.	Successful model of diesel engine developed.
	Yiddish actress Bertha Kalish emigrates to United States.	Paul Dunbar's *Lyrics of Lowly Life*.	Henryk Sienkiewicz's *Quo Vadis?*
	Weber and Fields open Music Hall; present musical burlesques of current Broadway successes.	Agricultural chemist George Washington Carver develops methods to make worn-out cropland productive by growing peanuts and sweet potatoes.	A. E. Housman's *A Shropshire Lad*.
			Anton Chekhov's *The Seagull*.

DATES	THEATRE EVENTS IN AMERICA	SELECTED HISTORICAL/CULTURAL EVENTS IN AMERICA	SELECTED HISTORICAL/CULTURAL EVENTS THROUGHOUT THE WORLD
1896	Oscar Hammerstein brings a vaudeville act from Iowa, the Cherry Sisters, to the stage. Known infamously as the "vegetable girls," they are pelted by debris from the audience.	John Dewey founds elementary school in Chicago to experiment with progressive education ideas.	The first modern Olympic Games held in Athens, Greece.
	New York has seven vaudeville theatres.	Artist Winslow Homer's *All's Well*.	Vladimir Nemirovich-Danchenko's *The Worth of Life*.
	Dramatic sketches become the rage in vaudeville.	Manufacturer Ransom Olds builds his first car.	Alfred Jarry's revolutionary play, *Ubu Roi*.
	The Afro–American Opera Co. makes its first appearance at Frieberg's Opera House in Chicago.	American Presbyterian evangelist Billy Sunday begins preaching.	
	The ghost of actor John McCullough dressed in the garb of Hamlet is reported to have been seen for the first time at the National Theatre (Washington, D.C.).	First advice-to-lovelorn column, written under pseudonym Dorothy Dix, appears in *New Orleans Picayune*.	
	Actors' Society founded but unsuccessful in gaining standard contract.	Adolph S. Ochs buys failing *New York Times* and turns it into successful paper. "All the news that's fit to print" first appears 25 October 1896.	
	Kliegl brothers' theatrical lighting company founded.	Sousa composes "The Stars and Stripes Forever."	
1897	Circus and museum impresario P. T. Barnum dies.	William McKinley inaugurated president.	First attempt to fly to North Pole is made in balloon by Swedish scientist S. A. Andrée. Remains of the party are not found until 1930.
	Elsie Janis, one of the biggest stars in vaudeville, debuts.	Gold rush in Klondike begins.	China leases Hong Kong to Britain for ninety-nine years.

1898

Mansfield plays Dick Dudgeon in Shaw's *The Devil's Disciple.*

Gaslight-illuminated marquees created by Strauss Signs.

Maude Adams first appears in Barrie's *The Little Minister.*

Bob Cole and Billy Johnson's original black musical *A Trip to Coontown* appears on Broadway.

Paul Laurence Dunbar and Will Marion Cook's *Clorindy; or, The Origin of the Cakewalk* premieres in a roof garden on Broadway.

Lew Dockstader and George Primrose begin most spectacular blackface minstrel troupe at turn of the century.

Madison's Budget, the first gag paper for professional comedians, is printed.

Musicians' Mutual Protection Union strikes in Seattle; first and only successful union strike in vaudeville history.

First Stanley steamer developed in Massachusetts.

Gugliemo Marconi achieves radio transmission over long distances.

World's largest refracting telescope in use at Yerkes Observatory.

First regular comic strip appears in *New York Journal.*

Boston subway opened.

Housing for Library of Congress completed.

Goodyear Tire and Rubber incorporates.

Spanish–American War breaks out; Theodore "Teddy" Roosevelt leads his Rough Riders at the Battle of San Juan Hill.

James Thornton's song "When You Were Sweet Sixteen."

United States gains control of Philippines and Cuba.

Holland VI, first successful military submarine, designed.

Bram Stoker's *Dracula.*

First turbine-powered steamship, *Turbinia,* is launched.

Shaw's *Candida.*

Theodore Herzl convenes first World Zionist Congress in Basel, Switzerland.

Oscar Wilde's biographical long poem *The Ballad of Reading Gaol.*

Nemirovich-Danchenko and Constantin Stanislavski found the Moscow Art Theatre.

Philippines ceded to United States from Spain for $20 million.

Russian physiologist Ivan Pavlov begins study on conditioned reflexes, using animals.

Paul Gauguin's *Two Tahitian Women.*

H. G. Wells's *The War of the Worlds.*

The Seagull, directed by Constantin Stanislavski at the Moscow Art Theatre, does away with most traditional histrionic techniques and is considered a success that modernizes the theatre, unlike staging two years earlier in St. Petersburg.

DATES	THEATRE EVENTS IN AMERICA	SELECTED HISTORICAL/CULTURAL EVENTS IN AMERICA	SELECTED HISTORICAL/CULTURAL EVENTS THROUGHOUT THE WORLD
1898	Klondike gold rush reopens many West Coast theatres.	Henry James's *Turn of the Screw.*	Radium and polonium discovered by Marie and Pierre Curie.
	Clyde Fitch's *The Moth and the Flame.*	Pepsi-Cola developed.	Peking University founded.
	Lottie Blair Parker's *Way Down East.*	First ragtime piano composition (by Scott Joplin) appears in sheet music form.	
	Joe Smith and Charlie Dale begin partnership as a blackface act.		
1899	*Ben-Hur* directed by Ben Teal, the first supercolossal production, complete with live horses on treadmills.	Supreme Court rules that segregated schools for whites and blacks are legal.	Boer War (1899–1902). British defeat rebels in bloody conflict in South Africa.
	Percy Williams builds vaudeville theatre the Orpheum in New York (later controlled by Keith–Albee).	Thorstein Veblen's *The Theory of the Leisure Class.*	Aspirin introduced in powdered form in Germany.
	George M. Cohan quits vaudeville and begins musical comedy career.	Special courts for juveniles established.	French filmmaker Georges Méliès, who pioneered stop-action camera techniques, expands on original peep-show format to film fictional narratives.
	Augustus Thomas's *Arizona.*	Kate Chopin's novel *The Awakening.*	
	David Belasco's *Zaza* with Mrs. Leslie Carter.	Campbell introduces canned, condensed soup.	
	Hebrew Actors' Union founded; recognized with collective bargaining in 1902.		
	Clyde Fitch's *Barbara Frietchie.*		
	James A. Herne's *Sag Harbor.*		
	William Gillette's *Sherlock Holmes* stars the playwright in title role.		
	There are eighty-seven productions for the 1899–1900 season.		

1900s	Comic acts in vaudeville shift from rough slapstick to character acts with emphasis on rapid-fire jokes.		
	Music publishers begin paying top stars to plug their songs by putting them in acts.		
	From 1900 to 1928 some eighty theatres are built in New York's Broadway district, 39th to 54th streets.	Farmers use sprinkler irrigation.	
1900	John Havlin and Edward Stair form popular-priced theatrical circuit, largely in Midwest; dissolved in 1915.		Umberto Cagni of Duke of Abruzzi's Italian expedition reaches record of 86°34' north latitude.
	Keith-Albee seek to monopolize first-class vaudeville through the Vaudeville Managers' Protective Association of the United States.	L. Frank Baum's novel *The Wonderful Wizard of Oz*.	
		Theodore Dreiser's *Sister Carrie*.	Italian King Humbert I assassinated by anarchist.
	William Morris head of the largest independent booking agency in the United States.	Catholic Church has 12 million members, following rapid growth among immigrants.	Boxer Rebellion in China (1900–1901).
	The White Rats, a vaudeville performers' union, formed by George Fuller Golden on 1 June.	Frank Lloyd Wright becomes famous for designing houses in "prairie style," characterized by low, horizontal lines and use of natural earth colors.	Photocopying machine invented in France.
	English import, *Florodora*, with Willie Edouin, runs for more than five hundred performances.		
	Belasco's *Madame Butterfly* with Blanche Bates.	A New Haven, Connecticut, restaurant owner invents the hamburger.	Joseph Conrad's *Lord Jim*.
	Shubert brothers begin "Independent Movement" to challenge Syndicate.	Vendor sells frankfurters from his cart, calling them "hot dachsund sausages," from which "hot dogs" is derived.	Sigmund Freud's *The Interpretation of Dreams*.

DATES	THEATRE EVENTS IN AMERICA	SELECTED HISTORICAL/CULTURAL EVENTS IN AMERICA	SELECTED HISTORICAL/CULTURAL EVENTS THROUGHOUT THE WORLD
1900	Censorious legal action taken against Fitch's *Sapho*. *The Theatre* (in 1917 changed to *Theatre Magazine*) founded (survives to 1931).	Baseball cards are packaged as bonus with cigarettes. There are 13,824 automobiles owned by private citizens. Former sportswriter Byron "Ban" Johnson announces plans for an American League baseball organization. Carry Nation, temperance advocate, denounces saloons and liquor and supports prohibition laws.	Palace of Knossos, center of Minoan civilization on Crete, located by Arthur Evans.
1901	Jane Addams and Mrs. Laura Dainty Pelham found the Hull-House Players in Chicago (to 1941), believing that good plays performed by amateurs could have a "salutary influence on the community." White Rats attempt strike against Keith–Albee control but are unsuccessful. Clyde Fitch's *The Climbers*. After a fire, New Orleans's St. Charles Theatre rebuilt as vaudeville house. First Spooner Stock Company founded in Brooklyn; survives until 1918. Phrase "Great White Way" coined. Shubert brothers open first Broadway production, *The Brixton Burglary*.	Teddy Roosevelt becomes president after the assassination of William McKinley. U.S. Steel incorporates. Marconi sends first transatlantic wireless radio message. Frank Norris's novel *The Octopus*. The U.S. Socialist Party is founded. Scott Joplin composes "The Easy Winners."	Sigmund Freud's *The Psychopathology of Everyday Life*. Paul Gauguin's *Golden Bodies*. Rudyard Kipling's *Kim*. Thomas Mann's *Buddenbrooks*. Samuel Butler's novel *Erewhon*. Practical technique for artificial insemination developed in Russia. Safety razor invented. Chekhov's *The Three Sisters*.

1902	Drama critic Henry Clapp publishes an overview of late-nineteenth-century Boston theatrical life.	Texaco organizes as The Texas Co.	Joseph Conrad's *Heart of Darkness*.
	Bert Williams and George Walker's black musical *In Dahomey* establishes them as stars.	Winslow Homer's *Early Morning after a Storm at Sea*.	André Gide's *The Immoralist*.
			Paul Gauguin's *Apparition*.
	Brander Matthews at Columbia University given title of Professor of Dramatic Literature, the first such post in the United States.	William James's *The Varieties of Religious Experience*.	William Butler Yeats and Lady Gregory's play *Cathleen ni Houlihan*. Strindberg's *A Dream Play*.
	Republic Theatre in New York opens (renamed Belasco).	American Anthropological Association (AAA) is founded; publishes journal *American Anthropologist*.	Russian playwright Maxim Gorky's *The Lower Depths*.
	Adaptation of Baum's *The Wizard of Oz* opens in Chicago with Montgomery and Stone; moves to New York following year.	Animal crackers are first sold in United States.	J. M. Barrie's play *The Admirable Crichton*.
		Brooklyn store owner develops the "teddy bear," named after President Roosevelt.	Aswan Dam built on Nile River in Egypt.
1903	Alexander Pantages builds the Crystal in Seattle.	J. C. Penney Co. begins.	Code of Hammurabi, first known set of laws, discovered engraved on tablets.
	First tour of Ben Greet Players from England company (continues until 1931).		Frenchman Georges Méliès's short film *A Trip to the Moon*.
	David Belasco and John Luther Long's *The Darling of the Gods*.		Hay-Bunau-Varilla Treaty grants United States rights to Panama Canal Zone.
	Children's Educational Theatre in New York, first venue designed especially for youth.	Era of "muckrakers" begins. Magazine and tabloid reporters expose corruption in business and politics.	Alaska boundary is set by joint Canadian–U.S. commission.
	Blanche Bates and George Arliss star in Belasco's *Sweet Kitty Bellairs*.	In *Champion v. Ames*, Supreme Court approves federal powers to prohibit as well as regulate commerce, thereby establishing so-called federal police power.	

DATES	THEATRE EVENTS IN AMERICA	SELECTED HISTORICAL/CULTURAL EVENTS IN AMERICA	SELECTED HISTORICAL/CULTURAL EVENTS THROUGHOUT THE WORLD
1903	Victor Herbert's musical *Babes in Toyland.*	Ford Motor Co. organizes.	Revolt establishes Panamanian independence from Columbia.
	Al and Harry Jolson join Joe Palmer to form a vaudeville trio.	Wright brothers achieve first successful powered flight of an aircraft at Kitty Hawk, North Carolina.	Russian socialists split into revolutionary Bolsheviks and gradualist Mensheviks.
	Actor Arnold Daly produces a highly successful version of Shaw's *Candida.*	Jack London's *The Call of the Wild.*	
	Raffi, an Armenian American drama group, forms in New York.	*The Life of an American Fireman* and *The Great Train Robbery* by Edwin Porter are first narrative films to portray successfully events occurring simultaneously at different locations.	J. M. Synge's *In the Shadow of the Glen.*
	Mrs. Fiske as Hedda Gabler. She and husband Harrison Grey Fiske lease Manhattan Theatre. Same year, Mary Shaw tours in *Ghosts.*	Boston Red Sox win the first World Series.	
	Iroquois Theatre Fire in Chicago on 30 December during Eddie Foy's performance in *Mr. Bluebeard.* Five hundred people die rushing to the exits.		
	Eva Tanguay introduces "I Don't Care" in *The Chaperones.*		
1904	George Ade's *The County Chairman,* followed next season by his *The College Widow.*	W. E. B. Du Bois's *The Souls of Black Folk.*	
	Comic Sam Bernard stars in *The Girl from Kay's.*	Mary Mallon – "Typhoid Mary" – found to be the carrier of the disease during a deadly epidemic in New York.	

Daniel Frohman opens (New) Lyceum Theatre on West 45th Street (Broadway's oldest operating theatre); Klaw and Erlanger open New Amsterdam on West 42nd Street.

George M. Cohan leaves vaudeville and writes and stars in musical *Little Johnny Jones*. Begins producing partnership with Sam H. Harris.

Arena publishes the influential symposium "A National Art Theatre for America."

Arnold Daly produces season of Shaw plays.

Winthrop Ames leader of art theatre movement at Boston's Castle Square Theatre.

Summer Chautauqua circuits begin; show business added soon thereafter.

David Warfield stars in Belasco's production of *The Music Master*.

E. A. Sothern and Julia Marlowe first appear together in *Romeo and Juliet*.

The Friars Club formed by theatrical press agents.

First ice-cream cone sold at Louisiana Purchase Exposition in St. Louis.

The Vanderbilt Cup Race, the first automobile-racing competition, on Long Island.

A woman is arrested in New York City for smoking a cigarette while riding in an open automobile.

Chekhov's *The Cherry Orchard*.

J. M. Synge's *Riders to the Sea*.

J. M. Barrie's *Peter Pan*.

Entente Cordiale resolves differences between Britain and France over colonial territories in Africa and the Far East.

Russo–Japanese War (into 1905).

Max Weber's *The Protestant Ethic and the Spirit of Capitalism*.

The Abbey Theatre in Dublin opens.

President Theodore Roosevelt proclaims his Roosevelt Corollary to the Monroe Doctrine, justifying intervention in Latin America on the basis of a U.S. responsibility to exercise an "international police power."

DATES	THEATRE EVENTS IN AMERICA	SELECTED HISTORICAL/CULTURAL EVENTS IN AMERICA	SELECTED HISTORICAL/CULTURAL EVENTS THROUGHOUT THE WORLD
1905	George Pierce Baker begins playwriting course English 47 at Harvard.	U.S. Supreme Court rules that minimum-wage laws are unconstitutional.	Canadian Northwest Territories region reorganized; provinces of Saskatchewan and Alberta formed.
	Shubert brothers begin seriously to challenge Klaw and Erlanger and the Syndicate.	Industrial Workers of the World (IWW), dubbed "Wobblies," founded to organize unskilled industrial laborers and dismantle capitalism.	Revolution of 1905. Shooting of demonstrators in St. Petersburg, Russia, begins period of strikes and political unrest.
	Maude Adams stars in Charles Frohman's production of *Peter Pan.*		Edward Gordon Craig's *The Art of the Theatre.*
	Shaw's *Mrs Warren's Profession* is a sensation in New York in October. Producer Daly and star arrested and acquitted.	First U.S. motion-picture theatre opens, in Pennsylvania.	Norway gains independence from Sweden.
	David Belasco's *The Girl of the Golden West.*	Forerunner of National Collegiate Athletic Association (NCAA) and football rules committee are founded.	Bernard Shaw's *Man and Superman* and *Major Barbara.*
	The theatrical trade paper *Variety* is founded by Sime Silverman.		
	Vaudeville dominates all popular entertainment forms.	Heavyweight Jim Jeffries retires undefeated.	
	The Hippodrome Theatre opens to house theatrical extravaganzas.	National Audobon Society meets for first time.	
	Julian Eltinge tours vaudeville and minstrel shows as a female impersonator.	Public outcry against increasing roughness of football follows season in which there are 18 deaths and 159 injuries in college competition.	
	Sam Scribner promotes clean burlesque with his Columbia burlesque circuit but faces racier competition from revues and vaudeville. Major competition comes from the Empire or Western Circuit.		
	Robert Motts opens the Pekin Theatre in Chicago, a mecca of black entertainment.	First "nickelodeon" (nickel theatre) opens in Pittsburgh.	

	Theatre	America	World
1906	George M. Cohan's *Forty-five Minutes from Broadway* with Fay Templeton.	San Francisco earthquake destroys four square miles of downtown district.	Norwegian polar explorer Roald Amundsen first European to navigate successfully through Northwest Passage.
	William C. DeMille's melodrama about Native Americans, *Strongheart*, opens to considerable success at the Hudson Theatre.	Playground and Recreation Association of America founded.	Simplon tunnel, longest railroad of its time (12.3 miles), links France and Italy.
	Langdon Mitchell's *The New York Idea.*	O. Henry's short story "The Gift of the Magi."	The Denshawi Affair, in which Egyptian natives are executed for the killing of a British army officer.
	William Vaughn Moody's *The Great Divide* with Margaret Anglin and Henry Miller.	Upton Sinclair's *The Jungle.*	British Labour Party formed.
	Keith and Albee found the United Booking Office (UBO) to handle bookings for the Keith and Orpheum circuits (and to control smaller independent circuits).	American inventor Reginald Aubrey Fessenden broadcasts first voice and music program via his wireless at Brant Rock, Massachusetts, on Christmas Eve.	John Galsworthy's play *The Silver Box.*
	Robert Motts establishes black theatre, the Pekin Stock Company, first in Chicago and later other Pekins in Cincinnati and Savannah.	The Rand School of Social Science is founded as Socialist Party organ for teaching of political and social science.	
	George Broadhurst's political melodrama *The Man of the Hour.*		
1907	Augustus Thomas's *The Witching Hour.*	Gulf Oil incorporates.	Pablo Picasso's *Les Demoiselles d'Avignon.*
	The Stuyvesant Theatre (current Belasco Theatre) opens.	John Sloan's *The Haymarket.*	
	The Charlotte Cushman Club in Philadelphia founded to offer lodging to actresses.		

DATES	THEATRE EVENTS IN AMERICA	SELECTED HISTORICAL/CULTURAL EVENTS IN AMERICA	SELECTED HISTORICAL/CULTURAL EVENTS THROUGHOUT THE WORLD
1907	Florenz Ziegfeld produces the *Follies of 1907*, the first in a series of annual revues.	*Three Weeks* by Elinor Glyn, a British novelist, causes scandal for its frank depictions of sexuality.	J. M. Synge's *Playboy of the Western World* and *The Tinker's Wedding*. The premiere of *Playboy* at the Abbey causes riots and outrage over the use of the term "shift."
	Franz Lehar's operetta *The Merry Widow* runs 416 performances at the New Amsterdam Theatre.		
	White Rats reorganized by Harry Mountford; Samuel Gompers gives them a national charter.	Democrats in Congress criticize government spending, which has doubled in past ten years to $1 billion per year.	*The Legend of the Invisible City of Kitezh and of the Maiden Fevrona*, opera by Nikolay Rimsky-Korsakov.
	Shuberts on 8 April declare an entertainment war on the Keith Circuit and the UBO but is unsuccessful.	William De Morgan's *Alice for Short*, Kate Douglas Wiggin's *New Chronicles of Rebecca*, W. J. Locke's *The Beloved Vagabond*, and Ellen Glasgow's *Wheel of Life* – all best-sellers.	Establishment of first day-care center, in Rome, by Italian educator Maria Montessori. Her teaching approach becomes known as Montessori Method.
	Mrs. Fiske as Rebecca West in Ibsen's *Rosmersholm*.		
	Playwright Martha Morton organizes Society of Dramatic Authors' Club because American Dramatists' Club refuses women members.		
	Clara Bloodgood appears as Becky Warder, role written for her by Clyde Fitch in his *The Truth*.		
	Blacks number 270 in vaudeville.		
1908	Edward Sheldon's *Salvation Nell*, with Mrs. Fiske, succeeds.	Bureau of Investigation, later FBI, established within Department of Justice.	Canadian Civil Service Commission established.
	Clyde Fitch's *Sapho*.		Gustav Klimt's painting *The Kiss*.

60

1909			
J. J. Shubert creates *The Mimic World* revue to compete with Ziegfeld's *Follies*.	In *Danbury Hatters case* (*Loewe v. Lawler*), Supreme Court rules against secondary boycott as restraining trade under Sherman Antitrust Act.	Robert E. Peary leads expedition to reach North Pole (6 April). American Frederick Cook claims to have reached it in 1908, however.	Kenneth Grahame's *The Wind in the Willows*.
5,000 nickelodeons nationwide, with twelve to eighteen showings a day, offer competition to live popular entertainment.	President Theodore Roosevelt holds conference to assess conservation of wildlife and natural resources.		
Seepage of blue material into vaudeville noted in public commentary.	Henry Ford introduces the Model T. It costs $850.		
Brooklyn Academy of Music constructs first multiple-theatre facility in the United States.	Mother's Day (10 May) first celebrated in the United States.		
30,000 mourn death of Yiddish playwright Avrom Goldfadn in Brooklyn.	National Board of Censorship formed.		
	D. W. Griffith directs his first film, *The Adventures of Dollie*.		
	Black stevedore Jack Johnson becomes heavyweight boxing champion.		
Opening on 6 November of the New Theatre, Central Park West, an art theatre devoted to permanent repertory, under the direction of Winthrop Ames. Fails within two seasons.	Sigmund Freud visits the United States; gives a series of lectures at Clark College in Worcester, Massachusetts.	Picasso's *Harlequin*.	
Edward Sheldon writes *The Nigger* for an all-white cast, to show the plight of blacks at the turn of the century.	William Taft inaugurated president.		
Belasco presents Eugene Walter's *The Easiest Way* with Frances Starr.	Sculptor Frederick Remington dies.	John Galsworthy's play *Strife*.	
The Dolly sisters become instant successes in vaudeville with their dancing routines.	Over 2 million Americans own stocks.	F. T. Marinetti publishes "The Founding and Manifesto of Futurism."	

DATES	THEATRE EVENTS IN AMERICA	SELECTED HISTORICAL/CULTURAL EVENTS IN AMERICA	SELECTED HISTORICAL/CULTURAL EVENTS THROUGHOUT THE WORLD
1909	First of Scottish music-hall performer Harry Lauder's twenty-two U.S. tours (last in 1932).		
	The Drama League is founded in Evanston, Illinois, by a ladies' literary society.	Jigsaw puzzles become enormously popular.	
	Dramatist Clyde Fitch dies at age forty-three, leaving behind thirty-three original plays and twenty-two adaptations and dramatizations; his *The City* produced posthumously.	The NAACP (National Association for the Advancement of Colored People) is founded.	
	Percy Mackaye's *The Scarecrow*.		
	William Winter retires as *New York Tribune* theatre critic; George Jean Nathan becomes critic for *Smart Set*.		
	Two-thousand small-time vaudeville houses in the United States begin to take over motion-picture-house business.		
	Toby, rustic "silly kid" role of tent shows, developed most likely by Fred Wilson.		
	Vaudevillian Blanche Ring debuts her most famous role, *The Yankee Girl*.		
	Providence, Rhode Island's theatre club The Players is founded (still in operation).		
1910–19	Small-time vaudeville strives for class and gains in popularity.		

62

1910

Hippodromes and airdomes spring up across America, capitalizing on vaudeville's success.

Albee begins to buy out competing vaudeville circuits. (Keith dies in 1914.)

R. H. Burnside begins fourteen-year career as director of spectacles at New York's Hippodrome.

Twenty-two vaudeville theatres operating in New York.

Ed Gallagher and Al Shean, Gus Van and Joe Schenck, form vaudeville teams.

Victor Herbert's operetta *Naughty Marietta*.

Ziegfeld discovers Fanny Brice in a burlesque show.

Seattle theatre pioneer John Cort forms National Theatre Owners' Association to exclude the Syndicate and the Shuberts on the West Coast.

Globe Theatre opens (in 1958 becomes Lunt–Fontanne).

William Vaughn Moody's *The Faith Healer*.

Variety blacklisted for all UBO acts by Albee.

Marie Dressler stars in *Tillie's Nightmare*.

Rachel Crothers's *A Man's World*.

International arbitration court settles Canadian–U.S. differences over Atlantic fishing rights.

First celebration of Father's Day, in Spokane, Washington.

Union of South Africa formed by uniting Cape of Good Hope, Transvaal, Orange Free State, and Natal.

Boy Scouts of America is incorporated.

Bertrand Russell's *Principia Mathematica*.

Artist Egon Schiele's *Dual Self-Portrait*.

Expressionist drama appears in Germany.

Freud and associates form International Psychoanalytic Association.

DATES	THEATRE EVENTS IN AMERICA	SELECTED HISTORICAL/CULTURAL EVENTS IN AMERICA	SELECTED HISTORICAL/CULTURAL EVENTS THROUGHOUT THE WORLD
1910	Jessie Bonstelle begins long career in Detroit theatre.		Rabinadrath Tagore publishes his most popular collection of poems, *Gintanjali.*
1911	William A. Brady produces *The Boss* by Edward Sheldon; with actress wife Grace George Brady opens the Playhouse on West 48th.	Ambrose Bierce's *The Devil's Dictionary.*	Henri Matisse's *The Red Studio.*
	David Warfield stars in Belasco's *The Return of Peter Grimm.*	Frances Hodgson Burnett's *The Secret Garden.*	Porfirio Diaz overthrown by Francisco Indalecio Madero. The Mexican Revolution ensues.
	Otis Skinner stars as Hajj in *Kismet.*	Edith Wharton's *Ethan Frome.*	Giorgio de Chirico's *Nostalgia of the Infinite.*
	Vaudeville Managers' Protective Association founded (VMPA).	The Urban League, a black social welfare organization, is founded.	
	Julian Eltinge's biggest hit in drag, *The Fascinating Widow* (plays four female and two male roles).		Carl Jung's *Psychology of the Unconscious.*
	Sixteen percent of New York's population attends a vaudeville theatre each week (700,000 persons in forty theatres).		
	The George M. Cohan Theatre opens.		Ernest Rutherford suggests model of atom consisting of nucleus surrounded by electrons.
	The Folies-Bergères, a restaurant theatre, founded in New York City.		Italo–Turkish War (ends 1912).
	The Winter Garden Theatre (second of that name) opens in New York.		
	Bothwell Browne, female impersonator, stars in the major musical *Miss Jack.*		
	The Teatro Hidalgo, an Hispanic theatre, opens on 10 September with its performance of *Zarzuel El Punao de Rosas.*		

1912

The Irish Players of Dublin tour the United States for the first time.

Sophie Tucker introduces "Some of These Days."

New Theatre's final production is Mary Austin's drama of Native American life, *The Arrow Maker.*

Wisconsin Dramatic Society founded in Madison and Milwaukee.

Philadelphia's Plays and Players, theatre club; still in operation.

Augustus Thomas answers Rachel Crothers with *As a Man Thinks.*

Organization of Authors' League of America, now Dramatists' Guild, to give legal protection to playwrights.

Maurice Browne's Chicago Little Theatre; Mrs. Lyman Gale's Toy Theatre in Boston; Arnold Arvold's Little Country Theatre in Fargo, North Dakota; San Francisco's The Players Club – all founded.

The number of medium-priced vaudeville theatres rises to 1,000, with an additional 4,000 small-time houses throughout the United States.

Max Reinhardt's company opens *Sumurun* at the Casino Theatre, introducing New Stagecraft to United States.

Winthrop Ames builds Little Theatre (now the Helen Hayes).

William James's *Essays in Radical Empiricism.*

French-made *Queen Elizabeth* becomes first popular full-length feature film in the United States.

Universal Pictures formed by mergers.

Marcel Duchamp's *Nude Descending a Staircase.*

Balkan Wars (1912–13), two wars that arouse nationalistic fervor in Eastern Europe and contribute to outbreak of World War I.

British liner *Titanic* collides with iceberg in North Atlantic (14–15 April); 1,513 die.

DATES	THEATRE EVENTS IN AMERICA	SELECTED HISTORICAL/CULTURAL EVENTS IN AMERICA	SELECTED HISTORICAL/CULTURAL EVENTS THROUGHOUT THE WORLD
1912	The Negro Players of New York is founded.	Mack Sennett's Keystone Kops films.	Thomas Mann's *Death in Venice.*
	Harvard Professor G. P. Baker establishes Workshop 47 as a laboratory for plays written in English 47.	Grand Central Station in New York City opens.	Marines land in Nicaragua and Honduras to protect banana barons; occupy the country until 1933.
	The Cort Theatre opens with J. Hartley Manners's *Peg O' My Heart* starring Laurette Taylor.	Campfire Girls and Girl Scouts are organized.	Bernard Shaw's *Pygmalion.*
	Beginnings of what becomes Theatre Owners' Booking Association (TOBA), chain of theatres for black entertainers.		Emile Durkheim's *Elementary Forms of Religious Life.*
	Eddie Cantor tours with Gus Edward's *Kid Kaberet*; includes young Georgie Jessel.		
	To better their revue competitors, burlesque performers begin to "strip" on stage.		Roald Amundsen first man to reach South Pole. British explorer Robert Falcon Scott reaches it thirty-five days after; dies with four companions of starvation and cold on return trip.
	P. J. Lowery's Circus Band, a sideshow attraction with the Hagenback and Wallace Circus, becomes a popular black musical group.		
	Comedians Willie and Eugene Howard begin legitimate career in revues.		
	Belasco's *The Governor's Lady* replicates a Child's restaurant on stage.		
1913	Actors' Equity Association is founded; first president actor-singer Francis Wilson.	Woodrow Wilson becomes twenty-eighth president.	D. H. Lawrence's *Sons and Lovers.*

The American Pageant Association founded (lasts into 1920s).	First Kewpie doll manufactured.	Marc Chagall's *The Musician.*
Shubert brothers open the Booth and Sam S. Shubert theatres, forming western wall of Shubert Alley.		Jacques Copeau founds the Vieux-Colombier.
Longacre Theatre built on West 48th Street.	Sixteenth Amendment to Constitution ratified, giving Congress power to impose income taxes.	Marcel Proust's *Remembrance of Things Past* begun (completed in 1927).
Martin Beck builds the Palace Theatre, the mecca for vaudevillians (ultimately controlled by Keith–Albee).	Federal income tax instituted.	Bernard Shaw's *Heartbreak House.*
Doris Keane stars in Sheldon's *Romance.*	The Armory Show in Greenwich Village, featuring modernist paintings, causes uproar.	
Actress Sarah Bernhardt appears at the Palace in May (at salary of $1,000 per night) and gives new venue respectability and currency. Also Horace Goldin is first conjuror to play this venue.		Igor Stravinsky's *The Rite of Spring.*
Eugene O'Neill copyrights his first play, *A Wife for Life.*	First modern bra developed by New York socialite Mary Phelps Jacobs.	Sax Rohmer publishes the first of his Fu Manchu novels.
Blurring history and drama, the Paterson Strike Pageant of 1913 is staged, reenacting the strike then taking place in Paterson, New Jersey, for an audience of about 15,000.		
Censorious legal action taken against George Scarborough's *The Lure.*		
George M. Cohan's *Seven Keys to Baldpate.*		
1914 First department of theatre founded at Carnegie Institute of Technology (now Carnegie–Mellon).	Red and green traffic lights utilized for first time in Cleveland, Ohio.	Archduke Francis Ferdinand assassinated in Bosnia by Serbian nationalist (28 June); Austria declares war on Serbia (28 July); World War I begins.

DATES	THEATRE EVENTS IN AMERICA	SELECTED HISTORICAL/CULTURAL EVENTS IN AMERICA	SELECTED HISTORICAL/CULTURAL EVENTS THROUGHOUT THE WORLD
1914	The Princess Theatre (New York City) is founded.	American Society of Composers, Authors, and Publishers (ASCAP) founded.	The U.S.-built Panama Canal opens.
	O'Neill enters George Pierce Baker's Workshop 47 at Harvard.	Federal Trade Commission organized.	James Joyce's *Dubliners*.
	Performers' salaries in vaudeville cut because of the influx of foreign acts.	Robert Frost's poems "Mending Wall" and "The Death of the Hired Man."	Germany invades Luxembourg (1 Aug.).
	Director Arthur Hopkins has first success with Elmer Rice's first play, *On Trial*, with Robert Edmond Jones's first Broadway-designed scenery.	Paramount Pictures founded as film-distribution outlet for a number of film-production companies.	Russia invades Prussia (13 Aug.).
		Luxury movie theatre, Strand (3,300 seats), opens on Broadway.	Battle of Frontiers (14–25 Aug.): French offensive is broken; troops bear heavy losses and are forced to evacuate Lorraine.
		Margaret Sanger indicted and ordered to leave the country for sending birth-control information through the mail.	First Battle of Marne: German attack on France falters twenty-five miles short of Paris.
		U.S. troops invade Mexico.	
1915	The Washington Square Players, based in New York and led by Lawrence Langner, produce the plays of Ibsen, Shaw, Chekhov, and new American talents.	*The New Republic* is founded.	W. Somerset Maugham's *Of Human Bondage*.
		Marcus Garvey's Universal Negro Improvement Association (UNIA) formed.	
		Edgar Rice Burroughs publishes *Tarzan of the Apes*.	
		Edgar Lee Master's *Spoon River Anthology*.	

The Provincetown Players is founded in Massachusetts and includes Susan Glaspell and George Cram Cook's *Suppressed Desires* on first bill.

Robert Edmond Jones's design for *The Man Who Married a Dumb Wife* promotes New Stagecraft.

Theatre impresario Charles Frohman perishes aboard the *Lusitania*.

The Lafayette Players, all-black acting ensemble, premieres in New York, founded by Anita Bush.

The Neighborhood Playhouse founded, a pioneering Off-Broadway theatre, founded by Alice and Irene Lewisohn.

Set designer Joseph Urban joins the *Ziegfeld Follies*.

Oscar Hammerstein's Victoria Theatre, known as the "freak house," closes, after a decade of success under Willie Hammerstein.

The new radio begins hiring vaudeville stars.

Boston Hippodrome is the first theatre in America to offer parking (free).

Sime Silverman of *Variety* and Albee negotiate and blacklist is lifted from the paper.

Alfred A. Knopf publishing house founded.

D. W. Griffith's film *Birth of a Nation*.

Hollywood becomes the center of American moviemaking by about this time.

The second incarnation of the Ku Klux Klan – the "Invisible Empire, Knights of the Ku Klux Klan, Inc." – born, lasting until 1944. William J. "Colonel" Simmons, a former Methodist circuit preacher, is responsible for the group's revival.

Sam Lucas is the first black to play a lead in a motion picture, *Uncle Tom's Cabin*.

T. S. Eliot's "The Love Song of J. Alfred Prufrock."

Franz Kafka's *The Metamorphosis*.

Marcel Duchamp's first Dada-style paintings seen.

Disastrous Gallipoli campaign in Turkey begins 19 February with landings by Allies.

German submarine sinks liner *Lusitania* 7 May off Irish coast; 1,195 passengers and crew are killed.

30,000 die in Avezzano, Italy, earthquake.

U.S. Marines land in Haiti and put down violent rebellions; they occupy the country until 1934.

DATES	THEATRE EVENTS IN AMERICA	SELECTED HISTORICAL/CULTURAL EVENTS IN AMERICA	SELECTED HISTORICAL/CULTURAL EVENTS THROUGHOUT THE WORLD
1915	Controversial and thesis one-act plays become popular in vaudeville.		
	Jerome Kern and Guy Bolton's musical *Very Good Eddie* (one of the "Princess Musicals" produced by Elisabeth Marbury).		
	The Knickerbocker Players organized in Philadelphia.		
	Granville Barker productions seen at Wallack's (New Stage Society of New York).		
	Shaw's *Major Barbara* produced by William A. Brady.		
	Folksbiene, longest-surviving Yiddish theatre in New York (still active), begins long history.		
1916	Provincetown Players produce first play by Eugene O'Neill, *Bound East for Cardiff*, and Glaspell's *Trifles*; in the fall move to New York.		Mexican rebel leader Pancho Villa raids Columbus, New Mexico.
	Sheldon Cheney founds the magazine *Theatre Arts* (first quarterly and then monthly).	John Dewey's *Democracy and Education*.	Secret Sykes–Picot Agreement provides for dividing up Ottoman Empire after World War I.
	Le Petit Théâtre du Vieux Carré, New Orleans's oldest modern performing-arts organization, is founded.	First U.S. supermarkets open in Tennessee.	Easter Rebellion in Ireland protests lack of home rule.

1917	Late fall White Rats strike vaudeville managers, in support of stagehands; managers (Keith–Albee in particular) counter with reactivation of VMPA (see 1911), formation of National Vaudeville Artists (a company union), and establish a blacklist.	General John Pershing sent into Mexico to pursue Pancho Villa.	Completion of 5,787-mile Trans-Siberian Railroad linking Moscow and Vladivostok, Russia.
	Chekhov's *The Seagull* produced professionally by Washington Square Players.	D. W. Griffith's film *Intolerance.*	Rasputin assassinated.
	Sam Hume's Arts and Crafts Theatre in Detroit and Frederick McConnell's Cleveland Play House founded.	United States purchases the Virgin Islands from Denmark for $25 million.	James Joyce's *A Portrait of the Artist as a Young Man.*
	Clare Kummer's *Good Gracious Annabelle!*		Dada artist Hans Arp's *Head of Tzara.*
	Will Rogers first appears in the *Ziegfeld Follies*; Ned Washburn directs the first of six editions of the revue.		U.S. Marines land in Santo Domingo, Dominican Republic, and occupy the country until 1924.
	The Broadhurst Theatre, commemorating English-born playwright, built by the Shuberts.	Frozen-food process developed by Clarence Birdseye.	Russian Revolution: Bolsheviks seize power after Czar Nicholas abdicates. Vladimir Ilyich Lenin in power as Soviet Communist Party head.
	The Morosco and Plymouth theatres are built.	Buster Keaton stars in *The Butcher Boy.*	Georg Kaiser's *From Morn to Midnight.*
	Fred and Adele Astaire's Broadway debut in revue *Over the Top.*		New Mexican Constitution is enacted; provides for agrarian reforms and separation of church and state.
	"Over There Theatres" formed by vaudevillians for the purpose of entertaining American troops overseas.		British occupy Palestine and issue Balfour Doctrine supporting Jewish national homeland.
	Shift to more movie theatre seats than vaudeville seats.		

DATES	THEATRE EVENTS IN AMERICA	SELECTED HISTORICAL/CULTURAL EVENTS IN AMERICA	SELECTED HISTORICAL/CULTURAL EVENTS THROUGHOUT THE WORLD
1917	Jacques Copeau's Vieux-Colombier Company residency at Old Garrick Theatre.		Colonel T. E. Lawrence takes Aqaba, inspiring Arab revolt against Turks.
	Vaudevillian Belle Baker's receipts tops those of all name performers in New York's Keith theatres.		Dutch dancer Mata Hari is executed in France on charges of spying.
	Eddie Cantor first appears in the *Ziegfeld Follies*.		First Americans in combat on Western Front in October.
	Mae Desmond Players, "popular-priced" stock company, founded; greatest success in Philadelphia in the 1920s.		Germany informs President Wilson on 1 February that unrestricted submarine warfare will be resumed.
	Raymond Hitchcock begins *Hitchy-Koo* revues (through 1920).		
1918	*Why Marry?* by Jesse Lynch Williams (opened 1917) wins first Pulitzer Prize for drama.	Socialist Eugene Debs is jailed under 1917 Espionage Act.	Women's suffrage enacted in Great Britain.
	Lionel Barrymore stars as Milt Shanks in Augustus Thomas's highly successful *The Copperhead*.	President Wilson presents his Fourteen Points, peace proposals advanced at Paris Peace Conference after World War I.	Former Czar Nicholas executed by Bolsheviks.
			In Red Terror, Communists murder tens of thousands of opponents after an attempt to assassinate Lenin.
	The Yiddish Art Theatre founded by Maurice Schwartz (Irving Place Theatre).	First U.S. airmail service between New York and Washington, D.C.	Mutiny by German sailors becomes full-scale revolt against monarchy.
	First black straight act (that is, non-comic), Sissle and Blake, appears on a vaudeville stage.	Earliest crop dusting by airplane recorded in the United States.	Czechoslovakia emerges as new nation in Europe under Treaty of Versailles.
	The Finnish Brotherhood League of Seattle, Washington, begins performing one-act plays and full-length productions of Finnish drama, like Teuvo Rakkala's	Raggedy Ann dolls first go on sale.	Yugoslavia created from former Austro–Hungarian lands of Serbia, Slovenia, Croatia, Bosnia, Herzegovina, Montenegro, Macedonia, and Kosovo.

1919			
Tukkijoella and Minna Canth's *Murtovarkaus*.	Willa Cather's *My Antonia*.		Baltic War of Liberation (1918–20). Estonia, Latvia, and Lithuania gain independence from Russia.
United Scenic Artists founded.			British occupy Ottoman territory that becomes Iraq.
Frank Bacon and Winchell Smith's *Lightnin'* begins three-year run.			Armistice ends fighting of World War I on 11 November.
Theatre named after vaudevillian Nora Bayes (later Forty-fourth Street Theatre).			Lytton Strachey's *Eminent Victorians*.
Pasadena Playhouse founded in California.			Tristan Tzara's *Dada Manifesto*.
Annie Russell retires to head drama program at Rollins College, Florida.			
Washington Square Players transformed into the Theatre Guild on 19 December, led by Lawrence Langner, Philip Moeller, and Theresa Helburn.	Labor unrests rock nation.		Bauhaus founded in Germany by Walter Gropius.
Avery Hopwood's *The Gold Diggers*.	Prohibition amendment (18th) ratified.		Spartacist revolt in Berlin.
Actors' Equity stages massive strike, demanding improved working conditions and unionization of acting profession.	Sherwood Anderson's *Winesburg, Ohio*.		Peace Conference at Versailles.
La, La Lucille is produced, George Gershwin's first complete musical score.	H. L. Mencken's *The American Language*.		
Produced by John Murray Anderson, *Greenwich Village Follies*, first of a series ending in 1928, applies New Stagecraft to the revue.	Austrian American violinist-composer Fritz Kreisler's *Apple Blossoms*.		Ireland granted home rule (it becomes Irish Free State in 1922). Northern Ireland created.
Booth Tarkington's *Clarence* stars Alfred Lunt and a young Helen Hayes.			Finland gains independence from Russia.

DATES	THEATRE EVENTS IN AMERICA	SELECTED HISTORICAL/CULTURAL EVENTS IN AMERICA	SELECTED HISTORICAL/CULTURAL EVENTS THROUGHOUT THE WORLD
1919	Brooks Costume Company becomes dominant theatrical costume shop.		
	St. Louis Municipal Outdoor Theatre built.	The "Black Sox" bribery scandal upends baseball.	
	Zoë Akins's *Déclassée* (her greatest success), with Ethel Barrymore.		
	Jewish Art Theatre founded by Jacob Ben-Ami.	A mass migration of black citizens to the North begins.	
	Ringling Bros. and Barnum & Bailey Circus created.		
	Pat Rooney Jr. introduces "The Daughters of Rosie O'Grady" at the Palace.	Race riots in Chicago.	
	George White produces first of thirteen revues (*Scandals*).	Jazz arrives in Europe.	
1920	Eugene O'Neill's *Beyond the Horizon*, written in 1918, wins Pulitzer Prize.	Nineteenth Amendment to Constitution is ratified, giving women right to vote.	
	O'Neill's *The Emperor Jones* with Charles Gilpin, designed by Cleon Throckmorton, produced.	Prohibition enacted.	
	Avery Hopwood and Mary Robert Rinehart's mystery-drama *The Bat* begins two-year run.	Edith Wharton's *The Age of Innocence*.	League of Nations commission named to study different forms of slavery world-wide.
	Arthur Hopkins, Robert Edmond Jones, and John Barrymore combine talents to produce *Richard III*.	Westinghouse Company establishes world's first commercial radio station, KDKA, in Pittsburgh; within eighteen months 300 stations in the United States.	
	Jerome Kern and Guy Bolton create the musical *Sally* for Ziegfeld star Marilyn Miller.		

The Poor Little Ritz Girl, musical by Richard Rodgers and Lorenz Hart.

Dramatists' Guild of America becomes separate branch of Authors' League of America.

World premiere of Shaw's *Heartbreak House* by the Theatre Guild.

Dallas Little Theatre founded.

By the decade of the twenties Chicano theatre flourished from Los Angeles to Chicago.

1921

Miss Lulu Bett by Zona Gale receives Pulitzer Prize.

Avery Hopwood and Wilson Collison's *Getting Gertie's Garter*, typical sex farce of the time.

Adult African American theatre company launched at Karamu House, Cleveland.

George S. Kaufman and Marc Connelly's *Dulcy* makes star of Lynn Fontanne.

All-black revues such as Noble Sissle and Eubie Blake's *Shuffle Along*, which helped make Florence Mills a star, gain popularity.

The Music Box Theatre opened by Irving Berlin and associates.

The National Theatre (now the Nederlander Theatre) built.

Lionel Barrymore fails in *Macbeth*.

Sinclair Lewis's *Main Street.*

Thoroughbred "Man O' War" retired to stud after winning 20 out of 21 races, including the Belmont and Preakness.

Henry Hadley opera *Cleopatra's Night.*

The United States population is 105,710,997.

Warren G. Harding, whose administration will be wracked by scandal, becomes twenty-ninth president. He dies in office.

Local telephone dialing service offered by Omaha, Nebraska, telephone system.

Scandal rocks Hollywood, as actor-filmmaker Roscoe "Fatty" Arbuckle is accused of killing actress Virginia Rapp in bizarre sexual incident.

Paul Klee's *Arctic Thaw.*

Four-Power Pacific Treaty among United States, France, Great Britain, and Japan recognizes their respective spheres of influence in Pacific.

Benito Mussolini organizes Fascist Party in Italy.

Treaty of Riga establishes boundaries of new Poland.

DATES	THEATRE EVENTS IN AMERICA	SELECTED HISTORICAL/CULTURAL EVENTS IN AMERICA	SELECTED HISTORICAL/CULTURAL EVENTS THROUGHOUT THE WORLD
1921	At least eight major black musicals open on Broadway, 1921–24.	Charlie Chaplin and Rudolph Valentino appear in *The Kid* and *The Sheik*, respectively, box-office successes that ensure the survival of cinema.	Adolf Hitler organizes the Nazi Party in Germany.
	The Tamiment Playhouse, a resident summer theatre that operates until 1960, is founded at Camp Tamiment, an adult summer camp, in Pennsylvania's Pocono Mountains. Growing out of such diverse influences as the American socialist movement, the Yiddish theatre, the burgeoning resort industry, and revue and burlesque comedies, it becomes the preeminent training ground for mid-twentieth-century dance, theatre, film, and television.	Jack Dempsey, the "Manassa Mauler," takes on Frenchman "Gorgeous George" Carpentier.	Widespread drought strikes USSR (to 1923).
	Blossom Time, libretto by Dorothy Donnelly and music by Romberg, opens at the new Ambassador Theatre; runs 576 performances.		Kronstadt Rebellion, in which Soviet navymen revolt over food shortages and Bolshevik political suppression.
	Ed Wynn stars in *The Perfect Fool*; becomes his nickname.		Spanish artist Pablo Picasso's *Three Musicians*.
	Ferenc Molnar's *Lilliom* stars Joseph Schildkraut on Broadway.		
	Musicians' Union, Local 802, chartered in New York.		Italian playwright Luigi Pirandello's *Six Characters in Search of an Author.*
	O'Neill's *Anna Christie*, with Pauline Lord; wins Pulitzer Prize in 1922.		Greco–Turkish War.
	Striptease becomes heart of burlesque.		

1922		
O'Neill's *The Hairy Ape* is produced, with designs by Robert Edmond Jones and starring Louis Wolheim.	Scripps–Howard becomes first newspaper chain in America.	In Five-Power Naval Limitation Treaty, United States, Italy, France, Great Britain, and Japan agree to limit size of their navies.
Anne Nichols's *Abie's Irish Rose* survives for 2,327 performances.	*Reader's Digest* is founded in Pleasantville, New York, by DeWitt Wallace.	Mexican government seizes 1.9 million acres to effect land reforms.
The Actors' Theatre organized as an affiliate to the Actors' Equity Association.	The Hays Code is adopted by film producers and directors as a means of self-censorship.	Mussolini's Fascists stage march in Rome as show of force. The government topples, and Mussolini is made head of state.
Austin Strong's *Seventh Heaven*.	"Rin Tin Tin" makes Hollywood debut.	First Congress of Soviets, held at the Bolshoi Theater, formally approves creation of USSR.
Rain, by John Colton and Clemence Randolph, based on a short story by W. Somerset Maugham, stars Jeanne Eagels.	The discovery of two bodies under a crabapple tree outside New Brunswick, New Jersey, institutes Halls–Mills case, first of the decade's "crimes of the century."	T. S. Eliot's *The Wasteland*. He founds the literary journal *Criterion* to showcase the poem.
John Barrymore in *Hamlet*, directed by Hopkins and designed by Jones; runs 101 performances.	The Mer Rouge murders in Louisiana: two sharecroppers' sons mutilated, allegedly by the strengthening Ku Klux Klan.	James Joyce's novel *Ulysses*.
		French poet-playwright-filmmaker Jean Cocteau's play *Antigone*.
	Hollywood Bowl opens.	Ludwig Wittgenstein's *Tractatus Logico-Philosophicus*.
		British archaeologist Howard Carter discovers tomb of Tutankhamen.
		German expressionist F. W. Murnau's film *Nosferatu*.
1923		
Icebound by Owen Davis wins Pulitzer Prize.	Calvin Coolidge becomes thirtieth president.	Hitler fails to start right-wing revolution in Bavaria in Munich Beer Hall Putsch. While serving eight-month jail term for incident, writes *Mein Kampf*.

DATES	THEATRE EVENTS IN AMERICA	SELECTED HISTORICAL/CULTURAL EVENTS IN AMERICA	SELECTED HISTORICAL/CULTURAL EVENTS THROUGHOUT THE WORLD
1923	The Adding Machine, experimental expressionistic social drama by Elmer Rice, with designs by Lee Simonson, stars Dudley Digges.	Teapot Dome scandal, involving corruption in Harding administration, begins to break.	Spain governed by military dictator General Miguel Primo de Rivera (to 1925), following coup.
	Lula Vollmer's Sun-Up staged at Provincetown Playhouse.		
	The Moscow Art Theatre's acting company travels to New York, brought by Morris Gest and F. Ray Comstock.	Experimental movie with sound imprinted directly on film is demonstrated.	
	The Shuberts' Imperial Theatre opens.	Philosopher George Santayana's Scepticism and Animal Faith.	Kahlil Gibran's The Prophet, a book that finds its most enthusiastic audience in the 1960s counterculture, published.
	Eddie Cantor stars in Kid Boots, his first musical.	Americans flock to stores to buy King Tut memorabilia, including hats, rings, and even home furnishings.	Mussolini seizes dictatorial powers as non-Fascist members of Chamber of Deputies walk out.
	The American Laboratory Theatre is founded by two émigrés of the Moscow Art Theatre.	The Charleston dance craze catches on. First record-dance marathon.	Joseph Stalin succeeds Lenin as Soviet communist leader.
	The first Little Theatre Tournament of one-act plays is held at the Nora Bayes Theatre, under the auspices of the New York Drama League.	Henry Luce founds Time magazine.	Irish playwright Sean O'Casey's Juno and the Paycock.
	Leon Gordon's White Cargo.	Release of The Covered Wagon, first of the "big" Westerns.	Noël Coward's The Vortex.
	Russian Theodore Komisarjevsky directs two productions for the Theatre Guild.		
	Willis Richardson's The Chip Woman's Fortune is the earliest nonmusical black play seen on Broadway.	Warner Bros. is founded.	British anthropologist Louis Leakey identifies the skull of Australopithecus africanus.

George Burns and Gracie Allen become a vaudeville team.

Earl Carroll begins his *Vanities* revues (through 1932).

Clare Tree Majors begins professional touring companies for youthful audiences (continue to her death in 1954).

John Howard Lawson's *Roger Bloomer*, early example of American expressionism.

Shaw's *Saint Joan*, produced by the Theatre Guild, has world premiere.

Minsky's New York National Winter Garden becomes paradigm for all burlesque theatres.

Jasper Deeter's Hedgerow Theatre founded in Moylan-Rose Valley, Pennsylvania.

Hell-Bent fer Heaven by Hatcher Hughes wins controversial Pulitzer Prize.

O'Neill's *All God's Chillun Got Wings* (brings Paul Robeson to national attention) and *Desire Under the Elms* (with Walter Huston and Mary Morris).

Maxwell Anderson and Laurence Stallings's World War I play, *What Price Glory*.

George Kaufman and Marc Connelly's *Beggar on Horseback*, satire on business.

French medico Dr. Emile Coué arrives in the United States preaching the therapy of Autosuggestion.

Wallace Stevens publishes *Harmonium*, a poetry collection.

Silent film star Harold Lloyd appears in *Safety Last*, doing all his own stunts.

Howard Hanson's *Nordic* symphony.

Demonstration of wireless transmission of photograph between New York and London.

Ban on dancing and theatregoing lifted by Methodist Episcopal General Conference.

Popsicles are first sold.

First crossword-puzzle book produced.

P. G. Wodehouse publishes *The Inimitable Mr. Jeeves*.

Lenin dies; Petrograd renamed Leningrad.

First Labour government in Britain.

André Breton's *Manifesto of Surrealism*.

Thomas Mann's *The Magic Mountain*.

1924

DATES	THEATRE EVENTS IN AMERICA	SELECTED HISTORICAL/CULTURAL EVENTS IN AMERICA	SELECTED HISTORICAL/CULTURAL EVENTS THROUGHOUT THE WORLD
1924	Operettas, like Rudolf Friml and Otto Harbach's *Rose-Marie* (with Dennis King) remain popular; Romberg's *The Student Prince*, the longest-running musical of the 1920s.	American publishers Richard Simon and Max Schuster found Simon and Schuster.	E. M. Forster's *A Passage to India.*
	Martin Beck Theatre built.	Columbia Pictures founded by Harry Cohn.	
		Metro Goldwyn Mayer formed by merger.	
	The 46th Street Theatre (later the Richard Rodgers Theatre) built by the Chanin brothers.	Nathan Leopold and Richard Loeb are convicted in the thrill-killing of fourteen-year-old Bobby Franks in Chicago.	
	Lunt and Fontanne brought together by Theresa Helburn in *The Guardsman.*	President Coolidge reelected on prosperity platform.	
	George and Ira Gershwin collaborate on their first musical, *Lady Be Good.*	Saks Fifth Avenue opens in New York.	
	George Kelly's *The Show-off* (successful revivals in 1932, 1950, 1967).	First Macy's Thanksgiving Day parade.	
	Norman Bel Geddes creates lavish designs for Max Reinhardt's *The Miracle* at Century Theatre.	*New York Herald-Tribune* founded.	
1925	*They Knew What They Wanted* by Sidney Howard (opened 1924) wins Pulitzer.	John Dos Passos's novel *Manhattan Transfer.*	Irish novelist Liam O'Flaherty's *The Informer.*
	The Marx Bros. appear in *The Cocoanuts*, by George S. Kaufman and Irving Berlin.	F. Scott Fitzgerald's *The Great Gatsby.*	Virginia Woolf's *Mrs. Dalloway.*
	The Goodman Theatre of Chicago, the second oldest regional theater in the country, founded.	Edward Hopper's painting *House by the Railroad.*	F. W. Murnau's film *The Last Laugh.*

Noted theatrical caricaturist Al Hirschfeld begins working exclusively for *The New York Times*, continuing into the nineties.

John Howard Lawson's *Processional*, "a jazz symphony of American life," opens, designed by Mordecai Gorelik.

The Prolet-Buehne, a New York worker's theatre, opens.

The Theatre Guild opens its own theatre, the Guild. Helen Hayes appears in *Caesar and Cleopatra*.

The Yale Drama Department founded by George Pierce Barker; designer Donald Oenslager begins fifty years of influence as teacher.

Vincent Youman scores a huge success with *No, No Nanette*; Friml's *The Vagabond King* also a hit.

James Gleason and Richard Tabor's *Is Zat So?*

Paul Robeson in revival of *Emperor Jones*.

Sunny, with music by Jerome Kern, opens at the New Amsterdam Theatre; runs 517 performances.

Surrealist Man Ray's photomontage *Clock Wheels*.

The New Yorker founded by Harold Ross.

Random House founded by publishers Bennett Cerf and Donald Klopfer.

Lon Chaney stars in his most successful film venture, *The Phantom of the Opera*.

The Scopes Monkey Trial debates the legitimacy of evolutionary theory and its propriety in the classroom.

Charlie Chaplin stars in *Gold Rush*.

The Freshman, a vehicle for Harold Lloyd, opens.

Anita Loos's *Gentlemen Prefer Blondes*.

Outline of History by H. G. Wells, *Story of Mankind* by Hendrik Willem Van Loom, *Story of Philosophy* by Will Durant, and *Story of the World's Literature* by John Macy, all best-sellers.

Buster Keaton stars in *The General*.

Franz Kafka's *The Trial*.

Epic theatre, revolutionary political dramatic style, appears.

Russian filmmaker Sergei Eisenstein's *Battleship Potemkin*.

DATES	THEATRE EVENTS IN AMERICA	SELECTED HISTORICAL/CULTURAL EVENTS IN AMERICA	SELECTED HISTORICAL/CULTURAL EVENTS THROUGHOUT THE WORLD
1925	Walter Hampden moves his company, founded 1918, into the Colonial (later Hampden) Theatre to do noncommerical plays.	Mrs. William B. Rose inaugurated governor of Wyoming, the first female governor.	
	Omaha (Nebraska) Community Playhouse established.	Alain Locke's *The New Negro.*	
1926	*Craig's Wife* by George Kelly, which opened in 1925, wins Pulitzer Prize.	Liquid-fuel rocket fired at Auburn, Massachusetts.	First flight to North Pole and back (9 May).
	O'Neill's *The Great God Brown.*	Carl Sandburg's *Abraham Lincoln.*	Stalin's chief opponent, Leon Trotsky, ousted.
	Mae West gains notoriety (and is arrested) for her role in her controversial play *Sex.*	Ernest Hemingway's *The Sun Also Rises.*	First transatlantic conversation via radiotelephone (New York to London).
	Ordet, by Kai Munk, the first Danish American drama, is performed in Danish.	Magician Harry Houdini dies.	British children's writer A. A. Milne's *Winnie-the-Pooh.*
	Broadway, by George Abbott and Philip Dunning, produced by Jed Harris.	People like Alvin "Shipwreck" Kelly begin the enormously popular flagpole-sitting fad.	Sean O'Casey's *The Plough and the Stars.*
	Sidney Howard's *The Silver Cord.*		Meyerhold's production of Gogol's *The Inspector General.*
	J. Frank Davis's *The Ladder.*	Middle-aged Edward West "Daddy" Browning marries teenager Frances Belle "Peaches" Heenan in ceremony that captures the nation's headlines.	German Fritz Lang's film *Metropolis.*
	Eva Le Gallienne founds the Civic Repertory Theatre in New York, which survives until 1933.	Movie actor Rudolph Valentino dies; mass hysteria accompanies the funeral.	*Days of the Turbins* by Russian writer Mikhail Bulgakov.
	Leftist group New Playwrights' Theatre founded.	Father Coughlin, a demagogue and anti-Semite, makes the first of his popular radio broadcasts (17 October).	Scottish poet Hugh MacDiarmid's *A Drunk Man Looks Into the Thistle.*

1927

Alvin Theatre built (now Neil Simon).

Mansfield Theatre built (now Brooks Atkinson).

Clown Lou Jacobs begins long career (until 1988) with Ringling Bros.

Karle Otto Amend begins six-year career as designer of Earl Carroll's *Vanities.*

Brooks Atkinson succeeds Stark Young as theatre critic for *The New York Times.*

In Abraham's Bosom (opens 1926) by white playwright Paul Green, with black actress Rose McClendon, wins Pulitzer Prize.

Romberg, Harbach, and Hammerstein II's *The Desert Song,* with Vivienne Segal, a hit at the Casino Theatre.

Robert Sherwood's *The Road to Rome* stars Jane Cowl.

Mrs. Fiske appears as Mrs. Alving in *Ghosts.*

Philip Barry's *Paris Bound.*

The infamous Wales Padlock Law is instituted in New York. The law upholds arrests of actors, the lock-up of theaters, and the banning of productions for performances deemed indecent.

Charles Lindbergh makes first solo transatlantic flight, from New York to Paris.

Thornton Wilder's *The Bridge of San Luis Rey.*

Martin Heidegger's *Being and Time.*

Women's hemlines rise sharply, to just below the knee, after slight rise in 1925.

Italian American anarchists Nicola Sacco and Bartolomeo Vanzetti executed for murdering two factory officials in South Braintree, Massachusetts. Petitioners around the world believe the conviction unfair, citing ethnic origin and anarchist political beliefs of the accused.

Canada is admitted to League of Nations Council.

Autumn Harvest Uprising, in which Chinese communists spark unsuccessful peasant revolt during Chinese Civil War.

Virginia Woolf's *To the Lighthouse.*

First Peking man fossil remains are found.

DATES	THEATRE EVENTS IN AMERICA	SELECTED HISTORICAL/CULTURAL EVENTS IN AMERICA	SELECTED HISTORICAL/CULTURAL EVENTS THROUGHOUT THE WORLD
1927	The Royale Theatre, Theatre Masque (1934 renamed John Golden), and Majestic Theatre are opened by the Chanin brothers. Abraham Erlanger opens Erlanger's Theatre (renamed St. James in 1932).	Talking motion pictures are ushered in with film *The Jazz Singer.*	
	Florenz Ziegfeld opens the Ziegfeld Theatre at 6th Avenue and 54th Street.	All-black Harlem Globetrotters team is founded.	
	Rodgers and Hart create *A Connecticut Yankee*; marks Busby Berkeley's debut as dance director–choreographer.	New York Yankees' Babe Ruth hits sixtieth home run in 154 games, a record until 1961.	
	George and Ira Gershwin's *Funny Face.*	In the sensational Dumbbell Murder, housewife is accused of killing her husband with a sash weight.	
	Jerome Kern and Oscar Hammerstein II's *Show Boat*, with designs by Joseph Urban, alters course of musical theatre; becomes a huge hit, integrating music, song, and dance.	Greta Garbo stars in *Flesh and Devil.*	
	Paul Sifton's *The Belt* produced, a synthesis of Marxist motifs, machine-age techniques, and native forms of popular entertainment.	Clara Bow achieves fame as the "It" girl.	
	Arthur Hammerstein opens Hammerstein's Theatre.	Vincent Sardi opens now legendary restaurant in Broadway theatre district on West 44th Street.	
	Keith–Albee Orpheum Corporation founded.		
1928	Eugene O'Neill receives third Pulitzer Prize for *Strange Interlude*. His *Marco Millions* is produced this year, as is *Lazarus*	United States and nearly every other nation sign Kellogg–Briand Pact, renouncing war.	First flight across Arctic Ocean is made by Australian explorers G. H. Wilkins and C. B. Eielson.

Laughed in a nonprofessional production at the Pasadena Playhouse.

Ben Hecht and Charles MacArthur's *The Front Page* marks directorial debut of George S. Kaufman.

Marx Bros. star in *Animal Crackers*.

Romberg's traditional operetta *The New Moon* is popular.

Holiday by Philip Barry is directed by Arthur Hopkins.

Shuberts open Ethel Barrymore Theatre.

Dorothy Parker founds the Round Table at the Algonquin Hotel in New York. Among its members are George S. Kaufman, Robert Benchley, James Thurber, and Harpo Marx.

Kaufman and Ferber's *The Royal Family* parodies the Barrymore family.

Novelist John Dos Passos's socialist drama *Airways* is produced.

The Lafayette Players, the first professional all-black stock company, forms in Los Angeles.

Eddie Cantor stars in *Whoopee*, which features the song "Makin' Whoopee."

Sophie Treadwell's unusual *Machinal* plays at the Plymouth Theatre.

American inventors build first quartz clock.

Color motion pictures first demonstrated, as is color television.

Stephen Vincent Benet's *John Brown's Body*.

Amos 'n' Andy debuts. The radio show is so popular by the early 1930s that movie theatres pipe in the program.

Steamboat Willie is the first Walt Disney Mickey Mouse movie feature.

William Butler Yeats's *The Tower*.

D. H. Lawrence's *Lady Chatterley's Lover*.

Virginia Woolf's *Orlando*.

German expressionist painter George Grosz creates his *Man of Opinion*, a startling prophecy of the rise of fascism.

Bertolt Brecht and Kurt Weill's *The Three Penny Opera*.

British physician Alexander Fleming discovers penicillin in molds.

DATES	THEATRE EVENTS IN AMERICA	SELECTED HISTORICAL/CULTURAL EVENTS IN AMERICA	SELECTED HISTORICAL/CULTURAL EVENTS THROUGHOUT THE WORLD
1928	Pioneer summer theatre, University Players, organized on Cape Cod.		
	Seattle Repertory Playhouse founded, modeled on Theatre Guild (survives twenty-three seasons).		
	After a two-year absence, black musicals reemerge on Broadway with the opening of *Blackbirds of 1928* on 9 May, which makes star of Bill Robinson.		
	Association of Theatrical Press Agents and Managers formed.		
1929	Elmer Rice wins Pulitzer Prize for *Street Scene*, with setting by Jo Mielziner.	Herbert Hoover becomes president.	First complete flight of airplane by instruments alone, including takeoff and landing.
	June Moon by George S. Kaufman and Ring Lardner.	Helen and Robert Lynd's *Middletown*.	FM radio transmission begins.
	John Drinkwater's *Bird in Hand* runs for 500 performances at the Booth Theatre (previously produced in London with Laurence Olivier and Peggy Ashcroft in leading roles).	Stock-market crash marks beginning of Great Depression.	Foam rubber developed.
		Thomas Wolfe's novel *Look Homeward, Angel*.	
	Preston Sturges's *Strictly Dishonorable*, a play dealing with feminine sexual mores, at New York's Avon Theatre.	Ernest Hemingway's *A Farewell to Arms*.	William Butler Yeats's *The Winding Stair*.
	Workers' Drama League formed.	William Faulkner's *The Sound and the Fury*.	German novelist Herman Hesse's *Steppenwolf*.
	Albee's vaudeville empire subsumed by RKO (the Radio–Keith–Orpheum Corporation).	John Dewey's *The Quest for Certainty*.	German World War I veteran Erich Maria Remarque's *All Quiet on the Western Front*.

1930		
The Bowery Theatre, which has become a Chinese vaudeville house, burns for the final time.	St. Valentine's Day Massacre in Chicago, the gangland killing of seven members of "Bug" Moran gang in dispute over bootleg liquor traffic.	Virginia Woolf's *A Room of One's Own*.
Composer Arthur Schwartz begins collaboration with Howard Dietz on series of revues, beginning with *The Little Show*.	First Academy Awards are presented for outstanding film performances.	
Century Lighting Co. founded.	Technicolor is introduced.	London Naval Treaty establishes permanent parity among American, British, and Japanese navies.
The Green Pastures by Marc Connelly and with Richard B. Harrison as De Lawd wins Pulitzer Prize.	National debt reduced to $16 billion.	Great Britain, France, and Germany hit hard during decade by Depression.
The Cherokee Night by Lynn Riggs performed at the Hedgerow Theatre, the first time a stage work by a full-blooded Native American has been performed.	Frank Whittle invents jet engine.	Noël Coward's comedy *Private Lives* produced.
The American production of Ashley Dukes's *Josef Suss*, a dramatization of Lion Feuchtwanger's *Power*, produced.	Hart Crane's long poem *The Bridge*.	Vladimir Mayakovsky's *The Bathhouse* staged in Leningrad.
Kenyon Nicholson and Charles Robinson's *Sailor, Beware!*	William Faulkner's *As I Lay Dying*.	Luigi Pirandello's *Tonight We Improvise*.
Workers' Laboratory Theatre founded.	John Dos Passos's *U.S.A., a trilogy*.	
P. Dodd Ackerman's tripartite setting for *Five Star Final* is one of earliest examples of simultaneous settings on Broadway.	Dashiell Hammett's *The Maltese Falcon*.	
Maxwell Anderson's *Elizabeth the Queen* produced by the Theatre Guild with Lunt and Fontanne.	Grant Wood's famed painting, *American Gothic*.	
	The yo-yo appears.	

DATES	THEATRE EVENTS IN AMERICA	SELECTED HISTORICAL/CULTURAL EVENTS IN AMERICA	SELECTED HISTORICAL/CULTURAL EVENTS THROUGHOUT THE WORLD
1930	New York's Colony Theatre renamed the Broadway; Hollywood Theatre opened, renamed Mark Hellinger in 1949.	About 3.7 million radios are operating in the country at this time. Popular programs like *The Shadow*, featuring elusive detective Lamont Cranston, attract large listening audiences nationwide.	Statute of Westminster grants autonomous government to Great Britain's former colonial possessions and creates British Commonwealth.
	Jed Harris's production of *Uncle Vanya* at the Cort Theatre is first commercially successful Chekhov in the United States.	James Whale's film *Frankenstein*, starring Boris Karloff, and Tod Browning's *Dracula*, starring Bela Lugosi, begin the monster craze for the American public and Universal Studios.	Second Spanish republic (to 1939) is established.
	The Gershwins' *Strike Up the Band* and *Girl Crazy*, the latter introducing Ethel Merman to Broadway.	Four million Americans are unemployed.	Spaniard Salvador Dali's *The Persistence of Memory*, the most notable surrealist work.
	League of New York Theatres incorporated.		Henry Miller's *Tropic of Cancer* written outside of native country (United States).
	Kaufman and Hart's *Once in a Lifetime* runs 406 performances.		
1931	Susan Glaspell's *Alison's House* (opened 1930) wins Pulitzer Prize.	The Empire State Building in New York is built. The most famous American skyscraper, it is the world's tallest building (1,250 feet) for more than forty years.	
	O'Neill's *Mourning Becomes Electra* stars Alla Nazimova and Alice Brady.	New York City's Rockefeller Center designed.	
	The Left Bank by Elmer Rice.	Alka-Seltzer marketed as a remedy for headaches and upset stomachs.	
	Reunion in Vienna by Robert Sherwood.	The Scottsboro Affair, in which black youths are wrongly accused of the rape of two white women.	

Harold Clurman founds the Group Theatre, after convincing New York actors and directors in twenty-five midnight sessions.	Gangster Al Capone is convicted on tax-evasion charges.	Englishman Harry St. John Philby makes celebrated journey into "empty quarter" of Arabia, Rugi al-Khali Desert, a land so desolate the Bedouin scarcely journey there.
House of Connelly by Paul Green and directed by Lee Strasberg is Group Theatre's first New York production.	The Nation of Islam, popularly called the Black Muslims, founded in Chicago by Wallace D. Fard.	
Katharine Cornell stars in *The Barretts of Wimpole Street.*	Singer Kate Smith makes radio debut; career lasts fifty years.	Aldous Huxley's *Brave New World,* a terrifying vision of the totalitarian state.
Minskys open the Republic burlesque house.		
Lynn Riggs's *Green Grow the Lilacs* (source for *Oklahoma!* book).	Supreme Court establishes protection against double jeopardy in cases in which the accused person has been previously acquitted.	Chaco War (1932–35), between Bolivia and Paraguay over disputed territory.
Of Thee I Sing (opened in 1931) by George Kaufman, Morrie Ryskind, George and Ira Gershwin wins Pulitzer Prize, the first musical so honored.	New York mayor Jimmy Walker resigns following investigation of graft and misuse of funds in Tammany Hall.	Saudi Arabia is created. First king is Ibn Saud.
Dinner at Eight, by George Kaufman and Edna Ferber.	Faulkner's *Light in August.*	
Radio City Music Hall opens, originally intended to cater to inexpensive vaudeville fare.		
Washington's Folger Library opens.	Painter Georgia O'Keeffe's *White Barn, Canada.*	
Motion pictures displace vaudeville in the Palace Theatre, marking the symbolic death of vaudeville.	Infant son of aviator Charles Lindbergh is kidnapped and found murdered.	

1932

DATES	THEATRE EVENTS IN AMERICA	SELECTED HISTORICAL/CULTURAL EVENTS IN AMERICA	SELECTED HISTORICAL/CULTURAL EVENTS THROUGHOUT THE WORLD
1932	League of Workers' Theatre established.	The Bonus Expeditionary Force marches to Washington to demand the enactment of a special bonus to provide pensions for veterans immediately.	
	Behrman's *Biography*, with Ina Claire.	Laurel and Hardy star in *The Music Box.*	
1933	*Both Your Houses* by Maxwell Anderson wins Pulitzer Prize.	Franklin D. Roosevelt becomes president. He will die in office, after being elected to an unprecedented fourth term.	Hindenburg appoints Hitler as chancellor. His capitulation to Nazi tactics paralyzes the German government.
	O'Neill's *Ah, Wilderness!*, his only domestic comedy, stars George M. Cohan.	FDR convenes special congressional session to halt wave of bank failures resulting from Depression. The New Deal program is subsequently introduced.	Operation of Nazi concentration camps begins for political opponents, Jews, and others.
	Elmer Rice's *We, The People.*	Twentieth Amendment to Constitution is ratified, changing terms of office of members of Congress, the President, and the Vice President to prevent "lame-duck" sessions of Congress.	Mexican artist Diego Rivera paints *Man and Machinery.*
	The Barter Theatre is founded in Abingdon, Virginia.	Twenty-first Amendment to Constitution is ratified, repealing Prohibition.	W. H. Auden's "The Dance of Death."
	The Pittsburgh Playhouse, a community theatre, is founded.	Severe drought in Midwest farming region, lasting into 1939, results in huge dust storms and migration of thousands of farmers from area.	Holocaust begins (ends 1945). Persecution and extermination of estimated 6 million Jews.
	The Theatre Union, one of the more successful of the groups dedicated to theatrical presentations of working-class problems, debuts.	Alcatraz prison opened.	
	Impresario Max Liebman assumes the directorship of the Tamiment Playhouse's social activities.	Banking crisis brought on by wave of failures.	

1934

The Thomas Davis Irish Players, the oldest Irish American drama group in New York, is founded.

The Drunkard opens in Los Angeles and plays 9,477 performances (closes in 1959).

Jack Kirkland's *Tobacco Road* (based on Erskine Caldwell's novel) begins seven-year run (3,182 performances) at the Masque Theatre.

Irving Berlin's *As Thousands Cheer.*

Gershwins' *Let 'Em Eat Cake.*

Emmett Kelly's tramp clown becomes popular in circuses.

Sally Rand's fan dance an enormous hit at the Chicago Exposition.

Kliegl lighting firm demonstrates ellipsoidal-reflector spotlight. Also three-scene preset controls installed in Radio City Music Hall.

Men in White (opened by Group Theatre in 1933) by Sidney Kingsley wins Pulitzer Prize.

O'Neill's *Days without End.*

National Industrial Recovery Act established to give minimum wage to workers, fair hours, collective bargaining, and the right to unionize.

Gertrude Stein's *The Autobiography of Alice B. Toklas.*

Nathanael West's *Miss Lonelyhearts.*

Tennessee Valley Authority (TVA) created to develop Tennessee River basin.

Screen Writers' Guild formed.

Engineer creates Monopoly board game.

First U.S. drive-in theatre opens in New Jersey.

Films *King Kong*, starring Fay Wray, and *Duck Soup*, starring the Marx Bros., open.

The avant-garde Black Mountain College opens.

F. Scott Fitzgerald's *Tender Is the Night.*

Anthropologist Ruth Benedict's *Patterns of Culture.*

Communist leader Sergei Kirov is assassinated. Bloody purges commence under Stalin.

Poet-novelist Robert Graves's *I, Claudius*, a fictionalized autobiography of the Roman emperor.

DATES	THEATRE EVENTS IN AMERICA	SELECTED HISTORICAL/CULTURAL EVENTS IN AMERICA	SELECTED HISTORICAL/CULTURAL EVENTS THROUGHOUT THE WORLD
1934	Maxwell Anderson's *Valley Forge*.	Bonnie Parker and Clyde Barrow shot dead near Shreveport, Louisiana, ending a two-year string of bank robberies and twelve murders.	French painter René Magritte's *Rape*.
	Left-wing melodrama, *Stevedore*, by Paul Peters and George Sklar, produced by Theatre Union.	Notorious bank robber John Dillinger dies in shootout with FBI agents in front of a Chicago movie theater.	Federico García Lorca writes *Yerma*.
	Cole Porter's *Anything Goes* with Ethel Merman, William Gaxton, and Victor Moore.	*The Partisan Review* begins publication.	
	The Civil Works Administration employs actors on relief for free entertainments.	Black nationalist Oscar Brown founds the National Movement for the Establishment of a Forty-ninth State.	Leni Riefenstahl's *Triumph of the Will*, a documentary produced as positive propaganda for Hitler's Nazis.
	Lawrence Reilly's *Personal Appearance*.	The summertime Berkshire Festival at Tanglewood in Lenox, Massachusetts, begins.	Russian poet Osip Mandelstam is imprisoned and exiled for poems denouncing Stalin and referring to the dictator as the "Kremlin mountaineer."
	Elliot Norton begins long career (retired 1982) as Boston theatre critic.	Thomas Hart Benton's painting *Going Home*.	André Breton publishes manifesto *What Is Surrealism?*
	John Houseman directs Gertrude Stein and Virgil Thomson's *Four Saints in Three Acts*, with lighting by Abe Feder (died 1997), one of his first credits.		
	First "New Faces" revue; sporadically through 1968.		
	Lillian Hellman's *The Children's Hour*, denied 1935 Pulitzer Prize because of controversial subject and leads to founding of New York Drama Critics' Circle Award.		

1935

The Old Maid by Zoë Akins wins controversial Pulitzer Prize.

Robert Sherwood's *The Petrified Forest* with Humphrey Bogart.

Maxwell Anderson's *Winterset*.

Clifford Odets's *Waiting for Lefty*, *Awake and Sing!*, and *Paradise Lost*, all produced by Group Theatre.

Langston Hughes's *Mulatto* becomes the most successful play by an African American playwright of the 1930s.

The Federal Theatre is organized by the Works Progress Administration (WPA) to create jobs for out-of-work theatre people.

The Apollo Theatre is taken over by Frank Schiffman and Leo Brecher; becomes historic showplace for black entertainers.

The New Theater League emerges, signifying radical leftist tolerance of the middle class in dramatic depictions.

The Prolet-Buehne produces *Scottsboro!*, about the framing of black youths by two white women.

Helen Hayes in *Victoria Regina*.

Vassar College professor Hallie Flanagan asssumes leadership of the Federal Theatre Project (FTP) in August.

First U.S.–Canadian reciprocal trade agreement is established.

Social Security Act established for unemployment compensation, retirement benefits, and state welfare programs for workers.

John L. Lewis founds Congress of Industrial Organizations (CIO).

Ansel Adams's *Making a Photograph*.

Wagner Act requires employers to accept collective bargaining.

Anthropologist Margaret Mead's *Sex and Temperament*.

Twentieth Century Fox is formed.

Heisman Trophy awarded for the first time.

Louisiana senator and demagogue Huey Long assassinated in Baton Rouge.

Germany reoccupies Rhineland.

Swastika made part of German national flag.

Italy successfully invades Ethiopia and annexes the country.

T. S. Eliot's *Murder in the Cathedral*, a celebrated verse play, is performed for the first time.

Karl Popper's *The Logic of Scientific Discovery*.

The Popular Front is created by Comintern representatives in Russia against fascism.

DATES	THEATRE EVENTS IN AMERICA	SELECTED HISTORICAL/CULTURAL EVENTS IN AMERICA	SELECTED HISTORICAL/CULTURAL EVENTS THROUGHOUT THE WORLD
1935	The Popular Price Theatre is established as New York adjunct of the Federal Theatre Project. The Managers' Try-Out Theatre is also formed to suit this purpose.	Babe Ruth quits the New York Yankees.	
	Old Globe Theatre opens in San Diego's Balboa Park; Oregon Shakespeare Festival founded in Ashland.		
	George Gershwin's opera *Porgy and Bess* (based on 1927 play *Porgy* by Dorothy and Dubose Heyward) produced by the Theatre Guild.	Middleweight Joe Louis defeats Primo Carnera.	
	John Cecil Holm and George Abbott's *Three Men on a Horse* with Sam Levene.	Alfred Hitchcock's film *The 39 Steps.*	
	Sidney Kingsley's *Dead End* begins 684-performance run; designed by Norman Bel Geddes.	*Butterfield 8* by John O'Hara.	
	Phil Silvers joins the Minskys as burlesque comic.		
	American National Theatre and Academy chartered.		
1936	*Idiot's Delight* by Robert Sherwood wins Pulitzer Prize.	Faulkner's *Absalom, Absalom!*	Edward VIII reigns briefly as British king.
	George Kaufman and Edna Ferber's *Stage Door.*	Hoover Dam constructed on Colorado River between Nevada and Arizona.	Spanish Civil War (1936–39).
	Orson Welles directs "voodoo" *Macbeth* for the Federal Theatre in Harlem.	National Baseball Hall of Fame established in Cooperstown, New York.	Oil found in Saudi Arabia.
	Living Newspaper production of Federal Theatre Project (FTP), *Triple-A-Plowed Under,* by Arthur Arent, deals with U.S.	*Life* magazine founded.	British Broadcasting Corp. begins first public high-definition television broadcasting.

agricultural problems and is conceived of as "a new American drama of the Depression era."

Irwin Shaw's antiwar play, *Bury the Dead.*

The Playreading Bureau is established, headed by Converse Tyler and Ben Russak, to provide written reports on the scripts sent to the FTP.

The Theatre of Action and the Theatre Collective cease independent operations and join the FTP.

Animal trainer Clyde Beatty forms his own big-top circus.

New York Drama Critics' Circle Awards established.

Brother Rat, a smash comedy by John Monks Jr. and Fred Finkelhoff, opens on Broadway.

Rodgers and Hart's *On Your Toes* features George Balanchine choreography (with Ray Bolger).

Under the FTP, Sinclair Lewis's *It Can't Happen Here* has twenty-three simultaneous openings on 27 October throughout the United States.

John Gielgud plays Hamlet to Judith Anderson's Gertrude in New York.

Clare Boothe's *The Women.*

Michael Chekhov begins the Chekhov Theatre Studio.

The January strike and sit-in of rubber workers at Firestone plant in Akron, Ohio, leads to massive regional workers' strikes.

Jesse Owens wins four gold medals at the Olympic Games in Berlin.

Margaret Mitchell's best-seller, *Gone with the Wind.*

Fluorescent lighting developed.

German critic Walter Benjamin's treatise "The Work of Art in the Age of Mechanical Reproduction."

DATES	THEATRE EVENTS IN AMERICA	SELECTED HISTORICAL/CULTURAL EVENTS IN AMERICA	SELECTED HISTORICAL/CULTURAL EVENTS THROUGHOUT THE WORLD
1937	American Educational Theatre Association founded (evolved into present Association for Theatre in Higher Education).		
	You Can't Take It with You by George Kaufman and Moss Hart receives a Pulitzer Prize (opened in 1936).	Ernest Hemingway's *To Have and Have Not.*	Arthur Neville Chamberlain is British prime minister (though 1940).
	Golden Boy by Clifford Odets.	Joan Miro's painting *The Circus.*	British academic J. R. R. Tolkien's *The Hobbit.*
	Rodgers and Hart's *Babes in Arms.*		Isak Dinesen publishes *Out of Africa.*
	Orson Welles and John Houseman create the Mercury Theatre, having resigned from the Federal Theatre because of the censorship and closing of the Federal Theatre's production of Marc Blitzstein's *The Cradle Will Rock.*	*Snow White and the Seven Dwarves*, the first full-length animated feature from Walt Disney studios.	Pablo Picasso paints *Guernica*, an anti-war piece.
	Burlesque houses in Times Square and other major theatre districts are closed. Reopening is contingent on the removal of striptease acts.	Amelia Earhart disappears on round-the-world flight.	Sino–Japanese War (1937–45).
	Rachel Crothers's *Susan and God.*		
	Negro Actors Guild founded; folds in 1982.		German dirigible *Hindenburg* explodes while mooring in Lakehurst, New Jersey; thirty-six perish.
	Harold Rome's satiric revue *Pins and Needles* runs for almost three seasons.		
	The Group Theatre produces *Johnny Johnson*, Kurt Weill's first Broadway musical.		
	Margaret Webster directs Maurice Evans		

in *Richard II*, *Hamlet* in 1938, and *Twelfth Night* in 1940.

The Lost Colony, Paul Green's first "symphonic drama" and impetus for subsequent outdoor dramas, staged in Manteo, North Carolina.

John Murray and Allen Boretz collaborate on *Room Service*, a farcical smash on Broadway, directed by George Abbott.

John Steinbeck's *Of Mice and Men* stars Broderick Crawford as Lennie.

Actress Maude Adams begins teaching career at Stephens College, Missouri (through 1950).

1938 Playwrights' Company founded (to 1961) by five playwrights; attempts to stage dramatists' productions despite economic hardships of Great Depression.

Thornton Wilder's *Our Town* wins Pulitzer Prize.

The Jewel Box revue, an all-drag burlesque, is founded in Miami and enjoys a successful eight-year run.

Hellzapoppin, a variety revue, is produced by Olsen and Johnson.

Maxwell Anderson and Weill's *Knickerbocker Holiday* stars Walter Huston.

Minimum wage for workers established under Fair Labor Standards Act.

H. G. Wells's *The War of the Worlds* is broadcast as a Halloween prank by Orson Welles's Mercury Theatre On the Air. Done as a series of on-the-spot news broadcasts, the show panics 1.5 million Americans.

The national membership of the American Communist Party reaches 55,000.

Nazis invade and take control of Austria.

Munich Pact between Germany and other European powers provides for German occupation of Czechoslovakia's Sudetenland. Hitler then nullifies pact, invading Poland and Czechoslovakia in 1939.

Sergei Eisenstein's film *Alexander Nevsky*.

DATES	THEATRE EVENTS IN AMERICA	SELECTED HISTORICAL/CULTURAL EVENTS IN AMERICA	SELECTED HISTORICAL/CULTURAL EVENTS THROUGHOUT THE WORLD
1938	FTP Living Newspaper, Arent's *One-Third of a Nation* with designs by Howard Bay exposes urban living conditions.		
	Chicago Negro Unit of FTP produces Theodore Ward's *Big White Fog*.		
	Paul Osborn's *Mornings at Seven*.		
	The FTP is investigated for alleged subversive activity by the House Committee to Investigate Un-American Activities and the Dies Committe on Un-American Activities. Among the so-called controversial works scrutinized are *Around the Corner, Chalk Dust, Class of '29, Created Equal, It Can't Happen Here, No More Peace, Professor Mamlock, Prologue to Glory, The Sun and I, Woman of Destiny, Help Yourself, Machine Age, On the Rocks*, and the musical *Sing for Your Supper*.		
	As lighting designer for Martha Graham, Jean Rosenthal begins to explore the art of stage lighting.		
	Rodgers, Hart, and Abbott's *Boys from Syracuse*.		
	Mary Martin's Broadway debut in *Leave It to Me*.		
1939	*Abe Lincoln in Illinois* by Robert Sherwood wins Pulitzer Prize (opened 1938 with Raymond Massey as first Playwrights' Company production).	Nathanael West's *The Day of the Locust*.	World War II begins as Nazi Germany invades Poland.

O'Neill's *The Iceman Cometh.*

Willard Quine's *Word and Object.*

Pact of Steel between Italy and Nazi Germany cements alliance.

George Kaufman and Moss Hart's *The Man Who Came to Dinner.*

Release of *Gone with the Wind,* one of the most successful movies of all time.

Italy occupies Albania.

S. N. Behrman's *No Time for Comedy* with Katharine Cornell.

John Steinbeck's *The Grapes of Wrath.*

The American Way by Moss Hart.

Denmark signs nonaggression pact with Germany but in April 1940 is invaded by Nazi forces.

Lillian Hellman's *The Little Foxes* with Tallulah Bankhead and designs by Aline Bernstein.

German battleship *Bismarck* is launched.

William Saroyan's *My Heart's in the Highlands,* produced by the Group Theatre, followed by his *The Time of Your Life.*

James Joyce's *Finnegan's Wake.*

Philip Barry's *The Philadelphia Story* stars Katharine Hepburn.

T. S. Eliot's play *The Family Reunion.*

The number of stage productions for the 1939–40 season is just eighty.

Russo–Finnish War.

Congress disbands the Federal Theatre Project.

Germany and Russia sign a treaty of mutual nonaggression (24 Aug.).

The Minsky brothers' burlesque theatres in New York are closed down.

German director Erwin Piscator heads the Dramatic Workshop in the New School of Social Research.

DeSylva, Brown, and Henderson's musical, *Du Barry Was a Lady,* stars Bert Lahr and Ethel Merman.

DATES	THEATRE EVENTS IN AMERICA	SELECTED HISTORICAL/CULTURAL EVENTS IN AMERICA	SELECTED HISTORICAL/CULTURAL EVENTS THROUGHOUT THE WORLD
1939	Lindsay and Crouse's *Life with Father*, designed by Stewart Chaney, runs for 3,224 performances, a record for four decades for a nonmusical show.		
1940	William Saroyan declines Pulitzer Prize for *The Time of Your Life*.	Ernest Hemingway's *For Whom the Bell Tolls*.	Leon Trotsky, exile from Stalinist Soviet Union, is assassinated in Mexico City.
	George Washington Slept Here, by Moss Hart.	Carson McCullers's *The Heart Is a Lonely Hunter*.	Cave paintings 17,000 years old are discovered at Lascaux, France.
	James Thurber and Elliott Nugent's *The Male Animal*.	Ezra Pound's *Cantos*.	
	The American Negro Theatre is founded in Harlem by Abram Hill and Frederick O'Neal.	Alice Neel's painting *T. B. Harlem*.	Olympic Games canceled for Tokyo and Helsinki.
	John O'Hara's story "Pal Joey," transformed into a musical by Rodgers and Hart, is first musical with truly mature subject (with Vivienne Segal).	Composer Paul Hindemith moves to United States.	
	José Ferrer achieves stardom in *Charley's Aunt*.	Saturday afternoon performances of "The Metropolitan Opera of the Air" begin.	
	My Sister Eileen, by Joseph Fields and Jerome Chodorov, produced by Max Gordon; 864 performances.		
	Pioneer arena theatre, the Penthouse, built at University of Washington.		
	Experimental Theatre, Inc., is founded in New York City; struggles along until 1948.		

1941

Hart, Gershwin, and Weill's inventive musical *Lady in the Dark*, directed by Hassard Short, stars Gertrude Lawrence and Danny Kaye.

Robert Sherwood wins third Pulitzer Prize for *There Shall Be No Night*.

Watch on the Rhine by Lillian Hellman.

Orson Welles directs Richard Wright's *Native Son*, with Canada Lee.

Joseph Kesselring's *Arsenic and Old Lace* runs for 1,444 performances at the Fulton Theatre; it is turned into a highly successful film, starring Cary Grant, three years later.

The Turnabout Theatre opens in Los Angeles under the auspices of the Yale puppeteers.

Group Theatre disbands.

Rose Franken's *Claudia*.

Patrick Hamilton's *Angel Street*, starring future horror-film star Vincent Price (and Leo G. Carroll), plays for 1,295 performances at the John Golden Theatre.

Stuart Davis's painting *New York Under Gaslight*.

Orson Welles's classic film, *Citizen Kane*.

Baseball great Lou Gehrig, who played 2,130 consecutive games, dies.

New York Yankees centerfielder Joe DiMaggio hits safely in fifty-six consecutive games, a major-league record.

Mrs. Ethel Leta Spinell becomes the first woman to be executed in California's San Quentin gas chamber.

Benjamin Britten's *Sinfonia da Requiem* premieres at Carnegie Hall.

National Gallery of Art opens in Washington, D.C.

Japan's sneak attack on naval base at Pearl Harbor galvanizes the U.S. response to the war, and the United States sides with the Allies.

Atlantic Charter adopted by United States and Britain, detailing policy for world peace and laying groundwork for United Nations Charter.

Noël Coward's *Blithe Spirit*.

Bertolt Brecht's *Mother Courage* staged in Zurich.

1942

Star and Garter, a mainstream burlesque, premieres at the Music Box Theatre.

Stars on Ice, a variety revue assembled by Sonja Henie and Arthur M. Wirtz, opens.

Roy Harris's *Folk Song Symphony*.

Congress of Racial Equality (CORE) forms to work for black equality.

Four hundred and ninety-one die in the Cocoanut Grove nightclub fire in Boston.

Ethiopia abolishes slavery; Liberia follows suit.

Oxford don and theologian C. S. Lewis publishes *The Screwtape Letters*.

DATES	THEATRE EVENTS IN AMERICA	SELECTED HISTORICAL/CULTURAL EVENTS IN AMERICA	SELECTED HISTORICAL/CULTURAL EVENTS THROUGHOUT THE WORLD
1942	Irving Berlin's *This Is the Army.*		Jean Anouilh's *Antigone.*
	Joseph Field's *The Doughgirls,* a farce dealing with the effects of war.		
	Burlesque officially banned in New York.		
1943	Thornton Wilder's *The Skin of Our Teeth* (opened in 1942 with Fredric March and Florence Eldridge) wins Pulitzer Prize.	CORE stages sit-in in Chicago to protest segregation.	French author Antoine de Saint-Exupéry's *Le Petit Prince.*
	O'Neill's *A Moon for the Misbegotten* written. Its first production closes out of town in 1947.	Race riot in Detroit, Michigan, in which twenty-five blacks and nine whites are killed.	Brecht's *Galileo* in Zurich.
	Paul Robeson appears as Othello.	Aaron Copland's *A Lincoln Portrait.*	Dmitri Shostakovich's Symphony no. 8.
	Rodgers and Hammerstein's *Oklahoma!* runs for 2,212 performances at the St. James Theatre; designed by Lemuel Ayers, with Alfred Drake as Curley and choreography by Agnes de Mille.	Paintings: Ben Shahn's *Welders;* Piet Mondrian's *Broadway Boogie-Woogie;* Grandma Moses's *The Thanksgiving Turkey.*	
	Moss Hart's *Winged Victory.*		
	Tomorrow the World by Arnaud D'Usseau and James Gow.		
	John Van Druten's *The Voice of the Turtle.*		
	Carmen Jones, adapted from the concert version of Bizet's *Carmen,* produced by Billy Rose. The Spanish gypsies in the first version become African Americans in this modernization.		
	G. J. Nathan begins his *Theatre Book of the Year* (to 1951).		

1944		
Lillian Hellman's *The Searching Wind*.	John Hersey's *A Bell for Adano*.	Greek Civil War (1944–49).
Tennessee Williams's *The Glass Menagerie*, co-directed by Eddie Dowling and Margo Jones, opens in Chicago; moves to New York in 1945, with Laurette Taylor as Amanda.	Death of illustrator John Dana Gibson.	Warsaw Uprising, in which Polish underground unsuccessfully attempts to capture Warsaw from Germans before advancing Soviets can take city.
	Walter Piston's second symphony.	French existentialist J. P. Sartre's play *No Exit*.
Big Top burns in Hartford, Connecticut, killing 168 people.	Popular songs of the day include: "Sentimental Journal," "Don't Fence Me In," "Rum and Coca-Cola," and "Swinging on a Star."	Argentinian Jorge Luis Borges's *Ficciones*.
On the Town by Leonard Bernstein, Betty Comden, and Adolphe Green; staged by George Abbott, choreographed by Jerome Robbins, and designed by Oliver Smith.		Massive Normandy Invasion 6 June begins Allied effort to retake continental Europe and totally defeat Nazi Germany.
Mary Coyle Chase's *Harvey* with Frank Fay and Josephine Hull; wins 1945 Pulitzer Prize.		W. Somerset Maugham's *The Razor's Edge*.
John van Druten's *I Remember Mama* features a young Marlon Brando.		Albert Camus's *Caligula*; Jean Giraudoux's *The Madwoman of Chaillot*.
Anna Lucasta, by Philip Yordan and produced by the American Negro Theatre with Frederick O'Neal, is the first nonmusical since *The Green Pastures* to feature an all-black cast to achieve a run of more than 500 performances (has a 957-performance run at the Mansfield Theatre).		

1945		
Memphis Bound!, a black musical adaptation of Gilbert and Sullivan's *H.M.S. Pinafore*, is brought to the stage.	Gross national product is $211 billion for the year, double the booming 1929 figure.	President Roosevelt, Prime Minister Churchill, and Premier Stalin meet at Yalta to discuss destiny of postwar world (4–12 Feb.).
Rodgers and Hammerstein's *Carousel* premieres.	Cars in the United States number 25 million.	Iwo Jima taken by U.S. troops (19 Feb.–14 March).

DATES	THEATRE EVENTS IN AMERICA	SELECTED HISTORICAL/CULTURAL EVENTS IN AMERICA	SELECTED HISTORICAL/CULTURAL EVENTS THROUGHOUT THE WORLD
1945	*The Glass Menagerie* wins New York Drama Critics' Circle Award.	Government establishes Operation Paperclip to lure German rocket scientists to work for the United States.	Hitler commits suicide in his Berlin bunker (13 April).
		Napalm developed to enhance effectiveness of incendiary bombing.	Germany signs surrender in Berlin (8 May).
	Elmer Rice's *Dream Girls*.	Vannevar Bush's *Science – The Endless Frontier* published.	The Economic and Social Council of the United Nations (ECOSOC) is established in New York (May).
	Arnaud d'Usseau and James Gow's *Deep Are the Roots*, directed by Elia Kazan, with Barbara Bel Geddes.	Saxophonist Charlie Parker records for first time with band under own name.	Truman, Churchill, and Stalin meet at Potsdam to make provisions in demilitarizing Germany (17 July–2 Aug.).
			Benjamin Britten's opera *Peter Grimes*.
	Lindsay and Crouse's *State of the Union* produced by Leland Hayward (wins 1946 Pulitzer).	President Roosevelt dies (12 April).	First atomic bomb, code named Trinity, is exploded near Alamogordo, New Mexico.
		B-25 bomber smashes into Empire State Building; fourteen die, including ten in the building.	United States drops bombs on Hiroshima and Nagasaki; 130,000 declared dead or missing (6 Aug.).
		Richard Wright's *Black Boy*.	Unconditional surrender of Japan ends World War II (14 Aug.).
			United States holds trial of Nazis for crimes against the law, humanity, and the tenets of the Geneva Convention.
		The United Nations Charter is ratified by the Senate (28 July).	Marshal Tito proclaims Federal People's Republic of Yugoslavia (29 Nov.).
		James Thurber's *The Thurber Carnival*.	Evelyn Waugh's *Brideshead Revisited*.

George Orwell writes *Animal Farm*, a scathing critique of Bolshevism.

Ezra Pound arrested in Italy by U.S. Army for pro-fascist broadcasts; writes *Pisan Cantos*.

Mussolini executed by partisans.

Arab League founded.

First attempt at manned rocket flight takes place in Germany; the pilot is killed.

Indochina War (1945–54).

1

The Hieroglyphic Stage: American Theatre and Society, Post–Civil War to 1945

Thomas Postlewait

Introduction: Death, Fire, and Wizards

EDITH WHARTON: In reality they all lived in a kind of hieroglyphic world, where the real thing was never said or done or even thought, but only represented by a set of arbitrary signs.

The Age of Innocence (1920)

WILL ROGERS (on the death of Florenz Ziegfeld): To have been the master amusement provider of your generation, surely a life's work has been accomplished.

The Autobiography of Will Rogers (1935)

VACHEL LINDSAY: . . . the wizards should rule, and the realists should serve them.

The Art of the Moving Picture (1915).

Inside and Outside of the Playhouse

The period of American theatrical entertainment to be surveyed here covers approximately three-quarters of a century, beginning in 1870 – though I will actually reach back to 1865 as my starting point – and ending in 1945. It is a rich, complex era of theatrical developments and transformations. During these decades American entertainment became one of the largest industries in the country, encompassing not only dramatic performances and musical theatre (from revues to opera) but also minstrelsy, vaudeville, amusement arcades and parks, circuses, and the new media of film and radio. In this chapter some of the defining traits of this broad array of entertainment will be outlined, and American theatre will be situated within the context of American cultural history (the political, economic, social, moral, and artistic aspects of the time). The events and conditions of the period serve as both a catalogue of the defining traits of American life and a measure of the theatre's accomplishments.

Typically, when dividing history into epochs, the beginning and the end of a period are identified by means of major events, including decisive wars and the deaths of important people. In the case of American history between 1865 and 1945, the deaths of two presidents, Abraham Lincoln and Franklin Delano Roosevelt, coincide with the culmination of two major wars and thus provide convenient and fitting period markers. The deaths also serve as points of transition between what has been and what will be, momentary gaps in the march of history. So identified, they become benchmarks from which we can survey the changes in both the political life of the country and the social and cultural affairs. Or so we assume.

For a history of American theatre, Lincoln's death is especially relevant – and troubling – because the actor John Wilkes Booth assassinated the president. In a perversion of its mimetic mission, the theatre in this case collapsed all distance between reality and imitation. Or, more to the point, Booth collapsed the distance in order to force political and theatrical events into an emblematic relationship. A national drama played itself out in Booth's disturbed mind according to the themes in Shakespeare's *Julius Caesar,* which he and his brothers, Edwin Booth and Junius Brutus Booth Jr., had acted together only a few months earlier. "What means this shouting? I do fear the people/Choose Caesar for their king." John Wilkes Booth, under the sway of his histrionic imagination, came to believe that a leader must fall in order to save the republic from imperial power. The theatre thus entered the realm of the real with terrible consequences.

Intriguingly, on the night of the Booths' *Julius Caesar* performance, 25 November 1864, a small group of southern conspirators set a series of fires throughout New York City in various hotels and other public buildings in the hopes of creating a chaotic inferno. Even if the city did not go up in flames (which it did not, because the fires were discovered and quickly extinguished), the conspirators wanted to demonstrate that northern cities were vulnerable to assault. If Atlanta burned, so could New York. Events inside and outside the theatre seem to coalesce, but there is no evidence that John Wilkes Booth, a southern sympathizer and incipient conspirator, knew anything about the plans for these fires.

It is noteworthy, however, that a fire was set in the building next to the Winter Garden Theatre, where the three brothers performed that night, though after Edwin Booth, playing Brutus, calmed the audience, the fires were contained, and the only deaths were theatrical, as Caesar, then Brutus fell. But five months later on 14 April 1865, Good Friday, John Wilkes Booth murdered Lincoln in Ford's Theatre, Washington, D.C. For weeks, while the nation struggled with anger and grief, the whole Booth family was under suspicion, though Edwin himself was not arrested. Still, he published a letter of apology to the nation, lamenting "this most foul and atrocious crime," then retreated behind draped windows, convinced that his acting career was over (Oggel, 19). In less than a year, however, he would return triumphantly to the stage as the melancholy Hamlet, his most famous (and most emblematic) role. The role became the man, the man, the role.

> O God! O God!
> How weary, stale, flat, and unprofitable
> Seem to me all the uses of this world.

Only tragedy offered sufficient measure of the national mood.

The elegy for Lincoln came, however, not from Booth or other theatre artists but from America's supreme poet, Walt Whitman, who saw Lincoln as the quintessential American, now transformed by death into the national martyr, as expressed in "When Lilacs Last in the Dooryard Bloom'd."

So commenced the new, troubled era, one that increasingly disturbed Whitman, who had embraced and celebrated the great American experiment in democracy when he published the first edition of *Leaves of Grass* in 1855.

By 1873, surveying his beloved country, Whitman had begun to doubt America's "democratic vistas":

> Shift and turn the combinations of the statement as we may, the problem of the future of America is in certain respects as dark as it is vast. Pride, competition, segregation, vicious wilfulness, and license beyond the example brood already upon us. Unwieldy and immense, who shall hold in behemoth? who bridle leviathan? Flaunt it as we choose, athwart and over the roads of our progress loom huge uncertainty, and dreadful threatening gloom. It is useless to deny it: Democracy grows rankly up the thickest, noxious, deadliest plants and fruits of all – brings worse and worse invaders – needs newer, larger, stronger, keener compensations and compellers.
> (Quoted in Morison and Commager, 3)

Whitman lived until 1892 (a year before Edwin Booth died), but little about the country in those last decades renewed his optimism. Lincoln's death and the Civil War had proved to be a turning point in the country's history, "purging, illuminating all." For Whitman, American history had crystalized in the murder of Lincoln, who proved to be "the leading actor in the stormiest drama known to real history's stage."[1] "Real history," tragic in dimensions, had brought an age to an end and set the nation on a new, unclear path. Yet what a terrible irony: This real event had occurred in that most unreal realm of theatre.

The attendant paradox is that both Whitman and Booth, from their different perspectives, and in accord with their different talents, tried to give voice to their tragic understanding by means of performance. At every opportunity in the last dozen years of his life, Whitman delivered his lecture on "The Death of Lincoln," attempting through imaginative reconstruction of the assassination to relive and release the national pain.

For example, on the anniversary night of the assassination in 1887, Whitman sat behind a small table on the stage of the Madison Square Theatre in New York. Caught in a circle of light and surrounded by darkness, he performed his reenactment of the tragic event, recalling and embellishing events for dramatic effect. Though he was not in Washington, D.C., on the day of the assassination, he now recreated (or invented) events as if he had been walking beside both Lincoln and John Wilkes Booth. He barely spoke loud enough for all to hear, and yet the effect was mesmerizing. In the audience were a number of famous Americans, including John Hay, former private secretary to Lincoln, James Russell Lowell, Charles Eliot Norton of Harvard, Frances Hodgson Burnett, Mark Twain, and Andrew Carnegie (who subscribed $350 for his seat). Whitman felt that John Wilkes Booth, that ranting actor and southern sympathizer, was a melodramatic villain, insufficient for the tragic role in which he had intruded himself. Only by recasting the whole event in terms of his own national vision could Whitman hope to present the real drama of the assassination as an act of tragic martyrdom. Through reenactment would come catharsis. He wanted to believe that Lincoln's death "belongs to these States in their entirety – not the North only, but the South – perhaps belongs most tenderly and devotedly to the South" (D. Reynolds, 443). But as he had to know, the events of the 1870s and 1880s belied any such dream of tragic resolution, reconciliation, and renewal. His performance of the death could not change conditions outside of the playhouse (see Kaplan).

Booth, by contrast, tried not to discuss the terrible event in public and instead used Shakespearean tragedy, especially *Hamlet,* to offer any chance of catharsis. In 1887 he was invited to perform in Washington, D.C., but he refused. He could not return to the scene of the tragedy. No redemption, no release, no resolution would come in that manner. Instead, he divided his responses to the assassination into public and private acts of atonement. Publicly, he played the role of Hamlet. It is the role he chose for returning to the stage after the assassination; it was his last role before retiring. The applause of the audience during those years provided a momentary benediction, but Booth continued to struggle with melancholy during the rest of his life. He could not purge or transform the "miserable affairs" of the assassination, so he tried to accept them as stoically as possible.[2]

Privately, he attended to the grief of his family. Seeking a proper burial for his brother, he appealed to President Johnson for the body, promising that no public demonstration would occur. On 1869 his request was granted; the body was transported to Baltimore for a burial in the family plot at Green Mount Cemetery. Only the family and a few friends took part in the grim ceremony. Then in the early spring of 1871, Edwin performed his own act of grief, and perhaps catharsis. Late one night, at 3 A.M., he went down to the furnace room of his New York theatre, and there, one by one, he burned all of John Wilkes's costumes. In the consuming fire the past became ashes, but of course Edwin never fully separated himself from the tragic stain of his brother's action (see Ruggles, 241). And in 1893 when he died, he was buried in Mount Auburn Cemetery in Cambridge, Massachusetts, not the family plot in Baltimore. A final act of separation.

Both Whitman and Booth had realized that a national tragedy had played itself out in Ford's Theatre. Yet despite their efforts to perform their versions of tragic suffering, neither of them could make the theatre a place of national conscience and renewal. Apparently, the stage, like the nation, did not quite know how to answer for the event. Lincoln's death had not resolved the national conflict; nor did it redeem the national mission.

A Theatre of Evasions

Ripped apart by a deadly war, which had been fought over not only the institution of slavery but the meaning and purpose of a democratic society, the United States attempted to put itself back together again in the coming decades while undergoing massive changes. Each of these changes tested the leadership of the country and the understanding of the people. Needless to say, both the leaders and the people were often found wanting as they struggled with numerous problems, including the challenges and failures of Reconstruction; the emergence of a segregated society (North as well as South); the rapid Western expansion, which doubled the size of the country; the Indian wars, which in some cases became acts of genocide; the Industrial Revolution; the crass money culture of the new plutocracy; the massive migrations into and across the country; the prejudicial actions against and between certain ethnic groups; the new factory systems and poor working conditions; the rapid urbanization; the growth of slum ghettos; the political corruption that went hand in hand with rapid urban growth; the series of economic crises (some of devastating proportions); the major shifts in social values and behavior; the various attempts to control or deny change with prohibitions (from Asian immigrants to alcohol); the new demands and ideas of women;

the inadequate, sometimes dim-witted response of most men to the sexual, ethnic, and racial challenges; the imperialist expansions and conflicts (where men could still be men); and – as a nightmarish culmination to these many disruptive, often radical changes in social and political order – the two world wars, framing a world depression.

World War II thus served as a hellish finale to the long, troubled era of eighty years. The age concluded as it began: a president dying in office, just after being reelected. Unlike Lincoln, Roosevelt did not get to see the end of his war, for he died on 12 April and the war continued until August. Nor was his death tied to the theatre (except the metaphoric theatre of war). So the date of 1945 may seem less than definitive for establishing the culminating point in an era of American theatre history. But if death is one of our bench-marks for epochs in American history, the 1940s must qualify as a major juncture that affected all aspects of society, including theatre.

World War II, like the Civil War, claimed over a half-million Americans on the battlefield. Horrible numbers, in two terrifying decades. Yet even these stark numbers seem insignificant when compared to the approximately 50 million people, soldiers and civilians, who died as a result of World War II, including 6 million Jews and 15 to 20 million Russians. Concluding the massacres, and as a coda to slaughter, over 200 thousand Japanese civilians died on 6 and 9 August 1945 in Hiroshima and Nagasaki, consumed in the ghastly firestorm of two atomic bombs. Finally the war was over with the dropping of those two bombs, which provided not only closure to an age but the defining concept and fearful condition for the next.

If all of these deaths are not enough to mark and stigmatize the period between 1865 and 1945, we must remember other bloody struggles, including World War I with 10 million lives sacrified on the battlefields, though the number of American deaths was only a small fraction of this total. Also, during this era the United States fought its Indian wars, which the theatre celebrated grandly for decades with Wild West shows (until film took over the popular narrative, shifting the white man's burden from Buffalo Bill and Pawnee Bill to Tom Mix and John Wayne). Completing the circle between theatre and country, Teddy Roosevelt was sufficiently inspired by Buffalo Bill's famous "Rough Riders" to create a cavalry unit of cowboys and college boys who fought under that banner during the Spanish–American War of 1898 (a war in which Tom Mix participated, but not as a Rough Rider).

And sadly, within the national borders another kind of war was waged after the Civil War by groups of southern men who founded secret societies, such as the Ku Klux Klan, the Knights of the White Camellia, and the Order of the White Rose. Inflamed by racism (yet another version of the white man's burden), members of these societies set in motion a series of guerrilla campaigns against black people, especially black men. These paramilitary attacks would flair up sporadically through the following decades. Thousands of homes were burned to the ground (the smoldering ashes serving as ghastly analogues to Sherman's scorched-earth march to the sea). Besides the many torched homes, approximately three thousand lynchings were carried out between 1865 and 1945. Very few of these cases were ever brought to trial.[3] Thus, an undeclared war was allowed to operate, often with tacit support from civic, business, and religious leaders.

These criminal acts and racial attitudes found their surrogate life in the theatre in the staging of Thomas Dixon Jr.'s popular novel *The Clansman* (1906), with Holbrook Blinn in blackface (that all-American tradition that characterizes popular theatre and embodies racial attitudes). The Klan's campaign to "save the south" was also glorified on film by D. W. Griffith as nothing less than the *Birth of a Nation* in 1915, the year the Ku Klux Klan reorganized and reinvented itself at Stone Mountain, Georgia. The film served as recruiting propaganda, though this was not Griffith's aim.

All in all, then, these eighty years were a very deadly era, not matched before or since. To frame the historical topic and problem in this manner is to suggest that nothing less than a tragic understanding of life and history could serve the task. Given the horror and suffering of these decades, anything short of a tragic vision would seem most inadequate for representing and expressing the age. But in great measure tragedy as a dramatic form lost its voice and purpose in the nineteenth century, with the exception of Shakespearean performance. In the place of tragedy the American stage put melodramas, minstrel shows, comedies, farces, circuses, vaudevilles, burlesques, operas, operettas, musicals, musical revues, medicine shows, amusement arcades, and Wild West shows – the whole hieroglyphic world of popular culture. And, in turn, most of the entertainment in the twentieth century on stage, radio, and screen continued to be presented in these popular modes, to the satisfaction of the majority of spectators. Of course, some theatrical artists attempted to represent the dark truths of the age, but in the main the great entertainment industry which grew rapidly with the country was quite satisfied to deliver an upbeat version of life and the times (see R. C. Allen; Fields and Fields; Kasson, *Amusing;* Lynes; Nye; Rourke; Toll).

What are we to make of this seeming failure or evasion of American theatre? How can we account for such an apparent disjunction between stage and age? Obviously, there is no law that requires theatre to be either the mirror of the nation or its editorial page. Nor must it put history on stage. In fact, the benefits of entertainment are normally not mimetic. We seek release from the daily grind and the image in the mirror. Whether we laugh or cry, we often want a different, more exciting version of life and self than what occurs within the domains of the real. As George Jean Nathan noted in his study of popular theatre in 1918, the vast audience for entertainment sought "horse-play, belly laughter, pretty girls, ingenious scenery, imported ladies of joy and eminent home talent, insane melodramas, lovely limbs, lively tunes, gaudy colors, loud humours, farce, flippancy, fol-de-rol" (quoted in David Nasaw, 42). In short, we prefer a theatre (stage, screen, radio, television, amusement arcade) that separates us from that elusive doppelgänger that Edith Wharton, Henry James, and the realist movement sought to understand.

Realism is fine (in short doses, we say), but we are more often pleased by an imaginative panoroma of life, those charming and bizarre acts of deception by the magicians and wizards of entertainment. We wish to experience the emotional satisfaction of seeing (and perhaps identifying with) clever conjurers who overcome or ignore difficulties by means of charm, cunning, beauty, and daring. From the skillful circus performer to the dashing hero in a melodrama, we want actions and personalities that fill us with awe and admiration. And who knows, perhaps in the process we are occasionally given a glimpse of the sublime (however tarted up).

If history is delivered, we want it in the persona of Buffalo Bill and the other heroes of frontier America. Or give us grand community pageants in city parks (such as those progressive allegories that blossomed everywhere in the nation at the beginning of the twentieth century). Or, most of all, we want to be entertained by the blackface performers who held stage-center during this era, from minstrel shows and *Uncle Tom's Cabin* to Al Jolson, Eddie Cantor, and Amos 'n' Andy. This is the way we want to negotiate race relations.

P. T. Barnum, the Ringling Brothers, B. F. Keith and Edward F. Albee, Oscar Hammerstein I, Charles and Daniel Frohman, David Belasco, Florenz Ziegfeld, the Shubert Brothers, Samuel Goldwyn, Walt Disney – these are the entrepreneurs who figured out how to create and satisfy our desires. Whether we approve or not, they are the main line in the history of American entertainment. Of course, the impresarios' success in mirroring or concocting our desires does not rule out a place or a need for a tragic, political, or realistic theatre, but it makes for very stiff competition.

Still, some playwrights, including Eugene O'Neill, tried to put the real thing onstage – the suffering, the struggles, and the self-deceptions of American lives. From crises to hypocrises, he charted his vision of the American scene – those vistas that began to trouble Whitman after the Civil War. And to some, O'Neill's achievement, however flawed, has suggested a line of development in American theatre: an arc of aesthetic improvement, moral seriousness, and social conscience that reflects upon the conditions of American life (and accords with the history of modernism in the arts).

In the twentieth century a number of dramatists joined O'Neill in the modernist campaign (including Susan Glaspell, Maxwell Anderson, Lillian Hellman, Elmer Rice, Sidney Kingsley, Clifford Odets, Langston Hughes, John

Howard Lawson, and Sophie Treadwell). Each of them wrote some powerful plays, especially on themes of domestic or urban life. These playwrights are often quite astute in their character studies, especially in the ways they focus on loneliness, entrapment, and hypocrisy in American life. Some of them achieved a gritty realism (for example, Rice's *Street Scene,* Kingley's *Dead End*) in language and scenic qualities, though melodramatic themes and idealistic dreams often underlie the action (as happens regularly in O'Neill too). Others are striking for their experimental techniques, usually of an expressionist nature (such as Rice's *The Adding Machine* and Treadwell's *Machinal*).

In addition, a handful of accomplished playwrights, whose works still get read and performed, captured aspects of life with ironic insight: Edward Sheldon, Rachel Crothers, Percy MacKaye, Paul Green, Sidney Howard, Marc Connelly, George S. Kaufman, Clare Boothe Luce, Philip Barry, Robert Sherwood, S. N. Behrman, William Saroyan, Thornton Wilder. Yet without exception, they lacked the kind of tragic vision and understanding that we associate with O'Neill. More to the point, whatever their approaches and topics, they usually turned away from the darker, more intransigent aspects of American life. In sensibility and vision, they leaned toward amelioration and sentimental accommodation. Or they became purveyors of ready-made allegories – morality plays about good and evil.

For instance, Wilder's *The Skin of Our Teeth* (1942), though written and performed during the carnage of World War II, is emblematic of a pervasive (if not pernicious) American desire to put the best spin on events, to offer reassurances that, though "living is struggle," the human race marches forward to a better life: "All I ask is the chance to build new worlds and God has always given us that."[4] Perhaps the American dramatic sensibility is essentially progressive, seeing the world in comedic or tragicomic rather than tragic terms. This sensibility does not rule out good plays, but it does raise questions about the ability of the theatre to take the measure of the country that Whitman and Booth experienced with the death of Lincoln, that O'Neill in his exceptional way engaged, and that other American writers, including novelists from Melville to Faulkner, saw outside the windows of their studies.

To note these attributes of American theatre is not to deny that serious historical events and conditions, including the wars, found their way to the stage. Indeed, each of our wars – the Civil War, the Indian wars, the Spanish–American War, World War I, and World War II – called forth a surrogate theatre of war, usually featuring patriotism, honor, bravery, and noble sacrifice.

In the case of the Civil War, three generations of playwrights dramatized it, but they avoided not only the horror of battle (most difficult to put onstage) but also the major issues and problems over which the war was fought. The demands of putting history on stage are seldom met. No one wrote a play like

Stephen Crane's novel *The Red Badge of Courage* (1895). Although O'Neill's *Mourning Becomes Electra* (1931) uses the Civil War to frame a tragic tale (which only indirectly is about the war), most Civil War plays such as Dion Boucicault's *Belle Lamar* (1874), William Gillette's *Held by the Enemy* (1886), Bronson Howard's *Shenandoah* (1889), Gillette's *Secret Service* (1895; revised 1896), David Belasco's *The Heart of Maryland* (1895), and Augustus Thomas's *The Copperhead* (1918) are popular melodramas that feature love, intrigue, spies, danger, patriotism, and fantastic *coups de théâtre* (horses galloping across the stage, a Northern spy sending crucial telegraph messages while Southerners descend upon him, and, best of all, a heroine swinging on the clapper of a huge bell to stop it from sounding an alarm).

As for World War I, though a handful of plays after the war spoke to the difficulties or impossibilities of returning to the prewar social order, the theatre's usual response to the war was moral uplift, evasion, and even silliness. For example, during the war George M. Cohan stirred up patriotism with his song "Over There," which won him a Congressional Medal and a signed photograph from President Wilson. The chorus girls of Ziegfeld and the Shuberts took part in patriotic extravaganzas and rallies for the war, parading in fetching costumes that suggested to the eye what we were fighting to protect. And a number of plays presented sympathetic yet sentimental stories about returning heroes who often struggled to find a place again in home and society. There were also dozens of plays, written before, during, and after the war, that featured evil German agents, spies, conspirators, and sympathizers, all exposed and defeated by the end of the play. With rare exceptions – *Aria da Capo* (1919) by Edna St. Vincent Millay, *The Inheritors* (1921) by Susan Glaspell, and *What Price Glory* (1924) by Maxwell Anderson and Laurence Stallings – the stage was not up to the task of seriously confronting the terrible conditions and moral issues of war. In contrast to the "lost generation" novelists, such as Hemingway, who tried to articulate the realities of war, the theatre usually pumped for heartfelt emotion. Or it just turned its attention elsewhere (see Wainscott, *Emergence,* 7–36).

To be expected, at the time of World War II, the German villains returned to the stage, once again taking their part in melodramatic struggles between good and evil. In most of these plays an earnest sense of imminent danger alternates with a moral tone of righteous resolve, though at the end of the war some plays, less given to preaching, attempted to reveal the psychological struggles of both those who went to war and those who remained at home. The difficulties of the returning wounded was a recurring topic, both on stage and screen. Robert Sherwood's screenplay for *The Best Years of Our Life* (1946) is the most striking example.

Yet, when surveying American drama during the war years (1939–1945), John Gassner wondered "what to make of a diminished thing." He found that serious plays about the war were only moderately successful in confronting the war and reaching a public. "The sober fact is that the American dramatist found varying degrees of difficulty in adjusting himself to the crisis. And it may as well be added that he received only scant encouragement or correction from the audiences that had grown accustomed to his old wares and were, besides, understandably avid for entertainment" (Gassner, *Best Plays . . . Modern,* xii). Of course, in a selective way we can identify some worthy plays by leading playwrights, but the abiding dichotomy between serious theatre and popular entertainment seemed to define the operations and struggles of American theatre.

Even the most accomplished playwrights of the time, such as Lillian Hellman, whose *Watch on the Rhine* (1941) received a request from President Roosevelt for a benefit performance, tended to write melodramas on the topic of war and evil. Earnest liberal outrage about the Russian invasion of Finland enlivens Robert Sherwood's *There Shall Be No Night* (1940), but this Pulitzer Prize–winning play is primarily a piece of propaganda against American isolationism. Likewise, though Maxwell Anderson co-authored a powerful drama in 1924, *What Price Glory,* he provided only a conventional melodrama in the case of *Key Largo* (1939).[5] And after the war, though some plays examined the evils of totalitarianism or the misery of war, they have not established themselves as major works of drama. Among the most effective was Sidney Kingsley's *Darkness at Noon* (1951), adapted from Arthur Koestler's novel.

Orson Welles: The New Wizard

Interestingly, the art of adaptation provided two of the strongest theatrical productions in the late 1930s and early 1940s. One of them put the conditions of racial conflict, suffering, and prejudice on the stage; the other confronted its audience with the horror of the fascist threat in Europe. There was no turning away from "the real thing" in these cases. The first production was a radical adaptation of Shakespeare's *Julius Caesar* (that play again); the second was the staging of Richard Wright's powerful novel, *Native Son.* The talents of Orson Welles and John Houseman were behind both productions.

In 1940 Richard Wright published *Native Son,* his searing novel about murder and racism in the 1930s. Houseman and Welles had read it with enthusiasm as soon as it appeared. Houseman then contacted Wright, and in a series of letters he encouraged Wright to work with him and Welles on the staging of the novel. At the same time Paul Green and Wright had begun to work on a playscript. When Houseman received a draft of their work, he had to force revisions, against Green's wishes, because Green had softened and sentimentalized key aspects of the story. Green threatened a lawsuit, but backed down when Houseman, Welles, and Wright stood their ground. Working separately with Wright, Houseman was able to maintain the harsh integrity of the novel (see both Callow and Houseman for details). Houseman also served officially as producer, tapping Welles, his colleague of the last five years in a number of stage productions, to direct the play. At that time Welles was putting the finishing touches on his first film, *Citizen Kane.* After reading the revised playscript for *Native Son,* Welles jumped at the opportunity.

Wright's novel presents the rage and confusion of a black man, Bigger Thomas, who accidentally kills a white woman, burns her body in a basement furnace, flees, is caught, and then is tried and condemned to death. Racial prejudice and hate, including self-hate, define the action. For Wright, the inferno of racial hate and struggle does not explode "next time," as James Baldwin would later warn; the fire burns now. The novel, an indictment of American racism, moves through a number of stark, dramatic scenes that Wright, Green, and Houseman were able to adapt to the stage effectively. Welles cast Canada Lee, ex-prizefighter and nightclub owner, as Bigger Thomas. Lee had played Banquo in Welles's "voodoo" *Macbeth* in 1936. Most of the other roles were taken by the actors who had been working with Welles and Houseman during the last five years at the Federal Theatre Project, the Mercury Theatre, and the RKO studio in Hollywood.

The Broadway production opened 24 March 1941 at the St. James Theatre and ran until July (then was revived for eleven weeks in 1942). During the preceding two decades a small handful of productions that featured black performers (rather than blackface actors) had reached Broadway, including some successful musicals by blacks, such as *Shuffle Along* (1921) by Noble Sissle and Eubie Blake. And several white playwrights had written and staged Broadway plays on black themes: Ridgely Torrence, *Three Plays for a Negro Theatre* (1917), Eugene O'Neill (*The Emperor Jones,* 1921; *All God's Chillin' Got Wings,* 1924), Paul Green (*In Abraham's Bosom,* 1926), Dorothy and Du Bose Heyward (*Porgy,* 1927), Marc Connelly (*The Green Pastures,* 1930), and George and Ira Gershwin (*Porgy and Bess,* 1935). But only a few serious plays written by black dramatists had reached Broadway (such as Willis Richardson, *The Chipwoman's Fortune,* 1923). An artistic renaissance was occurring in Harlem, but the doors to Broadway swung open only occasionally. One noteworthy exception was the production of Langston Hughes's *Mulatto* (1935), a powerful melodrama about racial struggle in the South that starred Rose McClendon.

During this period, then, a postminstrel theatre about blacks was beginning to develop in New York, but white playwrights were still prevalent and white producers were the norm, almost the reigning law. Predominantly, three images of blacks held the stage: (1) good-natured, simple blacks, (2) dancing, happy blacks, and (3) exotic, savage blacks.

Welles and Houseman continued the condition of white control (with Welles's fame serving to generate the funds). At the same time, they were prepared to push further than most others in taking up serious racial topics. *Native Son* was something new, a topic and an approach not seen on the American stage (with the possible exception of Theodore Ward's *Big White Fog,* performed in Chicago in 1938, but it was subsidized by the Federal Theatre Project).

Mixing realistic and expressionistic techniques in design and staging, Welles created a nightmare world of racial confrontations as Bigger moves from tenement room to his final jail cell. Enclosing yellow brick walls defined the action; sounds, such as the burning furnace, haunted and followed Bigger through his descent into his own hell. The murder of Mary Dalton, played by Anne Burr, was so violent that spectators gasped in fear and shock. Canada Lee was the very embodiment of Bigger Thomas, the defiant, anguished black man of the Chicago streets who is "crucified," said Welles, "by the Jim Crow world in which he lived" (quoted in Callow, 546).

The reviews were full of praise for the actors and the production (except for an attack from the Hearst's *Journal-American,* which complained about communist propaganda). And Richard Wright was just as pleased: "I cannot stress too highly my profound respect and admiration for Orson Welles, the director of this play. He is beyond doubt the most courageous, gallant, and talented director in the modern stage in the world today" (quoted in Brady, 298).

Broadway theatre at the time was still a white enterprise, fenced in by racial prejudice. But this production suggests that Wright, Houseman, Green, and Welles – along with the actors, especially Canada Lee, and the designers James Morcom, Andrea Nouryeh, and Jean Rosenthal – were able to create a partnership that delivered drama of the highest calibre, unlike anything else being written or performed on the American stage of the time. Only O'Neill was working at this dramatic level. But *Native Son,* starkly and powerfully realized on stage, had more to say about race in America than even O'Neill's plays were able to articulate. And the partnership of blacks and whites in this case almost overcame the persistent racism and paternalism that characterized so much of "black theatre" in the era. But, sadly, it was a one-time venture. And it did not help clear much ground for a self-sustaining black theatre in the professional world of Broadway.

As for the modern-dress production of *Julius Caesar,* which Welles adapted and staged in 1937, a strong case could be made that it was more successful in putting war, death, and suffering onstage than any of the new plays of the 1930s and 1940s.[6] It was also more effective than his "voodoo" *Macbeth* the year before (which was perceived by most white people as a gimmicky use of black actors – yet one more version of the "exotic" and "primitive" nature of black identity and culture).[7] The production of *Julius Caesar* at the new Mercury Theatre captured the imagination of the audience and the temper of the times. It presented both a general idea of the corruption of power and a specific conception of the moral and political concerns of the age, especially the threatening conditions in Germany and Italy.

The lighting design, prepared by Jean Rosenthal, Sam Leve, and Welles, suggested the look and feel of Hitler's Nuremberg rallies. The exposed stage wall was painted the color of dried blood. The conspirators' heavy boots on the raised platforms created the ominous drumming sound of soldiers marching. And the murders of Caesar and Cinna the Poet, played out in red, intense lights, were terrible, bloody moments, suggesting the unleashing of perverse human pleasures in the act of killing. As John Mason Brown wrote in his review in the *New York Post:*

> Something deathless and dangerous in the world sweeps past you down the darkened aisles at the Mercury and takes possession of the proud, gaunt stage. It is something fearful and ominous, something turbulent and to be dreaded, which distends the drama to include the life of nations as well as of men. (Quoted in Callow, 337)

For Brown and others, as they watched the production, "a map of the world" unrolled, "increasingly splotched with sickening colors." Emblematic of his aim, Welles created a subtitle for the play: *The Death of a Dictator.* The Nazi world appeared on stage, and step by step the noble Brutus, as played by Welles, became contaminated by the very disease he had tried to control and contain. A parable for the times.

Obviously, having just directed Marc Blitzstein's political opera *The Cradle Will Rock* in June 1937, Welles was sympathetic to the political agenda of leftist theatre in the 1930s. A few months earlier (11 April 1937) he had presented on radio Archibald MacLeish's antitotalitarian verse drama *The Fall of the City.* A strong polemic against fascism, the play was listened to by millions who were mesmerized by Welles's deep voice of threatening doom. So when he took up *Julius Caesar,* he decided to place its action within the context of "the lurid theatricality of the regimes of Mussolini and Hitler," as Simon Callow notes (324). Clearly, the marching, the bloody imagery, and the Nuremberg lighting effects expressed the threatening world of fascist power.

Re-creating this menacing, horrible world of fascism became Welles's primary aim. To achieve his theatrical concept, he shaped a production that ran without intermission for an hour and a half. The play was cut substantially (Act Five, for example, was reduced to one page). This tightened, lean version of the play was of great visual and verbal power, the action moving from death to death. Accordingly, the performance gained in political immediacy and emotional power, especially for an audience familiar with the images of fascism on the movie newsreels. But it also lost some of the complexity and tragic irony of the Shakespearean original.

This revisionist attempt to swerve away from the full play and its political meanings succeeded in setting up a tension or contradiction between Shake-speare's dramatic text and Welles's performance text. For example, on its own terms Shakespeare's play does not present Caesar as a dictatorial figure like Mussolini. Nor is Marc Antony a fascist henchman. As Richard France notes in his *Theatre of Orson Welles,* the implied "parallels with Mussolini should not be stressed too closely." France nonetheless believes the produc-tion was "Welles's highest achievement in the theatre" and calls it "a dazzling piece of propaganda, with the political equation so skillfully drawn that the spectator could not help but be partisan" (106–107).

Most reviewers and spectators were indeed partisan, enthusiastic about the production and its political impact. But the success of the production also raised some concerns. Stark Young, writing for *The New Republic,* was bothered by the cuttings, and he complained about the very thing others praised: the theatricality of the whole venture. The production was dazzling in its staging and emotional power, but Young felt that it created some con-fusing ideas in the process (Brady, 126). The visual effects were also criti-cized by *The Daily Worker,* the communist newspaper, which accused Welles of producing empty "formalism." We do not have to stand with *The Daily Worker* (which was prisoner to party slogans and an agitprop mentality) to see that Welles was a great magician of special effects and moods that he offered up with great pleasure (for himself as well as the spectators).

To be expected, then, Welles's substantial talent in production was brought to bear not just for realizing a political theatre but also for creating effective and seductive acts of theatricalism.[8] Indeed, Welles, the great magi-cian and seducer, was celebrated for the hypnotic power of his productions, especially the grandly staged moments. No doubt the *Julius Caesar* produc-tion created a threatening and pervasive sense of evil. In this it provided a similitude of foreboding reality and deservedly received high praise from many spectators. It rang true for them. But for others Welles's spectacular effects, such as the ominous lighting Rosenthal created at his behest, were theatrical tricks that not only distorted or simplified the text but also replaced political ideas and moral imperatives with theatrical wizardry.

Without doubt, Welles's powerful *Julius Caesar* was one of the most signifi-cant Shakespearean productions on the American stage, but the more the pro-duction succeeded theatrically, the more it raised questions about the power and purpose of theatricality. Here we confront an abiding controversy about Orson Welles. Perhaps John Houseman, Welles's partner in most of his great ventures between 1936 and 1941, expressed the terms of the dilemma best:

> Welles is at heart a magician whose particular talent lies not so much in his creative imagination (which is considerable) as in his proven ability to stretch the familiar elements of theatrical effect far beyond the normal

point of tension. For this reason his productions require more elaborate preparation and more perfect execution than most. At that – like all complicated magical tricks – they remain, until the last minute, in a state of precarious balance. (Quoted in Callow, 411–12)

As if to personally illustrate this "state of precarious balance," Welles was also doing radio shows at this time, playing the role of a man with a divided identity: Lamont Cranston, who is also The Shadow, who has "the hypnotic power to cloud men's minds so they cannot see him" (Callow, 321). And as if persona and person were one, Welles clouded minds as he performed his magic show. What is amazing is that he was only twenty-two years old, passing for a much older person. Another trick of high talent.

The point to be made here about Welles is not merely biographical. He was a great American artist and entertainer, on stage, radio, and screen. His career thus provides a window onto the American theatre, as Simon Callow astutely points out: "The conflicting and highly emotional ingredients of his artistic agenda go some way toward explaining why, half-audacious modernist, half-archaic dreamer, relunctant totalitarian and self-doubting star, he created such an extraordinary impact in the world of American theatre of the thirties" (320).

In many ways, Welles is a touchstone for us, a way of discovering how and why the apparent tension between "the real thing" and a confusing "hieroglyphic world" of "arbitrary signs" is at the heart of American entertainment. Indeed, I want to suggest that this tension (dichotomy, binary, contradiction, dilemma, or paradox) is a recurring aspect of American theatre throughout this entire era. Which is to say that the "state of precarious balance" that Houseman recognized in Welles is our topic – and not only in the case of Welles. It is the tablet on which is written some of the significant codes of the American theatre.

America the Spectatorium

RALPH WALDO EMERSON: Every man's condition is a solution in hieroglyphics to those inquiries he would put.
Nature (1836)

BARNUM CIRCUS PROGRAM, 1876 – the year of the United States Centennial Celebration:

> And the Star Spangled Banner
> In triumph shall wave
> O'er the grandest of shows
> Even Barnum e'er gave.

BRANDER MATTHEWS: Our actors are now less rhetorical and
more pictorial – as they must be on the stage of our modern
theatre.

On Acting (1914)

Theatrical Revolutions and the Lively Arts

Throughout the nineteenth century the American stage struggled to find and
realize its own identity. So argued a number of observers at the time; so we
have argued ever since, with some justification of course. After the Civil War
not a year passed without someone lamenting "the failure of the American
playwright" or calling for the "new American theatre" or the "future American
drama." Even the playwrights themselves, including Augustin Daly, Edward
Harrigan, Dion Boucicault, and Bronson Howard joined the campaign. As
Boucicault stated in 1890: "There is not, and there never has been, a literary
institution, which could be called the American Drama. We have produced no
dramatists essentially American to rival such workers as Fenimore Cooper,
Bret Harte, Hawthorne, Mrs. Harriet Beecher Stowe, and others of world-wide
reputation in the realms of narrative fiction" (quoted in Wolter, 209). A hundred years later, most of us agree with Boucicault, though our standard list of
well-known fiction writers would include Poe, Twain, Melville, and Henry
James as well. And, making one other minor correction, we would note that
in 1890 James Herne's *Margaret Fleming,* a precursor of modern realism, was
performed in Boston.

The emergence of theatrical realism (of which David Belasco's sets,
Stanislavskian acting, *Long Day's Journey into Night* are all hallmarks) is one
important aspect of the history of American entertainment. Indeed, when
realism is placed within the larger context of theatrical modernism, including
the symbolist and expressionist movements in design and playwriting, we
have the basic terms for our standard history of the expansion and ampli-
tude of American theatre.

Accordingly, we can identify a number of achievements that, taken together,
reveal a line of development from nineteenth-century popular entertainment –
especially melodrama, minstrelsy, and variety shows – to a modern "art of the
theatre," as Sheldon Cheney proclaimed in 1925 (in *The Art Theater*). This new
American theatre, benefiting from the Little Theatre movement, the universities, the plays of Ibsen, the directing talent of Max Reinhardt, and the ideas of
Gordon Craig, demonstrated that "the real progress of the American theatre"
could finally be charted (Cheney, *The New Movement in the Theater,* 177).

Most important, as Arthur Hobson Quinn declared, a "drama of revolt"
arrived in the 1920s (*American Drama from Civil War,* II, 208). By 1930, as
Oliver Sayler proclaimed, "the fact of revolt" was causing "in reality a vast,

overwhelming readjustment of values, involving not alone the arts as such but our whole understanding and conception of life" (13). Even American actors turned revolutionaries of a sort by successfully organizing Actors' Equity into a labor union that went on strike in 1919 against the Theatrical Syndicate, the Shuberts, Ziegfeld, and the other producers.

Clearly, American theatre had changed. At the beginning of this developmental history, in the postbellum era, we find Dion Boucicault, P. T. Barnum, and the United Mastodon Minstrels; at the end, by the mid–twentieth century, we have Eugene O'Neill (with Nobel Prize in hand), Robert Edmond Jones (the dean of design), and the Group Theatre – all emblematic of the triumph of art. Thus, within this period American playwriting is redeemed by modernist understanding; garish spectacle is tamed and refined by the "new stagecraft;" and the actor's craft, once a ragbag of clever techniques and cheap tricks, is transformed into a "fervent" program of social art and professional training. Similarly, the Bones and Tambo "delineators" of blackface minstrelsy give way slowly to an emerging African American theatre – clearly a moral as well as aesthetic improvement. (The fact that minstrelsy and Barnum might be more American than the Group Theatre's approach to theatre is something to be set aside in this progressive narrative.)

This history – one of several possible narratives that I want to consider – charts not only the aesthetic improvement of drama and theatre but also the upward mobility and hard-won respectability of theatre people in American society (see McArthur). In brief, theatre moved from a suspect enterprise, often seen as having little or no redeeming value (either artistic or moral), to the honored profession of accomplished performers, playwrights, designers, and producers.

For compelling reasons, then, this evolutionary narrative has established itself in our histories of American theatre. Of course recent scholarship, though acknowledging and honoring this triumphant history of the "art theatre," has enlarged the history to encompass several additional developments: (1) the role and place of women in American theatre, (2) the contributions of African American theatre and performers, (3) the place of ethnic and multicultural theatre, (4) the importance of American comedy (plays and performers), and (5) the central place of musical theatre.

Also, some scholars contend that popular entertainment is just as significant (and institutionally vital) as literary realism or theatrical modernism. Indeed, in opposition to Sheldon Cheney, Gilbert Seldes argued in *The Seven Lively Arts* (1924) that the definitive achievements in modern American entertainment should be credited to the popular artists: George M. Cohan, Al Jolson, Irving Berlin, Fanny Brice, the Marx Brothers, Flo Ziegfeld, Charlie Chaplin, George Gershwin, Cole Porter, Noble Sissle and Eubie Blake, and Florence Howe. For Seldes, much of the "high-minded art" of the modern era, which he identifies as serious drama, civic pageants, opera, and "pseudo-Greek" or classical dancing, is in service to "The Great God Bogus":

> The bogus arts are corrupting the lively ones – because an essential defect of the bogus is that they pretend to be better than the popular arts, yet they desperately want to be popular. They borrow and spoil what is good; they persuade people by appealing to their snobbery that they are the real thing. (309)

For Seldes, and many other champions of popular art, "the real right thing" (324) must be sought in the lively arts that stayed true to the Rabelaisian vitality of life: "our existence is hard, precise, high spirited" (318).

Striding defiantly to the cathedral of art, Seldes "nails upon its doors the following beliefs":

> That Al Jolson is more interesting to the intelligent mind than John Barrymore and Fanny Brice than Ethel; . . .
> That Florenz Ziegfeld is a better producer than David Belasco; . . .
> That the circus can be and often is more artistic than the Metropolitan Opera House in New York;
> That the civic masque is not perceptibly superior to the Elks' Parade in Atlantic City; . . .
> That the lively arts as they exist in America to-day are entertaining, interesting, and important;
> That with a few exceptions these same arts are more interesting to the adult cultivated intelligence than most of the things which pass for art in cultured society. (309, 349)

Seldes's spirited defense of the popular arts and artists serves as a necessary reminder that any history of the American theatre that fails to honor this rich theatrical tradition would be not only incomplete but myopic. For many observers this expansive tradition, stretching from minstrelsy, circuses, and vaudeville to the popular entertainment of the modern stage, screen, radio, and television, is the definitive achievement of American culture (on Seldes as cultural critic, see Kammen).

In making this case, however, we do not need to declare that everything about popular culture is wonderful and everything about modernist art is bogus. At times, in his polemical enthusiasm, Seldes sets up absolute (and finally false) dichotomies between low and high culture. But at his best he argues that "there is no opposition between the great and the lively arts." Both, in fact, "are opposed in spirit to the middle or bogus arts" (349). This method of identifying a third term is one way to open up the discussion, to get beyond the familiar binarisms.

In this spirit, I want to consider some additional achievements of American entertainment. Necessarily, then, I must express some reservations about the privileged place of the standard history that maps the chronological development of American theatre from popular entertainment to the triumph of realism and modernism. I counter this narrative not in order to dismiss "the real thing" but to enlarge and modify the historical registers that we use to identity, describe, and understand the history of American theatre.

In order to trace the lineaments of this fuller history, let us return to the 1880s, the era of Daly, Howard, Harrigan, and Boucicault. As we survey this transitional period, we want to note not only why the general complaints about the contemporary drama had some justification but also how and why other developments were changing the terms of what constitutes a "new American theatre." It is true, of course, that dozens of plays and adaptations from the European stage were performed in New York and across the country during this time. For example, the operettas of Gilbert and Sullivan dominated musical theatre in the 1880s. Also, people flocked to see the visiting stars from Europe. Thus, despite the familiar complaints, the American theatre had apparently accommodated itself to European culture. (Even the campaigns for a new drama were fought under the colors of European theatre, especially the plays of Ibsen.) By default, the American theatre had abandoned the jingoism that had contributed to the Astor Place riot of 1849. European culture reigned supreme. Or so it seemed. But let's look more closely at the theatrical scene.

The Triumph of Light

The year 1883 was one of celebration in New York City. The major event was the opening of the Brooklyn Bridge, which Walt Whitman praised, rather fancifully, as the fulfillment of Columbus's mission to create a linked world. That year also saw the opening of the Metropolitan Opera House, a tribute to new wealth and social status (as well as musical pleasure). Italian and French operas of the nineteenth century dominated the first season. The social elite showed little interest in the operas of Wagner (who had died in February that year).

One of the highpoints of the theatrical season was the visit of the British actors Henry Irving and Ellen Terry, who made the first of their many American tours. They presented *The Bells, Charles I, Louis XI, The Merchant of Venice, The Lyons Mail, The Belle's Strategem, Much Ado About Nothing,* and *The Captain of the Watch.* New Yorkers were given the opportunity to compare Irving and Edwin Booth when Booth returned to New York at the end of the year to present his standard repertory: *Richelieu, King Lear, Hamlet, The Fool's Revenge, Othello, Macbeth, The Merchant of Venice,* and *Katherine and Petruchio.* Everyone agreed that the scenic and ensemble values of Irving's productions were superior to Booth's rather drab presentations. But many observers felt, perhaps with touches of national pride, that Booth was the more poetic actor, showing a fuller tragic sensibility and talent. But unlike Edwin Forrest a few decades earlier, Booth made no attempt to generate patriotic fervor in his audiences. Nor did he select a repertory that might serve to put an American stamp on his talent and appeal.

Likewise, much of the New York theatre of 1883 showed little or no dedication to "a new American theatre." Oscar Wilde's *Vera; or, The Nihilist* played at Union Square, though it was not well received. When Wilde, who was also on an American tour, took a curtain call he was booed; the play was quickly withdrawn. Fanny Davenport, tapping another of Sarah Bernhardt's French roles, presented Sardou's *Fedora.* Davenport was generally praised, but most reviewers agreed that she lacked the emotional power of Bernhardt. Augustin Daly's company continued to have success with adaptations of German farces. Richard Mansfield's career was launched when he was chosen at the last minute to play a villainous Baron in Octave Feuillet's *A Parisian Romance,* adapted from the French by A. R. Cazuran. James O'Neill began his long career in *The Count of Monte Cristo.* Lillian Russell starred in an Offenbach opéra bouffe, *The Princess of Trébizonde.* And Helena Modjeska attempted to stage Ibsen's *A Doll's House,* retitled *Thora,* but the production failed.

On the American front, revivals provided the major contributions. Joseph Jefferson continued to present *Rip Van Winkle.* (He also starred in Sheridan's *The Rivals.*) Lawrence Barrett revived George Henry Boker's *Francesca da Rimini* with great success, and then played the role on tour. But Boker's play was hardly a sign of future developments. Also, Harrigan and Hart revived both *The Mulligan Guard Ball* and *The Mulligan Guard Picnic,* drawing audiences for weeks in each case. Harrigan was coming to the end of his series of plays about the Mulligan Guards, but his new work, *Cordelia's Aspirations,* was a great success, running for 176 performances. More than anyone else, he had been able to demonstrate that American plays on contemporary American topics had popular appeal. In this achievement, he anticipated the development of modern realistic drama (though the distance between his sentimental topicality and the critical force of modernist realism is quite apparent).

Another theatrical event in 1883 deserves special attention, in part because it bridges the European–American relationship in interesting ways, but more importantly because it captures a major new development. In midsummer two theatre impresarios, Bolossy and Irme Kiralfy, made a trip across the Hudson River to meet with Thomas Alva Edison at his Menlo Park laboratory. They wanted to see if he would allow them to incorporate his new invention, the electric light bulb, into a musical ballet called *Excelsior* that they were adapting for its American premiere at Niblo's Gardens. They also sought his guidance on how the magical lighting effects might best be accomplished.

Excelsior, a visual extravaganza of scenery, dance, and music, had been produced in Milan and Paris the previous two years. Choreographed by Luigi Manzotti, it was a celebration of the technological progress of humankind. The narrative, presented in pantomime, represented highpoints in human advancement, including the digging of tunnels through the Alps and the building of the Suez Canel. The production also featured the first steam engine to be put on stage. In a series of allegorical scenes, the forces of Light and Darkness battle one another. Of course, as the progress of science requires, the struggles culminate with the victory of the heroine Light over the villain Darkness.

In many ways the Kiralfy brothers were the appropriate, even ideal, producers for this spectacle, given their own life struggles and successes. For them the march of progress was an accurate, personal narrative of human development and opportunity. Born into a large Jewish family in Budapest in the 1840s, they became folk dancers in the 1850s in order to help their family survive after Austrian and Russian troops had defeated the Hungarian nationalists. Their father, a manufacturer of cloth, had provided uniforms for the revolutionary soldiers; when the nationalists failed, he lost his business. In order to escape reprisal, he changed the family name from Königsbaum ("King tree") to the common Hungarian name Kiralfy ("King's son").

The Kiralfy boys, who quickly became accomplished dancers, were soon invited to perform thoughout the Austro–Hungarian empire. By the 1860s the Kiralfy troupe (which had expanded to include more dancing brothers and sisters), toured and performed in many cities and towns of Europe. After successes in Paris and London, the eleven-member family troupe migrated to New York in 1869 to dance in George L. Fox's pantomime *Hiccory, Diccory, Dock.* In 1873 Bolossy and Imre made the jump to theatrical production when they rewrote and restaged *The Black Crook,* the dance and musical spectacle that had first captivated New York audiences in 1866 with its display of women's bodies. Their new production ran for one hundred performances at Niblo's Gardens and then toured the country for years. Following this successful venture, they staged three productions based upon Jules Verne's novels, including *Around the World in Eighty Days,* which featured a hot-air balloon, a suttee's funeral pyre, a sinking steamship, and an elephant (borrowed from P. T. Barnum). The production was revived in New York over a half-dozen times in the next fifteen years and also continued to draw audiences on several extended tours around the country.

In order to create an exciting visual effect for the finale of the new production of *Excelsior,* the brothers wanted to feature the incandescent light bulb, the ideal symbol for their heroine. Their proposal intrigued Edison, an impresario in his own right. Here was an opportunity not only to demonstrate the wonders of electricity but also to draw attention to the invention that Edison was in the process of capitalizing. Moreover, Edison had a special reason for joining forces with the Kiralfy brothers. Three years earlier, inspired by *Around the World in Eighty Days,* he had created extensive (and self-serving) publicity by sending his workers to Japan, the West Indies, and the Amazon region in search of the perfect natural material for the filament of the light bulb. Their reports on their travels and discoveries provided regular copy in the newspapers (and the death of one of them made the adventure of science even more exciting). While his workers traversed exotic and dangerous realms, Edison went off to London, followed by a trip to the Paris Exposition. In both capitals he set up theatrical demonstrations of his new electrical system.

Obviously, Edison understood as well as any theatrical entrepreneur that publicity drew the interests and the funds of the curious. He also realized that an accomplished impresario creates desires as well as new products. Indeed, as P. T. Barnum and other theatrical producers had demonstrated, creating the desire for something new is as important as creating desire's new objects – a double process directed at both speculators and spectators. So, from Edison's perspective, *Excelsior* would be a perfect way to illustrate and publicize the results of his research.

Quickly reaching an agreement, Edison and the Kiralfy brothers designed a production finale that was brilliantly illuminated by more than five hundred light bulbs, which were attached to the costumes of dozens of dancers and to the scenery, a representation of the new Brooklyn Bridge. Each chorus girl was also given an electric wand with a small bulb at the tip. Edison placed batteries in the corsets of the costumes, and he installed his fifty-five-volt dynamo in the theatre to generate the power to run the "novel lighting effects," as the theatre program stated (see B. Kiralfy; Boorstin).

The show, which opened on 21 August 1883, was an immediate hit. After its New York run, *Excelsior,* with its 108 performers, elaborate scenery, hundreds of light bulbs, and dynamo, was taken on the road, playing in most of the large cities of America, from Buffalo and Chicago to Denver and San Francisco. The wizards of spectacle and the "Wizard of Menlo Park" had taken the first step in the transformation of modern entertainment. Electric light would radically change stage lighting and the principles of scenic design. Even more significantly, electricity soon provided a whole new system for delivering entertainment, with the invention of the motion-picture camera, film, and projector.

Excelsior, which featured visual rather than verbal storytelling, became the model for a series of grand spectacles of light and motion that Bolossy Kiralfy staged in the coming years.[9] Using little or no dialogue, these visual extravaganzas, such as *The Siege of Troy, King Solomon, The Orient,* and *Constantinople, or The Revels of the East,* were not just a series of tableaux with panoramic scenery but grand flowing pageants of visual action and scenic transformation. Presented in Europe as well as America, the productions were the forerunners of the silent film spectacles made by Georges Méliès, Cecil B. DeMille, and D. W. Griffith (such as *Le Voyage dans la lune, The Ten Commandments,* and *Intolerance*). Even though he was not drawn to filmmaking, Kiralfy recognized, by the time he wrote his autobiography, that his work had been pointing in that direction: "Films seemed to be a logical extension of my career since by 1930 three of my American spectacles, including *Mathias Sandorf* and *A Trip to the Moon,* had been produced as motion pictures" (207).

In his own way, then, he had learned a basic principle that shaped not only stage spectacles and silent film but also the modern art of Isadora Duncan and the scenic design of Adolphe Appia. In Appia's words: "In space, units of time are expressed by a succession of forms, hence by movement" (7). That movement, organized by specific methods and techniques of each art (kinetic signs, montage, light, music), finds its meanings in the eye and consciousness of the spectator.

Kiralfy continued to stage large spectacles in the early years of the twentieth century, especially at world fairs and expositions where he could present grand pageants with hundreds of performers and splendid scenic effects. This was the period, between 1900 and 1917, when large stage spectacles and pageants were popular across the country. The highpoint was probably Percy MacKaye's *Masque of St. Louis* in 1914 and his *Caliban of the Yellow Sands* in 1916 (see Glassberg; Prevots). But after that, with a few notable exceptions (for instance, the outdoor pageants of Frederick Henry Koch and Paul Green), grand narrative pageants became much less popular on the stage. By 1915 the presentation of narrative spectacle had begun to shift from stage to screen, especially when multireel movies became the new norm. Silent film had transformed the visual codes of spectacle.

Thus, besides making major contributions to stage spectacle, Kiralfy had helped to forge the aethetics of film before the arrrival of film. His visual imagination, which located narrative in a flow of spectacular images and changing configurations, seemed to be made for film.

Obviously, Kiralfy was not alone in this visual endeavor. Nor was the development limited to America. Earlier in the century dioramas and panoramas were hugely popular (see Altick; Oetermann). And as Michael Booth has shown, spectacular theatre became prominent in England and Europe during the 1880s and 1890s. Also, in America Steele MacKaye was, in certain ways, more committed than Kiralfy to the new possibilities of a theatre of the eye. His grand project, the Spectatorium, was developed for the 1893 Columbian Exposition in Chicago. It was supposed to be 480 feet long, 380 feet wide, and 270 feet high – a grand room of optical wonders. Here spectators were to be immersed in a pictorial art of visual images and symbols that told the story of Columbus, the World Finder (see MacKaye, *Epoch*). Unfortunately, the financial support for completing the Spectatorium dissolved at the last minute, perhaps because the organizers of the Chicago World's Fair had the option of a much less costly spectacle on the topic of Columbus, provided by Imre Kiralfy.

So, the Kiralfy brothers and MacKaye began the transformation of American entertainment. Edison, completing the circle, would provide the missing technology for projecting light and motion when he created his Kinetoscope (1888, 1891) and the improved Vitascope (1896). In turn, Edison's Kinetophone (1891), which presented film in synchronization with a phonograph, laid the foundation for the talking and musical film. The rest is history – the triumph of Light over Darkness.

Eight Aspects of American Theatre

Of course, told in this manner, this narrative is yet another version of the evolutionary development of American entertainment. In this case, however, technology and the new codes of spectacle, rather than realism and the codes of modern art, become the "real progress of the American theatre." Does this mean that Sheldon Cheney got it wrong? If so, Kiralfy and Joseph Urban (the designer for *Ziegfeld's Follies* and the Metropolitan Opera) rather than Gordon Craig and Robert Edmond Jones, should be seen as the guiding spirits of the new stagecraft. And film spectacle, with all of its visual power and popular appeal, should be recognized as the apotheosis of American art.

This is hardly an argument that would appeal to the champions of modernist high culture. More troubling, it once again confines us to an overly neat binarism. But I do not raise the spector of *Excelsior* and popular entertainment in order to set up a historical reversal. Instead, I want to suggest that a number of different strands of American cultural development are woven into this historical development. Accordingly, with the visual spectacle of *Excelsior* as another touchstone, I want to identify and discuss eight strands or aspects of American entertainment. Then I will offer some concluding comments on America the Spectatorium.

Some of these strands, like the allegory of *Excelsior,* suggest a process of progressive change, carried forward not only by technological advances (electricity, new broadcast and film media) but also by an expansive capitalist system of production, distribution, and exhibition. The Kiralfy brothers, in the manner of other successful entrepreneurs (both inside and outside the world of entertainment), had developed new products and new consumer demands. Like Edison, they straddle the two eras of entrepreneurial individualism and corporate organization. And like Edison, as inventors and showmen they succeeded up to a point, yet failed to make the major shift to an incorporated capitalist system of horizontal and vertical integration (control of resources, including artistic ideas, actors, and technicans; control of production by means of a system of development; and control of distribution and exhibition). Just as Edison was closed out of the new Hollywood studio system, Bolossy Kiralfy was blocked by the Theatrical Syndicate.

Still, the careers of Kiralfy and Edison reveal many aspects of the capitalist transformation of entertainment into one of the largest industries in America. Along with other key wizards and entrepreneurs of entertainment, such as Steele MacKaye, B. F. Keith and Edward Albee, David Belasco, Charles and Daniel Frohman, Marc Klaw, Abraham Erlanger, the Shubert brothers, Frederic Thompson, Maurice Grau, Florenz Ziegfeld, Adolph Zukor, Cecil B. DeMille, Louis B. Mayer, Samuel Goldwyn, the Warner brothers, and Walt Disney, they helped to place entertainment at the center of the new American culture of leisure, advertising, consumerism, and mass production. That is one historical strand to follow.

The second strand is the representation and place of women in this entertainment juggernaut, which received worshipful adoration from the public. Kiralfy's productions, beginning with *The Black Crook* in 1873, were spectacles of young, dancing women. Obviously, these productions were explicit in their sexual messages. Indeed, when we survey the period between the 1870s and the 1940s, it seems that the whole era was committed to the display of women in scanty costumes – from Adah Isaacs Menken's supposedly nude horse rides in *Mazeppa* in the 1860s to Gypsy Rose Lee's stripteases in the 1930s and 1940s. And throughout the era the dancing chorus girls appeared. We can thus easily follow a line of development from Kiralfy's elaborate choreographies of dancers, presented in highly disciplined maneuvers, to not only Ziegfeld's methods of staging chorus girls in his *Follies* but also the visual wonders of the Busby Berkeley dance numbers on stage (such as *A Connecticut Yankee, Sweet and Low*) and on screen (the films made for Warner Bros.).[10] The electrically illuminated violins that Berkeley's chorus girls stroke in *The Gold Diggers of 1935* are the historical analogues of the electric wands in *Excelsior.*

Of course, the display, appeal, and commodification of young women is far from being the whole story of women in the theatre. Of major significance, hundreds of women playwrights, including Rachel Crothers, Susan Glaspell, Rose Franken, and Lillian Hellman, emerged in America during this era (see Shafer; Demastes). A number of women take leading roles as managers, directors, and producers. And a profound transformation of the place, power, and significance of actresses in American culture and society occurs, especially in the twentieth century (see Dudden; Chinoy and Jenkins; Robinson, Roberts, and Barranger). So the visual shows should be seen as one highly visible part of a series of changes in the identities, activities, and representations of women.

A third historical thread, tied to the first two, is the complex relationship between stage and screen. From the very beginning of film in 1893, when Edison built a little tar paper shack called the Black Maria (the slang term for a police van), theatre and movies have been yoked. There in that primitive film studio Edison filmed Annie Oakley, Buffalo Bill, and Eugen Sandow (the muscle man managed by a young Flo Ziegfeld). Within a few decades all aspects of twentieth-century theatre – performers, aesthetics, performance modes and themes, production, advertising, and business practices and decisions – would be influenced by and often tied to the development of film and the huge industry it generated. Thus, the history of the stage cannot (or should not) be separated from the history of the film industry (see Bowser; Mast; Musser; North; Sklar).

Perhaps one of the major accomplishments of film, helped along by radio, was its ability to create celebrities whose images and voices – far more than their actual presences – produce an aura of seductive appeal, sometimes of almost immeasurable power. Sexual charm was part of the story, but more important, the American stage and screen produced a group of stars who seemed to articulate and capture key aspects of the emerging American sensibility. In them we discovered not only attractive, desirable models for fashion and behavior but a complex set of signs and codes for national selfhood. This is the fourth historical strand to follow here, the culture of fame and influence that developed with the star system. The process began, of course, before the Civil War with the career of Edwin Forrest. And the growing fame of sports stars in the second half of the nineteenth century also contributed. But film clearly expanded the reach and impact of the modern culture of celebrities and the modern society of the iconographic personality (see Leo Brady; Dyer; Freedberg).

A fifth strand is the ethnic history of America. Overall, during the most extensive period of American immigration between the 1840s and the 1920s (the lifetime of Bolossy Kiralfy), a widespread transformation of American culture, including theatre, took place (see Bodnar; Higham; Nugent; Takaki; Thernstrom). On the one hand, ethnic theatre spread throughout the whole country, sometimes becoming, along with religious institutions and activities, the communal home of each ethnic group. Major theatrical activities occurred in the ethnic communities, including the Hispanic, the Scandinavian, and the East European communities (Polish, Latvians, and Lithuanians). On the other hand, key ethnic groups, including the Irish, Italian, and German communities, besides developing their own ethnic theatre, made major contributions to the development of a distinctive American theatre during this era. And as the Kiralfy case demonstrates, the emergence of Jews in the American entertainment industry is a central part of the narrative (see Erdman).

The sixth aspect of this history is the importance of theatrical touring, especially after the railroads had woven the country into a transportation network. Theatrical touring by rail became the financial imperative for individual careers and business operations, especially from the 1870s forward. Part of the story hinges on the displacement of the local stock companies by the many "combination" companies that came out of New York and moved around the country each year (see P. Davis). In turn, this development is at the heart of the changing business system for delivering theatrical entertainment. Only when film and radio provided new modes of distribution for entertainment did the great era of railway touring conclude.

A seventh strand, tied to touring, is the major demographic change in America from a rural to an urban society. In certain ways, by touring the country extensively, performers were able to connect the largest metropolitan centers to the smallest towns. Entertainers went everywhere. Even before the country was united by films and radio, touring performers were able to establish a national culture of shared experiences, from minstrelsy and circuses to popular stage stars and the latest musical delights. At the same time, it is crucial to note that a difficult, wrenching conflict between country and city was being played out in American society. America, despite its frontier ideology and its republican ideal of a piece of land for everyone, was actually becoming an urban society. But not without problems, doubts, conflicts, and suffering. The nation was changing rapidly, too rapidly for many people.

The American theatre community, quite sensitive to the many disjunctions between rural and urban life, offered up something for everyone. Sentimental evocations of country life remained popular for millions of people throughout this era, from homestead plays and Toby shows to communal pageants. At the same time, upbeat celebrations of city life were also popular, from the urban farces and comedies of Edward Harrigan and Charles H. Hoyt to the glamorous musicals and society plays that continued to draw audiences in the twentieth century. And a number of plays, most famously *Abie's Irish Rose* (1922), successfully combined ethnic comedy (Jewish–Irish conflict) and sentimentalism (the triumph of love).

But every action has a reaction. The stage also presented sharply critical dramas of both country and city life, especially from the pens of the modernist playwrights (for example, Susan Glaspell, Eugene O'Neill, Sidney Kingsley). And, in a balancing act between the sentimentalists and the hard-edged modernists, a group of mediators, such as Ned Harrigan, Will Rogers, George S. Kaufman, William Saroyan, Thornton Wilder, George Cukor, Ernst Lubitsch, and Frank Capra, offered their own idiosyncratic versions of American life and institutions that blended critical doubts about current conditions with a measured confidence in the country's future.

At least the mediators seemed to hold out the promise, once again, that Light would emerge victorious over Darkness. Thus, despite the turmoils of the age, American entertainment committed itself primarily to staging the many stories of successful struggle and happy resolution. This was part of the amazing appeal of George M. Cohan. But this recurring portrayal of Light triumphant, though obscuring and distorting the darker conditions of American life, did not completely wash them out. In fact, an often ambiguous and sometimes contradictory presentation of these dark conditions shadowed the positive visual codes of both stage and screen. Consequently, Darkness was everywhere present, acknowledged, and even celebrated in bizarre (sometimes comic) ways, yet paradoxically it was also everywhere invisible, denied, and condemned. In literal terms, it was denigrated. That darkness, most significantly embodied in the conditions and representations of African American life, is the eighth and final strand to be considered here.

The image of blackness, the absence of blackness – this dark dialectic operates at the heart of American entertainment, and it contains a number of the primary dualisms in American culture. Blackface performance, preeminent on the American stage, captured the imaginations of performers and spectators alike. Minstrelsy and *Uncle Tom's Cabin* were popular throughout much of the nation for decades, even into the twentieth century. And when traveling minstrel shows began to decrease in number (as did all road shows by the 1920s and 1930s) the New York stage and the Hollywood screen reconfigured the blackface image in the performances of the celebrities of popular culture: Sophie Tucker, Al Jolson, Eddie Cantor, Shirley Temple, Bing Crosby, and many others. Likewise, film continued to present the visual and verbal codes of the blackface tradition, from *Uncle Tom's Cabin* (1902) and *Birth of a Nation* (1915) to *The Jazz Singer* (1927) with Al Jolson and *Holiday Inn* (1942) with Bing Crosby. And on radio *Amos 'n' Andy* became one of the most popular shows in the nation (beginning as *Sam 'n' Henry* in 1926, and running for twenty-five years).

These images, conditions, masquerades, and commodities of racism defined much about the American theatre during the whole era. This blackface theatre was the heritage that black performers, composers, and playwrights attempted to join. Or perhaps it is more appropriate to say that this was the theatre and tradition from which black entertainers had to separate themselves. Working within but also subverting the blackface practices and ideologies, black theatre slowly began to assert its voice and to present (or repossess) its own images by the turn of the century. In doing so, black performers, playwrights, musicians, producers, and audiences challenged and changed (ever so slowly) a cultural practice that had determined the national perceptions and understanding of race.

In what follows, then, some key attributes of these eight major aspects of American entertainment will be identified and discussed, in a preliminary manner. Necessarily, many important events and figures of this era must be ignored or slighted. Yet perhaps, though a detailed, chronological survey is sacrificed, the benefit of a selective argument is gained. In taking this approach, I want to show that a theatre of the real thing and a theatre of hieroglyphic spectacle, instead of being mutually exclusive, are two dynamic, interrelated codes that operate within various forms and kinds of theatrical entertainment in American culture. Quite often the real and hieroglyphic codes are joined to create a singularly new thing, a theatre of visual seduction and virtuosity, extending from P. T. Barnum through Flo Ziegfeld to Robert Wilson. Among other things, I want to suggest that a theatre of the eye – an American spectatorium – unites many of the seemingly disparate aspects of theatre, culture, and society during this era.

Ethnic Theatre and Culture

In mid-nineteenth-century America, a genteel tradition of Protestant rectitude and social propriety continued to hold power over national attitudes and behavior, but with each passing decade the old values and certainties were slipping away. Though still strong in New England, the culture of gentility was waning, in part because a new economic and social order came into being after the Civil War. Tied to capitalist ventures in mining, railroads, manufacturing, publishing, urban building, and commercial development of new products for home and leisure, this new order spread rapidly throughout the nation, especially as the cities were transformed by the new industrial enterprises and the floodtide of immigrants. The changes were wrenching, as economic cycles of boom and bust became the pattern. And these many disruptions in the economic system not only put major pressure on social systems of family life and communal values but also brought about new cultural values, attitudes, beliefs, and behaviors (see H. Jones; Kasson, *Rudeness;* Lears, *No Place;* Schlereth; Wiebe).

Throughout the nineteenth century, and into the early twentieth century, Protestant ministers continued to preach the moral precepts of the genteel tradition. Their ideas and concerns would provide both a defense of the old order and the moral foundation for social activism in the progressive era (see M. Jones; Lears; Noble). During this period the established families and professional classes maintained their position in the social and cultural spheres, despite the emergence of the new economic class of businessmen, financiers, inventors, and technocrats. In Boston, for example, the Protestant elite held control over the banks, the education system, and the law profession (from the law schools to the political arenas). And from this economic and social foundation they also controlled the arts (especially the opera and the symphony), the private clubs, and the social season.

Yet despite the central power of the old Bostonians, a new social and political order emerged. Irish servants and workers began to gain control of city services and government; then they made their way along various social, educational, and economic avenues. And beyond Boston and the other citadels of gentility, a cruder and rougher social contract was being hammered out, especially in the new cities, such as Chicago, and the new territories of the West (see Cronon; Ethington).

The nineteenth-century stage willingly took up the task of representing the social world of genteel culture, but not often in the sophisticated and ironic ways of novelists such as Henry James and Edith Wharton. Augustin Daly had some success in putting aspects of the contemporary social world on stage, but many of the plays (such as *Divorce* and *Pique*), adapted from popular novels and European drama, confined social representation and critique within the basic theatrical conventions of romance and adventure, made popular by melodrama. A few writers turned to social comedy and drama, including William Dean Howells (a series of one-acts on Boston life) and Bronson Howard (*Young Mrs. Winthrop*). They stand out among the playwrights who attempted to present a critique of genteel society in a gilded age, but even their plays struggle rather unsuccessfully to capture the complexity of social conditions. So the basic issues were essentially evaded.

Unlike the Boston drawing rooms and private clubs, the stage welcomed the Irish and the Irish American. Indeed, beyond the popular Irish stereotypes, which sometimes were too plentiful and too predictable (cuddly drunks and cute lasses everywhere), the Irish helped to expand and modify not only their self-images on stage but also the parameters of the theatrical world. Though not always successful in resisting the stereotypes, Irish actors moved to the center of the stage in the nineteenth and early twentieth centuries. Among the most successful performers were Lawrence Barrett, James O'Neill, Dan Emmett, Edward Harrigan, Tony Hart, Annie Yeamans, John McCullough, George M. Cohan, and Laurette Taylor. Augustin Daly, Irish American himself, put together a company that featured an ensemble of great actors, including John Drew and Ada Rehan, both Irish. And Irish music and songs could be heard in a wide range of performances, from variety and minstrelsy to Victor Herbert operettas. Perhaps most impressively, Irish American playwrights, including Dion Boucicault, Edward Harrigan, James Herne, Philip Barry, and Eugene O'Neill, proceeded to transform the American stage with substantial success (just as they had done for the British stage since the Restoration).

So, though social values in America were still articulated by old Protestant families (especially those in Boston and Philadelphia), the new social and economic centers of American life were shifting to New York, Pittsburgh, Chicago, and other places across the map of the country. A new, different kind of American was stepping forward to lead the country. He was likely to be an industrialist, investment banker, engineer, or architect instead of a doctor, preacher, or educator. (Of course, lawyers continued to be prime players in the national development, including the political arena.) The sons of immigrants – some Protestant, some not – soon set the country on new tracks, including those of the railroad.

Throughout the nineteenth century the United States remained predominately a Protestant (if not Puritan) country, with Episcopalians and Presbyterians still operating as the social elite in the east. But as a sign of change within America's Protestant identity, 50 percent of the people in the 1870 census identified themselves as Methodist or Baptist. And the Catholic population was rapidly growing because of the immigration of the Irish and Italians, who provided a major part of the laboring class and urban poor.

A widespread distrust of Catholics and Catholicism operated in the country, but this was mild compared to the prejudice and sanctions against Mormons, who had taken refuge in the territory of Utah (not admitted as a state until 1896). The Mormon church had given women the vote in 1870, but the U.S. government intervened, taking this right away from them. Other Mormon activities, such as plural marriage, continued to draw attacks and sanctions. The contradictions within Mormonism were too much to abide for policy makers in Washington. Not surprisingly, in the popular press Mormons were often ridiculed and demonized, a practice that carried over to the popular stage (for example, Joaquin Miller's western play, *The Danites in the Sierras*, 1887).

In the 1870s small Chinese communities existed in the West, especially in San Francisco, Portland, and Seattle. Chinese laborers played a major role in the building of the western railroad, and many Chinese men worked in the mining camps. Others turned to agriculture, and as cities grew, some moved into small manufacturing (clothing, shoes, cigars). By 1870 there were 63,000 Chinese in the United States, mainly men and mostly in California (Takaki, *Mirror*, 194).

But as the Chinese communities grew, racial prejudice against the Chinese also increased. By the 1860s and 1870s the Chinese were being assaulted, sometimes by Irish and Italian workers, who were losing jobs (or feared losing jobs) to them. In 1882, as a wave of anti-Chinese attacks spread through the popular press and many communities, the U.S. government prohibited Chinese immigration, even though the Chinese constituted only .002 percent of the population (Takaki, *Mirror*, 206). Those who remained in the country created their own enclaves, in part for solidarity but also out of necessity, as racial prejudice against the Chinese limited their opportunities. Chinese immigration resumed in the twentieth century, but most Chinese continued to be isolated in the "Chinatown" sections of American cities. And this separatist condition also applied to most Japanese, Koreans, and Filipinos who immigrated before World War II.

In those enclosed Chinese communities, theatre was quite popular. As early as 1852 Chinese drama was presented in San Francisco by a visiting company. By the 1860s and 1870s theatre companies had established themselves in the city. Likewise, in Portland during the 1890s no less than three Chinese theatres were operating (Ernst, 96). Yet, Chinese theatre and performers were invisible to the general public. Instead, what people saw on the popular stage were caricatures of the Chinese, sometimes farcical, sometimes villainous. These stereotypes were always played by white actors made up to represent the racial type (see Moy). Of note, the Chinese were also portrayed occasionally by African American actors on the minstrel circuit. Thus a double parody of identity occurred, as a black actor, working within the self-denigrating codes of minstrelsy, invited laughter at the demeaning representation of a Chinese person.

Whites also represented Native Americans on the stage throughout this era. Before the Civil War some plays, such as *Metamora,* presented "Indians" as noble savages. But the western expansion and the Indian wars of the 1870s and 1880s changed the popular idea of Indians. In the mind of the general public Indians became ruthless savages: they killed General Custer, they attacked wagon trains and stagecoaches, they burned the homes of settlers, and they scalped innocent women and children. Accordingly, the American theatre provided an outpouring of plays set in the West that featured the struggle of civilization against savage Indians (see Berkofer; E. Jones; Slotkin; Wilmeth, "Noble or Ruthless").

The full mythology of the western expansion and manifest destiny, set against the resistance of savage Indians, found its fullest theatrical expression in the Wild West shows, especially that of Buffalo Bill. Sadly, for a short period Sitting Bull and a few Sioux warriors even took part in this travesty. Usually, though, Indians were represented by white actors in "typical" Indian attire.

To be expected, caricatures of all ethnic and racial groups were common on the American stage (especially Irish, Germans, Swedes, Italians, and Jews), but the stereotypes of the "colored" people – African Americans, Indians, and Asians – were the most prejudicial and longest lasting. In each case, the representation was developed in the nineteenth century and continued in the twentieth.

Besides the large communities of Chinese in the West, especially in California, there existed substantial numbers of Hispanic communities. Of course, much of the Southwest had been settled by Mexicans, so their situation was unlike that of the Chinese. Thousands of Hispanics had established successful ranches and communities before the 1840s, but the Mexican–American war and the subsequent statehood for Texas and California changed everything. Especially after the Civil War, when the Yankee land barons and railroad barons gained control of California, Spanish-speaking people became dispossessed "natives" (see Monroy; Pitt; Takaki, *Mirror*).

Thus, many Hispanic communities established their own versions of an enclave culture. Their communial situation was distinct from that of American Indians (reservations), African Americans (plantations, ghettos), and Chinese (Chinatowns), but nonetheless they faced yet another form of separation in the great American process of nation making.

Caricatures of Spanish-speaking people on the American stage were less prevalent than those of many other ethnic and racial groups. Perhaps because of their separation from eastern theatre centers during the nineteenth century, they were less often represented as stereotypical figures for farce or melodrama (though distance from the East did not exempt the Chinese). Whatever the case, the key story is the way that the Hispanic communities developed and maintained a rich ethnic tradition of performance that carried over into the twentieth century. From the mid–nineteenth century, when professional theatre groups moved on steamships up and down the California coast, a Hispanic theatre existed, presenting both Spanish and Mexican drama. Similar developments can be traced from the 1850s from San Antonio to Los Angeles. Texas was not as active as California, but a Hispanic theatre, with touring companies, can be traced throughout the Southwest. Then in the twentieth century, with the growth of Spanish-speaking communities along the eastern seaboard from Boston to Miami, a second major Hispanic theatre developed (see Kanellos).

At the same time that the remaining populations of American Indians were being isolated on reservations and Hispanics, Chinese, and African Americans were struggling to establish their independent communities (while yet attempting to enter the social, political, and economic order), the country was being transformed by new ethnic and racial groups, many of whom had recently arrived in America, and most of whom had little knowledge, sympathy, or concern for the struggles of American Hispanics, Indians, and African Americans.

These new American citizens, especially from northern Europe (Swedes, Norwegians, Danes, Finns, Poles, Slavs, Ukrainians), created communities that became conduits to new opportunities. Repeatedly, small-scale versions of the American success story were played out, as energetic, bright young sons made their way into careers. And to a lesser extent, some of the daughters too found and created new places for themselves. And some became active in the growing women's rights movements, though most contributed to the changes by becoming part of the growing female work force at the turn of the century. In time they also became the "matinee girls," who transformed theatre with their new power as a rapidly expanding audience (see Peiss).

One of the most striking features of the American theatre at this time is how much it mirrored the great variety of ethnic, immigrant populations. To be expected, popular character types and situations, based upon the stereotypes of ethnic life, continued to hold the national stage, especially in comedy. Harrigan and Hart were most successful in capturing the urban mix, especially the series of Mulligan Guard plays that were popular in the 1880s. Also, and perhaps more significantly, a broad-based ethnic theatre developed throughout the country, as had happened, for example, in the Spanish and Chinese communities. It was usually performed in the immigrants' native language before members of the community. Literally hundreds of ethnic theatre groups came into existence during this era. Theatre, like church activities and folk festivals, provided the essential shape and meaning for community activities. In this crucial role throughout the many ethnic communities, theatre helped people to hold onto their heritage while they were also accommodating themselves to the changing conditions in their new homeland (see Seller).

The German immigrants developed one of the strongest and most successful ethnic communities in America. Their numbers (Protestant, Catholic, and Jewish) continued to increase, especially after the 1848 disturbances in Germany. German communities expanded into a number of cities, especially in New York, Philadelphia, Cincinnati, Columbus, Louisville, St. Louis, Chicago, and Milwaukee. Like the Irish, they soon were making major contributions to theatre between 1865 and 1945: opera production, musicals, vaudeville, popular music, concert music, theatre building, management, and producing. In New York City, for example, the German community became the audience for a new opera company in the 1870s. And when the Metropolitan Opera Company in New York opened in 1883, the orchestra was primarily German (conductors commonly spoke in German to the orchestra).

The story of the Metropolitan Opera House is quite instructive. When it opened it was funded primarily by the nouveaux riches, including the Astors, Vanderbilts, Roosevelts, Goulds, Belmonts, and Morgans. Their aim in building the new opera house was social rather than musical: they wanted to have boxes at the opera, to be able to put their wealth and social status on display. So, the auditorium provided 122 boxes seating 750 people. The leaders of the new industrial elite had committed themselves to the new building because they had been unable to purchase boxes at the Academy of Music, the established opera house, which was controlled by people of old wealth (who determinedly held onto their 30 boxes).

Many of the box holders at the new Metropolitan Opera House had little interest in opera, and those who did preferred the familiar Italian and French operas of Rossini, Bellini, Donizetti, Verdi, Gounod, and Offenbach. Yet because they were unwilling to pay for the major deficits of the first season (brought on by competition with the Academy of Music), they found themselves confronted by a successful takeover of the company by the German musicians and audience members who wanted a venue for German opera, especially the works of Richard Wagner. So, between 1884 and 1891, the opera seasons at the new Metropolitan Opera House were dedicated to German opera. With four performances a week during the November to March season, there were 589 opera performances, of which 329 were the works of Wagner. The campaign for new opera (the first avant-garde movement in the modern theatre) thus was hatched in the house of the plutocracy by ethnic revolutionaries (though few thought of themselves in this light). And it was the large German audience, along with the musicians, who provided the campaign and support for the seasons of Wagner that transformed the Metropolitan for a few, telling years.

The guiding master was Anton Seidl, who conducted almost all performances and led the triumph of Wagernism in America, building upon the leadership of earlier Wagnerian advocates, including Leopold Damrosch and his son, Walter. In short, unlike Boston and Chicago, where the patrician leaders controlled classical music and opera, using "art" to define clear differences between not only high and low culture but WASP values and immigrant societies, New York City experienced a series of contending battles over who controlled culture. The German immigrant population (Protestant, Catholic, Jewish) played a major role in setting the agenda for opera and the idea of culture (see Dizikes; Horowitz).

Outside of New York City, ethnic theatre and audiences also grew rapidly. For example, up and down the Ohio and Mississippi rivers, theatre groups developed in the thriving American towns and cities. Because of the rich heritage of German theatre and performance, many Germans who came to America were quite familiar with the drama of Lessing, Goethe, and Schiller. In turn, opera was part of the experience of many Germans, and at the level of popular entertainment the plays of Kotzebue and many others who wrote melodramas and comedies were well loved. Also, Shakespeare's drama had become part of the German theatre and was performed regularly.

Germans in America actively established groups for amateur theatre (*Liebhabertheater*) to perform a wide range of plays and operas. By this means, German theatre served as part of a larger endeavor to use the German language for educational purposes, including the maintenance of a German heritage. The leaders of the German communities were often the ones who constructed the new "opera houses" in many towns and cities. These buildings were used not only by the resident company but also by visiting German performers. In addition, these theatres often became the stopping point for the combination shows, performing in English, that flowed out of New York City from the 1870s forward. So, what began as ethnic theatre became part of the acculturation process into the language and society of English-speaking America.

In the large cities (New York, Cincinnati, St. Louis, and Milwaukee) German professional companies developed. The level of production sometimes matched the best of the English-language theatres. The Neue Stadttheater in New York, the Deutsche Theater in Robinson's Opernhaus (German Theatre in Robinson's Opera House) in Cincinnati, the Stadttheater and later the Pabst theater in Milwaukee attained quite high professional levels of performance, and they introduced the production methods of the Meiningen Company of Duke Georg. At the end of the century, Ibsen, Hauptmann, Sudermann, and other modernists playwrights were presented in German productions at these theatres (see Christa Carvajal in Seller).

Yet despite all of this theatrical activity and professional experience, the German American theatre failed to have a direct and lasting influence on the American theatre, with the exception of opera production. The staging of modern drama, not uncommon in the German communities, did not contribute substantially to the development of modern American theatre. Schiller and Goethe did not make their way onto the English-language stage. Nor did the German American productions of Shakespeare seem to influence English-language productions. Still, German audiences in large numbers became audiences for the English-language theatre. And many German American performers, writers, and producers made the shift to the English-language theatre.

The Jewish contributions to theatre parallel some aspects of German activities because of the immigration of German Jews. As Jewish communities grew, especially in New York, the Jewish presence in theatre expanded at a fast pace. In 1850 approximately 50,000 Jews lived in the United States, a third of them in New York City. Between 1880 and 1910 about 1.4 million Jews moved into the city. By 1920 one-third of the city's population was Jewish (K. Jackson; Hertzberg; Higham; Howe).

Most of the Jews from Germany were Reform Jews, who assimilated to American life fairly quickly. Many of them had trades or professions. By contrast, the second major immigration of Jews between 1880 and 1910 came from Eastern Europe, especially Poland and Russia, where the Jewish communities had suffered from pogroms and economic discrimination. These Jews spoke Yiddish, tended to lack professional skills, and often resisted acculturation during the first and second generations. The two groups – assimilated German Jews, and Yiddish-speaking East European Jews – did not always see eye to eye. In fact, German Jews, for a while, tried to stop the development of Yiddish theatre, which embarrassed or appalled them.[11] A smaller Sephardic group also settled in New York City at the turn of the century, and some of them sponsored Judeo–Spanish theatre. For two generations, a vibrant and popular Yiddish theatre operated in New York. It also contributed performers to the English-speaking theatre, especially in the 1920s (see Lifson; Sandrow).

Despite their differences, the members of the Jewish communities made major contributions to American theatre along several different avenues: (1) German cultural entertainment, which encompassed the presentation of everything from opera to melodrama; (2) Yiddish theatre, which developed in New York and several other cities from the late nineteenth century onward; (3) a new American theatre, which included both popular entertainment (vaudeville, musicals); and many aspects of the new modernist theatre of the twentieth century (playwriting, theatre companies); and (4) film entertainment (performers, directors, technicans, management, and ownership).

These four major, often intersecting, paths of cultural development brought together an amazingly diverse range of theatre people who changed the direction of American theatre. For example, in 1869, when the eleven-person Kiralfy troupe came to the United States, Jewish presence in the American theatre was close to nil, excepting the occasional stage Jew who was at best a comic figure. But by 1932, when Bolossy died, the stage and screen had been transformed by Jewish talent, energy, and finance. Here are just a few names: David Belasco, the Frohman brothers, Marc Klaw, Abraham Erlanger, Otto Kahn, the Shubert brothers, Flo Ziegfeld, the DeMille family, Irving Berlin, Jerome Kern, Lorenz Hart, Oscar Hammerstein I, Oscar Hammerstein II, Weber and Fields, Rose Eytinge, Houdini, Jacob Adler, Al Jolson, Sophie Tucker, Fanny Brice, the Gershwin brothers, Moss Hart, the Marx brothers, Eddie Cantor, Elmer Rice, George S. Kaufman, Rudolph and Joseph Schildkraut, Maurice Schwartz, Clifford Odets, S. N. Behrman, the Group Theatre crowd, Ethel Merman, George Burns, and many other important Jewish people in the American theatre. In addition, the new Hollywood studio system was developed and controlled almost exclusively by Jewish entrepreneurs, including Adolphe Zukor, Louis Mayer, Samuel Goldwyn, and the Warner Brothers. As Houdini proclaimed quite appropriately about his own accomplishments: "Will wonders never cease!" – an assertion, not a question. By entering and transforming American entertainment, Jews became central to the development of all aspects of American theatre in the late-nineteenth and twentieth centuries. In key ways, then, the American theatre is part of Jewish history.

City and Country

Like much of Western Europe, the United States shifted from a rural to an urban society in the period between 1850 and 1950. Industrialization was a major factor in this development, of course, as jobs and money pulled people into the towns and cities. The forces of modernization – driven first by steam power (and coal furnaces that produced iron), then by electric power, steel manufacturing, and the railroads, and finally by gasoline power, the automobile industry, and a communications revolution – reordered all aspects of life and livelihood. Benefiting from these technological and economic developments, the cities grew rapidly. Moreover, the new systems of transportation and communication changed both the material environment and consciousness itself, as primary ways of conceiving and experiencing time, space, and movement underwent major transformations (see Kern; Giedion). These new developments created new political and social formations, economic orders, and psychological perceptions of self and others. In all cases, the many changes produced a new sense of opportunity, balanced by a pervasive condition of crisis.

Whereas no U.S. city was larger than thirty-five thousand in 1800, six cities were over one hundred thousand in 1850 (New York, Baltimore, Boston, Philadelphia, New Orleans, and Cincinnati), and ten were over three hundred thousand in 1900. By 1950 ten metropolitan areas had a million or more people. New York City (especially after it consolidated with Brooklyn and the other boroughs in 1898) became the largest city (3.5 million by 1900; almost 8 million by 1950). From 1860 to 1890 the urban areas increased from 16 percent to 33 percent of the country's population. Chicago trebled in size between 1880 and 1900, reaching 1.5 million. New York, Buffalo, Chicago, San Francisco, and a few other cities became magnet centers for the rapid developments in industry, transportation, communication, and finance. In turn, these large cities became hubs for a ring of smaller cities and towns within a two-hundred-mile radius. From the smallest town to the largest city, the country was increasingly interconnected not only by shipping and the rapidly expanding railway network (followed later by the automobile and airplane networks) but also by the new systems of communication (telegraph, telephone, film, radio, and television).

Besides the many aspects of industrialization and modernization, the United States was changed most by immigration, probably more so than any other country on either side of the Atlantic. Although it is debatable that the flow of immigrants justifies the popular "exceptionalist" view of America, it is still true that the number of immigrants who came into the United States between 1850 and 1914 profoundly transformed the demographics and the destiny of the nation, especially the cities. As Alan Brinkley notes: "By 1890, most of the population of the major urban areas consisted of immigrants: 87 percent of the population in Chicago, 80 percent in New York, 84 percent in Milwaukee and Detroit. London, the largest industrial city in Europe, had by contrast a population that was 94 percent native" (488–89). Twenty-five to thirty million people made the Atlantic crossing to the United States between 1850 and 1914 (four times the number of people who came to the United States between 1815 and 1865). In turn, a smaller but influential flow of immigrants came across the Pacific Ocean, especially from China during the nineteenth century. Overall, forty million immigrants arrived between 1820 and 1955 (Bodnar), and the vast majority settled in the cities. The economic, political, and social consequences of this immigration reached into every aspect of American city life, including the theatres.

Not surprisingly, as the nineteenth-century cities swelled with immigrants from abroad (and with people from the countryside as well), many lamented the changes, and some people poured out jeremiads about the evils of city life. These complaints took several different forms: spirited defenses of independence and self-sufficiency, Jeffersonian appeals for the nobility of owning and working a piece of land, Jacksonian rally cries for the rights of the common man, the farmer, and the laborer. Sometimes a strain of nostalgia ran through the complaints, expressing a longing for a supposedly simpler and more wholesome time in the nation's history. And increasingly by the end of the century the criticism revealed a widespread prejudice against various ethnic and racial groups, who were seen as a threat to established values and the sociopolitical order.

This population shift produced various clashes between country and city (also true in Western Europe). People complained regularly about living conditions and behavior in the cities (and about the encroachment of urban development and values on rural life), yet many of these same people could not stay away from the attractions and opportunities the cities offered. These changing conditions and dilemmas reveal that despite the contending ideas on where to live and what values to honor (such as Walden Pond and the frontier spirit versus urbanization) country and city were tied together in the development of the nation. Although those who remained in the country or moved westward were able to separate themselves from the daily rhythm and problems of the cities, they still found themselves dependent upon many of the same forces and conditions that were driving urbanization (for example, the railroads). From the farmer who became part of the new market economics to the cowboys who needed the trains to get the cattle to Chicago, the urban and capitalist transformation of the United States shaped most people's decisions, attitudes, and livelihood. Not only was the machine in the garden, it was demanding to be worshiped as the new secular arm of American deliverance.

The arguments about the railroads, like almost all the worries and debates over the forces of change, reveal an ambiguous, even contradictory set of attitudes toward the often raw forces of change. Many Americans living in the country looked with suspicion on the men of the Central Pacific and Union Pacific railroad companies who laid the railroad tracks across the whole West. Although technology fascinated most people (who, for example, flocked to see the new machines displayed at world fairs and expositions), the railroad titans were pictured as corrupt robber barons, and the railroads themselves were seen as the tentacles of the wealthy, strangling the innocent. Still, most communities fought to have a railroad line and its attendent financial benefits. This contradiction was common to the "antimodernist" protests that went with the rapid transformation of American life. As Jackson Lears notes: "Antimodernism was not simply escapism; it was ambivalent, often coexisting with enthusiasm for material progress" (*No Place,* xiii; see also Kasson, *Civilizing the Machine*).

In the cities themselves, the contradictions were just as severe. Centers of opportunity, the cities were also places of political corruption, vice, poverty, and disease. They were a strange mixture of grand homes and slum tenements, powerful businessmen and starving families, opera houses and saloons, imposing banks and dingy garment factories. In southern cities Jim Crow segregation established itself as the norm; in the northern cities ethnic and racial segregation likewise operated. The streets of the residential neighborhoods were filled with the immigrants who spilled out of the overcrowded tenements. For every mansion of a Stewart or Vanderbilt in New York City, hundreds of dilapidated shanties were pitched in parks and on vacant land. Ragpickers with small carts hauled by dogs roamed the streets. Children were everywhere, some sleeping outside, even in winter. And horses and their droppings filled the streets.

The smells and sounds of the cities were overpowering, including the garbage carts and barges that scavengers picked over and the noise of the new elevated railroads. Street confrontations, gang battles, and riots were common. Summer heatwaves and winter storms were terrible to endure in most cities. And even on the calmest of days the visual field was often chaotic: horses and trolleys, trains, signs and posters, carts lining the sidewalks and curbs, ethnic and racial diversity of unsettling dimensions, and movement everywhere, a restlessness that could be both exhilarating and exhausting. All of these various conditions caused even the strongest defenders of cities to long for escape to a simpler, idyllic country life.

And yet, the cities were also metropolitan pleasure zones for many people who enjoyed the parks, gardens, zoos, amusement arcades and centers, colonnades, clubs, department and merchant stores, restaurants, coffee shops, taverns, parades, fireworks, skating, horse races, baseball, swimming, dancing, museums, musical performances (both inside and outside), political gatherings and rallies, newspapers, journals, libraries, and colleges (on urbanization, see Barth; Boyer; Glaab and Brown; K. Jackson; Mohl; Monkkonen).

Unavoidably, the theatre of the era was drawn to the topics of country and city, but most representations featured neat oppositions (usually sentimental and moralistic) rather than complex contradictions and ambiguities. This was true of the negative as well as positive images of both places. And when a mediating representation emerged, it tended toward a meliorist position that safely evaded or contained rather than negotiated the sharp contradictions and unresolved ambiguities of life in both places.

Perhaps the frontier drama, which often translated the basic tensions between urban and country life into a geographic and moral conflict between the East and the West (such as *Davy Crockett*), was the most definite type of American drama during this era. Typically in this drama the West provides the testing ground for the character of "real" men and women. In this elemental world the veneer of civilization is removed, to reveal the basic traits of individuals. By contrast, when the East is represented or referred to, it is identified with urban life, genteel values, social hypocrisy, and corruption. This false or constricted civilization is thus set in opposition to the people and values of the frontier.

Frontier dramas, including Indian plays (see E. Jones; Wilmeth, "Checklist"), have had a long heritage in the American theatre. But after the Civil War, when the nation was expanding westward, frontier and western dramas, along with the Wild West shows, became quite popular (*Horizon, Davy Crockett, Ah Sin, My Partner, Arizona, The Virginian, The Girl of the Golden West,* and *The Great Divide*). Many successful playwrights contributed to the frontier genre, including Augustin Daly, Bret Harte and Mark Twain, Joaquin Miller, David Belasco, and William Vaughn Moody. With varying degrees of success, given the demands of melodramatic closure, these writers captured some of the powerful beliefs and myths about the American West that have continued to influence national identity to this day (see Bank; Berkhofer; Hall; Meinig; Merk; Meserve; Slotkin; F. J. Turner).

Also popular, yet serving a somewhat different function, were a series of country plays, such as *Rip Van Winkle* (a vehicle for Joseph Jefferson), *Kit, the Arkansas Traveller* (a vehicle for Frank Chanfrau), and *Shore Acres* (a vehicle for James Herne). Boucicault's Irish plays (such as *The Colleen Bawn*) also captured the spirit of countryside values that defines many of these works. Usually, the country plays offered sentimental and nostalgic evocations of the simple virtues of country people and family life, set against the threatening world of gamblers, thieves, loose women, selfishness, drunkenness, real estate swindlers, and urban evils. Often the hero, perhaps a misguided or misunderstood husband and father, must struggle against misfortune, temptations, and bad judgment in order to learn that home, sweet home is where he belongs.

These plays – and the actors who perfected the down-home roles – maintained a strong appeal throughout this era. The early Yankee character plays, popular before the Civil War, contributed to theme and characterization. But the plays written after 1865 were often less farcical or satirical, opting instead for easy humor and heavy sentiment. As the nation became more urbanized, there seemed to be a longing for the supposed lost harmony and innocence of country life. No play captured this feeling better than *The Old Homestead* (1876; revised 1886), Denman Thompson's celebration of New England rural charms, set in contrast to the evils of New York City. If we tracked the representations of country life over the following decades, from *The Old Homestead* to *Our Town* (1938) and *Oklahoma!* (1943), we can see that audiences continued to delight in the simple charms and abiding virtues of country life. Sometimes these plays provided an ironic perspective on the supposed virtues of country life, but audiences (and many performers) have generally preferred to ignore any shaded tones of contradiction or ambiguity.

Of course, the stage offered up some satirical and critical representations of country life, none more popular than the nasty and grotesque *Tobacco Road* (1933), which ran through the 1930s, to the delight of urban audiences (see Fearnow, *The American Stage*). And a darker, more tragic vision of country life can be found in such plays as Glaspell's *Trifles* and O'Neill's *Desire Under the Elms*. Just as certain novelists (Sherwood Anderson, *Winesburg, Ohio;* Sinclair Lewis, *Main Street*) were determined to show the dark side of small towns and country life, so some playwrights attempted to expose the loneliness of individuals and the suffering of families.

Likewise, despite the continuing popularity of frothy society plays (featuring love affairs and fashionable clothes) and social comedies (featuring the wit and charm of sophisticated urbanites), certain modern playwrights countered the celebrations of urban and society life with dark pictures of urban suffering: *Machinal, Dead End,* and *One-Third of a Nation.* A strong critique of urban ills developed in the nation from the progressive era onward (Lincoln Steffens, *The Shame of the Cities;* Upton Sinclair, *The Jungle*). Sometimes, when taking up these issues, the stage could not quite avoid sentimentalism (Sheldon's *Salvation Nell*), but a drama of social conscience and criticism did find its voice and audience, especially in the 1920s and 1930s.

Attempting to mediate between the sentimental, moralistic, and critical views of country and city, key performers such as Will Rogers, playwrights such as George S. Kaufman and Thornton Wilder, and filmmakers such as Frank Capra and Preston Sturges embodied and represented the ways that America could not only join some of the key values of country and city but also yoke the oppositions between past and present, individualism and democracy, nostalgia and hope, Anglo–Saxon Protestantism and multicultural diversity. Of course, it is an open question whether the mediators succeeded in their theatrical missions. Given that the nation was having a hard time reconciling the agendas and values of country and city, the theatre was equally hard-pressed to offer viable new ideas of community that bridged the divisive conditions of rural and urban America.

Touring and Transportation

In assessing the ability of American entertainment to mediate between country and city, it is important not to limit our perspective to dramatic literature. During the nineteenth and twentieth centuries the theatre established other ways to link country and city together, especially by means of the grand network of touring shows and performers. In order to appreciate just how significant this network proved to be in transforming the relations between country and city, we need to attend less to the subject matter of the shows and acts and more to the cultural processes by which entertainment (touring plays, stars, circuses, variety entertainment, Chautauqua presentations, tent shows, vaudeville) spread throughout the nation. By the end of the nineteenth century, performers had carried a shared national culture into almost every village, town, and city. This process of weaving diverse communities together by means of entertainment would culminate in the multimedia world of the present day, which provides the basis of a consumer society of shared tastes, values, and attitudes (for a majority of people).

If there is one real thing that all performers had in common during this era, it was touring. Everyone – and every kind of company – toured: famous stars, small family troupes, opera performers, Toby specialists, minstrel shows, vaudevillians, black performers on their separate booking circuit, and circuses. For theatre people America was comprised of, on the one hand, New York City – the mecca for the ambitious, the talented, and the lucky – and, on the other hand, the rest of the country, a grand network of theatre buildings, large and small, distributed almost everywhere. The great irony was that success in New York meant, almost invariably, that one must hit the road.

Of course, touring had its pleasures and rewards. But in addition to the applause, the profit, and the sightseeing, life on the road offered a series of train stops, delays, breakdowns, missed connections, boarding houses, cheap hotels, filthy rooms, poor restaurants, inadequately equipped theatres, incompetent musicians, bad weather, poor management, drunken companions, exhaustion, illness, social prejudice, and uncertain pay.

Until radio and film changed the whole method of delivering a performance to every city, town, and village of the nation, the road was the inescapable condition of life for performers. As Moss Hart learned early in his career, the massive Railway Guide was the "daily bible" of the theatre industry (38). No matter which circuit one was on – the grand star tour, a Syndicate or Shubert show, the Stair and Havlin popular-price circuit, the B. F. Keith and Edward F. Albee vaudeville circuit, the black Theatre Owners' Booking Association, the 10-20-30 circuit of low-budget melodramas organized by H. R. Jacobs and F. F. Proctor, or the Samuel Scribner's burlesque circuit – the Railway Guide was the great equalizer.

Everybody toured. Combination shows toured the latest New York hit, traveling the road for months until the play exhausted its ability to draw a crowd. Variety entertainment, popular throughout the nineteenth century, became even more popular by the early twentieth century, when tens of thousands of performers on the vaudeville and burlesque circuits crisscrossed the country, presenting their special acts. By 1915 there were approximately five thousand vaudeville houses in the country, one thousand of them for the main circuit and the other four thousand for small-price acts.

Also, thousands of actors made a living by performing melodramas, comedies, and farces on the popular-priced circuit. Many towns and cities had theatres that specialized in these cheap performances. For example, in 1895 the Burt Theatre in Toledo, Ohio, converted to a popular-priced melodrama theatre, offering seats for ten, twenty, or thirty cents. During that first year the average monthly audience was 45,000 people, who saw 488 performances of 64 different plays. In Toledo and across the country hundreds of touring companies provided the entertainment for these new popular-priced theatres. A number of playwrights, such as Owen Davis, got rich churning out formula melodramas (O. Davis, *My First Fifty Years;* Nasaw, 37).

Performers who failed to become stars had no choice but to tour. And stars, from Edwin Booth and Lotta Crabtree to George M. Cohan and Mrs. Fiske, were also obliged to tour. In 1905, for example, Richard Mansfield, at the height of his fame, toured the country with productions of *Richard III, The Merchant of Venice, Beau Brummel,* and *Dr. Jekyll and Mr. Hyde.* And Thomas W. Keene, though never attaining star status, toured the country in 1898, from Maryland to the Oklahoma Territory, the Dakotas, and Ontario, presenting a mix of Shakespeare and Bulwer–Lytton (*Richard III, Hamlet, Julius Caesar, Othello, Richelieu*). His tour went reasonably well, though some people found him to be decidedly old-fashioned. On 23 May 1898, unfortunately, Keene collapsed with an appendicitis attack while in Ontario, and though he made it home to Staten Island by train, he died on 1 June 1898 (A. Woods, in Conolly, 31–40).

Keene's career is instructive, demonstrating that most performers began on the road and many ended there. Between those two defining moments the road was often a series of one-nighters, though successful shows and performers could coax audiences into the theatres for several days without needing to move to the next town. Every town, large and small, built a theatre building (or "opera house"). For example, in 1885 the small community of Woodland, California, twenty-five miles from Sacramento, had a new theatre built in town at the corner of Second Street and Dead Cat Alley. The fifteen hundred people of the town had previously watched touring shows at Templar's Hall, Washington Hall, and Central Hall. But now they had a three story brick and iron opera house, which included four boxes, a raked auditorium, and a large stage. It opened with *The Merchant of Venice,* featuring Louise Davenport and W. E. Sheridan. Then for the next few years a steady mix of Shakespeare, melodramas, comedies, musicals, and farces held the stage, along with lectures and concerts, until it burned down in 1892. So much for brick and iron. Four years later a new opera house, also brick, rose from the ashes. It opened with Bronson Howard's *Saratoga.* Each year, for three decades, a steady stream of touring companies, not usually the major ones, came to Woodland for a day to a week, performing as part of a local season that stretched from September to June. Sometimes a major attraction appeared, as was the case with Kate Claxton's company, performing *The Two Orphans,* one of the most popular plays of the nineteenth century (McDermott and Sarlos, in Conolly, 57–76).

By 1876–77 already close to one hundred combination companies were touring the country (Bernheim, 30). And by the turn of the century there were twice as many shows on the road as were playing in New York. On average, 250–300 combination shows, originating in New York, crisscrossed the country each year between 1880 and 1910. And hundreds of additional companies, of a half-dozen to a couple of dozen performers, also toured the country, some providing one show (for example, *Uncle Tom's Cabin*), others presenting several plays at each stop. Thus, a medium-sized city, such as Little Rock, Arkansas, would be visited by fifty to seventy-five companies, which on average would present 3–4 shows. Each year the citizens of Little Rock would have 200–250 productions to choose from.

Extended tours of successful New York productions began even before the western railroad was in place. For example, the two longest-running productions in New York during the 1860s were *The Black Crook,* the melodramatic musical extravaganza with elaborate scenery and dozens of dancing girls in revealing costumes, and George L. Fox's *Humpty Dumpty,* the popular pantomime show. *The Black Crook* opened on 12 September 1866 and ran for 474 performances. *Humpty Dumpty* opened on 10 March 1867 and ran for 483 performances. Subsequently in the 1870s and 1880s, *The Black Crook,* in several different versions, toured for twenty years. Performers came and went, but *The Black Crook* continued to tour.

As for *Humpty Dumpty,* Fox pushed the show through several transformations and major tours, but by 1875 he cracked under the strain. The greatest pantomimist of his time, Fox had delighted audiences with his transgressive antics as the whitefaced Humpty. But the physical, mental, and financial strains of touring contributed to his breakdown. Between 30 May 1874 and 22 August 1875 he had presented "more than four hundred performances in one hundred and fifty separate engagements in twenty-six states or territories over the course of fourteen months" (Senelick, *Fox,* 198). The toll on Fox's health was too much, as were the continuing financial problems and the grief over the death of his brother Charlie, who had performed with him for decades. Despite his great fame Fox had to maintain himself by constant touring, which provided the necessary income and the equally necessary contact with audiences. But these needs drove Fox insane, just as they drove many actors to lonely suffering and death. The road giveth and taketh away.

Fox's last performances in November 1875 were in New York at Booth's Theatre (which Booth had just relinquished because of bankruptcy). The erratic behavior that had begun to threaten Fox's last tour now slipped over into deranged behavior on a nightly basis. His mind went, and he was carried off to Boston, not to home fires but to the ward at McLean's asylum. The expense of keeping him in the asylum put major strains on his wife, who begged in newspapers for help. Very little was forthcoming. Fox, like many aging actors, was at the mercy of charity and the generosity of other actors, few of whom had sufficient funds to help. Only in his last few days in late 1877 did he return home – taken in by his relatives, the Howard family, who had launched the most successful adaptation of *Uncle Tom's Cabin* twenty-five years earlier. After years of touring, they had settled in Cambridge. Fox died a broken, pathetic man at the age of fifty-two. (Senelick, *Fox;* see Roach in Vol. I, Chap. 4, of this history.)

Touring was always difficult, and often deadly. A few select performers found ways to anchor their careers in a particular city, but most performers had to tour regularly, no matter how famous they were. This was the case in the 1870s for Edwin Booth; it applied to George M. Cohan at the turn of the century; and it was still required of Mrs. Fiske in the 1920s.

Booth tried to escape touring by building his own theatre in 1869. But by 1871, struggling to cover the expenses, he leased the theatre for six weeks to Lotta Crabtree, who delighted her fans with a reprieve of *Little Nell*. Booth's next gambit was to convince Charlotte Cushman to come out of ten-year retirement to act with him in *Macbeth* and *Henry VIII*. She also performed her signature role of the witch Meg Merrilies in *Guy Mannering*. Despite this and other attempts to maintain the costly theatre (including leasing it to Italian star Tommaso Salvini in 1873 for his first American tour), Booth had to declare bankruptcy in 1874. The next two decades were given over to touring in order to pay debts and to support his family (including a mentally disturbed wife).

Booth did not go mad, though at times he seemed to be at the edge of not just exhaustion but mental instability because of the constant need to travel. Even though in the 1880s he had the luxury of a private "hotel" railcar that included an alcove for a bed, a sitting room, a piano, and a bookcase, he found the process of touring a terrible strain:

> I have that unhappy disposition to agonize over coming events, and even now I am weary of the possible next season's labors. Not the labor of acting but of travel and digesting the wretched stuff one is compelled to gorge in these handsome hotels. . . . My belly revolts. Oh! to begin before I've had a chance to ascertain if I can possibly endure the present, to arrange a future agony quite demoralizes me. (Quoted in Ruggles, 327)

Thirty years later Al Jolson made the same complaint in a letter to J. J. Shubert: "I have played thirty one-nighters in succession and I don't think I can stand it much longer. The food is terrible, the hotels worse; I have had one good meal this month" (quoted in McNamara, *Shuberts,* 73–74). If the food was that bad at the handsome hotels, imagine what it was like elsewhere.

Of course, performers have traveled throughout recorded time (and even longer), but there was something new about the flow of performers across the vast continent of America with the arrival of the railroad. Between 1850 and 1871, when the railroad land-grant policy ended, the railroad companies were deeded 175,350,000 acres on which to build the new transportation system (Foner and Garraty). Between 1850 and 1910 railroad mileage had gone from 9,021 miles to 240,293 miles. By 1905, when the United States possessed one-third of the world's railroad mileage, the country boasted 2,272 connecting railroad lines (Boorstin, III, 121; P. Lewis, 106; see also Chandler; Stover; Schivelbusch). Each day most of those lines were carrying performers. For example, in the expansive era of vaudeville, more than twenty thousand performers moved about each year. And, in addition, thousands of black performers, who were not normally allowed on the "white circuit," played their own theatre circuit. Black performers often faced special difficulties of travel, housing, and food in parts of the South, whereas out West, Hispanic troupes faced similar problems as they worked their own circuit from Texas to California. Both the black and the Hispanic performers learned to turn to their own communities for food and housing when hotels and restaurants were either closed to them or were too expensive.

The history of the Keith–Albee vaudeville empire of theatres and touring contracts illustrates how popular entertainment and new business practices were transforming American culture at the turn of the century. Like many of the successful entrepreneurs of this era, B. F. Keith began at the very bottom. Nothing about his early career suggested that he was going to become an empire maker. In the 1870s and early 1880s he made his living hawking portraits of Abraham Lincoln, selling gimcracks outside of a circus, making and selling brooms, working at Bunnell's Museum in New York (a showcase of freakish curiosities), and operating a dime museum in Boston that featured Little Alice, a tiny, prematurely born infant who had died. Then in 1886, with this apprenticeship behind him, he acquired the lease to the renovated Bijou Theatre in Boston. Determined to draw respectable, middle-class people into variety entertainment, Keith developed a "continuous show" of variety acts and musical selections. This formula, which P. T. Barnum and Tony Pastor had developed in New York, soon became the model for vaudeville, matching fast-paced "clean" acts to well-behaved audiences of men, women, and even children.

Successful in Boston, and aided by his cunning business partner Edward F. Albee, Keith began to build a vaudeville circuit. During the next twenty years the two men constructed and acquired theatres throughout the East, establishing their empire, which was helped along by their control over a booking office, an association for managers, and a union. Eventually the empire, which continued after Keith's death in 1914, grew to over seven hundred vaudeville theatres, including the Palace in New York – a circuit for twenty to twenty-five thousand acts each year. These acts, some in need of sanitizing (such as Mae West and the Marx Bros.), became the lively main line for popular entertainment in the period between 1890 and 1940. Thus, the Keith circuit shaped and dominated the touring shows of popular theatre (vaudeville, revues, musicals). In turn, it provided many of the performers for radio and film. The two new media benefited directly from the success of vaudeville, yet they also contributed to the rapid decline of the touring circuit. Empires rise and fall (see Robert C. Allen; Snyder).

For most performers touring was an adventure, but one that soon lost its charm. The positive side of trouping was voiced by Ethel Barrymore, who recalled her early days of touring with her uncle John Drew at the end of the nineteenth century: "I loved seeing America and I wanted to see it all. And it was a wonderful time to begin seeing America – just at the end of an era in which changes had been gentle and slow, just at the beginning of the changes that were to be so tremendous and so fiercely swift" (58). Likewise, before he settled in Hollywood, without any regrets about leaving the road, Cecil B. DeMille praised touring: "Playing on the road was not easy, but it gave one a feeling of and for America . . ." (quoted in Ann Edwards, 39).

Being on the road, striking out for new territory – this possibility of discovery has always been a powerful part of American experience and art. But as Bolossy Kiralfy knew, the difficulties of touring usually took the romance out of the adventure: "It was one of the unfortunate circumstances of a career in show business to be constantly moving from city to city, and in my situation, from land to land, giving up countless personal belongings and saying goodbye to friends" (*Autobiography,* 205).

Not only did Kiralfy's productions tour regularly across the continent and Europe (and he usually traveled with the shows, overseeing everything) but his career stretched from Budapest, Vienna, Paris, Brussels, and London to every large and small town of America. New York was his base, but much of the time he was elsewhere. Working a variation on touring, he also participated in a number of world fairs and expositions: Paris (twice, in 1867 and 1900), Philadelphia, New Orleans (where he advised William Cody on how to improve the management of the *Wild West* exhibition, which was commencing decades of touring), Brussels, Buffalo ("marred by one terrible event – the assassination of President William McKinley," but the production of *Constaninople* went well), St. Louis (where he presented the *Louisiana Purchase Spectacle,* a pageant representing the negotiations between Napoleon and Thomas Jefferson and the opening of the West), Portland (a 400-foot stage for two hundred performers and a broad canal for gondolas), Jamestown (where he staged *Pocahontas*), and Seattle. He missed the Columbian Exposition in Chicago, 1893, but only because his brother, Irme, got there before him with *Columbus and the Discovery of America* (a show that he had produced two years earlier in New York with P. T. Barnum).

How fitting it was in 1893 for the theatre to honor Columbus, who was a kind of patron saint for performers. Of course, travel in his time was more dangerous, a definite adventure of discovery. By contrast, travel in 1893, though still an adventure, was less a process of discovery than a well-scheduled activity, regulated by the Railway Guide and the profit motive.

Perhaps Thomas Edison's distinction beween discovery and invention is helpful here. He insisted that discovery was "more or less in the nature of an accident." It was a matter of chance, a role of the dice. That surely describes Columbus's voyage to the West. But an invention, Edison pointcd out, was a process of purposeful activity, an organized endeavor (Boorstin, III, 527). The modern wizard produced a new invention with two purposes in mind: to solve a specific problem and to fulfill a clearly defined aim.

The changes in theatre production and careers can be understood in these terms. Theatre was becoming less a process of discovering what will appeal and more a plan for inventing the product and creating the audience. *The Black Crook* may have started as an accident, but it quickly became the model for calculated production, as the Kiralfy brothers demonstrated. Of course, many performers were still operating upon the principle of chance, and they usually stayed on the tour, running in circles unless an accident propelled them in a new direction (which was usually just another circle). How fitting that the performers on the vaudeville circuit organized themselves into a union called the White Rats. But the major theatrical entrepreneurs were becoming inventors. In this they were learning to emulate not only Thomas Edision (and the other American entrepreneurs) but also P. T. Barnum, who had set the entertainment industry – and the country – on the path to the new organizational model of inventing, capitalizing, advertising, and delivering the products of the consumer society.

The Business of Entertainment

So, by the Gilded Age, though some aspects of American life and culture still seemed tied to midcentury practices, much had changed – or would soon change – in the nation. The familiar patterns and steady conditions (in particular, the almost continuous string of Republican presidents and Congresses after the Civil War), were quite misleading, for America was experiencing major, often radical changes in those decades. Soon the whole nation would move in directions that never occurred to Rutherford Hayes, James Garfield,

Chester Arthur, Grover Cleveland (the lone Democrat), Benjamin Harrison, or William McKinley. Of course, it was still possible to represent the country as a Currier and Ives landscape of tranquility and idyllic charm. But just beyond the country road, American life was in turmoil, and even country life was anything but peaceful and permanent.

Industrial growth, helped along by the railroads and new technology, transformed the country. Major advances in engineering, technology, and science created a new modern world of manufacturing. At first this system seemed committed to the exploitation of the earth and people. Yet despite its predatory traits, it also produced new resources and new capital. Consequently, opportunities and wealth spread rapidly. Of course, much of the new wealth ended up in the pockets of a few powerful men. But this economic and material development also rippled widely, if unevenly, through the country, affecting millions of lives. Some people were displaced, suffering in the process. Others benefited, more than they expected or quite understood. And some, besides benefiting themselves handsomely, became benefactors – or at least economic planners and social engineers – of a new society (see H. Jones).

For example, in the 1860s John D. Rockefeller had figured out how to refine petroleum into various kinds of fuel – kerosene, oil, and gasoline. Out of this discovery and his acute sense for business administration (controlling competitors, devising a capitalist trust), Standard Oil emerged. What also emerged was a corporate model that has maintained itself, with some modification and regulation, from Rockefeller and Standard Oil to Bill Gates and Microsoft. Rockefeller's business procedures were often rapacious, and his treatment of workers was sometimes ruthless. Yet, as an earnest Baptist who believed that he could not take it with him, he also redirected large reserves of his wealth into charitable contributions. In time he and his family gave $80 million for the creation and development of the University of Chicago. Likewise, millions went to the Rockefeller Institute and the Rockefeller Foundation.

This entrepreneurial model repeated itself with Andrew Carnegie, who came to this country at the age of twelve. Aided by the Scottish community, he found his way into railroad jobs and stock investment. Buying into the new Bessemer processing industry during the 1870s Depression, he built his new steel company into one of the most powerful industries in America. By the turn of the century, when he sold his holdings to J. Pierpont Morgan, he was one of the wealthiest men in the nation. United States Steel Company not only made him (and a handful of other people) very rich but also provided a factory system that was the foundation for the modern American economy: railroads, ships, tools, industrial buildings, skyscrapers. In the twentieth century the automobile industry, the partner of the steel industry, would provide jobs for millions and reshape American life profoundly (see Flink).

Carnegie's success was aided by the new kind of financier, such as Jay

Gould and J. Pierpont Morgan, who understood how to develop large trusts for new industrial opportunities and wealth, thereby funding a massive industrial revolution (and building their own fortunes). Like Rockefeller, Carnegie redirected some of his riches into philanthropy, developing research institutions, endowing universities, and building thousands of public libraries in towns across America.

By the turn of the century a number of entrepreneurs and financiers, successfully evading any significant regulation by the government, had built massive fortunes and grand industrial empires. In the process, they contributed to the modernization of the American capitalist system, which transformed production, economic systems, and daily life. Moreover, the complex process of modernization, international in scope, tied America increasingly to the economics and politics of Europe. Thus, despite an isolationist temperament, the American government soon was involved in the major upheavals of the modern age: labor unrest and collective organization, urbanization, imperial and colonialist projects, world wars, and depressions (see Boorstin; Chandler; Cochran and Miller; Licht; J. Matthews; Noble; E. Rosenberg; Taussig and Josllyn).

The struggles between business and labor were often mean-spirited and sometimes deadly, but during the first half of the twentieth century the labor movement was able to temper and restrain some of the abusive power of the new industrial order. And government, instead of being the arm of capital, began, in the progressive era, to put laws on the books that provided protection and rights for working people. Of course, as many immigrants learned (such as women in the garment industry, Irish miners, child laborers), exploitation of labor remained pervasive throughout the country (see Gutman; Higgs).

Necessarily, the theatre was directly affected by this new capitalism, which provided not only a new subject matter for drama but also a new model for the organization of the entertainment industry. Ironically, although the playwrights became increasingly critical of capitalism (especially during the Depression), American entertainment became a big business, primarily run by capitalist entrepreneurs.

Between the Civil War and World War I a number of plays celebrated the triumph of hard work, cunning, and integrity (including George M. Cohan's popular works). Many of these plays provided sentimental versions of the rags-to-riches story. Sometimes, after foiling a villain, the hero marries the rich man's daughter; sometimes he attains his sweetheart through his own industry. Whatever the case, success in love and enterprise went hand in hand. These popular plays (George Broadhurst's *The Speculator;* Owen Davis's *The Power of Money,* among others) still tried to honor American individualism, the integrity of the land (for example, country virtues), and wholesome family life, yet they also worked out an accommodation with ideals of

American success. A good job took on a patriotic aura – a duty if not a right of upstanding young men.

At the same time, but in a somewhat more critical mode, some social comedies and dramas offered a moral warning about the business world. These plays showed how profit and power might lead one astray, though by the end of story the protagonist usually recognizes, with the help of a loving woman, that there is more to life than profit. Plays by Bronson Howard (*The Henrietta,* 1887), Clyde Fitch (*The Climbers,* 1901), Edward Sheldon (*The Boss,* 1911), and Philip Barry's *Holiday* (1928) are representative of this theme.

In a darker, more adversarial mood, some playwrights used satire and wit to criticize capitalism, as in *Dulcy* (1921) and *Beggar on Horseback* (1924), both by George S. Kaufman and Marc Connelly. And other playwrights presented morality tales on the corrupting nature of commercialism and power: John Howard Lawson's *Roger Bloomer* (1923), Elmer Rice's *The Adding Machine* (1923), Lawson's *Processional* (1925), and Eugene O'Neill's *Marco Millions* (1928). Also, this darker version of capitalism sometimes carried a tone of sexual confusion or perversion, which emerges explicitly in certain twentieth-century plays and films (O'Neill's *The Hairy Ape* [1922)], Sophie Treadwell's *Machinal* [1928], and Welles's *Citizen Kane* [1941]). Following the Depression of 1929, a number of plays, many written from a leftist perspective, attacked capitalism and championed the working man (for example, Clifford Odets's *Waiting for Lefty*). Perhaps the most famous of these plays was Marc Blitzstein's musical *The Cradle Will Rock,* directed by Orson Welles.

Yet despite the criticism of capitalism in some plays, the American theatre itself was transformed by the new capitalist economics (see Poggi and Bernheim for economic histories of theatre). Two business models stand out. In the first case, some of the major impresarios such as P. T. Barnum and Flo Ziegfeld operated primarily as independent venture capitalists, creating and delivering a product (as well as the desire for that product). At times they did quite well, packaging everything from Jenny Lind, Tom Thumb, and Jumbo to dancing girls, Will Rogers, and *Show Boat.* Yet because they were gamblers (committed to the game of entertainment as much as the profit motive), they also hit bottom when bad judgment or bad luck (fire, depression) occurred.

Like Thomas Edison and Bolossy Kiralfy, Barnum and Ziegfeld were independent wizards, savvy inventors of theatrical enterprises. They also tended to be larger-than-life personalities whose exploits and accomplishments continue to fascinate us. Their lives were often as entertaining as their shows. Fittingly, Barnum's autobiography (Mark Twain's favorite book) was a best-seller that went through many editions, and Ziegfeld's life served as the basis for a popular movie in 1936 (four years after his death): *The Great Ziegfeld,* with William Powell in the title role. The film won the Academy Award that year, beating out, among other films, *Show Boat,* featuring Helen Morgan.

Ziegfeld had been the producer of the stage premiere of *Show Boat* in 1927 (in which Helen Morgan also appeared).

As for the second business model, it produced less colorful but more successful entrepreneurs, including B. F. Keith and Edward Albee, the members of the Theatrical Syndicate (though Charles Frohman had his charms), the Shubert brothers, and the film studio bosses. Like the new industrial capitalists, these men attempted, with varying degrees of success, to create networks of business entertainment that integrate all aspects of the industry into an expansive, unified system of production, distribution, exhibition, and reception.[12] The business task, as the major capitalists were demonstrating, was to gain control of all four aspects of the system. On this same model, the Motion Picture Patents Company was established in 1909 by Edison, Biograph, Vitagraph, Essanay, Selig, Lubin, Kalem, and the French producers Méliès and Pathé. This trust only succeeded for a few years until antitrust laws helped various independents to set up shop in Hollywood. Soon these new independent producers had created their own integrated studio system, which controlled film production until well after World War II (D. Robinson, 29–30).

Despite these differences, the two basic types of entrepreneurs shared the decisive talent for not only producing and delivering entertainment that was both popular and profitable but also creating new audiences for these entertainments. In many ways, Barnum set the agenda (and some of the standards) for the American show, although he was hardly the first of the impresarios (and occasional hoaxers). More effectively and extravagantly than anyone else in the nineteenth century, Barnum made the staging of curiosities and wonders the success story of American entertainment. He mastered techniques in presentation, publicity, and organization that served him quite well and guided other entrepreneurs who followed after him. The great success of his museum displays – and later the circus shows he developed in partnership with William C. Coup and James A. Bailey – demonstrated not so much that a sucker is born each minute (which he likely never uttered) as that almost no one can resist the opportunity to see "a big show." In a society of successful inventors and manufacturers, he invented and manufactured desires for an infinite market (see B. Adams).

Trafficking in desires, the theatrical world kept pace with – and sometimes led – the new consumer and leisure culture that realized itself most obviously in the birth of the "drug store" and the department store during this era: Walgreens, Woolworth's Five and Dime, Macy's, Wanamaker, Jordan Marsh, Marshall Field and Company, Lazarus, Hudson's. A world on display. Similarly, the catalogues of Sears, Roebuck and Montgomery Ward became feasts for the eyes in the new culture of acquisition and consumption. Thanks to the railroads, goods could find customers anywhere. If you couldn't come to the store, the store would come to you – just as theatrical performers did.

The display of merchandise, in the land of desires, turned consumption into spectacle (see Leach; Susman; Boorstin; Lears, *Fables;* Fox and Lears). When business became spectacle, it learned to operate as the world of theatrical entertainment did. The merchandising of desire was already a theatrical rule of operation. Shopping was just the continuation, by other means, of the public delight in curiosities, spectacles, and feats of wonder that were offered up in the world of entertainment. The whole urban environment was becoming an arcade in which the desirable was put on display: the tableaux vivants of department store windows, their merchandise aisles, amusement parks, arcades, theatre districts, roof gardens, cabarets, dancehalls, restaurants, nightclubs, new museums, and fairs. And inside the theatre buildings, the spectators saw even more splendid displays, from spectacular scenic wonders in the melodramas to continuous shows at the vaudeville houses, where each performer seemed more striking and curious than the one who went before. Soon, motion pictures arrived, creating yet another version of the continuous show of visual stimulation.

P. T. Barnum, B. F. Keith, Flo Ziegfeld, the Shubert brothers, Samuel Goldwyn – these and other entrepreneurs figured out how to create and partly quell, if not always satisfy, our desires. In this they are the teachers and allies of modern advertisers, who learned to generate needs we do not even know we have. But advertising, which some scholars wish to identify as the reigning principle of American culture from the Gilded Age onward, is but a simulacrum of the entertainment world. Indeed, modern advertising learned its task from nineteenth-century theatre entrepreneurs. And it also learned to attach itself to entertainment in order to deliver many of its products. Instead of the real, both entertainment and advertising learned how to deliver the hyperreal, the domain of desires. The entertainment world (with its culture of celebrities) is thus the first level of hyperreality or replication, and once this realm has established itself as a need, the processes of advertising expand the register of floating signs to give us another level of hyperreality. Both levels produce the desire in us to experience an already mediated reality, to take these alternative realities as satisfying substitutes. Or we learned to believe in them as the new reality (see Baudrillard on simulacra; also see Orvell).

Thus, Barnum and the other theatrical entrepreneurs, wizards of American desires, not only tapped our appetite for the bizarre but also created the procedures for packaging almost anything. Moreover, they helped to create something else – our concept of "leisure time." Our ancestors went to the dime museum, the circus, the follies, the amusement park; we go to the mall or Disney World. And we live within the hyperreal world of television.

Consequently, we all are Barnum's children. We work in order to have time to enter the hieroglyphic realms of wonder that he and his lieutenants have created for us. What does it matter that our mesmerizing desires have little or no foundation in need? Maybe we should say that our needs become all the more urgent when they become simulacra. Surely this development and its history, this transformation of life into a *theatre mundi,* must be understood as part of the history of American theatre.

Stage and Screen

The history of the stage in the twentieth century is also the history of film. Which is to say, it is impossible to separate stage and screen and still understand the history of American theatre. Tied together in various ways, each contributed substantially to the other's aesthetic and economic development.

In the first place, the early film industry depended on the melodramas and spectacles of the nineteenth-century stage. For example, most of DeMille's early narrative films, such as *The Squaw Man, The Virginian,* and *The Girl of the Golden West* were remakes of successful stage plays. The same is true of Adolph Zukor's early productions (*The Prisoner of Zenda,* with James K. Hackett; *La Reine Elisabeth,* with Sarah Bernhardt). By 1915, twenty-two films had been made of Boucicault's plays, not counting *Rip Van Winkle,* which had been made into eighteen different films by then (no doubt because of the popularity of Joseph Jefferson's stage version, to which Boucicault contributed). In that same year alone, six of Owen Davis's popular melodramas and seven of David Belasco's plays were converted to film (see Gifford). In brief, almost all film producers, companies, and directors turned to the stage for source material, as was the case with the agreement in 1913 between the Biograph Company and Klaw and Erlanger of the Theatrical Syndicate.[13]

In the following year the Shuberts also entered the film business, looking to counter the economic challenge of the film industry by turning their successful plays into movies. For a few years they made some popular films, but they were not able to compete with the emerging Hollywood system. By 1919 their days as film producers were numbered (McNamara, *Shuberts,* 75–80).

To be expected, most of the silent film actors got their start on stage. And in the early sound years many of the stars of screen musicals were troupers from the stage: Fred Astaire, Eddie Cantor, Ray Bolger, Marilyn Miller, Buddy Ebsen, Ruby Keeler, Busby Berkeley, Helen Morgan, Paul Robeson, Jeanette MacDonald, and, of course, Al Jolson.

And likewise, many of the popular film musicals of the 1930s and early 1940s were adapted from stage musicals of the 1920s and 1930s, including *Rose Marie* (on stage in 1924, on screen in 1936), *Lady Be Good* (1924–1941), *Big Boy* (1925–30, with Al Jolson in blackface, on stage and screen, playing

Gus the servant); *The Vagabond King* (1925–30); *Sunny* (1925–1930 and 1941); *The Cocoanuts* (1925–29, a Marx brothers' vehicle with book and music provided by Irving Berlin, George S. Kaufman, and Morris Ryskind); *Animal Crackers* (1928–30, more Marx Bros. mayhem); *The Desert Song* (1926–29, 1944, and 1953); Rio Rita (1927–29 and 1942, which opened the new Ziegfeld Theatre); *Good News* (1927–30 and 1947); *A Connecticut Yankee* (1927–31, with Will Rogers in the film of this Rogers and Hart version of Twain's novel); *Show Boat* (1927–36 and 1951); *Rain or Shine* (1928–30, as an early Frank Capra film with vaudevillian Joe Cook in both the stage and screen versions); *The Three Musketeers* (1928–39); *The New Moon* (1928–30, with Grace Moore and Lawrence Tibbett, and 1940, with Jeanette MacDonald and Nelson Eddy); *Whoopee* (1928–30, with Eddie Cantor in both versions); *Sweet Adeline* (1929–35).

At the same time that the new film industry was integrating stage plays and performers into the movies, the theatre world was also attempting to find a place for film. Indeed, on 20 April 1896 the first public showing in the United States of motion pictures occurred at Koster and Bial's Music Hall on 34th Street in New York. Fourteen short films, made for Edison's Vitascope, were featured. Two months later the Cinématographe of the Lumière brothers made its appeareance in New York at B. F. Keith's vaudeville theatre.

Then, in March 1897 Proctor's Pleasure Palace, a vaudeville theatre, joined stage and screen by presenting the Lumière Cinématographe. In the continous show short films were interspersed with various vaudeville performers, including Marie Dressler in her "farcical spasm" called *Tess of the Vaudevilles,* a burlesque of Mrs. Fiske's production of *Tess of the d'Urbervilles.* Vaudeville houses continued to feature short films until World War I, although the films were often used only as fillers between acts or chasers at the end of a show (see R. Allen, *Vaudeville and Film*).

More significantly, many performers took roles in films. Dressler herself, in 1914, starred in a film, *Tillie's Punctured Romance,* which she also directed. It also introduced an English music-hall comedian, Charlie Chaplin, who had just arrived in America. Soon, of course, he was directing and writing his own films. Dressler had some success with several silent two-reelers, featuring her character of Tillie, but the vaudeville circuit was her mainstay during these years. Then, in the early 1930s she became a top film attraction in *Anna Christie, Tugboat Annie,* and *Dinner at Eight.* The "ugly duckling," as she termed herself in her autobiography, showed that glamour was not the only ticket to Hollywood fame.

Of course, in the first few years of the twentieth century most people in the theatre world did not perceive films as an entertainment threat to the stage. The one-reelers, running only a few minutes, were mere novelties of visual action – bizarre projections of light that presented objects and people in a strange alternating pattern of sequence and suspension. Anything could appear or disappear in a second. Film, as Georges Méliès demonstrated, was the medium of the trickster, the wizard. It was a magician's art form. Thus, even though there were ten thousand Nickelodeon movie theatres across America by 1908, they attracted mainly the working class, especially immigrants. The stage was surely a superior art form because it followed basic rules of order and causality (that Aristotle had first spelled out). But soon D. W. Griffith and other innovators, transforming the poetics of the stage to the screen, turned moving pictures into narratives of great spectacle (see Bowser; Musser, *Emergence of Cinema*).

As films increased not only in formal sophistication but also in popularity, several stage producers attempted to find a place for their stars in the new medium. In 1914, for instance, Daniel Frohman, one of the partners in the newly formed Famous Players Film Company, produced a silent film version of *Tess of the d'Urbervilles,* starring Mrs. Fiske. The film, based upon her popular stage adaptation of Thomas Hardy's novel, was directed by Edwin S. Porter, who had left Edison. Although Mrs. Fiske was pleased by the film (including the way the soft photography made her look younger), it did not launch a successful film career for her. Her only other film, made a year later for Edison, was *Vanity Fair,* based upon her successful stage adaptation of Thackeray's novel. It lost money. Consequently, her last two decades were spent on the road, touring from coast to coast in old-fashioned star vehicles (such as *Mis' Nelly of N'Orleans*) and revivals of her most popular productions from decades earlier (*The Rivals, Ghosts, Becky Sharp*).[14]

The stage, though suffering from the technological and aesthetic invasion of cinema, maintained its entertainment identity and financial base for three decades by centralizing methods of production and distribution. Theatre also maintained its popular appeal by accenting its strengths: (1) words and songs, which film could not deliver until 1927; (2) vaudeville entertainment (offered cheaply, though the nickelodeons soon won that low-price battle); (3) live shows, with dynamic, beloved performers; (4) dancing girls in fancy, often revealing costumes; (5) the occasional Shakespearean production; (6) opera and musicals; (7) visiting international stars and theatre companies; and (8) the Little Theatre movement of serious, modernist intent and often "realistic" quality.

But the popularity of film began to change the audience demographics for the stage, especially on the touring circuit (see Lynd and Lynd). For instance, between 1900 and 1910 approximately three hundred productions, on average, toured the country each year. Most of them originated from shows that had premiered in New York City. By the 1920s the number of touring Broadway plays had dipped to approximately sixty-five shows annually. And in the 1930s, on average, the number settled at about twenty to twenty-five shows annually. These numbers do not measure the vaudeville, burlesque, and cheap melodrama circuits, but the same quick reduction hit them as well. By the 1920s the number of specialty acts dropped rapidly, and by the 1930s most of the various touring networks had collapsed.

To be expected, then, many of the theatre buildings used for road shows and popular entertainment became movie theatres. By 1929 at least eleven of the seventy-two legitimate theatres in New York were showing feature films ("talkies") instead of live shows. And another dozen or more theatres were alternating feature films with live shows. Short-term, this procedure of booking films helped the theatre owners cover costs, but soon many theatres had to convert to movie houses or close. By 1940 only thirty-two legitimate theatres were operating in New York (see Poggi).

In the midtwenties, however, theatre producers still believed in the golden future of live theatre. For example, in 1927 (the same year that the first sound film appeared) the new Ziegfeld Theatre had its grand opening. It was built specifically for staging musicals, something that silent films could not offer (until that fateful year). Funded primarily by William Randolph Hearst and designed sumptuously by Joseph Urban (an architect as well as a designer; see Chapter 8), it was the pinnacle of Art Deco style. The auditorium was egg shaped, with golden upholstery for rugs and seats, and it featured a grand mural designed by Urban (and executed by Lillian Gaertner) that swept up the side walls and across the seamless ceiling, celebrating, in Urban's words, "heroes of old romances." These heroes, often lovers, were distributed throughout a flowering pattern of colors, including a rich goldleaf that matched the rugs and seats. The ceiling included a secret window from which Ziegfeld, the goose who laid the golden egg, could watch the show. His hideaway room in the ceiling held up to 100 people (see Carter and Cole; Ziegfeld and Ziegfeld).

Show Boat had its premiere here, as did the *Follies* of 1931, but in 1933, four years after the Wall Street crash and one year after Ziegfeld died (bankrupt and owing Joseph Urban thousands of dollars), the theatre was converted into a movie house. In 1944 Billy Rose attempted to recapture its lost glory. He renovated it as a theatre house, but times had changed. So by the 1950s it was turned into a studio for NBC television. Then in 1966, the golden gem of New York theatres was demolished to make way for another bland skyscraper.

Economically, 1927 was the turning point for New York theatre. The number of new productions offered each season started to drop after the 1926–27 season (which had 263 shows) and the 1927–28 season (264 shows). Soon the "declines of the road and Broadway" (Poggi's central concern in his economic study of show business) became the defining condition of the theatre, especially as radio and film took over larger and larger aspects of entertainment. By the 1938–39 season the number of new shows had dropped to 96 productions;

by 1945–46 the number was 76 productions (*Variety,* 9 June 1971; quoted in McLaughlin, 271–73). Still, some savvy theatre producers, playwrights, and composers figured out how to build subsidiary sources into their contracts so that they made a profit out of film rights (even if a production lost money on Broadway). This procedure, especially for musicals, has continued to the present day (see McLaughlin).

By the 1930s and 1940s popular entertainment, in great measure, was provided by film, radio, and then television, despite the limited success of stage musicals, comedies, and the occasional upscale drama by such playwrights as Philip Barry, Clifford Odets, Lillian Hellman, S. N. Behrman, George S. Kaufman, and Thornton Wilder. Many of the stars of the stage in the 1920s began making the shift to the screen in the 1930s. Some never returned. Even most of the major playwrights, taking their cues from the performers, worked in Hollywood: Odets, Kaufman, Hellman, Wilder, S. J. Perelman, Maxwell Anderson, Sidney Howard, Elmer Rice, John Howard Lawson, Robert Sherwood, Albert Maltz, Garson Kanin, Charles McArthur, Ben Hecht, Zoë Akins, Sam and Bella Spewack (see Postlewait in Engle and Miller). They loved to complain about the place, usually to demonstrate that they could maintain their integrity while working for the evil empire, but we need to read between the lines. Stage and screen had become part of a large and increasingly integrated system of American entertainment.

Beyond economics, there is another important factor in the relation between stage and screen. The basic argument, put forward by Nicolas Vardac and others, claims that film became the best and most complete medium for realistic representation. Or in the words of Vardac: "[T]he cinema appeared when the theatrical need for the photographic ideal was greatest" (247). As we normally tell the story, stage realism, going as far as it could, passed the torch to film, which was ordained (by the laws of technological progress) to deliver a better product. D. W. Griffith, though drawing upon genres of romance and melodrama, refined film techniques "toward a more thorough realism" (Vardac, 201). In turn, as film developed, it found numerous new ways to achieve a realistic treatment of character. And film's expansive photographic detail transformed spectacle into lifelike visual representations.

D. W. Griffith and others demonstrated that the camera's eye could go anywhere and let us see anything. Even when Griffith adapted a stage play, as in the case of Thomas Bailey Aldrich's *Judith of Bethulia* (1914), the camera was able to present a "greater realism" (210) than the dwarfed stage could hope to achieve. The technology of film allowed it to integrate scenic realism and melodramatic spectacle in ways that the stage could never achieve. Film's control over motion, cutting, shot, and pictorial speed provided the difference. Thus, from Vardac's perspective, the hundred-year development of historical antiquarianism and realism on the nineteenth-century stage was actually a search for a mode of pictorial representation that only film could truly realize. The nineteenth-century stage, lacking the ability to achieve what it was aiming for, called forth its other, better self. In brief, the stage was yearning to become film. We can see, accordingly, that Steele MacKaye and the Kiralfy brothers were proto–film makers – not because of their imaginative reformulation of space and movement for the spectator's eye, but because of their supposed struggle toward the aesthetics of realism. Unfortunately, they were imprisoned in a lesser art form. Their sad fate was to be born too soon. "A greater perfection and elaboration" (Vardac, 243) of realism, pantomime, spectacle, narrative, and illusion arrived with film.

So, here again we have an argument for "the real thing." But we may doubt that the victory of motion pictures was primarily a matter of realism fulfilled. Granted, the aesthetics of realism and the techniques (or principles) of film support and complement one another in some telling ways, as some film theorists have argued (for a survey, see Andrew; Mast and Cohen; Rosen). But basically the processes and styles of film, from the modes of representation and codes of signification to the techniques of filming, editing, and audience identification, should not be confused with ideas of realism or the concept of verisimilitude (see Bordwell; Bordwell and Thompson). More to the point, realism is not the opposite or alternative to various kinds of theatricalized style; instead, it is yet one more kind of artistic style, one option among many styles in both theatre and film. Consequently, *Citizen Kane* is as stylized as Welles's theatre productions of the 1930s, not only because the film blends several modern styles, including realism, expressionism, and symbolism but also because both theatre and film cannot avoid being stylized media.

Film, as Vachel Lindsay argued in *The Art of the Moving Picture* (1915), is a spatial, temporal, and architectonic art of light and motion for arranging visual objects (including actors as objects) into some kind of associative or abstract formal order. The camera's eye, even when observing "real" places and "realistic" acting, selects and transforms them into a highly stylized artifact, produced by means of the registers and patterns of filmic art (film stock, lighting, editing, framing techniques and codes, shots and focus, sound, and so forth). In a sense, then, despite its referential codes and styles, film achieves something other than the real thing. Also, as Lindsay points out, filmic narrative, besides being an analogue of the world, serves as a mirror screen (65–66) of the spectator's dream world, a realm of hieroglyphic symbols. Film thus erases the neat division between not only realism and its supposed lesser alternatives (a false division) but also objective and subjective perception.

Interestingly, something similar happens with the modern stage. Part of what fascinates us about film is the ways it reconfigures time, space, and motion into narrative modes that are simultaneously realistic and symbolic, objective and subjective. Likewise, the modernist stage discovered its own techniques of simultaneity. Indeed, the development of realism in the theatre, as in film, should be placed within the context of new and renewed methods of pictorial and narrative simultaneity that emerged in playwriting and production, especially in the theatricalized methods of design, lighting, and movement (enhanced by the new possibilities of electrical lighting).

In brief, various theatrical and dramatic approaches to simultaneity can be identified in the modern era, beginning with Ibsen's complex method of yoking not only the temporal realms of past and present but the spatial domains of interior and exterior. In turn, various symbolist theatre artists, including Alfred Jarry, August Strindberg, and the surrealists, collapsed objective and subjective representation into a dreamlike, spacetime continuum. And in design Gordon Craig and Adolphe Appia spelled out many of the potentialities of simultaneity (architectonic forms in relation to space, time, and motion). Subsequently, key directors, such as Eisenstein and Meyerhold in Moscow and Piscator in Berlin, figured out how to articulate these artistic principles of simultaneity (see Postlewait, "Simultaneity").

On the American stage, simultaneous design became a paramount method for representing action, especially multiple locations (for example, Robert Edmond Jones's design for *Desire Under the Elms* and Jo Mielziner's design for *The Glass Menagerie, A Streetcar Named Desire,* and *Death of a Salesman*). These approaches to stage space also allowed for multiple or simultaneous time zones. In this theatre, realism may be one of the operating codes, but it is transformed into new visual codes, the hieroglyphics of simultaneity (see Postlewait, "Spatial Order").

Which is to say, the progressive march of theatre and film toward realism is an illusion – or, at best, a truncated, often myopic vision of the signs and significance of American theatrical entertainment. Vachel Lindsay had proclaimed that "the wizards should rule, and the realists should serve them" (264). Well, the history of film is the triumph of the wizards. But wizards also triumphed on the stage, some by adapting realism to a larger vision of artistic expression and meaning.

Women and the Theatre

Since the arrival of the Hallam company in 1752, women have been central to the professional history of American theatre. The company's first production in Williamsburg, on 15 September, was *The Merchant of Venice*. Mrs. Lewis Hallam, who had acted on the London stage, played the leading role of Portia. After her husband's death in 1755, she married David Douglass, and together they organized the American Company, which performed in various playhouses, up and down the Atlantic coast and in Jamaica. Until her retirement

Desire Under the Elms, designed and directed by Robert Edmond Jones, at the Greenwich Village Theatre, 1924. Mary Morris as Abbie, Walter Huston as Cabot, and Charles Ellis as Eben. Museum of the City of New York (Gift of Mr. and Mrs. Eugene O'Neill).

from the stage in 1769, she was a beloved, accomplished actress in both tragedy and comedy. Her contributions to management were important, but this aspect of her career remains in the shadows.

So began the professional history of women in the American theatre. During the nineteenth century, when few professional fields were open to women, the theatre continued to provide career opportunities, especially in acting but also management and playwriting (see Curry; Dudden; Kritzer). And when social and political conditions changed, especially in the twentieth century, women took up major roles in all aspects of the theatre: performance, design, choreography, management, directing, playwriting, and producing (though the top level of entrepreneurial control and activity remained closed to women, with the exception of Hallie Flanagan's reign at the Federal Theatre Project).

Also, as Bruce McConachie has shown (see Vol. I, Chap. 1, of this history; and *Melodramatic Formations*), women contributed to the changing nature of American theatre in their various roles as spectators. Their numbers, values, politics, and desires determined many of the agendas in the theatre, from aesthetic programs to economic decisions. Just as middle-class Protestant women of the mid–nineteenth century ensured the popularity of sentimental and moralistic drama (which often reinforced the cult of domesticity and the idea of a separate feminine sphere of virtuous influence), so too did other groups of women shape and reshape the continuing development of American theatre: the growing number of women managers; upper-class wives, who were often the catalyst for the building of the major opera houses; the immigrant matinee girls who flocked to the plays and silent films of the early twentieth century (see Peiss); the thousands of women who provided the organization and audience for much of the Little Theatre movement (see Blair); the actresses, such as Ethel Barrymore, who helped to organize Actors' Equity into a strike force; the hundreds of women playwrights who entered the theatre in the nineteenth and twentieth centuries (see Bzowski); and the community women across the nation who attended – and attended to – the popular pageantry movement.

Of course, whether onstage, backstage, or offstage, women often had to struggle for their opportunities and accomplishments in the theatre. Indeed, throughout this period most women in the theatre were anonymous contributors to the performance events, often unrecognized and unacknowledged. Behind the scenes, women performed a significant amount of the theatrical work, without much credit (and sometimes without pay). And even when visible, either onstage (the chorus girls) or in the auditorium (the matinee girls), they usually remained nameless.

Therefore, when charting the contributions of women in the theatre, it is important to give credit not only to the leading performers, playwrights, and producers but also to the many other women who constituted the American theatrical communities. In doing so, we should try to take the measure of the dynamic relation between the representations of women in American entertainment and the reception of those images by both men and women.

When we observe the images and displays of women in America, we begin to find a culture of visual images and codes that operated across all classes and all sections of the country. Of course, some parallels exist with developments in Europe, but often these American ways of representing or "imaging" women signaled a new, distinct project of realizing the "imaged idea of the American Girl" (Banta, xxxi).[15]

As Martha Banta has shown in *Imaging American Women,* the visual codes for representing women – photographs, sculptures, pageants, drawings in the many magazines, posters, advertising – went through major transformations in the era between 1880s and 1920s. Central to this process was the representation of women's bodies, fashions, and gender typologies on stage and screen. From the nameless chorus girls to the famous women performers, a revolution occurred in the images, ideas, and ideals of American feminine selfhood.

Obviously, not all women bought the package. And some worked to question, counter, and subvert the supposed ideal. In the theatre this alternative movement, which included a wide range of women with various political and social perspectives, provided the foundation for the major achievements of women in the modern (and sometimes modernist) American theatre. For this reason alone, there is much to celebrate in the careers and campaigns of women such as Olive Logan, Mrs. Drew, Clara Morris, Mrs. Fiske, Susan Glaspell, Anita Bush, Fanny Brice, Eva Le Gallienne, Gertrude Stein, Rose McClendon, Ethel Waters, Rose Franken, Katharine Cornell, Helen Hayes, Theresa Helburn, Cheryl Crawford, Jean Rosenthal, Aline Bernstein, Irene Sharaff, Lucinda Ballard, Lillian Hellman, Agnes de Mille, and Hallie Flanagan (see Robinson, Roberts, and Barranger; Wilmeth and Miller; also consult the many autobiographies and biographies that have been written). From our perspective today these women, and others like them, have pride of place in the development of American theatre.

But this central line of artistic excellence, discussed in some of the following essays, is also at the center of the expansive history of the idea of woman that was being worked out in the culture. From *The Black Crook* and Lydia Thompson to the chorus girls of stage and screen, American culture had become a visual culture for representing feminine identity.

Not surprisingly, no single idea of American womanhood dominated this extended era. Instead – from Barnum's "Gallery of American Female Beauty" to Ziegfeld's campaign of "glorifying the American Girl" – a series of possible representations held center stage. Yet despite the impossibility of identifying a single type, American popular culture generated an endless flow of images that offered a suggestion, even a promise, of the real thing. She had numerous manifestations: the Gibson girl, the Christy girl, the portraits by John Singer Sargent, Maude Adams, Julia Marlowe, Ethel Barrymore, the Gish sisters, Mary Pickford, and even Julian Eltinge, the female impersonator.

Especially during the era of mass immigration, a major campaign developed to present a preferred image of American identity for women – an American look that immigrant women were encouraged to admire and, if possible, to emulate. As long as one was "white," one could learn to pass. The melting pot thus promised an ethnic, not a racial, makeover (that is, a Jewish girl, off the boat from Odessa, but not a black girl, up from slavery, could at least dream of becoming representative). The campaign for the American girl – tied to beliefs in the superiority of white, northern European civilization (beliefs supported by "scientific" evidence from biological and anthropological studies of race) – was carried forward by many diverse individuals and institutions: scientists, doctors, teachers, psychologists, preachers, painters, and illustrators. And by advertisers, who glamourized all the products that would help one attain the dream (see Evans; Banta; Fox and Lears).

Both the stage and screen, joining the campaign energetically, packaged the visual formulas and personality types of the American girl. Most of the forms of theatrical entertainment – popular plays, musicals, revues, and burlesque shows – were committed to the display of women's bodies. These shows of beauty or sex, usually organized by men for the pleasure of men, are a crucial part of the history of the changing American theatre.

At the same time, we must remember that women as well as men flocked to many of these productions, which can be understood not only as acts of sexual exploitation but also as theatrical articulations of some of the emerging new codes of feminine identity, independence, and assertiveness in the new age of women's rights. We may feel more comfortable with the actors and playwrights, such as Olive Logan and Rachel Crothers, who took stances against the reductive sexual codes of a male society (see Logan). But then we might miss the full appeal and strategy of Mae West, who teased and exploited those sexual codes. Equally important, we would fail to understand how dancers and cheoreographers, such as Isadora Duncan and Martha Graham, developed new codes of the body and movement for women as they worked both within and against the new culture of the liberated eye. And we would fail to appreciate the ways that the thousands of nameless chorus girls and the millions of young female spectators contributed to the transformation of the American woman. The chorus lines, though certainly offering a less critical response to the cult of the American girl than was articulated by a handful of writers, were nonetheless more significant in the gender (as well as sexual) revolutions of this era.

Beyond Broadway, the pageantry movement, which swept the country in the 1910s and 1920s, put women on display as idealized American types. Often women were major organizers of these allegorical presentations, which usually celebrated American history and the possibilities for progressive change. In some cases pageants were used to campaign for women's suffrage. Seemingly far from the Broadway chorus lines, the pageants still shared in the national ideal of womanly grace and bodily charm. Through poses, tableaux, and dances (the same guiding principles of the chorus lines), the pageants represented the dignity, deportment, and beauty of women. Long, flowing Greek robes rather than scanty costumes served as the preferred attire, but the American girl was still on display (see Prevots; Glassberg).

Also, at the various world fairs and expositions in the United States, the "new woman" was to be seen not only in Bolossy Kiralfy's grand spectacles of hundreds of beautiful dancing girls but also in the exhibitions in "Women's Buildings" that featured women at work in domestic settings. Here American women demonstrated new kitchen implements (the latest "real things" that the technology could deliver).

Perhaps one set of images from the Columbian Exposition of 1893 in Chicago best illustrates the pervasiveness of this new cult of the American girl. Once again Thomas Edison (who demonstrated his new Kinetoscope at the Fair), electricity, and one of the Kiralfy brothers are at the center of spectacle.

Whereas the 1876 Centennial in Philadelphia had featured a massive, masculine icon as the quintessential representation of America – the Corliss engine with its long, stroking arm and powerful piston – the 1893 Exposition turned to images of women to capture the spirit of national identity. Large sculptural figures of the Republic and Columbia, suggestive of the Statue of Liberty, stood in the Grand Basin, a large pool at the center of the White City, which was presented as a utopian architectural world (see Kasson; Rydell; Burg). Around the basin, smaller murals with allegorical figures of women looked down on the scene. These murals of women, who were either draped in flowing gowns or nude, celebrated the spirit of electricity, industry, and progress. Fittingly, at night the murals and statues were ringed with electric lights that turned the whole scene into a grand spectacle: ". . . when the lights came up and the crown of the Republic shown and the Smith and Wellesley girls floated upon a sea of reflecting luminosity, hearts swelled and sublimity held dominion over the grounds of the Exposition" (Banta, 533).

The "Electricity Girls," represented in the murals and by the college girls, signified American progressive hopes. And in case anyone failed to read the message, the Exposition also offered Imre Kiralfy's "Gorgeous Spectacle *America*" in which the same images and themes of American progress and feminine beauty were joined (see I. Kiralfy). Electricity and the American dream girl illuminated the path to paradise. In perfect harmony with the message of the Exposition, Edison had demonstrated his new motion pictures that same year, thus showing yet another way that electricity and the American dream, attended by images of beautiful women, were to be joined. America the Beautiful.

And yet, we should note that the White City vision of unity and progress was an illusion, a sham. 1893 was also the year of an economic panic, with 550 banks closing and 150,000 businesses folding. Beyond the facade, a series of contradictions continued to define the country (and the theatre). Perhaps fittingly, a year later, on 5 July 1894, the whole White City went up in flames during a conflict between federal troops and striking railway workers. In two hours, "the World's Columbian Exposition, which had been conceived out of faith in a rebirth of order, ended in violence and flame" (Badger, 130). Just as well, because the White City, like its representation of women, was unreal. Which is to say, it was a dream that the twentieth century would discover how to re-create as fantasy realizations, from the dream worlds of film to Disneyland.

Celebrities and the American Ideal

Following the assassination of President Lincoln in 1865, actors lived under a dark cloud of suspicion and hostility (if not guilt by association). Edwin Booth was convinced that his career was over; other actors, though able to maintain their livelihoods, realized that they had to monitor their behavior and statements. But within a few months, as the nation began to redirect itself, this uneasy condition changed. People returned to the theatres, and Edwin Booth returned to the stage. The dark cloud lifted.

But actors still had to accept the fact that they lacked the respect and social status of most other professionals. Their talent and charm, though serving them well onstage, did not purchase them a central position in the public arena. Actors continued to exist at the margins of society, outside the social and political circles of most respectable people.

But some things change rapidly, and nothing more so than the status of actors in American society. By the twentieth century, actors had become major players in national politics, selling war bonds, entertaining troups, defeating entertainment taxes, and, most significantly, contributing fame and fortune to political campaigns. In 1932, for example, a number of stage and screen stars hit the campaign trail in support of Franklin Delano Roosevelt's run for president. By far the most influential was Will Rogers, who helped to solidify the support of common folk across the nation. His persona and voice spanned the country. Besides his stage work, Rogers starred in the movies (six films in 1931 and 1932), had a popular radio show, and wrote a syndicated political column for the newspapers. As the homespun philosopher of American values, he was immensely popular and trusted, so his political advocacy, greatly appreciated by Roosevelt, proved decisive for perhaps millions of voters (Yagoda, 298–300).

Twelve years later, in 1944, when running against Thomas Dewey (whom most newspapers supported), Roosevelt tapped Orson Welles as his celebrity supporter. Primarily because of the demands of the war (but also because of his paralysis and poor health), Roosevelt could not campaign around the country. So Welles became one of his surrogates, traveling to most of the states by railroad and airplane and delivering rousing speeches for Roosevelt and against the Republicans and their redbaiting. He and Roosevelt met on several occasions to plot strategy, and Roosevelt and his advisers contributed ideas for the speeches. When Roosevelt sent Welles on a secret political mission at this time, he called Rita Hayworth, whom Welles had just married, to assure her that Welles's disappearance for a week was for government service. And after winning the election, Roosevelt wrote to Welles: "I want to thank you for the splendid role you played in the recent campaign. I cannot recall any campaign in which actors and artists were so effective in the unrehearsed reality of the drama of the American future. It was a great show, in which you played a great part" (quoted in Brady, 375). Thus, long before the election of Ronald Reagan, American politics had become part of a celebrity culture of performers.

And we should note that Franklin Roosevelt was not the first president to draw upon the stars. In 1924 Calvin Coolidge tapped Al Jolson to sing his praises. Political pundits at the time estimated that several million voters were swayed by Jolson's energetic endorsement. Even earlier, D. W. Griffith campaigned for Woodrow Wilson by placing key statements of Wilson in his films. And George M. Cohan, singing "Over There," rallied the troops and American support for Wilson's war policy.

This political campaigning by celebrities, besides revealing a shift in national attitude toward entertainers and their place in society, signals a transformation in the ethical and social codes of the country. By the turn of the century, actors gained a new respectibility. They began to move from the margins of society to places of improved social status. A new professionalism developed (training schools, professional associations). Also, religious opposition to theatre decreased. And middle-class society began to accept actors as part of the American community. At the same time, American society was changing in major ways. As it became an urban, modernized culture, it also became a culture of leisure, advertising, consumption, and mass media. The Victorian codes gave way to new modern values. And the entertainment industry moved to the center of American life.

A new condition of fame for select stars coincided with the changing social status of performers in American society, but the celebrity culture also detached itself from standard codes of respectability in the twentieth century. Some stars were able to exist outside of the demands of standard norms, as Benjamin McArthur argues: "Concern about respectability devolved into the vagaries of image. Actors – as celebrities, as paragons of freedom, as models of lifestyle – epitomized the shift from an ethic of strict moral demands to one of permissive self-fulfillment" (226).

Celebrities became the objects of adoration and identification as the nation transformed itself from a Victorian morality of discipline and denial to a vague, new code of liberated selfhood and "personality" (see Susman). No longer limited by – sometimes not even tied to – rules of respectable behavior, select stars became emblems of the possibility of an emancipated existence, as the love affair between Mary Pickford and Douglas Fairbanks in the 1920s demonstrated. The Catholic Church might condemn them for freeing themselves of their spouses. But the public, thrilling to their liberation from social restraints and codes, acclaimed them. As Lary May notes: "Presumably, their breaks from the past had led to the happiness their films promised to millions" (144–45).

So, by the twentieth century some celebrities became the new icons of public fascination, desire, and admiration. Their fame thus served as both a condition of special privilege and a transferable quality that advertisers and politicians alike began to tap for their own substantial benefit. Of course, key actors in the nineteenth century were greatly admired for their talent, persona, or charm (prime examples are Edwin Booth, Joseph Jefferson, Lotta Crabtree, Ada Rehan). And a few – one thinks especially of Sarah Bernhardt – seemed to achieve something new (besides notoriety) in the firmament of fame. But in the twentieth century, as dozens and dozens of performers became national celebrities, artists achieved a status comparable to that of royalty in previous eras.

No doubt the flood of images of stars in magazines, newspapers, and films enhanced public interest in entertainers. Moreover, a growing publicity and advertising industry had developed nationally. And it seems apparent that the loosening of moral codes contributed to the new celebrity culture. But this supposed escape from the codes of respectability fails to explain the impact of such performers as Will Rogers or Orson Welles on the political process. And more important, this focus on the moral dimensions of social culture misses other forms of liberation and invention that modern entertainment has achieved.

Actually, in modern times two cultural processes of transformation – seemingly distinct but still related – have occurred for talented celebrities. In the first case, they have been granted (or have attained) a kind of separation from the norms of the real, including but not limited to the social codes of behavior. This distancing has allowed them to operate in a separate, fantastical realm that exists not only outside of the normal constraints of social and moral life but also beyond the principles of the mundane world. They became wizards and impresarios of fantastic possibilities – as we can see in the cases of Charlie Chaplin, Mary Pickford, and Orson Welles, the boy wonder. The real was not so much displaced as multiplied by the availability of images – a transformation in art and identity that many realist artists kept having difficulty understanding and representing because of their moral as well as aesthetic assumptions about real identity and truth. The real is not latent; the surface is not false.[16]

The supposed "real self," guaranteed in the past by the idea of moral character, has dissolved in the modern world into what Roland Barthes calls "the reality effect" and Martha Banta calls the process of "imaging" – the manufacturing of numerous typologies of visual representation. Indeed, presence, no longer tied to a single idea of the real self, has become an evocative suggestion – a promise of a fantastic selfhood (or a hitherto censored self). New realities are evoked by free-floating visual codes, the hieroglyphic signs of the world and selfhood. The image or aura of self becomes more substantial than actual selfhood (if indeed it can be found, even in diverse and multiple fragments).

Here, then, is one of the ironies of our history of American theatre. Although we sometimes want to see the American theatre of the 1920s as the triumph of the real, in a break from the fantasy of melodrama and sentimental plays, the major achievement of this era – as Gilbert Seldes intuited – was the creation of alternative worlds of art by highly talented celebrities who delivered something other than moralistic realism or formulaic genres.

One of the ways Americans dealt with the 1920s, the Depression, and World War II was to give themselves over to those artists who created and delivered versions of these alternative worlds: Maude Adams, Al Jolson, Charlie Chaplin, the Marx brothers, Fred Astaire, and Ginger Rogers. Likewise, certain dramatists, producers, songwriters, and filmmakers, such as William Saroyan, Thornton Wilder, Flo Ziegfeld, George and Ira Gershwin, and Frank Capra, captured aspects of these alternative visions. In design, Joseph Urban holds a special place (though he does not fit into our neat, modernist narrative, which requires that the development of design be charted through the modernist line of Gordon Craig and Robert Edmond Jones). And in the visual arts, above all, there's Krazy Kat. The issue here is not escapism, which still implies that the real is the moral home of truth. Instead, these alternative worlds are just that: alternatives to the binarism of the real and the false. Worlds of difference.

Yet at the same time, and seemingly in opposition to this freefall into alternative realms, other celebrities were able to collapse or mediate the distance between the real and the fantastic; in the process they became the emblems and the benchmarks of an American myth that passed itself off as reality. President Roosevelt's letter to Orson Welles suggests that he understood this new condition of creating or achieving the reality effect.

That is, while modern American society was in the process of displacing many of its foundational values, it also re-created (or held onto) a national ideal of the good American. And who else should embody this persona but the actor, especially those few actors who seem to be the very epitome of the American character: Buffalo Bill, Joseph Jefferson, George M. Cohan, Will Rogers, James Stewart, John Wayne, Orson Welles (until the 1950s), and, in time, Ronald Reagan. Set against this masculine line, but of course lacking the full aura of American identity, were the various installments of the ideal American woman: Maude Adams, Ethel Barrymore, Helen Hayes, and Katharine Hepburn.

Throughout this era, then, a rather vaguely defined but seductive idea of American goodness (or its likeness) held center stage. The resiliency, skill, charm, and decency of American individuals continued to be the abiding theme. Certain actors captured and expressed key aspects of this composite American persona. And a few performers, such as Will Rogers, Orson Welles, John Wayne, and Gary Cooper (as Sergeant York or Lou Gehrig), seemed not only to embody the central traits of the American identity but actually to become "the real thing." In other words, the hieroglyphic and the real worlds had merged – at least in the personae of a chosen few.

Befittingly, then, Will Rogers – whose persona and precursors included the Jonathan character in American drama, the iconic Abraham Lincoln, the witty Mark Twain, Joseph Jefferson, Buffalo Bill and the cowboys of his childhood, and Rogers's own partial heritage as a Cherokee from the Oklahoma Territory – became the national emblem of the American in the 1920s and early 1930s. At that time he captured the ambiguities and contradictions of the American desire to be true to both folk values and modern unrest (or patriotic sentiments and protective cynicism). Of course, it is open to question whether this kind of mediated image of country and city provided much more than a vague endorsement of meliorism. But there is no doubt about the popularity and influence of Rogers in the making of American cultural identity.

More recently, another performer, Ronald Reagan, embodied some of these same values and images that Will Rogers (as well as James Stewart and Gary Cooper) had represented, including the mix of manly virility and down-home attributes (the angularity of the body, the "natural" voice, the humor, the face of a trustful man, and the clothes or costumes of the land: jeans, hats, ropes, and horses). Like Rogers, Reagan spoke for the people and portrayed their idea of American character. Fantasy? Reality? Both – at one and the same time.[17]

Blackface and African American Theatre

Following the Civil War, the national leaders had the difficult task of finding ways to reunite the country. The divisions between North and South were substantial, and some issues seemed intractable.[18] The most immediate problem was the political program of Reconstruction, which for a few years swung open the doors of opportunity for the black population. But Reconstruction also made political, economic, and social reconciliation between whites in the North and South impossible to achieve. The political attempts to define the terms for equality and integration for blacks seemed to be irrevocably at odds with a political process of integration between white southerners and northerners. Racism was a key problem; it also remained a key condition for brokering compromises between the North and South. The rights and hopes of blacks were negotiable (see Foner).

By 1876, the centennial year of the country's independence, the northern commitment to Reconstruction was abandoned when Rutherford B. Hayes became president. In consequence of agreements hammered out behind closed doors, southern states delivered the decisive votes in the Electoral College. Soon after, Hayes withdrew the federal troops from the South, and those half-opened doors of opportunity for blacks began to close. Reconstruction was declared a flawed process, doomed to failure (or that's what white people wanted to believe in order to distance themselves from responsibility not only for past actions but also future endeavors to achieve racial justice).

This truce between white southerners and northerners was ratified in 1896 when the Supreme Court upheld the constitutionality of the segregation of the "white and colored races" (in the *Plessy v. Ferguson* case). Thus, a separate but equal doctrine (or legal travesty) became the justification for Jim Crow laws throughout the nation, not just in the south (see Woodword). In brief, blacks were sacrificed in order to achieve an accommodation between southern and northern whites. Not until 1954 (*Brown v. Board of Education* of Topeka, Kansas) would this tragic racial agreement begin to unravel in the courts and the political system (see Franklin and Moss).

The reconciliation between North and South remained an uneasy, troubled agreement with many flaws. Economically, the South failed to benefit from the major capitalist developments of the country (occurring mainly in the North and West). Politically, the Jim Crow arrangements proved to be retrograde, only delaying instead of facing an inevitable civil rights conflict in the South. And socially, the insularity of both whites and blacks retarded any mutual understanding that could have provided the basis for addressing the many problems of slavery and racism (e.g., the challenge of a new education system).[19]

No doubt there are many factors to consider in this historical condition. But there are three key points I want to make here: (1) This era, which began with the freeing of the slaves, proved to be a terrible time of segregation and racial injustice for the black population in the North as well as the South; (2) northern whites failed just as significantly as southern whites in the struggle to come to terms with the many conditions of racial prejudice (the suffrage movement, though allied with blacks before abolition, became strikingly racist by the turn of the century, pitting the rights of women against the rights of blacks); and (3) the failures to confront and solve key political problems of racism must be understood not in isolation from but as part of the overall national struggle to work out a new, integrated idea of the United States.

That is, the many struggles to create an integrated, united country, though failing miserably in the case of blacks (and, just as miserably, in the case of Native Americans), had some successes. Which is to say, the United States had some striking successes as well as failures. These achievements, albeit imperfect, included the processes of (1) linking the various parts of the country into one political system after a divisive civil war (though disfranchising blacks was a consequence of white unity); (2) making an equal place for women in the political order (if not the economic and social systems); (3) taking in and trying to assimiliate approximately 35 million immigrants during this era, mainly in the urban centers; (4) building and integrating four different transportation systems: the networks for trains, ships, automobiles, and airplanes; (5) creating a set of comprehensive communication systems: postal delivery, newspapers and journals, telegraph, telephone, and radio; (6) beginning a network of social services, especially in the Progressive and Depression eras; (7) overcoming the worst divisions between labor and capital (including the often reprehensible partnership between government and capital that contributed to bloody strife and suffering); (8) holding the country together through two world wars that destroyed a number of nations; and (9) shaping a shared language and culture that would integrate business, education, politics, social behavior, and, yes, entertainment. Of course, this national agenda was not without missed opportunities and political failures. Some of them held special moral power over the consciences and frustrations of U.S. citizens. Still, the country had experienced and achieved much, including a series of radical transformations of the national identity and social order. Even the political system had changed somewhat.

In order to understand the worst failure – the abiding heritage of racism against African Americans – we would have to place their history within the context of these various developments. In some cases, such as the integration of the national political system, blacks received few benefits until 1954. Yet in other cases, such as the new networks of transportation and communication, some blacks took advantage of the developments (such as the migration to northern cities, jobs on the railroads). But what about the development of unified cultural systems, including entertainment? The record is mixed, at best (see Lemann).

Following the Civil War, African Americans still lived mainly in the rural areas and small towns of the South, though substantial pockets of blacks were located in northern cities, and a few blacks had migrated west (including a number of men who joined the U.S. cavalry units; few become visible, however, in Wild West shows). Economic well-being was hard to come by, but slowly small numbers of blacks began to find places for themselves in farming, business, service jobs, and a few professions, helped along by the new black schools and colleges that were founded in the late nineteenth century.

At that time Booker T. Washington was a major influence on the new generation of blacks, including a number of educated blacks who emerged in the entertainment world in the 1890s. His version of pragmatism, which publically sometimes amounted to acquiescence to the status quo, provided a model for many black performers who had to please both white and black audiences simultaneously (see Krasner). The accommodation to blackface that black performers made, however relunctantly, was based upon the political understanding that Washington articulated. Also, his philosophy of self-reliance guided hundreds of black artists in establishing themselves professionally.

The new black educational institutions provided some of the first groups of touring black performers, including the popular Fiske Jubilee Singers. Other black performers, such as the Hyers Sisters and Sissieretta "Black Patti" Jones, also received professional training in music. Yet despite their obvious talents, which won the praise of whites and blacks alike, they discovered that roles in white musicals and operas were closed to them. Sadly, though the Fiske Jubilee Singers were invited to present a command performance for Queen Victoria in England and Sissieretta Jones was asked by President Benjamin Harrison to sing at the White House, they were not wanted on the white stage.

So, like other black performers in the decades after the Civil War, they had to make their way within the confining conditions of minstrelsy. The blackface tradition, by default, became their heritage. Minstrelsy proved to be both an avenue to professional opportunity and the dead-end of professional identity for most black performers until the mid–twentieth century and later.

Throughout the nineteenth century minstrelsy remained a major avenue for white and black careers. In New York City the highpoint of minstrelsy occurred between the 1840s and 1870s. At times a dozen different theatres were presenting minstrel shows in these decades. But after the 1870s minstrel shows gave way, in great part, to spectacles, such as *Around the World in Eighty Days,* and to the growth of musicals (for example, the craze for Gilbert and Sullivan in the 1880s; see Chapter 6). Out on the road, however, the story was different. White minstrel performers continued to have successful careers, and black actors used minstrelsy to perform for white and black audiences alike. Charles B. Hicks, a black man, organized the Original Georgia Minstrels in 1865; the Callender's Georgia Minstrels began touring in 1873; Henry Hart's Colored Minstrels appeared the following year. In 1879 Callender's Georgia Minstrels became Haverly's Colored Georgia Minstrels. In some cases these troupes remained under the control of the black performers, but some of the more successful ones were managed and acquired by white producers.

The Frohman brothers, for example, gained control of Callender's Georgia Minstrels by 1880 (see Marcosson and Frohman; Sampson, *The Ghost Walks*).

The minstrel shows and music, whether performed by whites or blacks, remained amazingly popular in the decades after the Civil War. For example, in the 1890s more than six hundred "coon songs" were published as sheet music. Many of these songs, including some written by black minstrel performers, sold over a million copies. And Fred Fisher's "If the Man in the Moon Were a Coon" sold over 3 million copies (Nasaw, 55).

From the 1870s onward the number of black performers increased. Toward the end of the century black shows were booked into the major white theatres in Chicago, Boston, Philadelphia, and New York, among other cities. Most black performers stayed within the conventions of minstrelsy, though they occasionally modified their routines, downplaying the more demeaning stereotypes and adding new routines. But blackface remained the norm for most black performers.

Then, in the late 1890s signs of change appeared. On 4 April 1898 Bob Cole and Billy Johnson premiered *A Trip to Coontown* at the Third Avenue Theatre. Starring Sam Lucas, who had established himself in minstrelsy and vaudeville, this show was the first black musical revue to appear on (or near) Broadway. It still had many of the characteristics of the minstrel show, but it had a plot. And more important it made overtures toward an ironic, even subversive, sensibility, because Cole played one of the characters, a tramp, in whiteface (see Krasner, 29–33; Riis; Woll).

That same year, on 4 July 1898, a one-hour musical revue called *Clorindy; or, the Origin of the Cakewalk* by Will Marion Cook (music, lyrics) and Paul Laurence Dunbar (libretto, lyrics) appeared at the Casino Roof Garden in New York City. This Independence Day revue, featuring syncopated music and "coon songs," starred Ernest Hogan, who had contributed to the popularity of coon songs in 1896 with "All Coons Look Alike to Me" (a signature song he came to regret). Roof-garden theatres (see S. Johnson) were popular late-night spots for a wide range of entertainment in this era, but this was the first appearance of African American performers in these trendy settings. Following a few weeks on the roof, the show toured during the rest of the year. Hogan had other obligations, however, so the comic team of George Walker and Bert Williams stepped in (see Krasner; Riis; Woll).

Four years later Cook and Dunbar (though now enemies who refused to meet together) provided the music and lyrics for one of the first successful black musicals on Broadway: *In Dahomey,* starring Walker and Williams, as well as Aida Overton Walker, who danced the cakewalk and provided choreography. The show, with book by Jessie Shipp, opened in Stamford, Connecticut, in September 1902, toured to a number of cities, and then, because of its success, opened on 13 February 1903 at the New York Theatre, a Syndicate theatre (which seated white spectators on the main floor, blacks in the balcony). *In Dahomey,* one of the turning points in the development of black theatre, is important because of its stars and where it played. The musical offered a series of songs and vaudeville skits, loosely tied to a plot about a trip to Africa. When the production was taken to London, the third act, set in Africa, was dropped. The comic skits, songs, and cakewalks were the main reason for the show's appeal. No doubt it provided different comic delights for white and black audiences, but *In Dahomey* was far from being subversive in any substantial manner (see E. Smith; Krasner).

During the 1890s and 1910s Williams and Walker developed into the most successful black comedy team in the business. Williams performed in blackface, Walker did not. (We might note, in passing, that in their politics and their approaches to entertainment Walker and Williams can be seen as analogues of W. E. B. Du Bois and Booker T. Washington, the one confrontational, the other accommodating.) Together they began the integration of the vaudeville circuit (though resistance from the White Rats, the union of white vaudeville performers, is another sad part of the racist history of American theatre). And they opened the path for black productions on Broadway. Walker's career continued only until 1909, when he began to suffer from paresis; he died in 1911. Williams turned to solo work in 1909, and in 1915 he accepted an offer from Flo Ziegfeld to appear in the *Follies.* Williams was the first black performer to join the *Follies,* where he starred with Fanny Brice, Will Rogers, and Eddie Cantor (often in blackface himself). Williams's career continued until 1922, when he died.

In the development of black musicals, a line can easily be traced from *In Dahomey* to the all-black musical revue *Shuffle Along* (1921) by Noble Sissle and Eubie Blake (on this history, see E. Smith; Woll; Riis; Krasner). Of note, when Langston Hughes decided to attend Columbia University in 1921, he counted *Shuffle Along* as well as the proximity of Harlem as decisive. Immensely popular with black and white audiences alike, the musical launched the careers of numerous black performers, including Florence Mills, Paul Robeson, Josephine Baker, Flournoy Miller, and Aubrey Lyles. Moreover, as Hughes would later argue, *Shuffle Along* became a catalyst for the Harlem Renaissance. "For nearly two years it was always packed. It gave the proper push – a pre-Charleston kick – to the vogue that spread to books, African sculpture, music, and dancing" (Hughes, "When Harlem Was in Vogue," *Town and Country,* July 1940; quoted in Woll, 60).

One consequence was that Florence Mills became the most beloved black performer of the 1920s. But her career ended abruptly on 1 November 1927, when she died at the age of thirty-two from appendicitis. She had just returned from Paris and London, where her revue called *Blackbirds* was a grand triumph. In it she danced seductively and sang wistfully her favorite song, "I'm a Little Blackbird Looking for a Bluebird." In London the Prince of Wales, completely captivated by Mills, saw the show at least a dozen times. But that engagement concluded her career.

The funeral in Harlem packed the Mother A. M. E. Zion Church, as the Hall Johnson choir sang spirituals to three thousand mourners. James Weldon Johnson, writing three years later in *Black Manhattan,* described the anguish and anger: "The Negroes of New York mourned her deeply, for she was more their idol than any other artist of the race. . . . Women fainted and men were unnerved. Under all there could be sensed a bewilderment, a resentment, at this act of God – Why did He do it? – we have so few – she was so young – she might have done so much more for us in the eyes of the world." Outside, 100,000 to 150,000 people lined the streets as the funeral procession slowly moved through Harlem. Above, an airplane circled low and released a flock of blackbirds, which quickly gathered and flew away (J. W. Johnson, 197–201).

Of course, despite the achievements of Howe and others, racial prejudice continued to make professional life difficult for black theatre artists. Nonetheless, a handful of talented writers, composers, musicians, and performers were able to make their way in the 1920s and 1930s. Willis Richardson, in Washington, D.C., began writing plays, influenced by Angelina Weld Grimke's *Rachel,* which he hoped to improve upon as a model. A few years later his play *The Chip Woman's Fortune,* which was produced on Broadway, fulfilled his aim. W. E. B. Du Bois and Alain Locke vigorously debated the merits of an art versus a social theatre. Du Bois founded the Krigwa Little Theatre Movement in 1926. Then in the 1930s Langston Hughes emerged as a dramatist with *Mulatto,* in which Rose McClendon starred (just before her untimely death). In the 1920s she had acted in *In Abraham's Bosom* and *Porgy and Bess.*

During this period a few black performers, besides McClendon, became stars, though always with some liabilities and scars to go along with the good fortune. In 1933, for example, Ethel Waters became the highest-paid woman on Broadway, performing in musical revues and singing such songs as "Stormy Weather," "Heat Wave," "I've Got Harlem on My Mind," and "Supper Time," which told of a woman preparing a meal for an absent husband who has just been lynched. As her autobiography reveals, though, her successes did not come easily (see Waters; Hill; Hay; Sanders; Woll).

As we look back on this vital history of African American theatre – which is beginning to be recovered by scholars today – we can see that thousands of black performers emerged between 1870 and 1945. Moreover, despite many difficulties, black artists, especially in music, dance, comedy, and acting, made major contributions to American entertainment during the era. Yet until most recently, we have failed to record and acknowledge their accomplishments.

Not surprisingly, then, *The New York Times* in its 1983 obituary on Eubie Blake, who composed *Shuffle Along* with Noble Sissle, credits Blake with basically being the first major black performer. Blake had spent much of his life trying to correct the record, but to no avail. In an interview in *The New York Times* just five years earlier he stated: "Now remember those names – Walker and Williams. They were great. My people forget the great ones they had. Everyone remembers Al Jolson. Who remembers Cole and Johnson? Miller and Lyles? Ernest Hogan? . . . These men were great and now nobody remembers them" (quoted in Woll, xi).

Perhaps Bert Williams best understood the problem of invisibility (in a culture of the visible). His signature song, "Nobody," became the comic yet poignant anthem for the age.

> When life seems full of clouds and rain,
> And I am full of nothin' but pain,
> Who soothes my thumpin', bumpin' brain?
> Nobody!
> I ain't never done nothin' to nobody,
> I ain't never got nothin' from nobody, no time,
> Until I get somethin' from somebody, some time,
> I'll never do nothin' for nobody, no time.

Wearing the American mask of minstrelsy, he could not actually be seen, even in the glare of the Ziegfeld spotlights. Fittingly, Ralph Ellison would take this cultural condition of being simultaneously present and absent as the dominant motif for his great novel, *Invisible Man.*

This problem of invisibility cannot be separated from what was always visible: those white performers in blackface. In other words, the mask of darkness always had two faces. A white man in blackface becomes somebody, a black man remains nobody. Perhaps, given the pervasiveness of blackface, even an actual face of a black person was almost completely invisible or unrecognizable – despite being right before the eyes of white spectators. The minstrel codes dictated the possibilities of identity. Or the lack of identity.

Like many black performers whose careers moved through the minstrel heritage, Bert Williams discovered that blackface simultaneously liberated and imprisoned him. Early in his career, in 1896, he first tried on the blackface mask: "Then I began to find myself. It was not until I was able to see myself as another person that my sense of humor developed" (quoted in Charters, 28). The trick of double identity worked. Williams put on the blackface at the beginning of his career and continued to cork up until the day he died. How appropriate and yet ironic, then, that Booker T. Washington, paying tribute to Williams, stated that "Bert Williams' humor strikes me as the real thing" (quoted in E. Smith, 145). Audiences – black and white alike – agreed about Williams's fine talent for doeful, pathetic comedy, but how can real black experiences find expression in the unreal, hieroglyphic mask of blackface? It would seem that Washington, besides admiring Williams's talent for creating an uncanny double or duplicitous identity, was recognizing the price one pays for certain accommodations to prejudice. Could it be that Washington, looking at a blackface artist, was also seeing himself as a masquerader? Black laughter becomes its own process of liberation and imprisonment.

Interestingly, Al Jolson claimed to have the same kind of liberation with blackface that Williams experienced. In 1904, trying to launch his career on the vaudeville circuit, Jolson took the suggestion of James Francis Dooley, a blackface performer, to put on burnt cork. Jolson gave it a try, and immediately the mask took over. "You looked, and *felt,* like a performer" (quoted in Goldman, 36). With growing confidence, he found his persona, in part by impersonating Bert Williams: that same year Jolson added "Nobody" to his routine. He worked his way up the vaudeville ladder (performing with Dockstader's Minstrels), and became a star with the Shubert organization. In the 1920s and 1930s, performing in blackface, he joined Will Rogers as one of the most popular entertainers in America.

Variations on this theme of liberation through masking recur regularly in the careers of blackface performers. Of course, masking has been central to the history of performance in many cultures. So, at one level, what Williams and Jolson experienced was what performers have always discovered about the double consciousness of acting. Here we have yet another version of the debate on the paradox of the actor.

But on another level blackface is not just one more possible mask to wear. Its visual codes and formal indeterminacies are tied to American racism, and its meanings are an essential part of the American experience. For over a hundred years, from the 1830s to the 1950s, the nation apparently needed the mask of blackness, which became part of the ethnic and racial history of the nation – from reworked Irish songs and plantation stereotypes to Jewish acts of assimilation and Elvis Presley's borrowed talent (see Bean, Hatch, and McNamara; Cockrell; Lhamon; Lott; Rogin; Toll). For many performers, who were part of the ethnic migration, blackface operated as a rite of passage – for them and their audiences. Obviously, not every performer put on the mask, but was there anyone who did not see and participate in the dramas of identity being played out in minstrelsy, *Uncle Tom's Cabin,* and the shows of Bert Williams, Al Jolson, Eddie Cantor, Shirley Temple, Bing Crosby, and thousands of other blackface performers? But what does it mean that one must become black in order to become American? How do we read those signs?

Both black and white performers who wore blackface were involved in racial and ethnic acts of transgression (and, sometimes, in gender acts of crossdressing). But what a difference it makes when the color of one's own skin is black instead of white (peaking out behind the mask). Whites passed through the mask into an assimilated world; blacks remained enclosed in the codes of darkness. By transgressing black identity, through racist codes, whites transformed themselves into Americans. Black performers could transgress the racial codes by acts of parody, irony, subversion, and reversal, especially when playing to black audiences, but the act of transforming their own images and identities for white audiences proved far more difficult. Not until the mask itself was no longer needed (by millions of immigrants, for example) did the country begin to set it aside in the 1950s. But that release only came when a new civil rights code and a new political system began to emerge. Until then, Jim Crow reigned – over the land, over the Congress, over the Supreme Court. And on stage and screen Jim Crow continued to jump down, turn around, and proclaim that being white was the best damn thing – the real thing – about being an American.

Conclusion

In 1946, seven decades after the Kiralfy brothers had presented their spectacular production of *Around the World in Eighty Days,* Orson Welles staged a "musical extravaganza," of his own devising, based upon Jules Verne's novel. Welles wrote the book (36 scenes, requiring 200 costumes), Cole Porter the music and lyrics (75 songs). Welles also directed and, in a series of disguises (such as Chinaman and cowboy), played a magician/villain who chases Phileas Fogg from country to country, trying to stop his progress.

The production of Welles's *Around the World* included an elephant, a complete Japanese circus, an onstage train racing across a bridge, dancing girls, a giant eagle that nightly plucked Fogg from a cliff, and Barbette, the French female impersonator (who performed on the trapeze and directed the circus acts). Welles also filmed five separate scenes, covering about thirty minutes (including the interior of the Bank of England and a ship at sea during a storm). These filmed sequences (shot in the old Edison film studio in the Bronx) were interspersed with the stage action.

When the show opened in New York, *Life* magazine commented: "Orson Welles has produced the most overstuffed conglomeration of circus, magic, movies, old-fashioned spectacle and penny peep shows that Broadway has seen since the days of Barnum's Museum" (quoted in Brady, 390). There we have it: the whole history of American entertainment, from Barnum to Welles, compressed into one madcap production, a cabinet of curiosities as it were. Even Edison and film had their moments.

Of course, such a history is a game of mirrors, a magician's trick. But then Welles was a magician and a wizard of entertainment. From the age of five, when he was taken to see Houdini perform, Welles had been fascinated by magic. In 1943, recalling his childhood, Welles stated: "I discovered [then] . . . that almost everything in this world was phony, worked with mirrors. Since then, I've always wanted to be a magician" (quoted in Brady, 6, 362). He got his wish. Throughout his career Welles operated in the realm of illusion and spectacle. For him, the desiring eye of the spectator was the beginning and end of performance.

All theatre is a hieroglyphic delight, a game for wizards, as I have argued here. The history of American entertainment from the mid–nineteenth century to the present can be understood, then, not only as a struggle between Europe and America, melodrama and realism, lowbrow and highbrow, stage and screen, country and city, natives and immigrants, men and women, whites and blacks but also, and more tellingly, as an overall process whereby a democratic or mass culture enters into a new kind of spectatorship, an optical culture defined by the reign of the eye and the seduction of images. Of course, because America's borders have been porous, much about American entertainment has been derived from Europe and elsewhere (see Altick; Booth; Oettermann; Schivelbusch). But what matters is not the problem of origins, which can be discovered in a hundred places, but the ways that American culture transformed itself into a spectatorium.

Not only did a new culture of leisure and consumption emerge after the Civil War; it proceeded to define almost all aspects of American life. That culture, as we have come to understand it, has been identified by various overlapping, sometimes contradictory concepts (e.g., by what is democratic, popular, lowbrow, mass, everyday, materialist, bourgeois, middle-class; by merchant, commercial, capitalist, shopping, tourist).[20] But what joins all of these identifying ideas of social order is the new role of the arbitrating eye in the process of consumption. This emergent and now dominant culture has been primarily a culture of new signs and codes. Indeed, since the Gilded Age, we have been immersed – perhaps drowning – in what Neil Harris calls "the flood of images" that define America (*Cultural Excursions,* 8). The images mediate between the words and things of life. In the process, the real thing and the facsimile cannot be distinguished from one another.

Today, in our total world of the eye – focused on a movie screen, a television, a computer – we may find it difficult to realize that this way of confronting and knowing the real is rather new. Aspects of its beginnings can be found in the early nineteenth century with the popularity of the panorama and diorama, which of course had their origins in Europe. Then, by the mid–nineteenth century, with the emergence of the era of photography, the eye takes over. The camera and plate provided a new process of seeing. From Daguerre (a French showman) to Edison (an impresario), the new image makers fixed and transfixed the world before our eyes, thus changing our sense of identity, time, space, motion, and the relations among them all. A new arsenal for conquering the world had come into being: daguerreotypes, tintypes, cartes-de-visite, stereographs, and stereoscopes, and Eastman photographs from Kodak box cameras (see Darrah; Jussim; Taft). With fascination, and occasionally with horror, we learned to behold the images of everyday life: individuals caught in a pose, soldiers dead on a Civil War battlefield.

This is also the era of lithography, photolithography, and photoengraving – processes that commercial printers, such as George Bellows, Joseph Pennell, Currier and Ives, and many others, used to produce millions of images that flowed into every corner of the civilized (and not so civilized) world. By the mid–nineteenth century, decades before the movies, the visual culture had already emerged, as Warren Susman argued:

> Early in the twentieth century, Vachel Lindsay argued that America was becoming a world of visual images, of signs and symbols – in short, a "hieroglyphic civilization." This transformation probably actually began closer to the 1850s, when Americans found themselves able to purchase as well as view an increasing number of inexpensive prints offered by companies like Currier and Ives and the special new images of life provided by the new profession of photography. (xvii)

By the late nineteenth century images and displays were everywhere: prints for the home, family albums of portraits, photographs for the stereoscope, postcards, posters for the shop windows and fences, illustrations for newspapers and books, department store windows, and the Sears, Roebuck, and Company catalogue. All offered new visual codes to see and interpret. These new codes were changing how one looked at the world, and they were reshaping what one saw.

Also, the mid–nineteenth century is the beginning of "World Fairs," which commenced with the London Crystal Palace Exposition in 1851 and have continued ever since. America fell in love with them, hosting twelve world fairs or expositions between 1876 and 1905, far more than any other country. The whole principle of a world fair is to overwhelm the eye with the cornucopia of the material world (and to demonstrate just how wonderful the host country is on the stage of the world). Building after building at each fair put on display thousands of wonders and enticements for the eye (even more curiosities than Barnum had offered). As Hamlin Garland wrote to his prairie parents at the time of the Columbian Exposition in Chicago in 1893: "Sell the cookstove if necessary and come. You *must* see this fair" (cited in Burg, 180).

Barnum had died two years earlier, but the Columbian Exposition seemed to be yet one more of his grand specacles. Clearly it demonstrated – with its White City spectacles and its Midway Plaisance of ethnic villages and honkytonk exhibits – that America had embraced Barnum and his entrepreneurial followers.

Origins are always uncertain, but the quintessential American starting point and homebase in this new alchemy of spectacle is Barnum's Museum, with its 100,000 curiosities. For us Barnum's Museum is the Rosetta Stone for reading the signs of the new hieroglyphic culture. But the code is impossible to read in any complete way because the museum burned down and the curiosities went up in smoke. And yet, we still have all of those photographs – the cryptic visual records of the lost wonderland. And just as intriguingly we have the historical record, often in visual documents, of the many impresarios and performers who followed after Barnum and carried on his methods. A fairly plentiful visual record is extant. What that record represents is open to question, of course; but in a sense its very condition, as a collection of visual objects, reveals its significance. That is, the key thing about the visual documents is that they are visual. From this perspective, what they represent is secondary (though they may well become primary in specific cases).

For example, *Frank Leslie's Illustrated Newspaper* began its amazingly successful life in 1855, continuing into the next century. Like the equally successful *London Illustrated News,* Leslie's pictorial magazine quickly became the popular model for how to present the news. The thousands upon thousands of images in this newspaper are an abundant record of earlier times. The images are irresistible to contemplate, each capturing a significant moment (if we can crack the visual codes). These images, in their collectivity, are also a sign that people of the time had this new visual relation to the world. Besides representing life or reality for the observers, the images created the new appetite to see things, and more things, to experience the abundance of the world. America became Emerson's transparent eyeball. Befittingly, Leslie got his start as an illustrator for P. T. Barnum in 1848. Barnum, of course, had already figured out that the spectator's eye must be enticed outside the theatre by visual publicity; then it can be satisfied inside the theatre by the many curiosities on display. We've been running previews ever since.

Another, related example: In the 1870s Daniel and Charles Frohman got their first professional jobs working for *The New York Graphic,* an illustrated newspaper in competition with *Leslie's Illustrated Newspaper.* For their second jobs, they became publicity agents for Callender Minstrels. Charles went ahead of the troupe on tour, postering the towns (setting up visual previews). Soon he took over ticket sales and management, learning to integrate the parts of the enterprise. Indeed, long before he had become an agent of the new theatre of images, Charles had been seduced by spectacle at the age of eight, when he saw a production of *The Black Crook,* his first experience with theatre. And even before this he had been enticed by the theatre posters of spectacles and minstrel shows in his father's cigar shop (see Marcosson and Frohman).

Following different routes, then, various artists and impresarios of light and motion discovered ways to transfigure modern American entertainment, which might best be appreciated and understood not so much as the achievement of putting real things on stage and screen but as the search for ways to seduce the eye with delights, curiosities, illusions, tricks, and spectacles. The theatrical artists have learned how to create and investigate illusions, especially as these illusions reach the mind through the eye (see Susman; Kouwenhoven; Toll, *Entertainment;* Lynes; Seldes; Kammen; W. Taylor). Realism, then, is not the opposite of spectacle in the American theatre. Instead, the real and the arbitrary sign, in Edith Wharton's terms, become two, interrelated parts of the larger scenic or hieroglyphic revolution. Like the magician's tricks, performance is all that matters. Thanks to Barnum and his followers, we have all become watchful connoisseurs.

Notes

1 From Whitman's speech, "Death of Abraham Lincoln," which he gave many times. Quoted in D. Reynolds, II, 3.
2 A letter to William Winter, 14 March 1876, in which he complained about a newspaper story, "a most brutal ghoul-feast," that discussed the assassination and the grave of John Wilkes Booth. In Watermeier, 58.
3 In America lynching has its origins and heritage in the era of the American Revolution. Charles Lynch, a soldier and judge in the area now called Lynchburg, Virginia, presided over the punishment of supposed loyalists by quick "justice" and "lynch law." The Ku Klux Klan followed his vigilante code, making lynching not only a mode of killing but also a means for instilling terror into a whole society, thus shaping attitudes and practices by a code of intimidation and fear that helped to define segregation and thereby institutionalize racial prejudice as the operating "law" of the land. Mob rule, by the minority, became the model for setting the agenda of the democratic majority.
4 This said, it is worth pointing out that Wilder's play and strategy might be compared rewardingly to Jean Giraudoux's *The Madwoman of Chaillot* (1945). Here too a seemingly fantastical action, with its charming characters and witty, often whimsical style, masks humanist concerns and hopes. Sometimes fantasy is the avenue to the real thing.
5 As Wainscott notes, it was Stallings, not Anderson, who went to war in 1918 and lost a leg. *What Price Glory* depends upon his experience and expresses his understanding.
6 Perhaps it is quite fitting, then, that this shoestring venture borrowed and adapted its costumes from the 1920s production of *What Price Glory.*
7 John Mason Brown, *New York Post,* 12 November 1937; quoted in Callow, 337.
8 Again, as Callow argues, "a great deal of the Mercury version, in fact, was devised for no other reason than to generate theatrical excitement" (324).
9 After a dispute, the brothers dissolved their partnership in 1887, and Irme moved to London, where he staged a number of extravaganzas.
10 Also, Kiralfy's outdoor spectacles at the turn of the century, such as *A Carnival in Venice* presented on Staten Island, contributed to the great popularity of pageantry, including the historical pageants in hundreds of communities and Percy MacKaye's democratic festivals. See Barker's introduction to her edition of Kiralfy's autobiography for comments on the filmic qualities of the productions.

11 Opposed to the new Yiddish theatre in New York, some German Jews in 1882 appealed to their Jewish cousins: "Go out into the country and become peddlars. Find decent work and don't bring shame upon your people with this foolery you call theatre" (Rosenfeld, 217–18).

12 See Musser, *Before the Nickelodeon,* on the important contributions of Edison and Edwin S. Porter to the development of film production, exhibition, and reception.

13 Popular novels, especially adventure stories, were mined as well. Of course, many novels, such as *The Count of Monte Cristo* and a number of Dickens's novels, had already been adapted for stage. Indeed, hundreds of stage-adapted novels also made their way into film.

14 A similar fate befell Eleonora Duse. On an American tour in 1923 and 1924 that would take her to California, she dreamed of seeing a real star: "Perhaps they will let me meet the little angel Mary Pickford." Duse, who was fascinated by film, had made one film in Italy in 1916. But like Mrs. Fiske, she was not successful in making the shift to motion pictures. The two great Ibsen actresses, famous for their realistic techniques and controlled emotion, seem somewhat melodramatic on film (though Duse less so than Fiske). Duse did not get to meet Pickford, who was out of town when Duse arrived. While in Los Angeles Duse had performed *La porta chiusa* by Marco Praga. Charlie Chaplin attended the performance and wrote a review, praising her restrained acting and her staging of the play: "If we could only direct pictures as this play was directed." A few weeks later Duse died of pneumonia in a hotel room in Pittsburgh (Woolcott, *Going to Pieces,* 75; Weaver, *Duse*).

15 This search and cult of the American girl proved to be one of the abiding themes in Henry James's fiction, though his critical eye caught the confusing consequences as well as the celebratory aspects of such an impossible ideal.

16 Ibsen and Chekhov, at their best, understood that they were offering a vision of life that was not simply a matter of surface hypocrisy and buried truth – the two-part formula of binary thinking. This formula allows the artist and the spectator to maintain an easy superiority over the dramatic characters and their illusions. Too often, modernist artists – including most "realist" writers, actors, designers – have settled for the illusion–truth opposition. But the best works do not let us off that easily.

17 Of note, Warner Brothers considered casting Ronald Reagan as Rogers in *The Story of Will Rogers* (1952). Instead, seeking authenticity, the studio cast Will Rogers Jr. in the role (see Yagoda, xi, xiv). They missed a golden opportunity (and misunderstood the nature of American authenticity).

18 Even the best patriotic oratory and flag waving failed for several decades to identify a common cause that would begin to overcome distrust, anger, and loss. Not until the Spanish American War and World War I would patriotism rally southerners to the Stars and Stripes. At the same time, and not incidentally, the nation developed a single model for the American flag, and the pledge of allegiance became a national ritual. New visual codes and symbolic acts succeeded in defining a national identity, even though the political and legal solutions remained quite elusive.

19 Obviously both whites and blacks in the North as well as the South created their own social and religious institutions, which provided many positive qualities to daily life, but the basic problems of integration were not part of a communal or a national dialogue.

20 On this general topic, see works by Susman, Trachtenberg, Neil Harris, Boorstin, and Leach.

Bibliography: Hieroglyphic Stage

As much as possible I have identified my major sources in the parenthetical notes in my essay. Those references point to the significant studies in American entertainment and social history that have guided me. In the case of the eight topics that I take up – including ethnic theatre and culture, blackface and black theatre, touring, and city and country – I have noted the relevant sources as I discuss each topic. The scholarship for each of these topics is extensive, so I have had to be quite selective in identifying sources. But of course many of the studies that I note in my references provide extensive bibliographies (see, for example, Ann Douglas's marvelous annotated bibliography of ninety pages in *Terrible Honesty: Mongrel Manhattan in the 1920s*). I thus urge the reader to move from my preliminary bibliography to the additional scholarship, primary and secondary, that appears in these studies.

For the most part I have not listed the many bibliographies, dictionaries, encyclopedias, collections of documents, and general histories that provide the foundation for any study of American theatre. Instead of cataloguing them here, I refer the reader to the valuable annotated bibliographies in Volume I of the *Cambridge History of American Theatre*, including Bruce McConachie's overview of "General Sources." Many of the studies of American cultural and social history that he identifies also guided me in my examination of theatre and culture between 1865 and 1945.

Bibliographies and Encyclopedias

I want to note, nevertheless, just a few valuable resource guides that I found indispensable. On American theatre: Silvester, Wilmeth and Miller, Bordman (*The Oxford Companion to American Theatre*), Durham (editor, *American Theatre Companies*), Robinson et al., and Salzman.

On reference sources for the study of literature in English, including American drama, see Harner's invaluable *Literary Research Guide*. More generally, on the topic of American history, every reader should be familiar with two valuable guides to sources: Prucha, *Handbook for Research in American History* and Mary Beth Norton (general editor), *The American Historical Association's Guide to Historical Literature*. Also helpful: Morris and Morris; Foner and Garraty; and K. T. Jackson. See Norton for many other bibliographies and encyclopedias on American history.

Norton also provides a good list of the major general histories of the United States. In addition to the recent ones (some quite popular today as college textbooks), two definitive histories written in the first half of the twentieth century should not be overlooked. They express many of the values, perspectives, and assumptions that operated in the United States during the era of expansive growth, progressivism, and international engagement: Charles A. Beard and Mary Ritter Beard, *The Rise of American Civilization* (1927); Samuel Eliot Morison and Henry Steel Commager, *The Growth of the American Republic* (1930). The Beard history was one of the most popular and influential of its era, and the Morison and Commager book, which went through four editions between 1930 and 1950, continues to hold its place in the history profession, with three editions since 1950.

Cultural and Intellectual History

In terms of cultural and intellectual histories of the United States, I found a handful of studies especially helpful, in particular those of Susman and Banta. Also most informative and challenging: Curti, Douglas (*Terrible Honesty*); Fox and Lears, H. M. Jones, N. Harris (*Cultural Excursions*), Lears (*No Place of Grace*), Leach, Levine (*Highbrow/Highbrow*), Kern, Noble, Schlereth, and Wiebe (*Search for Order* and *Segmented Society*).

Socioeconomic History

The scholarship on the social, economic, and industrial history of the era is also quite expansive. Among the many works available, these general studies proved especially insightful: Blumin, Boorstin, Chandler (*Visible Hand*), Evans, Franklin and Moss Jr., Glaab and Brown, Giedion, Gutman, S. P. Hays, Higgs, Kasson (*Civilizing the Machine*), Licht, Merk, Mohl, Orvell, Takaki (*A Different Mirror*), and Trachtenberg (*The Incorporation of America*).

Again, I recommend that the reader consult the Norton bibliography for studies on more specific topics: economic history, business, science and technology, labor, urban history, immigration, racial and ethnic minorities, Indians, women, and popular culture.

Histories of the Arts and Popular Entertainment

R. C. Allen (*Horrible Prettiness*), Denning; Dizikes, Kasson (*Amusing the Millions*), Kouwenhoven, Lynes, McArthur, McConachie, Nye, Nasaw, W. R. Taylor, and Toll (*The Entertainment Machine* and *On with the Show*). See also the sources provided in Chapter 5.

Film

In attempting to establish some working relations between stage and screen between 1890s and 1930s, I have found the following studies quite informative (even when I disagree with some of their arguments about the nature of theatre): R. C. Allen (*Vaudeville and Film*), Bowser, Bordwell, Fell, May, Mast (*A Short History of the Movies*), Sklar, Vardac, and Winokur. Especially impressive and comprehensive are two books by Charles Musser, *Before the Nickelodeon* and *The Emergence of Cinema*.

Contemporary Works

In my essay I have used a few key works from the era as touchstones, including Seldes, *The Seven Lively Arts;* Lindsay, *The Art of the Moving Picture;* Cheney, *The New Movement in the Theater* and *The Art Theater;* Johnson, *Black Manhattan;* Kahn, *Of Many Things;* B. Kiralfy, *Creator of Great Musical Spectacles, An Autobiography,* and Percy MacKaye, *Epoch.* I also recommend Kammen's recent biography of Seldes.

Autobiography and Biography

Central to any investigation of American entertainment are the autobiographies and biographies of performers. Many, perhaps most, of the autobiographies are unreliable documents, but they are also delightful and indispensable. And a few are classics, including Barnum, *Struggles and Triumphs,* Jefferson, *Autobiography,* Clurman, *The Fervant Years,* Hart, *Act One,* and Houseman, *Run-through* (as well as his subsequent two volumes). Several good biographies have been published in recent years, including Senelick, *The Age and Stage of George L. Fox;* Yagoda, *Will Rogers;* Fields and Fields, *From the Bowery to Broadway: Lew Fields and the Roots of American Popular Theatre;* Callow, *Orson Welles: The Road to Xanadu;* Peters, *The House of Barrymore;* and Duberman, *Paul Robeson.* And two interesting biographies of Fanny Brice showed up at the same time: Goldman, *Fanny Brice,* and Grossman, *Funny Woman.*

Also valuable are the large, illustrated books (some of them wonderful examples of bookmaking): Carter and Cole, *Joseph Urban* (an important book that will help to place Urban at the center of his age); R. and P. Ziegfeld, *The Ziegfeld Touch;* A. Edwards, *The DeMilles;* McNamara, *The Shuberts of Broadway;* and the Kunhardts' *P. T. Barnum.* Finally, concerning Barnum, who proved to be one of the paramount figures in my study, along with Kiralfy, Bert Williams, Ziegfeld, and Welles, I recommend Harris, *Humbug: The Art of P. T. Barnum* and Saxon, *P. T. Barnum: The Legend and the Man.* After reading the cultural historians and biographers, however, one should return to Barnum's autobiography (in its various manifestations). The voice and vision, if not the specific anecdotes, are the true story of American entertainment.

2

A Changing Theatre:
New York and Beyond

John Frick

A Changing Culture

The years between 1870 and 1945 were a time of radical restructuring in America – an inchoate era marked by a complex, often painful, transformation from a Victorian world to what we have come to regard as the modern one. During this period, Americans, caught up in the thrill of progress and the rush to modernity, experienced a bewildering kaleidoscope of events and developments – the disappearance of the American frontier in the wake of a pathology of uncontrolled expansion; the rise of the New South; secularized religion; an increasingly mechanized and compartmentalized daily life; the advent of the "New Woman"; commercialized recreation; countless labor union challenges to laissez-faire capitalism; the obliteration of regional divisions and differences, first by a national railroad system and later by the automobile, movies, and radio; and the standardization of American culture by a culture industry assisted by technologies of mass communication – to cite some of the more pronounced and dramatic examples. Although this list is by no means exhaustive, it is illustrative of the scope and range of the changes and the accelerating pace of innovation confronting Americans as the nineteenth century ended and they moved into the next. To historian Alan Trachtenberg, the sum of these changes amounted to nothing less than a total *cultural transformation* "so swift and thorough that many Americans seemed unable to fathom the extent of the upheaval" (5).

Economically, this period was practically sandwiched between two major economic depressions – the Panic of 1873 and the Great Depression of the 1930s – and was dotted with other financial crises, both large and small; yet it was also marked by unprecedented expansion in finance, manufacturing, transportation, and communication. During the 1870s and 1880s, the transformation from a simple agrarian country into a highly urbanized, industrialized one became a fait accompli; the small shop became an anachronism; incorporation became commonplace; and, roughly three hundred large corporations gained control of 40 percent of all manufacturing and directly or indirectly influenced 80 percent of America's commerce. During the same period, the railroads completed the links between America's small towns and major cities, creating the possibility of nationwide distribution of products and a national market for goods, either through catalogue sales or chains of stores like the Great American Tea Company which, by 1870, maintained sixty-seven stores throughout the country, selling everything from tea and coffee to fancy soaps and condensed milk. By the 1890s, the national scope of American industry, a relatively unstable economy, and a veritable mania for mergers created an environment that encouraged the consolidation of control in the hands of a relatively few men and culminated in a major realignment of the nation's economic power. In the waning years of the nineteenth century, centralization of organizational power became commonplace, and conglomerates exerted their influence upon all aspects of American life, from politics to family life and education to literature, the arts, and the use of leisure time.

If the period in question had been a response to industrialism alone, as Raymond Williams notes, it would have been far less unsettled; but, in fact, the restructuring of American culture that took place in the late nineteenth century required responses to new customs, values, public styles, and social developments. During the years between the Civil War and the end of the century, traditional preindustrial American culture gave way to a new culture, better adapted to urban, industrial imperatives and an emerging consumer society. The paradigm of America as a conglomeration of isolated "island communities" yielded to one of urban and national communities connected by innovations in communication and transportation, and the individual was "submerged" as relations became increasingly impersonal. In this *cultural reorientation,* hardly any realm of American life remained untouched.

America's Gilded Age was also an era during which social and recreational patterns were significantly restructured. Leisure time was effectively divorced from work time; public amusements became an integral part of commercial culture; and socializing with a "crowd" (what Gunther Barth labeled a "tumultuous encounter of everybody with everyone" [3]) supplanted socializing with a small circle of friends. Yet, nowhere was the cultural reorientation more pronounced than in relations between the sexes. By the end of the century, the Victorian ideology of spatial and psychological separation, the norm in nineteenth-century middle-class society, broke down, and antiquated notions about sexuality, female dependency, male power, and other aspects of gender relations were thoroughly renegotiated. As a result, America's New Woman, as she was labeled, boldly and publicly entered an increasingly heterosocial culture in which she smoked, rode bicycles, demanded political power, and insisted upon going to popular amusements, from the cabaret to first-class theatre.

Not surprisingly, the theatre, being subject to both economic and cultural forces in such a period of radical reorientation, was likewise transfigured. Throughout the final years of the nineteenth century and the early years of the twentieth, artists and entrepreneurs waged private wars for this most public of cultural institutions, and the changes they wrought, in the process, markedly transformed the structure of the American stage. The theatre, by the beginning of the current century, had become yet another American industry composed of a series of interlocking professions, each dependent upon the others, with its business operations centralized structurally and geographically. It had, in the course of the nineteenth century, become less democratic in both its administration and appeal and had assumed the role of manufacturer of a product prepared and packaged for nationwide distribution. The long run had become its principal goal; the star system and the star vehicle had become the means to that end; the combination company had become recognized as the standard producing unit of the commercial theatre; and the practices of theatre management and play production, once the domain of the actor-manager, had become discrete and separate endeavors.

Like other cultural institutions, the early-twentieth-century American theatre was composed of a nexus of practices developed and refined years earlier. Whereas most of these were developed after 1870, some (specifically, the star system and the long run) had been adopted during the stock company era prior to the Civil War. For roughly the first 120 years of the American theatre's existence, the basic organizational unit had been the resident stock-repertory company, which was functionally autonomous, generally identified with a specific theatre, and located permanently (or semipermanently) in a city with a population sufficient to support it. Adopted from the British and adapted for use in the United States before the Revolution, the stock company was organized as a resident acting company headed by a manager who assumed responsibility for selecting a season that would please local audiences, for hiring personnel, and for maintaining the theatre building.

In both its structure and daily operations, the early-nineteenth-century stock company was very much a preindustrial institution, ideally suited to its times. As Robert Wiebe observes, the entire nation at this time was composed of "island communities," each self-contained, self-sufficient, and loosely connected to other communities. Local autonomy was still the "heart of democracy," and any sense of a nation or a national culture, as we now know it, didn't yet exist (*Search for Order*, 3–4). In its decentralization, the stock company was fully consistent with Wiebe's model. Under the stock system, every local community with a theatre constituted an independent producing center, and, in fact, each individual company, in its organization, working relationships, and functional independence, was the theatrical equivalent of Wiebe's "island community." Accordingly, actors in stock companies normally led stable, settled lives and enjoyed working conditions comparable to workers in other fields.

Like the stock company, the star system, the first of the preindustrial practices later incorporated into the modern theatre, had been a common practice in the British theatre. The system gained a foothold in America in the late eighteenth century, when leading performers like Thomas Wignall, Thomas A. Cooper, and James Fennell realized that their popularity allowed them to move freely from one company to another and to dictate terms to the local manager. The star system attained additional respectability and moved closer to becoming a "mature" business practice with the 1810 "visit" of George Frederick Cooke, a leading actor at England's Covent Garden, who played to full houses both in New York and on tour. The economic lessons gleaned from Cooke's success were further reinforced in the 1820s by the popularity of a veritable "procession" of British stars (Edmund and Charles Kean, Charles Mathews, Junius Brutus Booth, Charles and Fanny Kemble, and others) and the rise of native-born stars like Edwin Forrest and James H. Hackett. From the 1820s on, it became common for a traveling star to be attached to a local stock company for at least part of a season, and increasingly American audiences came to demand nothing less than a star in every performance.

The long run, the second standard practice of twentieth-century commercial theatre, which had its genesis in the stock era, is conventionally believed to have been "discovered" in the 1840s and to have gained popularity in the 1850s. Although, as Rosemarie Bank has argued convincingly, the *concept* of a continuous run may actually have had its roots in business practices at the Bowery Theatre in the 1830s, it did not gain industrywide acceptance until *The Drunkard* (1844) and *Uncle Tom's Cabin* (1853), each of which ran for more than 100 consecutive performances, illustrated its full economic potential. Generally considered the forerunner of the long run in America, *The Drunkard; or, the Fallen Saved,* written by J. H. Smith and "a Gentleman," was first presented in 1844 at the Boston Museum. Capitalizing on the populist temperance activism of the Washingtonian movement in the forties and a "delirium tremens" scene that seldom failed to arouse an audience, *The Drunkard* ran for more than 140 successive nights in Boston and for an additional 198 performances at Barnum's American Museum in New York.

It was not until 1852, however, that the long run was generally recognized as the formula for Broadway success. On 27 September of that year, *Uncle Tom's Cabin,* adapted by George L. Aiken from the Harriet Beecher Stowe novel, opened in Troy, New York. There, a company headed by G. C. Howard performed the play until 1 December, when the show closed after the hundredth performance, having been witnessed by more than twenty-five thousand people. The same company opened at New York's National Theatre on 18 July 1853, and played almost continuously until 19 April 1854, a run of more than 300 consecutive performances. By the end of the 1850s, the phenomenon popularized by these two productions had become the established practice for managers seeking maximum profits from their investments. The long run was the acknowledged objective of stars such as Joseph Jefferson (as Rip Van Winkle), Frank Mayo (as Davy Crockett), and Denman Thompson (as the Yankee Josh Whitcomb in *The Old Homestead*), who toured with their own combination companies, as well as producers of spectacles like *The Black Crook*, which ran for 475 performances in 1866 and grossed $1,100,000 on an initial investment of $24,500.

Theatre as Industry: From Stock to Combination

The advent of the combination company marked the theatre's entrance into the modern, industrialized era. The American theatre began the 1870s as a stock company operation composed of independent, disconnected companies, and emerged from the 1870s as a traveling combination system boasting hundreds of New York casts bringing New York hits to audiences on "the Road," theatres grouped in circuits along major railroad routes, and specialized offices and agents whose sole function was the booking of tours for traveling companies. Accordingly, during the same period, New York's reputation as the nation's theatrical center, which prior to 1870 was due to the quality of its first-class stock companies and its ability to influence theatrical tastes, came to depend upon its role as the principal supplier of America's entertainments.

As it is most commonly defined, the combination company is a theatrical "package" or combination of performers (and often design and technical elements) in support of a star, formed or combined for the run of a single play. Once a tour has been completed or audiences exhausted, the combination ceases production, the performers seek work with other combinations, and the scenery and other technical elements are either put into storage or, more frequently, scrapped.

The concept of a star touring with supporting actors originated shortly after the advent of the star system itself, the impetus arising from traveling stars' dissatisfaction with the general lack of supporting talent in the stock companies with which they performed. From the 1830s on, local managers, eager to display the era's most popular stars to their public, had been forced to either reduce the size of their companies and/or to cut wages for supporting performers in order to meet stars' salaries. Since both practices adversely affected the overall quality of local companies, stars determined to appear with "competent" casts began touring with two or three performers, who assumed the principal supporting roles. Gradually, in order to ensure the overall quality of their productions, stars began to form entire companies to travel with them. At first, the companies supported the stars in a full repertory of plays; later in its development, the average combination company toured a single production.

While the early roots of the combination concept are identifiable, the precise origins of the modern self-contained traveling combination company, as Benjamin McArthur and others point out, are "clouded," with little agreement upon a single figure who can be considered its "originator" (see McArthur, 9). Credit is most frequently given to Dion Boucicault, who produced *The Colleen Bawn* with a combination company in London in 1860 and imported his new system to the United States in 1872; however, both Joseph Jefferson and Charles Wyndham claim to have toured with entire companies in 1868, and historians have isolated touring companies that may be even earlier examples of combinations.

The displacement of the stock system as the dominant mode of production by the combination system, when it occurred in the 1870s, took place with astonishing rapidity. During that decade, the number of first-class stock companies declined precipitously from fifty in 1872 to eight in 1880, whereas the number of traveling combinations rose from five in 1872 to nearly a hundred just four years later. So sweeping and complete was this transition that by the end of the century, not even the most famous stock houses – Lester Wallack's, Augustin Daly's, and the Union Square Stock Company in New York and the Arch Street Theatre company, the Walnut Street Theatre Company, and the Chestnut Street Theatre in Philadelphia – had survived.

In its suddenness, the transformation from a resident stock system to a traveling combination system was more in the nature of a rupture, an abrupt cultural shift or break, than it was a gradual evolution. Conventionally, historians have cited evolutionary processes as the prime causes for the decline of the stock system; however, these explanations fail to account for the rapidity of the change, nor do they take into account the unstable economic climate at the time of the transition. According to Peter Davis, a more plausible explanation for the shift lies in the economic Panic of 1873 and its subsequent effects. Davis points to studies that indicate that by 1870 the nineteenth-century stock company was becoming ill equipped to adapt to either the artistic or economic demands made upon it, was frequently a marginal operation, and hence was particularly susceptible to even slight economic pressures. Needless to say, a depression that caused upwards of ten thousand businesses to fail in a single year, as did the Panic of 1873, would account for the widespread closing of stock houses in a short time period.

In retrospect, the weaknesses of the nineteenth-century stock company were evident years before the Panic of 1873. From its inception, the long run had exposed the drawbacks of the stock-repertory scheme, which relied on the nightly change of bill. Nightly rotation required sets that were cheap, since scenery required periodic replacement because of the wear-and-tear of constant shifting or the ravages of time. In addition, scenery had to be relatively simple and light to facilitate moving and storage. By the early 1870s, the stock-repertory manager faced a dilemma: If he chose to continue the repertory system at his current level of production, he would be unable to compete with the elaborately staged long run next door; if, on the other hand, he chose to compete by upgrading his scenery, he would incur tremendous expenses, not only for the new sets, but for the additional stagehands required to move the more complicated scenery nightly, for the rental of additional storage space, and for the costs of transporting his elaborate sets to the storage area.

Besides the ever-escalating expenses of maintaining a stock company, managers had additional financial incentives for abandoning the stock system. Companies that were permanently located, even those situated in major cities and featuring a star in a vehicle replete with spectacle, faced ever-increasing competition for audiences. The Road, in contrast, promised a practically limitless audience, for traveling companies remained in a location only long enough to guarantee a profit. Road companies played "intermediate-sized" cities for no more than three nights and small towns (the so-called one-night stands) for one performance only, thereby minimizing the risk of exhausting audiences. Faced as they were with competition from the combinations, dwindling audiences, and financial pressures resultant from the Panic of 1873, it is hardly surprising that managers abandoned stock production to either convert their theatres to booking houses or to form combination companies.

Economics may undeniably have been instrumental in spurring structural changes in the American theatre of the 1870s, but the combination company offered *artistic* advantages as well. As a *New York Dramatic Mirror* editorial (17 January 1880) reported, audiences had, in fact, grown tired of paying to see "the same old faces" in a limited repertory. In contrast to the "sameness" and predictability of the local stock company, the traveling combination furnished spectators the era's most popular stars on their local stages, an ever-changing bill, the best supporting casts money could hire, and, since a combination company performed a single play repeatedly and employed specialists in both onstage and offstage positions, a more "polished" production.

Although the combination was better suited to a commercialized, industrialized culture than was its predecessor, its advent brought new problems. Initially, attempts to book upwards of 250 combinations into more than five thousand theatres in thirty-five thousand cities resulted in organizational chaos. Early in the combination era, business practices were still primitive, were conducted outdoors, and relied predominantly upon personal contacts and "gentlemen's agreements," which were sealed with a handshake. Each summer, the nation's managers were forced to journey to New York's Union Square, the hub of the nation's theatrical activity, to form road companies or book attractions into their theatres. There, on the south and east sides of the square, an area known in the profession as the "slave market," actors "at liberty" and seeking engagements searched for potential employers, and the out-of-town managers sought the attractions they believed would guarantee full houses. Once the necessary contacts had been made, critical negotiations were conducted on the benches that ringed the square, in nearby restaurants in the Morton House, the Hotel Hungaria and the Union Square Hotel, or in one of the theatrical bars nearby, with contracts often written on tablecloths or shirt cuffs (if written at all) and booking for an entire season recorded in a personal diary. At best, this method of booking each attraction separately was inconvenient; at worst, it was slipshod.

Booking was especially precarious for managers of the myriad one-night stands that dotted the routes between major cities, because their bookings were the least attractive. Assuming that company managers would not hesitate to cancel their bookings if a more "attractive" engagement materialized, small-town theatre owners routinely booked two attractions for the same evening. This procedure frequently resulted in two companies arriving to perform in the same theatre on the same night, and at the next town on the train route, a manager was burdened with an empty house.

One answer to the chaos created by competitive booking was the theatrical circuit, a construct that had existed as a formal, organized practice since the close of the Civil War. Initially a local business, a circuit was a group of contiguous theatres on a logical transportation route for a traveling company, usually a railroad line, that banded together for mutual protection. Since, in the laissez-faire days before centralization, small-theatre owners were the most vulnerable to performers' whims, a circuit significantly increased their bargaining power. As Alfred Bernheim states the case in *The Business of the Theatre,* an attraction could skip an engagement with a single theatre with little fear of penalty, but it would hesitate to cancel, knowing that an entire circuit of theatres between major cities might boycott it. The circuit offered an additional advantage in that it was considerably less expensive and far more convenient to book an entire circuit than it was to book each theatre separately, since just one man could handle the booking for many theatres.

Not coincidentally, the combination company's ascendance paralleled that of the American railroad network, which, by the 1870s, had already transformed the country from a collection of isolated, independent villages into an interconnected national community. America's railroads, little more than a broken skein of just 9,000 miles of track in 1850, had mushroomed into a national rail network after the Civil War – from 35,000 miles of connected track in 1865 to 80,000 miles by 1880. By the beginning of their second decade of existence, therefore, traveling combinations had access to hundreds of towns, both large and small, on rail lines from New York to San Francisco and from Minnesota to Texas.

Although independent circuits like Tom Davy's Louisiana circuit and Henry C. Jarrett's New England circuit had existed in the 1860s before the combination system, the circuit as a construct designed specifically to deal with traveling companies did not emerge until the seventies. The earliest circuits were true cooperatives composed of equal partners, but, gradually, circuits underwent an organizational transformation, as one person with enough wealth or power to assume control and set policy for the entire circuit gained domination. This centralization of power was reflected in the designations of the various circuits – the Mishler Circuit in eastern Pennsylvania, Schwartz's Wisconsin Theatrical Circuit, Craig's Kansas–Missouri Circuit, and Harry Greenwall's Lone Star Circuit.

The specialization inherent in the combination system contributed to a virtually unnoticed, yet significant, change in the American theatre: the effective divorce of the producing management from the theatre management (circuits and individual theatre owners). During the 1870s and 1880s, with the breakdown of the traditional stock system, many local theatre owners who once had maintained companies found that as they converted their theatres to booking houses rather than close their doors, they had, in effect, become little more than landlords. Consequently, as the touring combination gained ascendance, the organic link between the manager who produced the productions and the theatre manager, a given in the stock era, disappeared.

The chaos of the road and the growing power of circuits increased the demand for yet another specialized service industry: the booking office. Booking offices came into existence for the sole purpose of negotiating contracts between circuits and attractions, with the booking agent assuming the role of distributor of a product. Few figures symbolized the theatre's transformation into big business better than the booking agent for, like his twentieth-century counterpart, the nineteenth-century booking agent was a professional middleman who effected agreements between theatres seeking performers and attractions seeking routes, and, in turn, received a fee for his services.[1] Since he was not the manufacturer of the product he disseminated, the booking agent served as a facilitator, seldom a principal, in the transactions he negotiated.

During the early 1880s, the booking agent's role was transformed in a way that had widespread ramifications and permanently altered economic relations in the theatre. Through his booking agency, The Managers' and Stars' Agency, C. R. Gardiner undertook not only to negotiate contracts between performers and theatre managers but to gain control over which attractions were booked into which theatres. By controlling the stars' routes himself, instead of letting individual managers determine the paths of tours, Gardiner was able to force theatre owners to deal directly with him in order to sign attractions. This principle of "exclusive control" over the theatres and attractions – a principle later put into practice by the Klaw and Erlanger Exchange over a limited territory, and still later by the Syndicate over the first-class theatres of the entire country – was a significant step toward the centralization of the American theatre.

In actuality, the booking agent was not the theatre's first middleman but he was preceded by nearly a decade by a different type of agent, the dramatic agent, who, in the increasingly industrialized world of the theatre, served as a buffer between the artist and the "tougher" elements of the business. Before 1870, dramatic agencies were little more than clearing houses for talent – offices near the center of theatrical activity where managers could list their needs, either in person or by letter, and where actors and actresses could post their photos on the wall for a small fee. In the early days of dramatic agencies, often the agent was not involved in the final negotiations between actor and manager, a situation that often resulted in complaints from actors, who charged that even when they negotiated directly with the managers, they were frequently compelled to sign agreements at the agencies and to pay for services that were never rendered. Nevertheless, with an estimated two hundred thousand people in the United States connected with the theatre in 1870 (the majority of them actors), clearing houses for talent were rapidly becoming a necessity for the average actor and a time-saving convenience for the manager.

In the late 1870s, the hiring of actors moved indoors from the "slave market" to agents' offices, and the agent's role was redefined. When stars began hiring agents to handle their business transactions, often at salaries in excess of a hundred dollars per week, the talent broker was immediately placed in a strategic position. He alone decided for whom an important actor would work. Negotiating for the stars concentrated an enormous amount of power in the hands of a few individuals who could control not only the futures of the performers they represented but the fates of managers throughout the country. With power, money, and a certain prestige to be gained, often overnight if a major star was represented, scores of enterprising men entered the ranks of New York dramatic agents. Between 1875 and 1880 the number of agencies grew rapidly, and the agent's domain was expanded to include not only performers but scenic artists, stage carpenters, and property men as well.

Geographic Centralization

The breakdown of the stock system in the 1870s, in addition to influencing how the routine business of the theatre was conducted, played a role in the transformation of the nature and spatial organization of the modern city. Unlike the stock company, which had traditionally been attached to a particular theatre and had produced its own scenery, costumes, and properties "on site," the traveling combination company possessed no technical staff, shop facilities, or storage provisions. Sensing the voids left by the elimination of the stock company's backstage activities, astute entrepreneurs, some unemployed because of the reduction in stock production, responded with the creation of a full complement of theatrical service industries, ranging from scenery and costume shops to agents' offices to the small shops of individual artisans (wigmakers, theatrical shoemakers, props masters). Understandably, when these entrepreneurs selected locations, they chose to remain near the theatres they served, which, in New York in the 1870s, were located on or around Union Square, at the junction of Broadway, the Bowery, and Fourteenth Street.

The coalescence of theatrical businesses and the marked increase in activity in one area, when it occurred, did not go unnoticed. On Friday 19 April 1878, a headline in *The World* boldly proclaimed that "Theater, Newspapers, Actors and Play Publishers Capture Union Square." The column was less a revelation than a public acknowledgment of Union Square's status as New York's Rialto, the epicenter of the city's first district devoted exclusively to theatre and the prototype of later theatre centers at Madison and Times Squares. The streets on and adjacent to the square were dominated by some of New York's most renowned theatres and by the theatrical businesses that served them. Hotels and restaurants in the vicinity advertised that they catered to the "theatre crowd" and, in an age when stars still mingled with their public, were routinely patronized by the leading figures of the New York stage.

As Richard Hofstadter has observed, one of the identifying characteristics of urbanization was the rise in service industries composed of small units that organized themselves into discrete districts. Thus, the clustering of like business ventures on or near Union Square was but one manifestation of a citywide pattern of specialized commercial districts throughout New York City. According to the *New York Sun* in 1867, Wall Street was already given over to financial concerns, stock trading had settled between Hanover and William streets, wholesale grocers occupied Front Street, leather goods had settled on Ferry Street, tailors and small clothing shops lined Cherry and Catherine streets, fur dealers claimed Water Street, and fashionable women's

"Union Square in Midsummer, 1882." A chromo-lithograph showing numerous theatrical enterprises located on the square. The scene is surrounded by pictures of stars of the New York stage. From the *New York Mirror Supplement*. Museum of the City of New York (Gift of Morris Ranger).

shops were situated on a stretch of Broadway dubbed "Ladies' Mile," which began at A. T. Stewart's mammoth emporium between Ninth and Tenth streets and ended at Madison Square. Even the piano industry boasted its own district, Fourteenth Street, which became known throughout the city as "Piano-forte-eenth Street."

Earlier in the century, New Yorkers, with the exception of those wealthy enough to own their own carriages, had shopped, socialized, and sought recreation within walking distance of their homes. Thus, the neighborhood, with its complement of small specialty shops, crafts, theatres, and public gathering spots, served as the basic organizational unit in city life – an urban version of the self-contained rural community of times past. This lifestyle was gradually transformed in the decades preceding the Civil War by the introduction of the horsecar, the omnibus, and the streetcar, which allowed people to cross neighborhood boundaries to seek goods and recreation in areas of the city miles from their homes. The breakdown of neighborhood boundaries was facilitated by New York's "penny press," which daily advertised what was available throughout the city to a mass readership. The centralizing influence of cheap transportation, coupled with mass-circulation newspapers and the advent of specialized commercial districts, precipitated nothing less than a revolution in city life.

According to Gunther Barth, the ordering of urban space into distinct districts identified by specific function and connected by mass transit was a logical development in a city that historically had struggled with the management of its real estate. In its earliest days, growth was uncontrolled and the city spread in all directions from a limited number of governmental and commercial centers as topography allowed; however, by 1807, local and state officials realized the need for a method of structuring future expansion. The resultant solution, the Randel Plan of 1811, proposed rectilinear and rectangular streets and buildings that efficiently utilized space by eliminating odd-shaped, unusable tracts of land. This basic plan sufficed as the principal organizational model as long as New York remained a series of neighborhoods that ringed a downtown business center. Once the city outgrew its status as a residential, "walking" city, however, specialized districts that were rendered accessible by rapid transit became necessary. In the context of the age-old problem of ordering urban space, then, the districting of New York was yet another rational (albeit unplanned) means of bringing a degree of regularity or predictability to the spatial chaos that resulted from rapid expansion.

Even by contemporary standards, by the mid-1870s New York's first theatrical center was remarkably complete, with all of the necessary components for a specialized district in place. Union Square was accessible by trolleys that ran across town on Fourteenth Street and north–south on Broadway, while elevated lines crossed Fourteenth Street at Third and Sixth avenues. By the end of its tenure as a theatrical center in the late nineties, even inhabitants of the northernmost regions of Manhattan and the other boroughs could ride to the theatre by mass transit.

In the decade following its inception, the district contained the majority of New York's most famous theatres, including Booth's Theatre, the Fifth Avenue Theatre, Koster and Bial's Opera House, the Academy of Music, Wallack's, the Union Square Theatre, and the Fourteenth Street Theatre, the last four situated near the epicenter of theatrical activity. In the evening, theatregoers shared the sidewalks with concertgoers, for the neighborhood was home to a number of concert halls in the era before Carnegie Hall. Dodworth Hall, on Broadway just north of Grace Church; Chickering, Weber, and Knabe halls on lower Fifth Avenue; Steinway and Steck halls on Fourteenth Street; and Irving Hall on Irving Place, offered nightly fare ranging from solo piano recitals to full orchestral concerts. In the same area, anyone seeking popular entertainments could see a show at Robinson Hall on Sixteenth Street, the Columbia Opera House on Greenwich Avenue, Tony Pastor's New Fourteenth Street Theatre located in Tammany Hall on East Fourteenth Street, or the Hippotheatreon directly across the street from Pastor's. In the 1880s, spectators could wander through Bunnell's or Huber's Dime Museums, see a presentation at Meade's Midget Hall on Fifth Avenue, or visit the Cyclorama of the battle of Gettysburg at the north end of the square as well.

These performance venues were surrounded by the service industries that supported them. Eaves Costume Company, Kohler's Costume Shop, Jacoby and Company, A. Roemer and Son, Bloom's Theatrical Supplies Emporium, and Dazian's Theatrical Emporium furnished costumes for the New York stage, and Charles Meyer and Charles Winkelmann, Wigmakers, coifed its leading performers. Brentano's Literary Emporium, Christern's, and Samuel French and Son satisfied both the public's and the profession's need for new playtexts. *The Stage,* the *Musical Courier, The Dramatic News, Illustrated Dramatic Weekly, The Dramatic Times, The Dramatic Magazine, Leslie's Sporting and Dramatic Times,* and the *Dramatic Mirror* published from offices on or near the square. The center of America's music publishing industry (M. Witmark and Sons, Boosey and Company, Edward Schuberth and Company, and Gustave Schirmer, to list the more famous) was also located near the Square decades before Tin Pan Alley settled permanently near the Brill Building on West Forty-ninth Street and many of the era's theatrical photographers (Napoleon Sarony, Carl Hecker, Charles Eisenmann, the Bogardus Gallery, Feinberg Photo Studio, Andrew Jordan, Benjamin Falk, and the Pach Brothers' Gallery) maintained studios in the neighborhood in order to exhibit their work to the acting profession and the theatregoing public.

In the nineteenth century, an evening at the theatre was likely to be a culinary as well as an artistic experience. Theatres frequently maintained cafés where liquor, coffee, and cigars could be consumed, and some even operated dining facilities in their buildings. Restaurants in the vicinity of the city's theatres likewise catered to a clientele composed of managers, performers, and theatregoers. The more wealthy could dine sumptuously before the show at Delmonico's on Fifth Avenue, Taylor's Saloon at 365 Broadway, Louffre's on Pearl Street, the Maison Dorée on Union Square, or in the dining rooms of the Union Square Hotel or the Morton House. Less wealthy patrons could choose from a variety of oyster and chop houses; German *weinstuben,* which offered reasonably priced German cuisine and a wide selection of beers and wines; or Italian restaurants, where two dinners with wine cost less than a dollar. With the exception of Lüchow's on East Fourteenth Street, few establishments on Union Square achieved the fame of Rector's, Shanley's, Bustanoby's, or Sardi's, their twentieth-century counterparts; nevertheless, they were equally reliant upon the theatre trade, actively cultivated the patronage of the era's most popular performers, and acquired reputations as theatrical restaurants.

Consistent with the city's relentless northward progress, New York's theatrical center began moving uptown even while the district was still forming and, by the beginning of the twentieth century, Union Square had been super-seded as the city's Rialto, first by Madison Square, and then by Times Square. In 1883, the Metropolitan Opera House at Broadway and Thirty-ninth replaced the Academy of Music as the sanctioned home of grand opera, and by the early 1890s, theatres had already begun to cluster just below Forty-second Street. During roughly the same period, many of the service indus-tries that had prospered near Union Square during its Rialto period leased new quarters in the West Forties, Tin Pan Alley relocated to West Twenty-eighth Street, and the Morton House Café relinquished its reputation as the city's principal theatrical rendezvous to George Considine's Metropole Bar and Restaurant at the corner of Broadway and Forty-second Street.

Once started, the process of attrition gathered momentum. Although big-time vaudeville was still presented at Keith's Union Square Theatre and Tony Pastor's, and dime museums and Wild West shows continued to attract patrons, by 1900 Times Square had become universally recognized as New York's "white light district." Union Square nevertheless still clung tenaciously to a lesser place in the city's entertainment industry. The blocks on Second Avenue south of Fourteenth Street were given over to Yiddish drama, and the area was dubbed the "Yiddish Rialto," and many of the theatres and buildings formerly occupied by booking agents or script sellers were leased by the fledgling film industry. During the teens and 1920s, until the movies followed live theatre uptown, William Fox, Adolph Zukor, Marcus Loew, Mack Sennett, D. W. Griffith, and other movie pioneers, built their reputations and empires upon work done at Union Square.

While movies were moving into Union Square, New York's new theatrical center at Times Square, built upon the foundation of theatrical service indus-tries originally founded near Union Square, was becoming fully consolidated within an area between Sixth and Eighth avenues, Thirty-eighth Street and the low Fifties, roughly the same area occupied by today's theatre district. Although it would not diversify as much as it had when it was situated at Union Square, the Rialto at Times Square continued to grow for the first three decades of the twentieth century, until its expansion was ultimately limited by the scarcity of land available for building, skyrocketing real estate prices, the Depression, and other economic factors.

Structural Centralization

Although the American theatre was geographically centralized by the late 1870s, it would not become organizationally centralized until the mid-1890s. During the seventies, roughly the same period that it was settling around

"The Great White Way," Broadway. Day and night views from postcards (teens). Collection of Michael Gnat.

Union Square, the American theatre was in structural disarray. The opening of national markets for theatre, entrepreneurs willing and able to package the product for national distribution, and a vast railroad system to transport it quickly and reliably, although significantly expanding the economic potential of the theatre, dramatically increased the level of its organizational chaos and economic instability. Booking practices were still primitive and were effected outdoors, written contracts were a rarity, and everyone took whatever measures deemed necessary to protect personal interests, which resulted in universal distrust and a general lack of ethics in theatre practices. The net result of these haphazard practices and the laissez-faire philosophy that predominated was an unpredictable, "boom or bust" theatrical economy that was catastrophic for actors, managers, booking agents, theatre owners, and patrons alike.

Although the creation of circuits afforded the local theatre owner more authority in negotiating with booking agents and simplified touring considerably, the ultimate solution to the chaos of "the Road" lay in the consolidation of both booking and theatre management in the hands of a single manager, agency, or circuit that would exercise authority for the "good of the industry." By the late 1870s, such a solution was consistent with contemporaneous economic theories and industrial practices. Following the Civil War, regardless of whether the venture was oil, sugar, liquor, or theatre, the answer to economic chaos and instability was much the same: the creation of a monopoly or trust that could consolidate control in the hands of a few individuals and integrate all aspects of production and distribution.

To the post–Civil War businessman, the monopoly was an eminently rational concept. Faced with unstable prices for his products caused by fierce competition and periodic gluts of his markets, the clever postwar businessman quickly realized that to survive, he must rationalize marketing procedures and eliminate competition, either by negotiation, by forcing rivals into bankruptcy, or by buying them out. Once this had been accomplished, the newly created trust could control the supply of products, set prices, and even establish rates in industries forced to deal with it.

In the theatre, this concentration of authority took the form of the Theatrical Syndicate, which was formed in 1896 in the wake of the Panic of 1893, monopolized theatre booking for twenty years, and (along with the Shubert organization which eventually supplanted it) came to represent the highest degree of centralization in American theatre history. While it was, by no means, the inevitable development that some theatre historians claim, the Theatrical Syndicate was most certainly the "natural and logical" culmination of growth patterns established in the 1870s and 1880s and of business practices (booking, circuits, theatre management) common by the 1890s. The Syndicate was natural and logical, first, because similar monopolies in the business world (the Michigan Salt Association, the Distillers and Cattle Feeders Trust, the National Biscuit Company, John D. Rockefeller's Standard Oil Corporation) served as ready models for enterprising entrepreneurs willing to look beyond the theatre for solutions, and, second, because the chaos introduced into the theatre by the traveling combination company and irregular booking practices virtually invited the degree of intervention that would necessarily lead to a consolidation of power.

The Syndicate itself was composed of the (Marc) Klaw and (Abraham Lincoln) Erlanger Exchange, which owned theatres in the South on the route from Washington to New Orleans, held exclusive booking rights on an additional two hundred theatres, and assumed the duties of formally booking for the Syndicate throughout its twenty-year existence; the firm of Samuel Nixon and J. Fred Zimmerman of Philadelphia, which controlled the Broad Street Theatre, the Chestnut Street Opera House, and first-class theatres in Pennsylvania, West Virginia, and Ohio; Al Hayman, who either owned or controlled booking for a number of theatres in the West, including the Baldwin in San Francisco; and the producing manager Charles Frohman, who controlled theatres in New York and Boston. Between them, according to Monroe Lippman, writing in *The Quarterly Journal of Speech,* the members of the Syndicate "controlled nearly all the first-class theatres in the key cities throughout the country, in addition to enjoying exclusive booking control of more than five hundred first-class houses on all the best theatrical routes from the Atlantic to the Pacific and from Canada to the Gulf of Mexico" (275).

The Syndicate was legally conceived as a partnership (one of the only trusts in United States history to not incorporate) on 31 August 1896, for the express purpose of reducing the financial losses that resulted from indiscriminate booking of America's first-class theatres.[2] Syndicate members were bound by a contract that established the conditions under which attractions could play Syndicate houses, outlined how profits were to be pooled and divided, set forth the requirements for the future inclusion of theatres and managers in the trust, and included the requirement that Syndicate theatres be booked in conjunction with one another. The agreement further stipulated that managers who wished to book their theatres with the Syndicate must agree to book them exclusively through Klaw and Erlanger; provided similar exclusive booking imperatives for performers signing with the Syndicate; and listed the theatres either owned or controlled by the Syndicate. Then, with business alliances formalized, the theatrical trust began a campaign to secure control of the remainder of the first-class theatres in America, either through leasehold or by promises to theatre managers of the best attractions available. Their targets included theatres in Minneapolis, St. Louis, Cleveland, Detroit, and other major cities not yet under Syndicate control, theatres in towns that controlled the approaches to the big cities, and one-night-stand houses in between.

From the outset, there was nothing mysterious about the tactics the Syndicate employed to monopolize America's first-class theatres. When it first began operating publicly (evidence exists that it had secretly begun to position itself in the industry and seek allies several months prior to its legal inception), Klaw, Erlanger, and company represented themselves as the sole stabilizing force in booking, as the agency that would end the ruinous rivalries that threatened to bankrupt theatre makers. To the theatre manager, they promised a steady supply of the best available attractions, booking for an entire season without an expensive annual business trip to New York, and an end to empty theatres caused by performers' failure to appear without notice. To the independent producer and the performers who still booked their own tours, they promised efficient, economical routes composed of first-class theatres in any region of the country or even coast to coast. In short, the Syndicate offered everyone involved in the Road greater prosperity and security than they could attain on their own. For their services, the Klaw and Erlanger Exchange claimed a fee of 5 percent of a theatre's gross receipts.

As Syndicate members had hoped, theatre managers and booking agents flocked to the Klaw and Erlanger offices to sign contracts. In their first two years of operation, using little more than their ingenuity, persuasion, and their influence in the theatre, the Syndicate more than doubled the number of theatres it controlled, secured the contracts of stars with the stature of E. H. Sothern, Ethel Barrymore, Mrs. Leslie Carter, Blanche Bates, and Olga Nethersole, and developed into a monopoly in actuality, not just in intention.

With a strong nucleus of theatres and attractions, by 1898 the Syndicate was in a position to exercise its power overtly and to dictate terms to both theatres and performers. It therefore set out to gain control over houses and attractions that had not responded to its initial overtures. With its power and holdings consolidated, the Syndicate began to behave like any other monopoly – it threatened to withhold what it controlled from those who declined its terms. Theatre managers who refused to ally themselves with the Syndicate were unable to book high-quality talent or were forced to watch helplessly as the Syndicate built or leased a theatre nearby; meanwhile, recalcitrant performers might be routed from Cincinnati to Washington to Buffalo to Richmond with no intervening bookings, denied a route altogether, or, as in the case of Henrietta Crosman's 1901 tour of *Mistress Nell,* led to discover that a rival production (Ada Rehan in *Sweet Nell of Old Drury*) had been booked for the same route a week earlier. Thus, by controlling both sides of the booking equation – theatres and attractions – and threatening to withhold one or the other, Klaw, Erlanger, and company were able to force all but the most stalwart to capitulate to their demands.

As happened with the industrial trusts of the 1870s and 1880s, which initially received public support because the American public perceived them as necessary for restoring economic order and prosperity, initial reactions to the Syndicate, both from the theatrical community and the theatregoing public, were favorable. In its early years, the Syndicate was regarded as little more than a giant booking agency, and, with everyone reaping the financial rewards of a refined system, few (with the notable exceptions of Minnie Maddern Fiske and Harrison Grey Fiske, vigorous and vocal opponents of the Syndicate for the duration of its existence) had reason to complain. This mutual goodwill, however, was short-lived. In 1898, following a series of editorials criticizing the Syndicate in the *New York Dramatic Mirror* by its editor Harrison Grey Fiske, the trust faced its first public opposition in the form of an actors' uprising, the first of many it would face. Convinced that their artistic freedom was being curtailed by the Syndicate, the actors – Richard Mansfield, Francis Wilson, James O'Neill, William H. Crane, Fanny Davenport, Joseph Jefferson, and Mrs. Fiske – vowed to maintain their independence and to aggressively defy Klaw and Erlanger's dictates.

Although this rebellion ended, like all subsequent insurrections in the Syndicate's history, with the actors eventually capitulating to Syndicate pressure and their own instincts for self-preservation, it attracted the attention of the critics. For the remainder of the Syndicate's existence, a coterie of some of America's most respected critics and scholars, led by Walter Prichard Eaton and including John Ranken Towse, Sheldon Cheney, William Winter, and Norman Hapgood, indicted it, not just for the conventional industrial crimes (dictatorial management style, pressure tactics, and unfair labor practices) but for debasing the art of the theatre as well. In a series of reviews in *The New York Evening Post, Cosmopolitan, American Magazine,* and other publications, they charged, first, that the Syndicate destroyed the quality of American acting by keeping players in long runs, thereby preventing them from assuming the variety of roles necessary to develop artistic versatility, and by undermining the stock company that had traditionally served as the training ground for performers. Second, the critics claimed that the Syndicate discouraged native drama, favoring instead the foreign scripts preferred by Frohman. And third, they asserted that in order to appeal to the largest audience possible for strictly commercial reasons, it discouraged "serious" drama and mounted popular "fluff" like *The Soul Kiss, Miss Innocence, The Queen of the Moulin Rouge,* and *The Girl with the Whooping Cough.*

These allegations warrant attention here because, in the years since the Syndicate's demise, they have made the leap from critical opinion to historical fact. Further, they warrant mention because, upon scrutiny by Lippman and others, they have been shown to have been either exaggerated or erroneous. There is virtually no evidence, for example, to indicate that the overall quality of acting did, in fact, decline during the Syndicate's reign. While there admittedly may have been no Booth or Forrest during the Syndicate era, the rank and file of the profession (performers like Frances Starr, Holbrook Blinn, Ina Claire, and Jane Cowl) was clearly equal, both in talent and technique, to Kate Claxton, John Brougham, Charles Thorne, or Agnes Ethel of the great stock-company era. Nor can Klaw and Erlanger be blamed, even indirectly, for the demise of the stock company, for the shift from the stock to the combination system of production was a precondition of, rather than the result of, the Syndicate.

The critics' second assertion that the Syndicate single-handedly discouraged American dramaturgy is likewise a misrepresentation. Considering that William Dunlap, the oft-named father of American drama, once felt compelled to attribute a play he had authored to a foreign playwright to hide its "native origin" and render it respectable; that Palmer, Daly, Boucicault, and their contemporaries served the public a steady diet of foreign scripts; and that Lester Wallack billed his theatre as the American home of British high comedy, demonizing Syndicate members for the same attitudes and actions seems unduly harsh.

There is even less rationale for the critics' final charge: that the Syndicate failed to produce high-quality scripts. Although Klaw and Erlanger undeniably sought scripts for their box office potential, upon reflection, they were no more commercial than their contemporaries; nor were they appreciably more commercial than Wallack, Daly, and Palmer, all of whom reputedly chose scripts with profits in mind. Ironically, Klaw and Erlanger, through their production of works by James Herne, Clyde Fitch, Edmond Rostand, James Barrie, Bernard Shaw, Henrik Ibsen, and Oliver Goldsmith, as well as their series of Shakespearean plays featuring popular performers (Nat Goodwin as Bottom in *A Midsummer Night's Dream,* Johnston Forbes-Robertson as Hamlet, and E. H. Sothern and Julia Marlowe in *Romeo and Juliet, Hamlet,* and *Much Ado About Nothing*), may actually have done more to promote the classics than their reputedly more artistic predecessors.

In its twenty-year history, the Syndicate withstood numerous challenges to its authority from rebellious actors; from a rival booking conglomerate, the Independent Booking Agency, in 1902; and from an antitrust suit in 1907, which was dismissed when the judge ruled that, since the theatre was not a necessity, no "actual suffering" could result from changes in its nature. In the end, however, it was another theatrical monopoly, the Shubert organization, that ended the Syndicate's domination of first-class theatre.

The Shubert brothers (Sam, Lee, and Jacob J.) acquired their first theatre the year after the Syndicate was formed. Within five years, they controlled a chain of theatres in upstate New York and had leased the Herald Square in New York City. At first, relations between the Syndicate and the brothers were amicable, but, by 1905, as Bernheim notes, the Shuberts' rapid expansion in the first-class theatre market "awakened the Syndicate to the realization that [there] was an incipient rival whose power would have to be curbed before it reached unmanageable proportions" (64). When Klaw and Erlanger attempted to employ the tactics that had been successful against a host of earlier managers, the Shuberts' response was nothing short of a declaration of war.

Emulating the Syndicate's methods during the first decade of the century, the Shuberts continued to acquire theatres and entire circuits nationwide and, exploiting the rapidly growing discontent among managers and performers with the constraints imposed by Klaw and Erlanger, they offered to assist anyone who resisted the Syndicate. As a show of good faith, the brothers guaranteed an "open door" policy in the booking of Shubert theatres. After Sam's death in 1905, the remaining brothers became even more determined in their defiance of Klaw and Erlanger, and their underdog status attracted defectors from the Syndicate in ever-increasing numbers. By 1910, one decade after the Shuberts' arrival in New York, the Syndicate had been successfully challenged; during the subsequent decade, it was fully eclipsed by the Shubert organization, which, through continued growth and acquisitions, became a monopoly that was virtually indistinguishable from its predecessor in intent, methods, and scope.

Not coincidentally, the period of fiercest competition between the two conglomerates (1909–13) was also the period during which the Road began its legendary decline, with the number of traveling combinations shrinking from 289 in 1909 to 178 four years later. As Bernheim summarizes the situation, intensified competition brought an oversupply of theatres, as the Shuberts built or converted spaces in Syndicate towns to match their opponents house for house. The theatre glut, in turn, created a shortage of quality attractions. With vast chains of theatres to fill, panicky producers and bookers from both sides of the theatre war responded by cloning additional duplicate companies and billing them as "Straight from a Year on Broadway" with the hope that patrons in the hinterlands would not notice the ever-diminishing production values. However, spectators, perhaps remembering the great touring plays and players of earlier decades and refusing to be gulled by inferior productions despite advertisers' puffery, stopped patronizing the legitimate theatre, thus adding the final link in the causal chain that ultimately led to the decline of the Road.

Although the theatre war had an undeniable impact upon the Road, early in the century the American theatre was also at the mercy of a combination of intersecting social forces and events, many of them external to the theatre and hence beyond its control. Since the late nineteenth century, the legitimate theatre had encountered fierce competition from rival entertainments. Family vaudeville, begun in 1881 by Tony Pastor and promoted by B. F. Keith and Edward Albee, became an industry in its own right with the establishment of the United Booking Office (the vaudeville monopoly) in 1904 and increasingly usurped both theatres and patrons from the legitimate theatre. Likewise, movies, destined to reach maturity in 1915 with the first narrative film (D. W. Griffith's *Birth of a Nation*), siphoned off even more theatres and spectators.

The problems resultant from increased competition for audiences on the road were exacerbated by wartime railroad and labor rates so severe that they prompted the editor of *Theatre Arts* magazine (January 1920) to claim that "railroads are doing their best to annihilate English and American touring systems" (69). Added to soaring railroad fees that led to an 80 percent increase in transporting a traveling company by 1920, the Road was further plagued by the rising popularity of the automobile, which not only provided amusement on its own but allowed the theatre patron to avoid the second-rate road company at the local theatre in favor of a first-rate star or production in the "big city" just a forty-five-minute drive away. Not surprisingly, managers of one-night-stand houses, faced with poor-quality attractions and the desertion of their audiences for other pastimes, chose to convert their theatres to neighborhood vaudeville or film houses.

Intriguingly, the precipitous decline of "the Road," which affected the one-night-stand towns most profoundly, corresponded with a significant increase in stock-company formation and activity in the hinterlands. Generally operating on a scale of "10-20-30" cents, the popular-priced stock company offered both fare and prices tailored to lower-class tastes. Considered by Bernheim to have been a "compensating development" for diminished road activity, popular-priced stock was less a revolt against the Syndicate, the Shuberts, and the traveling combination company than it was a simple matter of survival. Local managers, either frozen out of the major circuits or unwilling to sign with the two trusts, turned to stock as their final opportunity to remain in the theatre. By leasing theatres left vacant by Syndicate–Shubert overbuilding, by producing Broadway hits from the previous year, by negotiating reduced royalties with playwrights or New York producers, by maintaining low admission prices, and by projecting profits upon smaller audiences than did traveling companies, the popular-priced stock companies of the early twentieth century were able to compete with the higher-priced combinations. This formula for competing with the Road proved so successful that, by 1910, there were in excess of a hundred new stock companies employing more than twelve hundred performers throughout the country.

Institutionalized Tensions

During the first decades of the twentieth century, the industrialization of the American theatre, the advent of the theatrical businessperson, and the widespread adoption of contracts led to a radical transformation in actor–manager relations. Historically, relations between actors and managers had been informal, with few social or business barriers existing between them.

Managers were, for the most part, fellow actors who had risen from the ranks through managerial ability and ambition, participated in a company's daily working routine, and consequently understood the problems and hardships of the profession. As a result, negotiations regarding wages or working conditions were settled informally after rehearsal or over drinks in a local tavern. During the transition from the stock to the combination system, this collegial bond between artists was supplanted by a legal and economic bond of employee to employer.

The rapid shift to contractual relations and clashing perspectives and business practices was accompanied by significantly worsened working conditions for the journeyman performer and, in many cases, wholesale abuses. Under the combination system, there was no limit to the number of free rehearsals a producer might require; performers were forced to pay their own transportation costs from New York to the first booking location and back to New York once a show closed; half salaries were paid during certain holiday weeks (Christmas, Easter, and so forth), although the usual number of performances was presented; wages might be reduced without warning or a reason given; managers could require up to fourteen performances per week without raising salaries; or performers could be terminated with just two weeks' notice, in many cases simply because managers deemed that they were "unsatisfactory" and hence had violated the "satisfaction clause" in their contracts. During the combination era, stories of performers rehearsing without pay for ten weeks only to have the production close on the fourth night (resulting in payment for only four nights of work) or entire companies being stranded on the road were legion and circulated widely throughout the profession. Because managers realized that the actor's only recourse was to "go to law" for breach of contract, an expensive and impractical course of action for someone who spent most of the year on the road, and because many managers had incorporated, thus insulating themselves from potentially injurious lawsuits, such abuses became increasingly frequent near the turn of the century.

To many, the solution to intolerable working conditions and adversarial relations lay in unionization. By the end of the nineteenth century, the resistance of "labor" to "capital" had become a common occurrence. Industrial expansion following the Civil War, coupled with a tide of immigration that flooded the market with cheap labor, contributed to diminished opportunities and rapidly deteriorating conditions for the average American worker. Between the depression of 1873 and the end of the century, a period so rife with labor unrest that historians nicknamed it the "Era of Upheaval," labor's accumulated grievances frequently boiled over into violence, and Americans witnessed some of the bloodiest strikes in United States history, including the Great Strikes of the late 1870s, the Homestead Strike, the Pullman Strike, and the Haymarket Square Riot. Invariably violent and horrifying to the public, strikes nevertheless effectively closed industries and exacted concessions from management.

Consistent with this trend, late in the nineteenth century, theatre workers began to unionize. In the 1880s, stagehands formed local unions to demand that managers employ them, not actors, to change scenery. These locals became the foundation for the National Alliance of Theatrical Stage Employees in 1893 and later of the International Alliance of Theatrical Stage Employees (IATSE). By the end of the century, Yiddish actors had formed the Hebrew Actors' Union (1899), stage painters had formed the Protective Alliance of Scenic Painters (1885), stage musicians had unionized, and actors had established The Actors' Society of America (1896), a bold but ineffectual organization that was quickly squashed by the emerging Syndicate.

In December 1912, eight actors held an organizational meeting to discuss the formation of an actors' union powerful enough to obtain a fair contract from the managers and institutionalize relations with their association, the United Managers' Protective Association (UMPA). Based upon preliminary plans from this meeting, 112 actors met at the Pabst Grand Circle Hotel in New York the following May and formed the Actors' Equity Association to serve as their advocate in future negotiations with managers. Although the officers of the newly formed union intended to rectify all of the grievances mentioned previously, they were most concerned with attaining the right to bargain collectively, recognition of Equity as the actors' authorized bargaining agent, and an eight-performance week.

Initial reactions to the new union were anything but favorable: the press reacted with skepticism, the public with indifference, and the managers with contempt. The UMPA opinion was expressed most succinctly (and honestly) in Lee Shubert's curt, "no person who delivers as little as the actor is paid so much" (quoted in J. Anderson, 28). Although the UMPA attitude was seldom this overtly derisive, throughout early negotiations in 1914 and 1915, managers continued to dismiss Equity as a serious threat to their sovereignty. In view of previous actor–manager relations, their position was logical. In the past, actors' uprisings had been quickly and easily suppressed, and employers' associations similar to the UMPA, utilized in labor crises in other industries since the mid-1880s, had been successful weapons against labor disturbances. Further, the UMPA was convinced that the actors would be unable to reach a consensus on affiliation with the American Federation of Labor (AF of L), a liaison that both actors and managers knew was necessary for Equity to form a power block equal to that of the managers.

From the outset, performers interested in affiliating with organized labor faced resistance from colleagues who staunchly maintained that they were professionals. During the last two decades of the nineteenth century, other vocations (law, medicine, engineering, architecture) were reconstituting themselves as professions with the intent of controlling access to their fields, prescribing training of new members, and attaining the respectability and prestige that accrued to a profession. Earlier actors, most notably Lester Wallack, Edwin Booth, and Lawrence Barrett, had achieved professional standing during their careers, and clubs such as The Players conveyed respectability upon their members. Consequently, a significant percentage of the acting profession feared the loss of status that they believed would result from being considered "labor" and lumped together with hod carriers, meat packers, and dock workers. The debate as to whether the actor was an artist or a laborer continued unabated until 29 May 1916, when the Equity Council voted 890 to 21 to affiliate with the AF of L, despite its first president's promise that "the Actors' Equity Association is not *per se* a labor union, and it will never become one" (quoted in McArthur, 218).[3]

Although Equity became part of organized labor in 1916, three years of fruitless negotiation with the managers elapsed before it was spurred to take collective action. In the end, it was the refusal of the Producing Managers' Association (the PMA had replaced the UMPA in the spring of 1919) to recognize the legitimacy of collective bargaining and Equity's role as the performers' legal representative, two long-standing grievances, that triggered an actors' strike.

On 6 August 1919, at a meeting attended by fourteen hundred actors, Equity members voted to strike any manager who was a member of PMA or who refused to honor the Equity contract. Despite frantic, last-minute negotiations, many of them orchestrated by E. H. Sothern, shortly after curtain time the following evening, Equity headquarters was informed that "*Lightnin'* has struck." The Gaiety Theatre, where *Lightnin'* was playing, was just one of twelve Broadway houses closed on the first night of the strike. By 16 August four more New York theatres had been closed, the strike had spread to Chicago and Boston, and the stagehands' and musicians' unions had walked out in support of Equity. At the beginning, in the face of a spreading strike, the managers maintained a defiant front, sought an endless series of injunctions against Equity, and even started a company union, the Actors' Fidelity League (Equity labeled its members "Fidos"); but by the end of August, with only five Broadway theatres operating, their battle tactics consistently failing, and Equity maintaining a united front, the PMA realized that victory was impossible.

The strike ended on 6 September with the managers recognizing Equity's right to bargain collectively on behalf of the actors and agreeing to rectify all of the actors' grievances. However, although tensions between PMA and Equity lessened after 1919, they did not end. Some managers continued to discriminate against Equity members and, during the eighteen months following the strike, union members formulated and instituted what they termed the

"Equity Shop," a form of the closed shop advocated by labor union organizers. Thus, although adversarial relations between actor and manager continued and tensions became institutionalized and hardened after the Equity strike of 1919, performers gained a strong advocate for their profession.

Alternative Theatre during the Teens

During the teens, while the battle for control of first-class theatre was raging and actors were asserting their independence from managers, a segment of the American theatre community was rediscovering the social and artistic dimensions of the stage. Throughout the nineteenth century, as Ethan Mordden points out, the American theatre had remained subservient to the popular taste and reinforced the dominant morality of the nation (vii). Theatre managers regarded themselves as both artists and businesspeople and felt no need to distinguish between the commercial, aesthetic, and social missions of their theatres. By the beginning of the twentieth century, however, progressive managers and writers, dissatisfied with the constrictions and decadence of the commercial theatre and spurred by the sudden and savage cultural transformation taking place around them, asserted their independence from the theatrical establishment, repudiated their middle-class benefactors, and created an alternative theatre culture. In spirit, ideology, and form, the influences upon these theatremakers were clearly European in origin, based upon the work done at "art theatres" like Paul Fort's Théâtre d'Art, André Antoine's Théâtre Libre, Lugné-Poë's Théâtre de l'Oeuvre, Jacques Rouché's Théâtre des Arts, J. T. Grein's Independent Theatre, Otto Brahm's Freie Bühne, Yeats's and Lady Gregory's Abbey Theatre, and The Moscow Art Theatre, as well as upon the theoretical writings of Richard Wagner, Adolph Appia, and Edward Gordon Craig.

One facet of their "revolution" was predicated on the belief that the theatre, like the other arts and like other cultural institutions, had roots in the social environment and hence was a proper vehicle for social action. As Emma Goldman envisioned it, Americans caught in the throes of cultural change were confronted with a choice – they could either become part of the process or be left behind. Those theatremakers who chose to become part of the process responded by creating a politics of art that challenged and often repudiated the dominant social mores of their time. Both by importing problem plays by foreign social critics like Ibsen and Shaw and by promoting the work of native-born playwrights like William Vaughn Moody, Eugene Walter, Edward Sheldon, and others, the American alternative theatre of the teens began to examine social issues and to reveal social truths to those willing to watch and listen.

Experimentation with theatrical form(s) was equally radical. During the first decades of the twentieth century, progressive American theatremakers like Maurice Browne, Arthur Hopkins, Robert Edmond Jones, and Samuel Hume "went to school" on the theories of Wagner, Appia, Craig, Georg Fuchs, the Symbolists, and other European artists who proposed alternatives to the Realism and Naturalism that had become popular in both European and American theatres. For those not fortunate enough to study in Europe, as Hopkins, Jones, and others had, the 1911 visit of Gertrude Hoffmann's ballet troupe, which exhibited methods of staging pioneered by Diagilev and the Ballets Russes; Max Reinhardt's Oriental pantomime *Sumurun* (1912), which publicly displayed Craigist principles; and the 1913 New York Armory show that featured works by Picasso, Matisse, Rouault, and Duchamp, brought the European art world to the showplaces of New York. American experimental productions, like Hopkins's staging of Eleanor Gates's *The Poor Little Rich Girl* and Alice Gerstenberg's adaptation of *Alice in Wonderland,* followed, as directors and designers attempted to create a theatre that, like its European counterparts, was mythical, evocative, suggestive, atmospheric, and sensual. In the process, they provided American theatremakers a viable alternative to the Belascoesque facsimile realism that was gaining favor on Broadway.

Like their European predecessors, American experimentalists likewise transformed their performance venues, creating an American counterpart of the "art" or "independent" theatre of Grein, Brahm, and Antoine. During the teens and twenties, small, out-of-the-mainstream theatres like the Toy Theatre in Boston, the Wisconsin Dramatic Society, the Plays and Players Club of Philadelphia, the Little Country Theatre in Fargo (North Dakota), and the Provincetown Players, the Washington Square Players, and the Neighborhood Playhouse in New York, were sites of vigorous formalist and/or ideological experimentation. Dubbed "little" theatres (after Maurice Browne's Little Theatre in Chicago), America's art theatres were predominantly amateur organizations consciously founded as an alternative to the "show shops" of Broadway and as sites for the type of theatrical experimentation impossible in the commercial theatre. As such, they were the forerunners of Off-Off-Broadway and today's regional theatres. Intriguingly, in their independence, decentralization, and local nature, they were also reminiscent of the preindustrial nineteenth-century stock company.

Alternative Theatre during the Thirties:
The Federal Theatre Project

During the 1930s, there was a second and especially fervid wave of alternative theatrical activity – a left-wing workers' theatre movement designed expressly to subvert the existing social system and its art. Inspired by the agitational theatres of the Soviet Union and Germany, groups of worker-artists organized into companies like the Theatre Union, the Labor Stage, and the Prolet-Buehne for the purpose of staging militant labor plays and pro-communist recitations in workers' halls and outside factory gates. Although these theatres had their origins in the twenties, they were virtually ignored until deteriorating economic conditions during the Great Depression attracted attention to their anticapitalist message(s).

Convinced of their mission as shock troops in the vanguard of the revolution and thoroughly schooled in the techniques of political agitation, the left-wing companies of the thirties employed some of the most common theatrical devices from the handbooks of revolutionary art – the mass recitation in which an entire theatre company (and frequently its audiences) chants or shouts preordained slogans; the conversion ending; and the agit-prop (agitation-propaganda play). The latter, regarded by Ira Levine as the most extreme artistic example of the principle of proletarianism and the staple of the communist theatre of the late 1920s and early 1930s, was the Marxist attempt to wed "form to content, specificity to didacticism, character to situation" (xv). Tied to communist dogma, which insisted that revolutionary theatre be an objective correlative to the social environment of the moment, left-wing play-makers looked to objectively verifiable sources and then attempted to present what Levine characterized as an "imaginatively rendered explication of the political truth," much as Clifford Odets did when he dramatized the 1934 New York City taxi strike in *Waiting for Lefty* (see I. Levine, 167). Ultimately, by the mid-thirties communist policy makers came to realize that Socialist Realism, not the agit-prop, represented the best marriage between form and content and was more effective as a vehicle for disseminating ideology. With its slogan-laden rhetoric, soapbox speeches, hortatory chants, and cartoonlike characters, the agit-prop, over time, grew too polemical and insufficiently entertaining to convert large numbers of workers to communist doctrine.[4]

Doomed by improving economic conditions and their own inability to reach the American working classes, the left-wing theatres of the thirties nevertheless helped to introduce Epic theatre into America, fostered the spirit of experimentation and innovation, continued to challenge the dominance of the American stage by what one activist termed a "shopworn naturalism," and illustrated the power and potential of a theatre committed to social action and change.

Perhaps the grandest American theatrical experiment of the modern era was conducted by the most unlikely of sponsors: the federal government. By the early 1930s, the advent and instant popularity of "talkies" and the onset of the Great Depression had significantly curtailed theatrical activity, both in the nation's major cities and its small towns. In New York alone, the picture was bleak; roughly half of the city's theatres were dark, Actors' Equity estimated that upwards of five thousand performers were without work, and total unemployment in the theatre was thought to be as high as twenty-five thousand. Similar conditions existed throughout the arts. To artists and nonartists alike, working conditions in the early 1930s represented nothing less than the wholesale collapse of the nation's arts economy.

In 1935, the Roosevelt administration responded to the crisis by including four relief measures under the aegis of the New Deal's Works Progress Administration (WPA). The arts programs promised employment and vocational support to writers, musicians, painters, sculptors, and theatre professionals. The theatrical branch of the WPA, the Federal Theatre Project, was designed not only to reduce unemployment but to increase the American public's access to entertainment during the financial crisis while ensuring that theatre artists' skills remained "sharp" until the economy improved.

To head the federal government's initial attempt at theatrical production, WPA chief Harry Hopkins selected Hallie Flanagan, director of the Experimental Theatre at Vassar College and an acknowledged expert on European theatre. In addition to personal attributes, which suited her for a leadership position (colleagues described her as fearless, indefatigable, and incorruptible), Flanagan possessed a keen insight into the nature of dramaturgy, attained at George Pierce Baker's 47 Workshop at Harvard, and a sound knowledge of state-subsidized theatre, which she had acquired in 1926–27 while a recipient of a Guggenheim Fellowship to study in Europe. One of Flanagan's first acts following her appointment was to convene a series of conferences in Washington to solicit advice from members of both the professional and the nonprofessional theatres and to form the cadre of the newly created Federal Theatre.

The theatre that Flanagan and her colleagues wrought, although federal in scope, was organized on a regional basis. Five separate districts were created, each with a capital city (New York, Boston, New Orleans, Chicago, and Los Angeles) that served as a production and playwriting center and provided retraining and support services for the region. Organizationally, the Federal Theatre Project was divided into five producing units – the Popular Priced Theatre, which mounted original scripts by new playwrights; the Experimental Theatre, which tested new staging techniques; the Tryout Theatre, which allowed commercial producers to try out plays that they deemed "risky;" the "Living Newspaper," which was designed to employ large numbers of performers and to dramatize social issues of import to the Roosevelt administration; and the Negro Theatre. Under the auspices of these units, an astonishing variety of entertainments – vaudeville, circus, puppet shows, Yiddish plays, children's theatre, minstrel shows, Gilbert and Sullivan operas, and classics from *Uncle Tom's Cabin* to *Julius Caesar* to Eliot's *Murder in the Cathedral* – were brought to the American public.

The "Voodoo" *Macbeth* directed by Orson Welles for the Federal Theatre Project, 1936. Library of Congress.

Of all of the Federal Theatre units, the Living Newspaper and the Negro Unit attracted the most attention – both from the general public and from the censors. The Negro Unit was designed to reemploy and train African American artists "of all kinds." It was divided into sixteen producing companies headquartered in large metropolitan centers like Atlanta, Seattle, and Los Angeles, with the majority clustered in the Northeast. Of these, the New York company, which was based at the Lafayette Theatre, was perhaps the most talented, energetic, and prolific. It was this company that staged one of the most spectacular productions in the Federal Theatre Project's short history – the "voodoo" *Macbeth,* in which directors John Houseman and Orson Welles shifted the scene from Scotland to Haiti and portrayed the witches delivering their incantations to the accompaniment of a combo of African drummers initially contracted to perform in the Living Newspaper's ill-fated *Ethiopia.* In less spectacular but in no less significant fashion, the Federal Theatre Project Negro Units throughout the country brought theatre to audiences that had never before attended the theatre; dramatized the lives and achievements of François Toussaint L'Ouverture, Henri Christophe, Jacques Dessalines, and other heroes; drew a new generation of talented African Americans to the theatre; opened previously unavailable theatrical positions to black artists; provided the training necessary to perform their new jobs; and commissioned and mounted new works like Theodore Browne's *Go Down Moses.*

Finale, scene 26, from *Triple-A Plowed Under,* a WPA (Federal Theatre Project) production staged in Chicago, 1935. Laurence Senelick Collection.

The Living Newspaper, arguably the most unique and controversial element of the Federal Theatre Project, was created to employ large numbers of theatre workers. The Living Newspaper format, which had its roots in the workers' theatres of Europe and America, political cabaret, Brechtian theatre, Russian prototypes, and the *March of Time* movie series of current events, combined dialogue, speeches, mime, film clips, offstage loudspeakers, dance, audience plants, placards, slogans, and slides in order to dramatize and comment upon sociopolitical issues and to construct an epic sense of the day's headlines. *Ethiopia* (1936) examined Mussolini's imperialism; *Triple-A Plowed Under* (1936) depicted the political and economic conditions affecting the farmer in the 1930s; *Injunction Granted* (1936) focused on the history of management–labor tensions in America; and *One-Third of a Nation* dramatized the atrocious living conditions in the country's slums.

Regardless of the founders' intentions when the Living Newspaper was created and despite repeated claims of objective reportage, from the outset the format proved to be an ideal platform for New Deal propaganda, and it was attacked accordingly. Claiming that *Ethiopia* was insulting to Mussolini and jeopardized United States neutrality, the State Department prevented its opening; *Injunction Granted* was flagrantly and embarrassingly one-sided in its pro-labor stance; and *Triple-A Plowed Under* was considered a thinly disguised attack upon the Supreme Court for its declaring the Agricultural Adjustment Act unconstitutional and was branded communistic because it urged the formation of a farm-labor party.

Given Flanagan's idealistic and social-minded nature, the social progressivism of the Roosevelt administration, the inclusion of doctrinaire communists and union members (albeit in relatively small numbers) in all branches of the WPA, and the politically charged climate of the 1930s, it was perhaps inevitable that the Federal Theatre Project's agenda would be a political one. At its inception, Hopkins had proclaimed that the Federal Theatre Project was to be "free, adult and uncensored"; yet, from practically its first day of operation, conservative critics challenged its collectivist approach to social issues, scrutinized its productions, and attempted to exercise social controls over its offerings. In addition to the Living Newspaper productions already mentioned, *Battle Hymn* (1936), *The Revolt of the Beavers* (a Marxist children's play that Brooks Atkinson dubbed "Jack and Jill lead the class revolution"), and most notably *The Cradle Will Rock*, Marc Blitzstein's musical indictment of American capitalism, drew conservatives' wrath and were deemed propagandistic and un-American. There were also critics of the Federal Theatre Project within the American theatre as well. Commercial producers resented the Roosevelt administration for its interference with private enterprise, and Actors' Equity expressed its displeasure for the Federal Theatre Project's employment of amateur, nonunion actors. In the end, however, it was the Federal Theatre Project's patron, the government, that killed it. In November 1938, the Dies Committee on Un-American Activities initiated an investigation of Flanagan and her theatre that resulted in its finding the Federal Theatre Project subversive and dangerous. As a consequence, on 30 June 1939, the Congress of the United States terminated the nation's first attempt at subsidized theatre.

Opinions about the worth and contributions of the Federal Theatre Project, which were mixed in its own time, are no less mixed today. Detractors contend that it left behind little of lasting value, noting that after its demise and the end of the Depression, Broadway assumed "business as usual." Others, ignoring the fact that the Federal Theatre Project was created to provide relief, not to serve as a theatrical showplace like England's National Theatre, dismiss it as a failed attempt to establish a lasting national theatre. In response, defenders stress that the Federal Theatre Project successfully accomplished the objectives established for it and claim that its legacy is an impressive one. It offered relief to thousands of unemployed theatre workers; introduced hundreds of new plays; mounted 63,729 performances of roughly twelve hundred productions; and brought theatre to audiences estimated at nearly 30,400,000. Furthermore, during its four years of operation, it presented works in an astonishing range of production modes and styles, kept admission prices low, and demonstrated a willingness to bring theatre to "nontraditional" venues, all of which were instrumental in attracting large numbers of first-time playgoers and lower-middle-class and working-class spectators who had never patronized the commercial theatre. A rare theatre collective, in that it was organized regionally and not headquartered in New York, the Federal Theatre Project serves to this day as the paradigm of an alternative theatre: It was decentralized in an era of centralization, and it was a people's theatre in an era of growing elitism in the commercial sphere.

Conclusion

The end of the Depression and the onset of World War II brought a temporary respite from the maelstrom of change that Americans had experienced since before the Civil War. The American theatre of the forties indulged itself with escapist "fluff" like *Abie's Irish Rose* and *Harvey* and draped itself in a jingoism that signaled a return to the sentimentalism of the nineteenth century, as good and evil (Americanism and fascism during World War II) once again became clearly delineated. Yet, by the end of the decade, change was already beginning anew – change that would bring an end to theatrical monopoly, new alternatives to Broadway, a regionalization of the professional theatre, the inclusion of previously disenfranchised groups, and a radical ferment during the sixties that would rival the activism and the innovation of the teens and the thirties. As America moved toward the postmodern era and as theatremakers explored new meanings and revealed undiscovered temporal and spatial patterns, new forms and ideas began to push the old aside, the pace of theatrical innovation accelerated, and, as if to prove Warren Susman's contention that history is composed of transitions and transformations, the theatre once again began the process of restructuring.

Notes

1 Although there is no shortage of antecedents to the businessman in the theatre, Stephen Price, manager of the Park Theatre, and A. M. Palmer, creator of the Union Square Stock Company, are often cited as examples of men who had no theatrical background before forming their theatre companies. Bernheim, on the other hand, claims that the booking agent represented the entrance, on a large scale, of the businessman into the field of legitimate theatre.

2 The original Syndicate agreement of 1896 has been reproduced by Don Wilmeth in *Theatre in the United States: A Documentary History* (1750–1915), edited by Witham. It is document 147 (incorrectly numbered in the text as 144), 184–87.

3 Equity was prevented from joining the AF of L until July of 1919 because the White Rats of America, the Vaudeville union, already held the union charter for the entertainment field.

4 This description of the agit-prop originally appeared in my article, "Staging Scottsboro: The Violence of Representation and Class–Race Negotiations in the 1930s," *New England Theatre Journal* 6 (Fall 1995): 5.

Bibliography

Although no single narrative can possibly encompass the myriad changes that took place between 1870 and 1945, *The Search for Order, 1877–1920* by Wiebe and *Culture as History: The Transformation of American Society in the Twentieth Century* by Susman, both sophisticated, insightful analyses of fin-de-siècle America, provide a good beginning to the study of cultural transformation. Boorstin's *The Americans: The Democratic Experience* complements these well, especially in the area of consumer capitalism, whereas Trachtenberg's *The Incorporation of America: Culture and Society in the Gilded Age* examines the implications and impact of incorporation, not only in commerce, but throughout the entire culture. Hofstadter's *The Age of Reform* remains one of the most incisive analyses of political responses to growth in the late nineteenth century (in particular, the trusts) and to social injustice. In the area of intellectual history, *The Origins of Modern Consciousness,* edited by Weiss, contains valuable analyses, most notably an essay titled "The Reorientation of American Culture in the 1890's" by John Higham. Stuart Hall, in his essay "Notes on Deconstructing the 'Popular'" in *People's History and Socialist Theory* (edited by Samuel), establishes the importance of popular culture as a barometer for measuring cultural transformation.

There is no shortage of excellent books on the transformations that took place in the world of public amusement. Ehrenberg, *Stepping Out: Nightlife and the Transformation of American Culture, 1890–1930;* Peiss, *Cheap Amusements in Turn-of-the-Century New York;* Dulles, *America Learns to Play;* Nasaw, *Going Out: The Rise and Fall of Public Amusements;* and Butsch (editor) *For Fun and Profit: The Transformation of Leisure into Consumption* all provide excellent insights into the entertainment revolution both before and after the turn of the century.

Bernheim's *The Business of the Theatre: An Economic History of the American Theatre, 1750–1932* and Poggi's *Theater in America: The Impact of Economic Forces, 1870–1967* remain the basic works on the economics of the theatre of the late nineteenth- and early twentieth centuries and on the centralization and commercialization of the American theatre. Although they are now somewhat dated and some of their conclusions have been challenged by contemporary scholars, they are nevertheless mandatory reading for students of the structure and economics of the American theatre. McDermott, "The Theatre and Its Audience: Changing Modes of Social Organization in the American Theatre," in *The American Stage: Social and Economic Issues from the Colonial Period to the Present* (edited by Engle and Miller) is an excellent brief analysis of organizational development of the American theatre. A concise overview of the long run is provided by Frick, "From Uncle Tom's Cabin to A Chorus Line: The Long

Run on the American Stage," while Rosemarie Bank, in an article titled "Antedating the Long Run: A Prolegomenon," argues that Thomas Hamblin at the Bowery Theatre in the 1830s may have begun the "custom of continuous runs for successful plays."

In the study of transition from the stock system to the combination system of production, Peter A. Davis, "From Stock to Combination: The Panic of 1873 and Its Effects on the American Theatre Industry," and Bank, "A Reconsideration of the Death of Nineteenth-Century American Repertory Companies and the Rise of the Combination," are especially valuable in that they challenge conventional notions regarding the development of the combination company. In addition to questioning earlier historians' tendency to directly attribute the decline of stock production to the rise of the combination company, Bank lists alternate definitions of "combination." Reardon and Bristow, "The American Theatre, 1864–1870: An Economic Portrait," outline the economics of the precombination decade, while Menefee, "A New Hypothesis for Dating the Decline of the 'Road,'" provides a statistical analysis of the Road era. Phillips's article on Arthur McKee Rankin's tour of *The Danites* in *Theatre Survey* provides a prime example of the American touring process. Anyone interested in antecedents to the theatrical businessman of the late nineteenth century should read Lippman's doctoral dissertation, "The History of the Theatrical Syndicate: Its Effect Upon the Theatre in America"; Hewitt's "'King Stephen' [Price] of the Park and Drury Lane," in *The Theatrical Manager in England and America* (edited by Donohue); and Pat M. Ryan Jr.'s "A. M. Palmer, Producer: A Study of Management, Dramaturgy, and Stagecraft in the American Theatre, 1872–96."

Mary Henderson's *The City and the Theatre: New York Playhouses from Bowling Green to Times Square* is still the most authoritative study of the growth of theatre in New York and provides the necessary background for understanding the districting of the 1870s to 1890s. Henderson's ideas about the formation of New York's first theatre district at Union Square are developed further by Frick in *New York's First Theatrical Center: The Rialto at Union Square,* which provides a detailed portrait of the district. *City People: The Rise of Modern City Culture in Nineteenth-Century America* by Gunther Barth affords a firm theoretical basis for the study of the modern city.

Considering its significant impact upon the American theatre, there is relatively little written about the Theatrical Syndicate. Lippman's dissertation remains the most comprehensive single source. This study can be augmented by the following articles: Lippman, "The Effect of the Theatrical Syndicate on the Theatrical Art in America"; Milo L. Smith, "The Klaw–Erlanger Bogeyman"; Klaw, "The Theatrical Syndicate: The Other Side," which offers an admittedly biased defense of Syndicate practices; and, Lee Shubert, "The Theatrical Syndicate and How It Operated" (edited by Maryann Chach), which provides an equally biased account by the Syndicate's staunchest adversary. Burnim in his 1951 Master's Thesis expands upon Lippman's study of the effects of the Syndicate, adding that it should be credited with improving the overall physical conditions of America's theatre buildings and making playwriting more remunerative. Wilmeth's section (1865–1915) of *Theatre in the United States: A Documentary History* (1750–1915), edited by Witham, contains numerous documents relevant to this chapter, including Charles Frohman's defense of the Syndicate. McNamara, *The Shuberts of Broadway,* and Jerry Stagg, *The Brothers Shubert,* are the basic works on the Shuberts. Durham, "The Revival and Decline of the Stock Company Mode of Organization, 1886–1930," offers an excellent account of the popular-priced stock phenomenon.

Although written over sixty-five years ago, Harding's *The Revolt of the Actors* remains the best single history of Actors' Equity. A concise, "readable" summary of events leading to the Equity strike is contained in Lynn Rogers's "The Actors' Revolt" in the September 1996 issue of *American Heritage*. The reader interested in the actor's place in American culture, however, is advised to begin study by first reading McArthur's *Actors and American Culture, 1880–1920*, which provides a remarkably comprehensive overview of the actor's life and social position in the nineteenth century.

The New Movement in the Theater and *The Art Theater*, both by Sheldon Cheney, trace the development of an alternative theatre, whereas Mordden's *The American Theatre* (55–64) offers a brief, yet insightful interpretation of the Art Movement in the American theatre of the teens. *Left-Wing Dramatic Theory in the American Theatre* by I. Levine and *Drama Was a Weapon: The Left-Wing Theatre in New York, 1929–1941* by Himelstein are both excellent accounts of the political, workers' theatre of the 1930s.

The Federal Theatre Project is too vast a subject to be fully covered in a single work. *Arena* by Hallie Flanagan, the director of the FTP, is required reading and can be complemented by Mathews's *The Federal Theatre, 1935–1939: Plays, Relief and Politics; Free, Adult, Uncensored*, edited by O'Connor and Brown; and Whitman's *Bread and Circuses*. The latter is well worth reading, but may be difficult to find. For those interested in specific aspects of the FTP (like the Living Newspaper or the Negro Unit) a number of focused studies are available. Scholars interested in the most detailed materials and primary documents are advised to consider research at the Library of Congress Federal Theatre Project Collection or the comparable archive housed at George Mason University. Finally, Welles's and Houseman's Mercury Theatre received good coverage in Houseman's *Run-Through* and in France's *The Theatre of Orson Welles*. See also sources on the FTP suggested in Chapter 3 (Murphy).

3

Plays and Playwrights

Plays and Playwrights:
Civil War to 1896

Tice L. Miller

Introduction

Melodrama dominated American drama in the post–Civil War period as managers sought to attract a large popular audience by offering spectacle, sensational plots, and topical subjects. Success was measured by the box office. The ability to anticipate and satisfy popular taste, then as now, was difficult and required from playwrights a keen sensitivity to changes in the social and moral order as well as skill in crafting their plots in broad strokes to hold the attention of the public. Playwrights responded to and influenced public taste, shaping the experiences of the spectator in an ongoing and interactive process.

Arthur Hobson Quinn in his history of American drama credits Augustin Daly with laying the foundations for the post–Civil War American drama in the 1860s and 1870s, but one can argue that these foundations were established in the decade before the Civil War as the public began to abandon the standard repertory of the American stock company – Shakespearean revivals, eighteenth-century English classics, and nineteenth-century pseudo-Elizabethan romantic tragedies – in favor of more contemporary dramatic fare. Several milestones appear important. The success of George L. Aiken's dramatization of *Uncle Tom's Cabin* in 1853 and afterward suggested to managers that a fortune was to be made from plays that dealt with contemporary events and dramatized subjects of concern to most people, especially if they included sensational scenes such as Eliza's crossing the Ohio River on blocks of ice. Also the new sensational French drama, especially Dumas fils's *La Dame aux camélias* (*The Lady of the Camellias*), which, as *Camille*, Matilda Heron popularized at Wallack's in

1857, made old war horses such as James Sheridan Knowles's *Virginius,* and Bulwer-Lytton's *The Lady of Lyons* and *Richelieu* seem old-fashioned. *Camille* offered novelty and sensationalism in dealing with the life and death of a courtesan, but it also made that experience an emotional and personal one for most audiences. Heron played to forty-six sold-out performances in seven weeks, a major success at the time. Ada Clare, the acknowledged leader of the bluestockings, wrote of *Camille* in 1859 that "the plain, unvarnished tale of a woman who knew how to love and to grieve . . . had struck one of the keynotes of the world's heart."[1] Heron's overt display of passion in the title role delighted audiences at Wallack's, where the play ran for a hundred performances before touring.

Looking Back at Boucicault

It was Dion Boucicault, however, who found the right combination of contemporary topics and sensational plot devices to most influence American playwriting in the pre–Civil War period. Boucicault first came to New York in 1853, staying until 1860, during which he wrote two hits, *The Poor of New York* (1857) and *The Octoroon* (1859). He had won early fame with the comedy *London Assurance,* first produced at London's Covent Garden Theatre in 1841, followed three years later with *Old Heads and Young Hearts* (1844) at the Haymarket. These plays, which created such stageworthy characters as Lady Gay Spanker and Sir Harcourt Courtly, made him a rising star. By the time he arrived in New York in 1853, he had lived in France, married and been widowed, applied for bankruptcy, acted in his own productions, and become adept at adapting French plays, English novels, and short stories into popular dramatic fare. He was prolific, ambitious, and had an ear and eye for what was topical and theatrically exciting, and his skill did not desert him in New York. In 1857 the financial panic helped turn *The Poor of New York* into a hit. A year later, continued popular interest in the relief of the British Garrison in India helped make *Jessie Brown; or, the Relief of Lucknow* successful. In 1859 Boucicault drew upon a novel (*The Quadroon*) and the feelings excited by the slavery issue to write a thrilling action melodrama, *The Octoroon; or, Life in Louisiana,* which offended neither side of opponents on the issue. The following year his adaptation of Gerald Griffin's novel *The Collegians* as *The Colleen Bawn; or, The Brides of Garryowen* portrayed a quality of Irish life onstage that seemed real to his audiences when compared to the stage Irish characters of the past. Later he wrote other Irish plays, the most famous *Arrah-na-Pogue; or, the Wicklow Wedding* (1864) and *The Shaughraun* in 1874, the latter first produced in New York. Gary Richardson argues that Boucicault's Irish plays spoke "eloquently for a group whose movement into American society faced significant misunderstanding and a certain amount of overt discrimination" (124). The plays struck "a blow for Irish independence" and helped recent immigrants in the process of assimilation.

Boucicault seemed able to fashion stageworthy plays from all materials. The critic A. C. Wheeler wrote that he tailored his plays "to the restless and superficial needs and moods of the public, not by being abreast of the thought of our time, but by being abreast of its desires" (quoted in McConachie, *Melodramatic Formations,* 211). In *Rip Van Winkle,* written with the actor Joseph Jefferson III, Boucicault began the play with Rip as a boy to make the elder Rip more sympathetic. His dramatization was played in both London and New York, with Jefferson performing the title role for the next forty years. Boucicault capitalized on the popularity of Charles Dickens by dramatizing a number of Dickens's novels and stories, including *The Cricket on the Hearth* and *Nicholas Nickleby,* both in 1859. In *The Poor of New York* he utilized sensational effects such as a burning tenement house onstage to attract and hold an audience. He understood instinctively what the crowd wanted to see and gave it to them. Joseph Francis Daly called him "the master of stage sensation" (74).

It is not surprising that Boucicault's melodramas were successful. The rapid change in American society after the Civil War had pushed the population from small towns and farms into the city to create a new and restless urban audience. Bruce McConachie argues that his melodramas helped create a sense of identity for bourgeois audiences troubled with questions of class and authenticity. They promoted middle-class values such as virtue, thrift, hard work, domesticity, and patriotism. And they put middle-class characters and concerns onstage. It was his methods in the decade following the Civil War that were to dominate, especially as practiced by Augustin Daly, who became America's most successful playwright and manager. (See Vol. I of this history for additional commentary on Boucicault.)

Augustin Daly

Born on 20 July 1838, at Plymouth, North Carolina, Daly moved to Norfolk, Virginia, in 1841 after his father died, and finally to New York City in 1849. There he developed a taste for theatre, first managing one in 1856. Like Boucicault, he was an astute judge of public taste and wrote and adapted plays with broad emotional appeal. Boucicault's success at tailoring plays for popular actors served as his model. However, in the 1850s Daly's attempts to write for Laura Keene, W. E. Burton, and Joseph Jefferson III failed. He then turned to journalism. Aided by his brother Joseph, Daly contributed to five newspapers over a nine-year period (1860–69) including the *Sunday Courier, Evening*

Express, Sun, Citizen, and *The New York Times.* He wrote about the theatre and reviewed opening nights. But this was only a means to an end, and in 1869 he left journalism to pursue a career in the theatre as a playwright and manager.

His observations and criticism of the theatre while working as a journalist were important later in developing his own principles and practices. That prominent contemporaries such as Bronson Howard and Bartley Campbell also began their writing careers in journalism would suggest that the ability to describe the passing moment in the daily and weekly papers served as a valuable apprenticeship for ambitious young dramatists. In addition to teaching them how to capture the essence of a story quickly and in few words, it exposed them to the most newsworthy events of the day, including murders, train wrecks, robberies and society functions. A. C. Wheeler regarded the drama as something like the newspaper, dependent upon the moods and tastes of the hour. "What we want is more nowness in the serious drama," he reasoned in 1886. The drama like the newspaper should provide the public with "the freshest of everything" (quoted in T. Miller, *Bohemians and Critics,* 143).

In covering the theatre, Daly learned about standard theatrical practices of his day: What kinds of plays were in demand by the stock companies? What kinds of roles did star actors want? What kinds of effects thrilled audiences, and with what kinds of situations could they identify? In his spectacular melodrama *Under the Gaslight* (1867), Daly's heroine, Laura Courtland, fights to retain her place in society, both economically and socially; McConachie suggests that her plight would have been especially meaningful to business-class audiences, who themselves were anxious about wealth, social position, and respectability.

Daly's journalistic experience should not be overlooked in analyzing his plays. He depicted scenes reminiscent of those graphically presented in the penny press and daily newspapers about low life of the city and violent crimes. To be expected were sensational scenes involving new technologies – for example, railroads and steamships – as they were common to both popular journalism and melodrama. The best-known scene in *Under the Gaslight,* if not in American melodrama as a whole, is the rescue from the railroad tracks of the trussed-up, one-armed Civil War veteran Snorkey by the plucky Laura Courtland. Stage directions indicate that this was accompanied by spectacular effects, with sounds from a steam whistle growing nearer, the rumble of a train approaching, and "locomotive lights" glaring on the scene. Then, as Snorkey is pulled from the tracks, the rush of the train of cars past with a "roar and whistle."[2] In *A Flash of Lightning; or, City Hearthsides and City Heartaches* (1868), Daly presents the burning Hudson river steamer *Daniel Doo* with his heroine Bessie Fallon trapped inside. She is rescued, of course – Daly had learned from Boucicault the value of a last-minute rescue for sensational and exciting fare. Joseph Daly noted that "the class of plays presenting some feature of physical peril and rescue were familiar, and usually called in disparagement the 'sensational drama'"(75). Such heroics remained a consistent and important part of popular theatre in the nineteenth and twentieth centuries, with little changing except the technology: Steamships do not blow up today, but spaceships do. Underlying the spectacle and sensational plot devices of Daly's melodramas were assumptions about respectability, domesticity, and the work ethic, which framed a middle-class ideology for his audiences.

Like journalism, popular melodrama of the day must not only be sensational, it must find novel ways of being sensational. In *A Flash of Lightning*, a necklace disappears in the first act, and suspicion is thrown upon Bessie Fallon, who, believing the real thief to be Jack Ryver, the man she loves, refuses to implicate him. In reality a bolt of lightning has entered the room and destroyed the necklace, a fact that Jack discovers and reveals in the last act. The credible gives way to the novel, a not unusual situation for melodrama. Daly manipulates similar sensational materials in *The Red Scarf; or, Scenes in Aroostock* (1868) with the last-minute rescue by May Hamilton of Gail Barston, whom his rival has tied to a log about to be sawed in two and set the mill afire to burn up the evidence. This scene maintains maximum suspense while bringing the play to the desired outcome. Daly also produced novel effects with local color, by placing onstage recognizable scenes from various neighborhoods throughout New York. Wilmeth and Cullen point out in *Plays of Augustin Daly* that in *Lightning*, "the audience sees a Greenwich Street house, a scene on Fifth Avenue, an all-night's lodging cellar called 'Jacob's Ladder', and a Hudson River steamer" (30). These familiar landmarks placed the action of the play within the experience of Daly's audiences.

First Dion Boucicault and then Augustin Daly had helped define public taste after the Civil War by writing sensational melodramas about urban life. In 1871 Daly turned to the American West and California, topics of interest for much of American society, due mainly to the stories of Bret Harte. (Daly's western melodrama *Horizon* will be discussed below under *Frontier Plays*.) However, in the same year, Daly also guessed correctly that the public was more than casually interested in the subject of divorce, and he borrowed heavily from Anthony Trollope's novel *He Knew He Was Right* for his social comedy *Divorce*. The hit of the season, the play opened on 5 September 1871, created "extraordinary interest," and ran a record 200 consecutive performances with Daly regulars Fanny Davenport, Clara Morris, and James Lewis in featured roles.

In *Divorce* Daly contrasts two marriages, that of Lu Ten Eyck and her sister, Fanny. The former is a May–December match and is treated comically; the latter makes the point that jealousy can ruin marriages. Three years after her marriage to Alfred Adrianse, Fanny has continued her friendship with an old admirer, Captain Lynde. Alfred is jealous. He orders her not to see Lynde again, to which she replies: "Do you know what your words mean? If I am fit to be told that I must not see any man living, I am not fit to be any man's wife."[3] Alfred is not willing to grant Fanny the independence she desires, at least not until the end of the play, which features the stratagems of a divorce lawyer and a private detective. Ultimately, both couples stay married, mainly in deference to current mores, and Captain Lynde turns out to be a cad, but not before Alfred has admitted he is wrong and offered his wife a separation. Although the ending of the play is conventional, the questions raised about marriage and divorce are important. Marriage is presented as something resembling an equal partnership, and both Fanny and Louise are seen as possessing a great deal of independence. Joseph Daly reported of the first performance that "the play exactly suited the temper of the public. It did not preach, it acted its moral. The causes of trouble lay on the surface of everyday life. The whole play was an appeal to reason, to fairness, to justice" (110). The critic for *The New York Telegram* (1 October 1879), however, was more skeptical about the play's intellectual content, suggesting instead that the "satin covered furniture of the scenes and the handsome dresses of the actresses" played a greater role in its success (quoted in Sturtevant, 76). In other words *Divorce* was fashionable.

From the subject of divorce, Daly turned to that of misalliance, borrowing the plot of a religious British novel, *Her Lord and Master* by Florence Marryatt Lean, for another major hit, *Pique,* which opened on 14 December 1875, at the Fifth Avenue Theatre. Catherine Sturtevant has noted that the last two acts drew upon a contemporary kidnapping and borrowed from Victor Hugo's *Les Miserables* (239). Critical reaction over the next ten years varied from "best American society play ever written" to "irritating mass of mawkish sentiment and emasculated sensationalism." In *Pique,* the haughty Mabel Renfrew (who "adores foreign life and manners") marries the worthy Navy Captain Arthur Standish in a fit of pique when the man she loves, Raymond Lessing, proposes marriage to her wealthy stepmother. Captain Standish's father was a factory overseer, and Mabel comes to believe that she has married below her station in life. Doctor Gossitt tells her (and the audience): "There is no such thing as rank in this country" (Act I). Arthur's father blames the aristocratic view that "love, marriage and duty" are subordinate to pride (Act III). After Mabel confesses to Arthur that she has never loved him, he goes back to sea. An encounter with Raymond then convinces Mabel that she does love her husband and after countless heroics, including the planned kidnapping of Mabel's son and the rescue by the family, all is forgiven. The sanctity of marriage has prevailed.

Daly raised timely questions about marriage and class in *Pique,* although his handling of these issues never seriously challenged conventional wisdom. His dialogue was realistic, with its liberal use of slang and colloquial expressions, whereas his plot was conventional, romantic, and funny. Daly aimed for a popular hit and succeeded. William Winter in the *New York Tribune* (14 December 1875) noted that it "blended comedy, sentiment, and sensation in a way that will not fail to please the average tastes." *Pique* ran 237 performances in New York, toured extensively, and in at least two versions was produced in London.

Bronson Howard

Following Daly's lead in the 1870s, Bronson Howard wrote social comedies set in the business world, with the American businessman as a major character. To Howard each country had its own subject, and in America that was business. Born and educated in Detroit, Howard, like Daly before him, learned his craft as a journalist, writing first for the *Detroit Free Press* as drama critic in the early 1860s before moving to New York City in 1865, where he wrote for the *Tribune* and *Evening Post.* His first play, *Fantine,* a dramatization of an episode in *Les Miserables,* was produced by the Detroit Theatre in 1864. Howard knew how to tie and untie intrigue with clever dialogue and suspense. With the success of his farce *Saratoga* at Daly's Fifth Avenue Theatre, 21 December 1870, he launched his New York career.

After a modest success with *Diamonds* in 1872, and a failure with *Moorcroft* in 1874, Howard revised an 1873 play *Lillian's Last Love* as *The Banker's Daughter,* which was produced at the Union Square Theatre by A. M. Palmer in 1878. In a lecture at Harvard in 1886 called "Autobiography of a Play," Howard explained how *The Banker's Daughter* was rewritten to satisfy what he called the "laws of dramatic construction." Dramatists should deal "with subjects of universal interest," he believed, and the strongest is "the love of the sexes." Next in importance the play must be "satisfactory" to its audiences, which meant to Howard that "In England and American, the death of a pure woman on the stage is not 'satisfactory,' except when the play rises to the dignity of tragedy."[4] In the earlier version of his play, the wife Lillian dies; in his new version she lives because she is pure: "The wife who has once taken the step from purity to impurity can never reinstate herself in the world of art this side of the grave." Few playwrights of the period challenged this maxim.

Howard wrote well-crafted social comedy-farces that appealed to his audiences. *Young Mrs. Winthrop,* which followed at the Madison Square Theatre on 9 October 1882, was considered a major achievement by Quinn because it "placed on the stage for the first time in America a group of characters whose actions are determined by the power of social laws and the interruption of social distractions without making the prevailing note one of satire" (*History of the American Drama,* 52). In effect, Howard writes in the vein of Henry James and Edith Wharton about the successful business class in American culture and the social class to which it belongs. In the play, Constance Winthrop occupies herself with the social scene, and her husband Douglas spends all his time involved in his work. Their marriage falls apart. They separate after their daughter, who has been ill, dies on her birthday while Constance is attending a ball and Douglas is away from home. In a sentimental ending, they reunite. Although Howard makes the point that preoccupation with business and society can destroy family life, he romanticizes his characters' situation by making them and their setting attractive. The drama ran for 190 performances and was successfully presented in London.

One of Howard's best social comedies, *The Henrietta,* is a satirical treatment of business, finance, and Wall Street. The play opened at the Union Square Theatre on 26 September 1887, its run cut short at 155 performances when a fire destroyed the theatre. *The Henrietta* is set in the richly appointed private residence of Nicholas Vanalstyne Sr. the "Master of Wall Street," who has bought a mine called Henrietta "on a three-hundred-dollar bluff, in a friendly game of poker." After incorporating the mine for $20 million, he "bought the whole town, including two newspapers and an opera house, and all the railways, not to mention the branch lines and a steamship company, to say nothing of six million acres of public land grants." To Vanalstyne Sr. the business of Wall Street is like a high-stakes poker game. He takes great delight when he has bankrupted an old friend but then extends to him a full line of credit. He competes with his minister for the affections of the widow, Mrs. Cornelia Opdyke. His city-bred children, however, lack his character. His daughter is to marry an effete English Lord. His son Nicholas Jr. is trying to bankrupt him while involved in an affair that has produced an illegitimate child. Another son Bertie has yet to find himself. Dr. Wainwright, the family doctor, draws the distinction between generations: Vanalstyne Sr. is in perfect health because he "was bred in the country. His nerves were as firm and as cold as steel before he ever came to the city." In contrast, "The furnace-bred young men of New York are pigmies . . . mere bundles of nerve, that burn themselves like the overcharged wires of a battery." The fast living of Wall Street, he explains, is like "wearing your life out in the greatest gambling hell on earth." He describes the floor of the New York Stock Exchange as a dangerous place: "No outsider has ever been on the floor . . . and come out alive."[5] Dr. Wainwright blames the "telephone and the stock indicator" for bringing death to the homes of fashionable society as well as the offices of Wall Street. Even as Howard shows that an obsession with business corrupts ethics, friendships, family life, and personal morals, he romanticizes the businessman and Wall Street as a place with high risks, excitement, and adventure. Such sentiments helped create the myth of big business in America.

Although borrowing from the form and plot devices of contemporary French drama, the comedy is rooted in the tradition of American comedy in which personal initiative and accomplishment outrank any title, and country life, not urban life, is lauded. Any attempt at affectation, especially of the English or French, is soundly ridiculed. The play contains traditional comic types, such as the liberal minister, The Reverend Dr. Murray Hilton, who is interested more in stock tips and widows than in saving souls (much like the Reverend Cream Cheese introduced by George W. Curtis in "The Potiphar Papers" in *Putnam's Monthly Magazine,* 1853). Edward G. P. Wilkins's *Young New York* (1856) presented a similar type in Needham Crawl, who is more interested in "two percent a month" than in caring for his flock.[6] The foppish English Lord had been a staple of American comedy from the beginning, and Lord Arthur Trelawney, who is married to Vanalstyne's daughter, is typical, with his eye glass and quaint English expressions. A younger son, Bertie, apes the manners of the English Lord at first but in the end gains independence and, with a satirical touch, shows how to make money on Wall Street by tossing a coin. The main comic device is the name of Henrietta, which some of the women characters suspect is a seductive ballet girl. An excellent craftsman, at the end of Act III, Howard builds suspense and excitement superbly with the ticking of the stock indicator as the market is first driven down, then up, when Nicholas Jr. attempts to win control of Wall Street from his father. The success of this play (according to Stephen Watt it grossed a half-million dollars in its initial run) would indicate that business values were taken for granted. Critic John Corbin identified *Henrietta* as the earliest of a new kind of drama, the business play.

Howard's most successful play, *Shenandoah,* was not a social comedy about American business but a romantic melodrama set against the background of the Civil War. It began inauspiciously at the Boston Museum on 19 November 1888 but was withdrawn, revised, and produced by Charles Frohman at the Star Theatre in New York the following year, opening 9 September for a 250-performance run. Quinn and others have suggested that it owed its success to William Gillette's *Held by the Enemy* (1886), although Boucicault's *The Octoroon* (1859) and *Belle Lamar* (1874) and Daly's *Norwood* (1867) dealt with issues surrounding the conflict.

Gillette's *Held by the Enemy* had opened in New York, 16 August 1886, at the Madison Square Theatre after premiering in Brooklyn. Set in the South in a city occupied by northern troops, the main plot concerns the love of two Union officers, Colonel Brant and Brigadier Surgeon Fielding, for Eunice (or Rachel) McCreery, who is engaged to a Confederate officer, Lieutenant Hayne. Arrested for spying, Hayne is tried at court martial; later wounded, he pretends to be dead so his "body" can be shipped through enemy lines. Surgeon Fielding examines Hayne, but he is saved from Fielding's villainous intent when Eunice whispers to Fielding that she will marry him. The conflict focuses upon which man Eunice will marry, not upon the significant issues of the war, and in the final scene Fielding and Hayne step aside to allow Eunice to marry Colonel Brant. With a public not ready to deal with the carnage of the Civil War, battles and deaths provided merely the background for romantic plots. William Gillette had begun work in the theatre as an actor in 1875, learning quickly the need of crafting plays with roles for himself. After writing and starring in *The Professor,* which opened in New York in 1881 and then toured the country the following year, Gillette worked on two adaptations before writing his first successful melodrama about the Civil War.

By the 1880s the ground rules for discussing the war placed sectional differences firmly in the background. Reviewing the opening night of *Shenandoah,* Nym Crinkle (A. C. Wheeler) in the *Dramatic Mirror* (14 September 1889), praised Howard for making heroism rather than partisanship the theme: "There is an evenhanded recognition of the bravery of Northern and Southern men that will make the play just as acceptable in South Carolina as it will be in Boston" (quoted in Hewitt, 255). Jeffrey Mason in *Melodrama and the Myth of America* notes how, by the time Howard wrote the play, the war had been framed in the nation's discussion to create the myth of the Civil War (see 155–86). Slavery and other sectional differences were not emphasized, but instead the characters on both sides of the conflict were depicted as fighting for liberty and independence. All soldiers were brave and all fought for a noble cause. Political issues were put aside for safer domestic and emotional ones, as the mood of the country – especially the North – favored reconciliation. The ideology of reconciliation associated the masculine ideal of the war with the North and the feminine with the Old South. Union officers and the Confederate women they loved became a cliché of Civil War drama.

The main plot of *Shenandoah* does not concern the war itself but lovers divided by the conflict. Colonel Kerchival West of the North is in love with Gertrude Ellingham, the sister of his best friend, Colonel Robert Ellingham of the South. Three other love stories are contained in the play, including that of Kerchival's sister Madeline and Robert; that of General Haverill and his young wife, Constance; and that of Jenny Buckthorn and Capt Heartsease. Howard avoided taking sides or, better yet, embraced both sides. When Madeline confesses to her brother that she loves the Confederate Colonel Robert Ellingham ("His people are my people his enemies are my enemies"), Kerchival tells her: "Every woman's heart, the world over, belongs not to any country or any flag, but to her husband – and her lover" (quoted in Watt and Richardson, 223). By 1889, and the theatrical success of *Shenandoah,* the national discussion had moved from partisanship to reconciliation, from division to unification, from two countries to union. Assessing truthfully the chaos and destruction caused by the war would await a later time and later writers.

Meanwhile, Howard had contributed to national mythmaking, as would William Gillette's *Secret Service* (1895) and David Belasco's *The Heart of Maryland* (1895), which also minimized the sectional conflict and depended upon sensational scenes and love interests.

Howard returned to social comedy in writing his last plays, although they never attained the success of *The Henrietta*. In his history of America drama Quinn notes that his *Aristocracy* was "moderately popular," his *Peter Stuyvesant* (written with Brander Matthews) had limited success in 1899, and *Kate* was never performed. *Aristocracy* (1892) contrasted a rich western capitalist with an old New York family and a Prince from Vienna. Contrasting America's self-made aristocrats with the titled nobility of Europe had been a principle concern of native comedy since *The Contrast* (1787). Arthur Beaufort in *Wheat and Chaff* (1858) believed that true aristocrats are charitable and needed no rank to "herald their munificence." Zachary Westwood in *Nature's Nobleman* (1851) exclaimed, "Aristocrats! It riles me to hear the word – it hadn't ought to pass American lips; we are borrowing the notions as well as the fashions of foreigners." Howard's comedies show how the natural aristocrats of farmers and soldiers in pre–Civil War America evolved into the businessmen of the post–Civil War era. Nicholas Vanalstyne Sr. is the new American aristocrat. Even as Howard moralized about the adverse effect of business upon domestic life, he romanticized the American business class. The first American playwright to make a profession out of playwriting, he was a co-founder of the American Dramatists Club in 1891.

Frontier Plays

Augustin Daly had catered to public taste in 1871 by setting his new play *Horizon* on the western frontier, but this was neither new nor innovative. The frontier had remained a popular concept in American culture throughout the nineteenth century as settlers pushed west from cities along the eastern seaboard to the Ohio and Mississippi River valleys and finally crossed the Great Plains to California and the West. The first appearance of a frontier character, Nimrod Wildfire in J. Kirke Paulding's *Lion of the West* (1831), had been based loosely on the historical Davy Crockett. Louisa Medina's adaptation of Robert Montgomery Bird's 1837 novel *Nick of the Woods*, successful in 1839 at the Bowery Theatre, featured the larger-than-life character of Jibbinainosay and spectacular events set in Kentucky. The shift of the frontier to the far West was brought about by the gold rush to California in 1849 and then to other western states between 1859 and 1876. Going west was the means to start a new life and become rich. Bret Harte migrated to California in 1854 and after some experience mining in the Mother Lode, moved to San Francisco and turned his attention to journalism. He became editor of *Overland Monthly* in 1868, in which he published "The Luck of Roaring Camp" and "The Outcasts of Poker Flat." These were local-color stories about life in the mining camps and were received with acclaim across the country. Influenced by Harte, Augustin Daly found the western theme attractive enough in 1871 to write *Horizon.*

The play is a melodrama about the West, where soldiers fought Indians and where settlers of uncertain origins from the eastern seaboard developed the land. The plot is filled with colorful characters and western types, for Daly drew in caricature. In Act I Mrs. Van Dorp of Waverly Place asks the politician Sundown Rowse Esq. about the West and if settlers "ever change their names, when they settle there?" The unscrupulous but farcical Rowse replies: "If they are absconders, they mostly do. If there ain't no debts, nor no trouble about the law, they don't. I know one town where every inhabitant's got another name. They take ranks there according to the amount of debts they ran away from. The worst insolvent is elected Sheriff" (in Wilmeth and Cullen, 112). Rowse is traveling west to inspect some new lands obtained in a Congressional land grant and accompanying Mrs. Van Dorp's adopted son, Alleyn, who has been dispatched to his new army post. They are to look for Mrs. Van Dorp's husband Wolf Van Dorp, who has kidnapped their daughter Med and fled westward. Later, they all meet up at a town called Rogue's Rest, where Wolf has joined other disreputable refugees from the East, including John Loder, a gambler who is described by Daly as "One of the reasons for the establishment of 'Vigilance Committees' in the peaceful hamlet of the Plains." The sensational scene – as noted earlier, a trademark of a Daly melo-drama – is the storming of the stockade by Indians. *Horizon* includes many of the stereotypes made popular by Bret Harte: Wannemucka, the stage Indian; Sundown Rowse Esq., the crooked but comic Washington politician; Med, the "white flower of the Plains"; John Loder, the gambler who sacrifices his own happiness to save her; and the "Heathen Chinee," a highly racist Chinese stereotype that Harte's "Plain Language from Truthful James," had done much to popularize in 1870 (see Mason, 150–51). Usually treated comically, the stage Chinese appeared regularly in Western drama and literature.

Following closely after *Horizon,* Frank Murdock's *Davy Crockett; or, Be Sure You're Right, Then Go Ahead* helped turn into myth the historical Davy Crock-ett who had died at the Alamo. Written for actor Frank Mayo, the play was first performed at the Opera House in Rochester (1872), opening in New York at Wood's Museum, 2 June 1873, with Mayo as Davy. The plot is conventional and turns on the love interest and sensational heroics of the hero and blackmail by the villain. Davy Crockett is presented as a "rough but honest backwoods-man" who loves a cultivated young woman, Eleanor Vaughn, who has returned from abroad. He prevents her from marrying the weak Neil Crampton, whose uncle Oscar Crampton is forcing the match by blackmailing her guardian, Major Hector Royston, with some promissory notes. At the end of Act II, Davy rescues Eleanor from howling wolves when he uses his arm as a bar to keep the door of his hunting lodge shut. Scott's poem of "Lochinvar" inspires Davy to abduct Eleanor at the beginning of Act IV; he takes her home and then marries her in Act V. In 1874 A. C. Wheeler sat through the play twice at Niblo's Garden and applauded the basic theme of the play: western vitality and virtue triumphing over eastern weakness and corruption (see T. Miller, *Bohemians and Critics,* 145).

Although Bret Hart influenced other writers, he had little success on his own as a playwright. On 30 August 1876 *New York Evening Post* critic J. Ranken Towse, gave his first play, *The Two Men of Sandy Bar,* a mixed notice: He praised Harte for writing "original and powerful" short stories that were "full of vigorous life, and abounding in grim humor and simple pathos"; he objected to a drunkard and gambler receiving heroic treatment and complained that Harte had tried to include too many incidents in his plot – "material for half-a-dozen melodramas." Harte was a good short-story writer but a poor playwright, Towse concluded, because he did not understand the demands of the stage.

Towse had the same complaint about Mark Twain, who failed to follow up on his literary successes by learning dramatic construction. *The Gilded Age; or, Colonel Sellers* (1874), which he wrote in collaboration with G. S. Densmore, possessed merit for its character study of Colonel Setters, but according to the *New York Evening Post* (17 September), as drama it was "essentially worthless." *Ah Sin,* written in collaboration with Bret Harte in 1877, failed for the same reasons. The influence of Harte can be seen in a better frontier play, *The Danites; or, the Heart of the Sierras,* credited to Joaquin Miller, and produced in 1877 at the Broadway Theatre. Stridently anti-Mormon, the plot involves a young woman hiding in a mining camp disguised as a boy to protect her from a secret society of Mormons (the Danites), who are attempting to find and kill her. Towse (not a fan of frontier drama) found the plot absurd and the play marred by excessive talking and moralizing. He especially objected to the coarseness in language and situations. *The Danites* presented familiar types, including the evil Mormon and racist stage Chinese, "Washee Washee." Gerald Bordman has noted that this play remained popular as long as Mormons were viewed as villains or as "unsavory comic" (*American Theatre 1869–1914,* 110). Miller wrote other plays with western subjects but none attained success.

Bartley Campbell also followed the lead of Bret Harte and wrote plays with western themes. He was more successful in the theatre, because he was a better craftsman and understood the demands of the stage. Mason argues that Campbell made the myth of the West attractive for an eastern audience taught to value both civilization and the wilderness: "In spite of the arrival of women, politicians, and organized religion, Campbell's characters remain eternally located on the frontier; they have their wilderness and their civilization, too" (*Melodrama and the Myth of America,* 140). Like Daly and Howard before him, Bartley Campbell began his career as a journalist. Born in Pittsburgh in 1840, he began writing for the *Pittsburgh Post* sometime in the late 1850s. From this time until about 1872 he served as dramatic critic, editor, reporter, and writer of stories and verse, also penning at least two novels while working for various papers in Pittsburgh, Louisville, Cincinnati, and New Orleans. After writing his first play in 1871, he gave up journalism and focused on his playwriting. He worked for Richard M. Hooley's Theatre in Chicago, going with Hooley to San Francisco in 1874, where he met Mark Twain and formed his own company in 1876 to tour his plays. He had little success until his melodrama of mining camp life, *My Partner,* opened for a short run at the Union Square Theatre on 16 September 1879 and established his career. Audiences preferred his more conventional melodramas: *The Galley Slave,* which opened a few weeks later (1 December 1879) at Haverly's Lyceum, and *The White Slave,* which resembled Boucicault's *The Octoroon* and which opened on 3 April 1882 at the Fourteenth Street Theatre.

Set in a mining camp in the West, *My Partner* dramatizes the deep friendship of two miners (Ned and Joe) and their love for Mary Brandon, the hotel owner's daughter. Ned (who has been to college and wears the finest clothes) is presented as the less worthy, as he is intimate with Mary out of wedlock and gets her pregnant before he is murdered by the villain Josiah Scraggs. Joe, the more worthy man, marries her even as he faces hanging, falsely accused of Ned's murder. In the end, through the efforts of Wing Lee (treated comically but sympathetically), Scraggs is revealed as the murderer, Joe goes free, and Mary and Joe are united. Although melodramatic and sentimental, *My Partner* offers a tight plot and colorful dialogue, which frequently rises to the level of poetry. One example is Joe Saunders's speech to the dead Ned Singleton in Act II:

> I couldn't go away without a feeling that we parted friends – when I got down dar in the canyon – where we worked together, I sat down to take a last look at the old familiar spot. The dry leaves were a-dancin' in the wind, the birds singing in the branches, and the creek laughing among the boulders, as if there were no such thing as pain or parting – Everything came back to me. The days we worked together, the plans we used to lay for the time we had made our pile, and could afford to let the pick grow red and rusty in the mine. All your good acts came a-crowding around me, making me ashamed of myself, that I'd refused a hand I'd often been glad to grasp when I warn't able to help myself – and so I'm here – here to offer ye my hand, and to ask yer pardon.[7]

At this point Joe discovers Ned has been murdered.

To its audience, the play presented a moral problem: Mary Brandon's marriage to Joe violated the contemporary notion that a woman who has surrendered her virtue before marriage must die by the end of the play. This question upset some critics, including Stephen Ryder Fiske, although Campbell's thoroughly native flavor prompted A. C. Wheeler to write on 27 January 1884 in the *New York World:* "There are touches in 'My Partner' that might have been written by Walt Whitman or [Henry Ward] Beecher. They never could have been written by Tennyson or Matthew Arnold." On the other hand, J. Ranken Towse thought that Campbell had written nothing new or important, although the play did offer local color or at least what the audience would accept as local. Where Wheeler found originality, Towse found convention. Fiske believed that *My Partner* had original ideas but that *The Galley Slave* (1879) was deficient in plot and that *The White Slave* (1882) was a rewritten *Uncle Tom's Cabin,* whose purpose was "catch-penny, not artistic" (see T. Miller, *Bohemians and Critics,* 116).

In the *New York Evening Post* Towse complained that playwrights of frontier plays devised new plots but their characters and situations were secondhand. In his review (15 February 1881) of a now forgotten melodrama, *One Hundred Wives,* at Booth's Theatre, Towse points to what had become clichés of the genre: "An abundance of miners in flannel shirts . . . the inevitable Chinaman, the sanctimonious Mormon elder. . . . The heroine . . . who has been lured from her home and her husband in England by the elder aforesaid . . . the efforts of the wronged husband to recover his wife and child. Virtue has a hard time of it at first . . . but is finally triumphant, thanks to a company of U.S. troops and the exigencies of the occasion." Towse thought the frontier play worthless as a reflection of human nature. Writing some forty-years later, however, Quinn praised Campbell for successfully producing a frontier drama: "For the frontier is in some respects the most significant element in American history" (*History of the American Drama,* 124). By Quinn's day, Frederick Jackson Turner's seminal address before the American Historical Association in 1893 on "The Significance of the Frontier in American History" had become the accepted way of thinking about the subject. Revisionist history in our own time has challenged Turner's thesis that the frontier was a positive experience for everyone, pointing to the harsh experiences of marginalized groups such as the Chinese, Indians, African Americans, Hispanics, and women.

Edward Harrigan and His City Plays

A. C. Wheeler was not alone in encouraging the writing of plays with American themes and characters. William Dean Howells and Hamlin Garland, among others in the 1880s, argued that literature and the stage must reflect the life of this country. The author of thirty-six plays, Howells promoted the realistic movement in his *Atlantic Monthly* and *Harper's Magazine* essays, especially as manifested in the plays of Edward Harrigan and James A. Herne.

Certainly Harrigan's ethnic urban types (Irish, German, Italian, and African American) also could not have been created by British authors. Harrigan was called both the American Charles Dickens and the American Goldoni. Born in New York in 1844, he traveled widely, beginning his theatrical career as an Irish comic singer in 1867 in San Francisco. Three years later he was back in New York and the following year met Tony Hart in Chicago. They performed Harrigan's vaudeville-like sketches, mainly of the immigrant class, which later were developed into full-length musicals. With Harrigan portraying the male characters and Hart the female, they produced comic sketches with songs and dialogue that attracted a large audience at the Theatre Comique in New York, beginning on 2 December 1872. Orchestra leader of the Comique, David Braham, composed the music.

Harrigan became famous for his Irish characters, which he presented in a series of plays, the first of which was *The Mulligan Guard* in 1873. Quinn notes that Harrigan's characters, of which Dan and Cordelia Mulligan are the best drawn, reflect a specific generation, the Irish who came to New York after the famine of 1848 and remained in the cities of the East (86). Harrigan explained that "the primary idea of the first Mulligan play was to take off the target companies that were formed by young fellows anxious to identify themselves with politics."[8] The hero of the series, Dan Mulligan, is addicted to drink and quarrels; he is a veteran of the Irish Civil War and is leader of his clan. He is brave, honest, loyal, courageous, impulsive, and likely to become drunk and disorderly at the slightest provocation, yet forgiving and generous to his enemies. His wife, Cordelia, faithful and helpful, is later brought low by social ambition. Harrigan drew upon real life for his characters, and Richard Moody points out that Dan Mulligan was "modeled on a tailor in the Seventh Ward" (*Ned Harrigan,* 45). In these plays, the Mulligans are joined by the German butcher, Gustave Lochmuller, Bridget his wife, and their daughter Katrina. Also depicted in these sketches and plays are the Skidmores, the African American types, such as the Mulligans' cook Rebecca Allup (played by Hart); the barber Simpson Primrose; and the Reverend Palestine Puter.

The Mulligans and Skidmores belong to feuding militia companies. With their inventive comic antics in military marching and drilling, they create havoc in *The Mulligan Guard Ball* when the Italian Mr. Garlic rents the Harp and Shamrock ballroom to both groups for the same evening. After the Mulligans have enjoyed several songs and dances, the Skidmores arrive and chaos threatens the evening. Garlic saves the moment by moving the Skidmores upstairs and deducting ten dollars from their rent. During the ensuing dance, according to stage directions, a "crash is heard and the ceiling falls with Skidmores on it. Grand crash." The play ends with more songs and a cotillion, and the tailors Sneider and Rosenfelt attempt to collect for clothes ordered for the ball. The final stage directions call for "a scrimmage . . . during which enter Lochmuller and six butchers with cleavers. General melee and curtain." As in vaudeville, Harrigan's productions depended upon the skills of the performers to enhance an underdeveloped script.

The *Mulligan Guard Ball* ran more than one hundred performances and prompted six other Guard plays, which followed over the next two years: *The Mulligan Guard Chowder* (1879), *The Mulligan Guards' Christmas* (1879), *The Mulligan Guards' Surprise* (1880), *The Mulligan Guard Picnic* (1880), *The Mulligan Guard Nominee* (1880), and *The Mulligans' Silver Wedding* (1880). Moody, who includes *The Mulligan Guard Ball* in his *Dramas from the American Theatre,* notes that the plays were "Like the serial dramas of television, each new play began where the preceding one left off" (540). Later came other plays, including *The Major* (1881), which abandoned the Mulligan characters and presented Harrigan as Major Gilfeather, a Yankee character who lives on his wits and cleverness in deceiving people. *The Major* was a hit, playing more than a hundred fifty performances in New York. Successful in 1882, *Squatter Sovereignty* dramatized the conflict between land owners and squatters near the East River. *Cordelia's Aspirations* (1883) and *Dan's Tribulations* (1884) brought back the Harrigan characters. After more plays and more tours, Harrigan revived Dan Mulligan for the last time in *Reilly and the Four Hundred* (1890). *The Illustrated American* (24 January 1891) reviewed the production:

> Dan Mulligan has returned to New York. He is the type of its streets. He is as truly the embodiment of its popular life as Pulcinella in Naples or Figaro in Madrid . . . he has really had more influence in directing the course of the contemporary stage than any fictitious personage of his time. . . . Sooner or later our managers will understand the lesson which Dan Mulligan teaches. They will see that American spectators care only for the portrayal of American life.

Other publications praised Harrigan for the depiction of American urban types with realistic detail.

William Dean Howells saw in Harrigan "part of the great tendency toward the faithful representation of life which is now animating fiction." Writing in *Harper's Magazine* (July 1886), Howells noted that "Mr. Harrigan accurately realizes in his scenes what he realizes in his persons; that is, the actual life of this city." Harrigan "shows us the street-cleaners and contractors, the grocery men, the shysters, the politicians, the washer-women, the servant-girls, the truck men, the policemen, the risen Irishman and Irish woman, of contemporary New York" (quoted in Witham, 294). Harrigan presented realistic characters in local settings, but his plots were little more than excuses for his characters to sing and dance. The American drama did not follow his lead. Barnard Hewitt suggests that the popularity of his characters depended more on production rather than on text, and Harrigan "never learned dramatic construction" (*Theatre U.S.A.,* 249).

Charles Hale Hoyt and Farce Comedy

Charles H. Hoyt has been compared with Harrigan for drawing broad character types and putting them into farcicial and witty situations that depend more on vaudeville routines than on the machinery of the well-made play. Born in Concord, New Hampshire, on 26 July 1860, Hoyt grew up in New England and pursued an early career in journalism, writing for a time for *The Boston Post* as dramatic and music critic. He attempted playwriting in the 1880s, demonstrating a forte for comedy and farce. In 1890 he achieved success with *A Texas Steer,* a satire aimed at Texans and congressmen. *A Trip to Chinatown* was a huge hit in 1891, running 657 performances at Hoyt's Madison Square Theatre in New York. Hoyt wrote crisp and witty dialogue, introducing such broad types as Welland Strong and Ben Gay, men about town in San Francisco. These characters needed little excuse from the plot to break into song; old favorites such as "Reuben and Cynthia" would be sung simply to create a festive mood. In *A Temperance Town* (1893), set in Vermont, Hoyt suggested that all the respectable citizens, including the minister, were corrupt and that the drunkards were noble and heroic. Stephen Ryder Fiske, writing in *Spirit of the Times* (23 September 1893) attacked the play's didactic nature and dismissed the plot as trash. Earlier he had praised *A Trip to Chinatown* for introducing the "quaint and original" character of Welland Strong. To Fiske, Hoyt had demonstrated artistic promise until sudden fame spoiled him.

Steele MacKaye

Plays with romantic plots yet with realistic touches in character and situation epitomized much of the transitional drama of the 1880s. American playwrights did not embrace the drama of Ibsen at this time because the American public was not ready to receive it. Audiences did want to see *Hazel Kirke,* a domestic melodrama by Steele MacKaye, which opened at the Madison Square Theatre on 4 February 1880. MacKaye eliminated the traditional villain and toned down the melodramatic excesses of character and plot in favor of understated actions and natural dialogue. Set in England, the plot is conventional and turns on the marriage of Hazel, daughter of mill owner, Dunstan Kirk, to Arthur Carrington, who in reality is Lord Travers, an English nobleman. She has been promised to an elderly squire, Aaron Rodney, who relinquishes his claims to Carrington, but her father refuses to accept this. Although she marries Carrington, the legality of the ceremony is cast in doubt because it is a Scottish ceremony on English soil. When she returns home her father disowns her. She attempts suicide but is rescued by Carrington, and the marriage turns out to have been valid. This play was a huge success, running for 486 performances on Broadway and touring the country with as many as fourteen duplicate companies from 1882 to 1883.

Steele MacKaye fashioned another hit in 1887, *Anarchy,* a romantic melodrama set during the French Revolution that offered the usual contrivances and last-minute heroics familiar to nineteenth-century theatre audiences but that also spoke to social unrest in the 1880s. Opening 24 December 1887, at the Standard Theatre, it deals with the chaos caused by the Reign of Terror in a complicated plot involving Paul Kauvar, a hero of the Revolution; his secret marriage to Diane, daughter of the Duke de Beaumont; his rescue of the Duke from the guillotine; his escape from the death cart, after which he joins the revolutionary army; his rescue of Diane and her father from the Republicans; accusations of his enemies that he betrayed the Revolution; and, with the death of Robespiere, the announcement of amnesty for all Frenchmen, which reunites him with Diane. A. C. Wheeler, who knew MacKaye, believed that he intended to comment upon the chaos that follows a revolutionary period, to contrast the differences between "Liberty under obedience and Liberty under license."9 Percy MacKaye would later suggest that the play was his father's response to the trial of the anarchists involved in the Chicago Haymarket Riot of 1886. After one performance and before the execution of the anarchists, he changed the title from *Anarchy* to *Paul Kavaur,* perhaps, suggests Richardson, to diffuse the publicity associated with the execution (179). Wheeler in the *New York World* (1 January 1888) praised the play's heroic characters, thrilling climaxes, great suspense, and "action, action, action." But he argued persuasively that the playwright's social message had taken second place to the love interest between Paul and Diane.

For an audience that wanted "action, action, action," MacKaye successfully created larger-than-life characters and situations. At the same time he rid his plays of the worst excesses of melodrama and considered themes that dealt with social issues of his day. He remains a transitional figure in American drama, remembered better for introducing the Delsarte system of restrained expression in American acting (see Chapter 7) and for building two stages that could be shifted by an elevator at the Madison Square Theatre in two minutes (see Chapter 8).

Denman Thompson's The Old Homestead

American audiences in the post–Civil War period through 1896 were senti-mental and nostalgic, filled with notions of equality, progress, and "uplift," believing despite facts to the contrary that everything would turn out well in the end. Like their grandfathers, they idealized rural life and the Yankee farmer who was simple and honest but could match wits with anyone from the city. Playwrights had been building plays around this character type for a century. One of the most endearing, Denman Thompson's *The Old Home-stead,* began as a sketch in 1875 before the author turned it into a three-act play, *Joshua Whitcomb.* By 1886 the play had been revised again into *The Old Homestead,* which opened to great acclaim at the Fourteenth Street Theatre in New York on 10 January 1887. With Thompson in the role of Josh, the pro-duction ran for the rest of the season and would remain in the actor's reper-tory until his death in 1911.

Set at the homestead farm of the Whitcombs' in New England and at the Hopkins' mansion in New York City, the play contrasts city and country life, idealizing the latter. The plot turns on Josh's search for his son, Reuben, who, falsely accused of a crime, has gone to New York City and turned to drink. Josh's trip to find him in the city is humorously depicted, with Josh staying at the mansion of his nouveaux riches boyhood friends and learning about big-city ways. In a highly emotional scene at the end of Act III, he finds his son. Stage directions suggest its pictorial and emotional appeal: "Enter Reuben staggering . . . Josh recognizes him. He falls into Josh's arms and then falls on his knees. Josh bends over him." Josh speaks: "My boy Reub! Reub! . . . Why, it's my boy Reub!" (Thompson, 62). After a second curtain, Reuben "stands with his head on Josh's shoulder." In the last act, Josh is back on the old homestead awaiting Reuben's return on New Year's Day, and the play ends as Josh throws a dance to celebrate the occasion.

The Old Homestead follows a long line of native comedies in which rural innocence and purity are contrasted with the corrupting influence of city life. It is sentimental and farcical but with quiet and understated dialogue and scenes of local color, including for example, Grace Church in New York. Stephen Ryder Fiske, writing in the *Spirit of the Times* (15 January 1887) called *The Old Homestead* one of the finest plays yet written on American life: "Anybody who has ever lived in the country has encountered just such peo-ple and heard just such talk. As most city folk were born and bred in the rural districts, the familiar scenes go right home to the hearts of the audience. . . . It is like an old cradle song, heard again in late life." Homespun and shrewd, Thompson's kindly farmer dates back to *The Contrast* (1787) and was a spe-cialty of comedians such as James H. Hackett, George Handel Hill, Danforth

Marble, and Joshua Silsbee in the period between 1820 and 1860. The character of the New England farmer remained a favorite of American audiences throughout the nineteenth century and has occasionally resurfaced in the twentieth.

James A. Herne: Early Realist

It was inevitable that an American playwright would move beyond the effort to write a popular success and tell the truth about men and women. Steele MacKaye and Denman Thompson did not take this risk because there was no commercial reward for doing so. A better writer than either, James A. Herne is regarded today as the best American realist playwright of the period. In the 1880s and early 1890s, he contributed several plays to the American stage that remain important milestones of realistic drama. Born in 1838 in Cohoes, New York, Herne learned his trade first as an actor in the 1860s, playing in theatres on the East Coast and in Montreal, before managing the Grand Opera House in New York, touring in the West and managing theatres for Tom Maguire in San Francisco. While in California, he met David Belasco, and they collaborated on several plays, none important until 1879, when they wrote *Hearts of Oak,* the plot borrowed by Belasco from an old English melodrama, *The Mariner's Compass.* After failing to attract an audience with the play in California, they opened it at Hamlin's Theatre in Chicago on 17 November 1879, later taking it to Philadelphia and New York and then touring it. Although *Hearts of Oak* was not successful, it suggested that Herne was aware of the realistic movement or at least aware that public taste was changing. The play lacked a villain and a conventional hero, and it offered simple and colloquial dialogue. Herne biographer John Perry has suggested that the playwright was "caught between two forces: the old popular school of Boucicault and his growing conviction that drama should truthfully mirror the lifestyle of common people" (60).

Herne's next play was totally different. Based on American history, *The Minute Men of 1774–75* (1886) drew upon a number of literary influences, especially the novels of James Fenimore Cooper. To Perry the play reflected the style of Cooper with "breath-taking escapes, last-minute rescues, savage villainies, poetic justice, and pale-faced colonists, all sketched against a wide panorama of early America's struggle for independence" (68). It was not successful, although the strong female role of Dorothy Foxglove that Herne wrote for his wife, Katharine Corcoran Herne, remains colorful and interesting.

Herne followed this play in 1888 with a temperance melodrama, *Drifting Apart,* which shows the effects of drinking upon family life. Thanks to the crusades of the American Temperance Society, temperance plays remained popular throughout the nineteenth century, especially in the 1840s and 1850s, when the best melodramas were written. The plot of *Drifting Apart* is simple: Jack Hepburne, "skipper o' the *Dolphin*" gives up sailing and drinking to marry his sweetheart, Mary, the fisherman's daughter. They have a daughter, Margaret. Jack suffers a relapse fifteen months later on Christmas Eve and falls into a drunken stupor. Unknown to the audience until the fifth act, the events following in Acts III and IV are in reality a nightmare in which Mary and daughter die and Jack goes mad. But on Christmas morning Jack wakes up to discover that it was only a dream and that his family is alive and well. Although it had a lengthy run of 250 performances, *Drifting Apart* was not considered financially successful. Katharine Corcoran Herne suggested that the audience resented being misled.[10] Hamlin Garland liked the play's local color and scenes of quiet realism. It was his promotion of *Drifting Apart* and of Herne that encouraged the playwright to write *Margaret Fleming,* which was to make his reputation as a serious dramatist.

With Katharine Corcoran Herne in the title role, *Margaret Fleming* opened at Chickering Hall in Boston on 5 October 1891, supported by leaders of the realistic movement and attended by the city's most distinguished citizens. The play quickly became a cause for critics such as William Dean Howells – an Ibsenesque American play. The plot moved forward in a quiet and thoughtful manner with simplicity of effect. The characters appeared true to life. Asides and soliloquies were absent. The dialogue was natural and understated. The subject concerned society's double sexual standard, and the play's frankness about the subject offended critics and audiences alike.

Central to the plot are the infidelity of Philip Fleming, the child born to him and one of the mill girls out of wedlock, and his wife Margaret's blindness when she discovers the truth about her husband's adultery. The play contained several shocking incidents for its first-night audience in Boston. For instance, when the child's mother dies shortly after childbirth, Margaret unbuttons her dress to nurse the baby. The original version of the play did not end with a reconciliation between Philip and Margaret, and some critics were offended that Margaret would not forgive her husband. William Dean Howells praised the play in *Harper's* (June–November 1891): "It clutched the heart. It was common; it was pitilessly plain; it was ugly; but it was true, and it was irresistible." Stephen Ryder Fiske in the *Spirit of the Times* (9 May 1891) dismissed it as "commonplace, abortive, immoral . . . a play of seduction, adultery, and delirium tremens." *Margaret Fleming* was given a matinee performance in New York at Palmer's Theatre on 9 December 1891. Although it was supported strongly by Howells and Garland, the major New York critics were repulsed by its focus on unpleasant subjects: "The life it portrays is sordid and mean, and its effect upon a sensitive mind is depressing," the *Herald* critic wrote (quoted in Perry, 170). The play received twelve performances the following summer in Chicago with a revised script that made it less objectionable to critics.

Margaret Fleming established Herne's reputation, but it did not make him any money. His next play, *Shore Acres* (1893), was a huge hit, which owed its success as much to his own portrayal as an actor of the gentle and wise Uncle Nat Berry as to the idyllic portrait of rural life in New England. Uncle Nat, drawn in the tradition of the stage Yankee, fought in the Civil War to protect the Union, and now lives with his brother Martin and family on Shores Acres, near Bar Harbor. He is fond of his granddaughter Helen, who is "high-spirited and proud, yet simple and direct." She is in love with Sam Warren, a young physician attracted to the advanced ideas of Charles Darwin. Sam's books provoke a violent reaction from Helen's father, Martin: "I won't hev yeh a-bringin' them books here! A-learnin' my daughter a pack o lies, about me an' my parents a-comin from monkeys –" (see Herne). Martin will tolerate no argument on the subject of religion and orders Helen and Sam off the farm. They marry, move west, and have a child. Uncle Nat remains the gentle protector of Shore Acres, buying presents for his grandchildren, bringing the family back together, and in the last act, using a war pension to rescue the farm from foreclosure. The final scene of Nat shutting up the house, putting out the light, and going upstairs to bed is played without dialogue. The play ran five years. Gary Richardson sums up the reason for its success:

> The picture of quiet country life with its deeply felt affinity for family and the soil, its festive turkey dinners with friends, and its enduring faith in tradition was greeted by the original audiences with such enthusiasm, one suspects, because the play's incidents were reminiscent of the origins of many in attendance who had left such an environment for the seemingly greater challenges and opportunities of the city. (203)

Herne ended his career with two commercial failures. A Civil War play, *The Reverend Griffith Davenport,* adapted from Helen H. Gardener's best-selling novel, *An Unofficial Patriot,* ran only twenty performances at the Herald Square Theatre in early 1899. Howells, however, liked it, noting that "It is an attempt, and a successful attempt, to put upon the stage a carefully studied passage of life once real, in which only such incidents as express character are employed, and no mere effects are sought for the sake of effects" (quoted in Murphy, 25). A year later *Sag Harbor,* a reworking of the *Hearts of Oak* material, also failed to find an audience. At his death in 1901, Herne was praised as a pioneer in the advancement of realism in America's drama.

Augustus Thomas and Regional Drama

Augustus Thomas contributed to the growing body of plays about American regional life in the 1890s with *Alabama* (1891), *In Mizzoura* (1893), and *Arizona* (1899). While his plots were conventional, he re-created regional scenes, characters, and dialogue with authenticity. Thomas, born in St. Louis in 1857, grew up in Missouri, working at a variety of jobs, including touring with a theatre company and newspaper reporting, before he turned to playwriting. In 1890 he was hired by A. M. Palmer, manager of the Madison Square Theatre, to serve as play adapter. The following year other failures prompted Palmer to produce *Alabama,* which became a hit and established his reputation. It opened on 1 April 1891. The play is set in Alabama after the Civil War and concerns the building of the railroad by a northern company through a bayou. *Alabama* makes the point that with the war over and the country reunited, old resentments should be put aside and the growth of a united country allowed to go forward. Northern capital and southern natural resources are the means by which this will happen. Symbolically this theme underscored in North–South marriages, including that of Captain Davenport with Mrs. Page and that of Armstrong with Davenport's daughter, Carey. Thomas keeps the focus of the play on the spirit of reconciliation and romance, not upon any problems besetting the new South.

Scenes of local color rather than big themes characterize Thomas's dramas *In Mizzoura* and *Arizona*. The former, written for Nat Goodwin and produced in 1893, concerns the efforts of the frontier sheriff, Jim Radburn (Nat Goodwin) to win the affections of Kate Vernon, a young woman he has paid to educate, a gesture unbeknownst to her. His rival is the polished and charming Travers, a bank robber. The plot is a cliché of melodrama; however, Thomas has drawn his characters with realistic detail and depicted local scenes with an eye for regionalisms. *Arizona* (1899) is regarded as Thomas's best play before 1900. The characters ring true, the dialogue is crisp, and the suspense builds admirably. The plot involves the attempted elopement of a junior cavalry officer with his colonel's wife and the issues of honor and self-sacrifice made by a younger officer who accepts blame to keep the colonel from knowing the truth. The army post and ranch life in Arizona are authentically drawn, perhaps as a result of Thomas's visit in 1897 to Arizona to prepare for writing the play.

The West and the Civil War as Subjects

Melodramas about the West were popular in the 1890s mainly because of the public's continued interest in Indian insurrections. In 1893 David Belasco, with the assistance of drama critic Franklin Fyles, wrote a powerful Indian-

and-army play, *The Girl I Left Behind Me*. Belasco, who had been secretary to Dion Boucicault and collaborator with James A. Herne in the 1870s, had learned how to create theatrically effective situations using romantic plots, realistic details, local color, and American characters. The play is set at Post Kennion in Blackfoot country in Montana. General Kennion of the American Army and John Ladru of the Blackfoot Sioux are engaged in a struggle over the disruption of the Indians' sun-dance ceremonies. Ladru protests that the ceremonies are religious in nature, but Kennion has orders from Washington to stop them. What begins as a sympathetic treatment of the Sioux vanishes in the third act, when they kill several soldiers, attack the fort, and threaten to kill the men and "do worse to the women." The Twelfth United States Cavalry rescues them at the last minute in a scene of great excitement. Kate and Fawn, the daughters of General Kennion and Ladru, play important roles in the battle, especially Kate, who is engaged to one officer and discovers she loves another. With the Sioux out of the way, the last act is devoted to tying up the loose ends of the romances. Belasco builds suspense superbly, creating highly effective, albeit conventional, theatrical situations that stir audience interest. The Sioux are seen as blood-thirsty savages, much the same as they are presented in the popular journalism and literature of the period.

The success of Belasco's *The Heart of Maryland* and William Gillette's *Secret Service* in 1895 indicated that audiences were still attracted to romantic melodramas about the Civil War. The plot of Belasco's play concerns the heroics of Alan Kendrick, a northern officer, and his love for Maryland Calvert, a southerner. Alan is falsely accused of spying and sentenced to be executed but is saved by Maryland, who clings to the clapper of the old church bell so it will not ring and warn the sentries that he has escaped. This was a scene that audiences loved and critics hated. The most interesting character in the play is the Iago-like Fulton Thorpe, dismissed from the northern army and now a spy for the South. When confronted by Alan for his treachery, he exclaims: "I don't care which rag I serve under. I fight for my own hand." Shocked, Alan tells him that he is "unfit to serve the States," to which Thorpe replies "Damn the States!" (see Hughes and Savage). *The Heart of Maryland* opened at the Herald Square Theatre on 22 October 1895 and ran for 229 performances.

Gillette's *Secret Service* proved to be his most significant play and one of the best of the Civil War melodramas. It originally opened in Philadelphia on 13 May 1895, then moved to the Garrick Theatre in New York on 5 October 1896. For the New York production, Gillette replaced Maurice Barrymore and played the leading role of Lewis Dumont, who, posing as Captain Thorne of the Confederate Army, is spying for the North. He has fallen in love with Edith Varney, daughter of a Confederate general, who obtains for him a commission in the telegraph service. Benton Arrelsford of the Confederate War Office, also in love with Edith, suspects him and sets a plan to expose him. At a crucial point, Edith produces the commission from Jefferson Davis to save Thorne. In one of the most dramatic scenes of the play, Thorne secures the telegraph to send a message to Union forces, whereupon Edith reminds him that she has acted to save his life, not for any other purpose. Love wins over patriotism, and Thorne does not send the message, a decision that saves his life when he is captured at the end of the play. Traditionally, it is a Confederate woman who sacrifices her country for the man she loves, but Gillette has reversed the situation, skillfully gaining audience sympathy for the choices of these characters. He builds suspense well and maintains continuous action. The play was successful in London, toured widely in the states, and was revived frequently by Gillette.

Conclusion

American playwriting between the Civil War and 1896 provides a kind of barometer for the social and cultural changes occurring throughout the nation. The sensational melodramas of Boucicault and Daly met the needs of their audiences, who were seeking some kind of validation of their roles as individuals within society and at the same time an escape from the harsher realities of daily life. Their melodramas and later those of Bronson Howard, James A. Herne, William Gillette, Augustus Thomas, and others, dealt with the issues of the day: slavery, the West, divorce and women's rights, the stock market and Wall Street, problems of urban life, nostalgia for rural life, reconciliation of the North and South, and the upheavals of social position and class. Although they introduced native subjects, little else in the dramas was original. Rather, playwrights borrowed and adapted plots and characters or whatever else they needed. They did not wean American audiences away from love stories with optimistic endings, James A. Herne and *Margaret Fleming* notwithstanding, because Americans did not want to believe in unhappy endings. It was not the reality but the myth of America that audiences wanted to see in the theatre.

Yet American drama made progress in the twenty-five years following the Civil War, especially in the proliferation of plays with native themes, native humor, native characters, and native environments. The realistic movement softened the excesses of romantic plots and made local color and realistic detail in productions fashionable, and native writers braver in challenging convention. Since playwrights aimed for commercial success, it was only logical that they set as their task to please the public, not offend it. The romantic plots, the love interests, the continuous tying and untying of intrigues, and the building of suspense – whether it was accomplished by the stock exchange ticker tape in *The Henrietta* or by the telegraph in *Secret Service* – represented the materials of the playwriting profession. James A. Herne may have been courageous in writing and producing *Margaret Fleming* in 1891, but his next play, *Shore Acres,* with its sentimental plot and Yankee character, was an obvious attempt to attract a popular audience and make money. It would be in the twentieth century and after a world war before an American audience existed large enough and mature enough to view the reality of America onstage.

Notes

1 See the *New York Saturday Press*, 27 August 1859. Ada Clare was an actress, feminist, lecture, and writer. She was part of the Bohemian coterie that met at Pfaff's Restaurant and Bier Saloon in the 1850s. This group included Thomas Bailey Aldrich, William Winter, and Adah Isaacs Menken.
2 See *Under the Gaslight* in Watt and Richardson, 189.
3 See *Divorce* in Sturtevant, 103.
4 Howard, 14. Portions of the essay are included in Witham, document 237.
5 See *The Henrietta* in Halline, 407–53.
6 See Tice L. Miller, "The Image of Fashionable Society, 1840–1870," in Fisher and Watt, 243–52.
7 Bartley Campbell, *My Partner,* in Wilt, 73–74.
8 Quoted in *New York Dramatic Mirror* (14 June 1911), 1.
9 *New York Dramatic Mirror* (4 June 1887), 1.
10 Cited in Quinn, *America's Lost Plays, vol. 7*, ix.

Bibliography: American Drama, Civil War to 1896

If Arthur Hobson Quinn were writing his monumental *A History of The American Drama from the Civil War to the Present Day* in our age, he would have an easier time of it than in 1927. The number of books, reference works, newspapers, periodicals, and American plays published or made available through microfilm has increased dramatically. Two recent books have been shaped by the cultural wars and by new methodologies, including feminism, deconstruction, semiotics, and Marxism. McConachie's *Melodramatic Formations: American Theatre and Society, 1820–1870* provides a largely Marxist analysis of the interaction of plays and audiences in the middle years of the nineteenth century. Of particular relevance to this period, he discusses the melodramas of Dion Boucicault and Augustin Daly and how they helped create a business-class ideology and contributed to the hegemony of that class in America. He explains what role they played in the political and social life of the age. The second book, Jeffrey Mason's *Melodrama and the Myth of America,* focuses on five plays, two from this period, including Bartley Campbell's *My Partner* and Bronson Howard's *Shenandoah.* Mason, like McConachie, is interested in how these plays contributed to American ideology and national mythmaking. He discusses questions such as, what did the concept of the West as the frontier mean to an eastern audience in the 1870s and 1880s?

And how did plays such as *Shenandoah* help create the myth of the Civil War? McConachie and Mason do not make the same arguments, nor do they offer the same conclusions, but they do suggest new methodologies by which we can make sense out of the commercial theatre and drama of the period.

Two other recent books acknowledge the cultural wars but provide a more traditional reading of American drama. Murphy's *American Realism and American Drama, 1880–1940* analyzes the melodramas of the 1880s and 1890s as the beginnings of the realistic movement in this country. She discusses the plays of Steele MacKaye, Bronson Howard, David Belasco, and attempts by Bret Harte and Mark Twain to write successful plays. Her book includes a chapter on realistic dramatic theory and covers several of the issues raised by McConachie and Mason. A fourth book, Richardson's *American Drama, From the Colonial Period Through World War I* is a clear and concise one-volume history and analysis of the most important plays and playwrights of this period. Richardson, like Murphy, Mason, and McConachie, is interested in the interrelationship of society and the theatre.

Of great value in locating information on American plays are recently published theatre encyclopedias, guides, and companions. Gerald Bordman's *American Theatre: A Chronicle of Comedy and Drama, 1869–1914* provides brief but helpful narratives, including plot summaries, casts, venues, dates, and length of runs for some of the period's most memorable plays. Wilmeth and Miller, editors of the hardcover edition of *The Cambridge Guide to American Theatre,* include entries on plays and playwrights, as does Bordman, *The Oxford Companion to American Theatre.* There is a useful section of documents on drama from this period compiled by Wilmeth in Witham, *Theatre in the United States: A Documentary History, 1750–1915.* Helpful in locating plays of this period are Hixon and Hennessee, *Nineteenth-Century American Drama: A Finding Guide;* Meserve, *American Drama to 1900: A Guide to Information Sources;* and Wilmeth, *The American Stage to World War I: A Guide to Information Sources.* The books above supplement but do not replace the standard works on American drama: Quinn, *A History of the American Drama, From the Civil War to the Present Day;* Moses, *The American Dramatist;* Moody, *America Takes the Stage;* and Meserve, *An Outline History of American Drama.* Also helpful are the standard histories: Hewitt, *Theatre U.S.A., 1668 to 1957;* Hornblow, *A History of the Theatre in America from Its Beginnings to the Present Time;* Hughes, *A History of the American Theatre, 1700–1950;* Morris, *Curtain Time: The Story of the American Theater;* and Garff B. Wilson, *Three Hundred Years of American Drama and Theatre.*

Most of the plays discussed have been published in anthologies and collections or else are available in microprint collections, including the twenty volumes of *America's Lost Plays* (general editor, Barrett H. Clark), published by Princeton University Press, 1940–41. Volume 21 was published by Indiana University Press in 1969. Other collections of note include: Clark, *Favorite American Plays of the Nineteenth Century;* Halline, *American Plays;* Matlaw, *The Black Crook and Other Nineteenth-Century American Plays;* Moody, *Dramas from the American Theatre, 1762–1909;* Moses, *Representative Plays by American Dramatists;* Quinn, *Representative American Plays;* Watt and Richardson, *American Drama, Colonial to Contemporary;* and Wilmeth, *Staging the Nation: Plays from the American Theatre, 1787–1909.* An important resource is the Readex Corporation's microprint collection, "American Plays, 1831–1900" (American Culture Series, II), on microfilm.

Other books consulted about individual playwrights and plays include Fawkes, *Dion Boucicault;* Hogan, *Dion Boucicault;* Thomson, editor, *Plays by Dion Boucicault;*

Joseph Francis Daly, *The Life of Augustin Daly;* Felheim, *The Theater of Augustin Daly: An Account of the Late Nineteenth Century American Stage;* Wilmeth and Cullen, editors, *Plays by Augustin Daly;* Fisher and Watt, *When They Weren't Doing Shakespeare;* Cullen and Wilmeth, editors, *Plays by William Hooker Gillette;* Moody, *Ned Harrigan, From Corlear's Hook to Herald Square;* T. L. Miller, *Bohemians and Critics, American Theatre Criticism in the Nineteenth Century;* Percy MacKaye, *Epoch* (the life of Steele MacKaye); Thompson, *The Old Homestead;* Perry, *James A. Herne, The American Ibsen;* James A. Herne, *Shore Acres and Other Plays;* Augustus Thomas, *Alabama* and *Arizona;* and Ronald J. Davis, *Augustus Thomas.*

Plays and Playwrights: 1896–1915

Ronald Wainscott

Introduction

American dramaturgy from 1896 to 1915 was dominated by the commercial control of the Theatrical Syndicate, which launched itself in 1896 and quickly declined, beginning with the death of Charles Frohman in 1915 and the challenge mounted by the brothers Shubert (see Chapter 2 for a detailed discussion). Using a larger arena for demarcation, we find that the period is bounded by warfare: U.S. difficulties with Cuba were escalating alarmingly in 1896, resulting in the Spanish American War of 1898, and our first world war erupted in 1914. Although America did not enter the war until 1917, the first American casualties were recorded in 1915 with the sinking of the Lusitania. The year 1915 may also be used as a watershed year for the appearance of well-publicized modern art in American theatre and drama through the efforts of the Provincetown Players, Washington Square Players, and Neighborhood Playhouse, as well as efforts by theatre artists such as Arthur Hopkins and Robert Edmond Jones. Experiment in structure was rare in this period, with Elmer Rice's *On Trial* (1914) and its flashbacks being a notable but late exception. Speaking in terms of aesthetics and subject matter, it might be fair to claim that nineteenth-century theatre practice and anglophilic tastes persisted as the norm in America until World War I.

The period 1896–1915 as expressed by playwriting is not easy to define with authority. Although superlative examples of stylish comedy and melodrama, social thesis plays, sensational mystery, rollicking farce, and sophisticated spectacle abound, with a sprinkling of poetic drama, the period is often overlooked or given short shrift by critics and historians. The vituperative condemnation heaped upon the "show-shop" practitioners like Clyde Fitch and David Belasco by playwrights and critics of the 1920s and 1930s have gone a long way toward burying the accomplishments of the playwrights of the early twentieth century who created some of the most theatrically effective examples of plays that reflect a culmination of most of the important developments of the nineteenth-century American theatre.

This period also saw the appearance of a host of successful women writing for the commercial theatre. The achievements of many female playwrights of the era were primarily the creations of vehicles for popular actors and often provided economic independence for themselves – no small feat, indeed, and "money without glory" in Felicia Londré's account (131). Nonetheless, the string of successes by Martha Morton, Lottie Blair Parker, Lillian Mortimer, Rida Johnson Young, and many others, created an environment a bit more welcoming for the next generation of women playwrights, beginning about 1915, who contributed remarkable artistic work for both the commercial and Little Theatres of America. Of course this era also experienced the early stunning plays of Rachel Crothers, which stand with the best work of the period.

Without a doubt postwar playwrights effected remarkable advances in dramaturgy, but many of the plays of the era of William Jennings Bryan reflect great technical skill, more sophisticated melodrama than usually seen in the earlier nineteenth century, and an overwhelming demand for or expectation of stage escapism. Nonetheless, some of these plays provide a cultural reflection of the era, even if indirectly. What is clearly missing in most of the work is a direct assessment of or confrontation with the obvious vicissitudes and tensions of the larger world surrounding the microcosm of the American theatre.

A large number of successful playwrights had another professional occupation in the theatre or elsewhere, considered at the time their primary job by either the public or the playwrights themselves. Most successful playwrights were actors, directors, or producers, and sometimes all three – in stark contrast to the comparatively large number of solitary playwrights of the 1920s and beyond who often attempted to make their living solely by the pen. Three of the biggest playwriting names of the era – Fitch, Belasco, and Crothers – usually directed their own plays, thus controlling the vision of their work, and both William Gillette and Crothers were actors, frequently in their own dramatic creations. Plays produced by the Syndicate, especially, were usually viewed as vehicles for star actors like Maude Adams, Ethel Barrymore, or Gillette, but to be fair this perception of the acting star being far more important than the play was typical of public responses throughout the nineteenth century. Audiences and critics usually sought out actors rather than plays, a majority of which were British imports.

During the early ascendancy of the Theatrical Syndicate, another actor-playwright, discussed in the first part of this chapter, James Herne, was completing his career. Although nearly all of his important work, most notably *Margaret Fleming* (1890) and *Shore Acres* (1892), appeared before 1896, this Ibsen-inspired, near-realist, with his detailed characterization, local color, and authentic staging – or "art for truth's sake" as he called it in an 1897 essay[1] – informed much of the scenic, environmental, and character detail that would follow in the most lasting prewar plays. Although most of his plays can be labeled melodrama in form and display a penchant for sentiment, he avoided villains and often engaged the emotions of his audiences, including his last foray in the New England drama *Sag Harbor* (1899), completed just two years before his death.

Although Herne did not herald a new era of Ibsenesque American drama, despite his best efforts, some of his concerns are quite evident in the plays of Belasco, Fitch, and many others at the turn of the century, who either worked for the Syndicate, or, like Belasco, fought it while promoting their own work in their own theatres. What most of the successful playwrights before World War I had in common was a dedication to environmental reality, the presentation of a believable society (both rural and urban), and carefully crafted language deemed appropriate for the time, place, and characters of the play. Although social issues would appear periodically in some of these plays, what kept most far from the frontiers of Ibsen was their approach to dramatic structure, selection of sensational event, and conventional conclusion to the central problem of the play. Nearly all of the American work that ventured into topical material in these years verified "traditional values" of the age. Rachel Crothers is the most obvious exception to this general observation.

David Belasco and Surface Reality

It is surely no coincidence that some of the formative work of David Belasco (1853–1931) in California and on the road was in collaboration with James Herne in both playwriting and staging. In fact, as noted in the last section, their domestic melodrama *Hearts of Oak* (1879) was the basis for Herne's later *Sag Harbor*. Once an independent producer, however, Belasco wrote or collaborated on the text of nearly every play he directed. Although it is appropriate to connect him to Herne in his scrupulous attention to scenic details and authenticity of stage action, Belasco usually avoided the domestic activity typical of Herne. Belasco should also be seen as a descendant of Dion Boucicault, with his remarkable presentation of spectacle and sensation.

Although Belasco was working regularly in New York in the 1880s, his independent career took off forcefully in 1895 and dominated New York theatrical aesthetics until about 1915. He continued to write and produce until 1930, but the heyday of his career corresponds almost precisely with the period of study in this portion of Chapter 3. After 1915, many critics and audiences began to find him old-fashioned, as stylization made itself more evident in American production at the same time that film was stealing the thunder of the stage's realistic style and spectacular verisimilitude with location shooting and historical re-creation in such movies as *Birth of a Nation* (1915). Before the usurpation of film, however, no one perpetuated melodrama more forcefully or effectively than Belasco, who at the same time used his plays to promote the stars he credited himself with creating: Mrs. Leslie Carter, Blanche Bates, Francis Starr, and David Warfield.

The Belasco model play could be found in a number of successful sensational dramas, including Belasco's first success, *The Heart of Maryland* (1895), set during the Civil War. The heroine, Maryland Calvert, finds herself torn between her duty to the Confederacy and her abiding love for a Union colonel, a dilemma popular in many Civil War plays both before and after this one, as was illustrated in the last section of this chapter in such plays as Bronson Howard's *Shenandoah* (1888) and William Gillette's *Secret Service* (1896). Belasco's Maryland seizes the dramatic initiative and stabs a villainous Confederate officer to protect her honor. Then in a brief scene with little dialogue in the third act we see Maryland save the life of her escaping colonel by preventing the sounding of the alarm. Having climbed into a belfry, "Maryland leaps and clings with both hands to the tongue of the bell" as the watch attempts to ring it from below. "The bell moves higher and higher; she is dragged backwards and forwards by the swing," but the bell never rings (Belasco, *Heart of Maryland,* 235–36). Climactic or sensational scenes dominated by action rather than dialogue or personal revelation are typical of Belasco's dramaturgy.

Belasco's penchant for the exotic was first made dynamically evident in his *Madame Butterfly* (1900). This drama inspired the Puccini opera, which Belasco was also the first to direct (on Belasco as director, see Chapter 9). His love of the distant and foreign perhaps reached its peak, however, when he collaborated with John Luther Long on *The Darling of the Gods* (1902). Although Belasco cast Caucasian actors, all the characters in this play are Japanese and often speak snippets of Japanese words. The noble heroine Yo-San falls in love with Kara, an outlaw prince, and their lives end in a double suicide in a red bamboo forest. But a supernatural happy ending is effected by having the couple ecstatically reunited in what Belasco calls an "intermezzo." After "a thousand years have elapsed" the soul of Yo-San enters "The First Celestial Heaven" and glides to the shining ghost of her lover (Belasco, *Six Plays,* 223–24). Belasco's love of the supernatural is also evident in one of his most popular plays, *The Return of Peter Grimm* (1911), which features a ghost, viewed by the audience but unseen by the characters. This device, of course, has been frequently resurrected in many screenplays and teleplays over the years, from television's *Topper* to the pop film *Ghost.*

The Girl of the Golden West (1905), however, is the best example for demonstrating the Belasco method and value system. It is also a benefit to compare this play to *The Great Divide,* discussed later. This vehicle for Blanche Bates celebrated American regionalism and individual enterprise. The western melodrama set during the Gold Rush allowed Belasco not only to enshrine his beloved California but to create numerous local-color touches in scenery, language, and event with his careful re-creation of a saloon, a mountain cabin, and "the boundless prairies of the West" (*Six Plays,* 402). This play has most of the elements so familiar to us now in television and film Westerns: melodramatic form, eccentric character and behavior, much comic relief punctuating dangerous environment and characters, and occasional forays into dramatic irony. A typical scene that demonstrates simultaneous danger and humor presents much overlapping drinking, argument, and joking in the saloon, interrupted by a shot ringing out from the next room. Everything stops until an offstage voice cries, "Missed!" Then all characters return to their normal business (319).

As with most of his plays, except those like *The Return of Peter Grimm,* written for actor David Warfield, Belasco centers the dramatic action on the emotional struggles of a female character, in this case Minnie, a savvy young saloonkeeper whom everyone calls simply "the Girl." She is always armed with a pistol and can hold her own as the only white woman in this rough mining community, yet she has "no suggestion of vice," and is a friend to all (*Six Plays,* 327).

Belasco maintains the hero–villain dichotomy, modifying it somewhat by making dapper Sheriff Rance the villain who would have his way with the heroine, while the gentlemanly outlaw Johnson is the love interest for the Girl. The primary conflict culminates in a second-act poker game. Rance discovers that the Girl is concealing the wounded hero in her loft when his blood drips from above onto the hand of the villain. While the hero lies wounded and unconscious beside her, the Girl plays three hands of poker with Rance in which the stakes are her lover's life versus her own body, which she must sacrifice to the villain if she loses. After splitting the first two hands and seeing that Rance has the winning hand, the Girl cheats by pulling a false full-house from her stocking. The otherwise virtuous heroine chooses to cheat rather than sacrifice her love. In another curious touch, Rance respects the Girl's victory and does not betray the whereabouts of Johnson as the posse searches for him.

Although Johnson is caught once again in Act III and nearly lynched, the Girl demonstrates to her miner friends that her love for the hero is genuine, and they (including Rance) allow the two lovers to escape. Unlike Yo-San, the Girl does not have to wait for a thousand years and the next world to be reunited with her love, but the conclusion is still very like that of *The Darling of the Gods.* All ends happily for the romantic couple, because the Girl has reformed Johnson with her virtue and simple honesty (save one cheating event, which he does not witness) in the midst of chaos. Life in the West of the Gold Rush days is always a remarkable gamble, the play seems to say, yet honest feelings find their reward. What Belasco offered was undoubtedly what most American audiences wished to experience in this period. They had balked at the uncomfortable Ibsenism of Herne, especially in *Margaret Fleming,* but they clearly enjoyed the physical realism of Belasco, with his minute authentic details in service to conventional structure and sensational but ultimately virtuous events. Belasco guaranteed serious conflict with a happy ending and a reinforcement of the values that remained firmly in place until the debacle of World War I turned American culture and values topsy-turvy.

The West of William Vaughn Moody

The American West locations, evident in *The Girl of the Golden West,* were fascinating to many playwrights in the late nineteenth century, such as Bret Harte and Joaquin Miller, but one of the most successful efforts of this period juxtaposed the untamed "lawless" West with eastern decorum and establishment. Or one might identify the center of the conflict as the free spirit versus the Puritan ethic, a theme that appeared periodically on the American stage since at least Frank Murdock's 1872 *Davy Crockett. The Great Divide* (1906), the work of William Vaughn Moody (1869–1910), an English literature teacher, is seen by many critics as the great hope of American drama, cut short by an early death. Although he maintained melodramatic form here and in his later less successful *The Faith Healer* (1909), he attempted to imbue American drama with meaningful subject matter, a leap made more complete in the domestic drama of Rachel Crothers.

Like Belasco's Girl, Moody's heroine Ruth Jordan, a brave nineteen-year-old from Massachusetts, is nearly raped by three drunken men who invade her Arizona cabin when she is alone. She is spared the gang humiliation by Steven Ghent, a rough but compassionate gold miner, whom Ruth talks into saving her. He bribes one man with a string of gold nuggets (a device that haunts each act) and wounds the other in a gunfight for possession of Ruth. After "purchasing" her, however, he does not rape her but holds her to a desperate promise made in terror, forcing her to leave with and marry him. She considers killing herself but cannot bring herself to do it; as a result she suffers much guilt, which leads to illness and despondency. Although against her will, Ruth is strangely attracted to Ghent – and had ironically told her sister-in-law earlier in the evening that she hoped one day to find a man who was strong but "unfinished" like the Western desert she loved – and she battles Ghent through eight months of marriage by refusing to take anything from him and making sure that his life is as unhappy as hers. Although his marriage to Ruth transforms him (much as Johnson is converted by the Girl), the misalliance leads to separation, as Ruth goes home to Massachusetts to rejoin her family. As she leaves Ghent she tells him that she sees in him "the human beast, that goes to its horrible pleasure as not even a wild animal will go" (quoted in Moody, *Dramas from the American Theatre,* 746).

"O, that dreadful West!" Ruth's mother intones in the final act. "If my children had only stayed where they were born and bred" (748). The beast image persists, and the idea is perpetuated that disparate cultures and values are impossible to bridge (hence the title). We learn, however, that division also applies to Ruth's emotional state: "Ruth is one of those people who can't live in a state of divided feelings," her sister-in-law observes (750). This is apparently the clue to the final scene, in which Ghent and Ruth reach an uneasy reconciliation, which, like the later *Anna Christie* of O'Neill, allows us to view the conclusion as either happy or disastrous, depending on the audience's point of view. Although the reunion of the final moments is a poor decision for Ruth, who in real life would be facing a lifetime of frustration and pain, the staging and popular performances of stars Henry Miller and Margaret Anglin all but precluded the image of a doomed ending. Despite the darker tone of Moody, he shared with Belasco the apparent need to lift the audience with hope at play's end. Moody, however, seemed to have a foot in each of two very different dramatic camps: sensational melodrama and social realism. The resultant product was constrained but intriguing enough to invite lamentations from critics that had Moody lived he would have revolutionized American drama, a feat O'Neill was later credited with achieving.

Moody, like Belasco and others, also flirted with presentations of the supernatural world in *The Faith Healer* (1909), in which he presents a genuine traveling faith healer, Ulrich Michaelis, who calls himself "a wanderer, almost a fugitive" (see Quinn, *Representative American Plays,* 7th ed., 782). Michaelis is near the beginning of his "great work" and undergoes a crisis of faith and loss of his powers when he falls in love with a young woman, Rhoda Williams. Challenged by skeptics, who are led by a minister and a doctor, Michaelis fails to help a dying baby soon after he has inspired a paralyzed woman to walk again.

Once again Moody was fascinated with the power of the West. Although the action takes place in the Midwest, Michaelis grew up the son of missionaries to Indians in New Mexico, and now Michaelis, after a sojourn in the wilderness, has raised a young Indian boy from the dead. The new Lazarus has become his mysterious, mute, traveling companion. After gossip of the arrival of Michaelis reaches the area, a multitude of sick and suffering people surround the house where he is boarding and set up a vigil, awaiting a healing visitation. The frequent offstage cries, murmurs, and hymn singing create a mysterious environment for the action of the play.

Rhoda reveals herself as a fallen woman, and the town's new doctor, who is both fascinated by and rejecting of the powers of Michaelis, turns out coincidentally to be the man who "ruined" Rhoda. When the doctor tries to force her to go away with him, Michaelis rises up in wrath, drives the doctor away, declares his love openly to Rhoda, and finds his powers and faith restored. So it is human love that enables the restoration of the healer. What begins as an intriguing dramatic study ends, unfortunately, as a pedestrian, formulaic piece, except for the presentation of Rhoda. By giving Rhoda promise of a happy life with Michaelis, Moody was clearly breaking with nineteenth-century tradition and with the Bronson Howard mandate of killing off fallen women before the final curtain.

The Supernatural and the West as Treated by Others

Moody's and Belasco's fascination with the supernatural took many turns in the work of other playwrights as well. Josephine Preston Peabody (1874–1922), a protégé of Moody, created a poetic drama, *The Piper* (1910), which flirted with symbolism and clearly reflected a fantasy world much like many Provincetown Players and Neighborhood Playhouse experiments that would appear a few years later. Poetic symbolism was also clearly at work in Percy MacKaye's (1875–1956) *The Scarecrow* (1910), a seventeenth-century fantasy featuring a living scarecrow built onstage by a witch, and devilish Dickon, called by the playwright "a Yankee improvisation of the Prince of Darkness" (MacKaye, *Representative American Plays,* 7th ed., quoted in Quinn, 814). The play is full of instantaneous vanishings, magic mirrors, and incantations. This shift in tone is not surprising, given the recent invasion of European symbolism in 1909–10 with *The Blue Bird* and *Chantecler* on Broadway stages. One of the most fascinating uses of such symbolism of the period, however, *Poor Little Rich Girl* (1913) by Eleanor Gates, was dominated by a dream sequence in which a sick little girl dreams that her duplicitous nanny really has two faces. In fact the whole household takes on bizarre transformations, much like later Disney animated features.

The American West, however, continued throughout the period to be mined for its myths, mysteries, danger, and excitement. As noted in the previous section, Augustus Thomas (1857–1934) produced a successful series of local-color plays named for territories and states, including *Arizona* (1899), *In Mizzoura* (1893), and *Alabama* (1891). More in the spirit of Herne than Belasco or Moody, Thomas downplayed or eliminated the villainy so prevalent in western melodrama. *In Mizzoura* presents the reverse of the formula of *Girl of the Golden West*. The Sheriff, as indicated by Tice Miller, is Jim Radburn, an unprepossessing hero whose understated bravery in the line of fire is matched by his unwillingness to hurt anyone when he can avoid it. Although he is admired by the educated young heroine, Kate Vernon, she is enamored of Robert Travers, a bright and also well-educated man who unfortunately turns out to be a train robber. Kate tells him that her honest, homespun, and sometimes silly family "made the mistake of sending me away to school. I've seen a bigger world than theirs. I like you . . . because you are a part of that bigger world" (see M. Moses, *Representative Plays*, 476). Jim's first proposal to Kate is refused, but in the play's crisis scene Jim's selfless act of compassion for Kate's plight begins to bring her to her senses. Travers shoots a Pinkerton and flees when he is recognized as the elusive outlaw. He goes to Kate to hide him but is discovered by Jim, who, instead of arresting him, gives him his own horse to escape the searching mob: "I give you my horse, but I'm *damned* if I shake hands with you" (507). Like Rance in *The Girl of the Golden West,* the sheriff frees the outlaw for the sake of the heroine, but in this case the romantic bandit does not get the girl. Ultimately Travers is killed, and Jim is recognized by Kate as the worthy man he is.

Like most of the well-written plays of this era, *In Mizzoura* is replete with detailed local color, painstaking descriptions of frontier furniture and behavior, and carefully wrought dialects. Only Kate and Travers, for example, speak standard speech, whereas other characters have frontier dialects that reflect limited or no education. The second act, which has much dramatic tension, takes place entirely during the fixing of a broken stagecoach wheel in a blacksmith shop, all the details of which are carefully described. Near the end of the scene the wheel is remounted to the coach onstage, which is then pushed off. The physical business is unrelated to the dramatic conflict, but has the effect of making the action seem genuine: Thomas created an illusion of realism.

Thomas was perhaps at his best in an urban play, *The Witching Hour* (1907), a work at the halfway point of the coverage of this chapter. It explored the popular infatuation with the supernatural, specifically, hypnotic suggestion and telepathy. Set in Louisville, Kentucky, in the home of a professional gambler, Jack Brookfield, the action centers on this unlikely hero, who discovers his telepathic powers and learns to his regret that he has unconsciously used his powers for years to win at gambling and unwittingly caused a fellow gambler to commit a crime. Thomas introduces much discussion of comparative morality in the law and love relations but focuses the dramatic events on the supernatural activity. Jack's friend Prentice, who helps him recognize his powers, tells us, "every thought is active – that is, born of a desire – and travels from us – or it . . . comes to us" from others (see Quinn, *Representative American Plays,* 7th ed., 747).

Even the plot's central problem, the hysterical murder of a drunken gambler by Jack's friend Clay, is linked to Jack's unnatural fear of a cat's eye jewel that we are led to believe is connected to the netherworld of the supernatural, until Jack demystifies it late in the play. While Clay is on trial for his life and likely to be convicted, Jack influences the jury with his telepathic powers to gain an acquittal for Clay. After Clay's release, Jack is threatened by a politician, Hardmuth, because Jack has rightly accused him in the press of orchestrating the murder of the governor of the state. At the climax of Act III Hardmuth tries to shoot Jack, but the hero and Prentice stop him with their hypnotic powers. Despite the obvious guilt of Hardmuth, Jack ultimately helps him to escape across the Ohio River because Jack believes that he unconsciously put the murder scheme in Hardmuth's head by telepathy.

Once again in this period, and not just in westerns, a hero helps a villain escape the law, apparently a popular event in melodrama of the period. It is clear from this play and many others mentioned here that by the end of the nineteenth century popular American playwrights were intent on suggesting authenticity by muddying the moral code of their heroes and heroines and humanizing the villains. Yet the melodramatic form remained supreme. *The Witching Hour* is replete with talk and events centered on the supernatural, yet all is presented with full attention to realistic detail. Yet again Thomas provides a believable field in which to convince his audience to accept sensation.

Eugene Walter

Although also an urban play, *The Easiest Way* (1909) by Eugene Walter (1874–1941) opens in a western setting, in which Laura Murdock, a kept woman and second-rate actress from New York, falls in love with the beauty and apparent purity of the unspoiled West and finds her ideal mate, "a *real* man," in her words, amid the rocky canyons of Colorado (see M. Moses, *Representative Plays,* 726; subsequent page references refer to this text). She is as enamoured of the West and its men as Ruth Jordan of *The Great Divide*. Reminiscent of the earlier Moody drama, the action of Walter's play traverses disastrous territory for the fallen woman who wishes to go straight. We can find precedent for this melodrama also in the early realism of the demimonde plays of Dumas fils and Augier, especially in the latter's *Olympe's Marriage* with its exploration of the notion of "nostalgia for filth."

The splendor of a terrace overlooking a canyon at twilight "beautiful in its tints of purple and amber" is foreground for a vista of "rolling foothills and lofty peaks of the Rockies" (725). This is in sharp contrast with the New York interiors described in meticulous detail that fill the remaining three acts. Most notable among these is the near squalor of a run-down room in a theatrical lodging house, which chronically depresses the almost penniless Laura of Act II as she struggles to remain faithful to her western love, John Madison. While in Colorado, Laura and Madison had confessed their pasts to one another (he has not been pure either), but both pledge to go straight, while Madison labors to earn enough money for them to marry and live well. In the world of the play this seems to take him eight months, some two months too long for Laura, who loses all control once she is down to her last dollar and has pawned all of her expensive dresses and jewelry. "Every day is a living horror," she laments (764). Once she falls again by returning to her old lifestyle, she perpetually lies both to Madison and to her wealthy sugar daddy, Will Brockton, a middle-aged stockbroker, to whom she returns, unable or unwilling to survive on her own as Madison attempts to prepare economically for their future in the West. Madison had ironically foreshadowed her fall in Act I, even as he declared his love for her: "the habit of life is a hard thing to get away from. You've lived in this way for a long time" (737). Brockton also predicts her return and considers her romantic ardor in the West a passing fancy: "She's full of heroics now," he tells Madison, "self-sacrifice, and all the things that go to make up the third act of a play" (743).

Laura's fall is also strongly connected to the urban environment, much as the personal corruption in Clyde Fitch's *The City,* discussed later, is linked to loss of small-town values and environment. In fact, Walter juxtaposes Laura's decline with the salvation of Laura's friend Jim Weston, a marginally theatrical advance man, who finds happiness by abandoning New York and moving his wife and children to a modest house and job in a tiny town in Ohio. We see Laura suffer when she learns of Weston's luck, because she knows she will never match his contentment.

Subtitled in the program of producer David Belasco as "concerning a peculiar phase of New York life," *The Easiest Way* supports the belief that depraved habits are difficult if not impossible to break permanently, especially for women. The sexism and paternalistic attitude of the two principal men, both conscious and unconscious, resolves itself in a "gentlemen's agreement," whereby each agrees to tell the other of Laura's success or failure in keeping her vow. As Brockton phrases it, "If she leaves you first, you are to tell me, and if she comes to me I'll make her let you know just when and why" (745). Laura's failure to be truthful with either man of course also undermines this agreement, which seems to anger the men almost as much as Laura's betrayal of each of them. Brockton's ultimate judgment of Laura is summed up in his parting speech: "My women don't mean a whole lot to me because I don't take them seriously" (811). It is Madison, however, who is cruelest in his assessment of Laura and her duplicity: "you're not immoral, you're just unmoral, . . . and I'm afraid there isn't a particle of hope for you. . . . With you it's the easy way, and it always will be. . . . And you'll sink until you're down to the very bed-rock of depravity" (812).

Walter's explication of the sexual nature of Laura's relationship with Brock-

Eugene Walter's *The Easiest Way* (1909), as staged by David Belasco, illustrating his scenic practice (in this case, the purchase of the contents of a boardinghouse transferred to the stage). Museum of the City of New York.

ton was surprisingly graphic for the era, with each act offering several direct references to their activity even as she continues to profess her love for Madison. Brockton, Laura, and her friend Elfie, another kept woman, refer to their activity as being "on the game," and when Brockton traps Laura in her lies in Act III, he bluntly calls her a whore who is no better than "all the rest of the women of your kind on the earth" who find it impossible to be honest (783). In this confrontation the playwright drives Laura to complete hysteria, but unlike his nineteenth-century models, Walter does not allow Laura to go mad. She recovers her control and after losing both men, bucks up and utters her famous exit line: "I'm going to Rector's to make a hit, and to hell with the rest!" (814). Although much of the play is disturbing and at least cosmetically realistic, it is ultimately a villainless melodrama with a sad ending for the heroine, who still tries to lift her own spirits at the play's conclusion. In numerous ways the tone and subject of this play were pointing toward some of the 1920s work of O'Neill and Sidney Howard, especially *Anna Christie* and *They Knew What They Wanted*.

Turn-of-the-Century Melodrama and Social Drama

William Gillette

Any discussion of melodrama in this period must include contributions of William Gillette (1853–1937), whose *Secret Service* (1896), discussed briefly in the previous section of this chapter, and *Sherlock Holmes* (1899) not only served the acting talents of the playwright but perpetuated the popularity of the sensational melodrama as thriller into the twentieth century. Gillette was masterful at capturing acting detail in his stage directions, creating a moment-by-moment explication of apparent reality, and even insisted that a telegraph message in Act III be accurately clicked out. In fact the action and stage business are as important as the dialogue and surely take up half of the printed text. Gillette is fond of lighting effects and creates two scenes, including a fight, in semidarkness.

The Civil War–action play, *Secret Service*, features a fake Confederate Captain Thorne (the Gillette role), who turns out to be a spy for the U.S. Secret Service and who through much of the action is glib, sarcastic, and cavalier. When he is caught by a Confederate Secret Service man sending a secret message to the Union in Act III, for example, the southern officer asks, "Do you know why I didn't kill you like a dog just now?" Thorne replies, "Because you're such a damn bad shot" (see Quinn, *Representative American Plays,* 7th ed., 599; subsequent page references refer to this text).

Gillette is skillful at creating tension as he mixes romance, military intrigue, dangerous suspense, and personal vindictiveness. The action is almost continuous, as the four acts span only two hours throughout. A comic and romantic subplot between the secondary lovers provides absurdity to break the tension of Thorne's capture in Act III, and the ensuing domestic confusion allows Thorne to escape. The subplots are unified with the main action in the final act of this masterfully crafted play.

Gillette appears to be undercutting the usual heroics of traditionally drawn soldiers. Wilfred Varney repeatedly demonstrates his own juvenile absurdity while being quite serious about his own excesses, and Thorne appears to be almost without feelings, even matter-of-fact when facing execution. As Gillette reminds us in a stage direction for this scene, Thorne's face remains "utterly atonic – no attitude or expression of bravado martyrdom" (614). Although Gillette was more adept at sustaining tension and less interested in traditional heroics than Belasco, his approach to detail, staging, and effect reflect an artistic kinship with this other master showman.

Clyde Fitch

Although melodrama was still king during the administrations of McKinley, Roosevelt, Taft, and Wilson, the popular commercial theatre was also busily presenting stylish social drama that relied heavily on devices of both melodrama and manners comedy. Such drama, which centered on the wealthy classes, is perhaps best exemplified in the work of Clyde Fitch (1865–1909), who remained at the top of the American playwriting profession for nearly twenty years, convincing many audiences and producers to look upon American playwriting with more respect. In age Fitch was a contemporary of William Vaughn Moody, but he had written *Beau Brummel,* a popular vehicle for Richard Mansfield, in 1890 and was an established playwriting star by the mid-1890s. Every season from this point until his untimely death abroad saw at least one new Fitch production and sometimes plays running simultaneously. Although working for the Syndicate, Fitch almost always directed his own plays in an autocratic manner and created a degree of physical detail unmatched by anyone other than Belasco and Gillette in his period.

The prolific Fitch seemed preoccupied with exploring matrimonial conflicts among the wealthy classes and had a knack for writing exciting roles for women in which the central conflict was geared to the personality or unusual characteristics of his Gibson Girl heroines. Although some of his characterizations are suspect, such as portraying the tendency to extreme jealousy as an inherited trait in *The Girl with the Green Eyes* (1902), he effectively depicted domestic issues, such as, in the same play, the impact of jealousy on marriage or pathological lying in *The Truth* (1907). These issues were topical because of the growing interest in psychology in Europe and America. Fitch's interest in and conclusions about heredity are not unlike some of the choices made by Ibsen in plays like *A Doll's House* or *Ghosts*. Despite the sometimes serious subject matter of Fitch's plays, one could count on a happy ending, even if essentially grafted onto the conclusion, quite likely as a requirement of Syndicate producers.

Two works, especially, reveal a sincere interest in social issues, not only playing well on the stage but providing commentary on turn-of-the-century American values. *The Climbers* (1901) and his final play, *The City* (1909), produced posthumously, aroused audiences and are arguably worthy of revival nearly one hundred years later. Both plays reflect Fitch's approach to realism: He endeavored, he said, to present reality with precision and authenticity and without distortion or dilution.

In *The Climbers* much of the focus is on a family of society women left without the fortune they expected when the patriarch dies. The women range from frivolous to level-headed, and one especially, Blanche, epitomizes the kind of woman Fitch seemed to admire. When her foolish husband tries to keep her from understanding his financial affairs she tells him in a gloss on Ibsen, "Doll wives are out of fashion, and even if they weren't, I could never be one" (517).

The play abounds with comments on social climbing – obvious and subtle. A cynical socialite tutoring a young man with money but no social position advises the appearance of ignorance: "You mustn't let society see that you *know* you're getting in; nothing pleases society so much as to think you're a blatant idiot. It makes everybody feel they're equal – that's why you get in" (536). An outrageously comic scene reveals the pretentious widow and her like-minded daughter on the day of the funeral selling their new, unworn winter frocks to other young society women, since mourning clothes must be worn for the rest of the season. The scene, all business and one-upmanship with occasional references to the death, displays a shift to pretense and false sentiment. The play's mixed tone and stylish combination of serious drama, intrigue, and comedy is reminiscent of Oscar Wilde's *The Ideal Husband.*

Fitch had an excellent sense of visual detail and verisimilitude, not only suggesting authentic action like Belasco and Thomas, but commenting ironically and incisively on the action the settings supported. In Act III, for example, there is a near frolic in the snow by a new husband and his daughter-in-law, followed by an agonizing, repressed love scene between Blanche and her would-be lover, as fresh snow begins to fall. As the emotional intensity of the scene escalates, their ardor is interrupted by her angry husband, Sterling, who senses betrayal. Another intriguing scene in Act II is played in complete darkness when Sterling is forced to confess his financial swindling of his friends and family. Although the cowardly Sterling admits his fraud in what amounts to a brief radio play, he tries to use the veil of darkness to escape.

In a twist from the expected, Fitch reverts to traditional values by having the horribly wronged Blanche decide against divorcing her unworthy, criminal husband when every instinct (but not conventional morality of the time) tells her to leave him. Fitch gets her off the hook, however, by having Sterling commit suicide with an overdose of morphine. Ironically, as the play is ending, Blanche thinks her husband is only sleeping on the couch, so her freedom from his oppression is known by the audience even as the heroine leaves the stage, thinking she is doomed to a life of unhappiness. Fitch seems prophetic in a statement uttered by Blanche's aunt when the big decision of Blanche still hangs in the balance: "We are all for ourselves; the twentieth century is to be a glorification of selfishness, the Era of Egotism!" (683). This statement could apply to an enormous number of American plays that trace the development of modern American culture.

An emotional fervor, rare in the theatre, surrounded the production of

Fitch's *The City* because of the death of the playwright shortly before the play went into production. Most recently such excitement was stirred by the musical *Rent* (1996), when its young creator, Jonathan Larson, died suddenly. At the opening of *The City* the press reported fainting and hysterics among female audience members in response to the intensity and language of the play, often claiming that "Fitchian" language exceeded all previous efforts to breach the gates of acceptable stage dialogue. This play reportedly introduced the words "God damn" to the American stage, but Fitch was careful to put the words in the mouth of a shady character, Hannock, who is blackmailing first Rand Sr. and then George. To the former he threatens to publish incriminating letters: "The anti-saloon paper, that hates you for not joining its movement, would be glad to get them and show you up for a God damned white sepulchre!" (see Moody, *Dramas,* 826; subsequent page references refer to this text). Ironically, Hannock does not realize the most damaging fact: that *he* is himself the illegitimate son of Rand Sr. Because no one tells him the truth, he seduces and elopes with George's sister and Hannock's half-sister Cicely and is unwittingly on the verge of committing incest with her when George finally reveals Hannock's parentage. This was surely the play's most shocking moment, culminating in Hannock's mad scene in which he shoots Cicely to keep her from discovering the truth.

In one respect at least this play fell outside Fitch's previous work, in which the female characters are repeatedly subordinated to male aggression. His women are always in a subordinate social position, as would be expected from a historical standpoint, but Fitch usually made his women prominent dramatically. In this play the men keep all of their business strictly from their wives. There is no Blanche Sterling here to discover the corruption of her husband. The typical melodramatic theme of a ruined woman in the past does surface, but only as reportage to demonstrate the inherited weakness of Hannock, who also turns out to be a drug fiend and the closest character to a villain in the play. Although Hannock sits in the antagonist's position, Fitch is careful to dirty up his hero George and many supporting characters in order to present a believable and complex cross section of family and business associates in his tale of rise and fall in the business world. In fact Fitch uses heredity and environment carefully to connect the corruption in George to his businessman father, George Sr., who turns out to be the out-of-wedlock father of the disturbed Hannock. "Following in father's footsteps, all right," Hannock says of George after discovering the son's crooked business deals, "and going Popper one better!" (832). The death of George Sr. from a heart attack in the first act sets in motion a severe reorganization of the family and contributes to the play's crisis, just as the father's death in *The Climbers* makes possible the play's dramatic development. This early scene allows the heart attack to develop slowly, unlike the sudden onstage stroke so typical of much dramatic fare. After the dying father stumbles offstage the playing space remains essentially empty as the family and servants panic over his attack. We hear much offstage dialogue and see occasional hurried comings and goings, as if we are voyeurs with an awkward watching place, trying to piece together the family crisis. This device, like the darkness scene in *The Climbers,* reflects Fitch's clever visual composition made manifest in the written text and his penchant for novelty in staging – which he most likely would be executing himself. Fitch also introduces an unusual scenic twist in the final act by returning to the location of the previous act but "seen from another point of view," like changing camera angles in a film (849). The audience now sees what had been the "fourth wall" earlier.

The major theme of the play is business corruption and the influence of urban life on the corruptibility of the young and impressionable. We must not overlook, however, the playwright's careful placement of a predisposition to evil and manipulation in his principal male characters *before* they move to New York. *The City* is probably the most hard-hitting of the business plays that appeared regularly from the 1890s until a new wave of even more caustic antibusiness plays between 1923 and 1929. Corruption in business was very topical because of frequent muckraking, trust-busting, and Theodore Roosevelt's campaign to undermine business and municipal corruption, the most famous being the excesses of Standard Oil. Many American writers and politicians were finally recognizing the failures of urban-industrial society. It is not coincidental that Upton Sinclair's *The Jungle* appeared in the same year as *The City.*

Ultimately, one might be disappointed by the play's moralizing, but its structure and tone are very consistent with a host of late-twentieth-century television dramas. Many of the play's major features also continue to dominate popular teleplays: divorce, profligacy, drug abuse, murder, near incest, and madness. Fitch's drug addiction scenes are the most graphic of its time, no doubt influencing efforts of many later playwrights of the 1920s who often used this theme. In the second act, for example, Fitch has Hannock onstage shoot up with a hypodermic just above his wrist, looking about furtively lest he be interrupted and "half grinning and murmuring to himself" (831), and late in the play Hannock has a mad scene in which he completely loses control and kills the woman he loves.

Mitchell's The New York Idea

The Fitchian elevated style and verve were approached, if not matched, in one play by Langdon Mitchell (1862–1935), *The New York Idea* (1906), which explores humorously the growing popularity of divorce among the moneyed elite of the most populous of American cities. As one character observes in a line destined for advertising, "New York is bounded on the North, South, East and West by the state of Divorce" (775). The play, with its edge and much stylish comic action, is not unlike the later *Private Lives* of Noël Coward with its mismatched couples, until the final act, when the mood turns sentimental and a high-spirited divorced couple is reunited.

Like Fitch, Mitchell provides considerable detail in stage directions, but most is dedicated to explication of character. Mitchell often complained about Broadway's scenic expense, yet he called for three different realistic interiors in the homes of socialites. And because one set is transformed for a wedding, he essentially called for four rich settings. Unlike most of his professional contemporaries, Mitchell's demands for physical verisimilitude are mostly implied by brief descriptions of the locales rather than painstaking details.

With characters, however, he often interjects delightful descriptions, resembling the efforts of Bernard Shaw and clearly meant to delight the reader or inspire the actor. Vida Phillimore, for example, when trying to pose for a would-be lover "is turned out in her best style for conquest" and "is smoking a cigarette in as aesthetic a manner as she can" (778). He calls one of his effete matronly characters "a semi-professional invalid, refined and unintelligent," and an officious, overbearing cousin of the central family "is and appears thoroughly insignificant. But his opinion of the place he occupies in the world is enormous" (762–63). Much of the comedy in the group scenes is at the expense of such characters.

Mitchell also laced the play with occasional political or other topical lines that lent a sense of immediacy and instant recognition for his audience but that unfortunately dated his material often only a few years later, much like the efforts of Charles Hoyt before him and Neil Simon well after. Some of the topical lines seem timeless, however. Philip Phillimore, for example, tells his fiancée that "the people insisted on electing a desperado to the presidential office – they must take the hold-up that follows" (766).

Mitchell's heroine, Cynthia Karslake, first played by Minnie Maddern Fiske, is clearly the center of the play, with her sporty behavior, deemed outrageous by the conservative elite (like her affianced Philip), who dictate the manners. Cynthia is remarkably strong-willed, is enamored of horse racing, and knows her own mind (except for her confusion in matters of love, without which the play would have no conflict). As an intrepid and intelligent, but ultimately suffering, heroine, she can be seen as a forerunner of Linda Seton in Philip Barry's *Holiday*. She is clearly unsuited for Philip, who waxes on about "the Halcyon calm of . . . second choice" (767), not an image dear to the fast-paced Cynthia. Mitchell places Cynthia in awkward situations in each act by chance or deliberate encounters with her ex-husband John, whom she claims to hate. After her jealousy is sparked by the interest in John of another divorcée, however, it is clear that Cynthia and John are a natural match.

Around this roller-coaster, second-chance romance, cynical and silly social conflicts take place that make parts of the play seem reworkings of Anna Cora Mowatt's *Fashion* and that recall various sensibilities portrayed in Restoration comedy of manners. The playwright places delightful but impossibly glib and clever people at the play's center, much like the rakes and lovers of the late seventeenth century. We can easily assume that the early-twentieth-century audience was likewise intended to admire the protagonists and probably fancied themselves as glib as the characters they observed.

A randy British sophisticate and modern good-hearted rake, Sir Wilfrid Cates-Darby, performed by George Arliss, courts two women simultaneously, even proposing to one in front of the other, and after being turned down, shifts his attentions to his second choice in nearly the same breath. Amazingly, he is successful in marrying his second choice. This bizarre character lends the play a streak of eccentricity while juxtaposing British and American manners. In the midst of courting Vida, who never stops talking, Sir Wilfrid finally intrudes firmly but civilly, "I was brought up not to interrupt. But you Americans. . . . if somebody didn't interrupt you, you'd go on forever" (782). His holding forth on the insubstantiality of many American women is often startling in its bluntness: "Some of your American gals," he tells Cynthia, "are the nicest boys I ever met" (799).

At the play's conclusion we discover that the Karslakes were never really divorced at all, because of a technicality in interstate laws. This is known for some time only by John, however, who plays games with Cynthia until it serves his purpose to reveal the truth. This same device was used in 1921 in the notorious sex farce *The Demi-Virgin* by Avery Hopwood, another socialite playwright whose style bears many resemblances to that of Mitchell and of Fitch. Although Mitchell wrote many other plays, most notably *Becky Sharp,* his adaptation of Thackeray's *Vanity Fair* (1899), his reputation in the period rests almost solely on *The New York Idea* and his working relationship with Mrs. Fiske and her Manhattan Theatre Company.

Race Relations

Except for the several important exceptions discussed later, for the most part race relations played a limited role in plays of this period, although many plays included jokes or comments about African American characters in small roles, especially step-and-fetch-it type servants. Cynthia in *The New York Idea,* for example, explains that her new cousin-to-be "couldn't have received me with more warmth if I'd been a mulatto" (766). Eugene Walter includes the significant supporting role of Annie, an African American maid who is a servant to Laura Murdock throughout much of the action of *The Easiest Way*. It is clear that Laura relies on Annie and often gives her little presents but must tolerate her stereotypical slowness and filching of small items from time to time. Ultimately, Annie is shown to be untrustworthy, but this revelation contributes nothing to the action of the play, not even comic relief. In Annie's first appearance she is described as slovenly and typical of black women in her position. Her opening scene demonstrates that she is nosey and always attempting to read Laura's private correspondence. Brockton calls her a "nigger" and worthless at her work, and even Laura in the final act says, "You've been about as honest as most colored girls are who work for women in the position that I am in. You haven't stolen enough to make me discharge you, but I've seen what you've taken" (803). In his character notes for the play Walter calls the character a "cunning, crafty, heartless, surly, sullen Northern negress, who to the number of thousands, are servants of women of easy morals, and who infest a district of New York" (722). Annie is the only character in the play without a last name and, of course, was played by a white actress.

Augustus Thomas frequently put black characters onstage, often with disparaging remarks about low intelligence. *In Mizzoura,* for example, is laced with racist language, and the abuse of the black characters is often quite painful to read today. For example, a half-witted black man, who throughout the play appears to be present for comic purposes, enters again during a showdown in the final act and throws in his running joke of trying to sell unwanted coke to the blacksmith. This time, however, one of the men abruptly calls out, "Shoot that nigger," whereupon his companion "smashes NIGGER in the mouth" (see Moses, *Representative Plays,* 515). Although missing the racial violence, *The Witching Hour* of Thomas includes several menial and comic blackface characters and has one gambler say, "your luck always stays by you if you divide a little with a nigger or a hunchback – and in Louisville it's easier to find a nigger" (see Quinn, *Representative American Plays,* 7th ed., 765). He goes on to suggest that it is bad luck, however, for a gambler to shake hands with a black man before gambling.

The major exceptions to the usual presentation of black characters are James Herne's *Reverend Griffith Davenport* (1899), which features a southern clergyman fighting against slavery during the Civil War (the play has survived only as a fragment); Moody's *The Faith Healer,* in which an ancient black prophet, Uncle Abe, is treated reverently; and Edward Sheldon's startling exposé *The Nigger* (1909). Sheldon's play is often noted as one of the first serious attempts to paint a more sympathetic portrait of the plight of African Americans after the abolition of slavery.

Edward Sheldon's The Nigger

Many aspects, however, of *The Nigger* as written and produced point back to the tradition of Boucicault's *The Octoroon,* wherein the center of the action and the heart of the crisis are geared to an apparently white character who is discovered to have black blood and who is therefore disenfranchised and ostracized. The characters are nonetheless all white and played by white actors. The horror of the play resides in its portrayal of the taint of mixed blood. Nonetheless the play represents a social advance over previous work and can be seen as pointing toward more sympathetic depictions of black characters that will appear after 1915, such as *Three Plays for a Negro Theatre, Porgy, All God's Chillun' Got Wings,* and others, all featuring black actors but written, produced, directed, and designed by whites and intended to entertain, instruct, and appeal to white audiences.

The action of *The Nigger* is set in the early twentieth century in an unspecified southern state where all the white characters seem to be preoccupied with the "negro question" (E. Sheldon, 18; subsequent page references refer to this text). The most common attitude among the whites is voiced by an older character woman: "The only way to make a negro straight is to knock him down" (68). The protagonist, Philip Morrow, who is a successful plantation owner and sheriff, is elected governor between Acts I and II, largely because of his stance against Prohibition and his knack of keeping the black population in hand. His major opposition has come from state senator Long, commonly called "the White Niggah" because he promotes equality for African Americans. Nonetheless, Morrow's attitude toward blacks is more humane than that of any other of the white characters in the play save Senator Long. In his own words Morrow claims, "while I'm good to my niggahs . . . I don't think they ought to have the franchise and I won't treat 'em as equals" (43). Morrow is clearly law-abiding, however, because he attempts to prevent a lynching of a young black man who admittedly raped and killed a white woman. This scene is the most horrific of the play, but much is done with offstage sound to create the sense of mob violence without seeing it. A similar effect is achieved in Act II through offstage race rioting led by angry white men trying to kill as many blacks as possible because of the mayor's hiring of black men for the police force. After Morrow is unsuccessful at preventing the lynching, his fiancée Georgie attempts to console him: "You couldn't help it, deah . . . and aftah all, you know, he's – well, he's only a negro" (100).

Before he discovers that his own blood is one-sixteenth black, Morrow feels a strong sense of paternalistic responsibility toward the black race. "We brought the niggahs ovah t' this country," he tells his cousin, "an' I reckon we're responsible for them while theah heah" (138). After passing through a crisis of self-loathing and loss of position as a result of learning the truth about his ethnic origin, Morrow experiences much guilt for his own racism and decides to announce his discovery publicly. "I don't want t' hate the niggahs," he tells the senator. "But – you see I was bawn an' brought up the othah way, an' somehow I can't shake it off" (209). The sense of responsibility and paternalism returns, leading Morrow to assume he should take a position of leadership among the disenfranchised. Nonetheless, even in trying to accept his own "blackness" Morrow assumes a hostile, condescending posture: "The niggah's not a man," he proclaims, "he's an animal – he's an African savage . . . it's monkey blood he's got in him, an' you can't evah change it" (212). Morrow at first loses Georgie, who is stricken with "a paroxysm of nervous horror" (193) when she hears the news, but rather unbelievably she comes to her senses in the final scene and returns to take a position beside her love. This shift is probably effective from the point of view of melodrama, ultimately the form for this play, but is weak in terms of realistic action.

In the final analysis Sheldon seems to assume that race relations were momentarily difficult but that in the foreseeable future equality would prevail. This optimism sounds much like some of Chekhov's forward-looking characters, who might speak thus if they had been graced with southern dialects: "I tell you, we'ah jes' se'vants o' the comin' generations – that's all! They'll enjoy ev'rythin' we've wo'ked an' thought an' suff'd t' give 'em." The senator goes on to dream of a country with "one people – jes' one people wo'kin shouldah t' shouldah fo' the common good an' the glory o' God" (214–15). Despite the optimism of the last scenes, Sheldon's efforts were very disturbing for white audiences who witnessed the play, and the play suggested an artistic greatness that might develop in American drama. Sheldon, however, never quite reached his potential.

Sheldon had also shown much promise in 1908 by shaking up the theatre community with his *Salvation Nell,* subtitled *Man's Extremity Is God's Opportunity* (see Gassner, *Best Plays of the Early American Theatre,* 557), a vehicle for Mrs. Fiske, which explored the urban world of whores, tramps, and drunks but attempted to show us human beings beneath the types. The action takes place first in the working environment of the Salvation Army, then travels from a barroom to a tenement apartment, and finally to a poor street on the Westside. Like Belasco, Sheldon worked for naturalistic environment, atmospheric effects, and emotional overflow, and crafted sustained silences on the stage. He also worked in the melodramatic form, but he can be seen as more successful in his depiction of contemporary character, much like Walter in *The Easiest Way.* In contrast to Laura Murdock, however, Sheldon's Nell Sanders proclaims that "it's Love that saves the world!" Her fervent faith in God and her steadfast attention to the fallen man she loves brings ultimate happiness, and as the two reunite the "Salvationists" sing "Heaven's morning breaks, and earth's black shadows flee" (see Gassner, op. cit., 616).

Rachel Crothers and the New Woman

A sharper dramatic edge, a more honest depiction of domestic life, and important social commentary with no easy solutions appeared in the early plays of Rachel Crothers (1870–1958). Two plays are of special importance for the period, *A Man's World* (1909) and *He and She* (1912). The only published version of *He and She* is a 1920 revision, but its subject matter and many of its characteristics date from the earlier production. As a commercial playwright Crothers was the most successful woman in this sphere until Lillian Hellman, and part of this success was due to Crothers's own active participation in the direction of her plays.

It is clear that Crothers sought social change, but she also recognized that serious alteration could only come with struggle and loss. She regularly addressed the topics of sexual freedom, women in the workplace, the double standard, and, like the best of Fitch, enduring marital problems. Simultaneously, her plays reflect the pull of new freedoms and opportunities for women in the early twentieth century and the lingering oppression of nineteenth-century conventions, stereotypes, and limitations for women. Like most of the men with whom she competed, Crothers followed conventional dramatic form while experimenting with subject matter. Perhaps because of her own life choices, Crothers did not think that marriage and career were reconcilable. A woman, she seemed to say, must choose.

The female protagonist of *A Man's World* is given a male name, Frank Ware, and, like Crothers herself, receives much attention in the art and literary world for her achievements as a writer with a social conscience and as a champion of downtrodden women. It is not surprising that many men, even of Frank's acquaintance, assume or suspect that a man is probably behind her work. It is difficult for them to believe that a woman could achieve great things on her own. Her friend Wells asks, "Where does she get her stuff, anyway?" Her French friend Emile answers, "A woman only gets what a man gives her" (see Barlow, *Plays by American Women,* 7). Even Crothers acknowledges that the influence of Frank's liberal father, who was also a writer, was probably essential in seeing that she was well educated and prepared for a career rather than domesticity. Frank explains: "I'm a natural woman – because I've been a free one. Living alone with my father all those years made me so. He took me with him every possible place" (20). Unlike most of her fellow artists and dilettantes, Frank, a devout realist, attempts to depict the world unsentimentally and exactly as she finds it. This "frank-ness" is clearly what attracts Gaskell (the love interest) to Frank, although it also creates most of the problems he ultimately has with her. Frank's attraction to Gaskell, however, is a bit more difficult to understand now, near the end of the twentieth century. She is attracted against her own better judgment, so perhaps we should assume overwhelming animal attraction on her part, but Crothers does not explore this in the play's text.

Despite the sexism, even in her artistic crowd, Frank is clearly a leader and charismatic, one of Crothers's "energetic and clear-sighted rebels," as Lois Gottlieb calls them ("Looking to Women," in Chinoy and Jenkins, 138). Nearly every one of her acquaintances wants to be close to her and offer advice; each friend seems to believe that he or she is the only one who truly understands Frank. All, including Gaskell, appear to be mistaken. Frank, on the other hand, understands the plight of several of her friends. Clara, in particular, is presented in stark contrast to the self-possessed Frank. Clara is an unattractive, would-be artist with marginal talent and no assertiveness. This sad woman admits that she would give up art and her attempt at a career if she could have a man to love her. Similar characters show up in many of Crothers's plays.

Though unmarried, Frank is raising a child she calls Kiddie, a seven-year-old boy she saved from the orphanage or worse when his mother, abandoned by the boy's father, died. In Act III the pitiful Kiddie overhears part of an argument between Frank and Gaskell in which Frank and Gaskell discover that Gaskell is Kiddie's missing father. Frank berates him, "I've loathed and despised that man . . . and it's you." The final stage direction of the act reads, "They both turn with horror, as Kiddie, in his night clothes, stands watching them, a little wondering figure" (see Barlow, op. cit., 63). With the discovery of paternity (perhaps Crothers is forcing coincidence here but there is much precedent for it in the theatre she knew), a period of crisis ensues, but, like much of realistic Ibsen, the reconciliation the audience probably expected does not occur. The double standard is attacked head on. Gaskell will not admit that he did anything wrong, because he assumes that the moral standards for men and women are different. Frank insists that he committed a crime and that he must confess he did or there is no possibility for reconciliation. The couple part ways. Like Walter in *The Easiest Way,* Crothers opts for an unhappy, unmelodramatic, tragicomic domestic conclusion that reflects the realities of her world.

Augustus Thomas brought further attention and fame to *A Man's World* when he attacked it in *As a Man Thinks* (1911), a play that attempted with apparent success at the time to defend the double standard on the grounds that it was necessary for the welfare of the world that women protect their virtue, otherwise men could never know if they were the father of their children. His arguments may seem absurd now, but they received much sage head-nodding at the time. Of course in *A Man's World,* Gaskell presents this argument himself: "A man wants the mother of his children to be the purest in the world" (601). Arthur Hobson Quinn, writing in the 1920s, praised Crothers for her courage, but unfortunately agreed with Gaskell and Thomas:

"There is no railing at mankind," he argued; the analysis of Thomas, he believed, was the "more profound" (*History of the American Drama*, 54).

With *He and She* Crothers pitted the roles of the career woman and the traditional mother-housewife, but this time the attempts to reject the double standard are seen to break down in practice. The arguments explore responsibility to self and self-expression as opposed to responsibilities to children. The conclusion of the play, at least in the 1920 version, is conventional.

The central action involves two married people, Ann and Tom Herford, both creative sculptors still very much in love, who have fallen into competition with each other. All those close to the family circle assume that Tom is the real talent, capable of the "big" work, whereas Ann is of course good but not quite in his league. Like Frank in *A Man's World,* Ann is very charismatic, and all see her as more inspirational than inspired. Tom is always supportive of Ann and very respectful of her abilities and criticism of his own work, but this fairmindedness is severely tested when Ann wins a $100,000 competition that Tom had also entered and expected to win. Predictably, the circle of friends and family feel sorry for Tom at losing and have no words of congratulation for Ann. At first Tom tries to support Ann's victory, but his deep-seated sexism rises to the surface, and he turns on her, demanding that she give up the commission for the sake of the family. Although he later repents his impulsive actions, the damage is done, and when their sixteen-year-old daughter Millicent runs away from boarding school with the intention of marrying a boy, Ann yields and gives up the commission, asking Tom to do the sculpture in her place.

Modern audiences are likely to find it disappointing that the wife assumes that tending to the problems of her daughter is her own responsibility, and not the shared responsibility of father and mother. This same assumption was made in 1919 by James Forbes in *The Famous Mrs. Fair,* in which a professional woman is placed in a similar position. Forbes has her give up her career to "save" her wayward teenage daughter. Crothers is probably demonstrating what we could expect to happen in such a situation, and the play clearly underscores her belief that career, marriage, and child raising do not mix with ease, and probably not at all. Although Ann's father, Remington, is essentially reactionary throughout most of the play, he may be speaking for Crothers when he tells Tom, "Men and women will go through hell over this before it shakes down into shape. *You're* right and *she's* right and you're tearing each other like mad dogs over it because you love each other" (see Quinn, *Representative American Plays,* 923; subsequent page references refer to this text).

Crothers makes her position even clearer in the subplot concerning Ann and Tom's family friends and colleagues Ruth and Keith, who are also much in love but not yet married. They argue endlessly about the importance Ruth gives to her career in magazine editing. This relationship finally dissolves because neither will yield to the antithetical demands or needs of the other.

Keith assumes that women can be creative and accomplished but are always somewhat below the level of talented men. It is their responsibility, he believes, to give up work outside the home once they marry. And Ruth reminds Keith that "it never seems to occur to you that I might be a little less tired but bored to death without my job" (902). A minor theme running through both plotlines of the play is an assumption by all the men, even when being sympathetic to women having careers, that women must do all the housework and cooking. Both Ruth and Ann attempt to tell them that many women in the twentieth century are fundamentally changing. "Men don't realize," Ann exclaims, "how deeply and fiercely creative women love their work" (905). For Ruth the ideal relationship for a woman and man is "for each to keep his independence . . . and live together merely because they charm each other. But somehow we don't seem to be able to make it respectable" (911). Unfortunately, she says, this only seems to occur in out-of-wedlock relationships. The battle lines drawn here in the early plays of Crothers continued to be breached throughout the next decade in numerous plays reflecting the effects, both reactionary and supportive, of the changing position of women in postwar America.

Just as the career of Crothers was gaining much attention, the number of plays written and produced by Americans was on the rise. In 1910, for the first time, more American than foreign plays appeared on the New York stage. Although the anglophilic prejudices of many American critics and audiences persisted, the burgeoning social consciousness of significant American playwrights between 1896 and 1915 helped to inspire a host of postwar dramatists. By the 1920s the drama of the United States was regularly and often predominantly exploring the problems, ideas and lifestyles of the American people. Unfortunately, the trend was not permanent.

Notes

1 An extracted version of Herne's "Art for Truth's Sake in the Drama" appears as document 236 in *Theatre in the United States: A Documentary History, 1750–1915,* edited by Witham and compiled by Wilmeth.

Bibliography: Plays and Playwrights, 1896–1915

Important discussions of these plays and sometimes their contexts appear in a number of books and articles that should be of interest to the student wishing to pursue these playwrights or the period in which they wrote. I include those most easily located in order of publication. Arthur Hobson Quinn's *History of the American Drama from the Civil War to the Present Day* (1927, revised 1936) is a conservative discussion of the major plays included here, but important as the first sustained examination of this drama. Hartman's *The Development of American Social Comedy from 1787 to 1936* includes examination of plays by Crothers, Fitch, and Mitchell. Gottlieb's "Looking to Women: Rachel Crothers and the Feminist Heroine" in *Women in American Theatre* (edited by Chinoy and Jenkins) examines the nature of Crothers's feminism. Richardson's *American Drama from the Colonial Period through World War I* discusses cogently (primarily as literature) many of the plays included here. Londré's "Money Without Glory: Turn-of-the-Century America's Women Playwrights" in *The American Stage* (edited by Engle and Miller) profiles successful commercial women writing professionally for the theatre in the period. Meserve's revised *An Outline History of American Drama* categorizes all of the plays discussed in this essay by type or theme and includes plot summaries and brief discussions of many important plays. Bordman's *American Theatre: A Chronicle of Comedy and Drama, 1869–1914* places all of the plays in the context of their production seasons and provides brief summaries and commentary. Yvonne Shafer's *American Women Playwrights, 1900–1950* provides discussions of many important and often neglected playwrights of the period.

Most of the plays discussed here are anthologized, although nearly all are out of print. I include here the anthologies and individual editions used to write this chapter, listing them alphabetically by editor or author. Barlow's *Plays by American Women, 1900–1930* is a well-introduced anthology that includes *A Man's World*. Select Gillette plays, including *Secret Service,* are in Cullen and Wilmeth, along with a lengthy introduction. Belasco's *The Heart of Maryland and Other Plays* has an introduction by editors Hughes and Savage. This volume contains five Belasco plays, including his famous *The Girl I Left Behind Me,* a collaboration with Franklin Fyles. Belasco's *Six Plays* are introduced by Montrose Moses, who also provides a Belasco chronology of famous productions to 1911. The collection includes *Madame Butterfly, The Darling of the Gods, The Girl of the Golden West,* and *The Return of Peter Grimm. Plays by Clyde Fitch,* a four-volume memorial collection of Fitch plays containing most of his hits from the period covered in this chapter, is edited by Montrose Moses. Gassner's *Best Plays of the Early American Theatre, From the Beginning to 1916* is an anthology with brief introductions for each play and an essay entitled "Before O'Neill." Plays included from the period in question are *Secret Service, The Great Divide, The New York Idea, The Truth, The Witching Hour, Salvation Nell, The Easiest Way,* and *The Scarecrow.* Moody's *Dramas from the American Theatre, 1762–1909* provides excellent introductions to the plays, which include three from this period: *The Great Divide, The New York Idea,* and *The City.* Moses' *Representative Plays by American Dramatists* is an anthology of plays with detailed introductions, often providing material by the playwrights themselves. *In Mizzoura,* for example, is accompanied by the playwright's account of his composition of the play, in which he explains creating the central character specifically for the attributes of the actor Nat Goodwin. Other relevant works include *The Moth and the Flame, The New York Idea, The Easiest Way,* and *The Return of Peter Grimm.* Sheldon's *The Nigger* (New York: Macmillan, 1910) was published alone. Quinn's *Representative American Plays* (for this chapter, the seventh edition) is an anthology with useful introductions that offers nine plays from the period, the most of any anthology: *Secret Service, Madame Butterfly, The Girl with the Green Eyes, The New York Idea, The Witching Hour, The Faith Healer, The Scarecrow, The Boss,* and *He and She.* A recent collection is Wilmeth, *Staging the Nation,* which includes *The City* and earlier plays from the nineteenth century.

Plays and Playwrights: 1915–1945

Brenda Murphy

Introduction

Two major developments in the theatre were extremely important for the creation of American drama during the period between 1915 and 1945: the emergence of Broadway as the center for creative activity in the mainstream commercial theatre and the growth of an alternative theatre movement in opposition to the mainstream (both topics are explored in the post–World War II period in individual chapters in Vol. III of this history). At the turn of the century, as theatrical monopolies strengthened their control of theatres throughout the country and regional stock companies disappeared, the growth in the production of new plays that emanated from Broadway was phenomenal. In the 1899–1900 theatrical season, 87 new productions appeared on Broadway. By the 1915–16 season, the number had increased to 115. During the prosperous twenties, this activity increased to a peak of 255 productions in 1925–26, leveling off again, as the Great Depression, the development of talking motion pictures, and World War II had their effect, to 76 in 1945–46 (Poggi, 47). From the perspective of the end of the twentieth century, Broadway in the twenties was a paradise for playwrights. New plays could be capitalized by one or two private producers and brought directly to New York, perhaps after one or two brief "tryout" engagements in Boston, Philadelphia, or New Haven. The potential audience was large and eclectic, and playwrights as different as Maxwell Anderson and George S. Kaufman, Owen Davis and Philip Barry, Rachel Crothers and Eugene O'Neill were easily able to find producers and accumulate fortunes from hit plays At the same time, groups of theatre artists, amateur and professional, were able to start companies based on their aesthetic, economic, social, and political ideologies and to maintain themselves for years, essentially through ticket sales. These included "art theatres," such as the Provincetown Players, which had an avowed purpose of encouraging new native playwrights, and the Washington Square Players, which did not, as well as social-protest theatres like the New Playwrights Company. During the thirties, while the depressed economy made things more difficult in the commercial theatre and the motion picture industry skimmed off many of the successful mainstream playwrights, a growing leftist theatre movement and the Federal Theatre Project (see Chapter 2) provided outlets for creative ways of theatricalizing a leftist critique of economic conditions and the sociopolitical system. At the same time, the mainstream theatre was reflecting a wide spectrum of American experience in plays that ranged from society comedy to naturalistic treatments of crime and poverty. It was a time of great vitality and creativity, the most prolific period for playwrights in the American theatre's history.

Eugene Gladstone O'Neill

Eugene O'Neill was literally born on Broadway, at the Barett House on the corner of Broadway and Forty-third Street, a family hotel in what was then a relatively quiet uptown neighborhood. His father, James O'Neill, was a well-known actor and successful manager of his own theatrical troupe, whose fame and success was largely based on his portrayal of the title role in Charles Fechter's *Count of Monte Cristo,* to which he owned the rights. Because of his father's profession and his mother Ella's morphine addiction, which began in the wake of Eugene's difficult birth on 16 October 1888 and lasted until 1914, he was raised largely by his nurse until the age of seven, touring with his parents during the theatrical season and spending the summers at the family cottage in New London, Connecticut – all experiences that were to inform his writing of *Long Day's Journey Into Night* (begun in 1941 but not staged until 1956). At age seven he was sent to a Catholic boarding school. He transferred to the secular Betts Academy in 1902, from which he graduated with a good record, but his education ended with his expulsion from Princeton University during his second semester for missing too many classes. He had begun drinking heavily in his teens, with his older brother Jamie's tutelage and example. Both brothers battled alcoholism throughout their lives; Jamie died of its effects in 1923.

After leaving Princeton, O'Neill worked briefly in New York and secretly married Kathleen Jenkins, a young woman who was pregnant with his first child, in 1909. With his father's help, he secured a place on a prospecting expedition to Honduras and left New York, essentially abandoning wife and child. Later he worked as a seaman, sailing to Buenos Aires, where he spent some time living from hand to mouth, and then to Liverpool. He returned to New York in 1911, staying in a waterfront flophouse where he attempted suicide in 1912 and later contracted tuberculosis, for which, at his father's expense, he was treated at Gaylord Sanatorium in Wallingford, Connecticut. His experience in the flophouse was the subject of *The Iceman Cometh* (written 1939; first produced 1946); it also provided background for the suicide of *The Exorcism* (1919) and for the sanatorium of *The Straw* (written 1919;

staged 1921). The most immediate product of O'Neill's time in "the San," as he called it, was that he began to write plays, which he did with extraordinary industry and productivity during the next three years, both on his own and as a member of George Pierce Baker's playwriting course at Harvard in 1914–15.

The products of O'Neill's early playwriting years are perhaps remarkable only for their diversity. They are the record of a young writer with considerable knowledge of the stage – derived from years of backstage loitering and free passes – finding his way in the drama and trying to adapt himself to the forms and venues that were available to him. O'Neill had read Strindberg, Shaw, and Ibsen while still in his teens and made it a point to see the touring Abbey Players even during his flophouse phase in 1911. In 1913 and 1914, he wrote eleven plays that reflect the range of the American theatre at that time, from vaudeville to avant-garde realism.

Among these early trials and experiments was *The Children of the Sea* (1914), revised as *Bound East for Cardiff* (1916), a realistic piece that Baker's class had told him was not really a play (Estrin, 194). It was the reading of this work that won O'Neill his debut with the Provincetown Players, inspiring Susan Glaspell's comment, "Then we knew what we were for."[1] *Bound East* was O'Neill's first-produced play, opening at the Wharf Theatre in Provincetown in July 1916, with a cast that included George Cram Cook, John Reed, and Wilbur Daniel Steele as well as O'Neill. Played in Provincetown, with the sound of the waves washing under the theatre, the effect on the audience of O'Neill's flatly realistic dramatization of the death of a sailor in his ship's bunk was extraordinary. It was played again in August, and in November it was on the first bill of the Players' new Playwright's Theatre in New York. The success of *Bound East* inspired O'Neill to write other plays based on his experiences as a sailor. They included the melodramatic *In the Zone* (1917), which examined wartime hysteria about spies; *Ile* (1917), a naturalistic study of the force of the environment on a character's psyche, and an early treatment of O'Neill's parents; *The Long Voyage Home* (1917), a naturalistic treatment of the sailor's futile dreams that would be developed fully in *Beyond the Horizon* (1920) and *Anna Christie* (1921); and *The Moon of the Caribees* (1918), which is remarkable for its evocation of mood and its lack of a conventional plot. The sea plays were consistently praised by critics for their natural, episodic quality, their realism, their deceptive simplicity, and their fullness of characterization. O'Neill was seen as pessimistic, but praised for his evocation of the sea as a force equivalent to fate for the seamen and for expressing the comradeship of these "common men" in the face of a hostile world. Grouped together as *S.S. Glencairn,* four of the plays – *Bound East, In the Zone, The Long Voyage Home,* and *The Moon of the Caribees* – were revived a number of times, and made into a film called *The Long Voyage Home,* by John Ford, in

1940. *In the Zone,* with its melodramatic exploitation of wartime anxiety about espionage, and *Long Voyage Home,* with its shanghaiing of a sailor in a waterfront dive, were the more popular successes, but O'Neill consistently valued *The Moon* more, although it was more conventionally plotted. As he said, "*The Moon* works with truth . . . while *In the Zone* substitutes theatrical sentimentalism. . . . I consider *In the Zone* a conventional construction of the theater as it is, and *The Moon* an attempt to achieve a higher plane of bigger, finer values" (quoted in Clark, *Eugene O'Neill,* 43).

O'Neill's remarkable productivity continued throughout the teens and early twenties, as he learned his craft and began to produce full-length plays. Most of these are important as early treatments of issues and characters that would absorb him later. *The Rope* (1918), *Where the Cross Is Made* (1918), and *Gold* (1920) all involve the driving force of greed, a subject that occupied him until the very end of his career. *The Rope* and *Diff'rent* (1920) are early explorations of the New England character and milieu that he was to use to great effect in *Desire Under the Elms* (1924) and *Mourning Becomes Electra* (1931). The one-act *Before Breakfast* (1916), based on Strindberg's *The Stronger,* pointed the way toward O'Neill's full-blown Strindbergian treatment of his second marriage, to writer Agnes Boulton, in *Welded* (1924). What made the years 1920 and 1921 decisive ones for O'Neill's career, however, was the writing of four important plays: *Beyond the Horizon* (1920), *Anna Christie* (1921), *The Emperor Jones* (1920), and *The Hairy Ape* (1922). These four plays were the first to be valued as the work of a mature playwright, and they earned O'Neill his first national and international recognition. They also defined a watershed that would determine the direction of his career as a playwright. *Beyond the Horizon* was meant for the Broadway theatre from the beginning. Its production was entrusted not to the Provincetown Players but to George C. Tyler, an old friend of James O'Neill's, and very much a denizen of the commercial theatre, and Richard Bennett, a matinee idol, who was to play the part of the romantic Robert Mayo, a character who dreams of a world "beyond the horizon" while he condemns himself to the drudgery of life on a New England farm because of a fleeting romantic passion for a young woman who is his brother's natural mate. After some trial matinees, *Horizon* received a full Broadway production, eventually running for 111 performances and winning the Pulitzer Prize. To O'Neill, whose father had died shortly after the premiere, "it was the greatest satisfaction [my father] knew that I had made good in a way dear to his heart. And I thank 'whatever Gods may be' that *Beyond* came into its own when it did and not too late for him" (quoted in Sheaffer, *Son and Artist,* 17).

Beyond the Horizon was overpraised by a group of drama critics who were eager for some evidence of substantial achievement by an American playwright. Typical of this feeling is Ludwig Lewisohn's hyperbolic pronouncement in the *Nation:* "The performance of Eugene G. O'Neil's [*sic*] tragedy 'Beyond the Horizon' at the Morosco theatre establishes America's kinship with the stage of the modern world. . . . Here at last is a full-bodied dramatic work which, whatever its ultimate and absolute value, exists in the fullest, in the richest sense today. . . . Mr. O'Neil is a naturalist. And that is fortunate" (Lewisohn, 241). Following upon *Horizon*'s success, *Anna Christie* was given an immediate Broadway production by the most literary of New York commercial directors, Arthur Hopkins. It ran for 177 performances on Broadway, winning the playwright his second Pulitzer Prize. O'Neill admitted later that, "in telling the story I deliberately employed all the Broadway tricks which I had learned in my stage training," claiming that, "using the same technique, and with my own experience as a basis I could turn out dozens of plays like *Anna Christie,* but I never cared to try. It is too easy" (quoted in Estrin, 79). In 1921, O'Neill was poised to become a successful Broadway playwright, recognized as perhaps America's most talented writer in what was then the style of choice for serious drama in the mainstream American theatre, a realism tinged with naturalistic pessimism, but to O'Neill this was working in a theatrical idiom that was facile and worn out.

At the same time that he had been pursuing the money and fame associated with a Broadway career, O'Neill had continued his work with the Provincetown Players and other "art theatres" in Greenwich Village, including the Washington Square Players, which became the Theatre Guild in 1919, and the Neighborhood Playhouse. O'Neill considered *The Emperor Jones* and *The Hairy Ape* too experimental for Broadway, at least to begin with. Both were naturally entrusted to the consciously experimental Provincetown Players, O'Neill's artistic home. Characteristically, George Cram Cook risked everything the Players had on *Emperor Jones* in order to match O'Neill's new methods for dramatizing protagonist Brutus Jones's subjective reality with a new stagecraft that was inspired by Edward Gordon Craig and Max Reinhardt in Europe. The Players built a plaster cyclorama, which, with proper lighting, could give the illusion of "infinity" to the tiny stage of the Players' MacDougal Street theatre, an illusion Cook felt was needed to convey the sense that O'Neill was looking for with his Great Forest, "a wall of darkness dividing the world" (O'Neill, *Plays,* I, 1,044). Against this primal environment were played a number of theatrical devices aimed at bringing the audience into Jones's subjective experience as he gradually sheds the trappings of civilization and retreats into a primordial world bred of mounting terror, pursued by the "subjects" he has exploited as "Emperor." Most notable are the "little formless fears," hallucinatory sluglike creatures that pursue Jones until he shoots at them, and "the faint, steady thump of a tom-tom, low and vibrating. It starts at a rate exactly corresponding to normal pulse beat – 72 to the minute – and continues at a gradually accelerating rate from [the end of the first scene] uninterruptedly to the very end of the play" (*Plays*, I, 1,041). Fleeing through the Great Forest, Jones sees a series of visions or hallucinations, which take him progressively back through his own life and then into the history of the African American and African people, a journey back through his conscious memory and the Jungian collective unconscious that forms part of his subjective reality. The shooting of Jones by his rebellious "subjects" coincides with his vision of being sacrificed to an African god, a recognition at some level of the deep violation he is guilty of in exploiting his own people.

O'Neill claimed not to have been influenced by European Expressionism in writing *Emperor Jones,* asserting, "the first Expressionistic play that I ever saw . . . was Kaiser's *From Morn to Midnight,* produced in New York in 1922, after I'd written both *The Emperor Jones* and *The Hairy Ape*" (quoted in Clark, *Eugene O'Neill,* 72). Although O'Neill acknowledged having read *From Morn to Midnight* before writing *The Hairy Ape,* he claimed it as "a direct descendant of *Jones,* written long before I had heard of Expressionism, and its form needs no explanation but this. As a matter of fact, I did not think much of *Morn to Midnight,* and still don't. It is too easy. It would not have influenced me" (quoted in Clark, *Eugene O'Neill,* 72). Since O'Neill often denied, or was not conscious of, his intertextual influences, his denial is not surprising, although it is difficult not to see the elements of European Expressionism in *The Hairy Ape.* Like *From Morn to Midnight, Hairy Ape* is a "station play," with the protagonist, a "common man," becoming alienated by his dehumanizing job and breaking away from it to search for some source of meaning in modern life in a series of short encounters with various segments of society. After trying and failing to get a response to his existence from a series of groups, ranging from the wealthy on Fifth Avenue to the International Workers of the World, Yank retreats at last to the apes in the zoo, where he thinks he belongs, but is crushed to death when he enters the cage, an everyman who is destroyed by the effort to connect with others. O'Neill was specific about his distinction from the Expressionists. Expressionism "denies the value of characterization," he said, "it strives to get the author talking directly to the audience" (quoted in Estrin, 62). O'Neill did not believe "that an idea can be readily put over to an audience except through characters" (Ibid.). Rather than creating characters that were abstractions, O'Neill sought emotional identification from the audience: "Yank is really yourself, and myself. He is *every* human being. But, apparently, very few people seem to get this. . . . His struggle to 'belong,' to find the thread that will make him a part of the fabric of Life – we are all struggling to do just that" (quoted in Estrin, 35).

The most surprising effect of these two consciously avant-garde experiments in a new modernist theatrical idiom was their popularity with the New York theatre audience. Both *The Emperor Jones* and *The Hairy Ape* were fortunate in their Provincetown Players productions; their designers, Robert Edmond Jones and Cleon Throckmorton; and their lead actors, Charles Gilpin and Louis Wolheim, who seemed in both cases to have been created for their parts. Both productions moved "uptown" to Broadway, where *Jones* had a run of 204 performances and *Hairy Ape* 127. Both were later made into successful films. The effect of this success on O'Neill's direction as a playwright is incalculable, for it demonstrated to him and to theatrical producers that he did not have to go on writing *Anna Christie*s for the rest of his life in order to have a successful career in the Broadway theatre.

O'Neill's rejection of naturalism coincided with his deepening friendship and professional association with designer Robert Edmond Jones and Kenneth Macgowan, a writer, editor, and theatre critic who was a convert to Jones's enthusiasm for avant-garde "art theatre," a theatre that would make full use of the new ideas about production that Jones had studied in Europe. In 1924, O'Neill, Macgowan, and Jones were to form the Experimental Theatre, Inc., out of the remains of the Provincetown Players after George Cram Cook and Susan Glaspell, the Players' founders and guiding geniuses, had left for an extended trip to Greece. "The Triumvirate," as it was called, would produce six O'Neill plays: *The Ancient Mariner* (1924), an adaptation of Coleridge's poem; *All God's Chillun Got Wings* (1924), a treatment of perceived inequality and self-hatred in a marriage, with race used as the symbolic divisive issue; *Desire Under the Elms* (1924), a mythic family tragedy of greed and sexual desire set in nineteenth-century New England; *Welded* (1924), the Strindbergian treatment of the love–hate relationship between men and women that was based on his marriage to Agnes Boulton; *The Great God Brown* (1926), a complicated treatment, relying heavily on masks, of the disjunction between public and personal identities; and *The Fountain* (1925), a romantic historical epic about Ponce de Leon's search for eternal youth.

The diversity of styles and subjects in these plays suggests the range of what is best characterized as modernism in the work of O'Neill and his collaborators. The background of their aesthetics certainly included the new European stagecraft, as Macgowan's *The Theatre of Tomorrow* (1921) and the book he and Jones wrote together, *Continental Stagecraft* (1922), make clear. It also included Jungian psychology and an anthropological interest in masks, evident in Macgowan's *Masks and Demons* (1923) as well as O'Neill's developing interest in the theatrical possibilities of masks in *All God's Chillun, Great God Brown,* and *Lazarus Laughed* (1928). Equally clear was an interest in Freudian psychology. Amateur analysis was a fad that took Greenwich Village by storm and that was ridiculed by the Provincetown Players in Glaspell and Cook's *Suppressed Desires* as early as 1916. O'Neill's serious interest in Freud intensified in the midtwenties, when he read *Beyond the Pleasure Principle*

and *Group Psychology and the Analysis of the Ego* and underwent psychoanalysis briefly. The plays of the period clearly show a developing acquaintance with Freudian psychology.[2]

In the early twenties, it was Jungian psychology and the theatrical potential
of masks rather than Freudian character study that interested O'Neill, and his
use of masks grew quickly in complexity and significance. In *All God's Chillun,*
a mask is introduced into an essentially realistic environment and freighted
with significance: "In the left corner, where a window lights it effectively, is a
Negro primitive mask from the Congo – a grotesque face, inspiring obscure,
dim connotations in one's mind, but beautifully done, conceived in a true religious spirit. In this room, however, the mask acquires an arbitrary accentua-
tion. It dominates by a diabolical quality that contrast imposes upon it" (*Plays,*
II, 297). Fixating on the mask as the signifier of her husband Jim's race, Ella
personifies the mask and, in a flagrantly theatrical gesture, stabs it in the final
scene, telling her husband that she had to "kill it" before it killed her. The use
of masks in *Great God Brown* is theatrically far more complex and more integral to the play, although O'Neill came to think that its thematic import was
too simple. Essentially, the masks represent the public personae that the characters present to the world in order to hide a vulnerable "self" they don't want
to reveal. Dion Anthony's wife Margaret wears the mask of a long-suffering and
happy wife to hide her disappointed and careworn reality from the world. His
lover Cybel wears the mask of a prostitute to shield her vulnerable "Earth
Mother" soul. In working out the relationship between the "bad boy" Dion
Anthony and the "good boy," Billy Brown, however, O'Neill's masking scheme
became prolix. Although the use of masks in *Great God Brown* is schematic
and complicated, sometimes demanding quick work on the part of the actors
to switch their identities, it is only on a small scale comparable to that in
Lazarus Laughed, subtitled "*A Play for an Imaginative Theatre*," O'Neill's most
elaborate work, created with the aesthetics of the "art theatre" in mind.
Though Lazarus, "freed now from the fear of death, wears no mask" (*Plays,* II,
542) and the other major characters wear half-masks, the play requires a
masked chorus on the Greek model, representing seven periods of life, and
within each period seven general types of character (the simple, ignorant; the
happy, eager; the self-tortured, introspective; the proud, self-reliant; the
servile, hypocritical; the revengeful, cruel; the sorrowful, resigned), forty-nine
different masks in all. The demands of this scheme are so great that it has
been virtually impossible to mount the play, either in the commercial theatre,
where the costs of cast and production would be very difficult to recoup, or in
the "art theatre," where there would never be money enough to mount the
production. Its first production was at the Pasadena Playhouse in California,
using a great deal of volunteer labor, and it has been revived only in university
theatres, where actors can work without wages.

Lazarus was the last of the mask experiments. O'Neill played with the idea of using masks in his trilogy constructed on the Greek pattern, *Mourning Becomes Electra,* but discarded them in favor of a less intrusive "life-like mask impression" (*Plays,* II, 897). As O'Neill left the Experimental Theatre behind and began what was to be his most significant producing relationship, with the Theatre Guild, his interests shifted, from external theatricalization of subjective reality and abstract ideas through the stagecraft of the art theatre to a dialogic representation of the conflict between his characters' external and internal personae.

O'Neill's association with the Theatre Guild began in January of 1928, with two momentous productions. *Marco Millions,* written in 1924 and clearly a product of O'Neill's art theatre years, was very much like Brechtian epic theatre, a combination of a *Babbitt*-like satire on American materialism and spiritual emptiness and a gorgeous historical chronicle of the adventures of Marco Polo. *Strange Interlude* indicated O'Neill's new interest, a Freudian-influenced, novelistic concentration on dialogue to reveal character. As early as 1920, O'Neill had "dreamed of wedding the theme for a novel to the play form in a way that would still leave the play master of the house" (O'Neill, "Letter"). *Strange Interlude* shows the influence of modernist fiction writers like James Joyce and O'Neill's Provincetown associate Djuna Barnes and the technique of "stream-of-consciousness."[3] The play requires the actors to establish two modes of dialogue, one that is recognized as regular speech to which the other characters respond and one that is recognized as what in film would be a "voiceover" – the character enunciating his or her thoughts – a dialogic strategy that had been used in the American theatre as early as Alice Gerstenberg's *Overtones* (1913). Although the play's psychology comes across as crudely Freudian today, O'Neill's novelistic dialogue has been consistently effective in the theatre. Despite the play's lengthy nine acts, played with a dinner break, the original Theatre Guild production with Lynn Fontanne as Nina ran for 426 performances, and it has been revived successfully as recently as 1984. Subsequent uses of what O'Neill called the "Interlude technique" were not so successful, however. In *Dynamo,* without the schematized dialogic dynamic of Nina and her three men – Sam, Darrell, and Charlie – the spoken thoughts are less controlled and appear more like a modernist mannerism than an integral technique. Early on in the writing of *Mourning Becomes Electra,* O'Neill decided against using the Interlude technique, reminding himself, "always hereafter regard with suspicion hang-over inclination to use 'Interlude' technique regardless – that was what principally hurt 'Dynamo,' being forced into thought-asides method which was quite alien to essential psychological form of its characters" (quoted in Bogart, *Contour,* 338).

Perhaps the most deeply modernist element of O'Neill's work during the twenties was his consciousness of the loss of religious faith and the lack of connection with the past in modern American culture, and his attempt to overcome these ruptures by remaking myth and mythicizing history. The late twenties was the time of O'Neill's search for what he called "god-replacements." Although written in styles that seem as far apart as one could get in the American theatre of the twenties, the two most interesting examples of O'Neill's search for meaning, *Desire Under the Elms* and *Dynamo,* are rooted in the same fundamental issues. Both plays depict attempts by their protagonists, Eben Cabot and Reuben Light, to transcend the forces that enslave them spiritually: sexual desire, the biological force that drives them; a patriarchal religion personified in their fathers; and sexual prudery born of jealousy, personified in their mothers. *Desire* is a naturalistic study of a historical subject, a New England farm family in 1850, which has as its deep structure the myth of Phaedra and Hippolytus, reflected in the tragic love of Eben and his stepmother, Abbie. *Desire* offers the more hopeful view of the human condition. In the end, the religion of Eben's father is cold, hard, and dead, a petty self-justification that finally constricts him rather than his wife and son, because he is unable to love. Eben's mother, whose force is concentrated in the "sinister maternity" and the "crushing, jealous absorption" (*Plays,* II, 318) of the elm trees that overshadow the farmhouse, is defeated when Abbie expresses her love for Eben. Abbie and Eben transcend their sexual desire when they agree to accept retribution for their crime and give up the farm, the symbol of greed and desire, because of their love for each other. In the spirit of the Greek tragedy it is based on, *Desire* implies that submission to the retribution of a more powerful force and renunciation of desire bring transcendence.

Dynamo presents a darker vision. Basing his play loosely on Henry Adams's opposition of the Dynamo and the Virgin in *The Education of Henry Adams,* O'Neill conflates the forces that are working upon Reuben Light – puritanism, a desire for religious faith, sexual desire for both his mother and his girlfriend, guilt, maternal jealousy, fear, electricity, and hatred for his father – into one unified force that comes into being when Reuben fetishizes the dynamo that produces electricity into a female idol representing the power of science in opposition to the patriarchal puritanism of his father. Projecting the sexual prudery of his mother onto his self-created god, Reuben is overcome with guilt for his own sexuality and immolates himself on the dynamo. The uncomprehending victim of forces that are more powerful than he, Reuben is hardly a tragic hero. The major import of the play is the futility of trying to replace America's outworn Puritan religion with a worship of power through science. The death of the spirit is the result of both of these forces.

O'Neill's "Catholic play," *Days without End* (1933), subtitled *A Modern Miracle Play,* and the biblical *Lazarus Laughed* are his most direct treatments of the religious quest. He resuscitated the Interlude technique and a variation on the masks of *Great God Brown* for *Days,* using two actors to represent the split consciousness of John Loving: the questing John, who finds spiritual salvation in love and self-renunciation, and the cynical, life-denying Loving, who is destroyed. The play ends with John standing over the corpse of Loving, who lies beneath the foot of the crucifix in a church, his arms outflung so that his body forms another cross. John holds his arms out so that he too is like a cross, and while this is happening, "the light of the dawn on the stained-glass windows swiftly rises to a brilliant intensity of crimson and green and gold, as if the sun had risen. The gray walls of the church, particularly the wall where the Cross is, and face of the Christ shine with this radiance" (*Plays,* III, 180). The play ends with John's line, "Life laughs with God's love again! Life laughs with love!" (*Plays,* III, 180), echoing the ending of *Lazarus Laughed,* when Lazarus calls out as he is being executed, "O men, fear not life! You die – but there is no death for Man!" (*Plays,* II, 624) and begins to laugh, ending with the transcendent, "Life! Eternity! Stars and dust! God's Eternal Laughter!" (*Plays,* II, 625). This seeming acceptance of conventional spiritual comfort was brief and unconvincing, both for O'Neill and for his audience. While the mythicized *Desire Under the Elms* was both a commercial and a critical success, running 204 performances in its initial production and securing a place in the literary canon of modern drama, the direct treatments of O'Neill's spiritual quest have not been considered effective either as theatre or as literature. *Dynamo* ran just 50 performances in its Theatre Guild production and *Days without End,* 57.

Critic Esther Jackson has noted the correspondences between O'Neill's treatment of history and Bertolt Brecht's, commenting that one factor distinguishing the epic forms of O'Neill from those of Brecht and other Europeans is "his attempt to create works expressive of the political, social, cultural, and moral values which have distinguished American society from earlier historical kinds" (E. M. Jackson, 36). This is certainly true of *Marco Millions,* which embeds a satiric treatment of American values within a historical chronicle of the adventures of Marco Polo. Like *Marco Millions, The Fountain* represents a protagonist with a divided soul, a pragmatic man of action troubled by the need for romantic love and spiritual fulfillment. *The Fountain* treats this dilemma with romantic seriousness. Its protagonist Ponce de Leon is driven to near madness by his striving for "the One" in the midst of division and hostility. Led by the beautiful Beatriz, whose name evokes the primal search for meaning in Dante's *Divine Comedy,* Ponce finds "the One" in eternal Love, a transcendent unity that obliterates age and decay as well as hostilities and divisions in human experience involving religion, politics, and family. While Ponce's search verges on obsession and madness, Marco's is treated with humorous satire. In fact, Marco is not aware of any search beyond the businessman's search for ever wider markets for his wares. As Kublai Khan puts it, "he has not even a mortal soul, he has only an acquisitive instinct" (*Plays,* II, 420). In *Marco Millions* O'Neill figures a division between the crass, commercial, grasping, and materialistic West, personified in Marco, who, like Sinclair Lewis's Babbitt, manages to be a "good guy" despite his spiritual poverty, and the contemplative East, which values wisdom and beauty above the material. Whereas Ponce is redeemed by eternal love, personified in Beatriz, Marco is unable even to perceive the love of the beautiful Princess Kukachin, who dies for unrequited love of him, and he is happy with his plump and healthy fiancée Donata and his crass display of the goods he has amassed in the East.

O'Neill's most effective treatment of history is in *Mourning Becomes Electra,* which brings together the two modernist strategies of mythicizing and historicizing to establish a context that endows contemporary human experience with transcendent meaning. *Electra* is a trilogy set in New England at the time of the Civil War and based on the Greek myth of the House of Atreus. It embodies a struggle between the New England Puritan heritage of the Mannon family and the "foreigners" who have the capacity to free America from its self-imposed oppression by the life-denying Puritan ideology. Like the United States, O'Neill implies, the Mannon family resists the attempts of "outsiders" – Ezra (Agamemnon) Mannon's young wife, Christine (Clytemnestra); the French servant-girl, Marie Brantôme; and her son, Adam Brant (Aegisthus) – to bring life into their tomblike house through love and a sensual appreciation of beauty. The younger generation of Mannons, Lavinia (Laodicea) and Orin (Orestes), are victims of the Electra and Oedipal complexes brought on by a culture of repressed sexuality and denial of emotion. Driven by their "unnatural" urges, they commit crimes that, as in the classical Greek versions of the myth, bring their inevitable retribution, self-inflicted in Lavinia's case.

O'Neill achieved his effect through careful evocation of the Greek theatre while maintaining a style of what he called "unreal realism" in the play. The faces of the Mannons give a "strange, life-like mask impression" in repose (*Plays,* II, 897), evoking the classical theatre without the insistent foregrounding of technique that was characteristic of O'Neill's "art theatre" period. All but one of the trilogy's fourteen acts take place, as in a classical Greek tragedy, before the exterior of a great building, the antebellum Mannon family mansion, a "white Grecian temple portico with its six tall columns" (*Plays,* II, 893). The house is freighted with significance, as O'Neill makes clear in Christine's early speech: "Each time I come back after being away it appears more like a sepulchre! The 'whited' one of the Bible – pagan temple front stuck like a mask on Puritan gray ugliness. It was just like old Abe Mannon [Atreus] to build such a monstrosity – as a temple for his hatred" (*Plays,* II, 903–904).

Eugene O'Neill's *Mourning Becomes Electra,* designed by Robert Edmond Jones (1931) with Alla Nazimova (standing) and Alice Brady. Courtesy Yale Collection of American Literature, Beinecke Rare Book and Manuscript Library.

Looming over the action of the play, the house is a constant statement of the failure of the Mannons, and of the United States, to overcome the failures of Puritan ideology, which, as a typical American modernist, O'Neill saw as moral hypocrisy and a life-denying repression of emotion, aesthetic response to beauty, and sexuality. Like the false face on the Mannon house, the overlay of a pseudo-classical civilization has served only to emphasize the ugliness of America's fundamental system of values. In the course of the three plays, Christine and Adam try to defeat the Mannons by escaping to a country where beauty and sensuality are not considered sins to be punished. In essentially murdering Ezra, however, they commit a crime themselves, which is avenged when Orin shoots Adam and Christine commits suicide. As retribution inexorably follows each moral violation, Orin in turn kills himself, and Lavinia is deprived of the freedom from the Mannon values she had hoped to win by violating them. She shuts herself up forever in the tomblike house, her denial of life a sacrificial atonement for her temporary rebellion.

O'Neill's most ambitious treatment of history was to be in his projected dramatic cycle about the history of the United States from 1775 to 1932, based on the story of a single American family, a union of the English Harfords and the Irish Melodys. The cycle's overall title, *A Tale of Possessors, Self-Dispossessed,* indicates O'Neill's point of view, essentially an indictment of America's greed and materialism and its failure to value spirituality or beauty. The number of plays in the projected cycle varied from five to eleven, and only two are extant, *A Touch of the Poet* (written 1942; produced first in 1957), the only one O'Neill carried through to completion, and *More Stately Mansions* (written 1939; produced 1962), a draft of which was spared accidentally when O'Neill and his third wife, actress Carlotta Monterey, destroyed the outlines and drafts of the cycle in his last year. Summing up the theme of the cycle in 1948, O'Neill told an interviewer:

> This country is going to get it – really get it. We had everything to start with – everything – but there's bound to be a retribution. We've followed the same selfish, greedy path as every other country in the world. We talk about the American Dream, and want to tell the world about the American Dream, but what is that dream, in most cases, but the dream of material things? I sometimes think that the United States, for this reason, is the greatest failure the world has ever seen. We've been able to get a very good price for our souls in this country – the greatest price perhaps that has ever been paid – but you'd think that after all these years, and all that man has been through, we'd have sense enough – *all* of us – to understand that the whole secret of human happiness is summed up in a sentence that even a child can understand. The sentence? "For what shall it profit a man if he shall gain the whole world and lose his own soul?" (Quoted in Estrin, 230)

O'Neill turned to autobiography as a break from his long labor on the historical cycle, on which he worked steadily from the early 1930s until he was forced by illness to stop writing in the midforties.[4] He wrote the first draft of *The Iceman Cometh* between June and November of 1939 and worked simultaneously on *Long Day's Journey Into Night,* finishing a draft in October of 1940. He finished the first draft of *A Moon for the Misbegotten* in January of 1942, returning to it for revision in January of 1943. In this short period of time, as a sideline to his more ambitious project, O'Neill wrote the three autobiographical plays that are universally recognized as major works in the world repertory and largely responsible for their author's continued standing as the United States's most significant playwright. O'Neill had written about his family, and particularly his parents, before, most ostensibly in his comedy, *Ah, Wilderness!*, which is set in the summer of 1906 and based on his youthful romance with Maibelle Scott in New London. Less flattering, and probably less deliberate, treatments of one or both of his parents occur in *Ile, Where the Cross Is Made, Gold, All God's Chillun Got Wings, Desire Under the Elms, The Great God Brown,* and *More Stately Mansions.* Probable allusions to his brother Jamie occur in *Beyond the Horizon* and *The Great God Brown.* The directly autobiographical plays were a concerted attempt by O'Neill to "face his dead at last," and to probe the mystery of his deeply ambivalent feelings about all three members of his family, as well as the depths of personal despair that he had plumbed in 1912, the year of his attempted suicide and his tuberculosis. Both *Iceman* and *Journey* are set in 1912, the first a study of the world – physical and psychological – that O'Neill inhabited during his flophouse days, and the second a probing of the family dynamics founded on the warring forces of love and hate, compassion and resentment, admiration and contempt and exacerbated by illness, drug addiction, and alcoholism. *Moon* is set in 1923, the year of Jamie's death from the effects of alcoholism. It is a play of understanding and forgiveness, a postmortem exorcism of the demon that drove him to self-destruction.

The Iceman Cometh was the only one of the autobiographical plays that O'Neill saw fully through the production process, its 1946 staging by the Theatre Guild his last for Broadway. Although this production, directed by Eddie Dowling, ran for 136 performances, its critical reception was not particularly positive. Many thought that the four-and-one-half-hour play was simply verbose, and treated O'Neill as if he were a dead issue. Elliot Norton wrote in the *Boston Post* (13 October 1946): "Although it has its tragic moments of pity and terror, this is no great play, but a tangled, grubby, fearsome, and fearful tract from a sick playwright who has given up hope and consigned humanity to despair; or drink, or dreams – or death. Let him come out into the sunlight." *Iceman* did not get the production it deserved until after O'Neill's death in 1953, with José Quintero's 1956 production at the Circle-in-the-Square Theatre in New York. With Jason Robards in the role of Hickey, the production ran for 565 performances and was largely responsible for the revival of O'Neill's reputation, which had been in decline since the early thirties despite his Nobel Prize for literature in 1936. It was this production that persuaded Carlotta Monterey to entrust *Long Day's Journey* to Quintero for its first American production later in the year, with Fredric March and Florence Eldridge as the elder Tyrones and Jason Robards and Bradford Dillman as the brothers, a production that ran for 390 performances and confirmed O'Neill's place as the great American playwright.

In a sense, *Iceman* is the endpoint of O'Neill's spiritual search for a higher meaning and an act of forgiveness for his younger self. Like Ibsen's *The Wild*

Duck, it is an acceptance of the "life lie" or sustaining illusion, what O'Neill's characters call their "pipe dreams." To the denizens of Harry Hope's saloon, a composite of three bars that O'Neill frequented in his youth (Floyd, *Eugene O'Neill at Work,* 260), the salesman Hickey comes with a promise of salvation. He will replace their sustaining illusions with reality and so, he imagines, free them to accept their failure at life and live in peace. In the course of the play, O'Neill shows that Hickey's claim to inner peace is itself an illusion, and that each of the characters needs a life lie in order to carry on. In the end, the group finds peace in the notion that Hickey is insane and that the "reality" he had forced them all to face was madness. There are two exceptions to this, the young man Parritt, who has killed himself out of guilt for turning his anarchist mother in to the authorities, and Larry, whose sustaining illusion was that he spent his life "in the grandstand" observing, and never became emotionally involved with people. Speaking with "horrified pity" of Parritt's death, Larry says, "God rest his soul in peace," and then, "with bitter self-derision": "Ah, the damned pity – the wrong kind, as Hickey said! Be God, there's no hope! I'll never be a success in the grandstand – or anywhere else! . . . I'm the only real convert to death Hickey made here. From the bottom of my coward's heart I mean that now!" (*Plays,* III, 710). Larry is partly based on O'Neill's old friend Terry Carlin, but the composite of Parritt's suicidal guilt and resentment and his own realization about his fundamental dividedness reflect O'Neill's own self-study. In *Iceman,* O'Neill asserts the necessity of the sustaining illusion to make life bearable for most people but also insists on his own recognition of reality.

Iceman achieves its opposition of the sustaining illusion and an unforgiving reality by means of its own gritty realistic style and the deep formal rhythms that O'Neill had been experimenting with since *Beyond the Horizon* and had fully mastered by the end of his career. While some of the play's directors, and many of its early critics, mistook the play's carefully constructed, rhythmic repetitions for mere verbosity, Quintero's skill as a director enabled him to bring out the play's deep structure. Each of the play's four acts is a series of conflicts between characters, building with ever greater duration and intensity toward a peak of tension that ends in one of Hickey's four disturbing announcements: that he has stopped drinking, that his wife is dead, that his wife was murdered, and that it was he who killed her. Within each act, O'Neill manipulates the tensions between the characters to a building crescendo that explodes with each climactic announcement, but the ending of the play is carefully calculated anticlimax, the cornerstone of realistic dramatic structure, which indicates that life is essentially unchanged by what seem overwhelming moments of decision or insight. *Iceman* begins and ends with the drunks in Harry Hope's saloon trying to kill their pain with alcohol and pipe dreams. Parritt's suicide and Larry's self-realization have changed nothing essential about this world.

O'Neill sent the finished typescript of *Long Day's Journey Into Night,* "written in tears and blood," as the dedication reads, to his publisher, Bennett Cerf of Random House, with instructions that it not be published until twenty-five years after his death. When Carlotta Monterey O'Neill, as his executrix, directed Random House to publish the play in 1955, Cerf decided to abide by the playwright's wishes and refused to publish it, whereupon the rights were given to Yale University Press, which published the play in 1956, an immediate best-seller. Its world premiere took place in Sweden before the Quintero production in November, 1956. The intense personal probing of the O'Neill family that was O'Neill "facing his dead" renders his tentativeness about making the play public understandable. Even in the context of the autobiographical self-absorption of many plays in the fifties by playwrights like Tennessee Williams, William Inge, Robert Anderson, and Carson McCullers, *Long Day's Journey* is a pitiless unmasking of a family's darkest secrets. It is also the most perfectly crafted play in the canon of American drama.

Like *Iceman, Journey* is built on a fundamentally realistic deep structure. An early note makes the play's two motivating forces, Edmund's tuberculosis and Mary's morphine addiction, clear: "The younger son has appointment p.m. with Doctor to hear results – the others already know because Father has talked with doctor over phone – The strain of knowing has been too much for Mother – has started her off again" (Floyd, 281). Like *Iceman,* the play has a four-act structure, but its rhythm is different. The play begins with escalating quarrels among the four characters. It builds, however, not to a series of climaxes, but to four sustained self-revelatory modified monologues, in which each of the characters reveals an essential motivating truth about him or her that provokes understanding and sympathy from the audience. Such truth also provides a moment of emotional connection with another character, but because that moment is shrouded in the forgetfulness of alcohol and morphine, the connection is fleeting. As Mary Tyrone's final monologue trails off into a fantasy of the past, and her husband and sons fall into alcoholic oblivion, O'Neill's implication is that their life will continue in an endless cycle of pain and escape, approach and avoidance. Although the audience comes away with new insight into the human condition and new charity for human failure, the characters do not escape being trapped. O'Neill's play honored the reality of his family's suffering through his reflection of its seemingly inescapable pattern of repetition.

While *Long Day's Journey* may have made O'Neill's peace with his parents, two other plays of the period, the short piece, *Hughie* (written 1941; first staged 1958), originally intended for a series entitled *By Way of Obit,* and *A*

Moon for the Misbegotten (written 1943; staged 1947), evoke his brother, Jamie, as he was in the early twenties, shortly before his death. Although it is surrounded by some expressionistic effects, *Hughie* is essentially a mono- logue that reveals the loneliness and insecurity of the Broadway "sport," who, like Jamie O'Neill, dreams of a perfect system for playing the horses and a life spent following them from racetrack to racetrack with the seasons. *Moon* is the more important play, a sympathetic coming to terms with Jamie's behavior after the death of his mother, just as *Journey* had dealt with his con- flicting feelings of love and hatred and his simultaneous impulses to protect and destroy his younger brother. O'Neill's mother, Ella, had died in 1922 in California, where she had gone with Jamie to dispose of some property. Jamie, who had been sober since his father's death in 1920, immediately began drinking heavily, and continued to do so until his death the following year. In *Moon,* Jim Tyrone tells the story of his having stayed drunk for three days on the cross-country train carrying his mother's coffin, while he sought forgetfulness with a prostitute. "It was as if I wanted revenge – because I'd been left alone," he says, "because I knew I was lost, without any hope left – that all I could do would be drink myself to death, because no one was left who could help me" (*Plays,* III, 932). The deep guilt he feels for his weakness and the unresolved oedipal feelings he has for his mother are exorcized for Jim when he tells the story to Josie Hogan, a young woman whose selfless love for Jim causes her to give up the thought of a sexual relationship with him in order to act as a forgiving Virgin Mother and absolve him of his sins. At the end of Act III, as Josie cradles the sleeping Jim in her arms, she speaks of "a dawn that won't creep over dirty windowpanes but will wake in the sky like a promise of God's peace in the soul's dark sadness" (*Plays,* III, 933), the same image of the *pietà* that closes *More Stately Mansions.* This play is not driven by sentiment or pathos, however. Jim's story is embedded in a lively comedy involving Josie and her father, Phil Hogan, who is based on a tenant of the O'Neills', "Dirty" Dolan. Josie's mostly satisfying life with her father on the farm will go on despite her loss of Jim Tyrone. Josie's final words in the play are an acceptance of life as well as a blessing for both Jim Tyrone and Jamie O'Neill: "May you have your wish and die in your sleep soon, Jim, dar- ling. May you rest forever in forgiveness and peace" (*Plays,* III, 946).

Having faced "his dead," Eugene O'Neill achieved a measure of peace with regard to his parents and brother, but the final decade of his life was far from happy. Unable to write because of his illness, he became increasingly depressed, and his marriage to Carlotta deteriorated markedly. They left Tao House, their home in the California mountains, and moved to Marblehead, Massachusetts. His relationship with his children was as tortured as that with his parents. His eldest child, Eugene O'Neill Jr., an alcoholic, killed him- self in 1950. O'Neill cut himself off from the two children he had with Agnes

Boulton, Shane and Oona, and disinherited them. Finally, he and Carlotta retreated to the Shelton Hotel in Boston. At one point in the last stages of his illness, "he suddenly struggled up to a half-sitting position and, staring wildly around the room, cried, 'I knew it I knew it! Born in a goddam hotel room and dying in a hotel room!'" (Sheaffer, *Son and Artist,* 670). He died there on 27 November 1953.

Folk Plays

One of the most unlikely phenomena of the worldly and rather cynical Jazz Age was the resurgence of the folk play. The romantic drama celebrating the virtues of domesticity and the cultural ideal of rural simplicity had been a staple of native American drama since the Yankee plays of the early nineteenth century. In the teens, such old standards as Denman Thompson's *Old Homestead,* James A. Herne's *Shore Acres,* and of course, *Uncle Tom's Cabin,* were still being played and appreciated outside of New York. The new wave of folk drama may be distinguished from the earlier plays by its academic origin and its cultural function. As the interest in cultural anthropology and the study of folklore developed in universities, the few faculty members who taught dramatic literature and playwriting began to see the "simple play about simple folk" in the light of these disciplines. The new writers of folk plays were educated, often university-trained, people who wrote with a consciousness of the cultural function their plays were to perform.

Two traditions of folk drama developed simultaneously during the twenties, based on the experience of Americans, both blacks and whites. Those with the clearest sense of mission were the African American writers, whose agenda was articulated by W. E. B. Du Bois, and two members of the Howard University faculty, who founded the theatre program there in 1921, Alain Locke and Montgomery T. Gregory. In his well-known statement on the occasion of the establishment of his Krigwa Little Theatre Movement in 1926, Du Bois articulated four principles for the drama of a Negro theatre. For Du Bois, the drama must be about, by, for, and near "the mass of ordinary Negro people" (Du Bois, 134). Whereas Du Bois favored and occasionally wrote "race plays," meant to educate African Americans about their history and the contemporary issues facing them, Locke and Gregory demanded freedom from the didacticism of this view of the arts. Locke promoted folk drama as "the uncurdled, almost naive reflection of the poetry and folk feeling of a people who have after all a different soul and temperament from that of the smug, unimaginative industrialist and the self-righteous and inhibited Puritan" (Locke, n.p.). Aware of the danger that placing black characters in the folk tradition could help to perpetuate the caricatures and stereotypes of the stage Negro hanging over from melodrama and the minstrel show, Locke contended that

> generations of enforced buffoonery and caricature have not completely stifled the dramatic endowment of the Negro; his temperament still moves natively and spontaneously in the world of make-believe with the primitive power of imaginative abandon and emotional conviction . . . as actor and as audience, the Negro temperament promises to bring back to a jaded, sceptical stage some of the renewing, elemental moods and powers of early drama. (Locke, n.p.)

During the twenties, encouraged by playwriting contests sponsored by the magazines *Crisis* and *Opportunity,* and largely through the creative efforts of Locke's and Montgomery's students and associates, such as Willis Richardson, Zora Neale Hurston, Mary P. Burrill, May Miller, Georgia Douglas Johnson, and Eulalie Spence, a substantial body of black folk drama was produced, although, access to the means of production being extremely limited for African Americans, only Richardson's plays *The Chip Woman's Fortune* (1923) and *The Broken Banjo* (1925) were produced on Broadway. The representation of blacks on the New York stage was overwhelmingly by whites.

The parallel development of the white folk tradition also had academic origins. Frederick Koch, who became professor of dramatic literature at the University of North Carolina in 1918, encouraged his students to develop their plays from the material of the Carolina "mountain folk" and took these plays on the road to be performed for rural audiences in the South. His most successful student was Paul Green, whose *In Abraham's Bosom* won the Pulitzer Prize in 1926 and who made a career of writing folk plays for the Broadway stage in the twenties and thirties. Lula Vollmer, whose *Sun-Up* (1923) was a success in both New York and London, was a native of North Carolina who studied under George Pierce Baker at Harvard. Hatcher Hughes, who won the Pulitzer Prize for his Appalachian folk play about fundamentalist Christianity, *Hell-Bent Fer Heaven,* in 1924, was on the faculty of Columbia University. Clearly this "folk drama" was not self-expression by the folk, but, as Koch defined it, "the work of a single author dealing consciously with his materials, the folkways of our less sophisticated people living simple lives. . . . the ultimate cause of all dramatic action we classify as 'folk,' whether it be physical or spiritual, may be found in man's desperate struggle for existence and in his enjoyment of the world of nature" (Koch, xv). In other words, like Locke's, Koch's "folk play" was a rather elitist representation of rural people as fundamentally and essentially different from the playwright and the middle-class theatre audience, because of a putative simplicity that made them more responsive to their natural environment and more susceptible to their own drives and passions than a more "civilized" person would be.

This distancing of the playwright and the audience from the characters of the play allowed for the representation of subject matter that would have been unproducible in the twenties if it had occurred in realistic middle-class drama – subjects such as miscegenation, incest, lynching, and religious hypocrisy. Although it was nearly closed down for obscenity, Eugene O'Neill's tragedy, *Desire Under the Elms* (1924), managed to treat adultery and religious fanaticism and to skirt incest, largely because it was cast within the conventions of folk drama. Similarly, the most successful of the plays by whites about blacks, *In Abraham's Bosom,* took on the highly charged issue of the color line, and specifically miscegenation. Green's point of view was based on racial essentialism; it was a version of the "tragic mulatto" theme in which the greatest tragedy of miscegenation was the battle of two conflicting "race" impulses within one nature. As one character puts it: "De white blood in him coming to de top. Dat make him want-a climb up and be sump'n. Nigger gwine hol' him down dough. Part of him take adder de Colonel, part adder his muh, 'vision and misery inside" (P. Green, 23). While Abe McCranie adheres to the doctrine of "racial uplift," trying to educate himself so that he can run a school and educate the community, he is thwarted by his own nature, which causes him to alienate the community by beating a student nearly to death, to lose his jobs because of his hot temper, and finally to beat his white half-brother to death, for which he is shot to death by a vigilante mob. The mob is given a measure of justification by the lines "what a bloody murder he done! . . . It's the only way to have peace, peace" (P. Green, 140–41). Although Green presents his tragic mulatto in a sympathetic light, the play's cultural message about miscegenation is that the mixing of white and black is dangerous and wrong because blacks are by nature more primitive, more violent, and less intelligent than whites.

In Abraham's Bosom was strongly influenced by O'Neill's *Emperor Jones;* scene 6 is a recreation of Jones's psychological journey back to his "primitive origins." Both plays also have a direct line forward to two plays by blacks that focus on the color line, Hall Johnson's *Run, Little Chillun* (1933), and the most commercially successful nonmusical play by an African American until Lorraine Hansberry's *Raisin in the Sun* (1959), Langston Hughes's *Mulatto* (1935). Hall Johnson is best known for the choir that bore his name and that was featured prominently in the white playwright Marc Connelly's representation of black folk-Christianity, *The Green Pastures* (1930). Connelly's play, which won the Pulitzer Prize, is a self-described "attempt to present certain aspects of a living religion in the terms of its believers" (Connelly, xv). When Johnson set out to write his own play featuring the choir, he composed a contemporary fable, closely allied to both *The Emperor Jones* and Countee Cullen's classic poem "Heritage," about the struggle for the soul of a young black man in the rural South between the Hope Baptist Church and the New

Day Pilgrims, a group that advocates the revival of African culture through what it imagines is a recreation of African religious rituals. In *Run, Little Chillun,* the African rituals are depicted as dangerously exotic orgies, unleashing the uncontrolled sexuality of the participants. The protagonist, Jim, is saved from this unleashing of his primitive side by the parson's daughter, Ella Jones, who brings him back to the Baptist fold, and the play culminates in an old-fashioned revival scene in which dangerous paganism is renounced in favor of jubilant Christianity. Like the plays by the white writers, *Run, Little Chillun* represents the African side of African American culture as primitive, uncontrollable, and dangerous, the black man's salvation as a simple, joyous Christianity.

Among the folk plays centered on the lives of rural blacks, Langston Hughes's *Mulatto* presents a unique perspective on the theme of the tragic mulatto and the issues of miscegenation and the color line. Like *In Abraham's Bosom,* Hughes's play focuses on the attempts of a young man to come to terms with his mixed heritage. Although Hughes relies on the tragic mulatto theme to give the play meaning, his use of it is unconventional. Robert Lewis's tragic end results from his rejection of his black heritage as well as his white father's rejection of him. He despises the black people of the town because the only way he sees to assert his own worth is to lay claim to his white heritage. What he fails to see is that his race is a social construct, not a biological fact. He wants to claim difference from other African Americans through his biological characteristics: "I'm not black, either. . . . Don't I look like my father? Ain't I as light as he is? . . . Ain't this our house?" (L. Hughes, 19). The fact that he has Caucasian characteristics and is his father's son does not make him "white," any more than it makes him heir to his father's possessions. Robert is black by the fiction of Jim Crow laws and social convention, but also because of his mother's heritage and the culture in which she has raised him. Exhibiting the double bind in which his protagonist is caught, Hughes suggests through Robert's suicide that he is a scapegoat for the irreconcilable contradictions in American culture. The only way to survive these conditions is to accept the inferior position to which African Americans are relegated in southern society, as Robert's brother William does, or to escape to the North and renounce half of one's heritage by passing for white, as his sister Bertha does. The tragedy of the mulatto here is not the mixing of the races, but the failure of Americans to realize that race is a fiction.

If the complex treatment of the tragic mulatto theme in *Mulatto* marks an endpoint for the black folk tradition, Jack Kirkland's adaptation of Erskine Caldwell's novel *Tobacco Road* (1933) may represent the final decadence of the white folk tradition. Paul Green followed *In Abraham's Bosom* with well-received representations of rural whites, in such plays as *The Field God* (1927) and *The House of Connelly* (1931), the inaugural production of the

Group Theatre. Like those of Hughes and Vollmer, these were serious efforts in the tradition of folk drama. *Tobacco Road,* the most successful folk play by far in commercial terms, offers a depiction of rural Georgia that goes beyond the primitive and as far as the grotesque. Kirkland's perspective pervades the opening stage direction:

> *It is a famished, desolate land. . . . Poverty, want, squalor, degeneracy, pitiful helplessness and grotesque, tragic lusts have stamped a lost, outpaced people with the mark of inevitable end. Unequipped to face a changing economic program, bound up in traditions, ties, and prejudices, they unknowingly face extinction. . . . Grim humor pervades all, stalking side by side with tragedy on the last short mile which leads to complete, eventual elimination. The pride and hope of a once aggressive group, pioneers in a great new world, thus meet ironic conclusion.* (Kirkland, 3)

The characters of the play, the Lester family, became a cultural icon for the decadence of self-enclosed American rural society. The play exists in a liminal space between horror and humor, where the audience is brought to view the world created on the stage as absurdly grotesque so that it can laugh at what would be unacceptable as a realistic representation of contemporary American life. Understandably, the production played up the comedy in this dialectic, and the audience accepted the play as a farcical representation of an alien culture from which it was clearly separate. *Tobacco Road,* which ran for 3,182 performances on Broadway, realized the end of the serious folk tradition in the American theatre.

Rachel Crothers: Review of Early Plays and Explication of Remaining Works

Rachel Crothers was born on 12 December 1870[5] in Bloomington, Illinois, a small town in the central part of the state, where her family was well known. Her father, Dr. Eli Kirk Crothers, was a friend of Abraham Lincoln, who once defended him successfully in a malpractice suit. The major influence on Crothers's work and ideas, however, was her mother, Dr. Marie Depew Crothers, who received an M.D. degree from the Women's Medical College of Pennsylvania in 1883 and encountered a good deal of resistance when she established her own practice in Bloomington, the first female physician in central Illinois. This experience no doubt influenced one of Rachel Crothers's best known plays, *He and She* (staged in Boston 1912; revised version first produced in New York, 1920), in which Ann Herford gives up a promising career as a sculptor because she decides that her teenage daughter, who has been exiled to boarding school, needs her. Dr. Crothers did not give up her career for Rachel, who was sent to live with an aunt in Wellesley, Massachusetts, while her mother studied medicine in Philadelphia.

After a severe attack of typhoid delayed her education, Crothers graduated from high school in 1891 and from the New England School of Dramatic Instruction in Boston in 1892. The death of her rather straitlaced father in 1893 no doubt freed Crothers to pursue a stage career that was frowned upon by her parents. In 1896, she moved to New York and attended the Stanhope–Wheatcroft school of acting, where she spent four years as a student, teacher, and acting coach, accumulating invaluable experience and knowledge for her future career as playwright and director. At the Wheatcroft School, Crothers later explained, "the practice that [she] had in every line of stagecraft gave [her] the opportunity to not only write plays, but to select the cast, rehearse them, and carry the performance through to the ringing down of the final curtain" ("Producing," 34). After several of the one-act plays that she wrote for her students to perform were produced in Broadway theatres, her first full-length play, *The Three of Us,* was produced professionally in 1906 to enthusiastic reviews, running for 227 performances in New York with Carlotta Nillson in the lead and achieving similar success in a London production with Ethyl Barrymore. Although it is essentially a domestic melodrama placed in the unlikely setting of a western mining camp, *The Three of Us* contained many of the elements of the social realism with which Crothers was to make her mark on the American theatre. It concerned one of her perennial themes, the double standard for sexual morality, and it introduced the typical Crothers protagonist in Rhy MacChesney, a strong, cheerful, independent young woman who is raising her two younger brothers and trying to live according to her own innocent standards of morality despite the community's hypocrisy and concern for appearances.

Crothers's next play, *Myself Bettina* (1908), a loose adaptation of *Magda,* launched her unique thirty-year career in the American theatre as what she called a "producing playwright." Crothers sold the play to Maxine Elliott, a powerful star who gave Crothers "the pleasure of producing one of [her] own plays entirely by [herself] for the first time" ("Troubles," 14). The success of the production established Crothers as a playwright "who not only writes the plays, and attends the rehearsals, but actually engages the company, directs all rehearsals, supervises the building of the scenery, selection of the costumes, and the lighting effects" ("Producing," 34). Although they had more in common with the Stanislavskian techniques that were to prevail in the thirties than with the "art theatre" concepts of the teens, Crothers's ideas on directing were definite and modern. She held that no one could be a better director for a play than its author, "if he has the ability and practical experience to do it," for "the author sees the finished production as a whole, the completed picture, as he creates, therefore no time is needed for experimenting. He goes straight at the thing as a whole. He knows every light and shade, every phase of character and its relation to every other character. Above all, he knows the tempo of each scene and of the whole play – and he starts each actor off in the right key at the first rehearsal, without letting him flounder in the wrong direction for some days" ("Troubles," 14). Like the later Method directors, Crothers believed that "directing means not only the mental understanding of characters, but the dramatic and theatric knowledge necessary to convey this understanding to the actor, and above all, the power to awaken the best in the actor, to stir latent fire he himself may not have known he possessed to use his individuality to the best advantage, calling upon all he has to give to the characterization both temperamentally and physically, and molding him into the living being which he must become for the play" ("Future," 13). Crothers went to great lengths to elicit authentic emotion from her actors. Believing that Helen Ormsby had "lost her first freshness and had grown hard and stilted in her scene of breakdown and tears" in *A Man's World* (1909), for example, she badgered her at rehearsal in order to "make her really cry, to make her go all to pieces herself in order to bring her back to her best work" ("Troubles," 14). Throughout her career, Crothers received great critical praise for the authenticity and technical perfection of her dialogue and characterization, qualities that probably had as much to do with her direction as her writing.

It was during the period of the Progressive Era that Crothers produced the plays for which she is best known today, dramas in the form of the Shavian discussion play that are at the heart of the feminist agenda for the Progressivist New Woman in the teens. *A Man's World,* the most frequently anthologized of Crothers's plays, which was discussed briefly in the preceding section of this chapter, gives full treatment to the question of the double standard. In an interesting twist on the question that was the standard fare in contemporary problem plays, what to do about the "tainted woman" after she has strayed, Crothers presents the issue from the perspective of a woman, Frank Ware, whose fiancé refuses to accept responsibility for having had an affair that has produced a son. In having Frank reject the man and keep the child, overturning the audience's expectations for a reconciliation, Crothers challenged the convention that a woman should accept a man's sexual promiscuity but be subject to condemnation by a man for having sex with him.

He and She, a play so important to Crothers that she played the lead in a 1920 revision of the play, which had failed in its 1912 production, is built on a more complex structure and presentation of ideas than is *A Man's World,* as suggested earlier by Wainscott. While the Herford couple debate the issues surrounding the wife's decision to accept the commission for a sculpting competition she has won and her husband has lost, two other characters show further perspectives on the question of combining career and marriage.

Through both dialogue and structure, Dr. Crothers's daughter, who remained a successful single woman throughout her life, suggests that marriage and career are fundamentally incompatible. One character decides not to marry because she realizes her career is her life; another gives up her career in a second to marry, claiming "there are lots and lots and lots of women taking care of themselves – putting up the bluff of being independent and happy – who would be so glad to live in a little flat and do their own work – just to be the nicest thing in the world to some man" (Crothers, quoted in Quinn, *Representative American Plays*, 3rd ed., 916).

The closest Crothers came to muckraking was *Ourselves* (1913), a treatment of what her contemporaries euphemistically called "white slavery," which concerns the efforts of middle-class women reformers to guide "wayward girls" away from a life of prostitution and into middle-class domesticity. The play depicts these efforts as futile, locating the causes for prostitution in economic and social conditions and also in aspects of both male and female sexuality, as well as in the unwillingness of middle-class women to accept responsibility for condoning the double standard.

Neither *He and She* nor *Ourselves* was successful commercially, and the reviews of *Ourselves* indicated that public interest in the Progressive agenda was waning by the midteens, prompting Crothers to reassess her own agenda as a playwright. The late teens found her experimenting with other modes of drama than social realism, as in, for example, the "gladness" plays, which were written on the basis of a formula blending comedy, romance, and sentiment (Gottlieb, *Rachel Crothers,* 76). These plays included an adaptation of Kate Douglas Wiggins's *Mother Carey's Chickens* (1917) and three commercially successful original scripts, *Old Lady 31* (1916), about an elderly man who lives in a home for elderly women so he can be with his wife; *39 East* (1919), based on Crothers's experiences in a boarding house when she first came to New York as an aspiring young actress; and *A Little Journey* (1918), about a penniless and despairing young woman brought up to be middle class and useless, and her regeneration, thanks to a young man from the West who gives her the chance to join him in a project to reform alcoholics by giving them wholesome work in the great outdoors on a ranch. As Lois Gottlieb has pointed out, *Little Journey* takes on greater significance when read as an early treatment of the postwar spiritual malaise of the lost generation (*Crothers,* 87–88), but its suggestion that the answer to Western civilization's collapse lies in a pastoral return to the regenerative powers of nature is simplistic at best.

More significant as an expression of Crothers's social interests in the teens is *Young Wisdom* (1914), which was seen by contemporary critics as a satire of the woman's movement and thus as a reversal of Crothers's earlier views on the New Woman and female emancipation. Written as a vehicle for the

Taliaferro sisters, the play treats the subject of trial marriage in a lightly satirical way. Having just returned from college, where she was filled with all sorts of "advanced" ideas, Victoria Claffenden convinces her sister Gail that she should resist the marriage that her parents have planned for her until she and her fiancé have lived together in a trial marriage long enough to know that their union will be a happy and lasting one. Crothers treats the situation with humor that is close to farcical, and the play takes a conservative stance on marriage, but it also contains enough discussion of the institution of marriage to engage its audience in serious consideration of some important issues. This was the essential plan of Crothers's social comedies in the twenties and early thirties, the plays that were most successful with audiences and that earned her the title of America's foremost woman playwright, plays like *Nice People* (1921), *Mary the Third* (1923), *Expressing Willie* (1924), *Let Us Be Gay* (1929), *As Husbands Go* (1931), *When Ladies Meet* (1932), and *Susan and God* (1937). In these treatments of the manners and mores of the American middle and upper classes, Crothers displayed an unerring sense of style and a mordant, witty dialogue similar to that of Philip Barry, Noël Coward, and S. N. Behrman, which became the recognized convention of the brittle American society comedies of the twenties and thirties. Combining a natural ingenuity with long years and practice as playwright, director, actor, and producer, she achieved a mastery of comic construction, pace, and tempo. She also managed to address the perennial social issues that interested her and her middle-class audience, primarily those related to marriage, divorce, the family, and the various social and intellectual fads that characterized the period, such as Freudianism, the cult of self-expression, and Buchmanism.

As in *Young Wisdom,* however, Crothers's main target during these years was the generation that came of age in the twenties and its various extremes and follies. In *Young Wisdom,* it is not the women's movement that is satirized so much as a new debased version of it, which rejected the social reform agenda of the Progressive movement and made the serious concerns of the New Woman – economic independence; the freedom to choose one's career and develop one's talent; the freedom to marry a husband of one's choice, or not to marry – into excuses for hedonism and irresponsibility. Crothers's attitude toward the Jazz Age generation is most evident in *Nice People,* a treatment of the flapper that followed F. Scott Fitzgerald's *This Side of Paradise* only a year later. *Nice People* featured the young Tallulah Bankhead, Katharine Cornell, and Francine Larrimore as three spoiled young flappers, who, in 1920, have allowances of twenty thousand dollars a year, and spend eighty dollars on a single night's spree. Crothers spends the first act displaying the vacuous materialism of these young women and then has the protagonist, Teddy Gloucester, rescued from her empty life by a young man who shows her the joys of a rural life of raising chickens. Like other Crothers heroines, Teddy discovers the satisfaction of independence, even from her own extremely wealthy family. When her father offers to buy her young man for her in the end, she replies: "I'd like to see you try. Why do you want to dispose of me? Let me do it myself. First of all, I want to be left alone – to think. Men aren't everything on earth . . . Regardless of you – or any other man in the world, I'm going to take care of myself" (Crothers, *Plays*, 184).

With *Expressing Willie*, Crothers beat F. Scott Fitzgerald by a year, anticipating Jay Gatsby in her Willie Smith, a young man who has made millions in toothpaste and is now surrounded by a crowd of social sycophants in his Long Island mansion. The target of the satire is the cult of self-expression arising from the popularization of Freudian psychology. After exposing the hypocrisy and silliness of this fad, Crothers leaves the audience siding with Willie's wholesome mother, who says "if we were all running around without any *suppressions,* we might as well have tails again" (72). The later social comedies attack the middle-aged rather than the youthful products of the new values of the Jazz Age. *Let Us Be Gay* takes on the values related to marriage and divorce among the upper class, and *As Husbands Go* examines the effect of Parisian freedom on two middle-aged women from Dubuque. Crothers's two most successful social comedies, *When Ladies Meet* and *Susan and God,* make use of her well-practiced formula of combining a topical social issue with recognizable society types as characters, witty dialogue, and a humorous comic plot. In this context, Crothers could get away with debating social issues that were as serious as those in her discussion plays of the teens without alienating an audience that was primarily interested in escapist entertainment. *When Ladies Meet* treats that stock component of the farce, the love triangle, from the neglected perspective of the "other woman" and makes a serious point. The play asks whether it is possible for a "decent" woman to fall in love with a married man, for him to fall in love with her, for her to discuss the situation with the wife, and for there to be a reasonably happy outcome for all. The play suggests that it is possible but also that the outcome is unpredictable – both women leave the man when they realize how he has treated the other woman.

Crothers's last produced play, and her most successful, was *Susan and God,* which, with Gertrude Lawrence in the role of Susan Trexel, ran for 288 performances on Broadway and won the Megrue Prize for comedy. It satirizes the attempt by the idle rich to import meaning into their empty lives by latching onto "spiritual" fads and enthusiasms – in this case, Buchmanism imported from England. In the course of the play, Susan finds that her newly found religious conviction is a sham but that she can fill her empty life by establishing a real family relationship with her husband and daughter.

Crothers also examined the values and mores of this world in more serious forms than that of social comedy, sometimes combining formal experimentation with a new perspective on the issues. She wrote a series of one-act plays in the early twenties that feature a cast of continuing characters in situations that expose their social and moral values. *The Importance of Being Clothed* (1920), which examines the effect of the fashion industry on social values and points out the exploitation of the garment workers and models, anticipates similar commentary in Clare Boothe's *The Women* (1936). Others in the series concern the clash of values implicit in the different codes of etiquette of the older generation and the younger and deal with several different aspects of the marriage-vs.-career question that preoccupied Crothers throughout this period.

The most skeptical of Crothers's plays, *Mary the Third* (1923), uses the device of the prologue, whereby a grandmother and mother, in the manner of 1870 and 1897, respectively, make the decision at the start of the play to give up their "soulmates" in order to marry men they are physically attracted to. The main body of the play presents Mary's struggle with the same issue in 1923, against the background of the unhappy marriages of mother and grandmother. At the same time that the play demystifies the cultural ideal of the traditional marriage by exposing the pragmatic motives for entering and continuing it, the ending suggests, through Mary's engagement to the young man she is attracted to, that marriage based on sexual attraction is inevitable in contemporary American culture, as is disillusionment of the cultural expectation that love and marriage will last forever. The only difference between Mary and her mother and grandmother is that divorce will be more socially acceptable for her, and along with her determination to be economically independent, will provide an escape when her marriage becomes intolerable.

Throughout her career, Crothers was primarily and fundamentally a theatre professional. She was among the first to adapt the Shavian discussion play to American characters and social issues. She brought American social comedy to a new standard of excellence, which she met consistently for twenty years. She was a significant force in defining the artistic and professional role of the director in the American theatre and in establishing its importance. Her plays provided a timely, intelligent, and often witty commentary on middle- and upper-class America from the underrepresented perspective of a woman negotiating the shifting economic and social conditions and cultural values surrounding the issues of marriage, divorce, sexuality, economic independence, family responsibility, class, generational conflict, materialism, and spirituality. Her plays are significant cultural documents that provide an extensive commentary on three generations of American life. After the success of *Susan and God,* she organized the American Theatre Wing Allied Relief Fund, serving as its president until 1950, and wrote at least three more plays, which were not produced on Broadway. She died at her home in Connecticut on 5 July 1958.

Realism

Rachel Crothers's career in the twenties and thirties was representative of the trends in Broadway theatre as a whole. During this period, the greatest number of plays by far were written in the mode of what is generally called bourgeois realism – they were representations of the middle class, concerned middle-class problems, and reflected a middle-class view of the world. These plays ranged throughout that great span of the population in the United States that identifies itself as middle class, from the simple small-town family in Zona Gale's *Miss Lulu Bett* (1920), in which the unmarried sister is tolerated because she does most of the housework, to the semidomesticated society people in plays by S. N. Behrman. These domestic plays could be light or serious, cast in the mode of comedy, melodrama, or that peculiar hybird of the period, comedy-melodrama. What distinguished them was their focus on marriage, divorce, and family life.

Although the play had a difficult time making it to the stage, Jesse Lynch Williams's *Why Marry?* received the first Pulitzer Prize for Drama in 1917. Williams had begun work on the play as early as 1910, but it was not until the rupture in traditional Victorian mores and values accompanying World War I that it could be found acceptable by the Broadway public. Williams's play was heavily influenced by Bernard Shaw. Like many of Shaw's plays, this one combines an improbable, nearly farcical, comic plot with a sophisticated, rather daring, and witty discussion of marriage, divorce, and the social values they represent. Although lines in the play were calculatedly shocking to an American audience in 1917 – "The object of marriage is not to bring together those who love each other, but to keep together those who do not" (62) – the comic plot places all three of the couples who are threatening the institution of marriage safely within its boundaries by the end of the play. It was a fitting beginning for the extensive treatment of marriage, divorce, and the family that was to be carried on in the Broadway theatre of the twenties and thirties.

In regard to the high-society end of the American social spectrum, two themes tended to dominate what was generally known as society comedy during the period: the destructive effects of too much money and the empty lives of society people. These notions appealed naturally to a Broadway theatre audience that was mainly middle class and frustrated in its desire to have the things the characters in the society comedies had. One of the earliest of these plays was by Philip Barry, a privileged young man who had gone to Yale, attended George Pierce Baker's playwriting workshop at Harvard, and then had two of the plays he wrote for Baker produced on Broadway. *A Punch for Judy* (1921) was followed by *You and I* (1923), which was a hit, launching Barry on a very successful career. In *Holiday* (1928), Barry depicted the dissatisfac-

George S. Kaufman and Moss Hart's *You Can't Take It with You* (1936), designed by Donald Oenslager. Vandamm photo. Billy Rose Theatre Collection, New York Public Library for the Performing Arts, Astor, Lenox and Tilden Foundations.

tion and frustration of the younger generation, who are in a sense imprisoned by wealth. Johnny Case, a self-made man who has accumulated a small fortune while still young, wants to drop out of the business world for a while and enjoy the freedom to live as he likes, away from the demands both of business and of the social world of high society. Linda Seton, a child of privilege, wants to escape from the strictures her social position places on her life choices. The two young people escape from their prison of wealth and society at the end of the play, going off to find freedom and fulfillment in what amounts to a largely symbolic rebellion against the values of their social group, since both have enough money to not have to work to support themselves.

The middle-class version of this rejection of the drive for material success and the social climbing that accompanied it was most energetically expressed in Moss Hart and George S. Kaufman's *You Can't Take It with You* (1936). In the midst of the Great Depression, the cultural fantasy of freedom from the need to accumulate money had been deflated considerably. The Sycamore family, consisting of Grandpa, his daughter and her husband, and his two granddaughters, one of whom is married, considers itself comfortably provided for on Grandpa's income of between three thousand and four thousand dollars a year. Only Alice, the younger granddaughter, works, mostly because she feels that she needs some contact with the outside world, away from her family, whom she loves very much but whom she recognizes as individualistic to a degree exceeding eccentricity. Kaufman and Hart create a farce by taking the values expressed in *Holiday* – personal fulfillment and freedom from materialism, social responsibilities, and social strictures – to their logical extreme. Thus the members of the family are deeply engaged in activities that serve no purpose except their own fulfillment: Grandpa goes to commencement exercises and raises snakes; his son-in-law makes fireworks; his daughter writes plays that are never produced; his granddaughter dances; and her husband prints slogans on a hand press. The comic plot involves the conversion of the conventional Kirby family to a moderate form of the Sycamore values, as young Tony is allowed to marry Alice and to find work that interests him rather than being forced into the family business, and his father is relieved of his chronic stomach trouble by relaxing among the Sycamores.

Barry continued to resist the values of his chosen subject, American society people, whether in comedies like *The Animal Kingdom* (1932) and *The Philadelphia Story* (1939) or in his more serious metaphysical and meta-theatrical efforts, such as *Hotel Universe* (1930) and *Here Come the Clowns* (1938), plays that were not nearly as successful with the Broadway audience as his comedies were. Besides Rachel Crothers, the other most significant chronicler of society people was S. N. Behrman, whose comedy maintained a cynical edge that never quite committed it to a point of view. Behrman's first play, produced by the prestigious Theatre Guild in 1927, was *The Second Man,* a witty comedy about a writer who is kept from any sincere commitment to romantic love or "higher values" by a skeptical "second man" inside him that constantly undermines these romantic notions. With the rather unconvincing exception of *Rain from Heaven* (1934), in which a character makes the decision to fight fascism rather than maintain a comfortable existence as a refugee artist, Behrman's plays maintain a noncommital position between two extremes, usually a self-interested and hypocritical Left and a vacuously materialistic and power-hungry Right. Even in *Rain from Heaven,* while the refugee returns to Germany to fight the Nazis, his liberal love-interest decides to stay in England, maintaining that "there is a genius for wandering and a genius for remaining behind. There is the shooting star and the fixed" (Behrman, 272). In a play like *Biography* (1932), in which the protagonist is trying to choose between marrying one extreme or the other, the final flight from both is depicted as an independent and empowering choice. Like one of Crothers's heroines, Marion Froude will make her own money and her own life, and, as an artist, she is free to exist outside the male power structure, on the fringes of political life, without making a commitment to any ideology. Behrman makes this position more overt in *No Time for Comedy* (1939), in which he presents an argument for writing entertaining escapist comedy in the face of the rising specter of fascism and war in Europe. In Behrman's plays, the rejection of conventional American cultural values, a sign in the plays of Barry or Crothers of a commitment to a more personal and more authentic value system, becomes an ideology in itself, a commitment to noninvolvement and personal freedom at the expense of personal relationships and civic responsibility.

Clare Boothe's satirical comedy *The Women* (1936) ran for 657 performances on Broadway. Many of the criticisms of society women that Rachel Crothers had conveyed in a gently satirical way in her series of one-act plays (1920–25) were repeated here with biting wit and somewhat heavy-handed humor. The empty lives of society women whose chief occupation was to enjoy themselves and to look as good as possible doing it, while their husbands earned money and servants raised their children and took care of their houses, are exposed by means of a series of vignettes: a bridge game in a fashionable drawing room, an exercise class, a beauty salon, a clothing designer's salon, a hotel in Reno for women who are awaiting divorces, a night club. Boothe exposes the uselessness and powerlessness of the women, and the manipulation and exploitation of their husbands that their position precipitates. Stripping to its essentials the struggle among the women for men who can support them, Boothe represents the salvation of the protagonist Mary in her willingness to meet the rival for her husband in a no-holds-barred contest that takes place in the ladies' room of a fashionable night club. Mary gets her husband back, and this comic closure reaffirms the values of Mary's society, but not without exposing the fraudulence and viciousness that underlies it. For the middle-class Broadway audience, this play served much the same function as Barry's *Philadelphia Story,* toppling the fantasy heroine of the hour, the wealthy young socialite, from her pedestal and exposing the emptiness of her life and the cultural values that supported it.

Despite the attraction of the sophisticated society comedy, on the stages of the United States between 1915 and 1945 middle-class domestic comedy was the most popular genre of the period by far, as is indicated by the incredibly long runs of some mediocre plays: *Life with Father* (1939), 3,224 performances; *Abie's Irish Rose* (1922), 2,327 performances; *Harvey* (1944), 1,775 performances; *The Voice of the Turtle* (1943), 1,667 performances; *Arsenic and Old Lace* (1941), 1,444 performances. For the most part, these plays used the conventional form of comedy to relieve various anxieties that were endemic to American culture during the twenties and thirties. As the rising tide of fascism made Americans fear the encroachment of tyranny on their lives and freedom, for example, in *Life with Father* the undercutting of a patriarchal domestic tyrant through humor and sentiment was reassuring. Father might rant and stamp on the floor, forbid money and hospitality, refuse to bow even to God, but the quiet and loving machinations of Mother would temper the extremes and domesticate the beast. The image of Father being led off to be baptized at the end of the play symbolized the ultimate civilizing influence of Christianity on a world being threatened by power-hungry dictators. Similarly, in a country that was increasingly troubled by ethnic prejudice, *Abie's Irish Rose* suggested that a new and happy future could be forged for America if its citizens could forget their petty ethnic differences and join together as one big family.

Three Pulitzer Prize winning plays suggest the possibilities of domestic comedy that were exploited effectively by a number of playwrights during the twenties and thirties. Zona Gale's *Miss Lulu Bett* (1920) is at once a depiction of the typically dreary hopelessness of the life of a single woman in small-town America and a comic affirmation of hope for the future. After living her life essentially as an unpaid servant in the home of her sister and brother-in-law, on whom she is dependent financially, Lulu wins her freedom by breaking the rules of her small-town world and eloping with a man she loves. Owen Davis's *Icebound* (1923) made effective use of the frozen New England landscape to represent the effects of inherited puritanism on the typical New England family: "It's like that half the year, froze up, everything, most of all the people" (O. Davis, 213). Because he has seen something of the world during his service in France, the World War I veteran Ben Jordan is able to escape the dreary imprisonment of his New England heritage and imagine a better future with his fiancée, Jane. George Kelly's *The Show-Off* (1926) was a kindly and humorous treatment of a typical twenties character, the egocentric young man who is convinced of his ability to make a fortune in business by "making an impression" – that is, bragging about money, possessions, and power that he doesn't have. After a good deal of resistance, Aubrey Piper is finally accepted by the Fisher family because he sincerely loves his new wife, Amy. Although the brash new success ethic is shown up as hollow, irritating, and undependable, it is also represented as harmless when under proper domestic control. Eugene O'Neill's *Ah, Wilderness!* (1933), a comic treatment of the autobiography that informs the tragedy of *Long Day's Journey Into Night*, managed to downplay the danger to the American family of alcoholism by having the alcoholic Uncle Sid care for young Richard during a humorous drunk scene and suggesting through the loving relationship of Uncle Sid and Aunt Lily that a drinking problem does not preclude sentiment or romantic love.

More sophisticated treatments of middle-class cultural concerns tended to be cast in the form of "social melodrama," an updated *drame bourgeois* that had its roots in Ibsen and the turn-of-the-century "problem plays." In keeping with larger cultural trends, the greatest amount of vehemence in these plays during the twenties was displayed toward the middle-aged wife and mother. As historian Ann Douglas has argued, "the writers who fought in the [first world] war threw off, in its name, all efforts to check their development or define their aims; open disillusion was the sharpest weapon they had in waging the real war, the war against Mother . . . the Victorian matriarch successfully attacked the Calvinist patriarchy, only to be hunted down in the twentieth century by the forces of masculinization bound together in that backlash we know as modernism" (*Terrible Honesty,* 220, 241). In the theatre, the serious war against the middle-class wife and mother was foreshadowed in a seemingly genial satire by George S. Kaufman and Marc Connelly called *Dulcy* (1921). The play is a farce based on what the authors conceived to be the representative suburban housewife in a character who appeared in the humor columns of Franklin P. Adams, Dulcy, an egocentric and mindless woman who utters a platitude "as if it were a wise and original thought" (Kaufman and Connelly, 528) and tries to manage the action around her in a way that will always place her at the center of attention. When things go wrong, her husband is about to divorce her for her childishness, and when they go right, he loves her because she has "the soul of a child" (567). Comic closure comes when the domestic power structure is rearranged; Dulcy's husband consents to stay with her on the condition that she keep out of his business interests and not try to exert any power over him.

Whereas Kaufman and Connelly could use the structure of comedy to imply that domestic and business order can be restored only when middle-class wives are kept in subordination to their husbands, some serious treatments of the middle-class housewife and mother by male playwrights represented her as a far more serious threat. The first of these, Lewis Beach's *A Square Peg* (1923), is an attempt at domestic tragedy. Rena Huckins is a domineering woman who keeps a fanatically clean but ugly and cheerless house. According to her daughter, "she was born a generation ahead of her time. She's had the wrong job. She should have been a modern business woman" (Beach, 120). Instead, she is a very unhappy housewife who has turned her daughter into a domestic servant, emasculated her husband, and driven her son to philandering, all of which behavior Beach tries to tie to Rena through Freudian psychology. Although the situation is potentially tragic, the play slides into domestic melodrama, with Rena as the villain threatening the health of the family, and through it, the well-being of American society. Her husband shoots himself; her daughter escapes from her domination with a married man; and her son joins the navy, leaving Rena to what the play implies is a well-deserved punishment, her own company.

A Square Peg set the tone for the two most successful attacks on the middle-class housewife, George Kelly's *Craig's Wife* (1925), which won the Pulitzer Prize and ran for 360 performances on Broadway, and Sidney Howard's *The Silver Cord* (1926). Kelly sets up Harriet Craig as a woman who believes that a marriage is a bargain. The wife's portion is the security and protection of a house and a husband, and, since the wife is "at the mercy of the *mood* of a *man*" (326), she has to secure her home by dominating her husband through stratagems and subterfuge. Walter Craig, on the other hand, is a self-styled romantic who believes that an ideal marriage will be founded on total honesty. Recognizing that his wife's attempts at controlling him are endangering his "manhood" and her possessions are "gods you had set up in the temple here, and been worshiping before me" (Kelly, 368), he asserts himself by breaking an ornament that is particularly dear to his wife and by scattering cigar butts on the floor. When Harriet refuses to support her husband in a murder case because it will endanger her position in the community, Walter walks out of the house, along with his niece, his aunt, and the servants, leaving Mrs. Craig to a life of well-deserved isolation in her empty house, the implication being that Mrs. Craig is despicable for valuing security over honesty and power over romantic love. Eleanore Flexner has pointed out the major weakness in the play's attack. Although he allows Mrs. Craig the explanation that her behavior results from her fear of economic dependence, "Kelly persists in treating Harriet as a *moral* phenomenon. She is dishonest; she is guilty of marrying a man without love and without trust; she is a pitiless nag. For these enormities she is punished. That she had been trapped . . . by forces beyond her control, is also beyond the dramatist's understanding" (Flexner, 238).

Sidney Howard's *The Silver Cord* did to the American mother what *Craig's Wife* did to the housewife. One of the most overtly Freudian plays of the Freudian twenties, *The Silver Cord* depicts the dangers of a smothering and domineering mother-love on the psychological development of sons. Mrs. Phelps, brilliantly portrayed by Laura Hope Crews in both the play and the film adaptation, was the frightening incarnation of the "unnatural mother." Throughout the play she manipulates her sons into a co-dependent relationship that places her at the center of their lives and does everything she can to break up the marriage of her elder son, Dave, and the engagement of her younger son, Robert. The play's climax is a lengthy speech by Dave's wife, Christine, a research biologist who is well-versed in the new Freudian psychology. Although there do exist natural mothers who contribute to their children's development and independence, she explains, Mrs. Phelps is not one of them. She has "swallowed up" Robert and has come close to destroying Dave as well. Through Christine, Howard is careful to imply that Mrs. Phelps is not a single exception but a cultural phenomenon: "And what makes you doubly deadly and dangerous is that people admire you and your kind. They actually admire you! You professional mothers!" (S. Howard, 672). Whereas Dave manages to escape from Mrs. Phelps's domination with Christine's help, Robert remains "engulfed forever" in his mother's love. In this play, Howard managed to overturn the most cherished icon of nineteenth-century American culture, the Angel in the House, and to replace a deeply entrenched Victorian value system centered on self-sacrifice and filial duty with a modernist one centered on freedom and self-actualization. Although the severing of the silver cord was the lost generation's grand gesture of freedom, it did not succeed in doing away with the domineering mother. Instead these plays established a dramatic type that was as alive in Bessie Berger of Clifford Odets's *Awake and Sing!* (1935) as in Mrs. Phelps or Rena Huckins. Resistance to matriarchal authority proved to be a perennial project of American playwrights in the twenties and thirties.

Although the American theatre of the twenties was preoccupied with domestic life, it did occasionally look outward to larger social issues. Susan Glaspell's *Inheritors* (1921) was an early treatment of the issue of free speech in universities and the persecution of leftist faculty members. Maxwell Anderson's *Gods of the Lightning* (1928) was an early "hard-boiled" melodramatic treatment of the Sacco and Vanzetti case, later the subject of one of his most significant verse plays, *Winterset* (1935). Augustus Thomas's *Still Waters* (1926) dealt with the evils of Prohibition. In the decade following World War I, however, the great social issue was war and its aftermath. The best known of the war plays was *What Price Glory* (1924) by Maxwell Anderson and Laurence Stallings, a play that was seen at the time as a realistic deflation of the romantic notions about war that had pervaded American culture before World War I. Largely because of the use of profanity and other "hard-boiled" language in its dialogue and the realistic depiction of the conditions in which the soldiers lived, the play was seen as a daringly realistic attack on war. The perspective of time revealed, however, as Frank O'Hara wrote in 1939, that in *What Price Glory*, "war, for all its sordidness and terror, still remains the romantic adventure" (O'Hara, 264). Despite their vaunted cynicism and their adolescent rivalry over women, alcohol, and fighting, the soldiers in the play reveal a courage, patriotism and honor that the audience is invited to admire. The play might aim, as Stallings said, to "tell the truth about war" (quoted in Brittain, 45), but it still glorified the soldier. From the perspective of the pacifist, Robert Sherwood contributed a witty and imaginative Shavian treatment of war in *The Road to Rome* (1927), which sets its argument against war in Rome at the time of Hannibal's invasion. Like others of his generation, Sherwood changed his stance on war as the fascist dictators in Europe threatened Western civilization during the thirties. In the allegorical *Petrified Forest* (1935), he predicted the death of a decadent European civilization through the shooting of the intellectual Alan Squier by the thug Duke Mantee, but he also presented an image of hope in the young woman Gabby, whose romantic idealism still has a chance of flourishing within the petrified forest. In *Idiot's Delight* (1936), another allegory of contemporary civilization cast in the mode of realism, Sherwood created a microcosm of Western society in a hotel in the Alps and represented the collapse of civilization with the advent of war. *Abe Lincoln in Illinois* (1938) depicted a reluctant young Lincoln making the decision to enter public life based on a moral imperative to act on the issue of slavery. In 1940, when he wrote *There Shall Be No Night*, there was no longer any doubt in Sherwood's mind where the civilized person must stand in the war against Hitler. The play is a straightforward plea for the United States to join the war in defense of small helpless democracies like Finland.

The Broadway theatre as a whole followed a line of development that was similar to Sherwood's. Antiwar plays such as Paul Green's *Johnny Johnson (1936),* Irwin Shaw's *Bury the Dead* and *Siege* (1937), Sidney Howard's *Paths of Glory* (1935), and Sidney Kingsley's *Ten Million Ghosts* (1936) were quickly displaced by antifascist plays that supported the United States's joining the war, such as Oliver Garrett's *Waltz in Goose Step* (1938), Burnet Hershey's *Brown Danube* (1939), Clare Boothe's *Margin for Error* (1939), Dorothy Thompson and Fritz Kortner's *Another Sun* (1940), Lillian Hellman's *Watch on the Rhine* (1941), and Maxwell Anderson's *Candle in the Wind* (1941). Once the United States entered the war, these plays were followed by a raft of war plays that represented the Allies' fight against Hitler as a clear contest between the forces of good and the forces of evil in which the soldier's moral choice had no shades of gray. These included John Steinbeck's *The Moon Is Down* (1942), Moss Hart's *Winged Victory* (1943), James Gow and Arnaud D'Usseau's *Tomorrow the World* (1943), Maxwell Anderson's *Storm Operation* (1944), and Arthur Laurents's *Home of the Brave* (1945). Though these plays may have helped the war effort, they were not particularly remarkable as literary contributions.

As important as the rise of fascism was to thinking Americans in the thirties, it was the immediate economic reality of the Great Depression that dominated the country's self-conception and that had to be faced in any realistic representation of American society outside the insulated enclave of high society. The pervasive effect of the Great Depression can be seen in the wide gulf that divides two self-conscious attempts to represent the lives of urban working-class Americans authentically on the stage. Elmer Rice's *Street Scene* (1929) is a tour de force of realistic dramaturgy, a play that contains both a melodramatic plot about a man's shooting his wife and her lover and a romantic love story but still manages to convey the larger rhythms of the characters' lives that surround these events, implying that the conventional story paradigms of drama do not contain or account for human life as it is lived. The play centers on the people who live in a Manhattan tenement at the end of the twenties, depicting their working-class lives as hard and the chances for escape as scarce and not always morally acceptable, but it depicts a world where there is hope for a better life and where the characters are free to make choices that will determine their future. Sidney Kingsley's *Dead End* (1935), written just six years later, captures in its naturalistic representation of a world where economic forces have restricted the characters' choices to dire poverty or prostitution and organized crime, the desperation and hopelessness of Americans about their society and the economic forces that have it in their grip. Whereas *Street Scene* focuses on two innocent young

Sidney Kingsley's *Dead End* (1935), designed by Norman Bel Geddes. White photo. Museum of the City of New York (Gift of the Burns Mantle Estate).

lovers, *Dead End* depicts the demise of the gangster Baby Face Martin and implies a similar future for the boys who provide the background for the action, swimming in the sewage of the East River and getting into trouble with both the gangsters and the police.

In the thirties, naturalistic melodrama provided the structure and the worldview for an ever-increasing number of plays about American society. The social issues they treated ranged from the infamous execution of the Scottsboro Boys in John Wexley's *They Shall Not Die* (1934) to the labor issues in a large number of plays inspired by Clifford Odets's *Waiting for Lefty* (1935) and Paul Peters and George Sklar's *Stevedore* (1934) to the evils of capitalism in Lillian Hellman's *The Little Foxes* (1939). Hellman also touched gingerly on the subject of homophobia in *The Children's Hour* (1934), a year after the Englishman Mordaunt Shairp's *The Green Bay Tree* had been produced on Broadway by Jed Harris in a version in which, as Burns Mantle put it, "all suggestion of degeneracy is carefully minimized and the play becomes the taut and fascinating contest of a man and woman for the affections of a young man who is the foster son of one and the fiancé of the other" (Mantle, 381). Under the aegis of the Federal Theatre Project, several significant naturalistic treatments of the urban life of African Americans were also produced during the thirties, particularly Theodore Ward's *Big White Fog* (1938) and Theodore Brown's *Natural Man* (1937). Paul Green and Richard Wright's effective adaptation of Wright's *Native Son* was produced on Broadway by Orson Welles and John Houseman in 1941 with Canada Lee in the role of Bigger Thomas.

Experiments

The period between 1915 and 1945 was an extraordinarily innovative time for Western drama generally. In Europe, expressionism was adapted from the visual arts and poetry to drama, developing particularly in Germany from the work of August Strindberg and Frank Wedekind to a spate of plays by Georg Kaiser, Walter Hasenclever, Ernst Toller, and others. In the United States, where realism was just coming into its own during the twenties, this new influence made for a unique combination of Freudian-influenced realism in characterization with staging, dialogue, and music that made use of American jazz rhythms as well as expressionistic distortion and exaggeration. In the thirties, the economic upheaval of the Great Depression created an audience for protest and agit-prop (agitation-propaganda) plays that again integrated some new German ideas about characterization, dialogue, form, and staging with a uniquely American message and point of view. And these were only the most conspicuous experiments. Among them, the art theatres, the Theatre Guild, and the socialist theatre groups produced a broad spectrum of dramatic experiments amid the bourgeois realism that dominated the American theatre during the twenties and thirties.

Susan Glaspell and the Provincetown Players

Susan Glaspell's career with the Provincetown Players is a good reflection of the broad spectrum of drama that qualified as experimental during the period. In its earliest years, the Provincetown distinguished itself by producing starkly simple realistic one-act plays about ordinary people. The best of these are O'Neill's plays about sailors, such as *The Moon of the Caribees* and *Bound East for Cardiff,* and Glaspell's *Trifles* (1916), which was based on a murder case she had covered as an investigative reporter in Iowa long before she had thought of writing plays. In *The Road to the Temple,* her memoir about her husband, and Provincetown co-founder, George Cram Cook, Glaspell described her process of sitting in the Wharf Theatre and visualizing the characters and the action of the play before she wrote it down, a process

Susan Glaspell's *Trifles.* Photo by White from *The Theatre,* January 1917.

she had gone through when visiting the scene of the murder years before, the house where a lonely farm wife had allegedly murdered her abusive husband.

In *Trifles,* the house becomes the key to the plot. Minnie Wright's cheerless kitchen, with its empty birdcage and dead canary, reveal the identity of the murderer and her motive for the act to the women who have come along with the men investigating the crime to get some of Mrs. Wright's belongings. Mr. Wright has killed the canary, wrung its neck, thus depriving Minnie, a former member of the church choir, of her one source of joy and comfort. Wright has been strangled in his sleep. Seeing a primal justice in Minnie's action that the law would not recognize, the women tacitly agree not to show the canary to the sheriff and the county attorney, allowing them to dismiss the women's interest in Mrs. Wright's life – a quilt she was making and her worry about her preserves freezing – as a typically feminine concern with "trifles." The county attorney leaves with no clear motive for the bizarre murder and worries that juries are not likely to convict women of murder without some definite piece of evidence to connect the suspect with the act. Throughout the play, Glaspell deftly manages her scheme of symbolism and metonymy so that the audience participates with Mrs. Hale and Mrs. Peters in their growing understanding of Mrs. Wright's situation and the desperate unhappiness that led her to kill her husband. The kitchen becomes a metonymic representation of Mrs. Wright's identity and the canary the symbol of the capacity for joy that Wright killed in her. In the end, the audience is complicit with them in seeing the men who represent the legal system as invaders in this psychic land-scape who cannot possibly understand its economy of motives.

The experimental plays that followed, such as *Bernice* (1919), *The Outside* (1917), and *The Verge* (1921) lack the carefully controlled technique of *Trifles*. Products of an ever more self-consciously "artistic" theatre in the Province-town, they exhibit both the risk-taking spirit and the aesthetic excesses of modernist experimental theatre. *Bernice* is notable mainly for Glaspell's tak-ing the technique of characterization that she used for Mrs. Wright in *Trifles* and making it the center of a full-length play. The whole action takes place after Bernice's death, and her character is gradually revealed to the audience as it is revealed to her family. Glaspell was to use the same technique for *Ali-son's House* (1930), a play that is loosely based on the life of the poet Emily Dickinson and that won Glaspell her only Pulitzer Prize. In both of these plays, the titular characters exert a stronger influence on the various mem-bers of their families after their deaths than they did while they were living, the implication being that it was only after their deaths that people took the time to examine these women and their lives closely – Bernice the wife and mother and Alison the "old maid" poetess – and to understand their signifi-cance. Like *Trifles,* these plays use an unusual approach to characterization to point out the significance of the lives of women who have traditionally been ignored or taken for granted in American society.

The Verge is the most daring of Glaspell's plays. Like *The Outside,* it is unabashedly symbolic, using only a thin veneer of realism in setting and characterization to provide the vehicle for a symbolic treatment of a number of issues surrounding the subject of human creativity. In a metatheatrical ref-erence to Glaspell's attempt to create a new dramatic form in the play, its pro-tagonist, Claire Archer, is a horticulturalist who is seeking literally to create new forms of life in the plants she develops – the Edge Vine and the Breath of Life. She is also in the process of choosing her appropriate mate among three men – Tom, Dick, and Harry. She has married her husband Harry because he is an aviator, and she was hoping to find in him the embodiment of flight. Since the reality has proven far more prosaic than her vision had been, she is having an affair with the aptly named Dick while she pursues a deeper intel-lectual and emotional union with Tom Edgeworthy, who understands, and to some extent, participates in her desire to break through barriers and create new life. When Tom asserts that he will become a shell for Claire that will keep her safe "from fartherness – from harm" (Bigsby, *Plays by Susan Glaspell,* 99), however, she strangles him as a "gift" to the Breath of Life, crying "You fill the place – should be a gate" (99). The play's dialogue is overwritten and its symbolism perhaps intentionally overblown. It is an attempt at the kind of theatre poetry that Tennessee Williams was to achieve with *Suddenly Last Summer* (1958), and it is a highly suggestive poetic drama, although more effective on the page than in the theatre. Glaspell's own plays never reached beyond the realm of the art theatre into the wider cultural landscape, but her experimental spirit and her willingness to challenge the prevailing limits of dramatic technique helped to make the new theatre of the succeeding generation possible.

Verse Drama

Although it is far from experimental in itself, the writing and production of verse drama was an experiment in the American theatre of the thirties. Although the art theatres produced an occasional play in verse and there were a number of commercial productions of verse "classics," such as Shakespeare's plays, full commercial production of new verse dramas by American playwrights was almost unheard of when Maxwell Anderson wrote *White Desert* in 1923, a play that closed after twelve performances on Broadway. It is not surprising that Anderson turned to collaborating on "hard boiled" realist plays such as *What Price Glory* and *Gods of the Lightning* immediately afterward. Anderson's real affinity, however, was more with Shakespeare than with Hemingway or Raymond Chandler, and he inspired a new interest both in poetry and in history on the American stage when his *Elizabeth the Queen* was produced by the Theatre Guild in 1930. The production, starring Lynn Fontanne and Alfred Lunt, ran for 147 performances, and *Elizabeth* is considered the first successful drama of the modern American theatre to be written in verse. It was followed by *Mary of Scotland* (1933), which ran for 248 performances in the Theatre Guild production starring Helen Hayes, *The Masque of Kings* (1937), about Crown Prince Rudolph of Austria, and *Anne of the Thousand Days* (1948), about Henry VIII and Anne Boleyn, which ran for 226 performances in its production by the Playwrights' Company. Although Anderson's historical verse dramas are sometimes dismissed as mere imitations of Shakespeare, they often combined blank verse with contemporary innovations, such as the metatheatrical approach of *Joan of Lorraine* (1946), Anderson's play about Joan of Arc, which combines the chronicle of the saint with a backstage drama about the actress who is playing her. Starring Ingrid Bergman, the Playwrights' Company production ran for 201 performances on Broadway.

Anderson's success enabled other playwrights to get a hearing for history plays in verse, the most significant of which is probably *Murder in the Cathedral,* T. S. Eliot's dramatization of the death of Thomas à Becket at the hands of Henry II, which was produced by the Federal Theatre Project in 1935. Eliot's play combined elements of the medieval morality play with modern metatheatrical devices to engage the audience in a contemplation of the issues of martyrdom and the abuse of power, significant issues for a citizenry

that was observing the rise of fascism in Europe. Anderson's great innovation, however, was the writing of verse tragedy about contemporary subjects.
Noting that none of the "great masters" of tragedy had written successfully
about their own time, Anderson wrote in his preface to *Winterset* (1935) that
the verse treatment of a contemporary tragic theme, the legacy of the unjust
executions of Sacco and Vanzetti, was an attempt "to establish a new convention, one that may prove impossible of acceptance, but to which I was driven
by the lively historical sense of our day" (M. Anderson, 54). *Winterset* has
become a classic of the American theatre. Not as well known, but equally
innovative, is Anderson's *High Tor* (1936), a comic satire about opposition to
the quarrying of a mountain in upstate New York that combined blank verse
with colloquial prose to create a play that only Anderson could have written.
Both of these plays received the New York Drama Critics' Circle Award, a
prize that was created partly to protest the Pulitzer Prize Committee's 1935
passing over *Winterset* and giving its prize to Zoë Akins's adaptation of Edith
Wharton's novel *The Old Maid.*

Other Experimentation

The dramatization of a character's subjective perception of reality that is the
central characteristic of expressionism could be found in plays by Americans
before the European expressionists were produced in American theatres.
Alice Gerstenberg's *Overtones,* which dramatizes the uncensored commentary by the "inner selves" of two middle-class women while they exchange
social lies during an afternoon call, was produced by the Washington Square
Players in 1915. The Provincetown Players produced O'Neill's's *Emperor
Jones* in 1920 and *The Hairy Ape* in 1922. It was the O'Neill plays, both of
which moved uptown to commercial theatres, and the Theatre Guild's production of two expressionistic plays from Europe, Georg Kaiser's *From Morn
to Midnight* and Karel Čapek's *R. U. R.,* in 1922, along with the film *The Cabinet
of Dr. Caligari* (1919), that familiarized American audiences with the expressionistic techniques for dramatizing subjectivity.

   Aside from O'Neill, the American who experimented most with the new
techniques was Elmer Rice, a playwright who in 1923 was best known for his
early success *On Trial* (1914), a potboiler that was based on the gimmick of
retrospective narration. Rice's *The Adding Machine,* produced by the Theatre
Guild in 1923, is probably the best known of the American expressionistic
plays. Like O'Neill, Rice claimed in his autobiography *Minority Report* (1963),
that he had not been influenced by the German expressionists, and that he
was not acquainted with their work when he wrote *The Adding Machine* in seventeen days during the summer of 1922. He suggested in a letter that "expressionism – a rather vague term at best – developed spontaneously and simulta-

Elmer Rice's *The Adding Machine* (1923), designed by Lee Simonson. Billy Rose Theatre Collection, New York Public Library for the Performing Arts, Astor, Lenox and Tilden Foundations.

neously in several countries and in the work of numerous writers as a result partly of the psychic dislocations that were a product of World War I, the impact of Freudianism, and the revolt (if that is the word) against the restrictions imposed upon the dramatists by the dominant Ibsenesque tradition of objective realism" (quoted in A. Coleman, 1). His goal is not a merging of the audience's consciousness with the artist's subjective vision (the vision the protagonist achieves at the end of the play) but a grounding in objective reality from which the audience can judge the protagonist's subjective perception. Rice invites the audience to judge his Mr. Zero, and the protagonist of *The Subway* (1929), Sophie Smith, from the point of view of a clear system of knowledge – that of Freudian psychology. His perspective is peculiarly American in rejecting the modernist phenomenology of the German plays and replacing it with an epistemology that is fundamentally pragmatic and positivist.

The other characteristic American aspect of Rice's expressionism is its humor. Rice's indictment of American society is primarily satirical. He uses the play to expose the materialism, the conventionalism, the snobbery, the hypocrisy, and the prudery of the lower middle class through grotesque exaggeration, inviting the audience to laugh at attitudes and values it shared. The same was true of the other expressionistic popular success, George S. Kaufman and Marc Connelly's *Beggar on Horseback* (1924), which was adapted at the request of producer Winthrop Ames from a rather somber German script called *Hans Sonnenstoesser's Höllenfahrt*. Worked over by Kaufman and Connelly, with the addition of jazz and humor, the play, as Alexander Woolcott wrote in his preface, represents "the distaste that can be inspired by the viewpoint, the complacency and the very idiom of Rotarian America. It is a small and facetious disturbance in the rear of the Church of the Gospel of Success" (Woolcott, "Preface," n.p.). John Howard Lawson's *Processional* (1925), which made use of jazz, vaudeville, and expressionistic techniques, also combined a love story, humor and entertainment with a heavy-handed message about the dehumanization of the worker and other injustices in American society.

These plays were more successful than the plays that were written with the intensity and desperation of the German plays. Lawson's *Roger Bloomer* (1923) was respected by critics but ran for only fifty performances. Rice's *The Subway,* a serious treatment of the victimization of a young female office worker in New York, was written just after *The Adding Machine* but was rejected by nearly every producer in New York before it was finally produced in 1929. Sophie Treadwell's *Machinal* (1928) was the most successful of the serious expressionistic plays, partly owing to its similarity to the notorious murder case of Ruth Snyder, the first woman to die in the electric chair. Treadwell had covered the case as a reporter, and although she denied that *Machinal* was about Ruth Snyder, the similarities are evident. This play is a melodrama, with the nameless Young Woman protagonist represented as the helpless victim of biological characteristics, environmental conditioning, heredity, and social forces and institutions over which she has no control. The single assertion of will the Young Woman makes, Treadwell implies, is the murder of her husband, an attempt at freeing herself that puts her behind bars and eventually in the electric chair. Treadwell's is a bleak depiction of modern life, particularly that of middle-class women.

Not strictly in the expressionistic mode, but making use of expressionistic techniques to create their own personal forms of drama, are two playwrights whose worldviews were at the opposite extreme from that of *Machinal,* Thornton Wilder and William Saroyan. Wilder and Saroyan came to the stage at the end of the thirties, when the depth of the economic depression and the advent of war in Europe made Americans eager for a hopeful point of view. This they both supplied. Saroyan's first play, produced by the Group Theatre and directed by Robert Lewis, was a fantasy about the value of art and cre-

Thornton Wilder's *Our Town* (1938) at the Morosco Theatre. Vandamm photo. Museum of the City of New York.

ativity called *My Heart's in the Highlands* (1939). Although most critics found the play confused and confusing, the production so impressed them and audiences that it was taken over by the Theatre Guild as a regular subscription offering. Saroyan's next play, *The Time of Your Life*, was produced by the Theatre Guild later that year with Eddie Dowling as Joe, the wise man at the center of the play, an alcoholic who sits in Nick's bar all day contemplating the way to a civilized life. The play was similar in design to Philip Barry's *Here Come the Clowns*, which Dowling had produced the year before, revealing through a collection of misfits who come together in a bar the fundamental human values that suggest some hope for a seemingly doomed civilization. An allegory for the condition of the world in 1939, the play depicts the destruction of the corrupt and fascistic police detective Harry Blick by Kit Carson, a tall-tale-telling hero of the old American West, as well as the eventual triumph of love, as Joe's loyal henchman marries the prostitute with a heart of gold. What Joe and the audience learn is a new faith in humanity and in the power of American vitality to overcome evil and corruption.

Thornton Wilder's two most significant plays, *Our Town* (1938) and *The Skin of Our Teeth* (1942), use expressionistic and other metatheatrical techniques to convey a similarly simple message. *Our Town* has three acts, which are about Daily Life, Love and Marriage, and Death in Grovers Corners, New Hampshire, a presumably typical American small town at the turn of the century. Contrary to the apparent view of Jed Harris, who produced the play with more realism than Wilder would have liked, Wilder explained in the preface to the published play that *"Our Town* is not offered as a picture of life in a New Hampshire village." Rather, it is "an attempt to find a value above all price for the smallest events in our daily life." In setting the village "against the largest dimensions of time and place," Wilder hoped to dramatize the idea that "our claim, our hope, our despair are in the mind – not in things, not in 'scenery'" (xi). In the interest of universalizing the action, Wilder insisted on a minimalist approach to scenery and introduced the metatheatrical device of the "Stage Manager," a narrator who constantly calls the audience's attention to the fact that it is witnessing a play, and who takes several of the parts in various scenes. In the first scene, the Stage Manager introduces characters who address the audience directly about the specific characteristics of the town, a strategy that suggests the typicality of the town at the same time that it particularizes it. Similarly, Wilder universalizes his characters by suggesting that their experiences of love, marriage, and family life are typical as well as particular instances of universal human experience.

Wilder's unique accomplishment in *Our Town* is his manipulation of realistic conventions of characterization and metatheatrical techniques in staging to evoke a sentimental identification from the audience and then to universalize it. As Christopher Bigsby has observed,

> Grovers Corners is essentially a literary conceit. Its origins lie less in New Hampshire than in a platonic world of literary paradigms. The figures self-consciously play dramatic roles at the direction of the Stage Manager because they are in origin as well as fact literary creations, and Grovers Corners a product of popular myth, sanitised, morally and socially simplified. (*Critical Introduction*, 266).

In *The Skin of Our Teeth*, Wilder turned from popular myth to biblical, from localized nostalgia to universal history. Acknowledging his literary debt to *Finnegan's Wake*, Wilder noted the dual time scheme of the play. On the one hand, the Antrobuses are a typical family in a New Jersey commuting suburb in the 1940s, on the other, they embody the history of the human race, from Adam and Eve to the near destruction of the earth by war – a universal human predicament at the same time that it is reflection of contemporary reality, as World War II threatened to destroy European civilization. Throughout his history of devastation, the perennially hopeful and ingenious Mr. Antrobus manages to survive and progress, inventing the wheel and the alphabet, going out to face the world while his wife keeps their children safe and the maid, Lily Sabina, supplies the sexual interest. The play combines a farcical pace and nonsensical logic that is similar to that in *You Can't Take It with You*. In the direct appeals of Lily Sabina to the audience, her ostensible refusal to play a scene in which Mr. Antrobus agrees to get a divorce and marry her, and the "replacement" of seven of the actors, who are reported to have ptomaine poisoning, with other employees of the theatre, Wilder adds a metatheatrical element that increases the audience's alienation from the fable on the stage but also intensifies its identification with the actors. The audience is drawn into trying to figure out the play that the actors seem compelled to present for it. The ultimate aim of Wilder's technique is identification with the actors and affirmation of the life cycle that the play celebrates.

While Saroyan and Wilder were using the new techniques to affirm the American way of life and universal human values, the New Theatre League, a combination of leftist theatre groups such as the New Playwrights Theatre, the Workers Laboratory (later, the Theatre of Action), the Artef Players, Theatre Collective, and the German Prolit-Buehne were combining expressionist techniques with the new agit-prop techniques being used by the labor theatres in Europe, and the Verfremdung (alienation) techniques of Bertolt Brecht to produce dramas that attacked the American socioeconomic system and questioned the fundamental values on which it was built. This movement was a national one, with theatre groups in Moline, Illinois, and Gary, Indiana, as well as urban centers like New York, Chicago, Cleveland, and Los Angeles. The high point of American workers' theatre was Clifford Odets's *Waiting for Lefty* (1935), which, working on the premise that the actors and the audience formed a taxi drivers' strike meeting, combined moving realistic scenes that dramatized several of the drivers' personal histories with direct appeals to the audience to join in the fight for justice and that climaxed in a call for action, as actors and audience joined in the chorus of "Strike! Strike! Strike!" (See Chapter 4 for additional discussion of the plays of Clifford Odets.)

Although the Federal Theatre Project (FTP) is most remarkable for its innovations in production, it also developed a surprisingly popular new dramatic form in the Living Newspaper. After learning about the Living Newspapers of *Zhivaya Gazeta* and the Blue Blouses during her trip to the Soviet Union to study the new theatre there, FTP director Hallie Flanagan had tried the form at Vassar College with success. Thus when Elmer Rice, the director of the New York FTP unit, appealed to her for ways to employ the many out-of-work actors in the city, she suggested the Living Newspaper as a highly labor-intensive endeavor, which it proved to be. The production of *Triple-A Plowed Under* (1936), the first Living Newspaper to reach the commercial stage, involved two hundred people, including about a hundred actors, forty research workers, and a staff of newspaper reporters, dramatists, directors, scene designers, and other stage technicians. As Hallie Flanagan put it, the Living Newspaper borrowed with fine impartiality from many sources: from Aristophanes, from the *Commedia dell' Arte,* from Shakespearean soliloquy, from the pantomime of Mei Lan Fang. . . . Although it has occasional reference to the *Volksbühne* and the Blue Blouses, to Bragaglia and Meierhold and Eisenstein, it is as American as Walt Disney, the *March of Time* and the *Congressional Record,* to all of which American institutions it is indebted. (Flanagan, "Introduction," xi)

Despite its claims to be "objectively" reporting the news, the Living Newspaper conveyed as strong an editorial point of view as any print newspaper. Like other FTP projects, it was plagued by conservative attacks on its leftist perspective from the beginning, when *Ethiopia* was suppressed before it had a chance to reach the stage and when the first performance of *Triple-A Plowed Under* was interrupted by two audience members, both WPA employees as it turned out, one of which started singing the national anthem and the other booing an actor because he played the well-known communist Earl Browder. To the surprise of most of the people involved, *Triple-A Plowed Under* was an instant critical and commercial hit, inspiring a number of FTP units, and even commercial producers, to try the form in such productions as *Power* (1937), *Spirochete* (1938), *One Third of a Nation* (1938), and *The Medicine Show* (produced by Carly Wharton and Martin Gabel, 1940). (For additional discussion of the Federal Theatre Project, see Chapter 2.)

Notes

1 *Road to the Temple,* 254. Glaspell's account, long accepted as factual reporting, has been challenged recently in the light of accounts by Harry Kemp and others. See Harry Kemp, "Out of Provincetown: A Memoir of Eugene O'Neill," and Gary Jay Williams, "Turned Down in Provincetown: O'Neill's Debut Re-Examined."

2 For a discussion of O'Neill's acquaintance with Freud, see Egil Törnqvist, "To Speak the Unspoken: Audible Thinking in O'Neill's Plays."

3 For discussion of the novelistic use of dialogue in *Strange Interlude,* see Törnqvist and Kurt Eisen, "Novelization and the Drama of Consciousness in *Strange Interlude,*" and the extended discussion in Eisen, *The Inner Strength of Opposites.*

4 O'Neill had a "familial tremor," from which his mother and brother also suffered, that got worse as he grew older. The tremor worsened, along with other health problems, in the early forties, until O'Neill was unable to write in longhand, his lifetime habit. Unable to compose on the typewriter or by dictating, O'Neill stopped work on his plays in the midforties, hoping to return to them when his health improved. It never did. With Carlotta's help, O'Neill destroyed much of his material for unfinished plays in 1943, finishing the job in 1952–53, when it became clear to him that he would never be able to complete them.

5 Crothers's birth date is usually given as 1878. Walter J. Meserve has discovered, however, that her date of birth is confirmed as 1870 by the 1900 U.S. Census and on her death certificate, provided by the Connecticut Department of Health. This birth

date clears up some confusion about her early history. She graduated from high school when she was twenty, not thirteen, and attended the New England School of Dramatic Instruction when she was twenty-one, not fourteen.

Bibliography: Plays and Playwrights, 1915–1945

The following general studies are suggested for further study. The most complete historical record of American plays for the period 1915–1945 can be found in the *Best Plays* series, the "Year Book of the Drama in America" edited by Burns Mantle, which includes brief chronicles of the seasons in New York, Chicago, San Francisco, and Southern California, and a complete list of plays premiering on Broadway in each season, including brief summaries of the plays, cast lists and data on the number of performances, as well as other information. Each volume also contains abridged versions of the ten plays that Mantle considered the best of each season. Other than Mantle's, the most useful reference work on American playwrights between 1915 and 1945 is *American Playwrights, 1880–1945: A Research and Production Sourcebook,* edited by Demastes. Useful one-volume histories include Quinn, *A History of the American Drama from the Civil War to the Present Day* (1936 revision); Toohey, *A History of the Pulitzer Prize Plays;* Atkinson, *Broadway;* Mordden, *The American Theatre;* and Henderson, *Theater in America.* An important source of information is Poggi, *Theater in America: The Impact of Economic Forces, 1870–1967.*

The major bibliographic sources for reviews and criticism include Eddleman, *American Drama Criticism: Interpretations, 1890–1977* and *Supplements* I, II, and III (1979, 1984, 1989, 1992); Charles A. Carpenter, *Modern Drama Scholarship and Criticism 1966–1980: An International Bibliography;* Salem, *A Guide to Critical Reviews, Pt. 1: American Drama, 1909–1982;* and Adelman and Dworkin, *Modern Drama: A Checklist of Critical Literature on 20th Century Plays.* More specific bibliographic sources include Bonin, *Prize-Winning American Drama: A Bibliographical and Descriptive Guide;* Peterson, *Early Black American Playwrights and Dramatic Writers;* and Duffy, *The Political Left in the American Drama of the 1930's: A Bibliographic Sourcebook.*

The best critical overview of the period is Bigsby, *A Critical Introduction to Twentieth-Century American Drama, Vol. 1: 1900–1940.* Others include Flexner, *American Playwrights;* Frank O'Hara, *Today in American Drama;* Downer, *Fifty Years of American Drama;* Bentley, *The Dramatic Event: An American Chronicle;* Krutch, *The American Drama Since 1918: An Informal History;* and the most recent, Miller and Frazer, *American Drama between the Wars,* and Wainscott, *The Emergence of the Modern American Theater, 1914–1929.* Wide-ranging critical studies include Sievers, *Freud on Broadway: A History of Psychoanalysis and the American Drama;* Golden, *The Death of Tinker Bell: The American Theatre in the 20th Century;* Porter, *Myth and Modern American Drama;* Cohn, *Dialogue in American Drama;* Greenfield, *Work and the Work Ethic in American Drama, 1920–1970;* Dukore, *American Dramatists, 1918–1945;* Murphy, *American Realism and American Drama 1880–1940;* and Adler, *Mirror on the Stage: The Pulitzer Prize Plays as an Approach to American Drama.*

Significant collections of contemporary theatre reviews are John Mason Brown, *Broadway in Review;* Downer (editor), *American Drama and Its Critics;* Atkinson and Hirschfeld, *The Lively Years: 1920–1973;* and Beckerman and Siegman, *On Stage: Selected Theater Reviews from the New York Times, 1920–1970.* Among recent critical treatments of particular aspects of the drama during this period are Schroeder, *The Presence of the Past in Modern American Drama;* Stowell, *A Stage of Their Own: Feminist Playwrights of the Suffrage Era;* Shafer, *American Women Playwrights, 1900–1950;* Schroeder, *The Feminist Possibilities of Dramatic Realism;* and Demastes (editor), *Realism and the American Dramatic Tradition.*

For the twenties, useful general studies include Dickinson, *Playwrights of the New American Theater;* Waldau, *Vintage Years of the Theatre Guild 1928–1939;* and Valgemae, *Accelerated Grimace: Expressionism in the American Drama of the 1920s.* Significant critical treatments of the playwrights of the New Negro Movement can be found in Abramson, *Negro Playwrights in the American Theatre, 1925–1959;* Keyssar, *The Curtain and the Veil;* Brown-Guillory, *Black Women Playwrights in America;* Sanders, *The Development of Black Theater in America;* and Hay, *African American Theatre: An Historical and Critical Analysis.*

For the thirties and early forties, general studies include Mersand, *The American Drama, 1930–1940;* Rabkin, *Drama and Commitment: Politics in the American Theatre of the Thirties;* Smiley, *The Drama of Attack: Didactic Plays of the American Depression;* Goldstein, *The Political Stage: American Drama and Theater of the Great Depression;* Jay Williams, *Stage Left;* Levine, *Left-Wing Dramatic Theory in the American Theatre;* Schlueter (editor), *Modern American Drama: The Female Canon;* and Scharine, *From Class to Caste in American Drama: Political and Social Themes since the 1930s;* and Fearnow, *The American Stage and the Great Depression: A Cultural History of the Grotesque.* Important studies of the Federal Theatre Project include Flanagan, *Arena: The Story of the Federal Theatre;* DeHart, *The Federal Theatre, 1935–1939;* Craig, *Black Drama of the Federal Theatre Era; The Federal Theatre Project: A Catalog-Calendar of Productions;* and Fraden, *Blueprints for a Black Federal Theatre 1935–1939.* See also sources suggested in Chapter 2.

Eugene O'Neill

The most complete edition of O'Neill's plays is Bogart (editor), *Complete Plays of Eugene O'Neill.* Additional plays include Bower (editor), *More Stately Mansions;* Floyd (editor), *Eugene O'Neill: The Unfinished Plays;* and Gellert (editor), *Lost Plays of Eugene O'Neill.* Valuable sources for research are Ranald, *The Eugene O'Neill Companion;* Bogard and Bryer (editors), *Selected Letters of Eugene O'Neill;* Bryer (editor), *"The Theatre We Worked For": The Letters of Eugene O'Neill and Kenneth Macgowan;* Commins (editor), *"Love and Admiration and Respect": The O'Neill-Commins Correspondence;* Roberts and Roberts (editors), *"As Ever, Gene": The Letters of Eugene O'Neill to George Jean Nathan;* Floyd (editor), *Eugene O'Neill at Work: Newly Released Ideas for Plays;* Gallup (editor), *Eugene O'Neill: Work Diary 1924–1943;* Estrin (editor), *Conversations with Eugene O'Neill;* Reaves, *An O'Neill Concordance;* and Black, *File on O'Neill.* Bibliographical tools include Jennifer McCabe Atkinson, *Eugene O'Neill: A Descriptive Bibliography;* Jordan Y. Miller, *Eugene O'Neill and the American Critic: A Bibliographical Checklist;* Bryer, *Checklist of Eugene O'Neill;* and Smith and Eaton, *Eugene O'Neill: An Annotated Bibliography.*

The standard biography of O'Neill is Louis Sheaffer's two-volume *O'Neill: Son and Playwright* and *O'Neill: Son and Artist.* Arthur and Barbara Gelb's *O'Neill* is also very useful, and Boulton's *Part of a Long Story* is a fascinating account of her marriage to O'Neill and his Provincetown period. Oscar Cargill et al. (editors), *O'Neill and His*

Plays: Four Decades of Criticism; Jordan Y. Miller (editor), *Playwright's Progress: Eugene O'Neill and the Critics,* and Ulrich Halfmann (editor), *Eugene O'Neill: Comments on the Drama and the Theater,* include contemporary criticism of the productions.

The first book-length critical treatment of O'Neill's work was Barrett H. Clark, *Eugene O'Neill: The Man and His Plays* (1927; rev. ed., 1947), which is still useful for its extensive quotation of O'Neill's comments on his work. The most important comprehensive study is Bogard, *Contour in Time: The Plays of Eugene O'Neill* (1972; rev. ed., 1988). Other good general overviews of O'Neill's career include Winther, *Eugene O'Neill: A Critical Study* (1934; rev. ed., 1961); Frederick I. Carpenter, *Eugene O'Neill* (1964; rev. ed., 1979); Raleigh, *The Plays of Eugene O'Neill;* Berlin, *Eugene O'Neill;* and Floyd, *The Plays of Eugene O'Neill: A New Assessment.* Important treatments of specific periods in his career are Alexander, *The Tempering of Eugene O'Neill* and *Eugene O'Neill's Creative Struggle: The Decisive Decade, 1924–1933.* Some significant critical studies among the many that have appeared in the last seventy years include Edwin A. Engel, *The Haunted Heroes of Eugene O'Neill;* Falk, *Eugene O'Neill and the Tragic Tension: An Interpretive Study of the Plays;* Timo Tiusanen, *O'Neill's Scenic Images,* Chothia, *Forging a Language: A Study of the Plays of Eugene O'Neill;* Manheim, *Eugene O'Neill's New Language of Kinship;* Robinson, *Eugene O'Neill and Oriental Thought: A Divided Vision;* Porter, *The Banished Prince: Time, Memory, and Ritual in the Late Plays of Eugene O'Neill;* Hinden, *Long Day's Journey into Night: Native Eloquence;* Eisen, *The Inner Strength of Opposites: O'Neill's Novelistic Drama and the Melodramatic Imagination;* and Pfister, *Staging Depth: Eugene O'Neill and the Politics of Psychological Discourse.*

Treatments of O'Neill's plays in production include Barlow, *Final Acts: The Creation of Three Late O'Neill Plays;* Wainscott, *Staging O'Neill: The Experimental Years, 1920–1934;* Vena, *O'Neill's* The Iceman Cometh: *Reconstructing the Premiere;* and Orlandello, *O'Neill on Film.*

Other Playwrights

Useful resources for the study of other significant playwrights of the period include Horn, *Maxwell Anderson: A Research and Production Sourcebook;* Shivers, *Maxwell Anderson: An Annotated Bibliography of Primary and Secondary Works;* Hazelton and Krauss, *Maxwell Anderson and the New York Stage;* Klink, *Maxwell Anderson and S. N. Behrman: A Reference Guide;* Gross, *S. N. Behrman: A Research and Production Sourcebook;* Reed, *S. N. Behrman;* Roppolo, *Philip Barry;* Gottlieb, *Rachel Crothers;* Lindroth, *Rachel Crothers: A Research and Production Sourcebook;* H. Simonson, *Zona Gale;* Kenny, *Paul Green;* White, *Sidney Howard;* Rampersad, *The Life of Langston Hughes;* Dickinson, *A Bio-Bibliography of Langston Hughes, 1902–1967;* Mikolzyk, *Langston Hughes: A Bio-Bibliography;* Emanuel, *Langston Hughes;* Hemenway, *Zora Neale Hurston: A Literary Biography;* Howard, *Zora Neale Hurston;* Newson, *Zora Neale Hurston: A Reference Guide;* Goldstein, *George S. Kaufman: His Life, His Theater;* Pollack, *George S. Kaufman;* Jeffrey D. Mason, *Wisecracks: The Farces of George S. Kaufman;* Hirsch, *George Kelly;* Shadegg, *Clare Boothe Luce: A Biography;* Sheed, *Clare Boothe Luce;* Fearnow, *Clare Boothe Luce: A Research and Production Sourcebook;* Sylvia Jukes Morris, *Rage for Fame: The Ascent of Clare Boothe Luce;* Elmer Rice, *Minority Report;* Durham, *Elmer Rice;* Palmieri, *Elmer Rice: A Playwright's Vision of America;* Heuvel, *Elmer Rice: A Research and Production Sourcebook;* Floan, *William Saroyan;* Aram

Saroyan, *William Saroyan;* Shuman, *Robert E. Sherwood;* John Mason Brown, *The Worlds of Robert E. Sherwood* and *The Ordeal of a Playwright: Robert E. Sherwood and the Challenge of War;* Dickey, *Sophie Treadwell: A Research and Production Sourcebook;* Burbank, *Thornton Wilder* (1961; rev. ed., 1978); Linda Simon, *Thornton Wilder: His World;* Goldstein, *The Art of Thornton Wilder;* Haberman, *Our Town: An American Play;* and Bryer (editor), *Conversations with Thornton Wilder.*

4

Theatre Groups
and Their Playwrights

Mark Fearnow

Foundation

If the nineteenth century was a century of star actors, then much of the twentieth century has been a century of groups. The lead in artistic innovation was taken over by a new communitarianism in theatrical organization that featured, at its center, a circle of collaborators who shared a vision of theatre and of society. Often at the center of the circle was a playwright or a nucleus of several playwrights, who generated, like the proton in the atom, the energy that drove the organization. Many factors fed this group movement in theatre, but most prominent were the influences of Marxist social philosophy, with its emphasis on egalitarianism and social identity (as opposed to hierarchical structures and personalism), and an older tradition of social cooperation, from which Marx borrowed, that is best observed in monastic and other utopian societies dating into the ancient past at least as far as the Essenes of ancient Israel and that could be observed in nineteenth-century America in such places as Oneida, New York; New Harmony, Indiana; and Lancaster County, Pennsylvania. The twentieth-century theatre groups that contributed so mightily to theatrical and dramatic innovation tended to combine, usually unconsciously, the Marxist and monastic–utopian visions of communitarian creativity. This vision is problematic in American culture, conflicting with American ideals of individualism, competition, and personal accomplishment. Part of the story of the group experience in twentieth-century American theatre is the inevitable tension between group identity and the drives toward personal fame and fortune.

If the philosophical foundation for the American groups was ancient, their more immediate models were found in Europe and Russia of the late nineteenth century. The work of Johann Wolfgang von Goethe and Friedrich Schiller at Weimar between 1790 and 1805 and of the Duke of Saxe–Meiningen with his Meiningen players from 1870 to 1890 had established a new ideal of ensemble playing and group discipline. The success of these companies was emulated by André Antoine's Théâtre Libre in Paris (opened in 1887), the Deutches Theater founded by Adolf L'Arronge and Ludwig Barnay in Berlin (opened in 1883), Otto Brahm's Freie Bühne (founded in 1889) in Berlin, and the Moscow Art Theatre, founded by Konstantin Stanislavsky and Vladimir Nemirovich-Danchenko in 1898. Key to the artistic success of these companies was their adherence to a unified style of acting, which promised both to assist actors in achieving dependably competent performances and to unify the ensemble, making it a flexible tool for the newly empowered stage director.

Whereas nearly all American theatre groups founded before 1945 would agree with the aesthetic goals of unity in acting and design and even on the necessity of a director in theatrical production, the issue of governance and social organization within the group would arise again and again as a major point of contention among group members. Unlike the company members of the European state theatres that had formed part of the group heritage, the Americans who joined groups saw their activities more as life missions than as jobs. Art for them was serious business, and the way in which it was pursued would be guided by a systematic social ethic. This crisis of power in group organization would prove second only to financial collapse in the list of causes for the groups' disintegrations.

The resident theatre companies that thrived across the United States before 1870 had largely disappeared beneath the onslaught of consolidation and industrialization of theatre production achieved by aggressive business interests in the 1870s and 1880s. Local theatre companies were liquidated as New York–based agencies purchased theatre buildings and substituted touring productions for locally produced work. By 1900, the agency or trust known as the Theatrical Syndicate controlled most legitimate theatre production outside New York. The Syndicate and, after 1905, the rival Shubert Organization, also wielded great influence in the New York theatre through the ownership of theatre buildings and through their near-exclusive control of "the Road." Whereas in 1870 the power to produce plays professionally had rested with hundreds of producers and star actors who were distributed widely around the country, by 1900 most of this power was concentrated in the hands of less than ten individuals in two organizations. This consolidation of power allowed the syndicates to dictate terms to actors, playwrights, designers, and technicians. (For a more detailed discussion of the Syndicate and the structure of American theatre, see Chapter 2.)

The artistic consequences of the consolidation of theatre production were grave. Having no tradition of government support for the arts, American the-atre had always been by necessity a commercial operation. At the same time, the sheer multiplicity of theatrical producers before 1870 fostered variety and innovation in both writing and production as well as a dialogue between theatre and community, the theatre being to some degree a showcase and forum for the community's working out its idea of itself. The industrialization of theatre and its centralization in New York City changed all that. Because theatre was now designed to sell tickets in Peoria as well as in Poughkeepsie, the tastes and interests of local audiences were irrelevant to the producers of the mass product. Over time, audiences were trained to want what the syndi-cates sent them, the advertising phrase, "as seen in New York," providing a golden imprimatur.

American intellectuals who looked at the state of the theatre in the early years of the twentieth century found this situation appalling. Playwriting, some believed, had been especially affected by centralization of power. The formu-laic commercial writing required by the syndicates held little allure for writers who saw themselves as serious artists and, to compound the situation, the monopolistic control of theatre production made it nearly impossible to make a reasonable living as a playwright, since there was little choice but to sell one's work at terms offered by one of the two syndicates. If a writer were to write a serious play, unconforming to a commercial formula, there would be virtually nowhere for it to be staged. When James Herne wrote his Ibsen-inspired drama *Margaret Fleming* in 1890, there was no conceivable commercial venue for it. The financial losses incurred by the playwright when he produced the play himself discouraged further such attempts at realizing "art for truth's sake," Herne's description for the kind of drama that America was lacking and a phrase titling an 1897 essay that became an intellectual rallying point for those who began to call for theatrical reform. Herne and his friends looked with long-ing and frustration to the art theatres of Europe.

The New Theatre

The first serious attempt to create an American art theatre was the establish-ment of the New Theatre in New York in 1909. The well-publicized and disas-trous history of this company would leave a mark on later group pioneers, who found in the New Theatre an example of how not to start an art theatre in the United States. The New Theatre was first conceived and proposed by Hein-rich Conried, then director of the Metropolitan Opera. Conried's plans for the theatre were grandiose: a national art theatre with a resident company main-taining a repertory of both opera and drama. The theatre was to be supported through gifts from wealthy individuals, who would ultimately provide an endowment so that operating expenses could be paid from interest. In 1906, after years of agitation and cajoling on Conried's part, a corporation was established called the New Theatre Company. The treasurer and leading force on the corporation's board was Otto Kahn, a wealthy financier who was extraordinary in his association with the founding of a series of experimental theatre groups between 1906 and 1930 (see Connors, "The New Theatre," 326).

Kahn and the other members of the board – all wealthy New Yorkers who wished to improve the cultural tone of the city – raised the money required to build a luxurious and enormous theatre at Sixty-second Street and Central Park West. After a failed attempt to woo the English director Harley Granville-Barker as artistic director, the board settled upon Winthrop Ames. The son of a railroad tycoon, Ames was experienced, having headed the successful Castle Square Stock Company in Boston, and his just-completed tour of European theatres had excited him with the possibility of quality repertory (ibid.). The board hired a full design, technical, and business staff and, as the centerpiece of the repertory idea, twenty-eight actors, including two stars of the era – Julia Marlowe and E. H. Sothern.

The hiring of Sothern and Marlowe was the first sign that the New Theatre was backing away from its repertory ideals before its first season had even begun. Not only did their high price tags escalate the amount needed to sustain the theatre (each was paid the amazing sum of $2,800 per week, compared to $379 per week for the next-highest-paid actor), but their presence called into question the whole idea of a play-based repertory (see Jennings, "A History of the New Theatre," 182). Sothern and Marlowe had special clauses written into their contracts giving them the right to refuse any role offered them and even to set their own blocking and stage business. As soon as the first season was announced, it became clear that the New Theatre would not be so new at all. It would be a high-priced version of the traditional star-centered stock company. When the theatre opened on 8 November 1909, New York's cultural elite gathered to witness a production of *Antony and Cleopatra* that was universally attacked by critics as sloppy and incoherent, and – after a dispute with Ames over their refusal to appear in the second play scheduled to enter the repertory – the stars resigned and returned to their successful careers in commercial long runs.

A second problem with the New Theatre was the unwieldy size of the building. A vast Italianesque structure seating twenty-five hundred patrons, the theatre was criticized from the outset as having terrible acoustics. This problem, along with the warping of the company toward stars and the inability to cast the number of productions promised to subscribers, led to the complete disintegration of the repertory idea during the very first season. The company was disbanded, and Ames scrambled to bring in productions already prepared by other producers. The New Theatre struggled on in this

The New Theatre (1909–1911). Courtesy of the Harvard Theatre Collection, The Houghton Library.

way for one more season and then ended its brief life in 1911. The founders leased the building as a spectacle house until it was razed to make way for an apartment building in 1930.

The wave of young radicals, intellectuals, and idealists who were to found the theatre groups that would have a lasting impact on American theatre witnessed the debacle of the New Theatre and learned to avoid its excesses and miscalculations. The New Theatre's board was driven by no particular aesthetic or intellectual mission. The project was initiated based on the vaguest notion of "theatre art," and its baser source was a species of culture envy: The founders were not sure exactly what this theatre should be like, as long as it was "as good as" theatres in Europe. A sense of the cultural meaning of the New Theatre can be discerned in the spectacle of its dedication ceremony. The fanfare of that day (6 November 1909) included speeches by the leading lights of government (Woodrow Wilson), business (J. Pierpont Morgan), science (Thomas Edison), literature (W. D. Howells), and education (Harvard's George Pierce Baker). The casting of this characteristically Progressive Era assemblage indicates a belief by those launching the venture that a theatre, a New Theatre, could be created full blown and in much the same way as a new and cleaner style of government could be instituted or a new light bulb could be invented: as the inevitable outcome of idea plus money plus effort. Like the *Titanic,* which was being built as the New Theatre opened, this emblem of progress and modernity had to be bigger and more luxurious than its old-fashioned precursors, an exemplar of comfort, quality, and the glory of the modern age, its very size and grandeur ensuring a majestic progress across oceans and through time. The New Theatre lasted only slightly longer than did the *Titanic,* both meeting disaster in their inaugural voyages.

By 1912, American culture was primed to produce the renaissance that Joseph Wood Krutch and other critics would see in the theatre and drama in the teens and twenties.[1] American intellectuals were frustrated by the commercialism of the mainstream theatre. European theatre had provided three rough frameworks within which American groups would be built: the art theatre, the subscription-based workers' theatre, and the radical mobile unit. Academia was contributing as well, with the establishment of George Pierce Baker's Workshop 47 in 1912, intended as a laboratory for staging the plays of his Harvard students and comprising the first American effort at training dramatic writers in the logic and technique of playwriting. Above all these factors hovered the hulking ghost of the New Theatre and its associated miasma of institutional failure. "Look out," it might have whispered, "icebergs."

What proved the best protection from obstacles for these new theatres was the determination to remain small. The wave of foundings of art theatres that swept the country in the teens (discussed as "Alternative Theatre" in Chapter 2 by Frick) came to be known as the Little Theatre Movement, and by 1917, when Constance D'Arcy Mackay wrote the first history of this phenomenon, *The Little Theatre in the United States,* she counted sixty-three such theatres, stretching in an irregular necklace from Hollis, Maine, to Portland, Oregon. Mackay put forward criteria to define Little Theatres: the organization must include a resident company, experimentation in staging techniques and literary choices, maintenance of a repertoire, and a subscription system (Mackay, 25). Mackay saw the Little Theatre Movement originating with Antoine in Paris and reaching the United States in 1911 with the establishment of Maurice Browne's Little Theatre in Chicago and Mrs. Lyman Gale's Toy Theatre in Boston. Other outstanding Little Theatres founded in the teens were Samuel A. Eliot Jr.'s Little Theatre of Indianapolis (1915), Sam Hume's Arts and Crafts Theatre in Detroit (1915), Frederick McDonnell's Cleveland Play House (1916), and Aline Barnsdall's Little Arts Theatre of Los Angeles (1916) (see Mackay, 159–63; 147–52; 153–55; 156–58).

Although the impulse behind many of the Little Theatres was aesthetic, others were founded more for the entertainment of the members themselves or for "self-improvement" through the social-artistic activity of staging plays. With the introduction of electricity into most urban and suburban homes by 1890, along with the rapid improvement in the gasoline engine between 1899 and 1908 (the year Ford released the Model T), a flood of labor-saving devices was unleashed upon an eager public. Women's magazines from the early teens are replete with advertisements for electric stoves, washing machines, vacuum cleaners, and other appliances, and magazines aimed toward men propose the advantages of power-driven saws, lawnmowers, and garden tractors. The result of all this invention and consumption was that middle-class people had more leisure time, and the Little Theatre Movement was one of a host of ideas put forth to assist people in achieving the richer, happier life that technology was supposed to make possible.[2] The playwright and producer Percy MacKaye in his books *The Civic Theatre* (1912) and *Community Drama* (1917) proposed amateur theatre as a form of "constructive leisure" that would – unlike the passive consumption of moviegoing – both improve the individual participant and strengthen the social cohesion of local communities.

The three theatre groups of the teens that would change the course of American theatre and drama were in their origins indistinguishable from the humblest Little Theatre. These theatres – the Neighborhood Playhouse, the Provincetown Players (discussed in Chapter 3 by Murphy), and the Washington Square Players – were featured prominently in Mackay's book on the movement. The creative energy of the period was abundant, and the Little Theatres met a variety of fates. A few, like the Washington Square Players and the Cleveland Play House, eventually transformed themselves into long-standing professional operations. Some would last only into the 1920s and then dissolve. Most of the sixty-three theatres listed by Mackay carried on for decades as amateur theatres, gradually becoming known as "community theatres" and continuing to fulfill the notions of "constructive leisure" set forth by Percy MacKaye in 1912.

The Neighborhood Playhouse

The most unusual combination of aesthetic goals and social purpose was found in the Neighborhood Playhouse, which grew out of the social work of Alice and Irene Lewisohn, wealthy sisters who came from a philanthropic New York family. The sisters accompanied their father in 1901 on a visit to the Henry Street Settlement House, a social-service center located among the crowded tenements and chaotic streets of Manhattan's Lower East Side (see Crowley, 6–7). The Settlement House was directed by Lillian Wald, an energetic social worker who believed that practical works of care and sustenance for poor immigrants should be combined with cultural activities, thus calling forth the best in people and helping them to avoid the despair and self-hatred that came with poverty and dislocation. The sisters began assisting in the Settlement House's program of lectures, arts and crafts, and cultural celebrations. When their father died in 1902, they applied all of their energies, and a considerable portion of their inheritances, toward the cultural program at Henry Street.

In their positions as "club leaders," the Lewisohns were responsible for groups of immigrant children, through whom they became acquainted with entire families. Presented with hundreds of children and their families from such places as Armenia, Greece, Italy, Russia, Hungary, Poland, Germany, Ireland, India, and China, people professing faiths including Judaism, various versions of Catholic, Orthodox, and Protestant Christianity, Buddhism, Confucianism, and Hinduism, the sisters mined their own interests in religion and psychology to find "symbolic imagery" that was meaningful to all of their clients, exploiting the "creative play instinct" in their actor-audiences to organize and choreograph the children and their families into ritual events that sometimes included as many as five hundred participants. A Midwinter Festival combined Hanukkah, Christmas, the Chinese New Year, and the winter solstice into one evening-long celebration of the mystery of light (see Crowley, 19–20). They were in essence creating new, ecumenical religious rituals that combined such ancient ritual elements as parading with icons, lighting of candles, distribution of flame, chanting, and processing. They organized these events in a carefully scripted way, as in most religious events, and Irene Lewisohn's choreography sought a form that was expressive of inner feeling and free from traditional movements of classical ballet.

The Lewisohns' Jungian-oriented approach to theatre became more explicitly dramatic in 1912 when they organized some older children into a dramatic club. The Lewisohns acted in these first plays, along with people from the neighborhood and volunteer actors from elsewhere in the city. The group chose an assortment of one-act plays by European and Russian authors, found in libraries or obscure periodicals by the sisters or their staff. As word of the work spread, theatre professionals began volunteering their services to take part in what must have seemed a refreshing idealism. Sarah Cowell Le Moyne, a well-known actress, came to work as director and acting coach; Agnes Morgan, a playwright and technician, came aboard to direct and evaluate scripts; Helen Arthur, a young attorney and employee of the Shubert organization, volunteered to manage the group's business affairs.

Witnessing the popularity of the group, which had named itself the Neighborhood Players, the Lewisohns took rapid steps to plan and build a new theatre and arts center. They began in 1913 to plan a simple but accommodating facility that had at its center an auditorium seating three hundred in the orchestra and ninety-nine in a shallow balcony.[3] The Lewisohns set off to teach themselves how to operate an art theatre by visiting outstanding examples in Europe, where they witnessed Max Reinhardt's work in Berlin. They also went to Hellerau, near Dresden, to experience the collaboration between Adolphe Appia and Jacques Dalcroze at the theatre and school especially designed by Appia. The sisters were influenced by Dalcroze's techniques in training actor-dancers through rhythmic movement (a system Dalcroze called Eurythmics), and they later adapted this method for training students at the Playhouse.

In February, 1915, the Neighborhood Playhouse opened at 466 Grand Street with a production of a biblical dance-drama called *Jephtha's Daughter.* The theatre's following grew steadily. Their carefully rehearsed productions of short plays by John Galsworthy, Lord Dunsany, Anton Chekhov, and Bernard Shaw, in addition to other lesser-known playwrights, began to attract critical attention to the unlikely location. Most of these productions were American premieres, and the Playhouse was influential in promoting the Little Theatre as a showplace for short plays, a genre virtually nonexistent on the commercial stage. As their dramatic theatre developed, the Lewisohns continued an array of other activities in the facility, including children's theatre, puppetry, the cultural festivals, and a film series, as well as classes in sewing, painting, and dance. Amateur groups such as the Workingman's Circle (a Yiddish cultural and political association) staged Yiddish plays, and the Irish Theatre of America presented a series of folk plays.

In 1920, the Executive Committee that had been formed to guide the Neighborhood Playhouse (the Lewisohns, Agnes Morgan, Helen Arthur, and designer Aline Bernstein) decided to organize a permanent professional company at the Playhouse. The committee reasoned that such a step would create a less hectic life for the volunteers and would provide better training for the students, who would work alongside the professionals. At the same time, the Lewisohns regretted the end of the "amateur era" in their theatre, giving up, as they saw it, the innocence and unsophisticated pleasure of those days. Though hundreds of actors from the commercial stage auditioned for the new company, the Playhouse struggled to recruit a group of actors "willing to search beyond the obvious form and character of the part . . . to enter into rapport with the orchestral values of a production" (Crowley, 100). This problem was never solved during the Playhouse's lifetime. In spite of the critical success that the professional company was to achieve, the Lewisohns saw an ever-widening gulf between their vision of the Playhouse and the increasingly well-polished artistic products that emerged on its stage. Though a coherent philosophy of theatre guided play selection and design choices, the lack of a unified acting system led to a constant schism between artistic idea and realization in performance.

In terms of critical and public recognition of its efforts, the formation of the professional Neighborhood Playhouse Acting Company was just the beginning. The company's first production was John Galsworthy's *The Mob.* The Playhouse had a history of performing Galsworthy's works, and the play's melange of social consciousness with near-expressionist depictions of "the mob" was an ideal fit with the philosophy of the Playhouse. So interested was Galsworthy in their activities that he arranged a visit to New York to see the production and meet the Lewisohns. Between the years 1920 and 1927, when the Playhouse company folded, the group staged forty-three productions. Most famous were their explorations into myth and religion, such as the ancient Indian play *The Little Clay Cart* in 1924 and the Yiddish drama *The Dybbuk* by S. Ansky in 1925.

At about the same time that the Lewisohns were organizing their amateur company on the Lower East Side, an assortment of intellectuals, artists, poets, dilettantes, and an energetic patent attorney were taking part in activities only a few miles away in Greenwich Village that would lead to the formation of two even more influential groups – the Washington Square Players and the Provincetown Players. Both groups had their origins in the fertile ground of the prewar Greenwich Village organization that called itself the Liberal Club, housed in a brownstone on MacDougal Street near Washington Square (see Langner, 65–71). This commodious space, sparsely furnished but equipped with open fireplaces, mahogany portals, and decorated with an array of modern paintings, served as a magnet for the writers, poets, painters, and politicos who were moving to the Village from across the country, seeking along its winding brick streets a mildly subversive haven from the perky optimism of the Progressive Era. They came to the Village as much for the cheap rents, picturesque architecture, and raucous basement restaurants as for, in Lawrence Langner's words, "the good companionship and exciting discussions of art, literature, sex, and psychology" (Langner, 67). The Club sponsored lectures and discussions on social topics, living up to its motto, "A Meeting Place for Those Interested in New Ideas" (Langner, 68). Langner, a young patent attorney newly arrived from London, was first taken to the Club in 1912, and he saw the Club's greatest value not in the "new ideas" per se but in the slow dancing, generous drinking, and kaleidoscopic coupling of the free-thinking men and women who made the place their headquarters.

The membership of the Liberal Club was an impressive roster of newly famous and about to become famous figures in American arts and politics. One evening at the Club might bring a visitor face to face with such writers as Alfred Kreymborg, Vachel Lindsay, Edna St. Vincent Millay, Upton Sinclair, Hutchins Hapgood, Neith Boyce, or Sinclair Lewis, and another night might present a person the opportunity to argue with Floyd Dell, Mary Heaton Vorse, Theodore Dreiser, or Susan Glaspell. The Club boasted political activists as well, with John Reed and Max Eastman representing communist and socialist tendencies and anarchist Alexander Berkman, who circulated and spoke in a low voice. The membership was rounded out by a variety of vaguely defined aesthetes (such as George Cram Cook), actors (such as Helen Westley), journalists (such as Lincoln Steffens), and publishers (such as Saxe Cummings).

The Washington Square Players

During the winter of 1914, the Liberal Club organized a "dramatic branch" that produced a romantic one-act by Club member Floyd Dell. Considering the project to have been inadequately conceived, Langner, Albert Boni, and Ida Rauh met in December at Rauh's home to plan the founding of their own theatre. Prominent among others who soon joined the effort were aspiring playwrights Edward Goodman, Philip Moeller, Susan Glaspell, George Cram Cook, and Floyd Dell; aspiring actors Helen Westley, Josephine Meyer, Ida Rauh, Dudley Tucker, Mary Morris, and Florence Enright; and scenic designers Robert Edmond Jones and Lee Simonson. The group, which soon selected the name Washington Square Players, was initially funded by contributions from Langner and Tucker, along with funds raised from a small group of subscribers. They rented the Bandbox Theatre, with a capacity of just 299, located on East Fifty-seventh Street near Third Avenue in Manhattan (see Durham, *American Theatre Companies, 1888–1930*, 461).

The group initially attempted to operate on a democratic basis, with every member having an equal vote in matters of play selection and casting. This system soon proved too cumbersome and chaotic, and the members elected a committee of five persons to make these decisions. Staff positions were defined, with Edward Goodman elected managing director and Langner and Albert Boni appointed business managers. Langner had observed that the German *Volkesbühne* and Maurice Browne's Chicago Little Theatre based their financial operations on the subscription method; he prompted the group to send out a manifesto designed to attract subscribers for what promised to be a new and unusual theatrical venture (see Helburn, 51). This document – written by Langner, Moeller, and Goodman – introduced the Washington Square Players as an organization "composed of individuals who believe in the future of the theatre in America" and who opposed the wretched condition of American drama. The Players believed that a higher standard could be achieved "only as the outcome of experiment and initiative" (quoted in Langner, 94). Through "hard work and perseverance, coupled with ability and the absence of purely commercial considerations," the Players hoped to bring about "the birth and healthy growth of an artistic theatre in this country" (ibid.). Their only policy in regard to play selection was that plays have "artistic merit." Preference would be given to American plays, but the group would also produce plays by "well-known European authors which have been ignored by the commercial managements" (ibid.). This declaration led to the pitch for financial assistance, offering tickets for fifty cents and subscriptions for five dollars.

The Players gave their first performance on 19 February 1915, with a bill of short plays juxtaposing European works with plays by the group's own members. Langner's *Licensed* was a drama about a pregnant bride whose intended husband died moments before they were to be married. This play was followed by *Eugenically Speaking,* by Edward Goodman, which satirized Bernard Shaw's ideas about intentional mating for the purpose of producing the Superman. Next was *Interior* by Belgian Symbolist Maurice Maeterlinck, followed by a comic send-up of Maeterlinck's play – a pantomime set inside a person's stomach instead of a mind, featuring members of the Players representing various items of food and drink, "swaying with a bilious rhythm" and finally rushing out of the stomach in an impressively peristaltic conclusion (Langner, 96).

The bill was well received by critics, and after the similar success of the second bill, three professional actors joined the group, bringing with them a higher standard of production as well as the expectation of being paid – a new issue for the Players, whose first bills were staged entirely by volunteers. The Players stepped up the tempo of their program, introducing a bill each month before taking a break over the summer. They continued assembling bills of plays by writers such as Chekhov, Schnitzler, Maeterlinck, Musset, and Wedekind, along with plays by Players members Langner, Moeller, and Goodman. Their seasons occasionally included new work by other American writers, such as *The Antick* by Percy MacKaye (October 1915); *Overtones* by Alice Gerstenberg (November 1915); *The Magical City* by Zoë Akins (March 1916); *The Girl in the Coffin* by Theodore Dreiser and *Neighbors* by Zona Gale (December 1917); and *The Home of the Free* by Elmer Rice (April 1918). Though there was sporadic interaction between the Washington Square Players and the Provincetown Players, the Washington Square group essentially lost the playwrights and actors who had been part of the Provincetown summer of 1915 (O'Neill, Glaspell, Dell, Reed, and Rauh) when George Cram Cook and Susan Glaspell organized the Provincetown group as a separate entity in September 1916, moving its operation from Cape Cod to New York. Launching its season on 3 November 1916 at 139 MacDougal Street, two years later it would find larger quarters at 133 MacDougal. Nevertheless, Cook's distinctly romantic philosophy of art would result in the Provincetown remaining deliberately amateur (until 1922), its focus almost exclusively on new American plays.

The Washington Square Players continued to produce through May 1918.

They attempted a few longer plays – Chekhov's *The Seagull* (May 1916), Andreyev's *The Life of Man* (January 1917), Ibsen's *Ghosts* (May 1917), Langner's *The Family Exit* (September 1917), and Shaw's *Mrs Warren's Profession* (March 1918). In June 1916, they moved to the Comedy Theatre, a larger house owned by the Shuberts and located near Broadway on West Thirty-eighth Street.

The major reason for the Players' demise was the fact that many of their number were drafted for military service (Langner, a British citizen, was exempted because of his essential work as a patent attorney in defense-related industries). Financial pressures on the group had also steadily increased. As the group became successful, their landlords increased their rents. They had paid only $35 a week for the Bandbox Theatre during their first season but were charged $8,000 for the nine months that comprised the second. Lee Shubert leased the Comedy Theatre to the Players for $32,000 per season, an expense that necessitated the company's raising their standard ticket price to the $2 that one critic had earlier said they were worth (see Durham, *American Theatre Companies, 1888–1930,* 461). As the Players expanded their activities, attempting to launch a school and sending out tours to a string of eastern cities, they stretched their resources beyond their capabilities. By the spring of 1918, the group was deeply in debt and depleted of personnel. The impetus that led to the group's creation was not dead, declared Langner in a letter to the New York newspapers in May 1918. The "doctors and wiseacres of Broadway and the newspaper offices who are busy analyzing the causes of the 'death' of the Washington Square Players" should not be surprised if "the corpse expresses its appreciation with a vigorous kick" (Langner, 113).

The accomplishments of the Washington Square Players over three and a half years of operation were impressive. They produced a total of sixty-two one-act plays and six full-length plays, taking the Little Theatre idea and transforming it into a semiprofessional, high-quality producing organization. Also important were their attempts to maintain a repertory and subscription list – ideals that many later groups would aspire to attain but would find unworkable amid a chaos of fund raising. Finally, the Players' organizational tactic of appointing a "Managers Committee" to make major production decisions would prove influential, being integral to the succeeding Theatre Guild as well as for the New Playwrights Theatre and the Theatre Union.

Most important, the Players provided a competent and high-profile home for "artistic" plays by American authors. As soon as the Washington Square Players announced their intention to form, American writers began sending them new work, suggesting a body of writers experiencing a hunger to write serious drama but who saw little point in doing so when none but the most formulaic and commercial products had any hope of being realized as high-quality productions. While some of these writers would fade from view without amassing a significant body of work, others would eventually emerge as major dramatists. Eugene O'Neill and Susan Glaspell turned away from the Washington Square group and devoted their efforts to their own Provincetown Players (the major plays of O'Neill and Glaspell are discussed by Murphy in Chapter 3). Zoë Akins would go on to win the Pulitzer Prize in drama and to enjoy a successful career as a Broadway playwright, as would fellow Washington Square Players alumnus Elmer Rice. If seasons had continued to feature mediocre plays by members of the company's executive committee, none of whom emerged as a significant playwright, the Players would likely have been dismissed by critics, audiences, and potential dramatists as a vanity organization of little merit. Langner and Theresa Helburn would later lament that they, along with Moeller, sacrificed their own budding playwriting careers to further the work of other writers. The question would be neatly solved for Langner, Moeller, and Helburn when their peers on the Board of Managers of the Theatre Guild insisted on a rule virtually banning production of plays authored by Board members (see Langner, 117; Helburn, 166, 248–49).

The Theatre Guild

Theatre histories have tended to consider the Washington Square Players and the Theatre Guild as two distinct organizations, but there are good reasons to see them as one continuous theatre that underwent a reconfiguration and renaming during a hiatus that lasted less than a year. The last Washington Square Players production closed in May 1918. The Armistice ending World War I was promulgated on 11 November of that year, and, on 18 December, Langner organized a meeting to start a "new" theatre built upon the foundations of the Players. Of the Theatre Guild's first Board of Managers, as they were to rename the executive committee, only Rollo Peters was not an alumnus of the Players (the other managers being Lawrence Langner, Helen Westley, Helen Freeman, Lee Simonson, Philip Moeller, and Justus Sheffield). One reason for the historical "remembering" of the Washington Square Players and Theatre Guild as distinct organizations is the success of Langner in his public relations efforts of 1918. Langner was a skilled managerial strategist, and the new beginning allowed him to institute various reforms. Langner was, moreover, a skilled legal strategist, and his declaration of the Theatre Guild as a distinct organization was the group's only protection from legal pursuit by the Shubert Organization and other creditors over the thousands of dollars of unpaid bills accumulated by the Washington Square Players. Both

Langner and Helburn are silent on the question of why Edward Goodman was not part of the reconstituted organization, and it seems likely that he was barred from the group for purely legal reasons. Goodman was listed on legal documents of the Players as Managing Director, and his continuation as an official of the Theatre Guild would have made implausible their legal claim of immunity from previous debts.

Langner wrote to Washington Square Players alumni in December 1918, envisioning the revitalized organization as "a little theatre grown up" (Langner, 115). The new theatre would, Langner promised, benefit from lessons he had learned from the Players' experience. These principles, added to those agreed upon by the Managers at a meeting on 19 December 1918, amounted to four guiding principles of the Theatre Guild:

1. The Guild would have a director but would be governed entirely by its Board of Managers.

2. The Guild would be a fully professional theatre, employing professional actors, designers, and technicians, thus making the Guild "entirely different from the Provincetown Playhouse type of theatre."

3. The Guild would produce only long plays, "which should be great plays."

4. The Guild would either lease or build a theatre "larger than the usual Little Theatre (between 500 and 600 seating capacity)" (see Langner, 115–16).

The founding group was soon supplemented by the addition of Maurice Wertheim to the Board, as a replacement for Justus Sheffield. Wertheim was an investment banker who had developed an interest in theatre when he took George Pierce Baker's playwriting course at Harvard. Theresa Helburn, also a Baker alumna and a drama critic for *The Nation,* was hired as Play Representative. After some heated argument, the Board accepted two additional principles that were to prove important in the Guild's success:

5. The theatre would be organized on a subscription basis and would be entirely supported by those funds and by the sale of individual tickets. This principle was insisted upon by Wertheim, who felt that market pressure would keep the theatre responsive to its audience (Eaton, 171–72).

6. The Guild would produce no plays authored by Board members unless the play received a unanimous vote of the Board, an event that was never to occur (Langner, 117, 119).

These principles proved lasting and beneficial, guiding the Guild through its most productive years of 1919–39. The autobiographies of Langner, Helburn, and Simonson are replete with accounts of the furious battles and well-nurtured grudges that animated the Sunday evening meetings of the Board. A pivotal argument during the second season was over the question of whether or not the Guild should be ruled by a strong director, as in the case of the Moscow Art Theatre and other European models, or whether the Board should rule on all serious matters. When the majority held the latter position, Rollo Peters resigned, along with Augustin Duncan (brother of Isadora), a recent Board initiate and the outstanding actor in the fledgling company. Their departures led to Helburn's being elected to the Board as a regular member, a crucial turn of events in that she possessed the talent and inclination for the day-to-day managerial work that would ensure the Guild's financial endurance.

The Guild's first production was *Bonds of Interest,* a fantasy in *commedia* style by the modern Spanish playwright Jacinto Benavente in a production that opened on 14 April 1919 at the Garrick Theatre on Thirty-fifth Street. The play was staged on a budget of $1,100, raised largely from Board members. The subscription list on opening night included only 135 persons, and when the play closed in its fourth week, only $19 remained in the treasury. Were it not for the fact that the Garrick's owner was the ubiquitous Otto Kahn, who agreed to accept rent from the Guild only when they could afford it, the group could hardly have contemplated a second production (see Helburn, 70–71).

The $19 production of Irish playwright St. John Ervine's *John Ferguson* became the launching pad for a mighty organization. Ervine's naturalistic drama opened to enthusiastic reviews on 12 May 1919. Its run was assisted by a general strike by Actors' Equity, which began in August and closed down all competing productions but which did not affect the Guild.

The financial and artistic successes of *John Ferguson* may have contributed to the Guild's decision to continue with a program of European plays. The complete list of their productions (see Langner, 473–80) does not show a season in which the majority of plays are by American authors until 1932 – the Guild's fifteenth season. Board members justified their choices by arguing that few American plays existed of the quality that the Guild required and that, moreover, the Guild's seasons of Strindberg, Tolstoy, Molnár, Shaw, Pirandello, Kaiser, Claudel, and Andreyev offered a kind of school for the degraded American authors whose only exposure had been to a crass commercial stage. This argument, an extension of one pursued by the Washington Square Players, was given out frequently in press statements by the Managers in the 1920s and is prominent in the memoirs of Langner and Helburn. "We felt that by showing our American playwrights the best of what was being done abroad, we were providing a valuable service," wrote Theresa Helburn, who went on:

> . . . providing our own writers with the stimulus of fresh ideas and new techniques, impressing on them the universality of theater, enabling them to weigh their own methods and achievement in the balance, to see them

against the terrific excitement of the experiments coming out of Russia and Germany, out of Italy and France. (99)

The claim that the Guild was to some degree responsible for the considerable flowering of serious American drama that occurred in the 1920s and 1930s is not entirely unrealistic. Playwrights such as Elmer Rice, Eugene O'Neill, Philip Barry, John Howard Lawson, Sidney Howard, S. N. Behrman, Maxwell Anderson, and Robert E. Sherwood emerged as prolific, confident, and skilled playwrights during the 1920s through plays produced at the Guild. But did Behrman, with his brilliantly discursive and serious comedies, come into existence because the Guild staged seven plays by Shaw between 1920 (*Heartbreak House*) and 1927, when Shaw's *Pygmalion* shared the season with Behrman's *The Second Man?* Was Rice able to write *The Adding Machine* (1923) because the Guild had previously staged two Expressionist plays – Strindberg's *The Dance of Death* in 1920 and Kaiser's *From Morn to Midnight* in 1922? In their autobiographies, both Langner and Helburn insisted that what might be called a cultural transference was self-evident. Writing from the vantage point of 1951, Langner extended the transference to include design as well as playwriting:

> As the years roll by, it seems clear that the Theatre Guild's early policy of importing the best artistic plays and production ideas of Europe, which was often bitterly opposed at the time, sowed the seeds which later bore a harvest of American plays and productions that have since then compared favorably with those of the rest of the world. (155–56)

American playwrights could, of course, read. That Shaw and Pirandello had to be staged in a Broadway-sized house before Americans could know that such a drama existed is highly questionable. The Guild's assessment of their own accomplishment includes a peculiar assumption of the United States as having been a hermetically sealed demi-continent before the Guild opened an artistic pipeline on Thirty-fifth Street in 1919. One thing can be asserted with some assurance of legitimacy: The Guild's existence may not have made it possible for these American playwrights to emerge in the 1920s, but the existence and flourishing condition of such a stage made it worthwhile to write unconventional plays, since for the first time it would be possible for them to be seen in a prominent space in one's own country. Had the Guild not existed, ambitious and sophisticated plays like Rice's *The Adding Machine* and O'Neill's sprawling *Strange Interlude* (1928) might never have been attempted. O'Neill did not write the novel-length *Mourning Becomes Electra* (1931) because the Guild had staged Shaw's twelve-hour *Back to Methuselah* in 1922, but he could indeed have seen a point in writing it because the Guild had shown the willingness to tackle massive experimental works. Their surprising success in attracting and retaining large numbers of subscribers and in generating ticket sales adequate to support this kind of theatre changed the commercial stage as well. By 1928, the Guild found itself competing with commercial producers for plays that previously would never have been considered potential sources of profit.

The Theatre Guild's literary, artistic, and managerial accomplishments between 1919 and the dissolution of the Board system in 1939 are impressive. Their original subscription list of 135 had grown by 1930 to include 35,000 subscribers in New York, as well as 45,000 subscribers in 132 cities and towns around the country – venues to which the Guild toured a complete season of plays, beginning in 1927 (see Langner, 222, and Waldau, 344). The Guild managed for a time to fulfill Langner's dream of a permanent acting company in an alternating repertory system. The acting company had as its core some of the finest actors in the American theatre – Alfred Lunt, Lynn Fontanne, Ina Claire, Dudley Digges, and Earle Larrimore – who rotated biweekly through a sequence of plays in two theatres in New York while also accommodating the many subscription cities across the country. The company and the repertory system were maintained for only two seasons (1927–29), collapsing under pressures from the stock-market crash and from playwrights, who were reluctant to offer their plays into a system that reduced the length of run.

The Theatre Guild expanded America's idea of a theatre as a full-service institution. The Guild operated a School of Theatre from 1927 to 1930 and published a glossy magazine from 1927 to 1932. These expansions were financed by income from a variety of sources: subscriptions, ticket sales, and film sales. Profits were partly invested in paying for the Guild's various buildings, partly set aside for future productions, and partly paid out as extra distributions to Board members, according to a vote of the Board itself. All of these operations were directed from the flagship Guild Theatre, an elegant 900-seat house specially built for the Guild in 1924–25 on Fifty-second Street. But the 1930s would take away much of what the Guild built up in the 1920s. They would lose their playwrights to break-away operations and to competing commercial producers. They would lose most of "the Road" as the Depression reduced their tour stops from 132 cities to a string of only the 6 largest (see Langner, 257). The Guild even lost their theatre when they failed during the late 1930s to make sufficient payments on the bonds that had paid for its construction, finally relinquishing the building in 1942. Financial pressures ultimately led to the dissolution of the Board system in 1939, pressures emphasized in Lee Simonson's ferocious verbal attack on Helburn and Langner for having paid themselves bonuses of $20,000 at the conclusion of the 1937–38 season, a season in which the Guild lost $120,000 (Waldau, 276). Most important, the 1930s took from the Guild what the original Board valued most – artistic prestige. As the next generation moved to build upon the Guild's accomplishments, the Guild could be seen as a floating relic of the 1920s and its Board a superannuated band of socially naïve aesthetes.

The Group Theatre

The most brutal challenge came from within. Among the scores of aspiring young people who found their first paying jobs within the Guild's gargantuan organization of the 1920s were three who would prove of particular importance and, to the Guild, a source of considerable irritation. All three were hired by the Guild in 1925. Harold Clurman, the brilliant and hyperarticulate son of a Manhattan physician, was employed as a bit player and wrote pensive dramaturgical articles for *Theatre Guild Magazine.* Lee Strasberg, an intensely private Polish-born actor, had been studying the Stanislavsky system with Moscow Art Theatre alumni Richard Boleslavsky and Maria Ouspenskaya at the tiny American Laboratory Theatre downtown on MacDougal Street. Strasberg was hired by the Guild as a bit player and assistant stage manager. Cheryl Crawford, a serious-minded young person who had once longed to escape her upper-middle-class home in Akron, Ohio, by becoming a Christian missionary, was employed by Theresa Helburn as administrative assistant and eventually as casting director.

These three unlikely collaborators first formed a sort of triad during rehearsals for the Guild production of Franz Werfel's *Juarez and Maximilian* in 1926. Clurman was playing several small roles in the play while Crawford appeared in crowd scenes and assisted backstage. Strasberg was not involved in the production, but Clurman's backstage harangues about the future of the American theatre captured Crawford's attention and she went with him to witness Strasberg's work with a group of amateur actors at the Chrystie Street Settlement House on the Lower East Side.

Clurman was a deep and deeply dissatisfied young man, and it was his profound dissatisfaction that would lead to the formation of something new and memorable, the most elaborate expression of the "group ideal" in American theatre. Clurman's reading of Gordon Craig, Jacques Copeau, and other visionaries of the modern theatre led him to question the value of the Guild's approach. He was working with the theatre organization widely recognized as the best and most serious in the country, yet he felt strongly that something was missing. What was wrong, for example, with the Guild's production of *Juarez and Maximilian?* The play was interesting in theme and built upon a solid plot. The production was artfully designed and cast with some of the best actors available in the American theatre, including Edward G. Robinson, Clare Eames, Arnold Daly, Alfred Lunt, Margalo Gillmore, and Dudley Digges (see Clurman, *The Fervent Years,* 4–15). Philip Moeller, the play's director, was experienced and skilled at creating meaningful stage pictures. Why, Clurman wondered, was the whole thing so lifeless and vague?

Clurman initially analyzed this problem in terms of the company's lack of connection with the play. The director had only a "vague literary feeling for it" and demonstrated no "organic sense" of what the play's theme really was (Clurman, *The Fervent Years,* 14). They selected plays, he charged, "the way lists of guests were drawn up for parties," mingling the charm of a Molnar play with the political jolt of a John Howard Lawson, the sweet sentimentality of an A. A. Milne, and the sprightly classicism of a Shaw (Clurman, *The Fervent Years,* 21). The Board "didn't want to say anything through plays," Clurman wrote in 1945,

> . . . and plays said nothing to them, except that they were amusing in a graceful way, or, if they were tragic plays, that they were "art." And art was a good thing. The board members were in favor of culture. As a result they chose plays of the most conflicting tendencies, and produced them all with the same generalized Broadway technique, though in better taste than the average. (Clurman, *The Fervent Years,* 26)

In what was perhaps the most damning critique possible for the generation that would come into maturity in the 1930s, Clurman described the Guild productions as "pretty" but with "a disguised middleclass stuffiness" that left them lacking "passion or pointedness" (ibid.).

Clurman saw in theatre nothing less than the salvation of humankind. The theatre has in it, he exclaimed one evening to his friend Aaron Copland, the potential for the perfection of humanity. Modern humans were busy, distracted, hysterical, no longer able to understand their dreams, constantly on the go but unable to feel their own motion, since motion had become identical with life. Despite their chronic agitation, they were actually passive, letting everything be done to them and not by them. So cut off were they from the dialectical bases of true action – objective thought and the meaning of dreams – that they simply "danced on maniacally, toward a place they did not know, for a pleasure they could not enjoy, for a purpose they did not seek" (Clurman, *The Fervent Years,* 30). But the intensely social art of theatre could draw people together into a new line, leading away from disaster, moving peacefully and gracefully toward a common ground. When that common ground was reached, "we must build our house on it," Clurman intoned, ". . . arrange it as a dwelling place for all decent humanity. For life, though it be individual to the end, cannot be lived except in terms of people together, sure and strong in their togetherness" (ibid.). Hearing all of this in 1926, Copland suddenly burst into tears, certain that his friend was in for a load of trouble.

During the years 1926 and 1927, Clurman built up a potent arsenal of ideas about what a *real* theatre would be when realized. Clurman's intensive reading of Walt Whitman's poems and essays and of Waldo Frank's *Our America* (1920) strengthened his belief that the artist and intellectual must tap into the vital energy that supported American culture, focus that energy and create a visible light. The artist must abandon postures of separation and aloofness and instead immerse himself or herself in the tumultuous energies of mass culture. Waldo Frank's influence on Clurman's thought intensified with the publication of his *Rediscovery of America* in 1927, wherein Frank asserted that, "with tragic need America needs groups" (quoted in Clurman, *The Fervent Years*, 20). Clurman theorized that the outward activity of a real theatre would be that of profound engagement in the deep life of the nation, a dialogue with culture made possible by the theatre's construction of its own distinct personality, a sense of self formed by the shared life of those who comprise it. The formation of this personality required both a shared artistic life (made possible by a shared artistic language) as well as a shared personal life. Clurman's genius was in combining his idea of a theatre as a vital cultural voice with the notions of unity and communion within the artistic organization itself, whereby the theatre's internal dialogue creates the sense of self and so propels the theatre's dialogue with the wider culture.

If Clurman's reading of Waldo Frank was a significant influence on the outward dialogue aspect of this model, his exposure to Strasberg and others at the American Laboratory Theatre contributed in a powerful way to his theory of theatre as a living and organic self. Watching Strasberg working with his amateur actors at Chrystie Street, using the techniques learned from the Moscow Art alumni at the Lab, Clurman was struck by the value of a company's sharing a common artistic language, one that denoted its understanding of a common artistic system. Strasberg was at this time working out his own version of acting technique, mingling Stanislavskian terms such as "the magic if" with Evgeny Vakhtangov's notion of "adjustments," a more daring technique by which the actor relied not only on imagination but also on memory. The actor would not simply ask, "What if I were this character?" He or she would make an "adjustment," which meant bringing into play a substitute reality to be held in the actor's mind during a particular moment. This reality was conjured not from the text and situations of the play but from the actor's personal history and was to be analogically applicable to the character's problem.[4] The value of these techniques and their potential to solve the problems that Clurman saw at the Guild was reinforced in Clurman's mind when he and Strasberg enrolled in Boleslavsky's directing course at the Lab in November 1926. The course proved doubly influential because it was there that Clurman met Stella Adler, who was the Lab's most serious, experienced, and questing student.

Adler's father was Jacob Adler, a star of the thriving Yiddish stage of lower

Manhattan and one of the actors who had mesmerized Clurman as a child. Stella Adler's brother, Luther, was also a well-known actor on the Yiddish stage, as were her sister, Julia, and mother, Sara. Stella Adler brought to her friendship and eventual romance with Clurman the whole tradition of the Yiddish theatre – a theatre that was already achieving the passionate connection between theatre and audience that Clurman longed to see on an English-language stage. Adler had acted in the Yiddish tradition since the age of five, when her father held her out to the audience at a curtain call, shouting, "She's yours, too!" In spite of the vital tradition behind her, Adler felt, like Clurman, that something was missing. She distrusted the elusive "inspiration" that was relied upon by her father and the other stars of the Yiddish stage and looked to the Lab for a dependable and practical technique.

Clurman's thinking was further affected by his encounter in the spring of 1927 with Jacques Copeau, who was brought in by the Guild to direct his adaptation of *The Brothers Karamozov.* Clurman assisted Copeau as translator and attended a series of lectures that the director gave at the Lab. In 1924, he had abandoned city life and his work at Paris's Théâtre du Vieux Colombier and had taken a company of actors to the countryside of Burgundy, where they lived an intensely shared artistic and personal life. This idea of communal living and artistic preparation in a serene retreat affected Clurman profoundly. If theatre was to be, in effect, a new and salvific religion – sustained by its own varieties of communion and witness – should it not be practiced in a setting that nourished this secular holiness, a kind of monastery with a stage at its center instead of a tabernacle?

Clurman also had before him the experiences of various American groups that had tried, in varying degrees, to combine artistic creation, social responsiveness, and communal living. The Provincetown Players had begun in such a setting, as an assortment of Greenwich Village intellectuals who isolated themselves in a fishing village for the summer of 1915. Eva Le Gallienne's Civic Repertory Theatre (1926–35) was managed cooperatively by an all-female staff, maintaining a repertory of modern classics at low prices in their Fourteenth Street Theatre. Clurman was also familiar with political theatre groups of the 1920s who pursued communitarian ideals. ARTEF (Yiddish acronym for Workers' Theatre Alliance) was founded in 1925 when a group of Leftist actors broke off from Maurice Schwartz's Yiddish Art Theatre. ARTEF (1925–39) followed elaborately egalitarian governance procedures (with an executive body of fifty representatives from multiple labor constituencies) and emphasized daily classes in acting and political theory.[5] The New Playwrights Theatre (1927–29) provided a model of a group-oriented theatre operating in a Broadway environment, as the collective management of six playwrights – Michael Gold, John Howard Lawson, Em Jo Basshe, Francis Faragoh, John Dos Passos, and Paul Sifton – staged ten Left-oriented plays under the sponsorship of Otto Kahn. Clurman was briefly employed as an actor by the New Playwrights for their production of Lawson's *Loudspeaker* in 1927.

Similar practices would be followed by other agit-prop groups in the 1930s, and their efforts would provide an abiding influence on Clurman's theatre, as members of the Group collaborated with less ambiguously Leftist organizations such as Prolet-Buehne (1930–34), the Workers Laboratory Theatre (1930–34), and the WLT's professionalized offshoots known as Theatre of Action (1934–36) and Theatre Collective (1932–36) (see Himelstein, 19–23). Also of continuing influence would be the Theatre Union, an explicitly Left theatre founded by Charles R. Walker, Michael Blankfort, Albert Maltz, Paul Peters, Victor Wolfson, and George Sklar in 1933. The Theatre Union made a name for itself with affecting Left-wing melodramas such as Maltz's *Black Pit* in 1933 and Sklar and Peters's *Stevedore* in 1934. The Federal Theatre Project (1935–39) brought together politically oriented groups, most notably the offshoot Mercury Theatre, operated by Orson Welles and John Houseman between 1937 and 1939.

Clurman and Strasberg got their first opportunity to try out their joined ideas in 1928, when Clurman persuaded businessman Sidney Ross to consider funding a new theatre. Ross agreed to Clurman and Strasberg's proposal that they assemble a group of actors and rehearse a play, eventually showing it to Ross for his consideration of the company as a commercial venture. The first three months of 1928 saw Clurman and Strasberg evaluating young actors whom they knew from the Guild, the Lab, and elsewhere as potential recruits for their group, which was to work on a new play called *New Year's Eve,* by Clurman's idol, Waldo Frank. Sanford Meisner was a twenty-two-year-old actor recruited from the Lab, where Strasberg had advised him to go for training when he expressed disappointment in the old-fashioned and unsystematic education he was receiving at the Guild School of Theatre. Franchot Tone was invited after Clurman saw him in John Howard Lawson's *The International* at the New Playwrights Theatre in January. Morris Carnovsky was recruited from the Guild. At twenty-nine, Carnovsky was the oldest of the actors that Clurman addressed in the rooftop garden above Riverside Drive in the spring of 1928. Clurman emphasized that they could expect no pay from the project but that – unlike most acting work – they would receive training during the rehearsal process and that the project might result in the formation of a new theatre. "We expected," Clurman recalled, "to link the actor as an individual with the creative purpose of the playwright" (Clurman, *The Fervent Years,* 23).

The group rehearsed Frank's play for four hours a day for seventeen weeks. When they presented it for Frank and Ross, both responded enthusiastically, but Ross decided that Clurman's idea of sustaining the company in the country for three months was too expensive and unlikely to succeed. He supported the group's efforts to rehearse a second play – Padraic Colum's *Balloon* – but this, too, produced no concrete financial offer. Clurman took a job as a staff playreader for the Guild in January 1929 and turned to other ways of making his and his fledgling group's dream into a reality.

Theresa Helburn provided the vehicle that would ultimately propel the Group Theatre when she called Clurman, Crawford, and stage manager Herbert Biberman into her office later that year. She told the three that the Guild's Board of Managers, in a move that mimicked the Moscow Art Theatre, had decided to launch a studio that would present experimental plays in extra performances on Sunday afternoons. She asked these three to head the project and gave them the play *Red Rust* by V. Kirchon and A. Ouspensky. It would be the first Soviet play presented by a mainstream theatre in the United States. The production was directed by Biberman. Clurman and Crawford recruited Franchot Tone and Luther Adler, along with Ruth Nelson and Eunice Stoddard (both students at the Lab) and William Challee (a Provincetown alumnus). The production was considered an artistic success, and the studio members were planning future productions when the Board informed them that the studio was being shut down. The production had lost the Guild $13,000 and had attracted a Left audience that the Guild found discomfiting.

A concurrence of events in late 1929 and early 1930 left Clurman and his collaborators determined to set out on their own. The stock-market crash confirmed in Clurman's mind that something was profoundly wrong in America and that the theatre was the way to repair the spiritual wound. The Guild's autocratic dismantling of the studio seemed a reaffirmation of the Board's reluctance to stray beyond the Middle European comedy, British fantasy, and ponderous American tragedy that had established the Guild a decade earlier. In March 1930, Clurman, Crawford, and Strasberg began holding a new series of meetings with potential recruits for a new theatre, an as yet invisible entity that they referred to simply as "The Group." They added to the personnel from the Ross project and the production of *Red Rust* such actors as Margaret Barker, Bobby Lewis, Dorothy Patten, Edward Bromberg, and Clifford Odets, accumulating a total of twenty-seven actors whom the Group's "directors" (as Clurman, Crawford, and Strasberg now called themselves) agreed would form a workable company.

Hearing about this "revolt from within" through newspaper reports, the Guild's Board of Managers summoned Clurman to appear before them. When Theresa Helburn recounted the meeting some thirty years later, a degree of bitterness was undiminished by time:

> It was true, he said, that they were working out some ideas of their own; something rather more far-reaching and profound than the Theatre Guild

had attempted. A technique of the theater, he explained loftily, had to be founded on life values. However, when they had selected their actors and completed their plans, they would be glad to tell the Guild Board of Managers what we could do for them. (Helburn, 219)

The Board was particularly alarmed by Clurman's talk of "collaborating" with playwrights. Despite the Board's own notorious "Managers Rehearsals" (known by the company as "the Death Watch"), at which the Board subjected playwrights to harsh questioning and demanded specific rewrites, and despite the pride taken by Helburn and Langner in "helping playwrights to rewrite their plays," the Board was appalled by Clurman's idea of a theatre shaping a playwright's voice to make it the voice of the theatre rather than of an individual artist (see Helburn, 239, 248–50; Langner 113, 166–67). "We want to establish a theatre," Clurman told the Board, "Not merely a production organization." When Lee Simonson asked him what he meant by that, Clurman responded: "A theatre is a homogeneous body of craftsmen to give voice to a certain point of view which they share with the dramatist, whose works might be described as the most clearly articulated and eloquent expression of the theatre's conscience." "Would you have anything to tell Eugene O'Neill?," Langner asked. "Certainly," answered Clurman (quoted in Helburn, 221–22). Clurman took advantage of the Board's stunned silence to ask them to fund the Group's first production "to prove that the theatre has a future, that something permanently valuable may still be accomplished" (quoted in W. Smith, *Real Life Drama*, 32).

In spite of their reservations, and showing steadiness in the face of Clurman's somewhat tactless approach, the Board voted to give the Group the rights to Paul Green's southern tragedy, *The House of Connelly* (on which the Guild held an option), and to contribute $1,000 toward the Group's preparation of it over the summer. They also voted to retain Crawford and Clurman as salaried employees as they organized the group and even released to them the services of Tone and Carnovsky, who were under exclusive contract with the Guild. Finally, the Board agreed to assess the Group's progress on *The House of Connelly* in the late summer and to consider financing its New York production. Crawford and Clurman managed to raise an additional $4,000 from playwrights Edna Ferber and Maxwell Anderson and on 8 June 1931, the three directors, twenty-seven Group members, and assorted non-Group actors, spouses, and children set off in the rain for Brookfield Center, Connecticut, where Crawford had rented a rustic resort for the summer. For many, it was the beginning of the most important work of their lives, work for which they would decline lucrative offers from Hollywood and for which they would suffer considerable mental torment, both from Strasberg's "emotional exercises" and from the rigors of protracted communal living. The months of isolation with his co-workers were, for Bobby Lewis, an experience that "except for two or three complete nervous breakdowns" did not touch him at all (R. Lewis, *Slings and Arrows,* 38).

The summer at Brookfield Center was both a paradise and an initiatory trial. Though many other actors would eventually work with the Group, including such luminaries as Frances Farmer, Leif Erikson, and Lee J. Cobb, only two actors who were not present that first summer – Elia Kazan and Roman Bohnen – were ever made Group members. "The feeling that's most completely satisfying," wrote Phoebe Brand in the Group's collective diary, "is the fact that I don't know where the work finishes, and life begins. . . . I believe – as I have wanted to believe for almost ten years – in some idea, person, thing outside myself" (quoted in W. Smith, *Real Life Drama,* 34). One person in whom most people came to believe that summer was Lee Strasberg. Anointed to direct *The House of Connelly,* he laid out in his meticulous rehearsal process what came to be seen as the essential foundation for the Group's shared method. In a 1976 interview, Strasberg insisted that Elia Kazan "does not really know the work," since he was not present that first summer at Brookfield Center. "Much of the work that people did later," Strasberg explained, "was based on earlier preparation" (quoted in Chinoy, 546). Hours were spent daily in the barn that the Group had taken over as a rehearsal space. Scenes from Green's play were worked and reworked, with Strasberg assigning the actors "exercises" intended to build an emotional underpinning for each moment. Afternoons were reserved for Clurman's talks on matters of aesthetic theory and the Group's dialogue with American culture.

By 25 August 1931, the Group had returned to New York, where they presented a run-through of *The House of Connelly* for the Guild's Board of Managers. The Board expressed mild admiration for the performances that Strasberg had drawn from most of the actors but were horrified to learn that the Group had persuaded Paul Green to change the play's ending. The play that the Board had read ended with the energetic young northern woman – who represented the hope of restoring life to the withered southern plantation – being smothered to death by the two black female servants. The Group had persuaded Green, who visited them at Brookfield Center, to revise the ending to a more "hopeful and positive" one. In the version that the Group performed, the young woman survived and showed some small progress in winning over her husband to a more constructive outlook. The Guild saw this change as a dilution of what had been the play's tragic power. Clurman muttered privately about what he saw as the Guild's simplistic idea that a depressing ending was the true measure of artistic worth. Theresa Helburn, in her memoirs, accused the Group of changing the author's intentions "to suit their needs." Such a procedure was artistically doomed, she insisted, because "with the best intentions in the world, they find themselves not serving a play or serving art; they are dishing out propaganda" (224). Unwilling to restore the tragic ending, the Group accepted the Guild's reduced offer of $5,000 and raised an additional $5,000 from Eugene O'Neill, Samuel French, Inc. (Green's publisher), and Franchot Tone, who controlled a portion of his wealthy family's money.

When the joint Guild–Group production opened on 29 September 1931, the adulation was immediate. The company was called back for twenty-two curtain calls, and Green received a stupendous ovation when Crawford persuaded him to mount the stage. Critics saw something distinctly new in the Group's ensemble performance. The *New York Times*'s Brooks Atkinson (30 September) compared the actors to "a band of musicians," and Gilbert Gabriel in the *New York American* (30 September) wrote that he had not seen "a more completely consecrated piece of work" since the last tour of the Moscow Art Theatre. Elated with this proof that the Group was viable as a continuing company, Clurman tried to embrace Strasberg, "but a certain rigidity in his posture made it difficult" (Clurman, *The Fervent Years,* 60).

Soon launched as an independent theatre, the Group began what would be its perpetual quest: for plays that were new, American, and that upheld a positive point of view about the nation's future. During the nine years that the Group was to endure, this quest would lead it to a few dramatic heights and to multiple artistic and financial failures. (For a complete listing of plays, casts, and artistic staffs for Group Theatre productions, see W. Smith, 430–33.) The Group's early hopes for a playwright who would meld with the Group and become its true voice settled on John Howard Lawson, whose "Expressionist vaudeville" *Processional* caused a sensation at the Guild in 1925 and whose other Left-oriented work had been shown at the short-lived New Playwrights Theatre (1927–29), of which Lawson had been a founding member. Lawson demonstrated unusual skill in the kind of socially conscious realism in which the Group excelled, and their much-praised production of Lawson's *Success Story* in 1932 fed their hopes for an artistic marriage. But Lawson was undergoing a highly public crisis in the early 1930s over whether or not he should join the Communist Party and write the clear, doctrinaire Socialist Realism that the party was beginning to require of its adherents. After the Group's failure in Lawson's promising but deeply flawed *Gentlewoman* in 1934, Lawson became a committed communist, and his manifesto-thumping work (such as *Marching Song* in 1937) found a more congenial home at the unblushingly Leftist Theatre Union.

Other playwrights groomed by the Group as potential voices were the young Irwin Shaw, who was eventually recruited by the Group and authored two of their late productions – *The Gentle People* in 1939 and *Retreat to Pleasure* in 1940 – as well as Robert Ardrey, whose *Casey Jones* (1938) and *Thunder Rock* (1939) failed to connect with audiences, despite Elia Kazan's skilled direction.

Maxwell Anderson, already an established Broadway author when the Group was formed, was eager to work with the company, but his *Night over Taos* (1932) was a financial disaster and may have blurred Clurman's vision regarding the merits of *Winterset,* which the Group rejected in 1935. They regretted the decision when the play made a fortune for Guthrie McClintic, its ultimate producer, at a time when the Group was desperate for operating capital. This situation arose with unpleasant frequency, the Group never succeeding in putting aside a sizable sum to support the company when ticket sales failed to materialize.

Clifford Odets

The playwright who would come closest to fulfilling the Group's idea of an artistic voice for and of the theatre was to emerge, as if willed by Clurman's rhetoric, from the Group itself. Clifford Odets had been seen by most Group members as a lovable but not notably talented actor who existed on the margins of the organization, a position from which he idolized Clurman, pursued Group women wholeheartedly and serially, and wished that he could somehow be Beethoven (see W. Smith, 47). Group members knew that Odets, stimulated by the constant presence of a skilled company of actors, had been writing scenes and monologues, which he occasionally asked them to read. The writing was not taken seriously by Group members, with the important exception of Clurman, who responded to Odets's work critically and encouraged him to write about what he knew – middle-class Jewish life in Philadelphia and New York.

Odets's work was eventually forced onto the Group's directorate as the result of a rebellion by the actors in 1935. For reasons that he never fully articulated, Strasberg disliked Odets's *Awake and Sing!* (originally titled *I Got the Blues*) from first contact. When the Group performed the second act of the play during their 1933 summer retreat near Warrensburg, New York, the company responded enthusiastically to these roles written especially for them, but the directors remained cool. Strasberg was the most dismissive, deflecting objections to his opinion with a characteristic shrug. Clurman considered the play flawed yet highly promising, but – intimidated by Strasberg's explosive temper – he declined to argue for the play. Crawford remained neutral, as was her habit when "the boys" (as she called them) were at serious odds. Hurt by this rejection by the "parents" among the people he had come to see as his family, Odets sold an option on the play to another producer and set about enjoying his earnings of $500.

In the autumn of 1934, representatives of the New Theatre League – a loose confederation of Left-wing theatre groups (which functioned between 1932

Clifford Odets's *Waiting for Lefty* (1935) with Elia Kazan at center. Vandamm photo. Museum of the City of New York. The Theater Collection.

and 1942) – paid a visit to a meeting of the Group's communist cell and asked them to contribute a short play to complete one of their "revolutionary" Sunday bills. The communist group within the Group was headed at the time by Joe Bromberg and included seven other actors, among whom were Kazan and Odets. Five Group members agreed to collaborate on a strike play, each actor writing one scene. As the date for the January performance neared, the Group risked embarrassment, since none of the actors had found time to write their scenes. To help the Group in saving face, Odets sequestered himself for three nights and wrote *Waiting for Lefty.* When the actors showed the play to Strasberg at a rehearsal, he shrugged (see Kazan, 112).

Waiting for Lefty was first performed on 6 January 1935, on the Sunday evening New Theatre League bill at Eva Le Gallienne's Civic Repertory Theatre on Fourteenth Street, rented for these occasions by the League. The evening became legendary and formed a defining moment for most members of the Group. The loosely structured play moves freely through time and space as members of a taxi drivers' union step forward to explain how they came to be radicalized. The response from the audience of Left-wing activists and questing theatre lovers, who had come prepared to applaud the usual array of doctrinaire political art, was immediate and overwhelming. Clurman describes a "shock of delighted recognition" that overtook the audience during the play's second minute. A "kind of joyous fervor seemed to sweep the audience toward the stage," carrying the actors along in an "exultancy of communication" such as he had never before witnessed. At the play's conclusion, when Elia Kazan rushed onto the stage and announced that Lefty (the insurgent union leader) had been found dead behind the car barns "with a bullet in his head," Joe Bromberg asked the assembled for the solution to their crisis, and the audience answered in a tumultuous roar, "Strike!" Clurman called this delirious moment, "the birthcry of the Thirties," and the voice of his generation's youth (Clurman, *The Fervent Years,* 148). "That was the dream all of us in the Group had," Kazan wrote, "to be embraced that way by a theatreful of people" (Kazan, 114).

Despite the success of *Waiting for Lefty* in successive Sunday performances, Strasberg remained set against Odets's work and resisted Clurman's timid though recurrent suggestions that the Group stage *I Got the Blues* – now retitled *Awake and Sing!* The issue of Odets's position within the Group was finally brought to a head just two weeks after the *Lefty* opening, when the directors called a meeting to inform the company that Melvin Levy's *Gold Eagle Guy* had to close – most of the company were already on half salaries – and that the directors had found no play with which to continue the season. They saw no recourse but to end the season at once, release the actors to find whatever outside work they could, and continue to look for a play to work on over the summer. The actors, under the leadership of an outraged Stella Adler, rebelled and demanded that *Awake and Sing!* be put into rehearsal. When Clurman and Crawford sided with the actors, Strasberg became furious and wished Clurman the best of luck in what would be his first directing assignment. This production, which established Odets as the hottest American playwright of the 1930s, the Group as a mature and expert ensemble, and Clurman as a viable director, alienated Strasberg from the Group to such an extent that it was the first step toward his eventual resignation from the Group in 1937.

The adulatory critical reception of Odets in 1935 brought him the kind of personal celebrity that he had never before experienced and that, as a Marxist, he was supposed to disdain. The press excitement over *Awake and Sing!* (which opened 19 February) was exceeded only by the Broadway staging of *Waiting for Lefty,* which was paired with *Till the Day I Die* (a short play that Odets wrote for the occasion) and opened on 26 March. Odets, who was being paid $35 per week as a minor actor in the Group, received offers as high as $2,500 per week to write screenplays in California. The Group also earned the admiration of the radical Left, who had earlier criticized its social ambiguity by calling it "the Grope Theatre" (W. Smith, 211). Across the nation, new theatre groups were formed for the sole purpose of staging *Waiting for Lefty*.

The fall of 1935 saw the Group at its peak. They had two Broadway productions running simultaneously, their homegrown playwright was the toast of New York, and the company was widely hailed for the depth and adaptability of its acting technique. But the seeds of discord and dissolution had already been sown. When the Group's production of Odets's *Paradise Lost* (opened December 1935) failed to attract audiences, Group members began to accept Hollywood offers. Franchot Tone had been the first to defect (in 1932), and the Group's new notoriety made such offers available to less prominent Group members. Joe Bromberg left for Hollywood in December 1935 and was quickly followed by Odets, who accepted a lucrative studio offer early in 1936. By January 1937, the Group had suffered multiple failures and defections. Clurman published an article in *The New York Times* (17 January) announcing that the Group was suspending operations. He and Kazan proceeded to Hollywood, where Cheryl Crawford was negotiating a film deal that could keep the Group actors intact in California and eventually fund stage productions in New York. A deal was signed in February, with Walter Wanger agreeing to pay Group members $750 a week. Despite this seeming abundance, the Group never fully recovered from the fragmentation and sense of defeat that overtook them that winter. The agreement with Wanger never resulted in a substantial film, and Group members were dismayed by the superficiality and dishonesty that they perceived in life in the film colony. Though "the Group" would resurrect itself under the leadership of Clurman and Kazan for the production of Odets's *Golden Boy* in November 1937, the productions from that point until the Group's final dissolution in 1940 included numerous non-Group actors. As far as many of the original members were concerned, the Group ended with the trip to Hollywood in 1937. The Group Idea – of a continuous and permanent working ensemble – ceased to exist thereafter, and the so-called Group became simply another producing organization, in existence for one production at a time.

The collapse of the Group left, in Kazan's words, a "void in [their] lives" so severe that "everything else seemed inferior, diffuse, without purpose." The Group had been "brought to life by a cause" and when the cause disappeared, their lives "seemed empty, and futile and rather meaningless" (quoted in Chinoy, 536). The longing to fill this void ultimately led to various attempts by Group alumni to recapture a part of the Group mystique for succeeding generations. Cheryl Crawford, Elia Kazan, Bobby Lewis, Harold Clurman, and Lee Strasberg would participate at various stages of the founding and operation of the Actors Studio, which opened in 1947. Sanford Meisner, who had begun teaching at the Neighborhood Playhouse School of Theatre in 1936, continued his work there in a legendary training program that he operated with few interruptions for nearly sixty years. Stella Adler went on to found acting studios on both coasts, and her teaching would exert enormous influence through her work with film stars such as Marlon Brando and Al Pacino. Bobby Lewis and Morris Carnovsky would also operate respected acting studios, Lewis serving as head of the acting program at Yale School of Drama from 1967 to 1976. Significantly, none of these actors attempted to found a continuous producing organization, apparently chastened by the financial realities that struck down the Group. Except for a brief and unsuccessful foray into production by the Actors Studio in the 1960s, the Group alumni focused on teaching technique, working scenes, directing occasional commercial productions, and producing in a traditional one-shot Broadway format (especially in the case of Crawford, whose producing career flourished in the 1950s and 1960s). As mature adults, most who had been in the Group seemed to desire to recapture the artistic commitment of the 1930s but had no wish to relive the strain and occasional misery of communitarian living.

Sanford Meisner seemed to speak for many former members of groups when he was interviewed in 1974, retaining a mixture of nostalgia for the intense group experience of his youth, along with a certain bitterness, as if the social intensity had been too filled with suffering to be borne. The continuous and high-stakes social interaction and artistic interdependency of group creativity seemed to intensify the already intensely social activity of theatre. The crucible of group life and work led members to occasional artistic and personal triumphs, but also toward a level of pain severe and wounding enough that its memory could cause shudders and tears. Meisner could not help urging his students at the Neighborhood Playhouse to get out of theatre altogether, if they were able. He found that most refused. Longing for the fulfillment of intense artistic and social activity, they accepted the pain of collective endeavor as a part of the work. Meisner, too, accepted that the lessons of youth had to be learned by the young and that pain was as much an inevitability in the creation of art as it was in life. Asking a committed young person to give up the intense social project of theatre was, he said, "like trying to get someone to give up living" (quoted in Chinoy, 505).

Notes

1 Joseph Wood Krutch, Introduction to *The Neighborhood Playhouse: Leaves from a Theatrical Scrapbook,* by Alice Lewisohn Crowley, ix.

2 See Susan Strasser, *Never Done: A History of American Housework* (1982) and James J. Flink, *The Automobile Age* (1988).

3 See Arthur McDonald, "The Neighborhood Playhouse," in *American Theatre Companies, 1888–1930,* edited by Weldon Durham.
4 See W. Smith, 19; and interview with Lee Strasberg in *Educational Theatre Journal* (*Reunion: A Self-Portrait of the Group Theatre*), edited by Helen K. Chinoy, 546–47.
5 For information on Jacob Adler and the Yiddish stage, see David F. Lifson, *The Yiddish Theatre in America,* and Lulla Rosenfeld, *Bright Star of Exile: Jacob Adler and the Yiddish Theatre.* Clurman authored the introduction to the latter book.
6 See Medovoy, 32–36.

Bibliography: Theatre Groups and Their Playwrights

Any consideration of artistic experiment in the first half of the century should include Alice Lewisohn Crowley's *The Neighborhood Playhouse: Leaves from a Theatrical Scrapbook,* an orderly remembrance of that organization by one of its founders. The formation and operation of the Provincetown Players are chronicled in *The Provincetown: A Story of the Theatre* by Deutsch and Hanau; *Jig Cook and the Provincetown Players* by Sarlos; and *Provincetown as a Stage: Provincetown, The Provincetown Players, and the Discovery of Eugene O'Neill* by Leona Rust Egan. Early plays performed by the Provincetowners are collected in *The Provincetown Plays,* edited by George Cram Cook and Frank Shay. The Provincetown Players in the context of the others arts and the times is dealt with effectively in *1915, The Cultural Moment,* edited by Heller and Rudnick.

For the Washington Square Players and Theatre Guild, major sources are Langner's *The Magic Curtain;* Helburn's *A Wayward Quest;* Eaton's *The Theatre Guild: The First Ten Years;* and Waldau's *Vintage Years of the Theatre Guild: 1928–1939.* Rare copies of early Washington Square Players texts can be found in two volumes of *Washington Square Plays* (1916 and 1918).

The difficulty of a playwright's life in contact with the Guild and the frustrations that led to the founding of the offshoot Playwrights Company are chronicled in Elmer Rice's *Minority Report: An Autobiography;* John Mason Brown's *The Worlds of Robert E. Sherwood, Mirror to His Times;* Gross's *S. N. Behrman: A Research and Production Sourcebook;* Shivers's *The Life of Maxwell Anderson;* and John F. Wharton's *Life Among the Playwrights.* The Guild's relations with Eugene O'Neill are detailed in Bogard and Bryer's *Selected Letters of Eugene O'Neill,* as well as in Sheaffer's *O'Neill: Son and Artist* and the Gelbs' *O'Neill.* The context and textures of the Guild's productions of O'Neill's work are found in Wainscott's *Staging O'Neill: The Experimental Years, 1920–1934.* Research on a Harlem Renaissance theatre of the 1920s is available in Ethel Pitts Walker's "Krigwa: A Theatre By, For, and About Black People." Paul Reuben Cooper's 1967 dissertation, "Eva Le Gallienne's Civic Repertory Theatre," is a comprehensive study of that venture and is complemented by Schanke's *Eva Le Gallienne: A Bio-bibliography* and his *Shattered Applause: The Lives of Eva Le Gallienne,* in addition to the biography by Helen Sheehy. Ronald Willis's dissertation, "The American Laboratory Theatre, 1923–1930" (University of Iowa, 1968), is a comprehensive source on the Lab.

An essential book on American theatre groups that operated during the 1930s is Goldstein's *The Political Stage: American Drama and Theater of the Great Depression.* He places the activities of that era in a detailed social and aesthetic context, showing the relations between the formation of such groups as diverse as the Theatre Guild and the Workers Laboratory Theatre. Goldstein deals concisely but comprehensively with the New Playwrights Theatre, the Prolet-Buehne and other proletarian organizations, the Group Theatre, the Theatre Union, and the Mercury Theatre, as well as commercial Broadway productions with political content. Other studies of Left-wing theatre groups of the 1930s are Himelstein's *Drama Was a Weapon: The Left-Wing Theatre in New York, 1929–1941* and Jay Williams's *Stage Left*. Books that focus more on Left-wing drama than on performance are Rabkin's *Drama and Commitment: Politics in the American Theatre of the Thirties* and Reynolds's *Stage Left: The Development of the American Social Drama of the Thirties*. For the Theatre Union, Weisstuch's 1982 dissertation is recommended. The most detailed working out of Left-wing dramatic theory by an American is found in John Howard Lawson's *Theory and Technique of Playwriting*, which he wrote in making the transition from Realism to Socialist Realism; Part II, Chapter I, titled, "Conscious Will and Social Necessity," is especially interesting in showing Lawson's attempts to derive a theory of drama from Hegel. Of related interest is *The Left Side of Paradise: The Screenwriting of John Howard Lawson* by Gary Carr, which deals as much with Lawson's playwriting as with his film work. A vivid critical picture of drama and theatre in the 1930s is found in George Jean Nathan's *The Theatre of the Moment* (1936) and of the 1920s and 1930s in Krutch's *The American Drama Since 1918* (1939). The short, tumultuous life of the Mercury Theatre is told vividly in John Houseman's *Run-through: A Memoir*. Information on Langston Hughes's repeated attempts to found the Left-oriented Harlem Suitcase Theatre and his association with the Hedgerow Theatre group are documented in Rampersad's *The Life of Langston Hughes, Volume I: 1902–1941*.

Members of the Group Theatre have been especially prolific. Clurman's *The Fervent Years: The Group Theatre and the Thirties* was the first book to be written on the Group and has become a classic in American theatre studies, remaining continuously in print. Additional recollections from a life in the theatre are available in Clurman's *All People Are Famous (Instead of an Autobiography)*. Clurman's telling of the Group's genesis and its relations with the Theatre Guild are supplemented by Crawford's *One Naked Individual*, Robert Lewis's *Slings and Arrows*, and Elia Kazan's *A Life*. The influence of the Yiddish stage on the Group through Stella and Luther Adler can be discerned from *Bright Star of Exile: Jacob Adler and the Yiddish Theatre* by Lulla Rosenfeld. The Group Theatre members recall their lives and work together in the invaluable interviews conducted by Helen Krich Chinoy and collected in *Reunion: A Self-Portrait of the Group Theatre*, a special issue of *Educational Theatre Journal*, December 1976. The Group's relations with Clifford Odets are considered in Weales's *Odets, the Playwright* and Margaret Brenman-Gibson's detailed psychological study, *Clifford Odets: American Playwright, the Years 1906 to 1940*; and from Odets's own point of view at a crucial moment in *The Time Is Ripe: The 1940 Journal of Clifford Odets*. The Group's effect on other playwrights can be gleaned from Shnayerson's *Irwin Shaw: A Biography* and Lee and Gifford's *Saroyan: A Biography*, whereas the Group's influence on the succeeding generation of playwrights is described in Arthur Miller's *Timebends* and in Leverich's *Tom: The Unknown Tennessee Williams*.

Wendy Smith's excellent and comprehensive study, *Real Life Drama: The Group Theatre and America, 1931–1940*, brings fresh interview material to the Group's story as well as the fresh eye of an outsider. A projected study by Chinoy is still promised. Copeau's influence on the Group idea is studied in "The Emerging Ensemble: The Vieux Colombier and the Group Theatre" by Richard Alan Whitmore. Assessments of Strasberg's role in the Group and his transition to the Actors Studio are available in Cindy Adams's *Lee Strasberg: The Imperfect Genius of the Actors Studio*, Garfield's *A*

Player's Place: The Story of the Actors Studio, and Hirsch's *A Method to Their Madness: The History of the Actors Studio.* (The Actors Studio is discussed by Foster Hirsch in some detail in Vol. III of this series.)

An invaluable resource book on radical theatre of the 1930s and beyond is *People's Theatre in Amerika: Documents by the People Who Do It,* edited by Karen Malpede Taylor, with a preface by John Howard Lawson. Taylor's collection includes rare documents that bring to life theoretical and production ideas from the hard-Left theatres of the 1930s, such as John Dos Passos's essay, "Did the New Playwrights Theatre Fail?"; founding documents of the Theatre Union; Mordecai Gorelik's essay explaining Brechtian theory to Americans; an essay (commissioned by the Group Theatre) by Soviet director V. Zakhava presenting a Marxist critique of the Stanislavsky system; and Theodorc Ward's 1940 manifesto for the short-lived Negro Playwrights Theatre. The book also includes agit-prop performance texts used by the Workers Laboratory Theatre, Prolet-Buehne, ARTEF, and others.

A second source of hard-to-find documents from the Left theatre of the 1930s is *New Theatre and Film, 1934 to 1937: An Anthology* edited by Herbert Kline. This sampling from the leading Left-wing theatre periodical of the era includes crucial essays by Clifford Odets, Albert Maltz, and Langston Hughes, as well as a Left perspective on mainstream playwrights such as O'Neill and Sherwood.

Among the many valuable reference books on groups in the period, most essential is *American Theatre Companies, 1888–1930,* edited by Weldon Durham. This volume includes entries on 105 theatre companies from the period, giving capsule histories as well as listings of personnel and repertory. Especially rare is the information on theatre companies outside of New York. Another reference work that proves immensely useful in research and writing is the series *The Encyclopedia of the New York Stage* edited by Samuel L. Leiter. Two volumes are available, listing virtually every New York production and providing plot summaries, critical reactions, artistic and production listings for productions from 1920 to 1930 (Vol. I) and from 1930 to 1940 (Vol. II). The plays are exhaustively indexed in each volume, not only by personnel but also by theme. Other valuable reference works are Shafer's *American Women Playwrights, 1900–1950,* which brings forward information on group-oriented playwrights such as Alice Gerstenberg and Zoë Akins; and the *Cambridge Guide to American Theatre,* edited by Wilmeth and Miller for its reliable information on a wide range of companies, plays, and individuals.

5

Popular Entertainment

Brooks McNamara

Orientation

The years between the conclusion of the Civil War and the end of the twenties represented a golden age of popular entertainment in America. In particular, the increased leisure time, improved transportation, and rapidly developing cities of the period helped spur the growth of a kind of performance that largely faded away later in the twentieth century, for the most part replaced by mass media. Live popular entertainment – amusements aimed at a broad, relatively unsophisticated audience – came to include a dizzying array of types, from the circus to vaudeville, the diorama to the amusement park. Most were European and already centuries old, but they were given a characteristic twist by American showmen.

Popular entertainment is difficult to separate neatly into categories or, in many cases, even into discrete periods or clearly separate types. Part of the reason for confusion is that there were so many relatively anonymous entertainers, who borrowed acts or parts of them without attribution. An example of this – often lateral – movement may be found in the words of a twentieth-century performer, Mae Noell, who came from a popular entertainment family. Her parents, she has written, performed in at least a dozen different kinds of entertainment during their long careers in show business, specializing in towns "too small for real theatre, nickelodeons or Chatauqua."[1]

It was common on the margins of the entertainment world to move between forms many times in one's career. An example of this type of performer was Harry Helms, a turn-of-the-century popular entertainer, whose specialties included magic, juggling, and playing various instruments. He worked, we know, in medicine shows, touring variety, circuses, and minstrel shows. In later life he wrote and sold comedy routines, magic tricks, and "how to" books, as well as pamphlets on show business, and sold such items as a "complete system" of hypnotism, a product somewhat ambiguously labeled "Sweet Sixteen Love Perfume, Greatly admired by the ladies," which men could carry in "pocket, chest, or trunk," and "The Greatest Tape Worm Secret in the World. Guaranteed to remove worm with head and all," advertising in such trade publications as *The Clipper* and *The Billboard* (see McNamara, *Step Right Up*, 162).

The famous and talented Bert Williams, one of America's greatest black stars, typifies another kind of movement common to some of the most talented popular performers – progression up through the various forms of popular entertainment to more elevated areas of the amusement business. Born in 1876 in the Bahamas, Williams got his start in a medicine show, eventually joining Martin and Sieg's Mastodon Minstrels in San Francisco in 1893. There he first worked with another talented black performer, George Walker, and the team of Williams and Walker played in several medicine shows and then appeared at Koster and Bial's Music Hall in New York, performing minstrel-style sketches, with Williams as the comedian and Walker as the straight man. By the end of the nineteenth century, the team had performed at the Empire Theatre in London and had graduated to musical comedies. Walker died in 1911, but Williams went on to become a great success in recordings, motion pictures, and various editions of *The Ziegfeld Follies*.

Of particular interest is a stock of sketches, jokes, recitations, and songs, some of which came from written sources but most of which were handed down singly by other entertainers. They appeared in different versions and represented a kind of common but unsystematic pool of source material. The same material would appear in different kinds of entertainment (say, both in vaudeville and burlesque), and it would appear in different configurations (here as a monologue, somewhere else as a sketch or joke or song). One sketch, for example, would be more or less like another, but subtly different. Thus in their travels Mae Noell's parents alternated between playing a well-known stock sketch called "Down on the Hats," in which the comedian "Jake" fell out of his chair and usually destroyed a hat, and, if cheap straw skimmers were not available or became too expensive to use at the climax of the act, they presented a variation called "Down on the Chairs."

The routing of material was not merely from professional to professional. It was also, as countless "minstrel guides" and joke books testify, from professional to amateur. For example, much of the material presented by professional minstrel companies in the nineteenth century was staged later by amateur minstrels. Conversely, a clear route flowed to professional popular entertainment from what have often loosely been classed as amateur forms – religious and school pageantry, club and lodge entertainments, and the like. And, of course, there was a relationship to other forms of popular art, as well as with much mainstream theatre and culture.

The appearance of pirated versions of such plays as *Ben-Hur, The Trail of the Lonesome Pine,* and *Little Lord Fauntleroy* in so-called tent repertoire companies, for example, demonstrates that cut-down versions of mainstream plays – which often originated as popular novels – moved easily into the arena of amusement. In addition, mainstream art and high-art works of many kinds were made the subject of parodies, as were situations facing the "ordinary Joe," always a staple of popular entertainment. In particular, the works of Shakespeare were relatively well known to many people in the nineteenth and early twentieth centuries and were often satirized and parodied. A vaudeville monologue, for example, begins:

> Last night the boss slips me a ticket
> For one of them opera shows.
> An' the name of the show is called "Hamlet,"
> So I digs up my glad rags and goes.
> Well, it's gloom from the minute it opens
> Till the time the theyayter shuts,
> An' the company's half of them looney
> An' the rest of the cast is plain nuts.[2]

Despite its complexity, live popular entertainment from after the Civil War to around 1930 – or in some cases later – can be divided roughly into four broad categories: variety entertainments, popular theatre, environmental entertainments, and optical and mechanical amusements.

Circus and the Wild West shows, as well as vaudeville, the burlesque show, and the minstrel show, are examples of variety entertainments. Like modern Happenings, they were "compartmented" – that is, made up of independent acts, or compartments, that were assembled into a show. Unlike the acts in a conventional play, the acts that made up these entertainments generally did not depend on a plot and had no thematic relationship to one another.

Although they might be bound together by some simple bracketing device, such as the blackface convention of minstrelsy, the organization of acts on a bill was governed by practical considerations about balancing the elements of a show, traditions about the location of certain kinds of material within the show's framework, and by attempts to create a "rising action" as the evening progressed that would build toward a climactic act at or near the end of the show. Beyond that, bill structure varied as tradition allowed. Although the compartments were usually arranged sequentially, as in vaudeville, some were given what could be called a simultaneous organization, similar to that of the American three-ring circus, in which action might play in several rings at the same time. In another example, the revue was a kind of cross between variety entertainment and the conventionally plotted play.

In a second major category of popular entertainment, "popular theatre," the organizational principle appears to be somewhat similar to that of the mainstream play. This category includes such traditional forms as ten-twenty-thirty melodramas (named for the low prices of admission), the Toby and Suzy show, spectacle drama typified by that produced at New York's huge theatre, the Hippodrome – all prominent early in the twentieth century – and forms "in miniature," such as the vaudeville playlet and the burlesque bit.

Although popular theatre seems to have been based on more or less the same structural model as the conventional play, that is where the resemblance ends. For one thing, works from the popular theatre possessed few of the artistic or intellectual pretensions common to the legitimate play. Instead, the emphasis, as in much modern television drama, appears to have been unabashedly on action, fantasy, and physicality. In fact, the written scripts that still exist seem, for the most part, to be little more than frameworks on which to hang improvisation, comic business, or spectacular events. It was not simply that these were bad plays but that they were usually malleable in ways that self-consciously "literary" scripts were not. The texts were fragmentary at best. Sometimes they were no more than transcriptions of remembered material and hence were downright incoherent. They were, indeed, often simply outlines for sheer action. However, onstage these outlines came to life when fleshed out with traditional gags and business by the performers. Popular plays and sketches, in effect, existed completely only in performance.

Variety entertainment implies organization of acts in a limited time onstage. But that is not true of all popular entertainment; some of it takes place over a longer time and over a considerable space. A carnival midway was – and still is – a very complex environment, and merely to describe each of its components without reference to the rest is not to describe it at all.

Classic entertainment environments of the period were of two basic types: those that redefined an already existing area for a time and those that were more permanent. The traveling carnival midway, for example, became a kind of temporary city with a specialized purpose – entertainment – and a distinctive brand of fantasy architecture, or "scenography." The amusement park – like its latterday descendant, the theme park – was essentially a more permanent version of the carnival, with more substantial and often more elaborate scenography, but with essentially the same objective.

To some extent, both "environmental entertainments" survive to the present day, and in both cases, they are made up of independently housed attractions, including rides, games, and a mixture of stands and booths, the booths sometimes containing simple shows of various kinds. All the booths, the stands, the rides, the games, and so on, operate simultaneously within the environment, and each spectator makes a unique selection from the available entertainments – or what appears to be a unique, uninfluenced selection. In most cases, organization of the environment is more carefully calculated than it appears, and spectators have rather less freedom of choice than they might imagine. Thus, the "shape of the event," in fact, becomes a kind of constant mediation between the patron and the powerful entertainment environment.

An aspect of carnival – and of many other popular entertainments – has always been the concept of "flash." The word has been used by many different kinds of popular show people in a number of different ways, but flash generally refers to an act, merchandise, a structure, or a place that is showy, highly visible, and extraordinary, in short, to something spectators would call "flashy." However, carnival show people do not necessarily see a flash item or act as vulgar or ostentatious but only as attention-getting because it stands out from the ordinary, asserts its authority in some eye-popping way, and is not constrained by conventional, middle-class "good" taste.

Areas associated to a considerable degree with popular entertainment – and also with such attendant pastimes as gambling, drinking, and prostitution – developed in many large cities, in particular, New York City. One such place, of course, was the famous Bowery. Around the turn of the nineteenth century, in fact, it became a kind of Ur-popular-entertainment district. Because of its reputation as a location in which the fleecing of unwary tourists took place, the Bowery inspired a famous turn-of-the-century song. The lyrics are telling:

> Oh, on the night that I struck New York
> I went out for a quiet walk.
> Folks who are on to the city say
> Better by far that I took Broadway
> But I was out to enjoy the sights,
> There was the Bowery ablaze with lights,
> I had one of the devil's own nights
> And I'll never go there anymore.[3]

Indeed, as the nineteenth-century historian James McCabe phrased it, the Bowery was "a paradise of beer saloons, bar-rooms, concert and dance halls." Mixed in, as in many other large cities, were "cheap theatres and low-class shows," often featuring boxing, Western, or, ironically, temperance melodramas (*New York by Gaslight,* 640).

Even Times Square evolved into an entertainment area of a sort. By the 1930s this area, the heart of Broadway theatre, was taking on many of the shoddy but exotic trappings of a cheap entertainment district. The 1939 *WPA Guide to New York,* for example, noted that an

> outer shell of bars and restaurants, electric signs, movie palaces, taxi dance halls, chop suey places and side shows of every description cover the central street. . . . Adjoining elaborate hotel and theater entrances and wide-windowed clothing shops are scores of typical midway enterprises: fruit

juice stands garlanded with artificial palm leaves, theater ticket offices, cheap lunch counters, cut-rate haberdasheries, burlesque houses, and novelty concessions.[4]

Finally, toward the end of the nineteenth century a burgeoning of optical and mechanical entertainments occurred that depended less on live performers than on painted or photographic images. Sometimes the images were projected, on occasion with movement. Broadly speaking, these entertainments included such forms as the peepshow, the magic lantern, the diorama, the panorama, and a host of other "orama" amusements. Clearly early film had strong roots in live popular entertainment. Could not so-called "precinematic" devices also be considered, in a sense, "post-theatrical"?

In effect, optical and mechanical amusements simply represented the application of a developing technology to the structural principles already present in live popular entertainment. Thus, for example, dioramas were often structured basically in the same way as popular theatre pieces, telling a story in a dramatic fashion. Magic lantern exhibitions, on the other hand, were often organized as variety entertainments, made up of a number of separate and unrelated groups of lantern slides. Of course the means of production of these amusements were very different indeed – different enough to set optical and mechanical entertainments off in a category of their own.

During the nineteenth century and the early years of the twentieth century, actors in general – and popular entertainers in particular – had a relatively low status in relation to "respectable" people. For the most part, popular entertainers existed outside the boundaries of polite society. In fact, traveling show people were generally felt to be immoral, quick to cheat, and slow to pay. Indeed, some outdoor amusement people were known to "burn the lot," that is, to indulge in such acts as shortchanging, "gaffed" (that is, rigged) gambling equipment, false advertising, or prostitution, which, once discovered, kept them from returning to an area. But many honest show people were unfairly labeled as little better than vagrants and criminals by locals, what carnival people called "towners." In reponse to the hostility, popular entertainers associated chiefly with their own kind.

The details of the private lives of many show people – particularly those who had achieved no particular distinction – were intentionally kept vague, even mysterious, to those not connected with show business. Indeed, show people often treated those not involved in the amusement world with a certain amount of calculation and not a little suspicion. Richard Harrity, who grew up in vaudeville, recalled that when his family came into a country town, "everything we did from the second we stepped down on the depot platform was carefully planned by Dad for one end: to lure as many cornfed customers as possible into paying increased admission prices to see and hear live actors on a stage" (11). But there always was clear prejudice on the other side, too. When, for instance, his sister Marie was "getting along fine with some other girls in . . . town, a lady would march out on her porch and call to her daughter, 'Come right in this house – and keep away from those show kids'" (58).

What Fred Allen said about his vaudeville days can be taken as typical of most popular entertainers. "A vaudeville actor," he wrote,

> could relax and enjoy himself only in the company of another vaudeville actor. . . . The herd instinct was a dominant impulse in the vaudeville actor's behavior pattern. When the season closed, the smalltimers congregated at vacation resorts to revel in each other's company. The smalltimer lived in another world. He thought and talked only about his act and about show-business. Nothing else interested him. (237)

In fact, show people usually formed strong bonds only with others who lived a similar kind of life. As an aspect of this self-created "sectarianism," a kind of obscure occupational language arose in the various branches of popular entertainment, typified by the prose found in early *Variety*. Workers in burlesque might know words and expressions that were, for example, slightly different from those used by workers in a circus. But a number of words were the same and were understood – or were at least comprehensible – to most show people. The ultimate function of so-called "Z-Latin" or "Z-Language," a derivative of pig latin used by many carnival workers, like that of any private language, was invented to keep outsiders from understanding what was being said.

Many of these rather self-contained and insular show people, as well as the somewhat rarefied live popular entertainments in which they worked, responded to increasingly intense competition from newer kinds of amusement either by emphasizing novelty and spectacle – and thus substantially increasing overhead in the process – or by retreating completely. In a way, perhaps, the decline of many live popular forms in the later twentieth century was summed up by the old medicine showman who protested that he could not tour a company of ten or a dozen people and compete successfully against a traveling film operator who unfairly carried his whole show in a tin can.

The Circus

The circus is likely the best known of the American variety forms. As it developed in the nineteenth century, it solidified certain characteristics that continue today in most of the several dozen remaining American shows. Circus, in fact, developed as a unique sort of variety entertainment, less dependent on language than some others, and for the most part centered on somewhat different performance values – agility, strength, ingenuity, and skillful handling of animals and equipment. Thus, circus has to some extent focused on what might be called "pure performing" rather than on acting in the conventional sense. In addition, unlike some other variety forms, the circus arena is more "place of performance" than theatricalized stage setting, and the relationship of spectators to the event is "looser."

In a sense, the circus was one of the casualties of increased technologization of society. By the Civil War Americans had been attending organized circuses for more than a half century. The period following the war, however, ushered in important changes in the shows. In general, the scope and size of traveling circuses increased. Many shows now moved by rail and, in later years, by truck, instead of in wagons or flatboats. As a result, by the turn of the century, circuses were able to cover far larger distances than the early shows.

In part as a result of their need for a larger work force and more performers, the biggest circuses in the post–Civil War period sometimes began to employ as many as several hundred staff members and performers, and their tents not infrequently housed a thousand people or more. Big-circus entrepreneurs were increasingly obliged to make sure that they always had something to engage and astonish spectators inside their ever-expanding tents.

In part as a result of their ballooning size, American circuses now began to include three rings – and occasionally as many as five or six. A typical big show might feature trained animals, acrobats, trick riders, jugglers, trapeze artists, clowns, and a host of other entertainers. Over the years, circuses not only increased in size but some also added related attractions, including concerts, menageries, sideshows (traveling versions of the ubiquitous dime-museum freak show), and elaborate street parades. The street parades (known as "dragging the town," a crude advertising device) were adopted by many other forms of itinerant popular entertainment, and many minstrel shows, medicine shows, and other live amusements used the device in the nineteenth and early twentieth centuries.

By and large, the relatively small stationary circus of the eighteenth and early nineteenth centuries had disappeared. In particular, the fad for huge multi-ring, traveling circuses under canvas was developed in the 1870s by the showman P. T. Barnum, who had previously made and lost several fortunes as a dime museum proprietor, and a partner, W. C. Coup. His "Barnum & Bailey Great Traveling World's Fair" was founded in 1871. Barnum split with Coup in 1875 and five years later joined forces with James A. Bailey and James L. Hutchinson. The venture reigned supreme among circuses in America until the 1890s, when it was challenged by a new firm, Ringling Brothers. In 1907, the Ringlings bought out the Barnum and Bailey Circus, and by 1918 they were advertising "Ringling Brothers and Barnum & Bailey Combined

Ringling Bros.–Barnum & Bailey Circus under canvas (12,000 capacity) pictured in Brooklyn, New York, in 1935. Courtesy: Circus World Museum, Baraboo, Wisconsin.

Shows." In spite of many attempts by other circus owners to shut them out, the Ringling show became the most famous three-ring circus in America – and probably in the world.

By about 1910, however, circuses generally were declining in size and scale, and there were fewer on the road. For the most part, the change came for a simple economic reason. Costs had skyrocketed, and there were now more readily accessible – and cheaper – competing entertainment forms. As a result circus profits were growing smaller, and, beginning in the early 1900s, circuses were starting to grow less elaborate. In 1905 Barnum & Bailey eliminated free street parades, with their elegant and costly wagons. Shortly menageries began to disappear, and eventually the famous canvas "Big Tops." A few circuses continue today, among them Ringling Brothers and Barnum & Bailey, but by World War I the golden age of the American circus was over for good.

Some of the characteristics of the circus as it arose in America, which to some extent continue to exist, are both unique to the form and illustrative of ideas that underlie all of popular entertainment. Specifically, circus paid little attention to traditional values. A "script" for a circus production is a purely technical document – a scenario or an organizational chart rather than a conscious work of art in its own right. By the same token, language becomes rudimentary, often serving only to provide continuity between acts. Much of the circus, in fact, is pure performance in which no attempt is made to create characters separate and distinct from the performers. When "acting" does appear – as with the clown routines or the themes that have developed in recent years with such shows as the Big Apple Circus in New York City – it tends to center on uncomplicated stock characters in simple, highly pantomimic scenes.

Like acting, design for circus tends to be "theatrical" and direct. The circus arena is constantly transformed by lights, costumes, and scenic pieces, but it always remains a totally practical working space. It contains purely functional equipment such as lights, rigging, cages, and so on, without any real attempt to conceal their function or to "integrate" them into some overall design scheme. Finally, circus creates a distinctive relationship with its audience. Instead of requiring the audience's rapt attention and concentration, it allows the spectator considerable freedom. One may watch some events and not others, talk to friends, or leave the arena at will. It makes little difference whether the spectator is involved in every moment of the circus.

The Wild West Show

The popular Wild West show, incorrectly assumed by some to be an offshoot of the circus, was, in a real sense, the live-action precursor of the Hollywood Western. In 1882, a former buffalo hunter and sometime actor, William F. Cody (known as "Buffalo Bill"), staged an open-air Fourth of July celebration near his home in North Platte, Nebraska. The following year he organized a show based on the North Platte celebration, which he called "Buffalo Bill's Wild West" (Cody abhorred the word "show") and took it on tour across America, playing in such large open-air spaces as baseball stadiums and fair grounds.

At the time, Americans had begun to believe that the frontier was closing and to view the so-called Old West with a certain nostalgia. As a result, Cody's show, a glamorized and highly stereotyped picture of western life, featuring heroic cowboys, "vicious" Indian attacks, and reconstructed stagecoach robberies and buffalo stampedes, delighted audiences throughout the United States and a number of foreign countries. One of Cody's featured acts was Annie Oakley (named "Little Sureshot" by Sitting Bull). Born on a farm in Ohio in 1860, even as a young girl she displayed remarkable ability as a sharpshooter with rifles, shotguns, and pistols. By the age of twelve she was already a well-known hunter, and by her teens she had beaten a professional marksman, Frank Butler, in a shooting match. Later she married Butler, and the two formed a professional shooting team and joined Cody's Wild West. Butler gave up his career to manage Oakley's, and for seventeen years she starred in Cody's show, shooting glass balls from the back of a running horse, drilling holes in the pips of playing cards, and knocking ashes off of cigarettes held in the mouths of fellow performers. Annie Oakley died in 1926.

BUFFALO BILL

Drawing of a young Buffalo Bill Cody. Cover of the Wild West Exhibition program for 1884. Wilmeth Collection.

By the early 1890s "Buffalo Bill's Wild West" had gained tremendous popularity and inspired many imitators, who also developed circuslike outdoor shows. Among the major imitations were Gordon Lillie's "Pawnee Bill Show" and the famous "101 Ranch Wild West Show," which served as backdrop for a number of western films. As the years went on and interest in the American West lessened, some, including Cody himself, introduced nonwestern elements in their shows, attempting to create a kind of novelty that would draw audiences. But the form faded from popularity by about World War I, in part because of rising touring costs and in part because of competition from the new kind of entertainment that was sweeping America, the motion picture, which offered more detailed and spectacular western stories.

Minstrel Show

A quintessentially American form and one of signal importance to the growth of the whole field of American entertainment, minstrel shows performed by white men in blackface did not disappear after the Civil War, but, as with the Wild West show, managers began to alter them to attract broader audiences.

New elements appeared. Shows increased in size and elaborateness, and a number of variations on the traditional minstrel-show format were tried out, such as "Hibernian" minstrels and the so-called female minstrels, who helped to originate burlesque. Yet traditional figures and the old stereotypes – the End Men, the Interlocutor, the ridiculous dances and racist songs – often remained important features of the shows. (See discussion of the early days of minstrelsy in Vol. I of this history.)

After the middle of the nineteenth century a growing number of foreign immigrants had begun to come to the United States, among them Germans and Irish, and, in later years, settlers from Eastern Europe and Italy. Many became laborers or servants, starting their lives in America at the bottom of the socio-economic ladder. Seizing on the presence of these new and somehow frightening immigrants, minstrel shows began to add jokes, skits, and comic songs ridiculing their incomprehensible languages and alien ways. At the time, many people accepted as appropriate and amusing both the old stereotypes about African Americans and the newer comic generalizations about the Irish, the Jews, and the Chinese. For instance, a parody of *Uncle Tom's Cabin* that probably appeared in late minstrelsy begins:

(*Enter Simon Degree.*)
DEGREE: (*Advancing down stage, slap stick in hand.*) B'gorry! 'tis a foine job I do be havin'. I have nothin' to do at all but lick the stuffin' out of Uncle Tom. (*Calls.*) Uncle Tom! Come out here; I want to beat ye up a bit. (*Strikes floor with stick. Enter Uncle Tom.*)
TOM: (*Walks slowly.*) Yes, mas'r, Ise comin', sah; Ise comin'.

(Newton in McNamara, *American Popular Entertainments,* 134)

After the Civil War some African Americans also turned to the minstrel stage. In a sense, it seems ironic that men who may have been former slaves would have chosen to perform songs and sketches that ridiculed their lives and culture and upheld the values of their former masters. But times were hard for black entertainers and, as one old African American performer phrased it, the minstrel stage was the only door open to blacks in the American theatre. Ironically, the black minstrel show was indeed to stand behind a whole series of African American–based popular entertainments and to serve as introduction to the field for many talented black performers who moved into other areas of entertainment.

By the turn of the century minstrelsy had been an American institution for some sixty years. But now several new forms of popular entertainment that were more interesting to American audiences began to appear around the country. All of these competing entertainments borrowed material – much of it frankly racist – from the traditional American minstrel show, although often the newer shows abandoned the old-fashioned blackface convention, leaving it increasingly to the amateurs. It would make frequent appearances in other, later forms, such as motion pictures.

Bean, Hatch, and McNamara summarize the social impact of minstrelsy thus:

> Among the major carriers of stereotyped images were later forms of popular entertainment – both live and recorded – that borrowed elements from the evolving minstrel show, among them vaudeville, burlesque, the revue, and later, film, radio, and television. Popular entertainments have great power. They tell us what is on the minds of ordinary people at any given moment – their concerns, biases and anxieties – and in turn refine them and restate them in a palatable, easily understood way. So it was with minstrelsy. . . . Does it come as any surprise, then, that the stereotypes brought together and codified in blackface minstrelsy before the Civil War have remained with us? If one explores the "performance genealogies" of this powerful entertainment form – if one traces its descendants in other entertainments – the answer should become increasingly apparent. (*Inside the Minstrel Mask*, xiii–xiv)

Concert Saloons, Dime Museums, Early Variety

Acts inherited from both the circus and the minstrel show had appeared for many years in concert saloons, the cheap beer-hall theatres found in many large cities, and in the exhibition rooms and "theatoriums" attached to dime museums. Concert saloons, for the most part, began to develop in the eastern states, particularly in New York, at around the middle of the nineteenth century. New York, in fact, could boast some three hundred after the Civil War, many of them located on the Bowery, in nearby Broadway, and in the so-called "Hell's Kitchen" neighborhood. Gradually, however, these saloon theatres, with acts borrowed at random from minstrel shows and other forms, and with clearly bawdy elements often added for their mostly male patrons, began to become more popular in other urban areas and to move westward with settlers. They became fixtures in a number of western towns and later were often used as models in the design sets of Western movies.

Although popular museums had been run by showmen before the Civil War – notably P. T. Barnum's famous American Museum in New York (see Vol. I, Chap. 6 of this history) – so-called dime museums flourished in the period between the war and the early years of the twentieth century, mostly in larger cities. They usually exhibited human freaks and curiosities, presented such popular melodramas as *Ten Nights in a Bar Room*, along with traditional acrobatic, freak, animal, musical, and comedy routines, and occasionally early films. The later wax museums, amusement arcades – and even the pornographic peepshows that were to appear still later – all had their roots in the dime museum.

Also influential were so-called variety companies and variety entertainers, which were ubiquitous in the years following the Civil War. There were many variations, from the "Musical, Concert and Comedy" companies that traveled together to independent performers moving between variety halls and other types of entertaiment. Their stock in trade was an informal melange of the popular songs of the day, acts taken from the circus and other sorts of shows, and sketches that often were borrowed from the minstrel show.

During the seventies and eighties a movement was started supposedly to "clean up" existing popular entertainments, though many showmen saw it less as moral reform than as an opportunity to attract something approaching a mass audience. It paralleled and was probably influenced by a similar movement in the English music hall of the day. Perhaps the best-known figure in the so-called American moral reform was Tony Pastor, whose career, in a sense, typifies the growth of the showman into a mass-entertainment entrepreneur. Pastor had begun as a circus performer. In the 1860s, he was associated with "444," a New York variety house of somewhat dubious reputation. In 1865 he opened Tony Pastor's Opera House on the Bowery, and in 1881 he took over the Fourteeenth Street Theatre. By this time he had cut most ties with the concert saloon tradition in which he had worked, discarded the serving of drinks in the theatre, and eagerly welcomed women and children to what had previously been primarily men-only entertainments. In the process he began to establish the roots of a new form, vaudeville.

Vaudeville

By the 1890s, material from the concert saloon, the dime museum, variety, and to a considerable extent, the British music hall, had more fully developed into the new, unobjectionable, systematically organized kind of popular entertainment that was vaudeville, which would remain an important force in America through the 1930s. Vaudeville continued to feature shows made up of a wide range of comedy, song and dance, and other specialties, impossible to illustrate in all their variety. However, comedy scenes known as "two acts," sometimes featuring a male–female comedy team, often appeared. A brief selection from a typical two-act runs as follows:

HE: Time seems to stand still when I'm with a clever girl like you.
SHE: Well, no wonder. You've got a face that would stop a clock.
HE: I suppose lots of things I say make you feel as if you could beat my brains out.

SHE: No, everything you say makes me realize there aren't any there to beat out.

HE: I read where a man ate twenty pounds of sausage in ten minutes. What would you call that? A record?

SHE: No, baloney!

(quoted in McNamara, *American Popular Entertainments*, 69–73.)

Although its material was obviously similar to, or borrowed from, earlier entertainments, a large difference marked the way the new form, vaudeville, was organized. The last years of the nineteenth century and the first years of the twentieth century made up a period of large-scale commercialization of entertainment in America. Legitimate theatre, for example, was being revolutionized by the Theatrical Syndicate, which, among other things, systematized booking. Now vaudeville performers – sometimes teams or whole families – typically began to tour on "circuits," moving from theatre to theatre, in chains of houses that were managed by such important figures in the field as E. F. Albee, B. F. Keith, Marcus Loew, F. F. Procter, and Alexander Pantages. It was an age of trusts and other shady business alliances, and the theatrical managers had formed conglomerates to protect their interests, as had legitimate theatre owners. The performers countered with a union, the White Rats, modeled on the one created by English music-hall performers.

Vaudeville circuits were of two kinds: big time, which played first-class theatres and offered relatively good salaries and working conditions, and small-time, which was concentrated in minor theatres, frequently in out-of-the-way towns, and often with backbreaking schedules and underpaid performers and staff. Because vaudeville people often came from poor backgrounds and lacked money and education, and because of the avowedly popular nature of their calling, those involved with the so-called "legitimate" theatre often looked down on all vaudevillians and their craft. As George Jean Nathan saw it in 1918, vaudeville was made up, "for the most part, of young men whose coat pockets are cut on a slant of ninety degrees and embellished with flaps fashioned in the shape of W's, and of young women whose speaking voices resemble that of Galli-Curci's cab starter" (*The Popular Theatre,* 193). A song of the day noted that "*Variety* won't notice us until the day we die," and added:

In Wichita, in Chickasaw, in Haverstraw and Niles,
In Kankakee and Laramee, we laid 'em in the aisles.
In Pontiac, in Fondulac, in Hackensack and Flint,
In spots that even Rand McNally never cared to print.
In rooming houses, boarding houses, broken down hotels,
Playing four a day and five a day, we went through fifty hells.
Our object and our aim,
The chance that never came.[5]

But vaudeville delighted audiences and spread across America in the first

Program for vaudeville at B.F. Keith's Palace Theatre, 19 May 1919. Wilmeth Collection.

years of the twentieth century. In the teens, ten to twenty thousand acts were seeking bookings, and more than five thousand theatres – both big- and small-time – presented vaudeville. Audiences flocked to vaudeville houses of every kind. About eighty theatres in large cities presented star attractions. The most famous was New York's Palace, which offered such stars as the magician Harry Houdini, and W. C. Fields, the renowned juggler and comedian. In part because a close relationship existed between big-time vaudeville and the so-called legitimate forms of entertainment, radio and film, the incomes for major or top stars, especially in the early years, were often huge. By the first years of the twentieth century, vaudeville had become one of several new forms of entertainment that had replaced minstrelsy in the affection of audiences. For the most part, it was light amusement, aimed at a mass audience and possessed no particular intellectual distinction; as a result, the form prospered, and the big managers, as well as many big stars, accumulated substantial fortunes.

Vaudeville's ultimate decline began with sound films and the Depression, and by the end of the thirties it was, as Brooks Atkinson pointed out, more or less complete. As he phrased it in 1938, "on the whole, there is nothing wrong with vaudeville except that it is dead."[6] For a few years motion picture "presentation" houses offered vaudeville, or sometimes a brief musical or dance spectacular, along with the film. But vaudeville was indeed dead, and its cousin burlesque was dying, too. Nightclubs, however, had begun to flourish after the repeal of Prohibition. By the forties, they had become big business. A few of the lucky vaudevillians and burlesque performers took their acts into the night-clubs or into presentation houses; many others left show business entirely; both sorts of performers, for the most part, departed for greener fields.

Burlesque

Many historians have pointed to the early origins of burlesque. Among the most significant were the concert saloon, which began featuring scantily clad female performers after the Civil War, and the incorporation of a stranded ballet company into an extravaganza, *The Black Crook,* presented at Niblo's Garden in 1866. In addition, as early as 1869, burlesques of popular books and plays, featuring scantily clad performers, were offered by a troupe called Lydia Thompson and Her British Blondes and later by imitators. Attesting to the importance of these influences, in the years after the war, all sorts of novelty shows featuring chorus girls in abbreviated costumes sprang up across America.

In any case, burlesque, seen by many people inside and outside the theatre world as a more plebian form than vaudeville, catered primarily to a male audience and came to trade on risqué jokes and sketches and scantily clad female performers. Besides other influences, burlesque, like vaudeville, however, probably had its origins largely in minstrelsy. Toward the end of the nineteenth century, minstrel producers, in search of some sort of novelty to promote flagging public interest in a seriously declining form, had added women to their shows and helped create a new kind of popular entertainment.

The first real burlesque entrepreneur was M. B. Leavitt, who, in the 1870s, combined material from the minstrel show, the concert saloon, and other popular forms and made it a new kind of theatre attraction. Within a short time, most of the shows had taken their standard form: variety acts; short comic sketches, or "bits"; and musical numbers with the ever-present scantily clad dancers. Leavitt founded the well-known Rentz–Santley Novelty and Burlesque Company and produced what may well have been the first real burlesque show, *Mme Rentz's Female Minstrels,* in 1879.

In the early years of the twentieth century, the comic was the center of the show. Ultimately, burlesque came in two basic forms. First, there was so-called "wheel" burlesque in which shows were sent out on the road, rotating from one theatre to another like spokes on a wheel. Unlike vaudeville circuits, shows usually traveled together as units, typically carrying a dozen or more girls, a comic and straightman, sometimes with a second comic-and-straightman team or a singing, dancing juvenile.

The three chief women performers in the shows were typically the prima donna, who was a singer; the soubrette, who was a dancer; and the ingenue, who played wide-eyed innocent roles. Wheel burlesque was the starting place for young male performers like Bud Abbott and Lou Costello, some of whom would later go on to to fame in vaudeville, musical theatre, motion pictures, radio, and early television. Among the most prominent producers of wheel burlesque was an initially fairly respectable organization, the Columbia Amusement Company, generally called The Columbia Wheel, founded in 1905 by Sam Scribner. Striptease was not an aspect of burlesque throughout most of the early twentieth century, but Izzy Herk's Mutual Association led the way in the twenties, with an increasing emphasis on sexual material of all kinds. Eventually the "striptease" became the center of most shows.

In the twenties, when burlesque ticket sales began to decline, an increasing number of theatres turned to the second basic form – so-called "stock burlesque." In fact, it was an old form, which had been around since early in the century, in a time when wheel houses would put together a stock company of burlesquers during the summer while the touring companies were on vacation. Later, however, these companies would play year round. In the twenties stock burlesque began to emphasize the famous striptease that would shock and outrage so many church groups and city officials.

Perhaps the most famous stock entrepreneurs were the Minsky brothers – Billy, Abe, Herbert, and Morton – whose New York theatres, first begun in the 1920s, featured striptease and broad, often "blue," comedy. Originally operating out of the famous National Winter Garden, the Minskys introduced burlesque to Broadway at the Republic on Forty-second Street. Controversy from neighboring theatres and other businesses in Times Square resulted in a number of battles between the owners and their critics.

By 1938, H. M. Alexander could write in *Strip Tease: The Vanished Art of Burlesque,* that "the operators can't use the tease; the off-color blackouts are forbidden; the word 'burlesque' is taboo. The Minskys aren't even allowed to put their own names on the marquee" (117). By 1942 Mayor La Guardia had refused to renew the licenses of burlesque houses, and the form essentially died in its capital, New York City. Although burlesque survived for some years in other cities, many of the comics and strippers often found employment in bars and nightclubs, occasionally in theatres, and frequently in totally unrelated fields. During the sixties, a form somewhat related to striptease arose with the live sex shows that appeared in many American cities.

Medicine Show

Like burlesque, medicine shows were a starting place for many performers who later moved into other areas of the theatre. And like a number of other American popular entertainments, the medicine shows grew up around the time of the Civil War and began to decline before World War II. If vaudeville and burlesque were types of performance associated with the city, medicine shows were primarily rural and small-town fare. In a way, they were the ancestors of later radio and television because they originated free sponsored entertainment. Some medicine shows were presented in vacant lots, occasionally with a so-called "airdrome" tent – canvas walls surrounding the stage and spectator area. Others appeared in roofed tents, or, in cold weather, in the ubiquitous "opera houses," the multipurpose theatres found in many small towns.

All had one thing in common – their owners could afford to charge spectators little or nothing because they peddled cheap cure-alls between the acts. Most presented an evening of variety acts of all kinds, interrupted by commercials and sales, and many ended the show with a comedy sketch that featured a blackface comedian called "Jake" or "Sambo," a character borrowed, along with the sketches, from the minstrel show.

As in burlesque, shows were of two basic types. Large firms like the Kickapoo Indian Medicine Company of New Haven, the Oregon Indian Medicine Company of Umatilla, Oregon, and the Hamlin's Wizard Oil Company of Chicago sent units out on the road, which presented shows and sold the company's products. But in addition there were a number of small independents, who usually had only a single show or two and who purchased their drugs from wholesalers or, especially before the Pure Food and Drug Act of 1906, stirred up their own medicines behind the stage. Both kinds of shows, in any case, were free or cost only a few pennies admission, with most of the profit coming from the sale of soap, salve, liniment, and a variety of other panaceas, and from candy sales.

The shows were generally similar in form, but over time they began to vary considerably in theme, consciously borrowing from other areas of popular entertainment. Some of the earliest were in effect free Wild West entertainments. They lasted from about the eighties until the teens. A Kickapoo Indian Medicine Show unit, for example,

> that included half a dozen Indians and five white entertainers played for six nights in the town hall in Colebrook, New Hampshire, during the winter of 1907–8. The show, which was interrupted about four times during an hour and a half for medicine pitches, consisted of singing, dancing, acrobatics, a fire eater, a so-called chalk talk, a lecture illustrated with chalk-board draw-

ings, and several afterpieces. As a special added attraction, patrons were treated to an early motion picture, *The Dream of the Rarebit Fiend.*[7]

Beginning in the teens, as the older Indian and western shows began to disappear, vaudeville-style shows became a more significant force in the medicine-show world. Basically, these were simple rural versions of the vaudeville shows that played in cities, and, like the western and Indian shows, presented a free or inexpensive entertainment in order to attract buyers for soap and medicine. Many shows were not, strictly speaking, vaudeville but simply catch-alls for miscellaneous variety acts. As one company phrased in its *Billboard* advertisement:

> *Wanted,* For the Ku-Ver-O Medicine Co.'s *Opera House Show,* all kinds of Medicine performers, who can make good for two weeks. Long engagement for right people. Kickers, Knockers, Boozers, and Managers save postage. Piano player to double on stage needed. Salary sure every Sunday morning; plenty of money behind this show, besides I always got the coin and do not close the year round. The Three Everetts, the Hermans, Walter Ross and Billy Vandy, write. Address Dr. W. D. Moore, Corner of Oliver and Central Aves, Cincinnati, Ohio. (Quoted in McNamara, *Step Right Up,* 120)

As country people became more sophisticated about doctors and medicine, however, as prosecution for medical fraud grew more severe, and as transportation improved, the shows gradually disappeared. A few lingered on in rural areas through the 1930s and 1940s, and occasionally into the 1950s, but the real heyday of the medicine show was over not long after World War I.

Chautauqua and Lyceum

A number of popular variety entertainments were aimed at rural and small-town audiences, such as "school shows," variety entertainments that took place in rural schoolhouses. Country musicians often performed in these school shows, frequently presenting traditional variety sketches between the musical numbers, a combination still seen to some extent at the famous Grand Old Opry. Tent or circuit Chautauqua was also a popular entertainment form seen mostly in rural areas. It was a product of the American penchant for mixing theatre and education with an emphasis on the educational aspects of the enterprise. This emphasis was largely out of deference to conservative Protestants and others who objected to the theatre on moral grounds but who relished any educational venture.

A forerunner, discussed in Volume I, Chapter 6, of this history, by Buckley, was the lyceum movement, founded before the Civil War by Josiah Holbrook for self-improvement and scientific or literary study, in part through lectures and debates. After the war professional lecture bureaus were organized using the name "lyceum," the most famous by James Redpath. They were clearing-houses for distinguished speakers and bore little or no resemblance to the institution originally organized by Holbrook.

The original Chautauqua Institution, which still exists, was founded in upstate New York in 1874 as a summer assembly designed to improve Sunday-school teaching. Some touring assemblies loosely based on the original took the form of tent or circuit Chautauquas. They were largely managed by the new lyceum bureaus, which booked them. By and large, these bureaus presented "lyceum" events in the cities during the winter. Their traveling "Chautauquas" took programs to smaller towns and rural areas in the summer. A whole range of lecturers, preachers, performers, and musical events traveled under the Lyceum and Chautauqua banner, but they were not well regarded by the sophisticated. The friends of lecturer Ida Tarbell, for example, who signed a Chautauqua contract in 1916, referred derisively to her future association with "bell ringers, trained dogs and Tyrolean yodelers" (Tarbell, quoted in Theodore Morrison, 191). The popularity of circuit Chautauqua trailed off after the midtwenties in the face of the changes taking place in American culture and its entertainment.

Toby, Tabs, Home Talent, and Popular Drama

Unlike Chautauqua shows, the majority of which featured variety entertainments, many other related types of shows were built around a group of plays. They focused on comedians generally known as Toby and Suzy; presented old standard plays; or put on so-called Tab Shows (an abbreviation for "tabloid"), often unlicensed versions of popular Broadway plays or other standard works. Frequently, variety turns by cast members were presented between the acts. The variations were endless: "tent repertoire," "opera house" shows, "circle stock" (which operated on a "wheel" basis from a large town or city). A great favorite was one or another version of the play based on Harriet Beecher Stowe's famous novel *Uncle Tom's Cabin,* with troupes of "Tommers" presented in tents and halls for years on end. Among the most popular traveling versions was that written by George Aiken and initially presented at the Troy Museum in 1852 (Vol. I of this history includes extensive coverage of *Uncle Tom's Cabin*).

"Home talent" shows were sponsored by companies that provided directors – often young women with a college drama department background – who were sent into small towns, armed with a playscript suitable for amateurs. The director would then cast the script with prominent local citizens, rehearse it, and present the show, usually benefiting some local charity. The well-known entertainer Cousin Minnie Pearl got her start in show business as a home talent director. By and large, the companies that sponsored these shows operated not unlike the professional firms that produced local amateur pageants.

For many years, American audiences – especially rural audiences – had seen country life as more healthy and honest than life in the city. As a result, the "Toby and Suzy" shows were great favorites with rural audiences in the Midwest and Southwest from about 1900 until the 1930s and 1940s. Some have been revived in recent years. As they were usually originally presented, they featured Toby, a freckle-faced country boy of indeterminate age, and his girlfriend Suzy, both uneducated rural characters. They possessed little sophistication, but the pair was always warm, generous, humorous, and down-to-earth. Usually, they were cast in plays in which rural and urban values and characters were contrasted – with rural standards eventually emerging as more satisfying and long-lasting.

In both the country and the city, cheap melodrama abounded. Not only did aged or pirated melodramas appear in rural rep shows, they were to be found in the so-called exhibition halls of dime museums and in the ubiquitous cheap theatres that flourished after the Civil War in down-at-the-heels, garish entertainment districts like the Bowery. By the turn of the century, the descendants of these cheap melodramas were to increase in popularity and be seen in various so-called ten-twenty-thirty (or popularly, ten-twent'-thirt') shows.

These shows were managed by such firms as Sullivan, Harris, and Woods and Stair and Havlin, as well as other entrepreneurs, and were written by popular authors like Owen Davis (who penned such turn-of-the-century thrillers as *In the Hands of the Enemy, Nellie, the Beautiful Cloak Model,* and *Convict 999*) and Theodore Kremer (author of works such as *Fast Life in New York, Slaves of the Orient,* and *The Great Automobile Mystery*). Ten-twenty-thirty shows often played in such popular New York theatres as the Star, near Union Square, the Third Avenue Theatre, and the old Academy of Music on Fourteenth Street.

The melodrama stock company was not unusual, but the touring production was most common. Popular melodramas and comedies often appeared first on Broadway, which was devoted to the so-called Box-Office play. In fact, it is clear that many Broadway shows of all kinds in the late nineteenth and early twentieth centuries were in fact popular entertainments and were often designed primarily for touring to small theatres outside New York at the end of their Broadway run. As I have suggested elsewhere about Lee and J. J. Shubert, producers who virtually dominated Broadway in the early years of the twentieth century (after the decline of Klaw and Erlanger's Theatrical Syndicate), they were "producers of popular entertainments, involved in show business rather than art. In many ways they fit more comfortably with the early motion-picture moguls – whom they undoubtedly influenced – than with such 'artistic' or socially committed producers as the Provincetown Players, the Theatre Guild, or the Mercury Theatre. In fact, their producing policies were precisely what such groups were reacting against from the teens onward" (McNamara, *The Shuberts of Broadway,* xxvi).

Other changes began to take place in American entertainment as early as the end of the century, in a time when ordinary people began to have more time and money to amuse themselves and their families outside the home. These amusements often were environmental and took advantage of the new technology that had grown up as the nineteenth century progressed. The novelty of carnivals and amusement parks – and, of course, early film – drew many people away from some of the more traditional amusements toward the turn of the nineteenth century.[8]

Carnivals and Amusement Parks

Traveling carnivals (called "fun fairs" in England) are a very old form, closely linked to agricultural fairs. Often they were "midway" adjuncts to a state or local fair, although they sometimes played – and continue to play – dates not associated with any kind of sponsorship or affiliation. In any case, American promoters gave the form a new lease on life toward the turn of the century.

Although they predated it, carnivals came into special prominence at the time of the Columbian Exposition, held in Chicago in 1893. Particularly featured in nationwide press coverage of the Exposition had been the gigantic Ferris Wheel, a pleasure wheel of a size and magnificence never seen in the United States before, and Little Egypt, an exotic dancer who may or may not actually have appeared at the fair. The spectacular "Midway Plaisance," the amusement area, today part of the University of Chicago campus, led to the appearance of similar amusement areas at later exhibitions and amusement parks, and helped popularize the carnival as an entertainment institution. All in all, there were many individual imitations of different kinds of the "Midway Plaisance."

Basically, the traveling carnival contained three types of attraction that – in spite of the decline of carnivals in recent years – are still featured today: rides (generallly broken down into such "major" types as the Ferris Wheel and "kiddie"or "punk" rides); shows (freak shows, fun houses, girlie shows, and so on); and concession stands selling food and souvenirs or featuring games of chance or skill, such as shooting galleries or penny pitching. Usually stands were, and still are, known as "joints" or "stores."

In general, the so-called back end of the carnival midway (the area farthest from the entrance) contains the shows; the rides are arranged down the center of the midway (often with the largest and most spectacular toward the back end); and many of the games and concessions are ranged down the two sides of the midway, from the gate to the back end, with a kind of "street" (sometimes referred to as a "midway") around the ride area. Thus, the overall shape of a typical lot is that of an extended loop or horseshoe, with the crowd entering at the front, moving down one leg of the "street," across the back end on another leg, and down toward the exit on a third.

The carnival lot, then, is not unlike a marketplace. It is divided into a network of structures, based on specialized kinds of entertainment or related "products." Broadly speaking, "open" structures at a carnival (rides, game, and food and souvenir joints, for example) may be participated in directly from the midway itself, whereas "closed" structures (the waxworks, the hall of mirrors, the fun house, and so on) must be entered by the spectator. At a typical carnival, dozens of different kinds of entertainment events are taking place simultaneously, both in view and in relative private, and the spectator creates his or her own unique organization of the total space through an individual – although highly directed – choice of certain open and closed structures in a certain order. The crowd is carefully guided through the midway, but ample options for certain individual choices are built in.

A more or less typical route through a carnival lot directs the crowd past the cheaper games and stands selling food and inexpensive souvenirs on their way to the more costly rides and shows in the back end. The premise is to "soften up" spectators gradually, and it is not unlike the approach of traditional medicine showmen who offered inexpensive soaps or salves early in their shows, saving the higher-priced remedies until the "tip had been turned" – that is, until the audience was in a spending mood.

Part of the appeal of the traveling carnival has long been its sense of disorientation. This "out-of-this-world" quality derives not only from traditional carnival "art" and advertising but also from highly creative, even bizarre use of light and sound and physical sensation. Sound, for example, never stops on the midway. Music from loudspeakers on the rides, pitches for the various shows, and the murmur of the crowd assaults the ears of spectators during their entire time at the canival. Normal speech becomes almost impossible. The rides exist to offer spectators controlled danger, physical disorientation, even the perverse pleasure of motion sickness. And their lights, especially, coupled to the eccentric movement of the rides, offer an extraordinary display.

The more permanent version of the traveling carnival is the amusement park. Amusement parks in the United States probably developed in part out of the many picnic grounds and pleasure gardens that sprouted up before the Civil War, with their simple swings and carousels. In the years following the war, trolley lines promoted the growth of such entertainment centers, as parks were constructed outside American cities to promote use of public transportation, especially on weekends. Their growth was also influenced by the increased need for cheap, easily accessible entertainment for the growing number of urban dwellers, as well as by amusement entrepreneurs, who saw opportunities for employing advanced entertainment technology in order to increase profits. Like the traveling carnival, the amusement park benefited from the immense publicity generated by Chicago's Columbian Exposition of 1893.

Among the many examples of amusement parks built around the United States, chiefly in the early part of the twentieth century, those at Coney Island stood out as the most lavish. Coney Island was not, in fact, a single amusement park but a beachfront area that eventually contained three major parks and entertainment areas. Its real beginning as a popular entertainment center was with the construction of Paul Boynton's Sea Lion Park in 1895. George Tilyou's Steeplechase Park followed two years later.

Then in 1903 two enterprising promoters, Frederick Thompson and Elmer "Skip" Dundy, bought out the failing Boynton park. With a lavish hand, they began to remodel it into a version of the "Midway Plaisance," the famous fairground entertainment zone. At Coney Island, Thompson and Dundy essentially re-created it on a more or less permanent basis. Their Luna Park offered visitors a madly eclectic environment that included an Eskimo village, a monkey theatre, a miniature railway, a shoot-the-shoots, and mock-Venetian canals, all illuminated at night by more than 250,000 electric lights. Luna Park was a tourist sensation, as was its rival, Dreamland, constructed at Coney Island the next year. If anything, Dreamland was an even more complex and compelling environment, with a 300-foot-high illuminated replica of the Giralda Tower of Seville, and the great spectacle "Fighting the Flames," in which a full-scale six-story building was burned while anguished tenants leaped from windows and actors impersonating firemen performed daring rescues.

Like the carnival, the amusement park depended heavily on the concepts of flash and disorientation mentioned earlier. Describing the impact of Coney Island in the twenties, for example, the poet e.e. cummings spoke with wonder at

> a trillion smells; the tinkle and snap of shooting galleries; the magically sonorous exhortations of barkers and ballyhoomen; the thousands upon thousands of faces paralyzed by enchantment to mere eyeful disks, which strugglingly surge through dizzy gates of illusion; the metamorphosis of atmosphere into a stupendous pattern of electric colors, punctuated by a continuous whisking of leaning and cleaving ship-like shapes; the yearn and skid of toy cars crammed with screeching reality, wildly spiraling earthward or gliding out of ferocious depth into sumptuous height or whirling eccentrically in a brilliant flatness. (See note 8.)

The function of the new electric light – as well as the extravagant use of fireworks – to create unique forms and colors was especially pronounced at Coney Island. In a famous quotation about the complex of amusement parks, Maxim Gorky found them seedy but, at the same time, exotic and extraordinary; they were, he said, all "pompous glitter." The remarkable uses of light particularly fascinated him. He saw

> thousands of ruddy sparks glimmer in the darkness, lining in fine, sensitive outline on the black background of the sky, shapely towers of miraculous castles, palaces and temples. Golden gossamer threads tremble in the air. They intertwine in transparent flaming patterns, which flutter and melt away in love with their own beauty mirrored in the water. Fabulous beyond conceiving, ineffably beautiful, is this fiery scintillation. (See note 8.)

Like the traveling carnival, the ambiance of amusement parks was frankly dedicated to the promotion of fantasy, which, at some level, seemed to be involved with images of speed, distortion, disorientation, controlled danger, and sexuality. It was a winning combination with the turn-of-the-century public. It was not long before the Coney Island complex began to serve as an inspiration for countless other Luna Parks and Dreamlands all over America, and soon the amusement park became a fixture of most sizable American cities. Their great era lasted from the turn of the century to about World War II. The competition from television and racial strife clouded their last years, but parks also became an early symbol of American family entertainment – only to be revived again in 1955 in a new, related, but sanitized form with Walt Disney's transformation of an orange grove in Anaheim, California, into Disneyland, the prototype for countless "theme" parks that would follow.

Optical and Mechanical Forms

So-called optical and mechanical entertainments, essentially marking the technological advances that led to modern media, were ubiquitous in the late nineteenth century and the early years of the twentieth century. For years the magic lantern had been a fixture of schools, homes, churches, and many theatres. But the period following the Civil War witnessed a number of improvements in projectors (including a reduction of prices for ordinary home lanterns, as well as greater variety) and in slides. A concomitant taste for moving images also helped to promote the increasing popularity of magic lanterns. This penchant for advancing technology would also be seen in a number of the other devices, such as the phonograph, and the increasing number of automated arcade machines that came into use during the period.

Similarly, dioramas and panoramas did not originate in late-nineteenth-century America. Various kinds were common in Europe and, indeed, in the United States during the early nineteenth century, and the two terms were often used interchangeably. By and large, however, panoramas were enormous canvases that were fastened to the inside of a circular building. They had a fundamentally documentary function. Spectators, in semidarkness in the middle of a viewing platform, gazed across a gulf of a dozen feet or more at a continuous, sometimes moving picture lit from above. Many that appeared in late-nineteenth-century America were of battle scenes from the Civil War, tourist attractions (such as a trip on the Mississippi river), or religious subjects. The audience could follow them using printed plans showing the building and the encircling picture, with notes on principal incidents or terrain features.

The diorama, on the other hand, was basically a series of gigantic, often transparent, pictures, exhibited under changing light in a theatre or other auditorium, frequently with background music and narration of some sort. The subject matter was fundamentally documentary and similar to that shown in the panorama. There were many variations of the diorama and the panorama, but both were essentially on the road to the cinema.

Another device that moved farther in the direction of film – and that was related to the magic lantern – was Edison's Kinetoscope. Many optical toys and other devices had long been popular in America, among them the Zoetrope, as well as the ubiquitous stereoscope. Edison was halfway to producing projected film, however, with his widely imitated Kinetoscope, an optical device based on the peepshow and often coupled to a variation of the phonograph, which was shown in professional Kinetoscope parlors. All of these advances, and many others, led to the taste for, and development of, projected film.

Perhaps the greatest entertainment sensation at the end of the century was a new type of technological advance in entertainment, the motion picture. First shown in America in the 1890s were various silent movies with or without subtitles – often scenes from plays, acts from live popular enterainments, or "actualities" (brief documentaries), accompanied by a piano player or sometimes, in the larger theatres, by a full orchestra. Movies appeared everywhere – in cities and small towns and in tents in rural areas. Many of the earliest appeared as attractions in the exhibition halls of dime museums and in vaudeville theatres. During the week of 10 March 1902, for example, in B. F. Keith's New Union Square Theatre in New York, a vaudeville house, one of the acts consisted of ten selections from "The American Biograph, The Most Perfect of All Picture-Moving [*sic*] Machines." According to a playbill in my possession, it included a "Comedy scene" and "The Queen of England playing with Olga and Titania, of Russia, and Marguerette and Martha, of Denmark, Fredensburg Castle, Denmark, September 10, 1901."

As motion-picture technology improved in the early twentieth century, longer and more complex story films added yet another challenge to traditional live popular entertainments. Although they were strongly influenced by live popular entertainments of the day, the movies also helped to make them obsolete. The talkies, too, appeared at the end of the twenties, and technicolor in the late thirties, adding to the lack of interest in live amusements.

Radio became a common form of home entertainment in the twenties and thirties. It also was strongly influenced by popular entertainment; in particular its format carried a hint of the medicine show's free sponsored entertainment. In any case, coming free directly to the living rooms of America, it added a new element of effortlessness to family amusement that had begun years before with the Victrola and some of the amateur optical and mechanical amusements. Beyond that, of course, later innovations such as television and the Internet have greatly extended the reach of the principles – and the material – that originated in live popular entertainment.

Extensions and Influences

Some final points about a few neglected aspects of classic popular entertainment and their influence on forms that survive to the present day are appropriate here. Street performing, for example, has clearly borrowed material from many areas of popular show business. Traditionally, between periods of working in the streets, practitioners, in fact, often performed in more formally structured popular entertainment – now in a medicine show, for example, next in burlesque, after that in a carnival. Thus, classic vaudeville turns were adapted in the streets, as were acrobatics and circus routines of all kinds. As a result, street performing – and it survives today in some towns and cities – has gradually become a unique distillation of material and techniques from various other forms of popular entertainment and is strongly influenced by many aspects of the urban environment. The street performer is essentially a kind of "environmental" entertainer. As Sally Harrison-Pepper points out in *Drawing a Circle in the Square,*

> Unlike much conventional theater, the street performer works in a "found" environment and must inscribe his meaning upon it. The competence of a successful performer can be partly measured by his ability to transform city "space" into theater "place." The performer must transform museum visitors resting on steps into an audience seated on bleachers. He must devise ways to invite the total participation of the environment, using its traffic, noise, and garbage as parts of the show. Not only must he allow the disruptions of urban space, he must also turn these potential disruptions into props, sets, actors for his show. (xv)

Amateur entertainments are also close relatives of traditional professional popular entertainments. At home, in a period before radio and television, for example, American family audiences amused themselves with a wide variety of amateur entertainments. Families presented all sorts of "parlor theatricals," simple plays, skits, and recitations, as well as magic acts, indoor games, and magic lantern slide shows. The magic lantern slides mentioned earlier, which often showed scenes from popular fairy tales, poems, stories, or documentary subjects, were sometimes accompanied by music from the piano or Victrola and by a narration read by a member of the family. The shows were extremely popular all over America and paved the way for the motion picture – and, in another sense, foreshadowed such amateur entertainment forms as home movies, 35-mm slide shows, and video presentations.

Amateur imitations of professional minstrelsy, vaudeville, the review/revue, and other popular forms have always been a staple of various kinds of school and community performance. Often they have featured parody of well-known songs, plays, films, books – or, in later years, radio and television programs. Amateur marching drills, skits, patriotic performances, and parades and celebrations of various kinds were ubiquitous in schools and settlement houses and in the streets of American towns and cities through the late nineteenth and early twentieth centuries, often connected with some holiday or other celebration. Simple religious plays or tableaux were performed by Sunday-school students. Some interesting remnants of the traditional amateur forms survive today.

It is just as well that some do not. Minstrel shows, in particular, were a standard form of both amusement and fund raising in schools, clubs, and lodges until the years following World War II, long after the professional forms that inspired them had disappeared from American stages, but before attitudes toward race relations had begun to change substantially in some communities. Of course, school entertainments, and the countless "beauty" and related pageants, are still important community-based shows. Amateur plays and shows more or less resembling vaudeville or the revue, but with a local slant and much burlesquing of local institutions, are still common in clubs, high schools, universities, and law and medical schools at the end of the twentieth century.

Curiously enough, an important influence from popular entertainment has probably been on the avant-garde of the 1960s and 1970s – and of later decades. The impulse, however, has been quite different in its aims. In an attempt to broaden the political and social spectrum of American theatre, and consciously to do battle with old ideas about structure and presentation, the avant-garde of the last half of the twentieth century has largely rejected conventional theatre, especially the kind of Broadway theatre that has emphasized well-made playmaking and the views of a middle-class audience. In doing so, some avant-gardists have seized on a return to certain elements of popular entertainment, but they have used them in new ways in order to make new social and artistic points, about such topics as capitalism, homelessness, or the war in Vietnam. Examples, among many, of their work include the productions of the San Francisco Mime Troupe and the Bread and Puppet Theatre as well as the broader-based New Vaudeville movement, all of which have used vaudeville-like comedy routines, juggling, magic, and puppetry to make quite different social and cultural points from those of traditional popular entertainment. (See Marvin Carlson's outline of alternative theatre in Vol. III of this history.)

Finally, it is also important to underline once again that the rapid growth of technology in twentieth-century America has been a major factor in the disappearance of traditional live popular and amateur entertainments and their replacement both by increasingly sophisticated media and by other technologically based amusement. One example might be the Disney and competing theme parks. Although it may be said that they are simply the descendants of the old amusement parks in the same way that those early environments were themselves the descendants of pleasure gardens, it is clear that modern theme parks have taken the technology of amusement to a new level and are catering to a new, late-twentieth-century audience.

It is true that in our day, of course, many of the older live forms of amusement have declined in popularity, and many have even disappeared, in no small part because of competition from such vital new mass-entertainment forms. Yet, if a number of the old live entertainments have virtually disappeared, it is nonetheless true that many traditional techniques and devices are still with us, still influencing such forms as the television cop show and the revue, the soap opera, the horror film, and the Disney park.

Notes

1 Mae Noell is quoted in McNamara, *Step Right Up,* 47. This has been a major source for my essay, drawing on research carried out at an earlier period.
2 This is an anonymous, undated satire of *Hamlet,* reproduced in McNamara, *American Popular Entertainments,* 45.
3 These lyrics are taken from the popular play *A Trip to Chinatown* by Charles Hoyt and from the song, "The Bowery" (music by Percy Gaunt), 1892, in Robert Freemont, ed., *Favorite Songs of the Nineties* (New York: Dover Publications, 1973), 42–46.
4 Quoted in McNamara, "Entertainment District," 182–83.
5 Quoted in Nelson, "Only a Paper Moon," 25.
6 Brooks Atkinson, quoted in McNamara, "Entertainment District," 185.
7 Stewart H. Holbrook *(The Golden Age of Quackery),* as paraphrased in McNamara, *Step Right Up,* 92.

8 The section on carnivals and amusement parks is based largely on an article and a catalogue essay: Brooks McNamara, "Come On Over," *Theatre Crafts* (September 1977), 33ff; and, by the same author, "A Canvas City . . . Half as Old as Time," in *The County Fair Carnival: Catalogue of an Exhibition by the Chemung County Historical Society*, 1992. Also useful was the author's "The Scenography of Popular Entertainment," *TDR* (T-61), 24, the source of e.e. cummings's quote in this section; Gorky, also quoted in this segment, is cited from a quotation in McNamara, "A Canvas City . . . Half as Old as Time," 17–18.

Bibliography: Popular Entertainment

A starting place for sources published up to the early 1980s, with assessments and bibliographic data, is Wilmeth's *Variety Entertainment and Outdoor Amusements* and his earlier *American and English Popular Entertainment*. These update an earlier bibliography by Wilmeth published in Matlaw's *American Popular Entertainment* and have, in turn, been updated in *Theatre History Studies* (1991 and 1998). The first source cited above, along with Wilmeth and Miller, *Cambridge Guide to American Theatre*, Matlaw (above), Toll's *On with the Show* and *The Entertainment Machine*, Green and Laurie's *Show Biz from Vaude to Video*, the Csidas's *American Entertainment: A Unique History of Popular Show Business*, Inge's *Handbook of American Popular Culture* (2nd ed.), Nasaw's *Going Out*, and numerous other basic sources discussed in the bibliographies mentioned above provide good overviews and introductions to most major forms of American popular entertainment. The material (skits, jokes, stump speeches, and so forth) of most forms can be found in McNamara's *American Popular Entertainments*, whereas the special vocabulary of performance forms and performers is covered in Wilmeth's *The Language of American Popular Entertainment*.

For the roots of American forms McKechnie's *Popular Entertainment Through the Ages*, though dated, is still useful. Among more recent studies, the following provide insights into the origin of many American forms: Altick, *The Shows of London* (on various exhibition forms, 1600–1862); Booth, *Theatre in the Victorian Age;* Jay, *Learned Pigs & Fireproof Women;* Kift, *The Victorian music hall;* Meisel, *Realizations: Narrative, Pictorial, and Theatrical Arts in Nineteenth-Century England;* and Speaight's *The History of the English Puppet Theatre*.

Sources on popular culture and the context for forms covered in this chapter are too extensive to include here. However, among recent studies Levine's *Highbrow/Lowbrow* has been especially influential. Also recommended are Butsch's *For Fun and Profit*, Harris's *Cultural Excursions*, and Peiss's *Cheap Amusements*. There are useful background essays in the three-volume *Encyclopedia of American Social History* (edited by Cayton, Gorn, and Williams) and *Encyclopedia of New York City* (edited by Jackson). The latter two contain a number of essays and entries specifically on entertainment.

For the origin of circus from the equestrian ring, Saxon's *Enter Foot and Horse* is a must. The history of the early American circus has most reliably been chronicled by Thayer in three volumes, ending his study essentially where this chapter begins but providing the necessary foundation for the golden age of the American circus. Other reliable historical essays can be found in *Bandwagon*, the magazine of the Circus Historical Society. Of published books on American circus, the best are recent. Three generally sound histories are Hoh and Rough's *Step Right Up!*, Culhane's *The American Cir-*

cus: An Illustrated History, and Eckley's *The American Circus.* Superior to many studies are those by Charles Fox (such as *Circus Baggage Stock* and *America's Great Circus Parade*) and Fox in collaboration with others (such as, with Parkinson, *Biller, Banners and Bombast* on circus advertising and *The Circus Moves by Rail*). There are hundreds of circus books dealing with specific aspects of the circus, many discussed in Wilmeth (see earlier) or found in Toole-Stott's five-volume world bibliography of the circus and allied arts. Space does not permit detailed listings, though more recent sources by the following are recommended: Bill Ballantine, John and Alice Durant, Richard W. Flint, F. Beverley Kelley, Gene Plowden, George Speaight, and Marcello Truzzi. The most thorough history of clowning remains Towsen's *Clowns.* The tag end of circus history within the scope of this chapter is well told by Hammarstrom in *Big Top Boss* on the Ringling operation, and, though outside of the coverage here, Albrecht's *The New American Circus* brings the story up to the present.

The Wild West exhibition, a form unique despite its frequent and misleading connection to the circus, has been dealt with adequately by Russell in *The Wild West or, A History of the Wild West* and has been attacked by Brasmer in two essays; Indians in the shows have been examined most thoroughly in L. G. Moses's *Wild West Shows and the Images of American Indians, 1883–1933.* There are numerous biographies and studies of the most prominent personality of this phenomenon, William "Buffalo Bill" Cody, the most reliable of which is by Nellie Yost, though Rosa and May's recent effort is superior for illustration. Thoughtful and provocative essays (and superb iconograpy) can be found in *Buffalo Bill and the Wild West,* an exhibit catalogue published in 1982.

Among variety forms, minstrelsy has received the most thorough coverage and perceptive study recently. A good starting point remains Toll's *Blacking Up,* but an equally useful introduction is *Inside the Minstrel Mask,* edited by Bean, Hatch, and McNamara. Provocative in its analysis is Lott's superb *Love & Theft,* and innovative in their examination of origins are Cockrell's *Demons of Disorder* and Lhamon's *Raising Cain.* Watkins in *On the Real Side* effectively places the minstrel show within the context of African American humor, and Emerson's *Doo-dah!* (life of Stephen Foster) provides useful background.

For variety entertainment, including the dime museum and vaudeville, sources are uneven. Among the few essays on the dime museum, those by Appleton and McNamara are excellent. Barnum, a show biz phenomenon and most intimately associated with the museum movement, has received a superb biography by Saxon; his promotional methods have been examined expertly by Neil Harris; and most recently the Kunhardts have produced a study of Barnum with extraordinary illustrations.

The concert saloon and early variety have received inadequate attention to date, especially among published books. Zeller's study of Tony Pastor provides some obligatory background, but, with few exceptions, overviews of variety and vaudeville remain dated and underdocumented, although the following are worth examination: DiMeglio, *Vaudeville U.S.A.;* Gilbert, *American Vaudeville: Its Life and Times;* Laurie, *Vaudeville: From the Honky-Tonks to The Palace;* and McLean's *American Vaudeville As Ritual.* Snyder's *The Voice of the City* is a worthy study of vaudeville as big business in New York; Stein's *American Vaudeville As Seen By Its Contemporaries* is a useful compilation; the Fields's mammoth biography of comic Lew Fields covers much of the period of this chapter; and Erenberg's *Steppin' Out* (along with Nasaw, above) examines the nightclub scene (1890–1930). The early use of vaudeville by the movies is examined in McNamara's "'Scavengers of the Amusement World'" and in Robert Allen's *Vaudeville and Film.*

The most thorough, albeit flawed, history of burlesque is Zeidman's undocumented overview. More stimulating certainly is Robert Allen's study of early burlesque, *Horrible Prettiness,* and more entertaining are Ralph Allen's essays. William Green is useful on the Minsky brothers. Pictorial histories (focused on the striptease) by Sobel, Corio, and Wortley are worth consultation.

The definitive study of medicine shows is McNamara's *Step Right Up,* recently revised. Among other standard works are those by Thomas Kelley and Violet McNeal. Young's *The Toadstool Millionaires* provides useful background on patent medicines.

For the phenomena of Chautauqua and lyceum, tent shows in general, and showboats, one could well begin with Morrison's *Chautauqua,* Bode's *The American Lyceum: Town Meeting of the Mind,* Slout's *Theatre in a Tent,* Graham's *Showboats,* and Hoyt's *Town Hall Tonight.*

For environmental-entertainment forms several key sources are suggested. For the American carnival, recommended are Easto and Truzzi's "Towards an Ethnography of the Carnival Social System," Truzzi's "Circuses, Carnivals and Fairs in America," Dembroski's "Hanky Panks and Group Games versus Alibis and Flats," Lewis's *Carnival* (though its veracity is sometimes suspect), and McKennon's *A Pictorial History of the American Carnival.* Although a definitive study of the carnival has yet to be written, these, along with the undocumented studies by Goldsack (such as *Work of Mirth Shows* and *Carnival Trains*), provide a sense of this unique American amusement. On the other hand, contemporary interest in the freak show (found in carnivals, circuses, and dime museums) has produced important studies, beginning with Fiedler's controversial *Freaks* and succeeded recently by Thomson's fascinating collection of essays titled *Freakery* and Bogdan's sociological study, *Freak Show.*

In contrast to the carnival, fairs (including world expositions) and amusement parks have received some good studies recently. Among the more thought-provoking are Kasson, *Amusing the Million* (the standard study now of Coney Island); Funnell, *By the Beautiful Sea* (on Atlantic City); Rydell, *All the World's a Fair* (on the Columbian Exposition) and *World of Fairs* (a more extensive study of the "Century of Progress" expositions); Blackburn, *Dawn of a New Day,* and Zim, Lerner, and Rolfes, *The World of Tomorrow* (both on the 1939 New York's World Fair); Harris, de Wit, Gilbert, and Rydell, *Grand Illusions: Chicago's World's Fair of 1893;* and Breitbart, *A World on Display* (1904 St. Louis World's Fair). An older but still useful study is Weedon and Ward's *Fairground Art.* A number of now standard sources can usefully be consulted as supplements to the above, including those by Badger and Burg on the Columbian Exposition; McCullough and Pilat/Ranson on Coney Island; Mangels on the outdoor entertainment industry in general; and Kyriazi on the amusement park. Recent books on aspects of the amusement park include Anderson's *Ferris Wheels* and Cartmell and Wyatt on roller coasters. Fraley's books on the carousel are outstanding, especially *The Great American Carousel.*

Other recent miscellaneous studies not discussed above but worth consultation include Davis, *Parades and Power* (Philadelphia street theatre); Fried, *America's Forgotten Folk Arts* (including carnival and fair art); Stanley Green, *The Great Clowns of Broadway;* Lawrence, *Rodeo;* Moody, *Ned Harrigan* (popular theatre); Senelick, *The Age and Stage of George L. Fox* (pantomime); and Silverman, *Houdini!!* (magic in vaudeville). And finally, among the numerous studies of early film and live entertainment, in addition to McNamara and Allen mentioned above, the following are suggested: Koszarski, *An Evening's Entertainment,* and Leyda and Musser, *Before Hollywood.*

–DBW

6

Musical Theatre

Thomas Riis

Introduction

Secular theatricals of various kinds became established in America about a century after the arrival of European colonists on the Atlantic coast and the Gulf of Mexico. Many, if not most, theatre pieces presented from the 1700s and early 1800s included music in some form, although the absence of a generous system of patronage prevented the wholesale importation of the materials required to mount major European works for the stage. Spanish informants described the playing of religious theatricals with music for Native Americans in Mexico in the middle of the sixteenth century. The presence of dances that originated in the New World were already being discussed in Spain in the 1590s. Because drama continued to flourish in the seventeenth century, during the golden age of Spanish culture, the plays of Lope de Vega and Pedro Calderón de la Barca were probably performed with their incidental music in the Spanish colonies during the 1600s and 1700s, although surviving musical evidence is sparser than one might hope. A play, entitled *El Rodrigo,* set to music by Mexican Manuel de Zumaya (c. 1678–1750), was probably mounted in 1708, and *La partenope,* a three-act opera also by Zumaya (based on Stampiglia's libretto, later used by Handel) greatly pleased the vice-regal authorities in Mexico City in 1711, well before any English and other continental works – ballad operas, Italian operas translated into English, English plays with spoken dialogue and songs, French melodramas (plays that used music to accompany action) – had been successfully transplanted. Because stage music in England in particular had long tended to be associated with low characters, light interludes, and foreign-language singers, by the 1830s no new genres had been encouraged to develop in the United States, although theatre buildings were built and American audiences avidly attended such productions as did occur.

The minstrel show – at first groups of whites in blackface makeup – developed as a new urban phenomenon in the 1840s, but it clearly had roots in unscripted, plebeian entertainments dating from much earlier that were not strictly racial parodies. The most important individual performer instrumental in developing a nationally recognized blackface persona as early 1828 was Thomas D. Rice, featuring his song "Jump Jim Crow." The central political issue of the United States in the nineteenth century – slavery – and all of its resultant oppression and disruptions, inevitably shaped the social commentary that took place on the minstrel stage, including the portrayal of race or racially defined characters, the position and relationship among blacks and whites in the larger society, and the place of both popular and high-class music within American culture as a whole. It also opened a door for the presentation of allegedly authentic slave music. Of course, all of musical theatre was not contained in the minstrel show, nor should the minstrel show be thought of as the only source of African influence on English theatricals in America, but it was the chief frame within which some folk elements appeared in an organized entertainment for paying spectators. Its audience and influence were widespread throughout the nineteenth century. It ultimately became a format, with an easily apprehended three-part structure (first part, olio, afterpiece) into which innumerable individual acts and routines could be worked (minstrelsy is discussed in more detail in Vol. I of this history and in Chap. 5 here).

More elaborate stage spectacles also developed in the mid–nineteenth century through the burlesques (defined as satires of previously known acts or actors) organized by British-born actress Laura Keene (c. 1820–73). In the late 1850s, Keene's legitimate experience, status, and talent for design gained her entrée into the theatre-managing business in America. In order to broaden her audience, suffering with the economic constraints imposed by the Civil War, she devoted less time to straight comedy, where she had made her first reputation, and more to creating dazzling stage effects for the enhancement of melodramas and burlesques featuring women in tight-fitting costumes. Her creation of spectacular finales – marvels of mechanical ingenuity called "transformation scenes" – were widely imitated and contributed to the success of many subsequent shows, most immediately *The Black Crook* of 1866. Unfortunately, the work of Keene's chief composer, Thomas Baker, was mostly unpublished. Very little of it is even extant in manuscript sources.

Stage effects, grand finales, dances, and movement in the shows of Keene and her contemporaries were enhanced by music, of course, but the music itself probably illustrated styles comparable to the dance tunes (waltzes, polkas, quadrilles, schottisches, and reels) and sung ballads (Irish melodies and Italian operatic airs) that survive as individual sheets. Melodramas included short sections of "action" music – loud chords, tremulous passages, or fast-moving scales – used to set the scene.

Minstrel shows and minstrel show music – mostly fast-sung tunes and pieces played on fiddles, banjos, tambourines, and bone castanets – dominated the middle decades of the nineteenth century, but a constant search for novelty and the arrival of shows imported from abroad, which could be both parodied and modified for local consumption, shaped developments in both book (plotted narrative) and variety (mixed act) shows.

Overview at the End of the Century: 1866–1895

No single feature can be said to define American musical theatre immediately following the Civil War. Neither Englishness nor ethnicity of any other kind, neither an attitude nor a musical style can be unambiguously tied to the full panoply of types of musical theatre of the post–Civil War period. American musicals after the late 1860s frequently possessed one or more elements perennially attractive to audiences. Whether a piece was called "musical comedy," "revue," "operetta," "extravaganza," "burlesque," "melodrama," or something else, it generally included glamorous and handsome actors and actresses, catchy or sentimental songs, elaborate stage effects, dialogue filled with plays on words, and a highly gestural acting style that was developed in parallel with melodrama and pantomime.

Witty topicality, the display of exotic locales, satire on familiar stage conventions, empathic nostalgia suffused through stories embodying widely shared values, and incidental music that consistently carried audiences along to periodic emotional heights were welcomed by all classes. Even sophisticated listeners with rather elevated standards tended to judge works on their overall effects, the degree to which they gave pleasure on first hearing, and the profit they eventually made for their producer.

The shadow cast by the Puritan-inspired disapproval of theatre in colonial times extended late into the nineteenth century. Much of what constituted the theatre – and its frequent accompanying vices, material extravagance, prostitution, and transvestism – simply could not be condoned within the religious ideology of early post-Revolutionary America. The relegation of much music to the domestic duties of women and the amusements of slaves also guaranteed that musical theatre would have very little acceptable definition for the American middle class until late in the nineteenth century. But with the rebuilding of the war-torn parts of the American South, the general prosperity following the Civil War, the exploration of the western American frontier, the completion of transcontinental rail links, impulses toward

national self-identification and unification, and the easing of religious crusades against the evils of the theatre, it is easy to see why audiences grew
and theatrical accomplishments are more fully documented across the country after 1870.

Tremendous population increases in eastern seaboard cities and the emergence of a comfortable if not wealthy professional class with more leisure
hours was also a condition that fostered the growth of theatrical institutions
in the 1880s and 1890s. Business and financial consolidation or monopoliza-
tion also occurred in the 1890s with the formation of the infamous trust, the
Theatrical Syndicate.

The emergence in the late nineteenth century of the professional actor and
the class-related linking of genres to specific theatre buildings in large cities,
especially New York, help make the historical description of the period from
1880 to 1920 somewhat easier to accomplish. Unfortunately, this state of
affairs may also give the erroneous impression that theatres in the decades
just prior to these never varied their offerings, feared experimentation, or
simply did not produce many musical productions. Nothing could be further
from the truth. As early as 1851 George Frederick Root (1820–1895) composed *The Flower Queen* as an operetta for children. John Hill Hewitt
(1801–1890) composed and presented nine operettas based on American
themes – especially genteel, southern ones – and dozens of other composers
followed in his wake before 1880. Records of over two hundred shows survive. Some such works were called "cantatas" or "concerts," yet their theatrical element is unmistakable, given descriptions of setting, costumes, and
blocking. Unfortunately, much of their music has been lost. Full-fledged
operas by native composers, though closely adhering to European models, as
well as imported works, were also mounted in this era, beginning with
William Henry Fry's *Leonora* (1845).

The Black Crook

The influence of specific large imported shows in the 1860s and 1870s on
American musical comedy proper has been much debated. (The term "musical comedy" was not used with any regularity or consistency until the 1890s,
although it was applied earlier to Edward R. Rice and J. Cheever Goodwin's
Evangeline in 1874.) *The Black Crook* (1866), an extremely long-running show
frequently interpreted as a landmark and credited with many "firsts," is a
unique work in virtually all respects. It partook of and resulted from a long
list of odd factors, so that it serves as an ambiguous touchstone at best.
Cited for its exceptionally long run (a record 475 performances in its initial
run at Niblo's Garden) and the flurry it caused at its New York opening, it
reflects the diverse strands that have come to characterize major landmarks:

foreign influence (in this case a visiting French ballet company in need of a performing space), a costly and sumptuous staging, alluring dancers in tight-fitting costumes, and a large talented cast of singers and actors. It enjoyed unparalleled success among all classes of theatregoer on the road and in revival. A film version was made of it in 1917.

The scene painting alone, because of the "dazzling transformation scene," was said to have cost $15,000. Fancy lighting effects and state-of-the-art machinery brought the total production cost to $50,000. Purely literary and musical values did not loom large in its success. On a stage crowded with monsters, fairies, demons, jewel-filled caverns, and abundant turbulence caused by fire and water, not to mention a plot driven by a plethora of melo-dramatic devices, *The Black Crook* literally provided something for everyone. Widely denounced from the press and pulpit as orgiastic, it also enjoyed the benefits of extraordinary pre-performance publicity. For all of these reasons, the show continued to attract audiences throughout an entire generation. But it did not so much point the way to the future as summarize all of the features characteristic of lavish spectacles in its own time. It revealed what the stage could accommodate if pushed to the limit of its producers' imagination and resources.

The context in which *The Black Crook* succeeded is quite clear. Coming out of a shattering Civil War, urban America wanted recreation, novelty, and escapist stories. Familiar with continental tastes and current fashions, they eagerly took up the *opéra-bouffe* of Jacques Offenbach in *La Grande-Duchesse de Gerolstein* (1867) and *La Belle Hélène* (1868), performed in the original French. Because these works were spoofs of European politics and classical mythology, respectively, they emphasized exotic as well as comic – and mildly naughty – elements. They were far removed from the tragic reality of recent American history. Any failure to understand the intricacies of a plot told in a foreign language would not have prevented widespread attraction to the vivacious tunes, scintillating orchestrations, scantily clad actresses, vig-orous dancing, and general effervescence. All of these features *The Black Crook* had in abundance.

Other Precursors and Influences

A Drury Lane genre that reached a popular peak in America in the late sixties was the pantomime. Now little known in the United States, though still done in Britain, pantomimes are holiday concoctions, featuring major stars in a variety of turns, elaborate staging covered by fairy-tale plots, and borrowed music. The runaway hit of 1868, George Fox's pantomime *Humpty Dumpty,* was perhaps the best such entertainment of its kind to be created by an American. It was revived in 1878, 1879, and 1904. Similar shows remained dependable box office vehicles at Christmastime through the early years of the twentieth century. (Major contributors to the spectacular side of pantomine were the three Kiralfy brothers – Imre, Arnold, and Bolossy – Hungarian dancers and mimes whose careers as producers of stage pictures dominated the period from 1875 to 1888. Their technical accomplishments in such shows as *Around the World in Eighty Days* [1875] were not duplicated until the 1920s.

Mature home-grown operettas were also composed in the 1860s. But hits like Julius Eichberg's *The Doctor of Alcantara* ((Boston, 1862; New York, 1866) were based on earlier models (British, French, and German comic operas) rather than Offenbach. With about fifteen musical numbers, including ensembles and finales, *The Doctor of Alcantara* had proportionately more music than *The Black Crook,* although the latter was a much longer piece. Eichberg wrote three other operettas, but *The Doctor of Alcantara* was the first work written in America to enjoy an international production. It surely made an impact on young, ambitious composers, although probably even at the time of its premiere it would not have been seen as a model of modernity.

American variety shows up until the 1870s had been chiefly erotic male-oriented entertainments, with negligible music. Fuller shows developed by H. J. Sargent and Tony Pastor played to more diverse family audiences in large cities and on national touring routes ("circuits"). Pastor, in particular, by cleaning up the language of his acts, offering household goods as premiums, and eliminating alcohol from the main seating areas encouraged an expanded family clientele, rather than an audience dominated by young "dudes," as had previously been the case. Michael B. Leavitt, sometimes credited with inventing the term "vaudeville," had already recognized the need for this new name to match the more refined audiences that the theatre promoters sought to appeal to. (See also the discussion of variety and vaudeville in the preceding chapter.)

Also during the 1870s, W. C. Coup, with the support and name of P. T. Barnum, developed what we have come to know as the traveling circus. With clowns, trained-animal acts, and acrobatics as the central activities but liberally accompanied by live musicians playing uptempo marches for wind instruments, these shows have survived up to the present day, although in their contemporary form are much scaled down from those of the late nineteenth century.

Callender's Original Georgia Minstrels troupe was put together in 1872, confirming the important role that African Americans themselves played in the blackface style of minstrel shows. Large troupes, like Callender's, and later Haverly's, provided essential professional opportunity for African Americans to train for a career in show business on both the theatrical and musical side. Individual black performers/songwriters such as James Bland and Sam Lucas also emerged in this period. In the late 1870s, with the advent of the Hyers Sisters' shows, *Out of Bondage* (1876) and *The Underground Railroad* (1879), black performers *without* blackface makeup appeared. The music of these shows consists of cues – some two dozen in *Out of Bondage* – that specified the performance of banjo tunes, spirituals, songs by Stephen Foster, and other contemporary popular songs, such as "I'se So Wicked" frequently used in *Uncle Tom's Cabin* productions.

The possibilities for presenting a range of ethnic character types in a fully plotted musical were realized by Harrigan and Hart in the 1870s. *The Mulligan Guards* comedies, discussed briefly in Chapter 3, with charming music provided by David Braham, were developed from a single sketch and song (1873) by Edward ("Ned") Harrigan. With his partner Tony Hart, Harrigan created cleverly contrived scenes – and eventually full-blown plays – which parodied the activities of neighborhood paramilitary organizations that he knew in the German, Black, Italian, and Irish neighborhoods of his youth. (Harrigan had grown up in an New York Irish ghetto in the 1850s.) Eventually he peopled his plays with characters intended to represent groups from most of the European and Asian ethnic communities of New York. The music included in his early acts reflected songs he had learned from his father, a sea captain, as well as African American songs and dances that his mother knew from her upbringing in Virginia. The songs composed by David Braham, chief composer for the Harrigan shows from 1873 to 1895, were generally recognized as simple and appealing in their use of familiar idioms – the Irish songs sound like traditional Irish tunes, the African American songs resemble minstrel show models, and so forth – as well as accurate in their retention of dialect. The rhythms used regular meters; the melodies were symmetrically shaped. Simple duple time was favored, and the songs reveal a high degree of phrase repetition. Because their popularity even outlasted their use in the Harrigan and Hart shows, a few were even recorded on disks in the twentieth century.

The farce-comedy, represented by such pieces as Nate Salsbury's *The Brook; or, A Jolly Day at the Picnic* (1879), can be viewed as another direct precursor to the musical comedy and revue to have emerged in the late 1870s. In this modest piece, an outing in the country for five friends provides the most minimal of narrative frameworks for a series of dances, songs, and specialty acts. (The happy picnickers carry in their picnic baskets not only their lunches but all of the costumes and props required for an amusing day. There is no other plot.) Utterly without pretension, this work made a hit because of its accessibility, pastoral slice-of-life directness, and rollicking good humor, free of high-class taint or any resemblance to established spectacles or leg shows. The music for *The Brook* has not been preserved but probably comprised familiar tunes or parodies. Perhaps the most socially significant aspect of the farce-comedy as a genre was its development and perfection outside New York. Only Salsbury's second theatre piece, it was first given as a brief skit in 1877 in St. Louis. By the time big-city entrepreneurs discovered it, *The Brook* had already won a national audience. Small, modestly equipped touring groups that performed farce-comedies proliferated in the next half-decade. The musical comedy proper of the 1890s was finally indistinguishable from a long farce-comedy with original music added.

In strong contrast to *The Brook,* with respect to both lyrical inventiveness and musical sophistication (but similarly chaste in language and theme), was the most influential English-language operetta of the decade, *H.M.S. Pinafore,* by the illustrious team of W. S. Gilbert and Arthur Sullivan. *Pinafore* was only their second collaboration but proved to be one of their most durable hits. Viewed all over America in 1878 and 1879, the show conquered audiences in a way few others ever have. It played for several weeks each in nearly a dozen major New York theatres, was widely parodied, and enjoyed renditions by all-female, all-black, and various foreign-language companies. It attracted singers to the dramatic stage and spurred the training of new talent when the supply of operetta singers fell short. The Boston Ideal Opera company was formed specifically for the purpose of performing *Pinafore.* Within a year of its London premiere, the show reportedly was produced dozens of times in the United States (often in pirated, abbreviated versions) by all varieties of groups – civic, church-related, and professional.

Many features recommended this show to Americans. The humorous critique of English society left nothing for politically sensitive Americans to take offense at. The language was clever but not off-color. Virtually all major characters had significant musical moments. The songs did not pose overwhelming difficulties, the choral writing was winning and solid – in the English tradition – and the dramatic effects, combined with the swift dialogue and crisp, clean humor set Gilbert and Sullivan's work as the standard to which others would aspire for at least fifty years after.

The high quality of Gilbert's libretti made Sullivan the envy of composers on both sides of the Atlantic for decades, despite Sullivan's personal disdain for the genre of operetta. But even with Sullivan's reservations about the possibilities within the form, the musical variety of *Pinafore* as well as the other successful Gilbert and Sullivan shows (especially *The Pirates of Penzance* [1880], *Patience* [1881], and *The Mikado* [1885]) included everything from ersatz madrigals – out of the English tradition of part-song singing – to genre-defining patter songs, such as "When I was a lad," to suave and efficient passages of recitative. Sullivan's command of harmonic gesture and the means to create dramatic continuity via his music achieved results that escaped other would-be writers of musical shows. He knew precisely how to treat the complex and witty verse of Gilbert (whose quality *without* the softening effect of music can sometimes be biting and sardonic).

Pinafore does not rely on improvised material, unspecified "business," or unnotated musical embellishment (although it often possesses topical allusions in the text that happily accommodate updating); it therefore could and did provide a clear model for other writers to emulate. Although other musical works enjoyed long vogues on the New York stage and on the road, none were so widely imitated. Nor were they capable of being so, since the publication of full scores was so much rarer at the time. For the vast majority of contemporary shows, the most that has survived is a stray script (usually without songs). Occasionally an especially popular tune or medley in a piano/vocal arrangement has come down to us, but few detailed musical arrangements survive with scripts.

Americans had been aware of European operetta prior to the arrival of *H.M.S. Pinafore,* but with this show and its immediate successor, *The Pirates of Penzance,* which had a U.S. premiere in 1880 (before its London debut, in order to prevent copyright piracy), Americans took a modern European product to their hearts more completely than ever before. The legacy of Gilbert and Sullivan is still strongly felt in the late twentieth century.

By 1874, another made-in-America work was produced to great success. *Evangeline,* written by J. Cheever Goodwin, with music by Edward E. Rice was, like *The Black Crook,* compounded of diverse elements. In contrast to *The Doctor of Alcantara* or other European works that succeeded in America, however, *Evangeline* prospered only in the United States and only after its component parts had become familiar to dozens of audiences outside New York. Among its defining elements were the inclusion of exotic sets, animal characters (a dancing cow and a lovesick whale), rhymed verse saturated with puns and allusions, an enigmatic mute known as the Lone Fisherman who served to provide interludes of comic pantomime, transformation scenes (with the multiple locales including Africa and the Wild West), cross-dressing roles for comic characters – the synonymous terms "travesty" and "burlesque" are commonly applied here – and a large number of popular-style songs, mostly ballads using sweetly high-toned language (such as "Thinking, Love, of Thee" and "Come to the Heart that is Thine") along with ensembles, choruses, and dances. The character names and a thread of the plot came from Longfellow, but that this is a parody of a well-known work is evident from start to finish.

The character of *Evangeline*'s success would seem to indicate that what Americans uniquely preferred in their comic musicals (or "opéra bouffes") of the late nineteenth century was a distraction from day-to-day reality, a look at the funny and the fantastic, accompanied by music that was strongly tinged with nostalgia, and lyrics containing a minimum of serious content, all presented within conventions whose roots were familiar, and staged in a manner that was as showy and grand as possible. Expertly executed foreign products found an audience, especially if their language were English or if their nontext components predominated over the need to understand a plot. There seems to have been no particular interest in musicals based on serious subjects (which would have seemed almost a contradiction in terms) or subtly developed plots.

Operetta prospered in the late nineteenth and early twentieth centuries despite a variety of factors that might be imagined to have prevented its rise. The union of tragedy and poetry that Shakespeare had created was a powerful model in the English-speaking world for centuries. Music on the stage had only rarely been allowed to rise to the high aesthetic plane occupied by tragedy. Musical theatre was by definition a mixed and therefore lesser genre. Even sung-through opera was developed relatively late in English-speaking countries, long after the Italian founders of the genre in 1600. Operettas filled a specific niche and found a paying audience that did not insist upon the purely through-sung devices of opera or the tunelessness of tragedy.

By the 1880s the elevation of opera was being achieved partly at the expense of operetta and all other types of musical theatre. The new Metropolitan Opera House, opened in 1883, was to be a temple of high art only. The added difficulty of finding both a first-rate playwright and a first-rate composer who preferred operetta to opera, not to mention the production costs, was a natural barrier to a profusion of durable pieces of operetta. Yet operettas gained in number and popularity. They did not make such great musical or dramatic demands on an audience as did opera, yet they were considerably more ambitious than farces, variety shows, and burlesques. In many ways they were the perfect entertainment for middle-brow tastes.

The 1880s was a decade of expansion and high aspirations in almost all theatrical genres and venues, artistic or popular, although it was not a time of blockbuster hits. Vaudeville circuits spread across the country, and individual theatres advertised continuous performances. Circuses featured three rings and huge crowds of performers. Technological advances led to better lit, more electrified, more mechanically sophisticated theatre buildings and stages – with elevators and roof gardens – that could accommodate more people in more scenically ambitious productions and larger orchestras. Ethnic theatres sprang up among German, Yiddish, and Lithuanian groups, among others. The Astor Place Company of Colored Tragedians presented an ambitious repertory of Shakespeare. The star system was well established, and the great heroes and heroines of the stage were popular from coast to coast.

The longest-lived show of the decade was Rice and William Gill's *Adonis*, featuring the handsome and well-built Henry Dixey in the title role. The piece was both a burlesque – the title page declared it "a perversion of common sense" – and a musical pastiche. Some tunes were composed by Rice (who dictated his tunes to a secretary because he himself did not read music), but at least a dozen others were borrowed, including parodies and excerpts from Mozart, Beethoven, Strauss, Offenbach, and David Braham. The central story involves a male statue of Adonis brought to life Pygmalion-style and adored by all women who see him. Over time Dixey expanded his role, which consisted of a series of recitations, impersonations, songs, and stunts, and the show proved so endearing to audiences that it achieved a record-breaking run of 603 performances in New York (September 1884 to April 1886) before setting sail for London, where it was much less successful. Rice's most memorable song performed by Dixey, "It's English, You Know," was taken up by other comedians of the time. The whole burlesque was itself finally spoofed by black-faced minstrel troupes and other individual performers.

The 1880s were a time of divergent tendencies within the theatre world as a whole. New York, America's leading theatrical city since the 1860s, was witnessing a period of massive immigration. By 1890 the two largest immigrant groups by far were the Germans and the Irish. German speakers made up over a quarter of New York's population of one and a half million. Not surprisingly, given this heavily Teutonic subculture, the 1880s also saw the embrace among New Yorkers of the music dramas by the great Richard Wagner. With this backdrop it seems surprising that Viennese operettas, such as Strauss's *Die Fledermaus* (1874), were not more successful than they were in the New World, but New York's German speakers were certainly not deprived of musical theatre when one realizes how much attention Wagner was getting. Too little is known about the makeup of audiences at the largest theatres at the time to be sure precisely how the ethnicity of composers may have influenced theatrical life as a whole, but the sheer numbers of Germans and Irish should alert us to probable themes and preferences.

Although several ethnic theatres and developments in them were brief and transitional, to sum up all of this activity as so many passing fads is to miss the manner in which New York's musical institutions were permanently shifted and had their repertories stabilized and standards raised. The 1880s saw growth in the sheer numbers of plays, shows, and audiences. But stability and continuity are also evident in the types of shows that were being viewed. Harrigan and Braham's plays (*Squatter Sovereignty* in 1882 and *Cordelia's Aspirations* in 1883) still dealt with class issues and social climbing while reaffirming democratic ideals and portraying a mixture of urban types (especially Irishmen) in farcical situations. English and French imports still drew well. J. K. Emmett's musical plays based on his stage character "Fritz, Our Cousin German" continued to appear in the 1880s, though not to such wide audiences or in such large halls as they had in the 1870s. If there was any stagnation in the comic musical theatre (as opposed to the opera) of the latter decade, it was most evident in the music itself. This all changed with the emergence of ragtime in the midnineties.

The Age of Ragtime: 1895–1915

With a fresh injection of syncopated rhythm, black dance, and dialect comedy, American musical theatre was reshaped permanently between 1895 and 1915. For the first time, a black vernacular style was brought full force onto the stage. Rather than the pale imitations of African Americans used by white professional minstrel entertainers, the repertory of ragtime was both created and presented by African Americans, and later by whites. There was no mistaking an imitation for the genuine article, and very quickly "everybody was doin' it." All major popular song writers had assimilated the essential black elements into their songs by 1905. Ragtime songs, such as Will Marion Cook's "Darktown is Out To-night," while considerably less complex than rags by Scott Joplin, James Scott, or Joseph Lamb, nevertheless signaled a clear departure from the older dance and ballad styles of popular music. A decade later the even more startling phenomenon of jazz would begin to be felt.

The 1890s saw the first large group of musical comedies so named, pieces speaking a sophisticated musical language that was directly indebted to Gilbert and Sullivan operettas but that also showed clear marks of the African presence in the Americas. Ethnic caricature was less dominant in the period than were attempts to create obvious "American" types of characters: stout-hearted young men bound for college or a business career, innocent ingenues who also exhibited a pert or saucy attitude, and venerable parents and other senior characters, all with respectable poor or middle-class origins, democratic impulses, and hearts of gold. Shows muted the effect of a growing ethnic mix of Eastern Europeans and Asians in American cities by developing and underlining a consciously American vernacular language, a proud dialect full of slang that was not only incomprehensible to many nonnative speakers (often the parents of the creators) but to Englishmen as well. Dialogue was delivered more quickly and naturally as plays departed from melodramatic models of the previous generation of operettas.

To the sassy and even irreverent sound of Tin Pan Alley songs and ragtime was added a sort of nationalistic fervor not yet soured by modern war. With the Civil War now a generation gone, young men and women of the 1890s celebrated the glitter of military uniforms and the glories of war rather than the mortal dangers of battle, aping and embracing as they did so similarly chauvinistic Viennese operettas. George M. Cohan became a mouthpiece of American patriotism in the age of Teddy Roosevelt and American interventionist politics, conceived at its most innocent and idealistic. Even the African American musicals, which were practically operettas, of J. Rosamond Johnson and Bob Cole, such as *The Shoo-Fly Regiment* (1907), picked up military themes with eagerness. In 1898 and 1899 American conflicts in the Philippines and Cuba were sufficiently short-lived and distant to provide the right amount of stimulus for the majority of Americans to enjoy the excitement but not suffer the pain of real military engagements.

The longest-running farce comedy of the century, *A Trip to Chinatown,* billed as an "idyll of San Francisco (musical trifle)," toured the country through much of 1890 and 1891, ran continuously in New York for two years (scoring some 657 performances), and achieved an unprecedented fame in subsequent touring and revival. No musical comedy surpassed its performance record for a generation. The plot, contrived by Charles Hoyt, was sufficiently loose and the music, composed and arranged mostly by Percy Gaunt, sufficiently general in mood that virtually all elements could be varied, updated, extracted, or deleted depending on the audience response of the moment. Filled with the American style of humor – zany, busy, fast-paced, and full of incident – the farcical side of farce-comedies was not slighted. Also, their remarkable flexibility allowed producers to refurbish a hit that would attract repeat audiences. Individual songs were interpolated at the whim of the director or the stars, and new skits, jokes, dances, and stage business were just as often used to spice up the show.

Robin Hood, by Harry B. Smith and Reginald De Koven, which premiered in New York in 1891, was the first American operetta to have a truly national reputation. It neither began nor flourished exclusively in New York, but its place in touring companies, particularly within the high-quality company of The Bostonians, who first produced it, guaranteed that its exposure would be wide. The special success of the song "O Promise Me" (with lyrics by the London critic Clement Scott), a favorite for weddings for over half a century, and the variety and appeal of the many other musical numbers by De Koven made it a sturdy vehicle apt for revival.

The basic plot of *Robin Hood* was as familiar as any could be, although the emphasis on comedy was clear in the characterization of the Sheriff of Nottingham (created by Henry Clay Barnabee) as a verbally clever and more-or-less reasonable fellow. The large number of disguises – it takes Maid Marian almost two acts to appear as herself – gender switches, and the calculatedly slow pace of the action placed the Smith–De Koven work firmly within the older Western European operetta tradition of the nineteenth century. It is an excellent work of its kind and was adopted by The Bostonians as worthy to be included within their Gilbert and Sullivan repertory.

Victor Herbert's first comic opera, *Prince Ananias,* premiered in 1894 and thus sustained an independent American operetta tradition along with the imports for another generation. His great hits, *Babes in Toyland* (1903) and *Naughty Marietta* (1910), made him a household name. De Koven, on the other hand, never equaled his success with *Robin Hood.* With the continuous production of new solidly built operettas the attraction of the genre for new composers was strong. Even the "March King," John Philip Sousa, among many others, tried his hand, although he did not succeed spectacularly in his several attempts, with the exception of *El Capitan* (the source of the march of the same name).

The chief beneficiary of *El Capitan,* however, was less the composer than the star, De Wolf Hopper, and it is Hopper's prominence that clarifies the importance of the star system as it existed at the time. Since the earliest days of opera, chief singers have tended to dominate if not embody the public image of opera. They have been far more visible than the authors of the shows in which they appeared. Composers, who were generally deemed deficient in literary skills, were even lower in the hierarchy of fame. The presence of music was assumed, but music writers were rarely given much credit. The collaborative process of making complex theatricals was less thrilling to contemplate than the appearance of the *prima donna* or the *primo uomo* for an audience. Musical comedy has been only slightly less performer dominated than opera in this century, and this was certainly true in the nineteenth century as well.

Probably because composer/lyricist collaborations have received so much more attention in the second half of the twentieth century than previously – the pairing of Richard Rodgers and Oscar Hammerstein II being the paramount example – the popular understanding and appreciation of musicals as singular products of star creators has obscured the long history of musical theatre as an unavoidably complex process, one always composed of multiple creative spirits.

Because the works of musical theatre in the 1890s depended so much on the quality and appeal of individual performers, they provided an opportunity for actors and singers from marginalized groups to make a pitch to middle-class audiences, even though collectively they included far more ticket-buying patrons than any single individual group. Jewish knockabout comedians Weber and Fields and African American cakewalk dancers Williams and Walker were two teams that epitomized the heights of fame and fortune to which a hardworking and talented act could rise within the world of theatre. Both teams achieved fame with their vaudeville skits and subsequently acquired the fame and resources with which to develop and help underwrite full-fledged musical comedies in the first decade of the twentieth century.

The entry of players like Lew Fields and Bert Williams into the front ranks by no means meant the demise of discrimination, prejudice, or racism against marginalized groups but rather reaffirmed that the stage of the late nineteenth century in America, as in so many other periods and cultures, could provide a safe place for the socially and economically disadvantaged to thrive. Both comic and tragic (or, at least pathetic) masks lured tired, bored, cultivated, and curious urbanites inside from the city street, placed them on plush and comfortable seats, and provided them with a welcome distraction from the troubles outside.

With an ever larger potential audience on which to draw, not merely the number but the types of musical theatre pieces proliferated. The first successful American revues appeared in the 1890s. George Lederer's influential *The Passing Show* (1894) attempted to provide an opportunity for Americans to enjoy an evening of entertainment that purported to review the recent stage hits as well as the political and social highlights of the year just past – but with no real plot. The show was filled with puns and parodies of other popular works and included a cast in excess of 100. The French spelling of the term "revue," which was slow to catch on, was a tip of the hat to the genre that English melodramatist James Planché claimed to have invented in the 1820s. It lent at least a few shows with modest trappings an undeserved air of sophistication and allure. As the years went by, however, American (and English) revues were notable less for their continental wit or subtlety than for glittering and extravagant production. The later long-running twentieth-century series of Florenz Ziegfeld, George White, Earl Carroll, and others epitomize the genre. Their music, like their lyrics, were dependent on the songs they reprised or burlesqued. *The Passing Show* itself included a medley of opera excerpts from *Carmen, I Pagliacci,* and *Tannhauser* and a musically old-fashioned topical song by Ludwig Englander, "Old Before His Time."

African American Musical Comedies

In the late 1890s, along with the general expansion of vaudeville – expansion with respect to the variety and length of acts, business organization, and sheer numbers of performers and theatre buildings – African American actors and a few actresses with minstrel-show experience began to band together to create full-fledged musical comedies. (The Hyers Sisters [Anna and Emma], of California, had formed a combination company with their father in the early 1880s to perform plays written for them with interpolated music, but their performances did not signal a trend and they did not score in New York.) By April 1898 Bob Cole and Billy Johnson's longish skit, *A Trip to Coontown* (featuring a tramp character, Willy Wayside, who appeared in whiteface makeup), had made it to Broadway. The run was brief, but its reception was fairly positive. Cole subsequently broke with Johnson but teamed up with a talented pair of brothers possessing university educations and conservatory music training. Cole and the Johnson Brothers (James Weldon and John Rosamond), after successfully pitching their songs to major vaudeville headliners, were noticed by Syndicate moguls, Klaw and Erlanger. Within two years their way to Broadway was paved. Since musical comedies were often little more than repositories for songs, dozens of Cole and Johnson songs were interpolated into major shows and became big sellers before the team's first full operetta, *The Shoo-Fly Regiment* (1907), was created. The music of this show was unusually syncopated for an operetta and lacked the standard European markers (waltzes, marches, and drinking choruses) – so it could be claimed as authentically American – but it stood uncomfortably between two worlds, a show too white in tone (despite its all-black cast) to satisfy a plebeian African American audience and too black to draw conservative middle-class European aficionados of operetta. Institutional racism also kept the touring cast from being booked into good houses on the road, and the show disappeared without a trace after one season, despite its string of excellent songs.

Will Marion Cook, who like J. Rosamond Johnson was classically trained and skillful in conducting and composing, had by 1903 created what would be the most familiar show of this mostly forgotten age of black musical theatre, *In Dahomey*. Cook's hiring of the vaudeville headliners, Bert Williams and George Walker, went far toward guaranteeing the ultimate success of the show, but it would not have made money for its backers without the powerful leadership from Cook and fine tunes he composed. (A bundle of European publicity that it accrued in a lengthy tour of England, including a royal command performance at Buckingham Palace, also proved indispensable.)

Cook's play, created with the help of poet Paul Laurence Dunbar and vaudevillian Jesse Shipp, was flimsy, but Cook's music amounted to symphonic ragtime and impressed its most sophisticated hearers. His ballads, choruses, and dances swing in a syncopated fashion, supported by rich and sonorous chromatic chords. Hints of the blues and even the not-yet-invented style called jazz can also be detected. *In Dahomey* possessed a rare combination of strong elements that contributed to the successful final product: a healthy dose of clever, clean comedy; a superb comic dancer-mime in the person of Williams; a block of solid choral songs and vigorous dances that showed off the performers to best effect at climaxes and finales; and a setting that exploited an exotic African locale. The use of spoken language and the style of humor in *In Dahomey* is also distinctively American. Slang and dialect abound. Audiences foreign and domestic loved it – even if they couldn't understand it. The road tour continued for two years, and about a dozen imitative sequels followed in its wake.

The vogue for black shows died along with several of their key business leaders and performers in about 1910. This premature decline was also helped by continuing financial and race-based restrictions. Bert Williams went on to become the first black star of the Ziegfeld Follies, and many other African American performers joined S. H. Dudley's Circuit, a precursor to the TOBA (Theatre Owners' Booking Association) Circuit, which developed road shows aimed primarily at black audiences in the South and a few large urban centers elsewhere. A revival of the big shows was only possible in the halcyon days following World War I. When *Shuffle Along* came on the boards in 1921, it acknowledged a debt of gratitude to *In Dahomey, The Shoo-Fly Regiment,* and others of their ilk.

George M. Cohan

Perhaps the most famous and successful vaudevillian to ride to musical comedy fame on a tide of national chauvinism and brash high spirits was George M. Cohan. In 1904 *Little Johnny Jones* was featured by Klaw and Erlanger in one of its smarter houses, the Liberty Theatre. The show was dominated by the uptempo tunes of Cohan's character, the American jockey Johnny Jones trying (but failing) to win the big English horse race, "the Derby." It possessed a consistent though highly melodramatic subplot and a cleverly constructed second-act finale, including a reprise of the show-stopping "Give My Regards to Broadway." This show achieved that oft-sought but rarely found element of "coherency" that bound its disparate song-and-dance parts together. It proved that a musical comedy could be more than merely an elaborate variety show.

The year 1907 saw several shows that confirmed the dominant forms in musical theatre for an entire generation. Florenz Ziegfeld produced the first of his annual Follies shows, which underlined the perennial drawing power of enticingly costumed women, first-rate comedians, and elaborate technical support. Franz Lehar's *The Merry Widow* ran for over four-hundred performances in New York, thus proving that operetta – even if it was imported – was far from dead. Indeed, the impact of *The Merry Widow* in the wider social world was probably unequaled until *Oklahoma!. Merry Widow*–inspired fashions and a mania for waltzing gripped the smart set like few earlier fads.

Many vaudeville and burlesque circuits thrived, bringing hundreds of different acts to huge audiences all over the country. (By 1911 one-sixth of New York City residents were said to be attending shows in a vaudeville theatre at least once a week.) The function of music in all of these forms was to support rather than dominate the story or skit, to avoid an appeal for itself alone, or to claim independent value. As had been true for the previous half-century, dramatists who sought to portray the most serious subjects shunned music (with its almost irresistible relationship to the broad gestures of actors) unless they chose to embrace grand opera, the ultimate melodramatic form with its complex collaborative requirements. Self-conscious opera composers for their part, by and large, did not write for the popular stage, although they were by no means unproductive. American opera composers of the period between 1892 and 1912 included Victor Herbert as well as the more academically oriented serious composers Frederick Converse, George Whitefield Chadwick, and Horatio Parker. Herbert was the most successful individual to bridge the gap, and his music is overdue close critical attention.

Besides the live theatre productions, moving pictures grew apace in the first decades of the twentieth century. Many silent films were accompanied by a pianist or small musical ensemble with the function of supplying music appropriate to the mood or activity. Many theatres hired orchestras numbering a dozen or more to play complete scores coordinated to the actions and attitudes of the screen.

The rage for ever larger and more impressive stagings in almost every venue was countered somewhat in the intimate and sophisticated plays made for the Princess Theatre (put up above a former livery stable by F. Ray Comstock in 1913). The auditorium, seating 299, in front of a modestly equipped stage, stood in sharp contrast to the glittering new Palace Theatre, also erected in 1913, the legendary goal of all vaudevillians, or the mammoth Hippodrome (constructed in 1905). The Princess played host to a raft of one-act plays and economical revues, as well as several witty musical comedies composed by Guy Bolton, P. G. Wodehouse, and Jerome Kern. (This same venue would later host such important productions as those of *The Emperor Jones* [1920], *Six Characters in Search of an Author* [1921], and *Pins and Needles* [1937].)

The New American Stage: 1915–1929

The conventions of the English popular stage and the new American ragtime style began to cross-pollinate closely after the turn of the century. (American minstrel-show performers had been touring successfully in the United Kingdom since the 1880s.) English music-hall shows composed by the likes of Leslie Stuart and Ivan Caryll enjoyed a vogue in America; and one American composer who would soon exert a powerful influence worked extensively on both sides of the water. Jerome Kern's (1885–1945) experiences as a young man in the London theatre scene shaped his taste and hence the nature of his productivity for years afterward. Kern's partnership with Englishmen Guy Bolton and P. G. Wodehouse represented a wedding of styles and technical means, together with a concentration on the musical and literary aspects of a show that fed American audiences well for over a generation. Partly as a result of the infusion of Anglo–American cooperation and Kern's ability to assimilate African American elements and popular dances within larger forms, musical comedy since 1914 has been universally identified as an *American* genre, distinct from English comic opera, operetta, or *opéra bouffe*. Within the United States, American productions, with only occasional borrowings from European sources, have been the trendsetters throughout most of the twentieth century. With the exception of a few blockbuster imports, by and large Americans have ceased to look to Europe for models of how to write musical comedies. Kern's accomplishment in particular is held in highest regard. His musical training was thorough and he could be a prickly and uncompromising collaborator, but he wrote an unusually large number of superb songs – in a variety of moods – for some thirty-six shows. The magnitude of his personal influence is striking.

Nobody Home – adopted from the British musical play *Mr. Popple of Ippleton* – the first Princess Theatre musical, was a modest success, running for 135 performances. *Very Good Eddie,* by Bolton, Kern, and lyricist Schuyler Greene, ran for over a year in New York before it began to tour. *Very Good Eddie* well illustrates the nature of the best musical comedy of the period as constructed by Bolton and Kern. The plot about love, marriage, and mistaken identities was plausible, coherent, and lively. The characters were individualized and endearing, and their foibles were recognizably part of everyday life. Sets and costumes were simple and modern. The comedy was topical – indeed, the show's title was borrowed from a familiar line in the hit of the previous season, David Montgomery and Fred Stone's *Chin-Chin* – and the songs were well built and singable, with an eye to the fad of the moment, in this case the hula dance.

The run of successful Princess Theatre shows by the team of Kern, Bolton, and Wodehouse included *Oh, Boy!* (1917), with its hit duet "Till the Clouds Roll By," and *Oh, Lady! Lady!!* (1918). The former borrowed the conventions of French bedroom farce and cleverly combined them with several winning songs assigned well across the uniformly talented cast. It played over four hundred performances in New York, toured successfully, opened in England as *Oh, Joy!,* and even became the subject for a 1919 (silent) film. *Oh, Joy!,* clearly intended as a sequel to *Oh, Boy!,* had little to do with it in any way other than the title and was considerably less successful. (*Oh, Lady Lady!!* is probably most famous for a song that was later lifted from it, "Bill," for use in *Show Boat.*) The success of *Oh, Boy!* was recognized as marking an important new direction in American music comedy. The term "masterpiece," rarely if ever applied even in the vicinity of musical theatre hitherto, was loudly echoed among the critics for this show.

The early 1920s have been characterized by one authority as "a baffling and abrupt creative slump" (Bordman, *American Musical Theatre: A Chronicle,* 362), by which he refers to a lack of quality works of the new type, especially

Scene from black musical, *Shuffle Along* (1921), with Flournoy Miller and Aubrey Lyles. Billy Rose Theatre Collection, New York Public Library for the Performing Arts, Astor, Lenox and Tilden Foundations.

by Kern. There was, however, no lack of activity, audience, or critical acclaim for the productions of the period, which witnessed the largest number of new shows in any decade to date. Once again the ineluctably collaborative nature of the theatre was apparent, and the understanding that a hit show resulted from a team of creative and business-conscious partners was fully appreciated. Audiences did not necessarily expect as tightly conceived a show as Comstock had produced with the combined talents of Kern, Bolton, and Wodehouse. But many other productions seemed to bring out the best from designers, choreographers, and performers, if not writers and composers.

Unquestionably, the most influential musical to come from the African American stage in the decade was Noble Sissle and Eubie Blake's *Shuffle Along* of 1921. While in some respects it represented a revival of the black Broadway shows of the 1898 to 1908 decade, *Shuffle Along* exhibited the formidable modern talent of ragtime composer-pianist Blake. Together with a workable and pleasant book, in a climate somewhat more receptive than before to black talent, Sissle and Blake led a sparkling cast that transported its audiences by sheer kinetic power. Few could gainsay the electricity of the piece: its constant movement, its verbal and melodic flexibility, its choreographic brashness. The frequent flattery of imitation produced a string of look-alike shows in the 1920s, not to mention several latterday revivals. The ease with which the conventions of black dramaturgy have been absorbed into other musicals that make no claim to ethnic statement has also somewhat obscured the importance of the show over time, and a succession of other styles of music has dimmed its memory within the black community. At a time when jazz was still a dangerous and undefined phenomenon – except for its evident association with working-class amusements, suspect popular music, and African American people – Broadway found for itself a protojazz artist who made a powerful impact on audiences. The pervasiveness of race as a preoccupation of Americans almost guaranteed that this show would convey an impression that was greater than the sum of its parts. It has still not enjoyed a full-scale recording.

The general legacy of black dance was felt throughout the decade of the twenties, and regular theatre patrons were conscious of the change. Ziegfeld beauty Gilda Gray noted that "pretty choc'late babies shake and shimmy everywhere" in her 1922 song "It's Getting Dark on Old Broadway." Because of the dance emphasis, many of the post–*Shuffle Along* revues resembled the Ziegfeld leg-show extravanganzas. *Strut Miss Lizzie* (1922) was about "glorifying the Creole Girl" – an obvious homage. However, dance shows served several purposes: They presented black talent in a setting that was both glamorous and virtuosic but avoided the pitfalls of stereotyped stories, minstrel-show anachronisms, and sexually or politically explosive dialogue. Black popular dances, such as the Charleston, could be displayed, professionalized, and commercially exploited without ever reminding white audiences how black dancers (or any other African Americans for that matter) struggled to survive when they were not performing onstage. Harlem shows of all kinds flourished, but consistent access to major Broadway houses remained difficult for black performers to achieve until the 1970s.

In 1924 the longest-running musical of the decade opened. *The Student Prince in Heidelberg*, by Dorothy Donnelly and Sigmund Romberg, based on an older play by Rudolf Bleichmann, gave hope to lovers of sturdy old romantic chestnuts in their Viennese operettas: student drinking songs, lusty choruses, serenades, and marches to accompany passionate stories of a romanticized past. Despite the producers' opposition at first – a musical without a happy ending or a female chorus line seemed the height of folly to the Shubert brothers – it was the biggest moneymaker they ever had. Its excellent quality and a frankly masculine fantasy appeal, with the disguised but dutiful prince doomed never to marry his true love, the show possessed qualities of both exuberance and seriousness that made it a draw for decades. It ran 608 performances in New York and more or less permanently on tour. Romberg's difficulties in getting the show mounted at all reveals that although a good composer could get his work produced, the expectations for musicals in general were fairly specific and rather low. No one had a lock on the formula for success, but there was no lack of formulas to be tried out. Then as now about three-quarters of all new shows flopped. There were just many more of them in the 1920s.

An emerging presence of the 1924 season was George Gershwin, whose *Lady, Be Good!* opened at the Liberty in December, the day before *The Student Prince.* The first show co-written with his brother Ira, *Lady, Be Good!* is also arguably the first Broadway show to convey a kind of jazz style that was deemed safe enough for white audiences. Earlier syncopated tunes masquerading under the name of ragtime had of course been around for decades. The new snappy rhythms and clever slangy lyrics by the inimitable Ira Gershwin, however, made this as different from *The Student Prince* as could be imagined. The pairing of the two shows – so close in time and place, and undoubtedly seen by many of the same viewers – suggests that New York audiences were receptive to the gamut of popular styles as long as the basic plots were diverting and the music was distinctive in tone. Gershwin's "Fascinating Rhythm" was only one of the best among many fine tunes in this show. The novelty of having two pianists in the pit guaranteed that Gershwin's new techniques would be audible. The art deco sets and the star quality of Fred and Adele Astaire also had something to do with the show's yearlong run. The plot, by Guy Bolton and Fred Thompson, was circuitous but ultimately harmless.

Just how far operetta could be made "American" was demonstrated in long-touring *Rose-Marie,* by Otto Harbach and Oscar Hammerstein II (book and lyrics) and Rudolf Friml and Herbert Sothart (music). A story of love and murder set in the Canadian Rockies, Hammerstein referred to his show as "an operatic musical play," an indication of the essential dramatic qualities that he sought to portray. A legitimate actress, Mary Ellis, who had sung minor parts at the Metropolitan Opera, was cast in the title role. The show's creators worked to avoid the impression that their work was a stereotypical musical comedy, and it was not so hard in 1924. An index of the show's novelty and popularity was the establishment of a road tour long before the closing of the New York run. It made a great deal of money for its creators. Extremely well received in London and Paris, where it set a record for the length of its run, *Rose-Marie* was made into a songless movie in 1928 as well as the more famous singing version with Jeanette MacDonald and Nelson Eddy in 1936.

The midtwenties was a fertile period for new shows of all kinds and the cluster of excellent shows between 1925 and 1928 included the work of master songwriters Sigmund Romberg, Rudolf Friml, Rodgers and Hart, the Gershwins, Jerome Kern, Oscar Hammerstein II, Irving Berlin: *No, No Nanette, The Vagabond King, Sunny, Oh, Kay!, The Wild Rose, Peggy Ann, Rio Rita, A*

Connecticut Yankee, Funny Face, The Desert Song, and everyone's favorite, *Show Boat,* were just the highpoints among the dozens of premieres.

Show Boat

The superlatives attached to *Show Boat* by commentators are innumerable and largely justified. The show has held the stage in some form since its opening (27 December 1927) and has suffered no significant dip in popularity or critical esteem from that time to this. For this reason it is widely viewed as the beginning of a type, as well as the epitome of the mature (or "well-rounded" or "integrated") bona fide American musical comedy. Although admitting the importance of precursors, virtually all histories of the genre take it as their first major touchstone. The superiority of *Show Boat* is easy to defend. While not as innovatory as some have claimed, it is a work of consistent quality. It adheres as closely to its literary model, Edna Ferber's novel of the same name, as any musical can be expected to and has been commended especially for retaining its incendiary subplot on the subject of miscegenation and family distintegration. Admittedly, the novel's somewhat dark conclusion, its focus on the materialistic Kim Ravenal, the death of Cap'n Andy, and the sad decline of Julie into prostitution were muted or removed in the musical version, but the show's musical integrity and vitality surmounted all other contemporary shows. It was a landmark in the careers of its creators, Oscar Hammerstein II and Jerome Kern, and a benchmark of American music and theatre. Its songs are readily grouped with those of much later shows without seeming quaint or dated.

Among its many strengths was the setting, a colorful riverside showboat, the *Cotton Blossom,* docked along the Mississippi. Scenes at the 1893 World's Columbian Exposition in Chicago also placed the show one nostalgic generation away from its first hearers and thereby allowed remarkable musical variety that encompassed the entire Tin Pan Alley heyday from the 1890s to 1927 (and making the inclusion of the old million-seller "After the Ball" dissimilar to a mere interpolation). The dramaturgy of the first act has been justifiably celebrated. From the backgrounding by the Mississippi River itself in the masterpiece song "Ol' Man River" to the contrasting opening black and white choruses to the brilliantly conceived love song–introduction of the romantic leads Magnolia and Ravenal ("Make Believe"), the scenes of the act move from strength to strength. Kern's unfailing ear for musical subtlety and the uses of continuous music and Hammerstein's powerful way of making words express high-flown sentiment work to fix this piece just before the modern day – whenever that might be. The setting is not and does not feel like the present, yet the emotions are easily sensed by an audience in the late twentieth century. The distancing exoticism of the Mississippi riverboat is paradoxically close to home, in the middle of America. If Joe and Queenie are less realistically drawn figures than some later African American characters, they are also more removed from the minstrel stereotypes that plagued the stage at the time. Although the "tragic mulatto" stereotype, which Julie exemplifies, had been a staple of nineteenth-century straight plays, the stark and unfair tragedy of Julie and Steve can be perceived without a historical guidebook to accompany the plot. Because stock characters and conventions are selectively cut (the villain is not really a villain, for instance) the tendency to reduce the play to a melodrama is avoided. The show within the show at the outset of the action adds a layer of perspective and credibility, rather than just an excuse for a song and a dance. The traditional choral opening draws the audience into the complex action on that most American of subjects, race relations. We find ourselves interested in the characters and involved in their story because the possibility of their development exists and because we know the reality behind their story. The return of compulsive gambler Ravenal to the *Cotton Blossom* at the end of the show, an obvious concession to sentiment, is not entirely pat or unmotivated by the other strands of the plot in the musical or in the novel.

Although modern audiences are apt to note the operetta qualities of *Show Boat,* the extent to which it strays from conventions of the operatic kind are just as remarkable as its avoidance of the free and easy side of earlier musicals. Kern never equaled *Show Boat. Sweet Adeline* (1929), also a collaboration with Hammerstein, with Helen Morgan of recent *Show Boat* fame, had possibilities. Its romantically haunted heroine was perfectly matched to Morgan's talents, but its run was slowed by the stock-market crash two months after opening night. Hammerstein worked twice more with Kern, but spent most of the thirties involved with shows that ranged from extremely modest successes to outright failures. Kern wrote more wonderful songs, including the famous "Smoke Gets in Your Eyes" for *Roberta* (1933), but died in 1945 at work in New York on a *Show Boat* revival.

The Varieties of Americana in the 1930s

Despite the stock-market crash, the onset of the Great Depression, and a precipitous decline in the number of new shows (a high of more than fifty in the 1927–28 season fell to a mere dozen shows – and mostly rather weak ones at that – in the 1935–36 term) and paid admissions (no show reached the 500-performance mark during the decade from 1929 to 1939), many artists and producers sought to imitate the 1927 success of Hammerstein and Kern. A fuller grasp of the necessity for marshaling a collaborative team, such as Kern had enjoyed with Bolton and Wodehouse, was evident. Moss Hart matched with Irving Berlin to make *Face the Music* (1932) and *As Thousands Cheer* (1933). Many individual song-and-lyric writer teams wrote dozens of good songs for forgettable books or revue medleys. George Gershwin, helped by his brother Ira, continued to generate a respectable income from writing songs for interpolation into a number of established annual revues, such as the *George White Scandals*. Director-producer George Abbott, whose remarkable career spanned this entire golden age of American musicals (the twenties to the sixties) became an important mentor and collaborator for Rodgers and Hart in *On Your Toes* (1936), *Jumbo* (1935), *The Boys from Syracuse* (1938), *Too Many Girls* (1939), and *Pal Joey* (1940). With the old monopolistic trust of theatre producers – the Klaw and Erlanger organization having been successfully challenged by the young Shuberts – new artistic teams were formed and reformed, so that a balanced mix of financial know-how and creative talent could be repeatedly combined to maximize profit. But it was finally the playwrights, composers, and lyricists who had to come up with the hits. Although the Shuberts were dominant in the field of theatre ownership and indeed witnessed the building of virtually all the theatrical houses that now constitute Broadway proper between 1900 and 1929, they developed on their own remarkably few quality shows of the new types in the years afterward.

Besides the disastrous economy, the advent of motion pictures also had a decisive impact on Broadway productions beginning in the 1930s. Audiences flocked to the musical films, leaving the live stage to those who could afford higher ticket prices. Hollywood lured away many good composers, such as Irving Berlin, Gershwin, and Kern – at least temporarily. Broadway producers decided that flimsy books would no longer suffice to serve as narrative frameworks. New story ideas reflected the leftist politics of urban intellectuals, and widespread cynicism was spawned by ineffectual or corrupt politicians. Faced by the continuation of a worldwide depression, writers made books more direct and biting than they had been at any time since the Civil War. Though only a few of these shows succeeded financially, their presence decisively affected the public attitude toward the theatre.

Revues flourished because short self-contained numbers featuring outstanding performers and inexpensive sets would still draw a crowd. Among the most popular of these was Moss Hart and Irving Berlin's profit-making show *As Thousands Cheered* (1933), which used newspaper headlines displayed on curtains as dividers for the various acts. In such a format a serious number, such as Ethel Waters's performance of "Supper Time" – her man misses supper because he has been lynched – was able to be placed side by side with a nostalgic song like "Easter Parade," lighter satires on evangelist Aimee Semple McPherson and John D. Rockefeller as "the world's wealthiest man," or Marilyn Miller's reportedly boisterous impersonation of Joan Crawford. The presence of several songs for Waters, notably the hit "Heat Wave," also revealed that Broadway could, at least in one of its formats, incorporate the artistry of black performers without requiring the trappings of old-fashioned minstrelsy or segregating a group of players in a farcical stereotypical setting. Black versions of older and safe standards included *Swing Mikado* (1939) and *Carmen Jones* (1943), by Gilbert and Sullivan and Bizet, respectively. (Small-scale black versions of European operas and Gilbert and Sullivan shows had also been mounted in the nineteenth century.) Along with the *Blackbirds of 1939,* these shows depended heavily on earlier material or formats with respect to music, but they redesigned dialogue and costumes to suit modern tastes. It was apparently impossible to generate the financial support for an original African American show.

The political climate also encouraged the use of contemporary satire in full-length shows as well as in revues, as long as they did not degenerate into bitterness or outright propaganda. *Pins and Needles,* a labor union show of 1937, with music by Harold Rome, was a surprise hit. Gershwin, Morrie Ryskind, and George S. Kaufman's *Of Thee I Sing,* musical comedy about politics, written before the election of Franklin Roosevelt, won the Pulitzer Prize for drama in 1931, a first for a musical comedy. The creative team's pacing and integration of the songs in the action – about a politician who talks out of both sides of his mouth, campaigns on a ticket advocating love ("Of thee I sing, baby!"), and whose vice-president is so forgettable that even his own party members don't know who he is – did much to assure that the political critique was evenhanded and palatable. Angry statements unleavened by sentiment or a spoonful of honey were bound to discourage audiences, and indeed books that seemed too partisan or spiteful, such as the sequel to *Of Thee I Sing, Let 'Em Eat Cake,* had short lives on the stage.

What amounted to creative committees headed by master artisans, working systematically, and benefited by careful financial underwriting, made the great shows of the 1930s and 1940s possible. Since extraordinary efforts were necessary to make a show pay – even one hundred New York performances in an earlier day would have resulted in a profit, but no longer – precise planning and collaboration were indispensable. This state of affairs also implied the need for a kind of political middle ground with regard to the specific details of the theme and plot.

The prohibitive cost of importing foreign shows in the 1930s encouraged the already growing tendency in the United States to develop shows with nationalist themes and contexts. Stories happened in recognizably American settings, usually urban spaces or suburbs, in a time close to the present, with characters and themes that did not so much recall the exotically tinged stages of Viennese operetta as they did New York City. The best of the lot included Cole Porter's *Anything Goes* (1934), the Rodgers-Hart-George Balanchine wonder *On Your Toes* (1936), the Gershwins' *Porgy and Bess* (1935), Rodgers and Hart's setting of John O'Hara's stories in *Pal Joey* (1940), Kurt Weill's *Lady in the Dark* (1941), and Leonard Bernstein's *On the Town* (1944).

Although foreign shows were inaccessible, the talents of recent immigrants from wartorn Europe were now available to Broadway. It received the works of Kurt Weill somewhat diffidently – his *Threepenny Opera* received only a dozen performances in 1933 – but after his permanent move to the United States both his command of the Broadway medium and his audience numbers improved. More recent viewers have recognized that many of Weill's pieces possessed a durability and a political character that has made them fit for revival. Like other superior classically trained musicians who turned to Broadway, Weill allied himself with established playwrights – Maxwell Anderson and Elmer Rice for *Knickerbocker Holiday* (1938) and *Street Scene* (1947), respectively – and with poets Ogden Nash for *One Touch of Venus* (1943) and Langston Hughes for *Street Scene* (1947). His earliest shows in Germany and in America were propagandistic – political theatre in the purest sense – but even amid *Knickerbocker Holiday*'s unappealing plot about old Dutch Manhattan, Weill turned out one hit tune, "September Song." Weill's command of symphonic and operatic language led him to experiment in interesting ways, and although in a purely commercial sense his impact on theatricals during his lifetime was small, his creative contribution viewed in retrospect has seemed to grow over time.

Weill's *Lady in the Dark* (1941), a story that drew on the popularization of psychoanalysis, cleverly uses music for its dream sequences only, as a foil to the spoken real-time dramatic action. Moss Hart's play is alert to modern sensibilities and sexual tensions, the root causes of the businesswoman-heroine Liza's problems. Ira Gershwin's experienced talent made the lyrics. Liza's fears and fantasies, more than mere passing nightmares or isolated dramatic moments, were explored in what amounted to (in Weill's own words) four "little one-act operas." In a way, perhaps, the words of this show were too good, almost too clever for the lilt of Weill's melodic idiom, which was at times even delicate. It featured the excellent "My Ship," Liza's theme song of fear and questioning, and a patter song for one of Liza's suitors, the eccentric Randall (Danny Kaye's first major Broadway role), based on a listing of Russian composer names (starting with "Tchaikowsky"). The dream sequence was not a novelty on the stage or even in a musical (Rodgers and Hart's *I Married an Angel* of 1938 featured a dream ballet in each of its two acts), but the strength of the ensemble, comprising rising stars Gertrude Lawrence, Victor Mature, Macdonald Carey, and Danny Kaye, created a powerful synergy that kept audiences coming for 467 performances. The war in Europe prevented what might have been an even more extended run abroad.

The successful shows of the period seemed to confirm that a critical balance of elements had to be maintained if a hit was to result. The parts of that formula included a tight structure so that the activity (and the plot if one existed) did not flag; music that exhibited the exuberance of syncopation in fast numbers and the proper harmonic language of modern sentimentality in the slower pieces; clever lyrics; and superior execution. Modern humor and a dash of political cynicism also helped.

The Songs of the 1930s

If Broadway in the thirties did not generate nearly so many musicals as it had in the 1920s, the number of high-quality theatre songs and excellent performers easily met and matched those of the earlier decade. A show with a weak book and pedestrian music was obviously doomed to a short life, but excellent songs, once launched from the stage, could have lives of their own after a show closed. It is important to note the theatrical origins of so many popular songs of the thirties, because the musical stage – along with the burgeoning movie musical – as a point of dissemination for American music was perhaps as powerful as it would ever be, and it set a pattern that has not changed appreciably during the remainder of the century, despite the overwhelming importance of sound recording as a medium.

Good songwriters were, almost by definition, writers of musical comedies. Though the reception of shows varied for many reasons, the consistently high quality in the music of Kern, Gershwin, Cole Porter, and Irving Berlin was sometimes enough to make a show viable. Expectations of a musical comedy plot were still modest enough that truly fine songs were essential to justifying the price of admission. All of the best songwriters were master craftsmen working in miniature. These men imbued the standard thirty-two-measure refrain (this was generally the most memorable part of a show song) with the harmonic suppleness of a technically modern style. Besides overcoming the well-known restrictions of the form, there was more to writing hits than merely "learning how to say 'I love you' in thirty-two bars." Chords that struck nineteenth-century listeners as dissonant, shatteringly disruptive, or even decadent were suavely assimilated during the 1930s in numbers small enough to be palatable (and even pleasantly distracting) within a rigid and highly predictable song form. Such a mix proved a formula for success, especially when it included a catchy new beat or dance rhythm. Having survived the modernities of ragtime and jazz, young audiences of the thirties embraced the coloristic chord palette of Jerome Kern and Richard Rodgers and the bluesy, syncopated style of George Gershwin.

When aided by good lyricists, as most of these were, the musicians were also adept at using a relatively small amount of basic music material to spin out and connect whole acts. Their songs within a show made structural con-

Rodgers and Hart's *Pal Joey* (1940) with Gene Kelly. Photo by Fred Fehl. Harry Ransom Humanities Research Center, The University of Texas at Austin.

tact with each other, so to speak, by sharing key melodic fragments or dramatic chord changes. Their songwriting blossomed into scene writing to the delight of thousands of unwitting but transfixed listeners. The oldest devices of melodrama – a tremolo here and a poignant chord there – were now being woven into larger tapestries. *Porgy and Bess* (1935), a work of this type, can lay claim to full operatic status, but its success over the years attests to its place in the line of mature musical theatre pieces as well.

When good lyrics and tunes were matched with innovative books, Broadway began to achieve exceptional results. The initial reception to *Pal Joey* (1940), based on stories about a sleazy night-club manager, which originally appeared in a personal letter format in *The New Yorker* magazine, provides an excellent gauge of American thinking about the proper domain of the musical comedy. Scored by many of its first critics as morally objectionable and musically meager, it nevertheless achieved a respectable run of 374 performances in its initial Broadway outing (making it a good but not remarkable commercial vehicle for the Rodgers and Hart team). Ultimately, in part because the show contained a song that had stood the test of time, "Bewitched, Bothered, and Bewildered," sung by the show's savvy antiheroine, Vera (originally Vivienne Segal), the 1952 revival had a greater impact than its first outing. (All of the principals' songs illuminated the plot and the characters in a fashion that surpassed the norm.) Still, by 1952 Joey's risqué amorality, the clever but brutally honest dialogue, the elements of promiscuity, exploitation, and blackmail that first struck even mature critics as offensive had become almost quaint or at least familiar. Still, at its premiere *Pal Joey* was different because it had an edge – one softened by wit and sentimental moments to be sure – that few other shows dared approach.

Rodgers and Hammerstein: Act One

After a famously mixed tryout in New Haven, *Oklahoma!* opened on 31 March 1943 at the St. James Theatre in the heart of Broadway. It continued to run at the St. James for approximately twenty-two hundred performances, over three times as long as the previous record holder for Broadway original cast musicals (*Irene* of 1919, which scored 670 performances; straight plays *Tobacco Road* [1933] and *Life with Father* [1939] had exceeded three thousand performances.) It toured continuously for a decade and has been acted and sung by hundreds of professional and amateur groups the world over, more or less without interruption, since that time. Its position in the history of the American musical in the twentieth century is therefore somewhat analogous to that of *Uncle Tom's Cabin* (1852), a phenomenally successful play (based on the Stowe novel) that remained in repertory for nearly a century, always liberally illustrated with musical interpolations. *Oklahoma!* is, of course, not the political document that *Uncle Tom's Cabin* was, yet in its own way it captured and crystallized the values that dominated in the United States during a time of national crisis (and conspicuous unity) and therefore made an impact that was felt well beyond the streets of New York. Again like *Uncle Tom,* it was a melodrama, a somewhat simplified version of its original play, Lynn Riggs's *Green Grow the Lilacs,* with music and lyrics that depicted gender roles in a formulaic fashion, albeit in a refreshingly uncynical and innocent manner. Enthusiastic and buoyant without being silly or utterly enslaved to recent Broadway conventions, *Oklahoma!* was a coherent, positive American show, yet far, far removed from the additive revue format, the pyrotechnics of operetta prima donnas, chorus girl kicklines, political satire, or just bad stories and pointless music that had characterized so many shows of the 1920s and 1930s. It is easy to tally *Oklahoma!*'s virtues, less easy to understand how they fit so perfectly together. The "open air" feeling of the opening number, "Oh, What a Beautiful Morning," the virgor and affirmation of the title song, the psychological sensitivity of Laurie's dream ballet, the craftsmanship of the love song, "People Will Say We're in Love," the avoidance of scenic extremes – all of these made for an extraordinary achievement.

Both of *Oklahoma!*'s principal creators had achieved Broadway successes beforehand, but they had never worked together. It was not clear that their first collaboration would be successful until it happened. Their subsequent work (covered in Vol. III of this history) put all others in the shade until Hammerstein's death in 1960. Rodgers's musical finesse and clarity and Hammerstein's poetic lyrics proved a brilliantly effective combination time after time. The full dimensions of their accomplishments were of course still to be seen in 1945. They also enjoyed the benefits of a supportive team of musical arrangers, stage designers, directors, actors, and dancers. The temper of the times and an expanding economy were with them.

Like the blithe and innocent *Oklahoma!,* the soberly moralistic story of *Carousel* introduced a dreamlike ballet in addition to well-used melodramatic devices. In the 1909 world hit *Liliom* (by Ferenc Molnár and later adapted by Benjamin Glazer, who had worked with earlier translations by Lorenz Hart), Rodgers and Hammerstein found a second Theatre Guild play (from its 1921 season) apt for musical adaptation. Others had sought to set it to music, but Rodgers finally won Molnár's consent. The story of Liliom/Billy Bigelow is that of the ne'er-do-well who tries and fails to reform his life for love's sake. Billy is a brutish carnival barker who falls for a poor mill worker, Julie Jordan. Both lose their jobs and their hearts almost immediately, but unlike most twenties musicals, when all would end happily, this pair is doomed to an unhappy and brief marriage that ends with a father's suicide and a hapless teenage daughter reliving the sad story of her father's ostracism and isolation. Although on the surface this sounds like a depressing story of female passivity and male abuse, it has proved to be a resilient vehicle, filled with some of Rodgers and Hammerstein's best material.

The superb lyrics and music were once again combined with the choreography of Agnes de Mille and the creative direction of Rouben Mamoulian – especially in the famous opening merry-go-round pantomime – and placed in an 1870s New England seaside setting that allowed for the development of the complex main characters, the unhappy lovers Julie and Billy. Their very inarticulateness, made explicit in the songs "You're a Queer One, Julie Jordan" and "If I Loved You" provided the perfect opportunity for music to give emotional expression to feelings that could not be spoken. The most celebrated addition to the original play is the famous "Soliloquy," about Billy's thoughts of his impending fatherhood, which provides him the necessary platform from which to earn the audience's sympathy.

The addition of a fantastic and somewhat pat final redemption for Billy has been scored as oversentimental, but Rodgers's restraint in the use of the ersatz hymn "You'll Never Walk Alone" and the highly economical use of both dialogue and other melodramatic music in the second act is far more deft than he is sometimes given credit for. The musical language itself – unusually modern chords and dissonances are introduced in the very opening measures of the infectious title waltz, and musical motives are subsequently woven through the work – show a marked advance in modernistic technique that sets it apart from *Oklahoma!*. Rodgers claimed that *Carousel* was his favorite among his own works, and it is easy to see why. Although its religiosity and the introduction of judgmental heavenly characters may strike some as embarassing or silly, these elements have not kept audiences away. They had proved themselves inoffensive in a "musical fantasy" of 1940, *Cabin in the Sky* (in which a similarly incorrigible husband, matched with a devout wife, is confronted by heavenly emissaries and given a second chance for redemption). *Carousel,* of course, eliminated the African American element – and with that the fine singing of Ethel Waters and Todd Duncan in the earlier show – although not the theme of outsiders finding their place. The American flavor is indeed especially evident in these associations and relationships, the more conspicuously with a Puritanical New England backdrop. Although the success of *Carousel* has never come up to the impressive heights of *Oklahoma,* it is now a classic.[1]

Carousel, because it was an unusually successful sequel to *Oklahoma!,* also encouraged the collaborators to pursue their favorite formulas again and again. As they established the techniques of effective integration of music and story, they also made money and ensured that their works would serve as models for others. That the team of Rodgers and Hammerstein became synonymous with "musical comedy" in the 1950s says it all. They stood for solid stories told about sincere good-hearted Americans, serious sentiments, beautiful vocal melodies, poetic lyrics, a smooth connection among all the constituent elements, and an insistence that functional entertainment music within the proper dramatic vehicle could aspire to the transcendance of art. Until the heyday of choreographers and directors dawned, their work was dominant. No composer came along until Stephen Sondheim, whose musical acuity would result in a comparable string of artistic achievements. Only Andrew Lloyd Webber has reached their commercial success.

Note

1 Editors' note: It is appropriate that this chapter end with a brief discussion of the Rodgers and Hammerstein collaboration and their innovative musical *Carousel*. It is just as fitting that John Degen's chapter on musical theatre in Volume III also begins with this collaboration and a more extended analysis of the importance of *Carousel.*

Bibliography: Musical Theatre

Books about musical theatre between 1900 and 1945 are numerous and mostly indiscriminately adulatory, long on reminiscence and opinion, short on analysis, although occasionally well stocked with period photographs. The critiques, such as they are, tend to be concentrated on a relatively small group of shows, or the most famous composers of the age, such as Kern, Berlin, Porter, Rodgers and Hammerstein, Gershwin, and Bernstein. The best of these biographies are Bergreen, *As Thousands Cheer: The Life of Irving Berlin;* Jablonski, *Gershwin;* and Gill's *Cole.* Kreuger, *Show Boat: The Story of a Classic American Musical,* is essentially a production history as well as a rare paean to a landmark show, prepared for its fiftieth anniversary.

No thorough and comprehensive history of the pre–*Show Boat* years exists, although the primary resources for examining these works are considerable. The sixteen volumes, with forty-eight separate works, from Garland Press, entitled *Nineteenth-Century American Musical Theatre* (1994, 1995), constitutes an extremely helpful collection – the first of its kind for American musicals in this period – in which both general reader and scholar can easily examine facsimile reprints of both plays and the music they contain in the same source. Deane Root, the editor of the series, has also produced his own *American Popular Stage Music 1860–1880,* a work that is well organized, highly informative, and copious in its discussion of musical detail. Cecil Smith, *Musical Comedy in America* (1950), is still the most interesting and detailed account of the fifty years before *Show Boat,* though far more anecdotal and less conspicuously scholarly than Root. His colorful, concrete, and opinionated work is an excellent survey, recording the assessments of an experienced theatregoer and observer. Despite his disclaimer of system or scholarly rigor, it is a fascinating and coherent account from the period between *The Black Crook* and *South Pacific.* Gilbert, *American Vaudeville: Its Life and Times* (1940), is a rich source, comparable to Smith for nonbook show entertainments.

The best and most thorough history that blossoms out of biography (but nevertheless supplies exhaustive details about turn-of-the-century developments) is *From Bowery to Broadway: Lew Fields and the Roots of American Popular Theatre,* by Armond and L. Marc Fields. Over 500 pages of lure, lore, and anecdote, along with extensive documentation and analysis, this labor of love grounded in the life and work of knockabout comedians turned producers, Weber and Fields, is far more than homage to the authors' forebears. Its subject is the detail within and the motivation for American vaudeville and variety from 1890 to 1930.

Among recent writers with a more skeptical turn of mind and less given to unqualified accolades, Bordman has most successfully summarized the entire panoply of musical theatre, with his several books, notably, *American Musical Theatre: A Chronicle* (revised, 1992). For all of its detail, it is far more than a mere list. Bordman provides excellent signposts in the form of chapter introductions, summaries, and inserted biographies, as well as a boldface entry for every show that he could lay his hands on between 1767 and 1990. Although not unique in its witty and trenchant style or taste for detail, this book is full of hidden riches in its compilation of astute musical observations and its assessment of historical context, but it is somewhat sparing in praise for modern musicals. Stanley Green and Lehman Engel were among the most prolific and respected Broadway aficionados, each with several essays, lists, books, and commentaries to his credit. For Green the most notable are *The World of Musical Comedy* (1960 and revised continuously), *The Great Clowns of Broadway, Ring Bells! Sing Songs!, Encyclopedia of the Musical Theatre, Broadway Musicals: Show by Show,* and *The Rodgers and Hammerstein Fact Book.* Engel, *Words with Music: The Broadway Musical Libretto,* examines the shape and dynamics of musical comedy construction from a conductor's viewpoint.

Gänzl, *The Encyclopedia of the Musical Theatre,* provides 1,600 pages of efficient description in over three thousand entries, most devoted to individual shows and their creators. Restricted to book shows (but not opera), and therefore neglectful of vaudeville, revues, extravaganzas, and other hybrids, this is an otherwise excellent compilation. Its use as a musical information source is limited. Mates, *America's Musical Stage* (1985), while summarizing "two hundred years of musical theatre" fairly efficiently, has largely been superseded.

Two books, both thoroughly documented, that discuss the history of African American shows at some length are Woll, *Black Musical Theatre from Coontown to Dreamgirls* and Riis, *Just Before Jazz: Black Musical Theatre in New York, 1890 to 1915*. The latter contains an appendix of eight musical scores. Toll, *Blacking Up* (1974), though chiefly devoted to the (mostly white) minstrel show in the 1840s and 1850s, is also helpful on sketching the history of "genuine" black entertainers at the end of the nineteenth century. Other useful references to black shows, printed reviews, and production data include Sampson, *Blacks in Blackface* and Peterson, *A Century of Musicals in Black and White: An Encyclopedia of Musical Stage Works By, About or Involving African-Americans*. The former is poorly edited and not entirely reliable. The latter is a model of thoroughness. See also sources on minstrely in Chapter 5's bibliographic essay.

Books by Abe Laufe, Ethan Mordden, David Ewen, Howard Taubman, Miles Kreuger, Martin Gottfried, and others are interesting but sometimes idiosyncratic and only spottily supported by scholarly citations. Typical is Mordden's recent *Make Believe: The Broadway Musical in the 1920s.* They are nevertheless well worth consulting, because all provide insights into the loyalty and enthusiasm that musicals have engendered since they arose in modern form during the 1890s.

Mast, *Can't Help Singin': The American Musical Comedy on Stage and Screen* is well documented, engagingly written, and, at times, highly provocative. (The bibliography of film musicals suffers from the same rhetorical overindulgences that plague writings about the Broadway musical stage, but there are signs of improvement for the future in a spate of recent articles.) The business history of musicals is supplied in Bernheim, *The Business of The Theatre;* Poggi, *Theatre in America: The Impact of Economic Forces;* and Rosenberg and Harburg, *The Broadway Musical: Collaboration in Commerce and Art.*

The music published from 1890 on is widely available in commercial facsimile reprints as well as in sheet-music archives in university libraries across the country (although determining a song's relationship to a show in the first place is not always easy). Appelbaum's edition of *Show Songs from the Black Crook to the Red Mill* contains sixty items in facsimile from 1866 to 1906, along with a helpful introduction, individual show biographies, and illustrations. Alec Wilder, *American Popular Song: The Great Innovators, 1900–1950,* is a highly specific musical analysis of some eight hundred songs by over two hundred composers and lyricists that nevertheless retains readability. Hamm, *Yesterdays: Popular Song in America,* is also an excellent and well-crafted narrative. The most musicological of books about the musical theatre is Swain, *The Broadway Musical: A Critical and Musical Survey,* analyses of fourteen hit shows from *Show Boat* to *Sweeney Todd.* While forbidding to nonreaders of music, and highly traditional in its formalist assumptions, Swain's is one of few books by a musician to examine the musical mechanics of successful Broadway shows and to explain convincingly the reasons that musical gestures work the way they do.

Among several other strong reference works on musicals, Kenneth Bloom, *American Song: The Complete Musical Theatre Companion,* is massive and superbly indexed. Suskin, *Show Tunes 1905–1985: The Songs, Shows and Careers of Broadway's Major*

Composers, is the most complete of several books of its type (providing data about the principle performers, runs, published songs, etc.). Raymond, *Show Music on Record: The First 100 Years* [1890–1990], is a specialized reference by an authoritative collector to the cylinders and discs created at the beginnings of sound recording history. The importance of recordings in assessing the performance practices and reception history of musical comedies has only begun to be recognized. However, an invaluable resource is the four-part, fifteen-hour-plus CD series on the Pearl Label (Pavilion Records, England) of *Music From the New York Stage, 1890–1920.* Recorded on twelve discs, an astonishing group of artists perform songs (some three hundred tracks) from most early musicals (indeed, virtually every extant original-cast performance is included).

A complementary bibliographic essay by John Degen appears in Volume III of this history.

7

Actors and Acting

Daniel J. Watermeier

Introduction

The period from the end of the Civil War to the onset of the Great Depression was the most dynamic in the history of the American stage. General economic prosperity and expanding urban populations fueled a demand for theatrical entertainment and an ever greater number of actors. Emerging young talents overlapped waning older stars. Traditional and new acting approaches and dramatic material jockeyed for audience attention and critical recognition. The acting profession, long held in disrepute, gradually attained an unprecedented level of social respectability. For the acting profession, it was a dynamic, progressive time, although not without significant organizational and artistic tensions and conflicts. Since other essays in this volume describe how organizational changes – the long run, touring combinations, managerial monopolies, and so forth – affected actors, this chapter concentrates principally on signal developments within the acting profession, on shifts in acting style, and on the leading, most celebrated actors of the era.

The Gilded Age: 1870–1915

The Profession Expands

After the Civil War, the number of actors steadily increased. The 1870 census reported two thousand actors and actresses; by 1890 this figure had grown almost fivefold. By 1912 there were more than fifteen thousand actors (see Winter, *Wallet of Time, I,* 28). This figure probably included only legitimate performers. If one adds professional showpeople – dancers, circus perform-

446

ers, and variety artists – there were possibly as many as thirty to forty thousand employed in some form of theatre or popular entertainment at the turn of the century. Regardless of the accuracy of the figures, that there was significant growth in the profession is indisputable.

Resident companies and the evolving combination system offered unprecedented job opportunities for Gilded Age actors. The larger New York companies employed as many as fifty players. At the beginning of the era, reflecting the standard repertoire of the day, a company usually contained twice as many actors as actresses. Later in the century, with the increasing popularity of English society comedy and French "sensation" drama, both largely centered on heroines rather than heroes, the number of women's roles was almost equal to the number of men's. By the turn of the century, actresses (or show women) comprised over 40 percent of the profession, far greater than the percentage of women in any other profession of the time (see McArthur, 30). Actors were hired on a seasonal basis, but one could reasonably expect to be rehired from season to season. Some actors remained with the same company much of their careers, most stayed only a season or two and then moved on. Turnover, even among the largest and most respected companies, was fairly high, often because of the lure of starring. Actors moved to secure better roles, higher pay, and perhaps greater attention and appreciation from a different audience, always hopeful that the next rung of the ladder would lift them to the heights of the profession.

In *The Wallet of Time* (1912), William Winter listed the names of dozens of star actors and actresses active during the period from 1871 to 1891 (24–27), many of whom earned princely incomes of $100,000 or more a season. Below the stars were numerous leading actors, comedians, character, and utility actors. In the period 1880–1900, leading men and ladies could make up to $250 a week; character actors, $100 a week; juveniles and ingenues, $75 a week; and general utility and chorus players, $18 a week. Salaries on Broadway were slightly higher than for touring; first-class combination companies paid more than second-class companies. There was no uniform salary scale; actors negotiated their own terms, and there could be a significant range of pay even for comparable roles.

Established performers who worked steadily had incomes that compared favorably with other middle-class occupations of the time. Most actors, however, regularly experienced periods of unemployment. There were more opportunities, but also more actors; competition remained keen. In 1900, with more companies touring than ever before, nearly 30 percent of the actors and 40 percent of the actresses reported they were unemployed. Comparatively few players, moreover, ever reached star or leading status, or even a role on Broadway or in a first-class combination. Many had to be content working in either provincial stock or touring in claptrap melodrama. Yet despite the uncertainty of steady employment, the rigors of touring, and almost certain career disappointment, with each new season an increasing number of aspiring actors were attracted to the stage.

Actor Training

Many late-nineteenth-century actors were born into theatrical families, although theatrical parents were not always eager to have their children follow in their footsteps. Junius Brutus Booth, for example, planned a medical career for his son Junius Jr., whereas Edwin was to become a lawyer or cabinetmaker. Even after both chose the stage, the elder Booth was not particularly supportive, but the Booth name undoubtedly opened doors that would have been closed to theatrical outsiders. Without family connections, or the support of a relative or friend in the profession, obtaining even an entry-level position was not easy. Usually aspiring actors petitioned managers or agents for an audition. If an audition was secured and proved successful, then an aspiring professional might with luck and diligence gradually advance in the company from utility roles to walking lady or gentleman, then to juvenile or ingenue, and finally to an established line of business as a principal character actor or leading man or lady. With each rung in this career ladder, players expanded their knowledge of the standard repertoire and honed their inherent acting talent and skills. Young actors might occasionally be coached by an older performer or take classes in elocution, singing, dancing, and fencing, but training evolved principally through observation, often imitation, and experience. It was not a systematic approach, but it had endured for decades.

With the decline of resident companies, there arose a need for a new approach to training. As early as 1871, fledgling actor Steele MacKaye (1842–1894) called for the establishment of an acting school, the American equivalent of the French Conservatoire. For eight months in 1869–70, MacKaye had studied in Paris with the teacher-theorist François Delsarte, who in the 1830s advocated that acting return to nature, to instinct and feeling, as its source of inspiration, and away from the imitative, studied, declamatory conventions taught at the Conservatoire. Over the next few decades Delsarte refined his course into an elaborate system of actor training, which though embedded in a complicated aesthetic philosophy, was based primarily on observations of human behavior. MacKaye, the leading exponent of Delsartism in America, developed in the 1870s and 1880s a notable career as actor, playwright, theatre manager, and visionary, and made a lasting contribution as an acting teacher. MacKaye's first acting school, the St. James School, was in operation for only six months, but MacKaye persisted. He founded two other relatively short-lived schools and then in 1884, in association with Franklin H.

Sargent, he organized the Lyceum Theatre School. A quarrel with Sargent, however, forced MacKaye to leave the Lyceum after a year. Under Sargent's leadership, it was renamed The New York School of Acting, and in 1892 The American Academy of Dramatic Arts, under which name it exists to the present day. With some of their own modifications and embellishments, training in the MacKaye–Sargent schools followed Delsartean principles and practices. The academy attracted numerous dedicated teachers, including not only Sargent but also the playwright-producer-director David Belasco and Charles Jehlinger, a graduate of its first class, who subsequently led the acting program until his death in 1951.

The American Academy of Dramatic Arts was the leading, but not the only turn-of-the-century acting school. Among other seminal schools were Charles W. Emerson's College of Oratory, Samuel Silas Curry's School of Expression, the Leland Powers School of the Spoken Word, the Stanhope–Wheatcroft School, which was connected with Charles Frohman's Empire Theatre, and F. F. Mackay's National Dramatic Conservatory. Several of these remained in operation well into the twentieth century. The College of Oratory, for example, evolved into Emerson College, whereas the School of Expression became Curry College – both today well-regarded liberal arts colleges, the former with a strong academic theatre program. Acting schools were not immediately embraced by older members of the profession for whom experience was still the best teacher. Gradually, however, criticism abated as an increasing number of school-trained actors succeeded in the profession. Between 1886 and 1925, nearly two thousand students graduated from the Academy of Dramatic Arts, many of whom became active in both the theatre and in the nascent film industry. As McTeague argues persuasively, at the turn of the century American acting schools were teaching and exploring techniques often thought to be introduced only after the arrival of Stanislavsky in 1923 (242–54).

Social Status

In midcentury America age-old prejudices continued to cling to actors, with reputations as drunkards and profligates, and actresses were supposedly women with loose morals. Constant travel, poor pay, periods of unemployment, and a certain clannishness among actors contributed to this social marginalization. The scantily costumed onstage performances and offstage escapades of Adah Isaacs Menken, the assassination of Lincoln by John Wilkes Booth, the scandalous divorce of Edwin Forrest and Catherine Sinclair, and other less publicized incidents reinforced negative public opinion. A few leading performers, however, earned a certain social acceptance. Actress Charlotte Cushman, for instance, counted among her friends numerous leading artists and writers. Generally, players might be applauded, even held in awe, but they were not considered a part of bourgeois society.

In the latter part of the century attitudes toward actors began to shift. A number of trends within society and the profession account for the change. With more disposable money and leisure time, as a result of a decreased work week, Gilded Age urbanites increasingly sought new recreational opportunities and venues. A range of sports and sporting events, outdoor pursuits, and theatrical entertainment were enthusiastically embraced. Recreation, no longer regarded as idle amusement, was a beneficial, integral part of life. Even the religious community, long a foe of theatre, now condoned and even encouraged the pursuit of amusement, as long as it was not carried to the extreme. Actors benefited from this attitudinal shift. Moreover, as their numbers expanded, and as theatrical organizations became more centralized and specialized, actors asserted a new professional self-consciousness.

Movement toward professionalism was evident in the founding of theatrical charities to aid distressed actors. The benefit performance, long the traditional method of aiding actors in financial need, was effective when the actor was well known. But ill, aging, or indigent common players were frequently neglected. Several charitable funds were established in the first part of the century, including the General Theatrical Fund (1829), the American Dramatic Fund Association (1848), and the Actors' Order of Friendship (1849). Yet membership in these organizations remained relatively small and their financial resources were limited. In 1882, the Actors' Fund of America was founded. Financed principally by an annual series of special performances, the Actors' Fund, in its first decade of operation, contributed over $160,000 to assist thousands of theatrical workers, from legitimate actors to stagehands. In 1902, the Actors' Fund Home was established on Staten Island to offer a final refuge to aged players. Maintaining a sound financial base for Fund activities was often difficult, but it continues to operate today.

The organization of professional actor associations was another step toward professionalism. In 1894, for example, the Actors' Society of America (ASA) was founded with the aim of promoting a professional image for actors and to address through collective action some of the employment problems continually facing them – such as the lack of standardized contracts and wages. ASA urged its members to contract only with its approved list of reputable managers and worked diligently to improve dressing-room conditions, end the common practice of play piracy, enhance communication within the profession, and raise performance standards. ASA also raised professional consciousness, and it was the foundation on which the Actors' Equity Association (AEA, or Equity), was built in 1916.

Professional life was also enhanced with the founding of theatrical social clubs in the nineteenth century. Numerous exclusive gentlemen's clubs existed in New York, but even notable, wealthy stars were generally excluded from these clubs. In the late 1880s, for example, Lester Wallack, Edwin Booth, and Lawrence Barrett were the only actor members of the Century, and Wallack was the only actor member of the Union Club. The Lambs Club, founded in 1875, was the first important New York theatrical club, but The Players, founded in 1888 by Edwin Booth, was the most prestigious. Booth wanted The Players to be a club in which actors would mingle with other artists, writers, and arts patrons. Having prominent businessmen, financiers, and political leaders as members, he hoped, would raise the social status of actors and the profession as a whole while association with other artists would win acceptance of acting as an art equal to other arts. With his own funds, Booth purchased a four-story residence at 16 Gramercy Park, an exclusive New York neighborhood at the time. He had the noted Beaux Arts architect Stanford White remodel it for a clubhouse. Booth also donated his own extensive collection of theatrical books to start a member's library. The dining room, lounges, bar, and billiard room were decorated with theatrical portraits and memorabilia, creating an atmosphere that was partly dignified gentlemen's club and partly theatrical museum. In 1904 a third theatrical club, The Friars, was organized. All three continue to operate to the present day.

These new actors' clubs were exclusively men's clubs. Women were not even admitted as guests or visitors, for example, to the Lambs Club. In the 1890s, however, actresses founded two clubs of their own: The Twelfth Night Club (1891) and the Professional Women's League (1892). The latter had a social function but also offered a range of services to actresses, including legal advice and classes on sewing, music, French, and stage dancing.

Professional organizations, acting schools, and social clubs encouraged solidarity and professional standards. An explosion of newspapers, photo engraving, and mass-market illustrated magazines brought actors widespread public recognition and social prominence. Inexpensive individual *carte de visite* photographs and photo albums of stars were sold in theatres and book stores. *McClure's, Cosmopolitan, Colliers,* and *Leslie's* regularly ran features – often promoted by professional press agents – about prominent actors. Public interest in the lives of stars seemed insatiable.

For some actors, prosperity coupled with celebrity brought a certain social and political influence. American actors historically were not active in politics or social-reform causes, with the notorious exception of John Wilkes Booth. Perhaps the itinerant nature of the profession and long-standing social exclusion were barriers to social and political engagement. Or, not wishing to offend audience members, actors avoided activities that could be controversial. However, in the latter part of the century, a number of actors and actresses worked for social-reform causes. Actress and writer Olive Logan was particularly active in the cause of women's rights. Julia Marlowe and

Minnie Maddern Fiske were among several prominent actresses who fought for suffrage and women's rights. Actor and playwright James A. Herne campaigned for several reform causes, including tax reform, and berated fellow actors for their political apathy. Most actors, however, remained politically disengaged. By the turn of the century, although segments of the population would retain an ambivalent attitude, actors and the acting profession had achieved a more widespread and much higher level of public respectability than had existed a generation before.

Acting Styles and Stars

Winter thought the era 1870–1912 a "Golden Age" of American acting, unequaled, as he wrote in *The Wallet of Time* (1912), "in the richness and variety of excellence in acting then visible" (27). Garff Wilson in *A History of American Acting* divides dramatic actors of the period into four major "schools": the Classic; the Heroic, a variation in large part on classical acting; the Emotional; and Personality. Comic specialists were a "school" unto themselves. Wilson's divisions do help chart the major stylistic variations in this histrionically fertile era, although they are somewhat problematic. There were, for example, leading performers who, over the course of their careers, played a range of roles, embracing more than one school, and, thus, they are not easily pigeonholed. Moreover, Gilded Age acting tended to veer between a late Romantic theatricalism and an emerging naturalism, or between the ideal and the real. Differences among actors in terms of style were determined by the roles they played, by their distinctive personalities, and by the degree to which their playing steered between acting traditions and conventions and the need to create an illusion of reality – that is, a recognizable, believable verisimilitude in gesture, vocal delivery, and emotional expression.

Acting in any age is largely defined by its stars. Within the confines of this chapter, profiling even a small percentage of the numerous leading actors of the era is prohibitive. Fortunately, sketches are readily available in contemporaneous accounts by Winter, Strang, Hutton, and others, and in a score of modern historical studies and biographies, many of which are cited in the Bibliography. I will focus, however, on a few major figures as representative of many Gilded Age stars and their stylistic permutations.

In the 1870s and 1880s, Edwin Booth was widely acknowledged to be the leading exemplar of the classical style, as well as the standard bearer of the profession. Although his career flourished, Booth was beset by personal shocks. Earlier in 1863 he had been devastated by the unexpected death of his wife Mary "Mollie" Devlin. His production of *Hamlet* won enthusiastic critical appraisal and played continuously for 100 performances, yet three weeks

Edwin Booth painted by John Singer Sargent (1890). The Hampden-Booth Theatre Library at The Players.

after the close of this *Hamlet*, misfortune struck again when his brother John Wilkes assassinated President Abraham Lincoln.

In 1866 the Winter Garden, which Booth then managed, and all of his stock of scenery, costumes, and properties was destroyed by fire. He set about building his own theatre, Booth's Theatre, which when it opened early in 1869 was one of the finest and most modern theatres of the era. However, poor business management, the duplicity of his business partner, and the financial panic of 1873 combined to plunge Booth into bankruptcy and the loss of his theatre.

Booth never again attempted management; instead, for the next twenty years, he toured, solidifying a reputation as America's foremost classical tragedian. His mature repertoire consisted of fifteen, mostly Shakespearean, roles that he played repeatedly, polishing them to diamondlike brilliance. He was at his best in the portrayal of brooding, melancholy characters like Hamlet – his greatest creation – or Brutus, or in capturing darkly sinister characters like

Iago. He was also successful in playfully comic roles, such as Benedick and Petruchio, or as the wily, histrionic Cardinal Richelieu in Edward Bulwer-Lytton's historical melodrama, *Richelieu* (1838).

One of the hallmarks of Booth's acting style was his vocal, physical, and emotional restraint, or "quietude," the chief quality that distinguished his acting from the emotional volatility of the earlier Romantic school. Mollie Devlin called his style, the "conversational, colloquial school." Booth himself thought his acting was "quieter" than his celebrated father's. He spoke Shakespeare's verse as if it were "natural conversation," mainly by using pauses and verbal emphases in a way that broke up the regular, formal meter but that created a new rhythm emphasizing meaning. Generally his physical actions also seemed to arise "naturally" and harmoniously out of the interplay between dialogue, character, and scene; they were planned, but in performance, they appeared spontaneous and dynamic. Booth was attentive to the details of realistic costuming and makeup, but the distinctiveness of his wide-ranging characterizations depended on much more fundamental factors. No matter whether the character was Hamlet, Petruchio, or Richelieu, he "naturalized" these extraordinary figures and made them seem recognizably human. Yet, although Booth's representation was natural, it was not "naturalistic." Indeed, Booth generally disdained a growing tendency toward "vulgar naturalism" as an approach inappropriate to great drama. He aimed – as Lewes wrote in *Actors and the Art of Acting* – to select, heighten, sublimate nature: "to represent ideal character with such truthfulness that it shall affect us as real, not to drag down ideal character to the vulgar level" (103).

Misfortune continued to plague Booth. During the 1880s, he suffered the death of an infant son; a generally unhappy second marriage; a near-fatal carriage accident; an assassination attempt; and the long illness, insanity, and death of his second wife. These personal traumas, however, seemed to deepen his artistry. In the Gilded Age, Booth was without peer as a classical actor. Working in his shadow, however, were several first-rate tragedians.

Lawrence Barrett's (1838–91) reputation was second only to Booth's, yet his acting frequently recalled aspects of the antebellum Romantic style, much more than Booth's more natural approach. Barrett was particularly adept at passionate outbursts that thrilled audiences, though some critics complained that they were old-fashioned, more calculated and planned than spontaneous. With deep-set, glowing eyes, and a high, broad forehead that evoked intellectual strength, Barrett was most effective in portraying characters close to his own often austere, ambitious, sometimes impetuous personality. Cassius, for example, fitted Barrett's temperament, appearance, and technique and his reading of the part was regarded as the definitive interpretation of his era. Unlike Booth, Barrett achieved considerable popular and critical success in a wide range of non-Shakespearean roles, usually in historical verse melodramas. His interpretation of the morose, physically deformed Lanciotto, in a revival of George Henry Boker's *Francesca da Rimini,* was among his acting masterpieces.

Barrett was also an outstanding theatrical producer. When he toured at the head of his own combination in the 1880s, his productions were noted for the quality of the supporting casts, carefully rehearsed ensemble effects, and handsome, historically accurate scenery and costumes. His successful management of Booth's five national tours (1886–1891), in three of which he also starred, was his crowning achievement as both an actor and producer. Barrett, a staunch champion of American drama, commissioned new plays, adaptations, and translations from many American writers. He also revived both American and European romantic dramas, presented the American premiere of Oscar Wilde's *The Duchess of Padua,* and encouraged Minnie Maddern Fiske to produce Ibsen's *A Doll's House.*

After Forrest's death in 1872, his protégé John McCullough (1837–85) became the principal exemplar of the "heroic" style. Like Forrest (discussed in Vol. I of this history), he was athletically built and classically handsome with a powerful voice. When he assumed several of his mentor's roles, including Spartacus, Virginius, and Jack Cade, comparisons with Forrest were inevitable. Some critics thought him a weak imitation, but others appreciated an emotional control and subtlety that was invariably lacking from Forrest's performances. In Shakespearean roles, although he fell short of Booth and Barrett, McCullough's more refined heroic playing served him well as Othello, Coriolanus – widely considered a definitive representation – and Lear. At the peak of his career McCullough was struck down by the ravages of advanced syphilis. With McCullough, the classic heroic style fell out of fashion. Some of the features of the style, however, were absorbed by a new generation of actors specializing in playing the dashing heroes of romantic costume melodramas, an increasingly popular genre at the turn of the century. James O'Neill (1874–1920), for example, became famous and wealthy playing almost exclusively the eponymous hero of Dumas's *The Count of Monte Cristo.* Romantic heroes also formed a large part of the early repertoire of Otis Skinner (1858–1942), although over the course of his long career, this remarkably versatile actor proved equally adept in classic, light comedy, or character roles.

When Charlotte Cushman retired in 1875, the void left in American classical acting on the distaff side was filled principally by two émigré actresses. Fanny Janauschek (1830–1904), born in Prague, was a recognized star in German theatre when she came to America in 1867. Initially she acted in German supported by an English-speaking company. (Bilingual performances of this sort were not unusual at the time.) She began to learn English, taking a leave of absence from performing for almost a year to do so, and in 1873–1874 reappeared as an English-speaking star. Although her accent remained noticeably pronounced, she nevertheless impressed American audiences with her powerful presence and fiery intensity as Lady Macbeth, Brunhilde (in a stage adaptation of the Nibelungen saga written especially for her), Queen Katherine in Shakespeare's *Henry VIII,* Mary Stuart, and Medea. However, public taste for her bravura, "old school" style of acting began to wane at the turn of the century.

In the 1860s and 1870s, Helena Modjeska (1840–1909) was one of Poland's leading actresses. In 1876, to escape political oppression and regain her health, she left Poland for America with her husband, a Polish nobleman, and a small band of fellow Poles who hoped to establish an utopian farming community in southern California; knowing little about farming, they soon found themselves in desperate financial straits. Modjeska resolved to try her luck on the American stage. After intensive English-language study, she made her American debut at the California Theatre in 1877. For the next several years, she toured in adaptations of French melodramas, such as Alexandre Dumas's *Camille,* Ludovic Halévy's *Frou-Frou,* and Eugène Scribe's *Adrienne Lecouvreur,* plays in which her accent would not seem out of place. Slender, with a sensitive beauty and a musical voice, she seemed ideally suited to such roles and quickly won widespread critical and public approval. After starring engagements in London in 1880–81, she gradually began to add a number of Shakespeare's heroines to her repertoire, including Rosalind, Viola, Beatrice, Imogen, and Isabella in *Measure for Measure,* the latter a play that had only rarely been seen on the American stage. In 1889, for her joint starring tour with Edwin Booth, she played Ophelia, Portia, and Lady Macbeth. Her Lady Macbeth became a mainstay of her later repertoire. Finally, in the last decade of her career, she added Queen Katherine, Queen Constance in *King John,* and, at the age of fifty-eight, Cleopatra. By the time she retired in 1907, she was widely recognized as America's foremost Shakespearean actress.

Mary Anderson (1859–1940) might have rivaled Modjeska as a classical and especially Shakespearean actress. Except for a series of private lessons with the veteran stager George Vandenhoff, she was entirely self-taught, modeling her style and ambitions on her idol Edwin Booth. In the late 1870s, she won acclaim playing traditional romantic heroines like Julia in *The Hunchback,* Pauline in *The Lady of Lyons,* and Shakespeare's Juliet. Audiences flocked to her performances by the thousands, and even older stars admired her talent and beauty. In 1883–84, she played two seasons at London's famed Lyceum Theatre. Despite harsh criticism, the Lyceum was crowded night after night. The poets Tennyson and Browning, the popular novelist Wilkie Collins, and the Prince and Princess of Wales sang her praises and befriended her. In 1885, playing Rosalind, she mounted a new, well-received production of *As You Like It* at Stratford-upon-Avon for the benefit of the Shakespeare Memorial Theatre. But when she remounted it in New York, most critics found her ineffectual in this classic comedic role; disappointed with this reception, Anderson returned to playing tragic heroines. In 1887–88, however, she revived *The Winter's Tale* at the Lyceum Theatre, boldly playing both Hermione and Perdita. When she brought it to America the following season, it was hailed as her finest accomplishment. Then, at age thirty, she abruptly retired from the stage, married an English solicitor, and moved to a village near Stratford-upon-Avon. Booth bemoaned the loss to the American theatre and the school of classical acting.

Indeed, in the last decades of the century, theatrical tastes steadily turned more toward contemporary light comedy and domestic or historical melodrama and away from classical drama. Among the new generation of leading performers, only a few would have careers solely playing a traditional repertoire. British émigré Robert Bruce Mantell (1854–1928), for example, who viewed himself as a bridge between the old and the new, successfully sustained the tradition touring in a repertoire that eventually was exclusively Shakespearean.

As a young trouper, English-born Frederick Warde (1851–1935) worked steadily in stock and on tour supporting many of the stars of the era, including Cushman, Booth, and McCullough. By the mid-1880s he was a popular draw on the cross-country touring circuit, often in partnership with Louis James (1842–1910), another all-round classical actor of the "old school." In the late 1890s, Warde and James played hundreds of towns and cities in a repertoire that included *Hamlet, Julius Caesar, Macbeth, Othello,* and *The School for Scandal.* Late in his career, Warde achieved distinction in two abbreviated, silent film versions of *King Lear* and *Richard III.* Unlike Mantell and Warde, most classically trained actors working at the turn of the century would have to extend their range into a different and more diverse repertoire.

After Booth's retirement, Richard Mansfield (1857–1907) was widely regarded as the leader of the profession. After several years of playing minor roles in England and America, Mansfield became an overnight sensation in 1882 with his richly detailed portrait of Baron Chevrial, an aging, physically and morally depraved rake, in an adaptation of Octave Feuillet's *A Parisian Romance.* Three years later, he struck out as a touring star at the head of his own combination company. Trained by his mother, a celebrated German opera singer, his acting style reflected in several respects the traditional, classical approach. On balance, he was more a bravura character actor than a classical tragedian in the fashion of Booth or Barrett. His forte was vivid, strongly theatrical or eccentric roles, whether comic or melodramatic. Conversant in several languages, he reveled in dialect parts. Among his notable portrayals, for example, were his tour de force performances as both Dr. Jekyl and Mr. Hyde, Ivan the Terrible, Beau Brummel, and Don Juan.

Throughout his career, Mansfield moved, not always comfortably, between traditional material and emerging modernism. In the 1890s he introduced Shaw to America, playing Bluntschli in *Arms and the Man* and Dick Dudgeon in *The Devil's Disciple,* but he was not prepared for Shaw's more modern plays. He produced Ibsen's *A Doll's House* so his actress-wife Beatrice Cameron could play Nora, but he was not particularly sympathetic toward modern, realistic drama. At heart, he was a mainstream Victorian and a romantic. Inspired by Booth, Barrett, and Henry Irving, Mansfield mounted scenically splendid productions of *Richard III, The Merchant of Venice, Henry V,* and *Julius Caesar,* but with the exception of Henry, his Shakespearean performances were judged only creditable. In 1898–89, however, he achieved tremendous public and critical success as Rostand's Cyrano de Bergerac. It was just the colorful, grand heroic role that ideally suited Mansfield's abilities and temperament. In the first decade of the twentieth century, he added to his reputation with performances as Molière's Alceste, Schiller's Don Carlos, and Ibsen's Peer Gynt. A tireless producer and trouper, crisscrossing the country each season, playing dozens of towns and cities, his premature death at age fifty left a gap in the profession that was never really filled.

"The School of Emotionalism" (also called "sensation" acting) was the exclusive domain of a number of Gilded Age actresses whose performances were characterized by seemingly uncontrolled emotional outbursts. For spectators, especially women, these moments caused frequent visceral responses, or "sensations." Instinct and the inspiration of the moment were keys for sensation actresses, often spurred on by the popularity of sensation melodrama with plots centered on distraught, imperiled, emotionally conflicted women.

After the death of Matilda Heron in 1877, the foremost "sensation" actress of the antebellum period, Clara Morris (1847–1925), emerged as the greatest emotionalistic actress of the era. In the 1870s, initially as a member of Augustin Daly's company, she established her reputation playing heroines in such sensation melodramas as *Camille, Miss Moulton* (a version of *East Lynne*), and *Divorce,* all of which revolved around women trapped in destructive love affairs and driven, as a consequence, to madness and death. Although often guilty of sexual transgressions, they were treated sympathetically as victims of male domination and abuse, society's double standards, betrayal, and their own conflicted passions. They sin, but they also suffer. It was a formula that touched a nerve in both male and female playgoers in a gender-unequal era.

Morris was unrivaled in her ability to realistically capture the struggles of such characters. Her face, for example, framed with a mass of golden hair, was often described as "girlish" or "innocent" but capable of projecting seductive allure. She was able to weep profusely on cue; a tearful voice, quivering lip, and heaving breast became her trademarks. She had an overwhelming, almost hypnotic stage presence that even riveted some of her onstage partners. She was regularly criticized for her physical awkwardness, mannerisms, and her faulty elocution, but these flaws were forgotten in the magnetism of her performances. Although she reigned supreme as the American emotional actress of her time, by the late 1880s chronic illness and morphine addiction had eroded her talent and popularity. But other actresses, two in particular, stood in the wings ready to create sensational effects equal to Morris's.

Tallish, youthfully radiant, with a charming onstage personality, Fanny Davenport (1850–98), the daughter of tragedian, E. L. Davenport, began her career playing classic, light comedy roles – for example, Lady Gay Spanker in *London Assurance* and Rosalind in *As You Like It.* As she matured, she extended her range to include dramatic roles. As Mabel Renfrew in Daly's *Pique,* for example, Davenport exhibited a range of intense emotional reactions, particularly in the climactic scenes in which she rescues her son from the clutches of thuggish kidnappers. After *Pique,* Davenport played various serious and comic roles in Daly's company, including Imogen, Beatrice, Lady Macbeth, and Lady Teazle. In the late 1880s and 1890s, as a touring star at the head of her own combination, she began to specialize as a sensation actress, playing for the first time in English in America various French volatile heroines. Although she never reached Morris's level of celebrity, much less Bernhardt's, Davenport had numerous admirers. Her premature death cut short her mature potential.

Mrs. Leslie Carter (1862–1937), born Caroline Louise Dudley, married at eighteen a prominent and wealthy Chicagoan; the marriage ended nine years later in a highly publicized divorce. Left without any means of support, but strikingly beautiful and blessed with a clear, mellifluous voice, she capitalized on her public notoriety with two undistinguished Broadway appearances in 1890–91. David Belasco, however, took Carter on as a student, and, in 1895, starred her in his play *The Heart of Maryland* as Maryland Calvert, a role specifically tailored to suit Carter's talent and abilities. Her emotional intensity, seemingly almost uncontrolled physicality, verging on hysteria, created a sensation. She played Maryland almost continually for the next three years in both New York and London, where thousands flocked to the performance. Belasco subsequently starred her in other sensational melodramas, including *Zaza* (1899), *Du Barry* (1901), and *Adrea* (1904), in which she had opportunities, according to William Winter, "to work herself into a state of violent excitement, to weep, vociferate, shriek, rant, become hoarse with passion, and finally to flop and beat the floor" (*Wallet of Time, II,* 327). She eventually broke with Belasco and starred on her own in *Zaza* and *Du Barry* as well as in *Camille* and *Tosca.* As popular taste turned toward less sensational, more realistic dramas, Mrs. Carter modified her style and achieved a notable success as Lady Catherine in Somerset Maugham's social drama *The Circle* (1921).

Gilded Age personality actresses generally exhibited a somewhat greater histrionic range than their emotionalistic sisters, although their repertoires

Ada Rehan as Lady Teazle in *The School for Scandal,* first seen in 1894. Sarony photo. Wilmeth Collection.

were still dominated by light comedies and romantic dramas, mainstays of the school. More than any other actresses of the era, the roles they played, and the personalities they projected through these roles, established the prototype of the starring actress for succeeding generations. Ada Rehan (1857–1916) and Maude Adams (1872–1953) were singular models of the school.

With an attractive, generously proportioned figure, masses of reddish hair and gray-blue eyes, and a voice most often described as "caressing" or "melodious" with perfect articulation or diction, Rehan captivated playgoers with her feminine loveliness, charm, and warmth, a requisite for personality players. Over the course of her career, she played over two hundred roles at Daly's, mostly in lively farces and romantic melodramas. In the 1880s, however, Daly showcased her talents in a series of scenically splendid revivals of Shakespeare's comedies, both in New York and London (Kate in *The Taming of the Shrew,* Helena in *A Midsummer Night's Dream,* Mistress Ford in *The Merry Wives of Windsor,* Rosalind, Viola, Portia, and Beatrice). In many respects, Rehan's acting prowess was completely dependent on Daly's skills as a director, play adapter, and promoter, and after his death, without Daly's coaching, her acting was seen as increasingly mannered and artificial. No longer youthful and unable to adapt to emerging realistic drama, she retired at the age of forty-five.

Daughter of a work-a-day stock actress, Maude Adams was on stage from the age of seven. In the early 1890s, she became a member of Charles Frohman's Empire Theatre company, playing characters that combined pathos and gaiety (most often described as "delicate," "heart-warming," "winsome," or "whimsical") and in which her natural sweetness and sympathetic charm shone through. She was pretty rather than beautiful, girlish rather than womanly, but her face easily registered pensiveness or mischievous merriment. The plaintive quality of her voice was frequently praised, and her laugh was considered uniquely infectious. In 1897, she played Lady Babbie in James M. Barrie's *The Little Minister,* which the Scots writer adapted from his novel expressly for her. The play offered Adams an opportunity to play a double role – a mysterious, beautiful gypsy, who is then revealed to be in actuality a well-born lady. Running for three seasons, Lady Babbie established Adams as a major star. She attempted to play a few classical roles – Juliet and Viola, for example – but these were judged failures. Her major successes continued to be in plays that Barrie wrote for her, including *What Every Woman Knows* (1908) and *Peter Pan* (1905), the latter certainly one of her greatest roles. She also was successful in two plays by Edmond Rostand – *L'Aiglon* in 1910 and *Chantecler* in 1911. For almost two decades, she proved to be a famously popular actress. The death of Charles Frohman, Adams's mentor and producer, was a traumatic loss for her. She was also seriously stricken during the great influenza epidemic of 1918. After her recovery, she decided to retire from the stage. An effort to make a comeback in 1931 as Portia to Otis Skinner's Shylock failed, but in 1937 at the age of sixty-five she began a teaching career as the founder of the drama department at Stephens College in Missouri, where she remained until 1950.

Julia Marlowe (1866–1950) had a versatility beyond that of the typical Gilded Age personality actress. As a teenager, she played minor roles in her hometown stock company; then for several seasons she toured with various combination companies. But ambitious and eager to improve, she left the stage to be tutored by a retired actress who subjected her to "genuine, old-

Maude Adams (and the children) from Act V of Barrie's *Peter Pan,* first seen in 1905. Hall photo. Wilmeth Collection.

fashioned stage training" (Strang, *Famous Actresses,* I, First series, 29). In the late 1880s, Marlowe launched herself as a star, touring in an exclusively Shakespearean repertoire as Rosalind, Viola, Juliet, Imogen, and Beatrice. She received good notices on "the Road" but could not succeed in New York. The powerful William Winter was unenthusiastic about her abilities; Daly, not wanting her competition, undermined her efforts. When Marlowe opened her *Twelfth Night;* or *As You Like It,* Daly countered with his own spectacular productions featuring Ada Rehan. Marlowe's manager pressured her into touring in more popular and lucrative historical romances; she was successful but artistically discontented with this repetoire. A turning point in her career came in 1904 when the manager Daniel Frohman teamed her with Edward H. Sothern (1859–1933) to tour a series of Shakespeare productions.

Sothern, son of the English comedian Edward Askew Sothern, was Frohman's leading man at the Lyceum Theatre, where, for a decade or more, he had specialized in gentlemanly light comedy roles and dashing romantic heroes in such plays as *The Prisoner of Zenda* and *The King's Musketeers.* Although highly successful, Sothern, like Marlowe, wanted recognition as a classical actor. In 1900, he played Hamlet in New York, garnering judicious critical praise and generating good audiences. For the next four years, he regularly played Hamlet; but, although he was undoubtedly interested, he did not attempt other Shakespeare roles – until he partnered Julia Marlowe.

E. H. Sothern and Julia Marlowe in *Romeo and Juliet* (c. 1904). Hall photo. Wilmeth Collection.

For twenty years, except for the war years, Sothern and Marlowe toured the country, playing mainly Shakespeare's comedies and romances, but including *Hamlet* and, after 1910, *Macbeth*. They became justly famous as the foremost Shakespearean actors of the era, noted for their graceful, studious, natural playing style with its light comic touch and tasteful sentiment. Their retirement in 1924, however, marked a final passing of the classical tradition in American acting.

Comic acting in the Gilded Age followed traditions established earlier in the century. Classic English comedies and Yankee characters, for example, remained as popular as ever. Certainly the most famous and popular traditional comic actor of the era was Joseph Jefferson III (1829–1905), also discussed in Volume I of this history. Jefferson, scion of an Anglo–American acting family that can be traced back to the age of Garrick, was onstage from age four. For three decades, he traipsed the country, initially with his family, then as a member of various stock companies from New Orleans to New York. With Laura Keene's company in the late 1850s, he scored successes as Dr. Pangloss in *The Heir-at-Law* and as Asa Trenchard in *Our American Cousin*. Following the death of his wife in 1861, Jefferson spent four years touring California and Australia, winding up in London, where in 1865 he first appeared as Rip Van Winkle, the role for which he was most noted during the next forty years, especially its exceptional naturalness, warmth, pathos, and whimsical humor. As Jefferson matured, Rip matured with him until the characterization was a polished masterpiece and Jefferson as Rip became virtually a one-role actor. He continued to play Bob Acres, Dr. Pangloss, and Caleb Plummer in *The Cricket on the Hearth,* but for some critics these were not distinctive characterizations, but merely Rip in different guises.

After Jefferson, William H. Crane (1845–1928) and Stuart Robson (1836–1903), were perhaps the most successful traditional comedians. After independent careers as comic stock actors, they became a starring team in the 1870s and 1880s appearing as the two Dromios in *The Comedy of Errors,* as Sir Andrew (Robson) and Sir Toby (Crane) in *Twelfth Night,* Falstaff (Crane) and Sender (Robson) in *The Merry Wives of Windsor,* and in Bronson Howard's *The Henrietta,* which was written especially for them. In the 1890s, they again struck out on their own in classic comedies and vehicles tailored for their talents.

Thousands of immigrants swelling America's cities in the 1880s and 1890s made ethnic comedy and character types even more relevant and appealing. Two of the most successful actors specializing in ethnic comedy were Edward Harrigan (1844–1911) and Tony Hart (1855–91). During the 1870s, Harrigan and Hart worked as a vaudeville team, presenting skits, written by Harrigan, centering on various urban ethnic characters and situations. Harrigan expanded these into full-length farces about an Irish pseudomilitary company the "Mulligan Guards," their rivals the German Lochmullers, and their various Italian and Negro neighbors and friends. The plays, a mixture of jokes, gags, songs, comic dancing, and knockdown, slapstick action, were also sharply etched satirical portrayals of life on New York's Lower East Side. With Harrigan as Dan Mulligan and Hart often in blackface drag as Rebecca Allup, the Mulligan Guard series was enormously popular not only with immigrant audiences, who recognized and laughed at themselves, but also with a number of New York's intellectuals, including William Dean Howells, who called Harrigan the "American Goldoni." (See also the discussion by Miller in Chapter 3.)

Foreign Stars in America

During the Gilded Age, the American stage was visited by numerous foreign stars. Faster and safer ships had reduced the hazards of transoceanic travel; thus a well-developed and organized touring circuit offered foreign stars, like their American counterparts, opportunities for enormous earnings. American impresarios were eager to promote these visitors. As in the past, some came and stayed in America, but most returned to their native countries.

English stars remained dominant. Among them were Charles Albert Fechter (1824–79); Adelaide Neilson (1846?–80), who visited four times in the 1870s; Lillie Langtry (1853–1929), who visited four times in the 1880s; Johnston Forbes-Robertson (1853–1937), who first came in 1885 to play in support of Mary Anderson, then returned as a star in his own right seven times between 1891 and 1916; Mrs. Patrick Campbell (1865–1940), who toured on numerous occasions from 1902 to 1916; and Herbert Beerbohm Tree (1853–1917), who visited in 1895, 1896, and 1916. In 1883, Henry Irving (1838–1905), regarded as England's greatest actor, came with his co-star Ellen Terry (1848–1928) and his entire Lyceum Theatre company, complete with splendid realistic scenery and costumes, and striking lighting effects for a half-dozen productions. American critics voiced reservations about Irving's merit as a great classical actor, but they praised his abilities as a producer – the quality of the ensemble and the high standards of his mise-en-scène, unmatched on the American stage, even by Daly. Critics and audiences were invariably bewitched by Ellen Terry. Irving and Terry would return eight more times, their last visit in 1905.

Several stars of the Italian stage were also regular visitors. Adelaide Ristori (1822–1906), one of the first continental stars to cross the Atlantic after the Civil War, gave in 1866–67 over 170 performances, mainly of *Elizabeth the Queen, Mary Stuart,* and *Marie Antoinette* in over a dozen cities from New York to Chicago and New Orleans. Ristori toured three more times in 1867–68, in 1875, and finally in 1885 on her last tour, she performed in English, including Lady Macbeth to the Macbeth of Edwin Booth. Tommaso Salvini (1829–1915), toured America five times – 1873, 1881, 1882–83, 1885–86, and 1889–90. Although he played several Italian tragic heroes – Alfieri's *Saul,* for example – he was lauded for his Shakespearean interpretations, especially for his powerful, passionate *Othello,* but also for *Macbeth* and *King Lear.* In 1886, Salvini acted Othello in Italian to Booth's celebrated Iago. In fact, after his first visit, Salvini always acted with an American company. These bilingual performances, strange by contemporary theatrical standards, were accepted by nineteenth-century audiences. In 1881–82, Ernesto Rossi (1827–96) tried to follow in Salvini's footsteps but failed to capture critical enthusiasm. A decade later, Eleonora Duse (1859–1924) came to America. She offered a repertoire of such standards as *Camille, Fédora,* and *Divorçons,* roles identified with her older rival, Sarah Bernhardt (1844–1923), and American Bernhardt imitators. Audiences did not warm to Duse's natural, subtle, modern approach. The taste was for the more theatrical, emotionalistic, Bernhardt style. When Duse returned in 1896 and again in 1903, with a repertoire of more modern plays, she was regarded in a different light. Familiarity and a shift in theatrical taste led to a new appreciation of her estimable style. Duse returned once more in 1923, but past her peak and ill, she could not recapture her earlier successes.

Americans never seemed to tire of Bernhardt. She made nine national tours between 1880 and 1918, playing a wide range of fallen women, femme fatales, historical figures, even a Frenchified and feminized Hamlet in 1900. Among other French actors touring America in the Gilded Age were the great comedian Constant-Benôit Coquelin (1841–1909), who, on his third tour in 1900, introduced Americans to Rostand's Cyrano de Bergerac. The noted tragedian, Jean Mounet-Sully (1841–1916), however, utterly failed in 1894 with a classic repertoire ranging from Corneille through Hugo. Gabriele Réjane (1856–1920), a gifted comedienne, touring with her own company from Paris's Vaudeville Theatre in 1895, had more success, enough to motivate a return in 1904. However, like Duse, Réjane was constantly compared to and frequently overshadowed by Bernhardt.

Among the distinguished stars of the German and Austrian stage playing in America in the last quarter of the century were Ludwig Barnay (1842–1924), Ernst Possart (1841–1921), and Adolphe von Sonnenthal (1834–1909). Invariably they performed only in the large, well-organized German language stock companies in New York, Chicago, Cincinnati, Milwaukee, St. Louis, and New Orleans. Bogumil Dawison (1818–1872), Polish-born, but a star of the German stage, did "cross-over" from German-language stock companies to the mainstream Anglophone stage when he performed Othello to Edwin Booth's Iago in the 1860s. It was, however, another bilingual affair: Booth and the ensemble in English, Dawison in German, and the Desdemona, German American actress Maria Methua-Schiller, alternating between German and English.

How influential these foreign performers – whatever their language – were on American stage culture is difficult to ascertain. Visiting English and continental actresses undoubtedly reinforced a taste for emotionalistic and personality performers. Irving's company inspired high standards for production and ensemble playing. At the least, these visitors contributed to the remarkably rich mix of acting styles and actors available to turn-of-the-century American playgoers.

Advancement and Decline: 1915–1945

By the teens, professional theatre in America was centralized in New York, controlled by commercially oriented producers and production companies. Typically, the New York – or Broadway (the terms had become virtually synonymous) – season was dominated by melodramas, light romantic comedies, farces, and lavishly staged musicals; classic and modern drama was marginalized. But new playwrights and alternative producing groups, in part inspired by modernist European theatrical trends, increasingly challenged Broadway's commercialism and its standard fare. Actors would be at the center of what would become an ongoing struggle between commercial and artistic interests in the American theatre.

Actors Organize

Theatrical producing was a risky business at the turn of the century; most productions failed. But the profits from a successful long run could be enormous. Most, though not all, Broadway producers seemed more interested in turning a profit than in elevating theatrical standards or fostering fair and equitable working conditions. Producers were regularly charged with abusive labor practices. Actors, for example, were expected to rehearse without pay, usually from six to ten weeks. They could be laid off without notice; their salaries cut without warning; the number of weekly performances increased without additional compensation. The ASA's efforts to lobby on behalf of the profession were generally ignored by producers. By 1912, the ASA was effectively dissolved, and a new organization, the Actors' Equity Association was founded. Led by its first president, comedian and singer Francis Wilson (1854–1935), Equity struggled for the next six years to negotiate a standard minimum contract for all classes of productions with the organizations that represented managers and producers – first the United Managers' Protective Association (UMPA), then in 1918 its successor organization, the Producing Managers' Association (PMA). But the producers steadfastly refused to make any concessions. Equity gradually overcame residual fear of unionization among its membership, and the opposition of the White Rats, the AFL-affiliated vaudevillian's union, to finally win AFL membership in 1919.

With producers still refusing to negotiate a standard contract, Equity, now backed by the powerful AFL, called a strike. It quickly spread to eight cities, closed thirty-seven plays, and prevented sixteen others from opening. The strike divided the profession, with actors on both sides of the issue. Musical star, playwright, and producer, George M. Cohan (1878–1942), particularly adamant in his opposition to Equity and unionism, went so far as to organize a rival association, the Actors' Fidelity League. But the strike held. In a show of union solidarity, actors were joined by stagehands, musicians, teamsters, and bill posters – all of whom had successfully organized in the preceding decade. The strike also had widespread public support. After thirty days and the loss of millions of dollars, the producers capitulated. They recognized Equity as the sole representative of professional actors in America and agreed to all points proposed in Equity's standard work contract. Over the next decade, Equity wrested other agreements from the producers, including minimum wage and minimum rehearsal pay provisions, and an important closed-shop clause, essentially enjoining its members to work only in companies in which all the actors belonged to Equity. (See also Chapter 2.)

Realistic Acting

As noted above, a tendency toward an ever more realistic, or "natural," style of acting steadily mounted through the last decades of the nineteenth century. Several factors account for the trend, the most prominent being a contemporary realistic drama, both native and foreign, that focused on ordinary people and, in particular, their inner, psychological lives. Realism of this sort was increasingly pervasive in American literature and art. The development of modern psychology with its interest in the complexities of consciousness was also a significant influence. Acting schools and acting teachers made their contribution. Playgoers were not immune to these influences. Old-style traditional actors, or the player queens of the emotional school, could still impress and thrill, but increasingly their approaches were considered mannered, artificial, and excessive. The largely middle-class, urban audience gradually began to prefer a more subdued, subtler, and introspective style.

Minnie Maddern Fiske (1864–1932), an early champion of realistic drama and of the acting style appropriate to its representation, in 1894, for a single-benefit performance, acted Nora in *A Doll's House.* She then included it in her repertoire and subsequently added *Hedda Gabler* (1903), *Rosmersholm* (1907), *The Pillars of Society* (1910), and *Ghosts* (1927), the last daringly staged in contemporary 1920s dress. Mrs. Fiske also enjoyed notable successes as Tess in an adaptation of Hardy's *Tess of the D'Urbervilles* (1897), as the eponymous *Becky Sharp* (1899), adapted from Thackeray's *Vanity Fair,* and in several new American plays, including Langdon Mitchell's *The New York Idea* (1906); two realistic plays by Edward Sheldon, *Salvation Nell* (1908) and *The High Road* (1912); and Harry James Smith's *Mrs. Bumpstead-Leigh* (1911), a comedy of contemporary manners.

In whatever she performed, whether somber realistic drama or contemporary social comedy, Fiske was invariably praised (and compared to Duse) for her naturalness and realistically detailed, telling business and gestures. Her attention to detail caused some to complain that she was a cold and intellectual technician. Her lack of vocal clarity also took some occasional dubbing, although she thought that the vocal flexibility was of paramount importance. Some critics thought she was a personality actress whose characterizations were never different or distinctive.

Throughout the early 1900s, critics would be divided about this new cult of personality, but audiences expected actors to project – both onstage and offstage – their distinctive personalities. In the public mind, at least, actors often became associated with their roles. To play oneself was the epitome of realism; not acting at all. Reinforced by movies in the twenties, thirties, and forties, the culture of personality would continue to profoundly affect actors and acting to the present day.

In addition to being a star, Mrs. Fiske also managed her own theatre and company, the Manhattan Theatre company. Functioning as a *régisseur,* overseeing all aspects of production (like Daly and Belasco), she promoted careful ensemble playing, advocated a science of acting, and urged her actors to give attention to detail and to be absolutely precise in execution. She had her share of failures, but Mrs. Fiske persisted. On Broadway and on tour she won thousands of converts to her artistry, although sometimes in vehicles beneath her estimable abilities. She was widely regarded by the late 1920s as the finest actress of her generation.

Unlike Mrs. Fiske, William H. Gillette (1855–1937) advanced a reputation for realistic acting, not in modern social dramas but principally in his own well-crafted melodramas. Gillette found his true métier as the cool-headed man of action, first as the Union spy Captain Thorne in his own Civil War melodrama *The Secret Service* (1895), and then even more successfully as the famous sleuth *Sherlock Holmes* (1899) in his own adaptation of Arthur Conan Doyle's stories.

Tall, slim, with chiseled features and a manner that projected a strongly intellectual, forceful personality, Gillette was ideal for such roles. He cultivated a complementary style of acting characterized by skillful underplaying and a repressed emotional intensity. He had a crisp, staccato way of delivering dialogue – which, of course, he had written himself – that seemed entirely natural, and true-to-life. But often it was not what he said, but what he did that proved suggestive. Critics commented on his economical but evocative gestures or business – for example, a twitching finger, a compression of the lips, his playing with a cigar or a revolver. Always, as Strang observed, his composure was "absolute" and "his mental grasp of the situation . . . complete" (175).

In 1910, in an address entitled "The Illusion of the First Time in Acting," Gillette declared that drama was essentially "life-simulation" and that the actor, as well as the playwright and producer, must make every effort to make the simulation spontaneous and believable. Playgoers must feel that they are "witnessing not one of a thousand weary repetitions but a life episode that is being lived just across the magic barrier of the footlights. That is to say, the whole must have that indescribable life-spirit or effect which produces the Illusion of Happening for the First Time" (quoted in W. Young, I, 429; document 77 in Witham). Gillette also endorsed the growing belief that personality was "the most singularly important factor for infusing the life-illusion into modern stage creations. . . . as no human being exists without personality of one sort or another, an actor who omits it in his impersonations of a human being omits one of the vital elements of existence" (Young, I, 429). Some critics believed that Gillette lacked versatility, that he projected the same persona regardless of the part. Gillette perhaps would have argued that he deliberately infused his personality into his roles, giving them as a result a high degree of vitality and believability. Over the course of his career, Gillette played dozens of roles in farces, light comedies, and melodramas. His notable successes included starring roles in Barrie's romantic fantasies *The Admirable Crichton* (1903) and *Dear Brutus* (1918), for which he garnered critical praise for naturalness and credibility. Sherlock Holmes was his mainstay, however; he played it more than thirteen hundred times. In 1928, he came out of an eight-year retirement to play Holmes one more time. Realistic acting was the norm; Gillette no longer seemed so innovative and modern, and the play was decidedly old-fashioned, but audiences and critics still found both winning (see Cullen and Wilmeth, 1–25).

Foreign influences also promoted realistic acting in America. The example of Duse has already been noted. The Irish actors from Dublin's Abbey Theatre impressed many with their natural style during their tours in 1911 and 1915. The tours of the celebrated Moscow Art Theatre (MAT) between 1923 and 1925 had even more widespread and lasting influence. Although they played in Russian, they were heralded for their realistic, ensemble acting. During the course of the MAT's American visits, Stanislavsky published an English version of his autobiography *My Life in Art* (1924). Although hastily written and in significant instances misleadingly, ambiguously translated, it was widely read as an introduction or "preface" to Stanislavsky's famous system of actor training. (The 1936 American, English-language publication of Stanislavsky's *An Actor Prepares* was even more influential, although it was but a fragment of the Russian version published two years later, and filled with inaccurate translations as well.)

On arriving in New York in 1923, the MAT was greeted by Richard Boleslavski (1887–1937), a former company member who had fled Moscow in the wake of the Revolution, winding up in America in 1922. Shortly after the MAT opened its New York engagement, Boleslavski presented a series of lectures at the Princess Theatre outlining Stanislavsky's system. During his lectures, Boleslavski was approached by two wealthy arts patrons to head an American version of the MAT. With the assistance of Maria Ouspenskaya (1881–1949), a MAT member who had decided to remain in America, Boleslavski set up the American Laboratory Theatre (ALT). Until it was disbanded in 1933, the ALT offered Stanislavsky-based acting courses, as well as classes in voice and movement. Among the students who studied at the ALT were Lee Strasberg (1901–82) and Stella Adler (1903–92).

In 1931, Strasberg, Harold Clurman (1901–80), who would subsequently become an important director and critic, and Cheryl Crawford (1902–86) founded the Group Theatre (see Chapter 4). Dedicated to developing a systemized approach to actor training, based on the Stanislavsky model – what Strasberg would later refer to as the Method – and to the production of new realistic plays, the Group Theatre became an important theatre organization until it disbanded in 1941. Dozens of actors were associated with the Group, including Stella and her brother Luther Adler (1903–84), Morris Carnovsky (1847–1992), and Lee J. Cobb (1911–76). The Group's training methods, in one form or another, would continue to be refined and taught from the 1940s through the 1980s by Stella Adler at her own studio and at Yale University, by Sanford Meisner (1905–97), another member of the Group, at the Neighborhood Playhouse, and, most influentially, by Strasberg at the Actors Studio, founded in 1947 by Cheryl Crawford and former Group members Elia Kazan (b. 1909) and Robert Lewis (b. 1909–97). There are those, including some of its original members, who believe that the training methods pioneered by the Group and then refined by Strasberg at the Actors Studio have not had a salutary effect on American acting. Strasberg's "Method," especially with its emphasis on the actor's own emotional resources – on personality or temperament rather than character – arguably produced actors who were much too self-involved and limited. But the Method did produce a style of acting that was remarkably natural, emotionally compelling and charged, and universally recognized as the quintessentially American style, the triumph of the realistic techniques called for by Mrs. Fiske and Gillette at the turn of the century. (For a discussion of the impact of the "Method," see Hirsch in Vol. III of this history.)

The Royal Family of Broadway

Between 1920 and 1940, the reigning stars of the American stage were not, however, associated with organizations like the Group Theatre, nor had they heard of (or if they had, they were not particularly interested in) the Stanislavski system. In many respects, they were the direct descendants, the heirs of the bravura stars of the Gilded Age. They were not systematically trained; rather they were instinctive actors who had learned their craft from observation and experience in stock companies, on tour, or in commercial Broadway productions. They possessed compelling or winning personalities – forceful, charming, dashing, glamorous – which, when combined with an essentially representational or realistic acting technique, proved effective in various roles. If they seemed less versatile than their predecessors, it was more from a lack of opportunity than talent. The prevailing taste, after all, was for comedy, romance, and melodrama. But over the course of their careers, many of these new stars would occasionally, but effectively, test their mettle in classics or serious modern plays.

John Barrymore as Hamlet (1922). Irving Klaw photo. Michael A. Morrison Collection.

The Barrymores – Lionel (1878–1954), Ethel (1879–1959), and John (1882–1942) – were models of this new breed of Broadway star. Children of actors Maurice Barrymore (1847–1905) and Georgianna Drew (1856–93), they grew up in Philadelphia's Arch Street Theatre, which was managed by their grandmother, Mrs. John Drew (1820–97), one of the most celebrated actor-managers of her day. By the 1920s, each had attained a position as a major Broadway star. Collectively, they were viewed as the American stage's "royal family."

Lionel made his debut in 1893 in his grandmother's road tour of *The Rivals*. For fifteen years he played a range of roles, mainly in stock, on the vaudeville circuit, and in the emerging film industry, where he appeared in dozens of one-reelers. In 1918, he achieved Broadway prominence as the simple Illinois farmer Milton Shanks in Augustus Thomas's Civil War drama *The Copperhead*. The role required Lionel to age forty years between Acts I and II. His remarkable physical transformation from middle to old age, and the emotional depth of his performance proved a triumph. He then success-fully co-starred with his brother John in *The Jest* (1919), a historical melo-drama. But Lionel aimed higher. In 1921, he acted Macbeth in a production directed by Arthur Hopkins, one of the outstanding producer-directors of the late teens and twenties. But Broadway's critical establishment was not impressed by Lionel's unconventional, psychological approach to the Thane. He rebounded to win acclaim in a French social drama called *The Claw* (1921) and as Tito Beppi, a Pagliacci-like figure, in another historical melodrama called *Laugh, Clown, Laugh* (1923). There then followed a series of disastrous productions. Disappointed with the New York stage, still smarting from the failure of *Macbeth,* and beset by personal difficulties, Lionel left Broadway for the less stressful and more lucrative fields of Hollywood, never returning to the stage.

John played in a series of vapid comedies in the early 1900s, rising to stardom in *The Fortune Hunter* (1909), an above-average play about a young man's pursuit of an heiress. Like Lionel, John also appeared in a number of inconsequential plays and silent films. In 1916, he gave a distinguished and surprising performance as the check-forging clerk William Falder in John Galsworthy's searing social drama *Justice.* Despite his matinee-idol good looks, devil-may-care manner, sexual buccaneering, and terrible bouts with demon rum, John gained an overnight reputation as a serious actor. He even went on the wagon. Notable successes followed, in Edward Sheldon's adaptation of George du Maurier's popular novel *Peter Ibbetson* (1917; Lionel co-starred as Colonel Ibbetson), in Tolstoy's *Redemption,* and in *The Jest.* In all three, John was commended for the psychological depth and subtlety of his characterizations. He advanced to a higher rung as an actor with his triumphal performance as *Richard III* (1920), which critic Arthur Hornblow hailed as "brilliant, daringly bold, and insistently fascinating" (quoted in Peters, 201). Two years later, he enhanced his mounting reputation with an innovative performance as Hamlet.

Barrymore's Hamlet – more sexually conflicted, more darkly modern than previous Hamlets – seemed inventive and distinctive. Alexander Woollcott commended the natural delivery of the soliloquies, which "seemed for once just a lonely, unhappy man's thoughts walking in the silent darkness" (quoted in Bordman, *American Theatre: A Chronicle of Comedy and Drama, 1914–1930,* 193). For many playgoers, Barrymore was the finest Hamlet of his generation; and as if to underscore his standing, *Hamlet* was repeated for 101 consecutive performances, breaking Booth's record of 100 nights. A cross-country tour in 1923–24 was followed by a London engagement in 1925. London's critics were even more enthusiastic. Laurence Olivier, aged seventeen, saw the performance and remembered it as "burningly real." He even confessed to emulating Barrymore for his own celebrated interpretation in 1937 and later in his 1942 screen version (see Peters, 260).[1]

Then at the peak of his career, Barrymore perversely abandoned the stage for Hollywood. He became a movie star, earning thousands of dollars, but spending even more. He appeared with distinction in films such as *Grand*

Hotel (1923), *Reunion in Vienna* (1933), and *Twentieth Century* (1934), but mainly squandered his talent and ruined his health with drink.

Ethel as a teenager had planned to be a concert pianist but, drawn into the theatre by her grandmother, soon was stagestruck. Unlike her brothers, she took her career seriously. At age fourteen, she was touring in *The Rivals* as Julia. Before she was twenty-one, she had played in New York at the Empire Theatre, and in London with Henry Irving and Ellen Terry. In 1901, she became one of Charles Frohman's major stars as Madame Trentoni in Clyde Fitch's society comedy *Captain Jinks of the Horse Marines*.

Like other personality actresses of the day, Ethel had the requisite physical attributes: Tall, willowy, with huge blue eyes, wavy ash-blond hair, and a distinctive, throaty voice, Ethel captivated as much with her beauty as with her talent and natural, seemingly effortless acting style. An avid reader interested in new ideas, she also exuded intellectual independence and strength – a modern young woman of the new century. Frohman followed *Jinks* with other light comedies that capitalized on his new star's looks and personality, including James Barrie's *Alice-Sit-By-The-Fire* (1905) and *The Twelve Pound Look* (1911), in which Ethel rivaled Maude Adams. As she matured, Ethel refused to be pigeon-holed as a light comedienne, opting for more serious roles in Edna Ferber's *Our Mrs. McChesney* (1915), Zoë Akins's *Déclassée* (1919), Gerhart Hauptmann's *Rose Bernd* (1922), Arthur Pinero's *The Second Mrs. Tanqueray* (1925), and Somerset Maugham's *The Constant Wife* (1926). In 1925, she played Ophelia and Portia to Walter Hampden's Hamlet and Shylock. In 1928, a critic dubbed Ethel the "First Lady of the Theatre." Although she hated the title, it stuck. In the same year, the Shubert's named their new theatre the "Ethel Barrymore."

Throughout the thirties, Ethel added to her reputation on Broadway and on tour, including notable successes in an adaptation of Canadian novelist Mazo de La Roche's popular family epic *The Whiteoaks of Jalna* (1938) and Welsh actor and writer Emlyn Williams's autobiographical *The Corn is Green* (1940). Unlike Lionel and John, she did not desert the stage for the movies, although she starred with them in the film *Rasputin and the Empress* in 1923. In the mid-1940s, however, Ethel, now in her sixties, succumbed to Hollywood, appearing with distinction in over twenty-five films.

Tradition Redux

Walter Hampden (1879–1955) was the most representative and successful classical actor of the twenties and thirties. Born in New York, he received his early theatrical experience in England, where he was a member of Frank R. Benson's distinguished classical repertory company, playing dozens of roles in London and the Provinces between 1901 and 1904, followed by appearances at London's Adelphi Theatre and in Glasgow for several years. In 1907, he returned to America, engaged by actor-manager Henry Miller to play second leads to the Russian émigré star Alla Nazimova in a repertoire of Ibsen and other modern plays. After a brief engagement supporting personality star Viola Allen, he achieved prominence playing the Christ-like butler, Manson, in Charles Rann Kennedy's allegorical drama *The Servant in the House* (1908) which had a long run on Broadway. Hampden subsequently appeared in other contemporary plays, including Clyde Fitch's *The City* (1909), special matinee performances in 1913 of Strindberg's *The Stronger, Pariah,* and *Miss Julie* – Strindberg was rarely produced at the time – and Eugene Walter's *Just a Woman* (1916), and he regularly revived *The Servant in the House* in the late teens and twenties.

Hampden was particularly interested in Shakespeare and poetic drama. In 1916, he played Caliban in a Shakespeare tercentenary production of *The Tempest* at the Century Theatre, receiving good notices for the power of his performance. Two years later, with assistance from several wealthy patrons, he formed his own company in New York, producing and starring in *Hamlet, Macbeth,* and as Marc Antony in *Julius Caesar.* Hampden then toured this repertoire successfully for several months, deciding to alternate limited New York runs with touring for the next four years, including a transcontinental tour in 1922–23.

In 1923, his company took up residence in New York, first at the National Theatre, then at the Colonial Theatre, which he renamed Hampden's Theatre. Perhaps sensing that his Hamlet was eclipsed by Barrymore's, he revived Rostand's *Cyrano de Bergerac.* His interpretation was hailed as superior to Mansfield's – even to Coquelin's. It ran for over 250 performances and became a fixture in Hampden's repertoire. For the next seven years, Hampden continued to stage new romantic historical plays, often reflecting his personal interest in theosophy, and revivals of Shakespeare and modern classics (*Othello, Hamlet,* and *The Merchant of Venice* [1925]; *Caponsacchi* [1926], adapted from Robert Browning's "The Ring and the Book"; Ibsen's *An Enemy of the People* [1927]; *Henry V* [1928]; and Bulwer–Lytton's *Richelieu* [1929]). Hampden maintained a large company, and his productions were often lavish. He was able to remain financially solvent by covering any losses with always profitable revivals of Cyrano (which he reportedly played over a thousand times, twice as many as Coquelin). The onset of the Depression, however, forced him to disband the company in 1930.

Throughout the twenties, Hampden was one of the few New York commercial actor-managers regularly producing classic and poetic drama and maintaining an almost traditional stock company. He continued to perform in various productions through the early fifties, earning a reputation as a thoughtful and consistent performer, widely respected in the profession, yet never becoming a star of the first magnitude.

Like Hampden, Eva Le Gallienne (1899–1994) also had an idealistic, high-minded idea of theatre, tempered by an acute practical sense. Born in London, educated there and in Paris, Le Gallienne came to America in 1915. After several years playing minor roles, she had a notable success as Julie in Ferenc Molnár's *Liliom*. In the mid-twenties, she also achieved success in Molnár's *The Swan,* Schnitzler's *The Call of Life,* and Ibsen's *The Master Builder* and *John Gabriel Borkman.* Inspired by Duse, whom she had seen first in London, Le Gallienne also developed a style of playing that was quiet, controlled, and emotionally restrained. It served her well in the modern roles she preferred; she was widely admired, although some critics complained that her performances were too intellectual or emotionally detached.

In 1926, Le Gallienne established the Civic Repertory Theatre (CRT), a turning point in her career. Located in an old theatre on Fourteenth Street west of Sixth Avenue, forty blocks south of the Broadway theatre district, the CRT combined a European art theatre ideal with a popular-priced American stock company organization. For almost a decade, Le Gallienne produced, directed, and starred in a series of notable productions of classics and new American and foreign plays, ultimately over thirty productions. Plays were presented in repertory fashion, at popular prices, largely to a neighborhood audience. Although frequently in difficult financial straits, Le Gallienne, proved that high-quality drama, as well as the repertory system could be successful. When a serious physical injury, however, which necessitated months of recuperation, combined with the effects of the Depression, Le Gallienne was forced to disband the CRT in 1933.

Until the early eighties Le Gallienne remained a forceful presence in the American theatre as an actress, producer, and director. She continued to promote modern drama, especially the plays of Ibsen and Chekhov, and to espouse the repertory ideal. Her American Repertory Theatre, founded in 1946, failed after a single season, but the National Repertory Theatre, which she founded in 1959, successfully toured until 1965. In the last decades of her career, she was celebrated for her lifelong committment to the highest standards of theatre art.

The Lunts

After the Barrymores, the husband–wife team of Alfred Lunt (1892–1977) and Lynn Fontanne (1887–1983) were among the more prominent and successful stage stars of the 1920s and 1930s. Lunt's theatrical apprenticeship was served in Boston's Castle Square Theatre company, where, between 1912 and 1915, he played a range of roles in dozens of melodramas and farces and an occasional classic. Observing many of the leading actors of the day when they toured Boston, Lunt was particularly impressed with Mrs. Fiske and her company, whose acting style seemed, as he wrote to a friend, not "acting," for "they all just live it & the 'fewness' of their gestures would startle you" (quoted in Jared Brown, 57). In 1919, after several seasons touring as a supporting player, he joined producer George C. Tyler's Washington, D.C., company, whose members included a young English actress – Lynn Fontanne.

As a teenager, Fontanne had the good fortune to have been given acting lessons by Ellen Terry, who also arranged Fontanne's professional debut in a pantomime. There followed minor roles in various touring productions and finally a series of London engagements. In 1915 the American actress Laurette Taylor, starring in London in *Peg O' My Heart* (1912), recruited Fontanne for her American company, in which she played for several tours. Then she landed a leading role in George S. Kaufman's first play, *Someone in the House* (1918), produced by George C. Tyler. Fontanne received rave reviews, but a flu epidemic prematurely ended the run. Tyler persuaded his new star to join his Washington, D.C., company until he could develop her next vehicle.

Tyler, perhaps intuiting their compatibility, featured Lunt and Fontanne in the same plays. Despite an immediate physical attraction and a remarkable performance chemistry, it would be several more years before they became "the Lunts." They rose to major stardom in separate vehicles – Lunt in Booth Tarkington's *Clarence* (1919) and Fontanne in George S. Kaufman and Marc Connelly's *Dulcy* (1921). In 1922 they married but continued to pursue independent careers, finally brought together by the Theatre Guild's 1924 production of Molnár's high comedy *The Guardsman,* in which they achieved resounding success.

For the next thirty-five years, the Lunts acted almost exclusively together, becoming one of the most successful and respected acting partnerships in the history of the American theatre, particularly admired for their natural, nuanced approach to sophisticated comedy, their meticulous attention to the details of characterization – from costumes to stage business – and, when called for, their witty sexual byplay. In their years of playing together, they developed a unique technique of overlapping their dialogue that heightened the naturalism and sometimes the comic effect of their acting. Several contemporary playwrights were inspired by the Lunts. Plays written specifically for them include S. N. Behrman's *The Second Man* (1927) and *Amphitryon 38* (1937; adapted from Jean Giraudoux's play), Robert Sherwood's *Reunion in Vienna* (1931) and *Idiot's Delight* (1936), Noël Coward's *Design for Living* (1933), and Howard Lindsay and Russel Crouse's *The Great Sebastians* (1956). The Lunts were also acclaimed for their performances in *The Taming of the*

Shrew (1935) – a performance that years later inspired the musical *Kiss Me, Kate* (1948) – and as Madame Arkadina and Trigorin in *The Seagull* (1938). They had versatility; they might have appeared in other classic comedies or serious dramas, but opportunity confined them mainly to a type of urbane contemporary comedy at which they had few equals. Their last stage appearance was in Duerrenmatt's ironic modern drama *The Visit* (1958), directed by Peter Brook, which proved to be one of their greatest successes. Despite offers to make films and appear on television (which they did a few times), the Lunts remained quintessential stars of the stage.

First Ladies of the Stage

Notwithstanding the achievements of John and Lionel Barrymore, Walter Hampden, and Alfred Lunt, the American theatre from the mid-twenties to World War II was dominated by star actresses. In the late twenties, for example, Ethel Barrymore's eminent position – held for nearly two decades – was challenged by several rising younger stars, including not only Fontanne, but notably Katharine Cornell (1893–1974) and Helen Hayes (1900–1993).

Cornell served her theatrical apprenticeship with the Washington Square Players, then in 1918 joined the stock company (Buffalo and Detroit) of Jessie Bonstelle, who cast Cornell in the pivotal role of Jo March for a London production of *Little Women,* which Bonstelle had first produced in 1911. Cornell's Jo received glowing reviews from London's pundits. Returning to New York, Cornell received good notices for roles in a number of contemporary romantic dramas, yet it was the title role in Shaw's *Candida* (1924) that established her as a star. Tall and slender, with a dark, exotic beauty, and a soft but resonant voice, she added to her reputation, playing intelligent but vulnerable heroines such as Leslie Crosbie in Somerset Maugham's *The Letter* (1927), Countess Oleska in an adaptation of Edith Wharton's *The Age of Innocence* (1928), and the poetess Elizabeth Barrett in *The Barretts of Wimpole Street* (1931).

In 1921, Cornell married Guthrie McClintic (1893–1961), a young actor turned director, whom she had met in Detroit. In the early thirties, they organized their own production company with Cornell as star and McClintic as director. Like the Lunts, Cornell and McClintic would be highly successful partners for almost thirty-five years. Season after season, they mounted a series of distinguished productions of contemporary plays and classics – twenty-nine, in all – including *Romeo and Juliet* (1933–34), Shaw's *Saint Joan* (1936) and *The Doctor's Dilemma* (1941), Maxwell Anderson's *The Wingless Victory* (1936–37), *The Three Sisters* (1942), *Antony and Cleopatra* (1947), and Christopher Fry's *The Dark Is Light Enough* (1955).

Like the Lunts, Cornell and McClintic usually toured their productions widely after a New York run. By the onset of World War II, Cornell was widely held to be the most distinguished actress in the American theatre – the lead-ing lady of her time. Also like the Lunts, Cornell refused movie roles, but late in her career, she also appeared on television, notably in a production of *The Barretts of Wimpole Street* in 1955. When McClintic died, Cornell retired from the stage.

Helen Hayes made her first stage appearances as a child actor. Petite, cute, and vivacious, even her early adult roles tended in the direction of stereotypi-cal teenagers – the winsome "girl next door" or a mischievous twenties flap-per – in light romantic comedies, including Tarkington's *Clarence* (1919) with Alfred Lunt. In the mid-twenties, Hayes succeeded in redirecting her career toward a more varied repertoire with roles such as Constance Neville in *She Stoops to Conquer* (1924), Cleopatra in the Theatre Guild's staging of Shaw's *Caesar and Cleopatra* (1925), Maggie Shane in a revival of Barrie's *What Every Woman Knows* (1926), and Norma Besant in George Abbott and Ann Preston Bridgers's tragic social drama *Coquette* (1927), in which Hayes's emotional range ran from the coquettish to the suicidal. Hayes subsequently triumphed in two historical roles, *Mary of Scotland* (1933) and, most notably, *Victoria Regina* (1935), a tour de force in which she portrayed Queen Victoria from a newlywed young woman to a widowed, aged empress.

For the next forty years, Hayes proved to be a remarkably resilient and flexible leading actress, appearing in plays as wide ranging as the historical drama *Harriet* (1943), about Harriet Beecher Stowe, to the comedy *Mrs. McThing* (1952), in which she played a society lady turned charwoman, to Eugene O'Neill's tragic *A Touch of the Poet* (1958). In the sixties, sponsored by the Department of State, she embarked on several extensive international tours, playing a repertoire of American plays such as *The Skin of Our Teeth* and *The Glass Menagerie*. Sustained by a solid, realistic technique, emotional range, and an unaffected manner, as she matured she made a graceful transi-tion from "leading lady" to character roles. Long after other player queens of her generation had peaked and retired, Hayes continued to have an active and successful career. And, unlike other stars of her era, she moved easily between Broadway and Hollywood, winning her first Oscar in 1932 and her second in 1970! Until she retired in the late seventies, she was an inspiration to, but also a respected colleague of, a new generation of actresses entering the theatre after World War II.

Black Stars on Broadway

At the turn of the century, a number of African American actors organized companies to serve their communities in cities such as New York, Chicago, Cincinnati, and Detroit. Among the more prominent was New York's Lafayette Players, located at the Lafayette Theatre in the Harlem section of Manhattan, where they presented hundreds of abridged versions of popular Broadway comedies and dramas between 1915 and 1928. A few black actors did perform on Broadway in all-black musicals and revues and in vaudeville. Black entertainer Bert Williams, for example, was a star of the Ziegfeld Follies. But racist attitudes and practices kept black actors off the legitimate stage. Black characters were invariably played by white actors in blackface.

In 1920, however, one of the Lafayette's leading players, Charles Sidney Gilpin (1878–1930), won the title role in O'Neill's *The Emperor Jones,* produced by the Theatre Guild. Initially presented Off Broadway at the Provincetown Playhouse in Greenwich Village, *The Emperor Jones* quickly transferred to Broadway. Its success was credited not only to the innovative, expressionistic structure of the play, but also to Gilpin's riveting performance as Brutus Jones, the ex-Pullman porter become dictator. Like many black performers of the day, Gilpin had moved from black minstrelsy to vaudeville to a range of roles in the Pekin Stock Company of Chicago, a pioneering turn-of-the-century black company, and then to the Lafayette Players. Between acting engagements, he took various jobs as a printer, barber, and Pullman porter. In 1919, he landed his first Broadway role as the slave Custis in English playwright John Drinkwater's *Abraham Lincoln. The Emperor Jones,* one of the earliest Broadway productions by a white playwright to feature a black performer, was not the first: In 1917, three short plays about Negro life by white poet Ridgely Torrence were presented on Broadway with an entirely black cast. But Gilpin was the first black actor to achieve prominence on Broadway. In 1926, *The Emperor Jones,* again with Gilpin in the title role, was revived for a successful short run. Talented and experienced, but bedeviled by alcoholism and hampered by limited opportunities, Gilpin never again performed on Broadway.

The Emperor Jones and Gilpin pried open the Broadway door for at least a few other black actors. Rose McClendon (1884–1936), trained at the American Academy of Dramatic Arts, had leading roles in Paul Green's *In Abraham's Bosom* (1926) and in Dorothy and DuBose Heyward's all-black cast *Porgy* (1927), the source for George and Ira Gershwin's opera *Porgy and Bess* (1935). *Porgy,* produced by the Theatre Guild, ran for nearly four hundred performances. McClendon appeared on Broadway in numerous plays throughout the thirties, most notably in the Group Theatre's production of Paul Green's *The House of Connelly* (1931), the distinguished black poet Langston Hughes's *Mulatto* (1935), and in Archibald McLeish's *Panic* (1935). Richard B. Harrison (1864–1935) achieved widespread fame on Broadway, and later on tour, as De Lawd in Marc Connelly's biblical folk drama *The Green Pastures* (1930). Canada Lee (1907–1952) appeared notably in Paul Peters and George Sklar's left-wing antilynching drama *Stevedore* (1934), as Banquo in Orson Welles's celebrated all black-cast "voodoo" *Macbeth* (1936), as Bigger Thomas in Richard Wright's *Native Son* (1941), and as Caliban in director Margaret Webster's revival of *The Tempest* (1945).

Paul Robeson (1898–1976) was the most prominent black star of the era. Although trained for the law at Columbia University, Robeson's outstanding baritone voice and natural acting abilities led him to a career as a concert singer and actor: Brutus Jones in revivals of *The Emperor Jones* in 1924 and 1925 and the lawyer Jim Harris in O'Neill's controversial *All God's Children Got Wings* (1924). In the late twenties Robeson went to England, where he played in the London production of *The Emperor Jones* and triumphed as Joe with his moving interpretation of "Ol' Man River" in Jerome Kern's *Show Boat* (1928). While in London, he also played Othello, the first African American to do so since Ira Aldridge's appearances in 1865 (see Roach, Chap. 4, Vol. I, of this history). Robeson had no previous experience acting Shakespeare, and critical notices ranged from "magnificent" to "disappointing." The production had a respectable six-week run, however, and then briefly toured the provincial circuit. It laid the foundation for Robeson's subsequent Othellos and asserted a view of Othello as a black African rather than as an Arabic Moor, as the character had traditionally been played. Returning to New York, Robeson reprised Joe in Florenz Ziegfeld's revised and updated revival of *Show Boat* (1932). In the 1930s, Robeson achieved international renown as a concert singer. He also appeared in a number of movies, mostly adventure melodramas set in colonial Africa. In 1943, he returned to Broadway as Othello in a successful production directed by Margaret Webster with Uta Hagen as Desdemona and Puerto Rican–American actor José Ferrer as Iago. Robeson was the first African American to play Othello in America with a white supporting cast. Some critics complained about his technical shortcomings as a Shakespearean actor, but overall Robeson and the production were judged a resounding success. With this performance Robeson claimed Othello for future generations of African American actors and furthered progress toward racial equality and a recognition of black acting talent. An outspoken activist engaged in various social and political causes, particularly human rights, and sympathetic with leftish organizations, Robeson's career faltered in the virulent anticommunist atmosphere of postwar America. He was essentially blacklisted from Broadway and Hollywood. The Department of State revoked his passport, so international travel was also impossible. He continued to give concerts, however. In the late fifties, Robeson's passport was returned, and in 1959 he reprised his Othello at Stratford-upon-Avon. Robeson garnered high praise from critics and numerous friends and admirers for his powerful, stately interpretation. Had social conditions been different, Robeson might have become a major stage and screen star. But his achievements as a singer, actor, and political activist were significant and an inspiration to the postwar generation of African American actors.

The Lure of Hollywood

Beginning in the early 1900s, movies became increasingly popular. Estimates vary, but Bernheim, for example, noted that in 1909 there were seven thousand movie theatres nationwide, increasing by the late twenties to over twenty thousand. He also calculated that in 1925 weekly movie attendance was 130 million compared to legitimate theatre weekly attendance of 2.3 million (87). With the arrival of "talkies" in 1927, the appetite for movies grew substantially, first surpassing and then replacing vaudeville and popular-priced stock as the leading form of popular entertainment. By the end of the thirties, Hollywood was producing over four hundred feature films a year, four times the number of theatrical productions of all kinds available in New York.

As a class, actors were disdainful of the dramatically vapid, cheaply made early "flickers," and – at least initially – movie salaries, roughly comparable to stock salaries, offered no incentive for compromising one's talent. Nonetheless, most early silent-film stars were stage trained, often with decades of experience in stock companies, touring, and on Broadway before they turned to films. When the nascent film industry was centered near New York, actors might easily divide their time between film shooting and stage performance. The industry's relocation to Hollywood in the early teens, however, made such a schedule difficult, with actors moving to Hollywood permanently or foreswearing the movies – a rare few would succeed as both stage and screen stars.

As the quality of films improved and financial rewards increased, few actors could resist a Hollywood offer. In the late twenties, a few top legitimate stars could command $1,000 to $1,500 a week (musical and vaudeville stars even more); leading supporting players might make as much as $500; common players, $100. Hollywood salaries were substantially higher, especially for stars. After his triumph as *Hamlet* in London in 1925, John Barrymore, for example, was offered over $76,000 per film. Furthermore, if the shooting schedule went beyond the usual three weeks, he was paid an extra $7,625 per week. By the early thirties, Barrymore was earning a half-million dollars a year (Peters, 264). Hollywood also held out the lure of national celebrity and a glamorous, sybaritic lifestyle, formerly available only to the wealthy social elite and never to mere players. Numerous promising and experienced actors were gobbled up by Hollywood producers, insatiable for new stars to feature in the hundreds of films produced annually.

From Hard Times to Limited Prospects

The Broadway stage, weakened by Hollywood and by its own mounting organizational tensions and practices, was further crippled by the Great Depression (1929–40). Established stars, some companies like the Theatre Guild, and a few commercial producers managed to survive. How the Depression directly affected the acting profession is difficult to determine. Actors, as a rule, were perennially unemployed. In the late twenties, there were about ten thousand members of Equity. During the peak 1927–28 season, of six thousand New York performers very few averaged more than fourteen weeks work in the theatre (Bernheim, 124–26). By 1934, Equity reported that in New York there were five thousand unemployed actors, roughly half its membership. In Hollywood in 1932, twenty-two thousand actors registered with casting bureaus, but most were probably inexperienced laypersons looking for work as extras in one of the few industries with jobs (Flanagan, 14, 20). One might assume, however, that in the 1930s, with a significant decline in the number of Broadway productions, stock companies, and touring combinations, employment opportunities for legitimate actors were even more limited than usual. Certainly many of Broadway's established and most promising stars opted for the relative financial security of Hollywood, largely immune to the country's economic woes. Most would never return to the stage.

The establishment of the Federal Theatre Project (FTP) in 1935, discussed elsewhere in this history, was a boon to many common players. Although the weekly base pay of twenty-three dollars was about half the Equity minimum, FTP offered hundreds of jobs, across the nation, in a broad range of theatrical productions from revivals of the classics, to original docudramas, to plays for children. Sniped at by Equity and commercial producers for "amateurism" and unfair competition and eventually closed down in 1939 by anti–New Deal congressmen, the FTP gave jobs to over twelve thousand people, five thousand in New York alone, during its four years of operation, many presumably actors. The opportunities that it presented to minority and local performers was unprecedented. By 1938–39, as the economy slowly improved, thousands of FTP "graduates" returned to jobs in theatre, the film industry, and radio.

The onset of World War II stimulated industrial growth, created jobs, and ultimately broke the back of the Great Depression. The number of new productions increased marginally, but acting opportunities in the legitimate theatre remained severely limited. After the war, Hollywood would continue to flourish, and new venues for actors would be established Off-Broadway, in a growing number of regional professional theatres, and in the new medium of television, but the heady, expansive days of the Gilded Age and the twenties would never be recaptured.

Note

1   Michael A. Morrison in a recent book, *John Barrymore, Shakepearean Actor* (1997), reconstructs Barrymore's Richard III and Hamlet in the most detailed analysis to date.

Bibliography: Actors and Acting

To date, there is no definitive, comprehensive history of American actors and acting. Students of American actors and acting must mine a variety of primary and secondary sources. This chapter drew on a number of different sources, including, in particular, two excellent modern studies. Garff B. Wilson's *A History of American Acting* (1966) is a seminal survey of notable actors and their performance styles with an emphasis on the nineteenth century. Wilson's chapter-length treatment of twentieth-century acting trends, is cursory yet informative. Benjamin McArthur's *Actors and American Culture, 1880–1920* (1984) is an authoritative examination of the acting profession against the social and cultural background of the time. Duerr's remarkable history of acting from ancient Greece to the present times, *The Length and Depth of Acting* (1962), is useful for placing American actors and acting styles against both their English and continental counterparts and the general aesthetic movements of the day.

Theatrical biography and autobiography proliferated at the turn of the century as public interest in the lives of actors mounted. The critic and theatrical chronicler William Winter, a prolific leader in the field, authored full-scale biographies of Edwin Booth (1893), Ada Rehan (1898), Richard Mansfield (1910), Joseph Jefferson (1913), and Tyrone Power (1913); and his various theatrical memoirs, including *Brief Chronicles* (1889), *Other Days* (1908), the two-volume *The Wallet of Time* (1913), the three-volume *Shakespeare on the Stage* (1911–1916), and *Vagrant Memories* (1915), sketch the lives of numerous Gilded Age stars. Profiles of notable actors can also be found in the following collections: Strang's *Famous Actresses of the Day, Famous Actors of the Day,* and *Players and Plays of the Last Quarter Century,* collectively covering numerous turn-of-the century examples; Matthews and Hutton's five-volume *Actors and Actresses of Great Britain and the United States* (1886); Moses's *Famous Actor-Families in America* (1906); Clapp and Edgett's *Players of the Present* (1899–1901); and McKay and Wingate's *Famous American Actors of Today* (1896). Although usually anecdotal and lacking in critical and historical perspective, and sometimes factually unreliable as well, actors' autobiographies and reminiscences are important sources of information. John Drew's *My Years on Stage* (1922), Clara Morris's *Life on the Stage* (1901), Otis Skinner's *Footlights and Spotlights* (1924), and Frederick Warde's *Fifty Years of Make-Believe* (1920), are but a few examples of the genre.

As movies brought celebrity status to many actors, public interest in their lives escalated with an increase in frequently gossipy or "confessional" accounts that often reveal more about actors' private lives than about their craft; but as sources of insight into sometimes unique personalities, their potential value should not be discounted. For the most part, modern biographies of American actors have been weak in narrative and critical approach; theatrical biography simply has not consistently achieved the high level of its counterpart in literature, music, or art. But a number of generally well-researched, eminently readable narrative lives have fleshed out our knowledge of many late-nineteenth and early-twentieth-century stars. The life of Edwin Booth, for example, has been chronicled in several sympathetic studies, including Lockridge's *Darling of Misfortune,* Kimmel's *The Mad Booths of Maryland,* and Ruggles's *The Prince of Players.* Shattuck's exemplary *The Hamlet of Edwin Booth* and my own *Edwin Booth's Performances* (1990) have added concrete details about Booth's signal performances and their significance in Gilded Age culture. Other traditional but meritorious biographies include Binns's *Mrs. Fiske and the American Theatre,* Coleman's *Fair Rosalind: The American Career of Helena Modjeska,* Patterson's *Maude Adams;* Kotsilibas-Davis's *Great Times, Good Times: The Odyssey of Maurice Barrymore,* Tad Mosel's *Leading Lady: The World and Theatre of Katharine Cornell,* Kenneth Barrow's *Helen Hayes,* Jared Brown's *The Fabulous Lunts,* and Lambert's *Nazimova. The House of Barrymore* by Margot Peters, an experienced literary and theatrical biographer, is a well-documented, thoughtful, and lively group portrait of Lionel, Ethel, and John Barrymore against the heyday of Broadway and Hollywood.

In recent years, the influence of feminist studies has critically informed a number of insightful works on nineteenth- and early-twentieth-century actresses, including Johnson's *American Actress: Perspective on the Nineteenth Century;* Auster's *Actresses and Suffragists: Women in the American Theatre, 1890–1920;* the invaluable *Notable Women in the American Theatre,* superbly compiled and edited by Robinson, Roberts, and Barranger; Shanke's *Shattered Applause: The Lives of Eva Le Gallienne;* and Helen Sheehy's *Eva Le Gallienne.* Martin Bauml Duberman brought both his perspective as a distinguished historian of modern America and his special sensitivity to "otherness" and oppression to create in *Paul Robeson,* the definitive biography of the great black singer, actor, and political activist, as well as an illuminating history of a turbulent era.

Several recent studies of actors and acting interweave cultural history with biography. Shattuck's *Shakespeare on the American Stage: From Booth and Barrett to Sothern and Marlowe* vividly recovers dozens of Gilded Age Shakespearean actors while tracing the gradual decline of traditional, classical acting. Erroll Hill's *Shakespeare in Sable: A History of Black Shakespearean Actors* is a pioneering, substantial contribution to the subject. The visits of various foreign actors to America are covered in a chapter of Shattuck's *Shakespeare on the American Stage.* Knepler's *The Gilded Stage: The Years of the Great International Actresses* focuses mainly on Ristori, Bernhardt, and Duse; Carlson describes the tours of Ristori, Salvini, and Rossi in *The Italian Shakespearians. Trouping: How the Show Came to Town* by Philip C. Lewis, a trouper himself as a young man, is a delightfully entertaining and informative account of nineteenth-century theatrical touring.

The development of acting schools is thoroughly covered in McTeague's *Before Stanislavsky: American Professional Acting Schools and Acting Theory, 1875–1925.* Hornblow's *Training for the Stage* (1916), subtitled "Some Hints for Those About to Choose The Player's Career," is an interesting and informative essay on the opportunities, options, and pitfalls facing an aspiring actor at the turn of the century. Edwards's *The Stanislavsky Heritage* reports on the visits and influence of the Moscow Art Theatre. J. W. Roberts's *Richard Boleslavsky: His Life and Work in the Theatre* is the only book-length account in English. Several informative essays on the influence of Russian actors and acting on American acting can be found in *Wandering Stars: Russian Emigré Theatre, 1905–1940,* edited by Laurence Senelick. Wendy Smith's *Real Life Drama* is a detailed history of the Group Theatre, including its efforts to develop psychologically real, politically charged acting techniques. Hallie Flanagan's memoir *Arena* and Matthew's *The Federal Theatre, 1935–1939* remain important works on the Federal Theatre Project (see also suggestions in Chapters 2 and 4). Hirsch's *A Method to their*

Madness: The History of the Actor's Studio is a provocative account of this influential training school (the Hirsch chapter on acting in Vol. III of this history provides additional coverage).

Several recent reference works provide important primary data and guidance for further information on American actors. *American Theatre Companies,* edited by Durham, is particularly useful for information about actors' changing company affiliations, their repertoires, and salary scales. Both Leiter's multivolume *The Encyclopedia of the New York Stage: 1920–1950* and Bordman's three-volume *American Theatre: A Chronicle of Comedy and Drama* [1869–1945] reliably date and excerpt critical reactions to the performances of numerous actors. Archer's *American Actors and Actresses: A Guide to Information Sources* is a standard bibliographic guide to the subject. Bryan's *Stage Lives: A Bibliography and Index to Theatrical Biographies in English* and *Stage Deaths: A Biographical Guide to International Theatrical Obituaries* are valuble sources, especially to secondary or minor players. William C. Young's *Famous Actors and Actresses on the American Stage* and Donald Mullin's *Victorian Actors and Actresses in Review* excerpt selections from often hard to find contemporary memoirs, biographies, and critical reviews. Standard reference works, such as the *Dictionary of American Biography* and the *National Cyclopedia of American Biography,* are sometimes the only sources to certain actors's biographies. Older general histories of the American theatre, such as *The American Stage* (1929) by Oral Sumner Coad and Edwin Mims Jr. and *A History of the Theatre in America* (1919) by Arthur Hornblow, also contain information about individual actors not available in other sources.

It is surprising that so few first-rate biographies of notable stars of the past exist. Often a wealth of primary material can be found available in one or more American theatrical collections. Feminist and critical studies suggest, furthermore, new biographical approaches. Several stars of the past seem to merit renewed attention, including Mary Anderson, John Drew, Clara Morris, Julia Marlowe and E. H. Sothern, and Walter Hampden. Perhaps a new generation of scholars might be encouraged to explore this potentially rich field.

8

Scenography, Stagecraft, and Architecture

Mary C. Henderson

Architecture

The post–Civil War years ushered in an era of unprecedented and widespread theatre building in the country. By 1880, according to the most often quoted estimate by the critic William Winter, there were approximately five thousand theatres in thirty-five hundred cities and towns across America. Disparate forces – evolutionary and revolutionary, internal and external – abetted the proliferation of theatres and were responsible for an extended period of growth that lasted more than fifty years. In the immediate postwar years, the now united country was on the verge of enormous change. The steady flow of population pushing west predicted the time when the geography of the country would extend from the east to the West Coast. When the Gold Rush of 1849 propelled the sleepy California territory into a state the following year, it was even more imperative that the country be united. Fortunately, the means to accomplish this event were at hand or in the process of being developed.

When Congress passed the Pacific Railroad Act and the Homestead Act in tandem in 1862, the spectacular growth of the country was assured. Thousands of miles of railroad track were being added each year and would meet in 1869 in a remote area in Utah to unite the country from coast to coast. The population followed the railroad and "cities sprang up where nature once reigned." History repeated itself again and again in the westward push as settlement became town and town became city along the route of the railroad. Prosperity brought civilization and leisure time, and they, in turn, pulled the theatre, the principal medium of entertainment outside the home, into the mainstream of life in the emerging towns and cities.

Almost simultaneously, events in theatrical history would begin to dovetail with these external influences. The most important and far-reaching of them was the creation and consequent spread of the "combination system." When increasing profits loomed large in the life of nineteenth-century managers, they realized that greater gains could be had by sending a hit show with its complement of actors to not just one or two nearby theatres but a dozen or more by railroad. The touring company carrying its own scenery replaced the centuries-old stock-repertory company resident in its own theatre, which was transformed into a "booking house," a playhouse to be rented out to the traveling shows.

A logical outgrowth of the combination system was the creation of the "duplicate company," one or more spawns of the original show that could be sent out on "the Road," usually from New York, with a *different* complement of actors but with enough of the show left intact to qualify it as a hit "Direct from Broadway." In time, hundreds of companies would take to the Road, setting up competition among rival attractions, which encouraged the building of multiple playhouses in the larger cities. A further development was in the creation of "first class" theatres for booking plays and musicals and "second class" playhouses for vaudeville, minstrel, or specialty shows. In 1897, Baltimore had six "first class" theatres; Cincinnati, seven; Philadelphia, eleven; San Francisco, four; and St. Louis, seven. Each of these cities also had one or more "second-class" theatres.

By the turn of the century, New York, with its near-two-million population, had close to thirty "first-class theatres" and seven "second-class" theatres. Since 1875, with the establishment of a theatre district around Union Square, New York had assumed the role not only of principal purveyor of theatrical products for the country but theatre architecture as well. Shows originating in the city's theatre district were soon sent on the road for the rest of the country to enjoy, and theatres built in New York were models for those in the hinterlands.

Like everything else in American society, economic cycles had an impact on theatre building. The Panics of 1873 and 1893 may have temporarily slowed the growth of the theatre and the building of playhouses, but in their wake came renewed spurts of building and often changes in direction. The Panic of 1873 helped the combination system consolidate its position because it proved to be more efficient and economical than the stock-repertory company, despite the miseries it wrought on actors and other theatre professionals who found themselves out of steady jobs. The Panic of 1893 helped to bring forth the Theatrical Syndicate, an oft-referred-to phenomenon in this volume and the inspiration of six theatrical managers who, when they looked at the industrial practices of the time, realized that industrial monopolies worked well and could weather hard times. They plotted to control both the theatrical productions and the playhouses from coast to coast. And for a while, they almost succeeded. Only the cunning of the Shubert brothers, who began to build their own theatres opposite or close to Syndicate-controlled playhouses, weakened the hold of the infamous six. The competition only added to the proliferation of theatres across the country.

Among the thousands of theatres built from 1870 to 1930 in America were examples of good and bad, conventional and innovative architecture. At the beginning of the era, the deep stage, proscenium boxes, and horseshoe auditorium prevailed, but by 1900 they were supplanted by the shallow picture-frame stage and the smaller fan-shaped auditorium with boxes on the side walls above the orchestra. The addition of a tall stage house to encompass the fly gallery, where scenery could be hung above the stage, altered the profile of the exterior. Throughout the era, theatres continued to be included as a part of larger buildings that contained stores and other commercial enterprises, whose rents provided a financial cushion for the owners. In 1880, when the Madison Square Theatre in New York attached a marquee at the entrance, the playhouse was no longer hidden or dominated by other parts of the encompassing structure. Some social historians believe that the playhouse became an architectural statement on the status and achievements of the society it served. In the more prosperous communities, architects, the more prestigious the better, were solicited to design the theatre. Their mission was to add some magic to the facade or the ornamentation of the interior. The basic arrangement of the proscenium theatre remained intact.

Up to 1870, with the exception of one architectural firm, J. B. McElfatrick and Sons, no architect or architectural firm could make a respectable living designing theatres. From the founding of that firm in 1855 until it went out of business in 1922, the McElfatricks, father and sons, made theatre design almost an exclusive specialty, receiving 228 commissions to build theatres in more than ninety cities and towns from coast to coast. Despite the fact that the founder, John Bailey McElfatrick (1828–1906), had received his training as a carpenter and architectural assistant without benefit of study abroad or in one of the burgeoning architectural and engineering schools in America, he produced workable plants that provided good sight lines and acoustics. (Curiously, they located their New York office in the Knickerbocker Theatre building, a Carrère and Hastings creation.)

The typical McElfatrick theatre was a boxy structure housing a fan-shaped auditorium with side boxes and one or two balconies, a proscenium stage, and adequate, if not remarkable, backstage space and dressing rooms. The McElfatricks were also able to fit the theatre into available plots without sacrificing too many amenities. There were always a lobby and lounges in a McElfatrick house as well as fire safety equipment (their theatre complex, the

Olympia, was equipped with an automatic sprinkling system, an innovation for the time). Without doubt they tailored the degree of decoration both inside and out to the purses of their clients.

For Oscar Hammerstein's Olympia, McElfatrick's most impressive accomplishment, built in 1895 with a blockwide frontage on Broadway, they designed a monumental facade that borrowed heavily from the French Second Empire style (popular in the post–Civil War decades) but added such McElfatrick touches as a row of round porthole windows in the middle of the building and on the sides. Originally, it had been conceived as a kind of entertainment mall, but it evolved into two theatres, one (later named the Criterion) for dramatic spectacles and the other larger hall (later named the New York Theatre) principally for musical attractions, with a roof garden theatre perched above it. A color scheme of light and dark blue and a liberal use of Italianate ornamental plaster, marble, large murals, and other ornate touches dominated the interior decoration.

The McElfatricks and their successors made prompt use of the technological advances outside the theatre. Developments in construction – such as structural steel and reinforced concrete, the improved cantilever, the invention of the elevator, the introduction of the electric light, and the production of flameproof materials – altered forever the architecture of theatres, making them safer and more flexible. For the first time in America, engineers as well as architects began to study the special problems of acoustics, then an infant science, in theatrical construction. In 1896, the publication of William B. Birkmire's book, *The Planning and Construction of American Theatres,* covered not only construction and acoustics but also heating and ventilation, the available means of fireproofing, and building codes. It symbolized the long way that the theatre building had traveled since the days when it was regarded by Puritan colonists as the "devil's playroom."

The dominant influence in the architecture of theatres came from abroad. Beginning in the middle of the nineteenth century and extending well into the twentieth century, many aspiring American architects were educated at the famed Ecole des Beaux-Arts (Ecole Nationale Supérieur des Beaux-Arts) in Paris. They carried home not only the basic styles promulgated by the school but also its practical philosophy of construction, which involved symmetry, balance, and a mathematical precision in laying out plans for each building. The design had to be wedded to practicality, the selection of materials to the logic of the structure.

Stylistically, the school's teachings favored the academic and conservative. Classical Greek architecture was assiduously studied, but other eras were also revisited. Evolving from the school was a welter of eclectic Beaux-Arts styles variously described as Italian Renaissance, French Second Empire, Near Eastern, Oriental, Gothic, Romanesque, and Victorian. One prevailing characteristic of the Beaux-Arts styles was a horror of undecorated surfaces, which resulted in a mixture of styles in one building. Among the Americans who studied at the school and later designed theatres were Louis Sullivan (1856–1924), John Merven Carrère (1858–1911), Thomas Hastings (1860–1929), Whitney Warren (1864–1943), Henry Herts (1871–1933), and Hugh Tallant (1869–1952).

Louis Sullivan designed the Auditorum Theatre in Chicago, the theatre that is most often cited as revolutionary by architectural experts. Opening in 1889, its influence was not immediately felt despite its unique elements. Like Wagner's Festspielhaus in Bayreuth, it contained innovations that were not readily adopted by theatre architects and builders of the time. The Auditorium was co-designed by Dankmar Adler (1844–1900), Sullivan's partner in the engineering and architectural firm that gained prominence in the surge of building after the Chicago fire of 1871. Although the firm designed ten theatres during its existence, it is the Auditorium that has survived and made its reputation in theatrical architecture. (Threatened with destruction during the forties, the entire building complex is now the property of Roosevelt College, which has restored the theatre as faithfully as possible with municipal and private support.)

In physical construction, the theatre was unremarkable. Before the age of structural steel, the entire structure was built with the usual brick load-bearing walls faced with granite and limestone. The arches of the facade borrowed from the heavy Romanesque style of H. H. Richardson. Within the building itself, the newer system of cast-iron trusses and beams was used extensively. The theatre itself was part of a larger complex containing a hotel, offices, and stores, which almost entirely encased it. It was a big theatre (the largest in America to that time) with a capacity of more than forty-two hundred seats, which could be pared down to about twenty-five hundred seats when the upper two balconies were closed off by iron shutters. The proscenium opening, too, could be reduced in size from a width of forty-seven feet from seventy-five feet. (Even with a smaller capacity and smaller proscenium opening, it did not suit the kind of plays and musical attractions that were coming into vogue at the time.) It was, in effect, a multipurpose auditorium, several generations before its time.

Several of the Auditorium's features were noteworthy. At a time when the science of acoustics was still being studied, Adler was a pioneer in applying the principles that he himself had explored and defined. The orchestra floor rose seventeen feet from front to back, based on what Adler called the "isocoustic curve," the better to carry the sound from front to back. The balconies also had steep rakes. The two upper balconies became an integral part of the roof rather than hanging off the back wall. Surrounding the orchestra were two levels of boxes to complete the interior arrangement. Above, Adler's acoustical

ceiling completed the curve of the auditorium. Few right angles are immediately discernible in the theatre.

Sullivan, who was responsible for most of the design, made liberal use of
arches to carry forward the curve that Adler used as the basis for acoustics.
He also averred that he had been the first to make decorative use of electric
lighting, which became part of the ornamentation of the Auditorium's interior.
Sullivan's color scheme of gold and old ivory in graded tones was enhanced
by lightbulbs studding the ceiling. Three large murals, one over the proscenium and one on each of the two side walls, were allegorical and inspired by
Sullivan's lifelong obsession with music, particularly Wagnerian opera. The
Auditorium was a superb opera house and concert hall but less successful as
a theatre for drama.

Several architectural firms in New York, although not specialists in theatre
design, made a number of (and it turns out, lasting) contributions to theatre
architecture. When they designed theatres in the city's emerging theatre district, they had to accept certain limitations. The first was the plot size, which,
because of the increasing scarcity and cost of available building sites, might
be of unusual shape or of severely constricted dimensions. The second was
the New York building code, the most stringent in the nation. Because of theatre fires in the city (some thirty during the century), regulations were
enacted to protect the public. In the wake of the fire in Brooklyn at Conway's
Theatre in 1876, and in Chicago at the Iroquois Theatre in 1903, the two worst
fires in theatrical history, which claimed many lives, building codes were
enacted nationally in 1905. By 1927, the regulations became uniform and
international, covering such architectural elements as the number of exits,
the flammability of building and ornamental materials, easy egress to the
street, built-in fire-fighting equipment, and other essentials that had to be
absorbed into the design of the playhouse.[1]

The sheer number of theatres built from 1893 to 1928 within New York's
confined theatre district, as well as the fact that the men who controlled
these theatres also had interests throughout the nation, made New York's
theatre architecture the paradigm for the country. The leading producers of
the time turned to some of the most prestigious architectural firms for the
design of their theatres. Among them were the firms of Herts and Tallant and
Carrère and Hastings.

Carrère and Hastings, who had previously designed the Knickerbocker Theatre (1893), a boxy structure on Broadway and Thirty-eighth Street, with a large
stage intended for big musicals and spectacles, were commissioned by Charles
Dillingham to design his flagship playhouse. More in the spirit of Beaux-Arts,
the handsome Globe theatre (renamed much later as the Lunt–Fontanne) was
built on Broadway and Forty-sixth Street. The architects chose Italian Renaissance for the exterior and French Louis Seize for the interior treatment, but the

house itself, with its fan-shaped auditorium and picture-frame proscenium, was unique only for its inclusion of a sliding panel in the ceiling. During warm weather, it could be opened to ventilate the house and make it viable for productions during the summer months. (No record exists to affirm whether it was ever used as intended.)

Herts and Tallant as a firm, and later Henry Herts alone, made major contributions to the architecture of the theatre district, utilizing the latest advances in structural engineering. Their first joint commissions were for the New Amsterdam and the Lyceum, both of which opened within a week of each other in 1903. The New Amsterdam was notable for its extensive use of Art Nouveau in its decoration and for its complex construction, which united a ten-story office tower with a main theatre surmounted by a roof-garden theatre. In the interior construction, Herts and Tallant employed the largest steel cantilevers ever used in theatres to bear the weight of the balconies and the roof-garden theatre atop the main auditorium. The cantilevers also did away with the support posts that obstructed the view of the stage from many seats.

The interior ornamentation of the New Amsterdam – all sinuous leaf, flower, and vine entwined with allegorical, Shakespearean, and Wagnerian themes – was unique in theatrical decoration. It was combined with a color scheme of muted mauve, green, lilac, and aluminum leaf, unheard of in those days of gilt and red interiors. Commissioned by Daniel Frohman, the (new) Lyceum, with its stately columned facade, was typical of Beaux-Arts architecture, but its inclusion of a seven-story wing devoted to such facilities as a paint frame, scenery construction, prop, and costume shops harkened back to nineteenth-century repertory playhouses. By the time it opened in 1903, they were rendered obsolete in the new system of single-show bookings.

Busily acquiring sites in the theatre district, the Shuberts had commissioned Henry Herts to design their Sam S. Shubert and Booth theatres in 1913. One of the associates in the Herts office, a young man named Herbert J. Krapp (1887–1973), was probably encouraged by the Shubert brothers to strike out on his own. From 1916 to 1928, Krapp was to design twelve theatres in New York as well as scores more west of the Hudson. (He was also kept busy altering hundreds of existing theatres both in New York and throughout the country.) In addition to the Shubert houses, Krapp designed nine other Broadway houses. Most of his theatres are still standing.

Always inhibited by the budget-minded Shuberts, Krapp built compact playhouses on limited plots with restricted public amenities. In most cases, the almost lobbyless theatres used the street outside the doors as their public gathering spaces. The decoration of Krapp-designed theatres was usually restrained and eschewed the ornate Beaux-Arts in favor of the simpler Georgian and Federal styles. When Krapp designed for the Chanin Construction

Company between 1924 and 1927, he appeared to have more latitude (and money) in his designs for six theatre commissions. The Chanin theatres were somewhat better built than the Shubert houses, and Krapp introduced in the first of them, Chanin's Forty-sixth Street Theatre, a sharply raked orchestra floor, reminiscent of Adler and Sullivan's Auditorium. It had the effect of pulling the audience in the rear seats closer to the stage. However, a deep balcony overhang also partially obstructed the view of the rear orchestra seating. Whatever their faults, the Krapp-designed shoebox theatres have been pronounced among "the best performance halls known."

Away from Broadway, other developments were shaping theatre architecture. As an outgrowth of the community and amateur "Little Theatre movement" during the twenties, playhouses were being built in large and small cities and on college and university campuses to serve special audiences. Unlike commercial booking houses, where most of the equipment had to be rented and brought into the theatre, college and community theatres had the virtue of subsuming up-to-the-minute backstage equipment into the architecture and could indulge in limited experimentation in the actual building. The Pasadena Playhouse (1925), the Cleveland Play House (1927), and the Kalamazoo Civic Auditorium (1931) are outstanding examples of architecture that was bent to the needs of the permanent company and the community.

All three were proscenium houses with limited seating capacities (500–800 seats) and incorporated built-in lighting and scenery-handling equipment; storage facilities; a warren of shops for scenery, props, and costumes; offices; and amenities for the audience. The Cleveland Play House originally had two theatres in its complex, one for use as a laboratory stage. Taking its community mission seriously, the Pasadena Playhouse included a school for training actors on a year-round basis, which added classrooms to the main structure. Although all were undistinguished architecturally on the exterior, they were deliberately designed to fit within the community ambiance – from the red-brick Cleveland Play House to the California mission style of the Pasadena Playhouse.

With the emergence of the study of drama and theatre as a separate academic discipline, several universities saw the need to provide students with a practical workplace for advancing their study. In 1926, Yale University brought George Pierce Baker to its campus from Harvard to found a graduate school of drama and to build a theatre to serve his needs. Behind a facade of brick and stone to blend with the Collegiate Gothic style of the campus there was a simply arranged auditorum seating approximately seven hundred in the orchestra and balcony and an unadorned proscenium stage without an orchestra pit. The building, as befitting its purpose, continues to house lecture rooms, a library, and faculty offices, in addition to the complement of shops for making scenery and costumes.

Not all universities clung to the proscenium stage. In 1914, designer Raymond Sovey set up a temporary theatre-in-the-round in the gymnasium of Columbia University's Teachers College. In place of the traditional arrangement of separate auditorium and stage, Sovey placed the audience in a ring around the stage. Arena staging was simpler and more economical than proscenium staging and required just a large space, not expensive new architecture. Only minimal scenery and lighting were necessary; the rest of the usual theatrical panoply was left to the eye of the beholder. According to the adherents of theatre-in-the-round, what the audience missed in visual spectacle was more than compensated by greater interaction and intimacy between audience and players.

Before the Pasadena Playhouse was built in 1925, Gilmor Brown had also tried arena staging and later built the Bandbox, an arena theatre, for his experiments as an adjunct to the main theatre. But it was at the University of Washington that the virtues of arena staging were convincingly displayed. In 1932, Glenn Hughes, head of the drama department, began to apply arena staging successfully to realistic plays; and, in 1940, the university built the Penthouse Theatre, an architectural theatre-in-the-round for his work. A low, single-story building with a central dome covering the theatre, it embraced a simple arena with three rows of stepped-up seating. The actors moved within a circle, scenery-less except for appropriate props, and entered from doors in the surrounding walls. Other academic groups followed the lead of the University of Washington, but not until the post–World War II years did theatre-in-the-round become a potent architectural form.

What can be best described as a movement *against* theatrical architecture occurred in the dozen or so years preceding America's entry into World War II. In those pre-air-conditioned years, when the well-off could flee to the countryside away from urban heat, producers would set up stages in barns, mills, old inns, abandoned factories, fish houses, churches, meeting houses, and any other buildings providing a large unencumbered space. One end would be fitted out with a stage and the rest of the space would be devoted to the discomfort of the audience, most of whom sat on hard benches or folding chairs. Located most often in resort or rural areas, these makeshift theatres, drafty and uncomfortable, managed to charm not only audiences but stars idled by Broadway's summer shutdown.

One of the oldest survivors of this era is the Cape Playhouse in Dennis on Cape Cod in Massachusetts. Founded by Raymond Moore in 1927, it was a transformed Unitarian meeting house that Moore bought for a few hundred dollars and had moved to a three-and-a-half-acre open field, for which he paid $1,200. He lured designer Cleon Throckmorton from New York to organize it into a proper theatre and design such necessary components as a stage, proscenium, and fly gallery, which were added to the north end of the building.

Throckmorton retained the ecclesiastical feel of the interior by constructing church pews in place of regular seating. Moore's investment was a staggering (for the time) $40,000. Eventually a scene shop was built and, still later, a restaurant, a souvenir shop, and other audience attractions. With a seating capacity of under six hundred (in the orchestra, balcony, and two loges), Moore and his successors had no trouble in keeping it afloat during the Depression and after. In a way, the Cape Playhouse and its sister summer theatres in the northeast represented a return to the improvised architecture that had ushered in theatrical activity in America.

Scenography and Stagecraft

During the last decades of the nineteenth century the building of theatres underwent pronounced changes not only from social, economic, and historical causes but also from a slow transformation of theatrical practice. As public taste for the oft-repeated Shakespearean dramas, spectacles, and melodramas began to wane, managers began to replace them with a different kind of dramatic fare, which demanded special and unusual (for the time) scenic investiture. Inevitably, theatrical architecture reflected the changes. Gone were proscenium doors, the extended apron, the deep and raked stage, and the high proscenium opening, all of which did not suit the domestic dramas and storybook operettas that were gradually replacing the old fare.

As usual, the first intimations of change came from abroad. At midcentury, Charles Kean and his company arrived in America in productions of Shakespeare unlike any seen before on U.S. stages. Kean's obsession with verisimilitude in scene and costume to fit the time and place of the drama created a stir among managers and audiences alike. A generation later, in 1883, his countryman Henry Irving added a new chapter to the trend toward realism by giving more three-dimensionality to the settings. Audiences could not help but be impressed by the completeness of Irving's productions: the ensemble acting combined with realistic settings and atmospheric lighting. Compared to the artificial painted trompe-l'oeil scenery and indifferent lighting with which they were accustomed, Irving's productions were a revelation of how realism could be made not only palatable but attractive to audiences.

The "new" American stagecraft demonstrated by Charles Witham, the scenic artist who had been responsible for the success of Edwin Booth's stage in 1869 (see Vol. I of this history), sounded the death knell of the wing-and-drop setting on a raked and grooved stage. Theatres began to be built with flat floors, the better to accommodate the pieces of scenery ("flats"), now lashed together and braced on the floor to form interiors or walls or confined spaces on the stage. A system of "traps" or openings in the stage floor could be utilized not merely for the appearance of Hamlet's ghost or Macbeth's witches but also for special effects. In 1884, borrowing from the European "Asphaleia system," a series of hydraulic lifts that penetrated the stage floor in "cuts" to vary the stage planes, Louis Sullivan went beyond the simple trapped stage in the Auditorium Theatre in Chicago to create a more plastic stage environment.

With the gradual demise of the stock company came a change in the status of the late-nineteenth-century scene painters and their art. The combination system, followed by the rise of the Theatrical Syndicate, forced scene painters out of their heretofore safe berths as well-paid members of the company staff into the hurly burly of competition. Although managers might have had their favorites among the artists who built and painted the scenery, the drive for increasing profits set aside sentimental attachments. The more entrepreneurial members of the profession set up their own scene shops to accept work for hire. Others who preferred to freelance found themselves employed from job to job by either the scene studios that submitted the lowest bids to producers shopping for scenery or directly by the producers.

Scenery-producing factories that supplied generic sets of scenery sprang up wherever there were multiple playhouses in a city or region. Among the earliest was the Armbruster Scenic Studios, founded in Columbus, Ohio, by a German-immigrant scene painter named Mathias Armbruster in 1875. Advertising his wares, he soon established a thriving business supplying scenery to managers, stars, traveling minstrel shows, and hundreds of theatres, both professional and amateur, throughout the country. Catalogs mailed to customers listed prefabricated scenery to represent Victorian hotels and lobbies, southern swamps, South Sea Islands, Atlantic City, Arizona desert, and Japanese gardens as stock pieces along with interiors for whatever social stratum deemed suitable for the characters of the plays. Complete sets of scenery were sent by rail to customers – the only rule applying was that all units of scenery could not be more than five feet nine inches in any one dimension. Since freight-car doors had a maximum opening of six feet, all scenery had to fit through the doors for touring.

The studios also produced scenery to order when special designs were submitted to them by managers. Most often, the scenery consisted of curtains and drops on medium-weight muslin painted with aniline dyes or with opaque distemper (pigment mixed with water and size, a light glue or starch) on heavier weight muslin or linen. Dyes and distemper could be combined on one drop to allow light to drift through the dye-painted portions to create moonlight, sunset, or other atmospheric effects. Cut-outs or profiles of foliage or interesting architectural details might be designed for drops or other pieces, all of which were hung or fitted together on site to create the complete scene. Although drops painted with dyes could be folded for traveling, the pieces

Drawing of a late-nineteenth-century paint shop from *Harper's Weekly,* 30 November 1878.

painted with distemper had to be shipped flat, usually on wooden frames. Everything was painted with small, feathery brush strokes (particularly after the advent of electric lighting) in a style that can only be described as romantic realism. To complete the settings, managers bought three-dimensional pieces from shops specializing in the manufacturing of props or furniture.

Of course, not all of industrializing of scenery was greeted with universal enthusiasm. The loss of status among the scene-painting profession combined with the seriously deteriorating working conditions spurred the artists to band together to form the Protective Alliance of Scene Painters in 1896, which later metamorphosed into the Scenic Artists Assocation in 1912. (It became part of the United Scenic Artists in 1918, which since 1923 has served as the parent organization for contemporary scene designers.) Scenery continued to be the province of the scene painter and the stage carpenter until the end of the nineteenth century. It should be noted, however, that the term "scene painter" was applied loosely. These artists were in fact the designers of the scenery within the conventions of the time.

Toward the end of the nineteenth century, the new realistic play began to take the stage in America. Tightly constructed, with fewer characters than the old-fashioned melodramas and with the action often narrowed to rooms in homes, the plays needed and received a different kind of setting. The "box set," representing three walls of a room, was already in existence as a scenic device but became imbued with new importance. With roots that went back several centuries, it finally took hold when it proved to be the right medium for the "well made" play rapidly coming into vogue. Its staunchest and most influential practitioner was the producer David Belasco (1859–1931).

Belasco, who had served his theatrical apprenticeship in California, arrived in New York in 1895, ready and eager to put his accumulated ideas for stagecraft into action (for Belasco as director, see Chapter 9). For the next twenty-five years, he created the benchmark in realism on stage. It was frequently imitated, but rarely bested. When the curtain rang up on a Belasco set, the audience saw completely appointed rooms, real props, practicable windows and doors, solid-appearing walls, all made to appear as if real people lived or worked in them. Stories about the lengths that Belasco traveled to provide realism have become legend. The contents of a theatrical boarding house, down to the torn and soiled wallpaper, an entire restaurant interior, pine needles from the far West shipped to cover the floor of the stage so that the aroma of pine wafted into the audience every time an actor walked on them, fresh flowers in window boxes, real food cooked on real stoves – all these and more were employed by Belasco. His two loyal stage artists, Wilfred Buckland and Ernest Gros, fulfilled his every demand.

While the illusion of reality suited the frequently meretricious plays that Belasco (and others) brought to the stage, it could not be transported to other kinds of theatrical fare from the 1890s to the teens of the new century. The musical comedy and the revue, which were gaining popularity as lighter forms of entertainment, demanded flights of scenic fancy. The man who best achieved this was Joseph Urban (1872–1933), a Viennese artist-of-all-trades, who was hired by Florenz Ziegfeld Jr. to provide the scenic magic for his series of revues known as the *Follies* and also his productions of musical comedies. Urban did not travel from Europe alone; he brought his finest scene painters with him, who eventually formed the core of a scenic studio founded by the artist. They introduced the practice of painting scenery on the floor rather than hanging from the back of the stage or a large paint frame. Urban was probably the first to be given full credit as the "designer" (not the painter) of the settings and was listed on the first page of the credits of the programs.

Urban designed sets in vivid colors in a romantic pictorial style and lighted them exquisitely. Among his achievements in stagecraft, he introduced a system of painting the scenery canvas in layers of colors, which were spattered in different-colored flecks, much like the pointillism of the impressionist painters. When white light was trained on the canvas, it took on a textured feeling; when colored light was directed on it, one of the flecked colors became dominant. Urban's sets, which shimmered in his carefully wrought lighting, provided the fantasy to the performances that Ziegfeld devised.

Another of Urban's improvements was in his methodical planning of the scenery from sketch to model to built and painted units, a system that came to be universally accepted by later designers. Nothing was left to chance. When the finished scenery arrived on stage, it represented the perfect fulfillment of the designs as originally approved by the producer. Urban supervised the installation and placement of the lighting during special rehearsals so that every scene change and light cue were synchronized during the progress of the actual performance.

Because of the increasingly complicated nature of the scenery, it became imperative to devise a means to change the sets more rapidly to suit the action of the plays, revues, or musicals. In the eighteenth and most of the nineteenth century, with the old wing and drop system, the settings were changed in full view of the audience, who were obviously willing to accept the noise and the mishaps that were a usual occurrence. Whether late-nineteenth-century audiences became less tolerant or whether the producers and managers in collaboration with the stage technicians wanted improvement, the changes in scenery began to be effected behind the curtains, creating the "stage wait." (The stage wait became the bane of all designers.) Improvements in construction and stage technology led to more efficient ways to change scenery – and shorter stage waits. Some of them were descendants of previous eras in stage history

Joseph Urban design for 1917 *Ziegfeld Follies* (a patriotic number marking the U.S.'s entry into World War I). Joseph Urban Collection, Columbia University.

and adapted for contemporary use. They remained experiments until after the turn of the century, when the use of the electric motor supplanted human muscle power.

Hydraulic-lift systems had been installed in Booth's Theatre as early as 1869, and later (as noted) in the Auditorium Theatre in Chicago and the New Amsterdam in New York. Whole sections of the stage could be sunk out of sight, dressed for the next scene, and lifted to stage level or above it. But it was Steele MacKaye (1842–94) who had demonstrated the possibilities of changing complete scenes on double stages, one above the other, then raising one of them to stage level, hiding the other in the stage house. His rebuilt Madison Square Theatre opened in 1880 and contained an elevator stage, among other innovations, which in most cases were slow to spread to the rest of the profession. (The elevator stage proved to be noisy, cumbersome, and slow to operate. It had to wait for future generations to make it technically viable.)

Several other innovations were, in reality, versions of devices tried in other

[Entered at the Post Office of New York, N. Y., as Second Class Matter.]

EKLY JOURNAL OF PRACTICAL INFORMATION, ART, SCIENCE, MECHANICS, CHEMISTRY, AND MANU

No. 14. [PRICE.]   NEW YORK, APRIL 5, 1884.   [$3.]

MOVABLE THEATER STAGES

few years back, or since Richard Wagner first
put the Niebelungen lied at Bayreuth, the tendency
of theaters and opera houses has been to greater
on of the scenic details, the more vivid representa-
the surroundings connected with the plot of the
play or opera. It was on this account that a temple was
specially built in which to present the best illustration of
the "music of the future." Thus also has Mr. Henry Irving
obtained phenomenal success in England, and won great
favor here, by the hard study and unstinted labor he gives
to the perfecting of the scenery and stage equipments for
the setting of his plays. Yet in all of the
now demanded of stage managers, there h
aid extended by inventors, and but few th
patented. The illustration we herewith
affords a view of an improved practic
Madison Square Theater in this city, whic

The elevator stage at the Madison Square Theatre. From *Scientific American,* 5 April 1884. Wilmeth Collection.

ages. The revolving or turntable stage, which had roots in the court theatres of Europe during the late Renaissance and in Japanese theatre, proved to be a serviceable alternate to drawing the curtain for a long stage wait. (In Germany, Karl Lautenschläger reinvented the turntable stage, which became standard equipment for most of the major opera houses and theatres in the country.) Two or more settings could be erected simultaneously, each turned toward the audience at the proper moment. In the early part of the period, its most serious drawback for producers was that the scenery designed for it could not be sent on the road intact. Turntables were installed in 1912 in the Little Theatre and in 1909 in the New Theatre in New York. When they could be made portable and electrically driven, they began to be used extensively and became part of the design vocabulary.

The movable or wagon stage, which was also used in court theatres for tableaux and could probably trace its history to the *eccyclema* of Greek theatre, was a sliding platform mounted on rubber wheels. Scenery could be mounted on it, then pulled to the wings to allow another dressed wagon to take its place. Since they had to be pushed and pulled manually, wagons remained an alternate to the tried-and-true methods. They proved to be as unadaptable for trouping as the other movable stages until the time arrived in the first half of the twentieth century when they, too, could be made portable. Eventually, they would be electrically driven, traveling on grooves built into stage or platform floors.

In the nineteenth century, scene painters and carpenters were joined by machinists and the men who worked the gas table, whose task it was to engineer such special effects as treadmills, roaring locomotives, waterfalls, erupting volcanos, and the like. They used all the resources available to them, adapting them to special usage on the stage. Lighting was the most important component of their scenic effects. For this, they relied on gas power, an energy source that persisted almost to the end of the nineteenth century. Although experiments in producing atmospheric or special lighting were taken as far as they could go in the age of gas illuminants, significant progress in manipulating light did not arrive until the advent of electric lighting. Like gas lighting, electric illumination evolved slowly until the power for it could be brought to the buildings through wires suspended in the streets instead of individual on-site generators. In 1885, Thomas Alva Edison supervised the installation of a complete system of electric lighting in Steele MacKaye's Lyceum Theatre in New York. Even after its demonstrated success, many theatres throughout the country continued to be built to include dual systems of gas and electric lighting.

Except for the pioneering efforts of Steele MacKaye, the aesthetic qualities of electric lighting were yet to be explored. The heralds of the new age of scenic lighting appeared in Europe with the pronouncements from the Swiss-born Adolphe Appia and the English-born Edward Gordon Craig, whose theories did not immediately cross the ocean. World War I and slowness in communication were perhaps the contributing factors in preventing their explorations from being known more rapidly in the United States.

The man who should have been the flag bearer in America for the new age in scenic art and lighting was Livingston Platt (1874–1933), an artist by training whose experiments in scenery and lighting began in a little theatre in Bruges, Belgium, in 1903. When he returned to the United States in 1911, he was hired to create settings for the tiny stage of the Toy Theatre in Boston. Employing elemental architectural components, without regard to realism, on a twelve- by twenty-foot stage, he projected suffused lighting against a neutral backdrop, making no attempt to create false perspective. The simplicity of his settings and his imaginative use of lighting to unite all the elements of a production brought him to the attention of the actress Margaret Anglin, who engaged him to provide the scenery for her Shakespearean presentations. Platt's use of lighting as a scenic element rather than simple illumination became the prelude to the new aesthetic in America that was quickly evolving after the war.

By far, the most influential designer to appear on the American scene was Robert Edmond Jones (1887–1954). Trained in the fine arts at Harvard, where he took Professor George Pierce Baker's soon-to-be famous "47 Dramatic Workshop," Jones joined a circle of young avant-gardists in New York, who were rebelling against the tight hold of Belascoism on the American stage. Rebuffed in his attempt to get an audience with Gordon Craig during a sojourn in Europe, Jones went to Berlin to study the methods of Max Reinhardt, who was then conducting his own experiments in stagecraft. Returning to America in 1914, Jones developed into the most passionate and articulate voice in the promulgation of what came to be known as the "New Stagecraft."

In 1915, he designed a setting for *The Man Who Married a Dumb Wife* for the English director Harley Granville-Barker at the Garrick Theatre in New York. The memory of the play has largely faded, but the scenery that Jones created lives on as the fountainhead of the avant-gardist movement. The setting was all right angles and geometric simplicity to represent "the door, two windows, and a room," that Granville-Barker requested. Jones designed it in silvery gray tones and black outlines with vivid color provided by the costumes, which he also created. Jones's setting drew enormous attention and approval and, together with the work of his contemporaries Lee Simonson (1888–1967), and Norman Bel Geddes (1893–1958), changed the course of American scenography forever.

The New Stagecraft designers worked in no set style, attempting to adapt their designs to the plays and musicals that they were commissioned to do. Simonson worked for many years as the principal designer of the Theatre

Robert Edmond Jones's design for Anatole France's *The Man Who Married a Dumb Wife* (1915). Wilmeth Collection.

Guild, which was founded in 1919 and became the most influential producing organization in the country (see the discussion on the Theatre Guild in Chapter 4). Although at its inauguration it focused on European plays, once it was well established, the Theatre Guild eventually attracted many of the outstanding American playwriting talents emerging in the country. They provided rare raw material for the New Stagecraft designers. Of the three seminal stage artists, Bel Geddes was perhaps the most visionary, encompassing the design of theatres to provide a total environment for the production. Unfortunately, most of Bel Geddes's theatrical architecture remained on the drawing board.

The manifesto of the New Stagecraft is embodied in Jones's book *The Dramatic Imagination,* in which he synthesized his ideas over twenty-five years. It is not a how-to-do-it book as much as a setting forth of a philosophy of stage art in very personal terms, a kind of mystical and poetic unfolding of ideas without much regard to the very real world of paint and canvas and the practical considerations of the stage. About as close Jones got to practical advice is embodied in his statement that "the aim of stage designing [is] to bring the audience into the atmosphere of the theme or thought. Any device will be acceptable so long as it succeeds in carrying the audience along with it" (136).

An audience saturated with the photographic realism of Belasco and his imitators and, before that, a skillfully painted stage that fooled the eye but remained all artifice, was perhaps ready for the New Stagecraft. First of all, the scene designers felt liberated. In their hands, realistic clutter for its own sake was banished from the stage. In its place were transmutations of realism. First, there was an abbreviated realism: a park bench to signify an entire park. Taken to its extreme, it could be further distilled, as it was in the setting for Thornton Wilder's *Our Town* (1938), which was set on a bare stage. At the beginning of the play, the character of the Stage Manager, the narrator, brings chairs and tables and sets the stage, explaining their significance to the audience. Despite the lack of solid scenery, its seeming artlessness was itself the design.

Another type of realism, impressionistic or poetic realism, had its greatest exponent in Jo Mielziner (1901–76). In 1935, he designed Maxwell Anderson's *Winterset,* a grim play set in the shadows of the Brooklyn Bridge in New York. The bridge that Mielziner created bore no semblance to reality, but its looming presence not only suggested a bridge but served the play, making a metaphor of the aspirations of the principal characters. Exaggerated realism, in which one or more scenic elements are deliberately enlarged or made dominant, became another way realism could be transmuted for effect. Lee Simonson's setting for Eugene O'Neill's *Dynamo* (1929), a construction of a hydroelectric power plant, contained overblown realistic elements within the fantasy setting and was intended to diminish man in the face of man-made power.

Whenever and however it was used, realistic scenery was necessary to serve the realistic plays that were becoming (and have remained) the modern American dramatic idiom. In the hands of the New Stagecraft designers it took many forms, but American stage artists ranged among many styles to create the most accurate physical and psychological environment for the play or musical. Although what they did could not rival the photographic realism of movie sets, they used whatever means were available to effect changes of scenery in cinematic fashion. Wagon stages, pivoting stages, turntables, scenes that nested within each other that could be lifted into the flies – every device at hand and more to come – now could accomplish the more rapid changes demanded by the playwrights and the designers themselves.

When they could be more creative, they eschewed realism and ventured into other territories. The "unit set" was a favorite of New Stagecraft designers. It consists of a sculptural mass or construction on stage that can serve many scenes by the addition or subtraction of scenic elements. Actors can bring necessary props on stage, small wagons can move into place at its edges, curtains can be hung on parts of the set, screens can be set up rapidly by stagehands, or an inner turntable can be used to alter or adapt the central unit. The set was

Jo Mielziner's design for Maxwell Anderson's *Winterset* (1935). Courtesy, the Estate of Hilda S. Kook.

considered ideal for Shakespeare and the classics, or for modern episodic plays, and New Stagecraft designers used it whenever they were given the determining choice of style. Another of their predilections was the "simultaneous set." When the curtain rises on a simultaneous setting, all scenes are in full view. By the use of lighting, only the scene that is being played is illuminated, with the rest of the stage left in relative darkness.

New Stagecraft designers wanted nothing less than to create the visual essence of the heart and soul of the play or musical. Jones, Simonson, and Bel Geddes were followed by a fresh generation of designers, most of whom had served in the studios of one or the other of them. Donald Oenslager (1902–75), whose career as a designer spanned fifty years, went one step further. As a former Jones assistant and later as an instructor at the School of Drama at Yale University, he was responsible for disseminating the ideals of the New Stagecraft to wave after wave of young aspiring designers over his long career at the school. Many of them went into professional theatre, not only in New York and regional theatres but combined careers in academia on university campuses. The New Stagecraft torch was passed to yet more generations.

Lighting

Nothing helped the New Stagecraft designer more in his quest to provide the play with the quintessentially correct stage setting than lighting. In Europe, both Appia and Craig had extolled the aesthetic principles of lighting beyond its usual function of illuminating the set. With the advent of electricity, the means were at hand – or soon developing – to use lighting to unite play, scenery, and actor. Although stages and theatres were still lighted by gas, the possibilities of manipulating light were limited, and although the gas technicians were able to achieve all manner of special effects, the lighting emitted was still soft and fuzzy and difficult to control. The only means to achieve brilliant illumination came from the limelight, which came into vogue in the mid–nineteenth century. By heating a stick of lime to a high temperature with an oxyhydrogen flame and placing it in a box fitted with a reflector and lens, a shaft of brilliant light could be directed to the stage. The limelight, too, was an effect that required a special operator to handle it. Other experiments in lighting were performed during the nineteenth century, but all were inherently limited by the cumbersome technique required to produce them.

Electric lighting seemed to provide easy solutions, and the technology developing outside the bounds of the theatre was quickly adapted to theatrical use. As the first incandescent bulbs began to be replaced with longer-lived lamps and the means to control the amount of electric current to them was developed, the possibilities of stage lighting seemed limitless. In his quest for realism, David Belasco was responsible for making lighting a paramount and indispensable element of scenery. With Louis Hartman (1877?–1941) at his side, Belasco conducted painstaking experiments in lighting workshops set up at both the theatres that he controlled from 1902 until the end of the twenties. His technical rehearsals often lasted for weeks as he adjusted intensities and colors to achieve realistic effects. Hartmann was so resourceful that when Belasco called for an effect for which the technology had not yet been invented, he invented it himself.

Although the New Stagecraft designers decried the literalism of his effects, they respected Belasco's achievements and his comprehension of the value of lighting in play production. But they wanted more than realistic lighting. Jones wanted it to live. In *The Dramatic Imagination,* he describes a moment during light rehearsals when he was overcome by the "livingness" of light. "As we gradually bring a scene out of the shadows," he wrote, "sending long rays slanting across a column, touching an outline with color, animating the scene moment by moment until it seems to breathe, our work becomes an incantation. We feel the presence of elemental energies" (113). For New Stagecraft designers, the problem was not to illuminate the setting but to illuminate the drama.

This they did with a practical system that consisted of strips of lights above the stage ("border lights"), a row of lights set within the apron of the stage ("footlights"), lamps set in portable boxes ("strip lights") to be positioned where they are necessary to illuminate a part of the scenery or stage, a cluster of lights ("bunch lights") set within a reflecting head and mounted on a stand, a high-powered lamp within a reflector set on a telescoping pole ("flood light") to spread light over large areas, and lamps of high intensity fitted with a lens ("spotlights") to pinpoint an actor or a special section of the stage much as the limelight did in an earlier age. Lighting was confined behind the proscenium until Belasco began to mount instruments on the face of the balcony to light the actors' faces in place of footlights. Although footlights persisted until almost the middle of the twentieth century, Belasco and his successors avoided using them because they either washed out or distorted facial features.

In the early years of electric stage lighting, colored light was achieved by two means: dipping the lamps into stains or covering the face of lighting instruments with colored media in frames. Silk in various hues was eventually replaced by thin sheets of colored gelatin as the preferred medium. Although the gelatins could be produced in an almost limitless array of shades, hues, and intensities, their major drawback was fragility. Because the heat of the lamps eventually melted or cracked them, they had to be replaced frequently during the run of a production. (Much later, with the advent of heat-resistant plastics, they became durable and long-lasting.) As early as 1911, experiments in color and light were conducted by Monroe Pevear in Boston. He broke stage light into its own primary colors: red, green, and blue, and recombined them as "white light." Pevear's studies with optics resulted in the invention of special lighting instruments that improved the quality and control of lighting.

Of course, the most important piece of equipment in the lighting of the stage was the control board, or "switchboard," the equivalent of the old gas table in a previous era. This has been the one element that has undergone enormous change from one era to the next as improvements in controls have been invented. Simply stated, the control board was and remains the brains of the lighting system, capable of controlling individual instruments, banks of lights, projections, house lights, and so forth, through a bank of dimmers. (Only the follow spotlight remained under individual control, operated by a stagehand usually on a small platform in the auditorium.) Set up usually in the wings of the theatre, the switchboard required several stagehands to man the levers to alter the intensity and placement of lighting as cues were given to them. Usually, working in the blind, they relied on their watches and plans ("light plots") to adjust the lighting as needed.

The work of several men on university campuses led to profound changes in both the size of the switchboard and the ease with which lighting could be controlled. In the thirties, George Izenour (b. 1912) and Stanley McCandless (1897–1967) at Yale University's School of Drama and Theodore Fuchs (b. 1904) at Northwestern University began experiments both in engineering and the aesthetics of lighting that led to the shrinking of the size of the switchboard and the establishment of a system and vocabulary for the stage. Their pioneering efforts carried over into professional theatre, which quickly adapted their discoveries and methods into the manufacture of better lighting equipment by specialized companies. The Kliegl and Century lighting companies were in the forefront of supplying lighting systems both to the commercial and amateur theatres throughout the country.

After World War I, other advances in stagecraft in Europe quickly crossed to America. Most of the continental state-run theatres and opera houses were equipped with permanent plaster "cycloramas," structures that filled the rear of the stage. Special effects could be projected on the neutral surface from large painted slides, which had the added advantage of being easily changeable. The cycloramas effectively replaced the nineteenth-century painted backdrops. However, in America, permanent cycloramas were not practical. Instead, a curtain on a curved track, which could be lifted out of sight when it was not needed, was devised as a substitute. Projected scenery, the darling of the New Stagecraft designers, had to wait until a later age and better technology to become totally effective on the American stage.

The designing generation between the world wars acted as their own lighting designers with the help of skilled stage electricians. Although Jones, Simonson, and Bel Geddes had their favorite helpmates in the electrical department, each jealously guarded the actual lighting design, verbally dictating the colors, effects, intensities, and other lighting variables required for every moment of the production. Rarely were they given program credit for the lighting, except when it was blanketed into the statement "production designed by. . . . " Although Jo Mielziner had been designing the lighting as well as the scenery for his many shows for almost a decade, it was only in 1935 that he was finally listed in the program for *Panic* as the lighting designer.

Inevitably, the functions of designer and lighting technician would be combined in one person and, just as inevitably, he or she would establish the role of lighting designer as the full collaborative partner in the mounting of a stage production. If anyone could be said to have invented the role on the American stage, it would be Abe Feder (1909–97). Arriving in New York in 1930, he made lighting his province and his passion. With a strong belief that it was a mixture of science and art, he gave it both. Leaving nothing to chance, he invented a system of numbering the lighting instruments on charts so that he could tell the stage electricians exactly what type of instrument was to be used, where it was was to be placed, what color gelatins and intensities it should have, and what was to be done with it during the progression of the scenes. Whenever he found that he could not achieve an effect that he wanted, he invented the equipment to achieve it. He lit scores of Broadway shows, designed permanent lighting systems in theatres, and set up a firm (Lighting by Feder) that branched out in industrial and commercial lighting design.

Feder's improvements were almost immediately augmented by his one-time assistant Jean Rosenthal (1912–69). Attracted by the theatre but, more particularly, by what went on in back of the curtain rather than in front of it, she enrolled in the Yale School of Drama, studying stage design with both Donald Oenslager and Stanley McCandless. Working with various dance companies and the Federal Theatre Project during the midthirties, she was able to extend her theatrical education and gain invaluable experience. Inevitably, Broadway beckoned. Her first credit, for lighting the John Houseman production of *Richard III* in 1943, brought her to the attention of many designers. She soon became the leading lighting designer in New York.

Although her many contributions live on, Rosenthal's principal legacy was in making lighting design a precise, yet flexible, art. Improving on Feder's system of numbering the lighting equipment, she invented symbols for the instruments and colors and formulated detailed and exact light plots on paper as a blueprint for the stage technicians to follow. She insisted on separate lighting rehearsals to test all the cues so that nothing was left to chance or error. But more than these, she gave shape, color, and movement, making it breathe the way Jones predicted it could. The summum bonum of both Feder and Rosenthal was to create scenery from lighting and transform lighting into palpable emotional scenery.

Jones had predicted that the time would come when Americans would lead the world in stagecraft. On the eve of World War II, American designers had begun to fulfill his prophecy.

Note

1 For coverage of theatre fires in this period, see Witham (editor), *Theatre in the United States: A Documentary History, 1750–1915,* in particular documents 195–200, compiled in Wilmeth's section, 1865–1915. Among the items included are the ground plan of the Iroquois Theatre, the verdict of the coroner's inquest for the Iroquois fire, the assessment of exits for that theatre, and notes on fire safety at Proctor's Twenty-third Street Theatre in 1904.

Bibliography: Scenography, Stagecraft, and Architecture

Two general bibliographic sources for the subjects covered by this essay are Stoddard's *Stage Scenery, Machinery, and Lighting* (1977) and *Theatre and Cinema Architecture* (1978) – both have ample sources of information on individual theatres and scene designers in American theatre.

Although there are no specific histories of American architecture, several general studies include information about it, including Izenour's *Theater Design* and his lectures published as *Theater Design and Modern Architecture*. Other studies to be consulted are Glasstone's *Victorian and Edwardian Theatres;* Mullin's *The Development of the Stage;* Steele's *Theatre Builders;* the Leacroft's *Theatre and Playhouse;* Mielziner's *The Shapes of Our Theatre;* and Tidworth's *Theatres: An Architectural and Cultural History.* Limited aspects or specific eras of theatre architecture are embraced in Birkmire's *The Planning and Construction of American Theatres* (1896); Sexton and Betts's *American Theatres of Today* (1927); Carlson's 1989 *Places of Performance: The Semiotics of Theatre Architecture; Architecture for the New Theatre,* a series of essays edited in 1935 by Edith J. R. Isaacs; Macintosh's 1993 *Architecture, Actor and Audience.* The two volumes of *Famous American Playhouses: Documents of American Theatre History,* edited by William C. Young, contain accounts of theatres as they were reported on or reviewed mostly in newspapers and periodicals to 1971.

Sources on New York's theatres include Henderson's *The City and the Theatre;* Dimmick's *Our Theatres To-Day and Yesterday* (1913); and Van Hoogstraten's *Lost Broadway Theatres* (Princeton Architectural Press, 1991).

Except for Carter and Cole's book on Joseph Urban, information on theatre architects is difficult to come by and is found only in monographs, encyclopedias, or all-inclusive chapters in larger histories. Commentaries on the work of Henry B. Herts and Hugh Tallant, for example, can be found by Abbot H. Moore in the *Architectural Record* (January 1904) and by Bill Morrison in *Marquee* published by the Theatre Historical Society (Number 4,1990). Macmillan's *Encyclopedia of Architects* contains brief biographies on a number of architects who designed theatres, chief among them is the entry on J. B. McElfatrick by Craig Morrison. Bill Morrison wrote on Herbert J. Krapp in the spring number (1993) of *The Passing Show.*

For studies on the design and construction of theatres, including acoustics and lighting, see the six-part series of articles by Roi L. Morin in *The American Architect* (December 1922 to February 1923); also Lee Simonson's "Basic Theatre Planning" in *Architectural Forum* (September 1923); William Albert Swasey's "A Few Essentials in Theatre Construction" in *The American Architect* (22 January 1913); and Hugh Tallant's "The American Theatre: Its Antecedents and Characteristics" in *The Brickbuilder* (December 1914).

Two invaluable resources for listings of theatres built during the era covered by this essay are the yearly editions of Julius Cahn's *Official Theatrical Guide,* 1896–1921 and the *National List of Historic Theatre Buildings* compiled by Carlton Ward.

Sources that offer historical backgrounds, both general and specific, include Bernheim's *The Business of the Theatre* (published originally in 1932); Poggi's *Theater in America: The Impact of Economic Forces;* Morison's *The Oxford History of the American People;* Furnas's *The Americans: A Social History of the United States 1587–1914;* John Hoyt Williams's *A Great and Shining Road;* and Andrews's *Architecture, Ambition and Americans.* Peter Davis's essay "From Stock to Combination: The Panic of 1873 and Its Effects on the American Theatre Industry" is a thoughtful analysis on the interaction between commerce and art.

Chapters on both theatre architecture and scene design can be found in various anthologies and histories: *The American Theatre: A Sum of Its Parts,* edited by Williams; *The Theater of To-Day,* by Moderwell; *Our American Theatre,* by Sayler; *Theatre Arts Anthology,* edited by Gilder; *Theatre: Essays on the Arts of the Theatre,* edited by Isaacs; *Play Production in America,* by Krows; and *Theater in America,* by Henderson.

Although there exist studies on specific designers and periods of design, there is no complete history of either American scenography or stagecraft. Krows's book (cited above) examines his own limited period and is the best source for late-nineteenth-century and early-twentieth-century stagecraft and scene design. Larsen's *Scene Design in the American Theatre from 1915 to 1960* continues the history with numerous illustrations. Oenslager's *Stage Design: Four Centuries of Scenic Invention* presents a worldview but includes American innovations. Although it was intended primarily as a textbook, Howard Bay's *Stage Design* examines the state of American design, both past and present; and *Theatre Backstage from A to Z* by Warren C. Lounsbury defines terms of modern stagecraft technology in understandable language. Lee Simonson's *The Stage Is Set,* a landmark book, embraces world theatre.

By far, the most influential sources have been written by designers themselves. First on the list is *The Dramatic Imagination,* by Robert Edmond Jones, and *Continental Stagecraft,* by Jones and Kenneth Macgowan. *The Theatre of Robert Edmond Jones,* edited by Ralph Pendleton, examines the contributions of the most seminal figure in American scenography. Several outstanding designers wrote personal accounts of their own evolution in scene design: *Part of a Lifetime* by Simonson; *The Theatre of Donald Oenslager* by Oenslager; *Designing for the Theatre* by Jo Mielziner; and *Miracle in the Evening* by Norman Bel Geddes. Although it focuses strictly on the English theatre, R. Southern's *Changeable Scenery* is nonetheless a fascinating study not only of the methods of changing scenery through the ages but also of the shifting attitudes toward the function of scenery within play production. Much of both are reflected in the American theatre.

The subject of lighting in the theatre is covered by several important sources: Izenour's *Theater Technology;* Bentham's *The Art of Stage Lighting;* Fuchs's *Stage Lighting;* Hartmann's *Theatre Lighting;* and McCandless's *A Method of Lighting the Stage. The Magic of Light* by Rosenthal and Wertenbaker includes the personal history of Rosenthal but also examines the art and craft of lighting.

9

Directors and Direction

Warren Kliewer

Introduction

In 1870, playbills did not credit a "director" or designate a work as being "staged by" someone. Yet, as we know, vast numbers of shows were mounted and, human nature being what it is, we cannot reasonably suppose that a group of artists and artisans, lacking a leader, would coalesce by itself into a satisfying performance and open on time. Even in 1870 someone had to cast, call the rehearsals, instruct the crews, interpret the play, and pace the production.

In 1945, playbills routinely named directors, whereas producers issued them with separate contracts. Reviewers knew, or believed they knew, what directors had contributed. Actors courted them, believing they could bestow stardom, or at least a job. Indeed, by 1945 some directors viewed themselves as seminal artists, using the labor of others as the raw material for fulfilling the grand vision of an *auteur.*

The evolution from anonymity to adulation, a slow process of reassembling variously assigned directorial tasks into a job description separable from other theatrical chores, is the subject of this chapter. The discussion will dwell on the participants in that evolution, sometimes examining their best-remembered work but more often their responses to economic, social, or technological changes that affected the production process. If plays of enduring value are not mentioned often, it is because, as George S. Kaufman put it tersely, "Good plays have a way of being well directed." That is, they direct themselves. Conversely, a weak script needs very fine direction to make it work. And so, examining directors' work on flimsy texts or even catastrophic failures can lead to useful insights. Finally, this chapter will explore the ways in which these people combined directing with other jobs: theatre administration, writing, acting, stage managing, or teaching. People who directed exclusively were rare indeed, which remains true today.

The Power of Tradition

American actors in the early decades of this period had inherited unified, well-articulated traditions, providing them with insights and performance techniques that we moderns, coming from widely different ethnic, educational, and linguistic backgrounds, have to spend rehearsal time developing. The contrast was illustrated in Margaret Webster's *Don't Put Your Daughter on the Stage* (1972). She had to bring in British actor and tradition-bearer Dennis King to teach snuff taking and moving and sitting while wearing a sword. "Dennis had learned it," she says, "when he was a 'call boy' at the Birmingham Theatre from an older actor who had learned it from Samuel Phelps, whose father was of a generation which did all these things as part of daily living" (242).

In this tradition-driven theatre there were three basic rehearsal systems, the most common of which we might call the "promptbook system." In the stock companies, especially, rehearsal authority resided in a detailed record of a successful previous production, not in the person conducting rehearsals: a stage manager or even a lowly prompter, sitting at a table at stage right and reading aloud the stage directions and notes. If an actress asked, "Why should I snap my fan on this line?" the correct answer was, "Because it's always been done that way." Lest one be tempted to condescend to that "uncreative" way of directing, it should be remembered that the "promptbook system" is still the most popular method of directing shows, not only in amateur theatres using published acting editions of plays, but even in some professional theatres and, most especially, opera companies. Productions in the 1870s had an added advantage, which we lack, of actors' acute awareness of the living traditions, of which the promptbook was merely a reminder.

Almost as common was direction by the visiting star, who had jobbed into a resident stock company and was expected to direct the supporting roles. Here, too, tradition informed the work. Katherine Goodale in *Behind the Scenes with Edwin Booth* (1931) remembered that "any actor engaged to support Mr. Booth would know enough to drop below him and not take the centre of the stage unless he was instructed to" (85). But she also discovered that Edwin Booth had more than star tricks in his repertoire of directorial skills. Whether directing from onstage in starring roles or working with actors backstage, Booth gave each one solid grounding in the role, coached each one in areas of deficiency, and maintained control of the quality throughout the run.

The star system of direction has likewise survived to this day – overtly in films, in which transforming oneself from a young star into a middle-aged director of oneself has become an acceptable way to move the career forward, and covertly in live theatre. Anyone hired to be the titular director of a "star package" must be a diplomat prepared to deal with the stars' needs and

opinions and carry them out. Even though a playbill says, "Directed by . . . ,"
the star is frequently an uncredited co-director.

The third method was that used typically by a stock company manager,
usually an actor or actress playing not leading but supporting roles while
directing from onstage. This was combined with offstage responsibility for all
financial and administrative management, and often building management as
well. In these circumstances directing a play was not considered a separate
job but rather the artistic aspect of theatre management.

Among the most eminent of the actor/actress-managers was Mrs. John
Drew (1820–97), whose typical day, as outlined by C. Lee Jenner in "The
Duchess of Arch Street," is astonishing:

> Promptly at nine o'clock, she reviewed accounts, handled bills, heard
> reports, . . . inspected both public and backstage areas, made arrangements
> for forthcoming plays, and handled the printing and distribution of pro-
> grams. . . . At ten o'clock, sometimes even on Sundays, a four-hour rehearsal
> of one or more plays began, always under Mrs. Drew's direction. . . . When
> the acting company was dismissed to memorize lines, she usually put in
> another office hour before she drove home for her midday dinner, followed
> by her own script study. Most nights she was on stage; if not, she monitored
> the action from the private box to which she alone had the key. And she
> watched . . . "with a hawk's eye that nothing escaped." On Saturdays she
> herself distributed salaries and often played in the matinee as well as the
> evening show before she finally took a late supper at home. (34)

That is, she carried out the duties of what we now call producer, artistic
director, company manager, facilities manager, production manager, actress,
and of course stage director. This was not a schedule for the fainthearted.

New Technologies

Certain technological innovations, especially electrical lighting, upset traditional theatre practice during the last two decades of the century. Electrical
stage lighting was irresistible, once it had become practical, but the problem,
as Tim Fort points out in "The Introduction of Electrical Incandescence into
American Theatres," was that electrical lighting "in its general diffuse bright-
ness lacked artistic effect" (see 21–28). Somehow the shadows, gradation,
variety, and color had to be controlled, but no one could teach these new
artistic techniques, since no one knew what they were. The new technology
had created the need for specialists. (See Chapter 8.)

Or perhaps the theatre needed a universal genius. Steele MacKaye
(1842–94) filled the bill. Not content to be a few things, such as playwright

and director, he also worked as actor, theatre manager (unsuccessfully), acting teacher, and designer of impossible-to-realize theatre structures and useful gadgets – "circa 100 patented Stage-Inventions," according to his son and biographer Percy.[1] When he opened his 1885 Lyceum Theatre with his play *In Spite of It All,* directed by himself, his miraculous inventions were also on display: completely electrical lighting, an asbestos fire curtain, traverse curtains, a two-leveled stage elevator for fast scene changes, audience seating with fold-up seats, and coupon tickets with detachable stubs. By immersing himself in new inventions and technology, MacKaye expanded the director's job description to include new areas of expertise, and added new words to a director's vocabulary, such as "amps" and "ohms." In mastering and unifying all these disciplines, MacKaye demonstrated that visual unity is attainable.

A Search for Unity

A contemporary of MacKaye, Augustin Daly (1838–99), sought for another kind of unity. He created an enduring acting ensemble in order to achieve productions that were vocally and physically, as well as visually, unified. To that end, he issued only long-term contracts, usually three to five years, did not hesitate to use intimidation or legal proceedings to enforce his contracts, and was infamous for posting detailed company rules in the greenroom, including stiff fines for any malefactors.[2] It is no wonder that George C. D. Odell described him as a "martinet-manager."

The objective – to break down the stereotypical "lines of business," the specialties stock-company actors depended on – could be attained, Daly believed, only if he kept his people for long periods of time. He succeeded most clearly with the actress Ada Rehan, who remained in his company as leading lady from 1878 until his death in 1899, but there were other loyal actors as well who throve in this mutually beneficial relationship. He had a parallel relationship with his brother Joseph, a judge in the Court of Common Pleas in New York, who was the principal collaborator on most of the plays and adaptations credited to Augustin, and was quite willing to keep the secret. As producer-director, Augustin Daly provided the opportunity and the vision. His collaborator and loyal actors took advantage of the opportunity and fulfilled his vision to his satisfaction.

Since Daly did not perform, he was able to reposition his directorial vantage point. Mrs. Drew, Edwin Booth, or other actor-directors would have had to spend part of their rehearsal and performance time on stage with the other actors. As a nonperformer, Daly was freed of this obligation and was able to move his directorial vantage point out into the house. This shift of just a few yards made possible a radical reconception of what directing is, enabling Daly as director to see the whole show from first rehearsal to closing night with the eyes of the audience.

To learn how Daly worked one must go not to one of his loyal actors but, ironically, to one of his defectors, the observant Clara Morris, whose autobiography, *Life on the Stage* (1901), devotes a chapter to "A Study of Stage Management." When she believed herself miscast as a sixteen-year-old naif, the title role in *Alixe,* she told Daly, "She is a little convent-bred bit of innocence – a veritable baby of sixteen years! Dear Mr. Daly, don't you see, I should ruin the play?" He persisted. She reports that she fretted and studied and worked on her costume, then went back in memory to her "first sweetheart," who had said "the foolish old words that never lose sweetness and novelty." This, she realized, was enough. "I won't act at all! I'll just speak the lines sincerely and simply and leave the effect to Providence" (358). Daly approved, encouraged her to pursue her approach, and even changed the emphasis of the production to feature Morris's character. The "martinet-manager," it seems, was capable of responding to and guiding his actors' process of discovery after all.

A Mania for Perfection

If Daly's Theatre set a new standard of ensemble and visual unity, David Belasco (1853–1931) pushed his quest even beyond that. As Lise-Lone Marker asserts in her thorough study, *David Belasco: Naturalism in the American Theatre* (1975), his grand vision of the theatre embraced urban realism, such as Eugene Walter's *The Easiest Way* (1909); such "vivid, colorful panoramas of western life" as *The Girl of the Golden West* (1905); romances and extravaganzas in exotic settings, such as *Madame Butterfly* (1900); and "the crowning achievement of his artistic career," *The Merchant of Venice* (1992), his only Shakespearean production.

Unlike MacKaye, Belasco was not blessed (or cursed, if you will) with early success. By 1895, when he mounted *The Heart of Maryland,* his first independently written and produced play, he had served an apprenticeship of twenty-four years. Having worked in actor-managed companies, taken direction from visiting stars, and constantly educated himself in all theatrical areas – arts, business, and technologies – he was able to gather into his creative sphere the production's finances, administration, artistic direction, ownership of the theatre, development of the script, and all aspects of production design.

Generalizations, however, do not convey the fervor with which Belasco worked. In "David Belasco: The Last of his Line," an interlude in *These Things Are Mine* (1947), playwright George Middleton vividly dramatizes the fact that

Byron photograph of David Belasco in his studio (and pajamas) at the first Belasco Theatre (c. 1902). Wilmeth Collection.

"Belasco thought in immediacies. He was not interested in arrival, only in going." Middleton reports that "in a costume play he wanted a lady to call a man a coward. Belasco felt the straight phrase lacked period subtlety." And so he called for his trusty propmaster.

> "Matty, Matty! Get me a fan – a large fan, with feathers; yes white feathers.'" Presto – it arrived. Then Belasco gave it to the actress. "Here. . . . You have been fanning yourself . . . before . . . so . . . so . . . it won't seem like a device. . . . See? Fan slowly. . . . See, this way. . . . Now . . . when he speaks – what is the line? Oh yes! When he hesitates to go to fight for his country. . . . You smile . . . Lady on top – claws underneath. . . . See? Now – fan yourself. . . . That's it. . . . Look at him . . . Look at the fan. . . . Yes. . . . Now you get an idea. . . . See? Feather? See? It's a white feather. . . . See? Now you pluck one out. . . . No emotion. . . . Brain. . . . Yes. . . . Wait. . . . Now throw it

into the air. . . . No, blow it up – over your head! . . . Yes. Natural – as though amused. . . . See? Now fan it. . . . Not too much. . . . Fan it – and watch it as it settles slowly to the ground. . . . You both watch it. Now. . . . you speak." He turned abruptly to the playwright: "Now get me a line there for her to say." (281–82)

In this and other vignettes Middleton captures Belasco's ability to give lessons in dramatic writing, help actors build an inner life, redesign the set decoration, rewrite the prop list, instruct the stage crew, and assess the audience's perception of the flow of the action – all this at once in an intense directorial outburst.

Underneath Belasco's direction, his prop business, his long lighting rehearsals, according to Marker, lay "A sense of the harmonious and the conciliatory, . . . a sense that appears everywhere in his work and comes to expression in all phases of his theatrical activity" (56). If so, then the credit, according to Belasco's own statement in *The Theatre Through Its Stage Door* (1919), should go to nature, which served as his raw material and which, in turn, he and his production served. When he uttered his credo – "He who goes direct to nature for the effects he introduces on the stage can never go wrong" – he was speaking abstractly about his "faith in realism" but also specifically about the basis of his set and lighting designs and his coaching of the actors (quoted in Marker, 118).

Enter the Businessman

Prior to the 1870s the person who directed a production was normally the employer, as in the case of Mrs. Drew, who directed and acted with her company and also distributed the salaries. It is not hard to understand why that arrangement makes actors willing to take direction. This tidy formula was about to break down in 1872 when lawyer and librarian A. M. Palmer (1838–1905) allowed his fascination with the theatre to draw him into active participation. Since he had no professional theatrical experience, he hired directors to mount his productions, though it should be added that some of the accomplished directors he used – Dion Boucicault, Steele MacKaye, William Seymour, Eugene W. Presbrey – complained that Palmer loved to come into late rehearsals and add a few "finishing touches." More comfortable was the arrangement Palmer worked out with John Parselle, a compliant director who knew his place, liked receiving regular paychecks, and kept his job for a long time.

The importance of this management innovation cannot be overemphasized. By separating direction from management, that is, artistic authority from hiring power, Palmer initiated a major shift in theatrical structure. Direction was becoming a job assigned to an employee, a person who may or may not retain the power to recast a production and who is himself subject to termination. Under Palmer's tasteful guidance, the producer–employee relationship resulted in fine productions, and a director who considered Palmer's tinkering intrusive could always find work somewhere else.

The situation became grimmer in 1896 when six theatrical managers – Erlanger, Klaw, Frohman, Nixon, Hayman, and Zimmerman, men not gifted with Palmer's taste (with the possible exception, on occasion, of producer Frohman) – signed the contracts constituting the Theatrical Syndicate (see Chapter 2). They created a virtual monopoly, the most serious challenger of which was the Shubert trio – Sam, Lee, and J. J., who organized an even smarter, stronger, and more aggressive nationwide chain of theatres. During this period from 1896 until well into the 1930s, there were few attractive alternatives to being a director-for-hire in an unmistakably commercial theatre. Traditional power structures and job descriptions had been completely rearranged. The intimate family structure of actor-manager companies was replaced by corporate hierarchies. Women, who under the traditional systems could take on administrative-management responsibilities if they chose to, were excluded from the monopolies, except in subordinate positions.

This consolidation of economic power under the control of a few individuals was not an isolated phenomenon. It was a nationwide restructuring, in which, according to financier Thomas W. Lawson's *Frenzied Finance* (1905), "Americans found they could . . . so take advantage of the laws of the land and its economic customs as to create for themselves wealth . . . without the aid of time or labor or the possession of any unusual ability coming through birth or education" (quoted in Morison, 763).

Once these robber barons and other newly rich Americans had accumulated wealth, they had new problems: how to spend the money, how to live in their elevated social class? In his essay, "The Education of Everyman," Dixon Wecter makes vivid a new American passion for self-education, an enthusiasm for lectures, self-improvement societies, home-study correspondence courses, morally uplifting fiction. It paid off, says Wecter. "Illiteracy declined from 17 per cent of our population in 1880 to 13 per cent in 1890, despite the influx from Ellis Island" (803). The urge to aspire touched even some of the robber barons and captains of industry, who endowed such universities as Drew and Vanderbilt and built Carnegie libraries throughout the country.

The second generation, however, was in a better position to turn industrial wealth into high culture. Winthrop Ames (1871–1937) used his substantial inheritance, derived from his father's New England railroad fortune, to educate himself in architecture and design, to build two exquisite intimate theatres, and to set out to stretch the imagination of American audiences with plays by the likes of Maurice Maeterlinck, Bernard Shaw, John Galsworthy, and

Granville Barker. With that background of careful education and cultivated taste, Ames evolved into a director who prepared meticulously and treated his actors as honored colleagues. One of his former apprentices, Guthrie McClintic, recorded in *Me and Kit* that Ames "was quiet, courteous, concerned if the performer felt at ease or not – 'Could you pass the drink with your left hand?' always followed by the questioning sound 'H'm.' 'If you're not comfortable, please let me know' was his constant solicitation" (123–24). Ames had devised a civilized alternative to commercial entrepreneurship.

The Inner Conflict

Not all theatre artists resolved the conflict as gracefully as Ames did. Take the case of Mrs. Fiske (1864–1932), known earlier as the child star "Little Minnie Maddern," and her husband Harrison Grey Fiske (1861–1942). Neither one had intended to become directors, but his attacks, as crusading editor of the *Dramatic Mirror,* on the Theatrical Syndicate would have made it impossible for her to work for the Syndicate – if she had wanted to, which she did not. So they formed their own company and took shows on the road, playing in whatever second-class venues had escaped Syndicate control. They directed as a team in a manner not unlike the husband-and-wife companies of a previous time. In this case he, whereas keeping his New York editing job, coordinated the production elements, while her work was "the psychological analysis and the rehearsal of the actors," and both shared in various ways in the financial responsibilities (see Binns, 174).

Indeed, Mrs. Fiske was a fierce perfectionist, particularly about casting, as she explained when interviewed by Alexander Woollcott for his volume, *Mrs. Fiske* (1917).

> I cannot begin to tell you how many times Mr. Fiske and I virtually dismissed an entire company; how over and over again we would start with an almost entirely new company, until every part, from Holbrook Blinn's down to the very tiniest, was perfectly realized; how much there was of private rehearsal; of the virtual opening of a dramatic conservatory; how much of the most exquisite care before *Salvation Nell* was ready. (21–22)

This production, she said, was the only one in fifty years that satisfied her.

A bolder but equally uncomfortable response to the monopolies was that of James A. Herne (1839–1901), whose career as a director is not as well documented as his acting and his playwriting (see Chapter 3). He struggled mightily to reconcile the need to make a living in commercial theatre with his aspirations to a "higher," that is, more truthful form of theatrical expression, and managed to do excellent work in both areas. His biographer, John Perry, points to a revealing moment of irony in 1891. After the struggling production of Herne's play, *Margaret Fleming,* in Boston's Chickering Hall, Herne went on to his next job directing *The Country Circus* at the huge Chestnut Street Theatre in Philadelphia. Herne, after hearing the author read the script to the cast, exclaimed, "Oh, God!" And who wouldn't? In every way a director's logistical nightmare, the script was little more than an excuse for putting a circus on stage – with horses, dog acts, monkeys, clowns, acrobats, sawdust – the works.

But Herne was up to the task, according to Perry. Not only was the staging "highly imaginative," with an onstage audience on bleachers backed by an oversized mirror reflecting the paying audience in the house, but Herne stayed with the show, working onstage in circus uniform to maintain the quality and safety throughout the Philadelphia run and then another one hundred performances in New York. It is not easy to be an artist with a conscience during times of radical economic change (see Perry, 167–68).

Herne's adaptability was exceeded only by that of William Seymour (1855–1933), who worked as an actor, resident stage manager for several large theatres (a job that at that time also included production management), occasional play doctor, and regular contributor to the *Boston Evening Transcript* theatre page. And of course he directed. His title for this job at first was "stage manager," followed by "acting manager," and then, after 1900, the "General Stage Director" of Charles Frohman's Empire Theatre. Was this a change in the job description or merely terminology? On one level the answer is that the title changed but the work remained the same.

But the public perception of direction did change during Seymour's seventy-year career. Directing became honorable, a quality that American democratic traditions had not conferred on the job. A probable source of the new, higher status of "The Director" was the foreign-language theatres that had been organized wherever immigrant enclaves were stable enough to support theatres in their languages. German actors in the Germania, the Thalia, and the Irving Place Theatres in New York, for example, had no qualms about vesting authority in a strong artistic leader. Their history, after all, revered the multi-talented Goethe, who was for a time an expert stage director. In Jewish communities, according to David S. Lifson, the Yiddish language was the bond that brought these multilingual immigrants together, indeed was "a dialect of the Jewish Soul" (31). It followed that Yiddish theatre directors had to be, or to become, ministers to "the Jewish soul," not mere staging technicians. In the twenties a series of Russian visitors and emigrés arrived, beginning with Konstantin Stanislavski. Although he was wildly enthusiastic about Belasco's 1923 production of *The Merchant of Venice* and confessed, "I have often wondered why the Americans praise us so much" (quoted in Marker, 179), it was Stanislavski, not Belasco, whom Americans adopted as the prophet of the future theatre. Then, when foreign-language directors such as Heinrich Con-ried, Maurice Schwartz, and Richard Boleslavsky crossed over into English-language theatre, they brought their directorial traditions with them. It is not unlikely that public recognition of directors' authority was hastened by these Eastern European influences. Playbills began to divulge the names of directors.

Bigger Is Better

With the monopolies' emphasis on exploitation for maximum profits, a new menu developed for the commercial stage, aptly described by Mary C. Hen-derson in *Theater in America:* "Light romantic comedies and frothy musical comedies, overproduced spectacles and modern melodramas, chic revues and star vehicles" (32). This taste for the lavish created a need for new kinds of directing skills, maybe even a new kind of directorial personality. A big-budget production with a cast of dozens or hundreds of stars, musicians, chorus girls, plus horses, multiple costume changers, and tons of scenery hanging in the flies: such a production needs a traffic cop – brisk, efficient, and unaware of the fine points of etiquette. Enter Ben Teal (1862–1917) who was, according to Henderson, "without peer in his ability to move large num-bers of extras around onstage" (101).

All eyewitnesses agree that Teal was always brusque and often insulting to his casts, especially to women. But there is also much evidence to suggest that many of the minor performers Teal dealt with, and even some stars, had much to learn about rehearsal discipline. His regrettable character flaw, if that is what it was, was exactly what the big, overproduced shows needed. If a show calls for precision in a chorus kick line, for example, then sloppiness is a crime against the art of the show. Even more urgent was the matter of safety. Cast in the crowd scenes of Teal's fiftieth New York show, *Ben-Hur* (1899), were half-trained, part-time extras, including children, playing on the same stage as the horses on treadmills. Many directors tremble at the prospect of putting horses or children on stage – *Ben-Hur* had both. If Teal barked out his orders, it was as a drill sergeant reminding the troops that "it's dangerous out there."

In such extravaganzas as Florenz Ziegfeld's *Follies* (begun in 1907) and J. J. Shubert's *The Passing Show* (1912–14), and the even more lavish *Artists and Models* (1923–42), there was no time for the passionate coaching of a Mrs. Fiske or David Belasco. Instead, directors of extravaganzas had to become the administrators of artistic hierarchies and to delegate to subordinate spe-cialists. When R. H. Burnside (1870–1952), for example, directed *A Trip to Japan* (1909) at the New York Hippodrome, a venue with a seating capacity of 5,240 and a raked stage that measured 114 by 110 feet, his staff included a composer, a musical director, an assistant musical director, an equestrian director, a ballet master (that is, choreographer), and a small army of stage managers. The directors of the *Follies* and Shubert's revues, Julian Mitchell (1854–1926) and Ned Wayburn (1874–1942), worked on a smaller scale but on the same principle. They redefined direction as administration. Mammoth productions had made bureaucracies obligatory.

The Independents

Though the two great producing giants, the Syndicate and the Shuberts, controlled much of the market, a few intrepid entrepreneurs, who were able to read a balance sheet or a box office statement as readily as a playscript, realized that one could find directing work not as an employee but as one's own employer. Among the ambidextrous producer-directors who emerged in the early twentieth century, Arthur M. Hopkins (1878–1950) stands out as a solid businessman and humane director, with a philosophical talent as well. "Except in the case of certain intellectual plays," he argued in *How's Your Second Act?* (1918), "the theatre is wholly concerned with the unconscious mind of the audience. The conscious mind should play no part" (8). In practice this meant that he eliminated any visual elements that might impede the audience's perception of the inner life of the play. The actors too were called upon to simplify. "Every moment on the stage should mean something. . . . I want the unconscious of the actors talking to the unconscious of the audience" (ibid.). He carried out his theory in eighty-two Broadway productions, defining his job as the elimination of the unneeded. "I finally become a censor," he wrote. "I must say what shall not pass – and therein I believe lies the whole secret of direction" (15–16). Cold theory notwithstanding, Hopkins carried out his work with such generosity of spirit that Brooks Atkinson described him as "the most modest and lovable man who ever produced on Broadway" (Broadway, 127).

Jed Harris (1900–1979), on the other hand, was arguably the most arrogant and unloved. A self-taught genius gripped by an intense love–hate relationship with the theatre, producer-director Harris brought his internal warfare into rehearsals with him and used his contradictions as the instrument on which he played in order to create. Whereas Hopkins built an enduring production team by developing rather than exploiting his designers and actors, creating first-rate artistic teams of loyal followers of a gentlemanly leader, Harris succeeded in alienating many of his most talented collaborators, including Thornton Wilder, Ruth and Augustus Goetz, and George Abbott. His heavy-handed rewriting of *Our Town* (1938), for example, was so extensive that he asked Wilder for co-authorship credit, which was refused, and Harris's temperament drove the normally benign Wilder into a screeching rage on opening night. Even though the human cost was high, the play and Harris's production stand as monuments of theatrical art.

If Hopkins raised astute esthetic questions, Harris's example raises fascinating ethical questions. How far can a director go in imposing his will on a playwright? Is it legitimate to use temperament as a method in rehearsals, a time when actors are inevitably vulnerable? Is directorial autocracy justifiable? Harris replied that his instincts were trustworthy and actors trusted him. In case anyone still doubted, he included testimonials from two of his former stage managers in his autobiographical *Watchman, What of the Night?* (1963). Besides, he added, he was risking no one's money but his own. The growing power and authority of directors during the twenties and thirties gave these ethical questions urgency.

Many of Harris's contemporaries believed there must be a better way to conduct one's life in the theatre: Brock Pemberton (1885–1950), for example, primarily a producer with a brief directing career; his thirty-year collaborator, Antoinette Perry (1888–1946), one of the few women directing on Broadway; and John Golden (1874–1955), whose direction was incidental to his work as a producer. All three carried their conciliatory attitudes offstage as well, volunteering in social-service organizations such as the Stage Relief Fund and in resolving labor disputes such as the Actors' Equity strike of 1919.

Their attitudes, their ability to negotiate and to sustain long-lived partnerships, are not merely interesting character traits. Eagerness to collaborate is the foundation of the method of a director seeking to induce teamwork within a cast and crew. Guthrie McClintic (1893–1961) makes this principle explicit in *Me and Kit* (1955), his entertaining account of his career and that of his wife, actress Katharine Cornell. Although she starred in only twenty-eight of his ninety-four productions, their collaboration was the core of his career. But he goes even further back to credit Winthrop Ames, with whom he apprenticed, and actress Blanche Bates, whom he directed, for pointing him in the right direction. Bates, he says, was "real theatre": "She always played for the next fellow's line. This is the test by which I determine the true generous spirit of the artist in the theatre. Playing for the next fellow's line is the simple honesty of reading which makes the reply following inevitable" (259). In directing, generosity begets generosity.

Power Plays

Playwrights, the textbooks tell us, should never direct their own plays. Daly, Belasco, Herne, Cohan, and dozens of others, who learned by apprenticeship, not textbooks, routinely directed their own scripts, all of them having established their directing credentials independently of their writing. The case of Clyde Fitch (1865–1909) was somewhat different. His unique style – what Montrose J. Moses in *Representative Plays by American Dramatists* calls "the Peter Pan quality" – made his plays "a commodity, coveted by the theatrical manager" (524). His unique ability to translate this quality from the page to the stage made him irreplaceable as a director, a negotiating strategy that playwrights have copied ever since.

Playwright direction was common during the first decade of the century and again during the thirties, when the Depression made producers eager to save money and made playwrights eager to parlay one salary into two. This was the frame of reference in which George Abbott (1887–1995) began his long career. As an apprentice in the John Golden office, he was assigned as assistant stage manager to playwright-director Winchell Smith (1871–1933) on the 1918 production of *Lightnin'*. "It was an invaluable school for a young director," he reports in his lively autobiography. Smith was "crystal clear. There was no posing, no nonsense, just 'this is how we do it.'" Once when Ruth Gordon experimented with one of her best laugh lines, Smith warned her, "No, no, dear. If you've got lines that don't go, then you can fool around with them. But when you get lines that do go, just say it, dear, just simply say it" (92).

Abbott followed the same rule. After his first acting job in 1913, and until 1945, the end of the period this chapter covers, a time in which he worked on seventy-one productions as author, director, play-doctor, producer, or some combination of these jobs, he began his process with establishing a sound script. At times this became overt collaboration, and he became the co-author or play-doctor. At other times, he said, the director's contribution was "influence upon the shape of the play, . . . the decision as to just how much to do or not to do, at what point to leave one scene and get into another, and for the actor, how much to express and how much to imply" (264). Once a script was solid, he asserted, a director would be able to administer Smith's advice: "just simply say it."

At a time when no women were directing on Broadway, Rachel Crothers (1878–1958) took on the challenge of directing her own plays (see Chapter 3). But she first prepared herself, as she explains in "The Producing Playwright," by learning "every line of stagecraft." Emphasize "every." Skill in casting not only by type but also against type, the ability to handle not only women's settings but also "the smoking room of a man's club," "a knowledge of color values," a working knowledge of all aspects of production from electricity to "temperament," not to mention "a large grasp of the entire machinery" and "the ability to gather the multiplicity of detail into the balanced whole": all these skills, she said, a woman director needs to know – and, for that matter, a man does too (34).

Whereas Crothers had learned her trade while mounting numerous productions at the Wheatcroft School of Acting, George S. Kaufman (1889–1961) had an equally strenuous apprenticeship in the newspaper business, contributing to humor columns and writing reviews. Indeed, basic journalistic values governed his work throughout his career. He believed, for example, that terser is better and that "A play is supposed to simulate life." Kaufman elaborates on this last point – tersely, of course – in a statement reprinted in Teichmann's biography of Kaufman. "The best direction is that which is so effortless and natural that it simply isn't noticed at all. Once it begins to call attention to itself, something is wrong" (126). As a dictum for directors this is as revealing for what it omits as for what it includes.

But Kaufman evolved from being a word-martinet into being a director who handled the human aspects expertly as well. In his production of *My Sister Eileen* (1940), for example, he allowed Shirley Booth, a seasoned professional, to go her own way. But since Jo Ann Sayers in the title role had youth, charm, and innocence, but little experience and no skill, he kept her occupied with prop business – cleaning, ironing, folding, carrying. As a result, both actresses seemed thoroughly expert (Teichmann, 127).

Directors with Agendas

Ingenious theatre people found another way to sidestep commercial theatre by forming independent companies. As early as 1896 Chicago's Hull-House proposed an "art theatre" based on European models, and became itself a model for the Neighborhood Playhouse in 1915, the year that also saw the birth of the Provincetown Players and the Washington Square Players. Late in 1925 Artef (Arbeiter Teater Farband, or Workers' Theatre Group) was formed. All these alternative theatres had goals and purposes – in other words, agendas.

From a director's viewpoint, an agenda – whether it be bland ("amusing the members"), social ("improving the community"), or political ("advancing the proletarian revolution") – must be incorporated into the production process. Indeed, the agenda governs the production and sometimes overrides all other considerations. Violations of the companies' purposes often provoke extreme responses. George Cram Cook, for example, abandoned the Provincetown Players when it outgrew the amateur spirit in which he had founded it. Benno Schneider, Russian-trained director of most of Artef's productions, had no compunctions about bending the material to further his agenda. When one playwright objected to script revisions, Schneider responded:

> Artef is a revolutionary theatre group, and to make the play consonant with our ideas and those of our audience, certain changes had to be made. . . .

[Y]our pet character, . . . Harriet, is not the leader of the oppressed, but a typical liberal who wants to help the oppressed lest they help themselves at the expense of the ruling class, her father's class. (Quoted in Lifson, 453)

If Artef's rules were harsh and intimidating, they were at least clear: A director must be a believer among believers. Philip Moeller (1880–1958) – one of the founders of the Washington Square Players, which was reorganized in 1919 into the Theatre Guild, of which he was the principal director – found himself directing in circumstances that were not only complicated but unclear. The Guild's mission was to produce the best of the world's best dramatic literature with the best production values (see also Chapter 4). But what does "best" mean? Once that question is settled, if it ever can be, how does one execute that definition? The Theatre Guild, which evolved from a collaboration among friends into an institution, was governed by a Board of Managers in control of financing, administration, and artistic direction. Its committees selected the plays, directors, and casts, criticized run-throughs, and appointed its members as ad-hoc production supervisors. At the same time director Moeller was a member of the Board of Managers, and so was one of the supervisors as well as the one continually supervised. To the long list of skills a director must possess, the institutional Theatre Guild added another one: the ability to find one's way through a labyrinthine bureaucracy.

Working within these complexities, Moeller led more than seventy plays to fruition in twenty years. Most were comedies, including ten of Shaw's, but some were serious dramas, including O'Neill's *Strange Interlude* and *Mourning Becomes Electra.* O'Neill described Moeller's as "the most imaginative directing I've ever seen." Eva Le Gallienne (1899–1991) thought him the worst director ever inflicted on her – totally unprepared and passive, she reports in pyrotechnical prose in *With a Quiet Heart* (97–101). Most of her own direction was done from 1926–33 in her Civic Repertory Theatre under a policy of high theatrical aspirations and low ticket prices. Reverting to the actress-manager system of Mrs. Drew, Le Gallienne was producer, director, designer, production manager, actress, dramaturg (and often translator of Ibsen), and general factotum. Surely her experience as an overworked laborer-in-the-fields colored her opinion of Moeller.

A fairer judgment would suggest that complex, institutional theatres attract directors who need support and control. Le Gallienne, pursuing her ideal of theatre for "the forgotten public," did not need institutional structures, or believed she did not. Moeller knew that he did, and he never freelanced except within the complex bureaucracies of Hollywood. The pattern he established of working within committee structures has been followed by hundreds of not-for-profit, institutional theatre directors during the rest of the twentieth century.

The phenomenon of theatres with agendas is an anomaly, since most American theatre artists throughout our history have been reluctant to theorize until long after they had gained experience. Herne, MacKaye, Belasco, Hopkins, and others reasoned deductively. Harold Clurman (1901–80) and the Group Theatre changed all that and reasoned inductively, projecting a theatre not yet realized, an art form based on ensemble as a central aesthetic value and modeled on their impressions of Stanislavski's Moscow Art Theatre. Clurman carried out the same a priori approach in his rehearsals as he demonstrates in his volume *On Directing* (1972), which includes several promptbooks, scored not only for physical business but also for the characters' intentions. That is, the inner lives of the characters and the actors were determined long before the cast arrived for the first rehearsal.

If Clurman had a theory, Lee Strasberg (1901–82) was a convert to Stanislavski's training methods as disseminated by Richard Boleslavsky and Maria Ouspenskaya. Strasberg adopted these ideas with religious fervor, evolved "The Method," and applied it to each of his productions. In an early one, a play entitled *1931,* according to Clurman in *The Fervent Years* (rev. ed., 1975), Strasberg coached one of his extras. "A crowd reaction – even off stage," says Clurman, "had to be as true as anything in the play. . . . A half-hour or more of very quiet work went on while the company of thirty-five sat around and watched with keen interest" (73). Clurman does not report having asked the extras how keen their interest actually was.

As compared with other major directors of the period, Clurman, Strasberg, and a third Group alumnus, Robert Lewis (1909–97), did not direct a large number of plays. Instead, by turning their attention to writing, lecturing, and teaching – conducting their thought processes publicly – they constructed a philosophical frame of reference that future directors have been free to accept or reject but could not ignore.

The precocious young mind of Orson Welles (1915–85), while looking for work in the barren market of the Depression, did not have a single agenda. He had many agendas, or more precisely, "directorial concepts." When hired by his partner, John Houseman, to direct for the Negro Theatre Project of the Federal Theatre of the WPA, Welles accepted literally within hours with a concept to direct *Macbeth* set in Haiti, and within a week he had a fully developed set design. Under the aegis of the Mercury Theatre, typically founded on an impulse and capitalized at $100, he mounted his famous *Julius Caesar* (1937) as a melodrama, with Romans costumed as modern fascists. His work schedule was always excessive, and his manner suggested that he was driven by a relentless demon. He directed everything, including the combat scenes, designed and sometimes built and painted and shopped as well, and more often than not, played a starring role.

Welles did not serve playwrights; they served him. When his radically edited texts were strong enough to withstand the pressures his concepts exerted, Broadway audiences saw unforgettable performances and imagery. But what about productions of weak scripts? John Houseman in *Unfinished Business* (1989) analyzes the Mercury production of *Danton's Death,* "a very young man's play with a fragmentary and defective structure" (189). The production failed miserably and virtually destroyed the Mercury Theatre; the play was warped beyond recognition, actors were injured, the theatre building was damaged, the stage manager had a breakdown, and the designers' health was put at risk. All this and more, according to Houseman, Welles considered an acceptable sacrifice to his artistic vision.

Setting aside this ethical problem, one must still acknowledge that Welles took the evolution of the stage director to another level by introducing the notion that a director need not be merely an interpreter or stager. His vision of the director as seminal artist and of direction as an art form on its own terms has inspired countless imitations – some of them brilliant, some ghastly, most lacking Welles's genius. The metamorphosis of the director from simple facilitator to omnipotent ultimate artist could go no further.

Depression and War

During the Depression of the thirties the number of Broadway productions fell from 280 in the 1927–28 season to 80 in the 1939–40 season. To directors this meant that in twelve years the number of job opportunities had been reduced by 71 percent, and most of the jobs remaining were taken by the established directors, playwright-directors, and producer-directors. The high-profile Broadway stage was no longer an open market for beginners, who found they had to develop aggressive job-hunting skills. For the first time finding a directing job was more difficult than doing the work. And whereas Abbott and Kaufman had apprenticed on Broadway, it now became necessary to go somewhere else to prove oneself. A pair of Princeton University do-it-yourselfers, Bretaigne Windust (1906–60) and Joshua Logan (1908–88), were typical. They turned amateur work in college into a summer stock company (the University Players), which they then parlayed into Broadway debuts.

Both men evolved into directors who, unlike Welles, respected the playwright's text – Windust a little too much, perhaps. Bringing an actor's sensibility to rehearsals, he accepted the script as the reality that an actor must make the most of. When confronted with a weak script or a floundering playwright, Windust's respect for the text was self-defeating. But when handed finished work, such as *Life with Father* (1939) and *Arsenic and Old Lace* (1941), the result was a palpable hit, for such work freed him to focus on making things work for the actors. Logan, on the other hand, considered himself on the job long before rehearsals began, working with the script and the playwright to build a strong foundation. This pattern he established in 1938 while helping Paul Osborn to reshape the imperfect script of *On Borrowed Time.* Directing and writing, he said in an interview, "are pretty well mixed up together" (see Logan, *SSDC Journal,* 5–23). This view became the basis of a long career.

However, his career was interrupted by military service during World War II. Indeed, during the late 1930s, long before this country entered the war, ominous hints of an impending European conflict affected American theatre people. In her autobiographical *Don't Put Your Daughter on the Stage,* British emigré Margaret Webster (1905–72) vividly dramatizes the extent to which she worked with a double consciousness, with one eye on the growing war and the other intently on Shakespeare. But with a British determination to reaffirm tradition (for she was, after all, of the fifth generation of her family in the theatre), she launched her Broadway career under Maurice Evans's actor-management with their 1937 *Richard II.* After an interlude of four forty-minute versions of Shakespearean comedies for the 1939 World's Fair, she mounted four more of the Bard's plays, culminating in her 1945 *The Tempest.* Even to attempt to mount Shakespeare in the commercial setting of Broadway would have been a bold gesture. But she did more; she succeeded where others had failed, because, she said, she trusted Shakespeare's expertise. She regarded him as a fellow craftsman who knew well the job of an actor and the psychology of the audience. "It is generally a good idea," she advised, "to look very carefully for the reason, the theatre reason, why he put such and such scenes where he did, or made them the length they are" (437). Blank verse did not drown out the radio broadcasts of Hitler's speeches, but Webster hoped her reaffirming tradition would keep him at bay.

As the United States was drawn into the war, the theatre acquired a new purpose outside itself: "the War Effort," reflected not only in topical plays but also in the many efforts to entertain the troops, such as the USO's "Stage Door Canteen." The Webster–Evans Production of *Hamlet* was trimmed down and toured to army bases as the *GI Hamlet.* A young black director who seemed headed for a major career, Owen Dodson (1914–83), spent part of the war years as author-director of mundane instructional plays at the Great Lakes Naval Training Station. Universal conscription depleted the male talent pool, creating gaps to be filled by women (such as Webster), rejectees (such as Orson Welles – flat feet), and refugees.

One foreign director, too old for the draft, found his way into the mainstream by taking on projects no one else trusted (such as *Porgy* in 1927) and by conceiving a format he considered "typically American." Rouben Mamoulian (1897–1987) was in search of properties capable of being shaped into his vision: "the total integration of dialogue, singing, dancing, and dramatic action," as he explained in an extraordinary interview (see Mamoulian, *SSDC Journal,* 1986). He found what he was seeking in Lynn Riggs's *Green Grow the Lilacs,* and his composer and writer, Rodgers and Hammerstein, concurred, though his choreographer, Agnes de Mille, needed some coaxing. "I don't want a 'ballet' here," he told her. "This should be part of the action . . . should tell as much of the story . . . as any dialogue scene. And don't kick the principals upstage. They're going to be principals in this, too, no matter what they do, even if it's just little steps" (*SSDC Journal,* 8). The result, *Oklahoma!,* which had seemed headed for disaster, succeeded beyond anyone's wildest hopes, breaking Oscar Hammerstein's ten-year streak of failures and rescuing the Theatre Guild from almost certain bankruptcy. The work of the director had once again been redefined: The production process became the working out of the director's (not the author's) aesthetic principles – with the consent of the governed, one might add.

Epilogue

Mamoulian's innovations raised more procedural questions than they answered. The same was true of the unstable conditions of wartime. Would women and minority directors have a future after the war? Should directors start looking outside New York for employment? For that matter, just exactly what is a director? The duties and possibilities kept changing as circumstances changed, and will continue to do so as long as playwrights hand us unsolvable staging problems, teachers devise new methods of actor training, theatre technology develops irresistible new techniques, and theatre economics devise new ways to do old tasks. The story of the evolution of the director did not end in 1945. At the end of the century, the Society of Stage Directors and Choreographers still has not written an official job description.

Notes

1 See Percy MacKaye, Introduction, to *An Arrant Knave and Other Plays,* xvii.
2 A sample Daly contract is included in Wilmeth's compilation for 1865–1915 (Witham, ed., *Theatre in the United States: A Documentary History, 1790–1915*) as document 146; a list of rules, similar to Daly's but for the Boston Museum in 1880, appears as document 144.

Bibliography: Directors and Direction

The classic anthology of directors' position papers, Cole and Chinoy's *Directing the Play: A Source Book of Stagecraft,* a "why-to-do-it as well as a how-to-do-it book," is still a fine introduction to the way directors think about their work. The excerpts should lead a reader to original sources, especially Hopkins's *How's Your Second Act?* and Belasco's *The Theatre Through Its Stage Door,* one chapter of which, "The Evolution of a Play," is as good a manual on direction as any ever written. A portion of this essay appears as document 178 in Witham, *Theatre in the United States,* which includes a number of additional primary sources relevant to this chapter.

The study of specific directors' work might well begin with *Theater in America,* in which Mary C. Henderson's agile prose and exquisite illustrations bring to life some twenty directors and choreographers of the 1870–1945 period. Two recent encyclopedic collections – Frick and Vallillo's *Theatrical Directors: A Biographical Dictionary* and Leiter's *The Great Stage Directors: 100 Distinguished Careers of the Theater* (Leiter is the author of the comparable chapter on direction in Vol. III of this history) – provide capsule summaries of the directors' lives, careers, and production histories, as well as basic bibliographies. The *Cambridge Guide to American Theatre* (Wilmeth and Miller) and *The Oxford Companion to American Theatre* (Bordman) include briefer biographies. A periodical, *Journal of the SDC Foundation* (formerly ". . . of the Society of Stage Directors and Choreographers"), specializes in interviews with mid- or late-career directors and choreographers. A model of how to write a scholarly study of a theatre artist, C. Lee Jenner's "The Duchess of Arch Street" in *The Drews and the Barrymores: A Dynasty of Actors,* expands on Mrs. John Drew's privately circulated autobiography.

Not surprisingly, theatrical biographies and autobiographies are usually written to entertain but often contain valuable shoptalk as well. Chapter 37 ("A Study of Stage-Management") in Clara Morris's *Life on the Stage* is a vivid account of Augustin Daly at work on stage and in the office. Other firsthand accounts are cited in Wilmeth and Cullen's edition of select Daly plays. Mrs. Fiske also had her Boswell in Alexander Woollcott, whose *Mrs. Fiske: Her Views on Actors, Acting, and the Problems of Production* articulates her working principles. When he allows himself to become serious, John Golden reveals himself as an insightful professional in *Stage Struck* (1930). Guthrie McClintic's *Me and Kit* and George Abbott's *Mister Abbott* are lucid and unsparing in presenting the authors' triumphs and failures. Less gentlemanly, as one would expect, are Jed Harris's *Watchman, What of the Night?* (1963) and *A Dance on the High Wire* (1979), though the epilogue of *Watchman* consists of two sober assessments of Harris's work as director. Eva Le Gallienne's fullest account of the Civic Repertory Theatre appears in *At 33.* Margaret Webster's theories of directing in *Shakespeare without Tears* are made vivid in *Don't Put Your Daughter on the Stage,* in which she recreates the social and political context of her work.

Directors with agendas are likely to extend them to their writing, and so a bit of sales resistance is in order. Harold Clurman's often-reprinted *The Fervent Years: The Story of the Group Theatre and the Thirties* and *On Directing* are well-reasoned but not objective accounts of a specific school of directing. Houseman's *Unfinished Business* includes a not-at-all dispassionate revisionist history of the Mercury Theater. Richard France's *The Theatre of Orson Welles* and *Orson Welles on Shakespeare* are basic for any understanding of Welles the director.

A scholar who understands directorial concerns, Lise-Lone Marker, covers an entire career in *David Belasco: Naturalism in the American Theatre.* More often, book-length studies of playwright-directors emphasize texts rather than production, as in Felheim's *The Theatre of Augustin Daly;* Perry's *James A. Herne: The American Ibsen;* and Goldstein's *George S. Kaufman.* Sometimes one has to read between the lines. But Teichmann's *George S. Kaufman: An Intimate Portrait* includes a whole chapter devoted to Kaufman's direction. Helen Sheehy's *Eva Le Gallienne* looks at both the directing and acting careers.

Literary and dramatic expressions of the nineteenth-century waves of immigrants are sympathetically covered by Henry A. Pochmann in "The Mingling of Tongues," *Literary History of the United States,* including an overview of German-language theatres. Lifson's chronicle, *The Yiddish Theatre in America,* includes directors in his survey. The complex genealogy of Stanislavski's influence on directors would be worth a volume by itself. A good place to start exploring would be Paul Gray's "Stanislavski and America: A Critical Chronology."

The Journal of American Drama and Theatre, as the title suggests, covers all aspects and all periods, including directors, as in Lewis E. Shelton's "Mr. Ben Teal." The Shubert Archive, a rich source of information about the major figures of the mammoth productions, publishes a newsletter, *The Passing Show,* with information impossible to find elsewhere about past directors.

The best way to get inside the skin of a past director is to frequent the special theatre collections of the New York Public Library, the Shubert Archive, the Harvard Theatre Collection, the William Seymour Collection of the Princeton University Library, the Walter Hampden Library of the Players Club, and any other library that preserves directors' promptbooks, notebooks, contracts, floor plans, sketches, or other records that provide clues for reconstructing what went on in rehearsal rooms.

Bibliography

(The sources below include those mentioned in the text, in notes, and in bibliographical essays at the conclusion of each chapter.)

Abbott, George. *Mister Abbott.* New York: Random House, 1963.

Abramson, Doris E. *Negro Playwrights in the American Theatre, 1925–1959.* New York: Columbia University Press, 1969.

Adams, Bluford. *E Pluribus Barnum: The Great Showman and The Making of U.S. Popular Culture.* Minneapolis: University of Minnesota Press, 1997.

Adams, Cindy. *Lee Strasberg: The Imperfect Genius of the Actors Studio.* New York: Doubleday, 1980.

Adelman, Irving, and Rita Dworkin. *Modern Drama: A Checklist of Critical Literature on 20th Century Plays.* Metuchen, N.J.: Scarecrow Press, 1967.

Adler, Thomas P. *Mirror on the Stage: The Pulitzer Prize Plays as an Approach to American Drama.* West Lafayette, Ind.: Purdue University Press, 1987.

Albrecht, Ernest J. *The New American Circus.* Gainesville: University Press of Florida, 1995.

Alexander, Doris. *The Tempering of Eugene O'Neill.* New York: Harcourt Brace and World, 1962.

_____. *Eugene O'Neill's Creative Struggle: The Decisive Decade, 1924–1933.* University Park: Pennsylvania State University Press, 1992.

Allen, Fred. *Much Ado About Me.* Boston: Little, Brown, 1956.

Allen, Frederick Lewis. *Only Yesterday: An Informal History of the 1920s.* New York: Harper and Row, 1931.

_____. *The Big Change: America Transforms Itself, 1900–1950.* New York: Harper, 1952.

Allen, Robert C. *Vaudeville and Film, 1895–1915: A Study in Media Interaction.* New York: Arno Press, 1980.

_____. *Horrible Prettiness: Burlesque and American Culture.* Chapel Hill: University of North Carolina, 1991.

Altick, Richard D. *The Shows of London.* Cambridge: Belknap Press of Harvard University Press, 1978.

Anderson, John. *Box Office.* New York: Jonathan Cape and Harrison Smith, 1929.

Anderson, Maxwell. *Off Broadway: Essays about the Theatre.* New York: William Sloan, 1947.

Anderson, Norman. *Ferris Wheels: An Illustrated History.* Bowling Green, Oh.: Bowling Green State University Popular Press, 1992.

Andrew, Dudley. *Concepts of Film Theory.* New York: Oxford University Press, 1984.

Andrews, Wayne. *Architecture, Ambition and Americans.* Rev. ed. New York: Free Press, 1978.

Appelbaum, Stanley. *Show Songs from the Black Crook to the Red Mill.* New York: Dover, 1974.

Appia, Adolphe. *The Work of Living Art.* Trans. H. D. Albright. Edited by Barnard Hewitt. Coral Gables, Fla.: University Press of Miami, 1960.

Archer, Stephen M. *American Actors and Actresses: A Guide to Information Sources.* Detroit: Gale Research Press, 1983.

Atkinson, Brooks. *Broadway.* Rev. ed. New York: Macmillan, 1974.

Atkinson, Brooks, and Al Hirschfeld. *The Lively Years: 1920–1973.* New York: Association Press, 1973.

Atkinson, Jennifer McCabe. *Eugene O'Neill: A Descriptive Bibliography.* Pittsburgh, Penn.: University of Pittsburgh Press, 1974.

Auster, Albert. *Actresses and Suffragists: Women in the American Theatre, 1890–1920.* New York: Praeger, 1984.

Badger, R. Reid. *The Great Amusement Fair.* Chicago: Nelson Hall, 1979.

Bailyn, Bernard, et al. *The Great Republic: A History of the American People.* 4th ed. 2 vols. Lexington, Mass.: D.C. Heath, 1992.

Bank, Rosemarie. "Antedating the Long Run: A Prolegomenon." *Nineteenth Century Theatre Research* 13 (Summer 1985): 33–36.

   "A Reconsideration of the Death of Nineteenth-Century American Repertory Companies and the Rise of the Combination." *Essays in Theatre* 5 (November 1986): 61–75.

   "Frontier Melodrama." In Dunbar Ogden, Douglas McDermott, and Robert K. Sarlós, eds., *Theatre West: Image and Impact.* Amsterdam: Editions Rodopi, 1991.

Banta, Martha. *Imaging American Women: Idea and Ideals in Cultural History.* New York: Columbia University Press, 1987.

Barker, Barbara M. (See B. Kiralfy).

Barlow, Judith E., ed. *Plays by American Women, 1900–1930.* New York: Applause, 1985.
   Final Acts: The Creation of Three Late O'Neill Plays. Athens: University of Georgia Press, 1985.

Barnum, P. T. *Struggles and Triumphs: Forty Years of Recollections.* Buffalo, N.Y.: Warren, Johnson, 1872.

Barrow, Kenneth. *Helen Hayes, First Lady of the American Theatre.* Garden City, N.Y.: Doubleday, 1985.

Barrymore, Ethel. *Memories: An Autobiography.* New York: Harper and Row, 1955.

Barth, Gunther. *City People: The Rise of Modern City Culture in Nineteenth-Century America.* New York: Oxford University Press, 1980.

Barthes, Roland. *Image-Music-Text.* Trans. Stephen Heath. New York: Hill and Wang, 1977.

Baudrillard, Jean. *Selected Writings.* Ed. Mark Poster. Stanford, Calif.: Stanford University Press, 1988.

Bay, Howard. *Stage Design.* New York: Drama Book Publishers, 1974.

Beach, Lewis. *A Square Peg.* Boston: Little, Brown, 1924.

Bean, Annamarie, James Hatch, and Brooks McNamara, eds. *Inside the Minstrel Mask.* Hanover, N.H.: University Press of New England (Wesleyan University Press), 1996.

Beard, Charles A., and Mary Ritter Beard. *The Rise of American Civilization.* 2 vols. New York: Macmillan, 1929.

Beckerman, Bernard, and Howard Siegman, eds. *On Stage: Selected Theater Reviews from the New York Times, 1920–1970.* New York: Quadrangle, 1973.

Behrman, S. N. *4 Plays by S. N. Behrman.* New York: Random House, 1952.

Bel Geddes, Norman. *Miracle in the Evening.* New York: Doubleday, 1960.

Belasco, David. *The Heart of Maryland and Other Plays.* See Hughes and Savage.

Six Plays. Boston: Little, Brown, 1928.

The Theatre Through Its Stage Door. Ed. Louis V. Defoe. New York: Harper, 1929.

Bentham, Frederick. *Stage Lighting.* London: Pitman House, 1980.

Bentley, Eric. *The Dramatic Event: An American Chronicle.* New York: Horizon, 1954.

Bergreen, Laurence. *As Thousands Cheer: The Life of Irving Berlin.* New York: Viking Press, 1990.

Berkhofer, Robert F., Jr. *The White Man's Indian: Images of the American Indian from Columbus to the Present.* New York: Random House, 1978.

Berlin, Normand. *Eugene O'Neill.* New York: Grove Press, 1982.

Bernheim, Alfred L. *The Business of the Theatre: An Economic History of the American Theatre 1750–1932.* New York, 1932; rpt. New York: Benjamin Blom, 1964.

Bigsby, C. W. E. *A Critical Introduction to Twentieth-Century American Drama, Vol. 1: 1900–1940.* Cambridge: Cambridge University Press, 1982.

Bigsby, C. W. E., ed. *Plays by Susan Glaspell.* Cambridge and New York: Cambridge University Press, 1987.

Binns, Archie. *Mrs. Fiske and the American Theatre.* New York: Crown, 1955.

Birkmire, William H. *The Planning and Construction of American Theatres.* New York: John Wiley, 1896.

Black, Stephen A. *File on O'Neill.* London: Methuen, 1993.

Blackburn, Sara, ed. *Dawn of a New Day: The New York World's Fair 1939/40.* New York: Queens Museum and New York University Press, 1980.

Blair, Karen J. *The Torchbearers: Women and their Amateur Arts Associations in America, 1890–1930.* Bloomington: Indiana University Press, 1994.

Bloom, Kenneth. *American Song: The Complete Musical Theatre Companion.* 2 vols. New York: Facts on File, 1985.

Blumin, Stuart. *The Emergence of the Middle Class: Social Experience in the American City, 1760–1900.* New York: Cambridge University Press, 1989.

Bode, Carl. *The American Lyceum: Town Meeting of the Mind.* New York: Oxford University Press, 1956.

Bodnar, John. *The Transplanted: A History of Immigrants in Urban America.* Bloomington: Indiana University Press, 1985.

Bogart, Travis. *Contour in Time: The Plays of Eugene O'Neill.* Rev. ed. New York: Oxford University Press, 1988.

Bogart, Travis, ed. *Complete Plays of Eugene O'Neill.* 3 vols. New York: Library of America, 1988.

Bogart, Travis, and Jackson Bryer, eds. *Selected Letters of Eugene O'Neill.* New Haven, Conn.: Yale University Press, 1988.

Bogart, Travis, Richard Moody, and Walter J. Meserve. *The Revels History of Drama in English, Vol. VIII: American Drama.* London: Methuen, 1977.

Bogdan, Robert. *Freak Show: Presenting Human Oddities for Amusement and Profit.* Chicago: University of Chicago Press, 1988.

Bonin, Jane F. *Prize-Winning American Drama: A Bibliographical and Descriptive Guide.* Metuchen, N.J.: Scarecrow Press, 1973.

Boorstin, Daniel J. *The Americans: The Democratic Experience.* 3 vols. New York: Random House, 1958–1973.

Booth, Michael. *Victorian Spectacular Theatre, 1850–1910.* London: Routledge and Kegan Paul, 1981.

Theatre in the Victorian Age. Cambridge and New York: Cambridge University Press, 1991.

Bordman, Gerald. *The Oxford Companion to American Theatre.* 2nd ed. New York: Oxford University Press, 1992.

———. *American Musical Theatre: A Chronicle.* 2nd ed. New York: Oxford University Press, 1993.

———. *American Theatre: A Chronicle of Comedy and Drama, 1869–1914.* New York: Oxford University Press, 1994.

———. *American Theatre: A Chronicle of Comedy and Drama, 1914–1930.* New York: Oxford University Press, 1995.

———. *American Theatre: A Chronicle of Comedy and Drama, 1930–1969.* New York: Oxford University Press, 1996.

Bordwell, David. *On the History of Film Style.* Cambridge, Mass.: Harvard University Press, 1997.

Bordwell, David, Janet Staiger, and Kristin Thompson. *The Classic Hollywood Cinema: Film Style and Mode of Production to 1960.* New York: Columbia University Press, 1985.

Bordwell, David, and Kristin Thompson. *Film Art: An Introduction.* 4th ed. New York: McGraw-Hill, 1993.

Boskin, Joseph. *Sambo: The Rise and Demise of an American Jester.* New York: Oxford University Press, 1986.

Boulton, Agnes. *Part of a Long Story.* London: Peter Davies, 1958.

Bower, Martha Gilman, ed. *More Stately Mansions.* New York: Oxford University Press, 1988.

Bowser, Eileen. *The Transformation of Cinema, 1907–1915.* New York: Scribner's, 1990.

Boyer, Paul. *Urban Masses and Moral Order in America, 1820–1920.* Cambridge, Mass.: Harvard University Press, 1978.

Brady, Frank. *Citizen Welles: A Biography of Orson Welles.* New York: Scribner's, 1989.

Braudy, Leo. *The Frenzy of Renown: Fame and Its History.* New York: Oxford University Press, 1986.

Breitbart, Eric. *A World on Display: Photographs from the St. Louis World's Fair, 1904.* Albuquerque: University of New Mexico Press, 1997.

Brenman-Gibson, Margaret. *Clifford Odets: American Playwright, the Years 1906 to 1940.* New York: Atheneum, 1981.

Brinkley, Alan. *An Unfinished Nation: A Concise History of the American People.* New York: Alfred A. Knopf, 1993.

Brittain, Joan T. *Laurence Stallings.* Boston: Twayne, 1975.

Brown, Jared. *The Fabulous Lunts: A Biography of Alfred Lunt and Lynn Fontanne.* New York: Atheneum, 1986.

Brown, John Mason. *Broadway in Review.* New York: Norton, 1940.

———. *The Worlds of Robert E. Sherwood, Mirror to His Times.* New York: Harper and Row, 1962.

———. *The Ordeal of a Playwright: Robert E. Sherwood and the Challenge of War.* New York: Harper and Row, 1970.

Brown-Guillory, Elizabeth. *Black Women Playwrights in America.* Westport, Conn.: Greenwood Press, 1988.

Bryan, George B. *Stage Lives: A Bibliography and Index to Theatrical Biographies in English.* Westport, Conn.: Greenwood Press, 1985.

———. *Stage Deaths: A Biographical Guide to International Theatrical Obituaries.* Westport, Conn.: Greenwood Press, 1991.

Bryer, Jackson R. *Checklist of Eugene O'Neill.* Columbus, Oh.: Merrill, 1971.

Bryer, Jackson R., ed. *"The Theatre We Worked For": The Letters of Eugene O'Neill and Kenneth Macgowan.* New Haven, Conn.: Yale University Press, 1982.

Conversations with Thornton Wilder. Jackson: University Press of Mississippi, 1992.

Burbank, Rex J. *Thornton Wilder.* Rev. ed. Boston: Twayne, 1978.

Burg, David. *Chicago's White City of 1893.* Lexington: University Press of Kentucky, 1976.

Burge, James C. *Lines of Business: Casting Practice and Policy in the American Theatre, 1752–1899.* New York: Peter Lang, 1986.

Burke, Billie, with Cameron Shipp. *With a Feather on My Nose.* New York: Appleton-Century-Crofts, 1949.

Burnim, Kalman. "The Effect of the Theatrical Syndicate upon the American Drama." Master's thesis, Indiana University, 1951.

Butsch, Richard, ed. *For Fun and Profit: The Transformation of Leisure into Consumption.* Philadelphia: Temple University Press, 1990.

Bzowski, Frances Diodato, ed. *American Women Playwrights, 1900–1930.* Westport, Conn.: Greenwood Press, 1992.

Cahn, Julius. *Official Theatrical Guide.* New York: Empire Theatre Publications, 1896–1921.

Callow, Simon. *Orson Welles: The Road to Xanadu.* London: Jonathan Cape, 1995.

Campbell, Bartley. See Napier Wilt.

Cargill, Oscar, et al., eds. *O'Neill and His Plays: Four Decades of Criticism.* New York: New York University Press, 1961.

Carlson, Marvin. *The Italian Shakespearians: Performances by Ristori, Salvini, and Rossi in England and America.* Washington, D.C.: Folger Shakespeare Library, 1985.

Places of Performance: The Semiotics of Theatre Architecture. Ithaca, N.Y.: Cornell University Press, 1989.

Carpenter, Charles A. *Modern Drama Scholarship and Criticism 1966–1980: An International Bibliography.* Toronto: University of Toronto Press, 1986.

Carpenter, Frederick I. *Eugene O'Neill.* Rev. ed. Boston: Twayne, 1979.

Carr, Gary. *The Left Side of Paradise: The Screenwriting of John Howard Lawson.* Ann Arbor: UMI Research Press, 1984.

Carter, Randolph, and Robert Reed Cole. *Joseph Urban: Architecture, Theatre, Opera, Film.* New York: Abbeville Press, 1992.

Cayton, Kupiec, Elliot J. Gorn, and Peter W. Williams, eds. *Encyclopedia of American Social History.* New York: Scribner's, 1993.

Chandler, Alfred D., Jr. *The Railroads: The Nation's First Big Business.* New York: Harcourt, Brace, and World, 1965.

The Visible Hand: The Managerial Revolution in American Business. Cambridge: Belknap Press of Harvard University Press, 1977.

Charters, Ann. *Nobody: The Story of Bert Williams.* New York: Macmillan, 1970.

Cheney, Sheldon. *The New Movement in the Theater.* 1914. Rpt. Westport, Conn.: Greenwood Press, 1971.

The Art Theater. 1916. Rev. ed. New York: Alfred A. Knopf, 1925.

Chinoy, Helen Krich. "Reunion: A Self-Portrait of the Group Theatre." *Educational Theatre Journal* 28 (December 1976).

Chinoy, Helen Krich, and Linda Walsh Jenkins, eds. *Women in American Theatre.* Rev. ed. New York: Theatre Communications Group, 1987.

Chothia, Jean. *Forging a Language: A Study of the Plays of Eugene O'Neill.* Cambridge: Cambridge University Press, 1979.

Clapp, John Bouve, and Edwin Francis Edgett. *Players of the Present.* Series 2, Vols. IX, XI, XII. New York: Dunlap Society, 1899–1901; rpt. Benjamin Blom, 1969.

Clark, Barrett H. *Eugene O'Neill: The Man and His Plays.* New York: Robert McBride, 1927; rev. ed. New York: Dover, 1947.

Clark, Barrett H., ed. *America's Lost Plays.* 20 vols. Princeton, N.J.: Princeton University Press, 1940–41; rpt. Bloomington: Indiana University Press, 1963–65; Vol. 21, 1969.

   Favorite American Plays of the Nineteenth Century. Princeton, N.J.: Princeton University Press, 1943.

Clurman, Harold. *The Fervent Years: The Group Theatre and the Thirties.* New York: Harcourt Brace, 1945, 1957, 1975; Da Capo Press, 1983.

   On Directing. New York: Macmillan, 1972.

   All People Are Famous (Instead of an Autobiography). New York: Harcourt Brace Jovanovich, 1977.

Coad, Oral Sumner, and Edwin Mims Jr. *The American Stage.* New Haven, Conn.: Yale University Press, 1929.

Cochran, Thomas, and William Miller. *The Age of Enterprise: A Social History of Industrial America.* New York: Harper and Row, 1961.

Cockrell, Dale. *Demons of Disorder: Early Blackface Minstrels and Their World.* New York and Cambridge: Cambridge University Press, 1997.

Cohan, George M. *Twenty Years on Broadway.* New York: Harper and Row, 1925.

Cohen-Stratyner, Barbara Naomi, ed. *Performing Arts Resources.* Vol. 13. New York: Theatre Library Association, 1988.

Cohn, Ruby. *Dialogue in American Drama.* Bloomington: Indiana University Press, 1971.

Cole, Toby, and Helen Krich Chinoy. *Directing the Play: A Source Book of Stagecraft.* Indianapolis and New York: Bobbs-Merrill, 1953.

Coleman, Ann. "Expressionism – 40 Years After" *CEA Critic* 27 (June 1965): 1, 7–8.

Coleman, Marion Moore. *Fair Rosalind: The American Career of Helena Modjeska.* Cheshire, Conn.: Cherry Hill, 1969.

Commins, Dorothy, ed. *"Love and Admiration and Respect": The O'Neill–Commins Correspondence.* Durham, N.C.: Duke University Press, 1986.

Connelly, Marc. *The Green Pastures: A Fable.* New York: Farrar and Rinehart, 1929.

Connors, Timothy. "The New Theatre." In Weldon Durham, ed., *American Theatre Companies, 1888–1930.* Westport, Conn.: Greenwood Press, 1987.

Conolly, L. W., ed. *Theatrical Touring and Founding in North America.* Westport, Conn.: Greenwood Press, 1982.

Cook, George Cram, and Frank Shay, eds. *The Provincetown Plays.* Cincinnati, Oh.: Stewart and Kidd, 1921.

Cooper, Paul Reuben. "Eva Le Gallienne's Civic Repertory Theatre." Diss., University of Illinois, 1967.

Craig, E. Quita. *Black Drama of the Federal Theatre Era.* Amherst: University of Massachusetts Press, 1980.

Crawford, Cheryl. *One Naked Individual.* Indianapolis, Ind.: Bobbs-Merrill, 1977.

Cronon, William *Nature's Metropolis: Chicago and the Great West.* New York: Norton, 1991.

Crothers, Rachel. "Troubles of a Playwright." *Harper's Bazaar* 15 (January 1911): 14, 46.

   Ourselves. Unpublished ms. 1913. University of Pennsylvania Library.

   "The Future of the American Stage." *The New York Times Magazine* 3 (December 1916): 13.

   "The Producing Playwright." *Theater Magazine* 27 (January 1918): 34.

Expressing Willie and Other Plays: Expressing Willie, 39 East, Nice People. New York: Brentano's, 1924.

Crowley, Alice Lewisohn. *The Neighborhood Playhouse: Leaves from a Theatrical Scrapbook.* New York: Theatre Arts Books, 1959.

Csida, Joseph, and June Bundy Csida. *American Entertainment: A Unique History of Popular Show Business.* New York: Watson-Guptill, 1978.

Culhane, John. *The American Circus: An Illustrated History.* New York: Henry Holt, 1990.

Cullen, Rosemary, and Don B. Wilmeth, eds. *Plays by William Hooker Gillette.* Cambridge and New York: Cambridge University Press, 1983.

Curry, Jane Kathleen. *Nineteenth-Century American Women Theatre Managers.* Westport, Conn: Greenwood Press, 1994.

Curti, Merle Eugene. *The Growth of American Thought.* 3rd ed. New Brunswick, N.J: Transaction, 1982.

Daly, Augustin. See Catherine Sturtevant; Don B. Wilmeth.

Daly, Joseph Francis. *The Life of Augustin Daly.* New York: Macmillan, 1917.

Darrah, William. *Cartes de Visite in Nineteenth Century Photography.* Gettysburgh, Penn.: Darrah, 1981.

The World of Stereographs. Gettysburgh, Penn.: Darrah, 1977.

Davis, Owen. *Icebound.* In Kathryn Coe and William Cordell, eds., *The Pulitzer Prize Plays.* New York: Random House, 1935.

My First Fifty Years in the Theatre. Boston: Baker, 1950.

Davis, Peter A. "From Stock to Combination: The Panic of 1873 and Its Effects on the American Theatre Industry." *Theatre History Studies* 8 (1988): 1–9.

Davis, Ronald J. *Augustus Thomas.* Boston: Twayne, 1984.

Davis, Susan G. *Parades and Power: Street Theatre in Nineteenth-Century Philadelphia.* Philadelphia: Temple University Press, 1986.

DeHart, Jane Sherron. *The Federal Theatre, 1935–1939.* Princeton, N.J.: Princeton University Press, 1967.

Demastes, William W., ed. *American Playwrights, 1880–1945: A Research and Production Sourcebook.* Westport, Conn.: Greenwood Press, 1995.

Realism and the American Dramatic Tradition. Tuscaloosa: University of Alabama Press, 1996.

Dembroski, Theodore M. "Hanky Panks and Group Games versus Alibis and Flats: The Legitimate and Illegitimate of the Carnival Front End." *Journal of Popular Culture* 6 (Winter 1972): 567–82.

Denning, Michael. *The Cultural Front: The Laboring of American Culture in the Twentieth Century.* New York: Verso, 1997.

Deutsch, Helen, and Stella Hanau. *The Provincetown: A Story of the Theatre.* New York: Farrar and Rinehart, 1931.

Dickey, Jerry. *Sophie Treadwell: A Research and Production Sourcebook.* Westport, Conn.: Greenwood Press, 1997.

Dickinson, Donald C. *A Bio-Bibliography of Langston Hughes, 1902–1967.* Hamden, Conn.: Archon, 1972.

Dickinson, Thomas H. *Playwrights of the New American Theater.* New York: Macmillan, 1925.

DiMeglio, John E. *Vaudeville U.S.A.* Bowling Green, Oh.: Popular Press, 1973.

Dimmick, Ruth C. *Our Theatres To-Day and Yesterday.* New York: H. K. Fly Co., 1913.

Dizikes, John. *Opera in America, A Cultural History.* New Haven, Conn.: Yale University Press, 1993.

Douglas, Ann. *The Feminization of American Culture.* New York: Doubleday, 1978.
   Terrible Honesty: Mongrel Manhattan in the 1920's. New York: Farrar, Straus, Giroux, 1995.

Downer, Alan S. *Fifty Years of American Drama.* Chicago: Regnery, 1951.

Downer, Alan S., ed. *American Drama and Its Critics.* Chicago: University of Chicago Press, 1965.

Dressler, Marie. *The Life Story of an Ugly Duckling, An Autobiographical Fragment in Seven Parts.* New York: McBride, 1924.

Drew, John. *My Years on Stage.* New York: Dutton, 1922.

Duberman, Martin Bauml. *Paul Robeson.* New York: Alfred A. Knopf, 1988.

Du Bois, W. E. B. "Krigwa Little Theatre Movement." *Crisis* 32 (July 1926): 134–36.

Dudden, Faye E. *Women in the American Theatre: Actresses and Audiences 1790–1870.* New Haven, Conn.: Yale University Press, 1994.

Duerr, Edwin. *The Length and Depth of Acting.* New York: Holt, Rinehart, and Winston, 1962.

Duffy, Susan. *The Political Left in the American Drama of the 1930s: A Bibliographic Sourcebook.* Metuchen, N.J.: Scarecrow Press, 1992.

Dukore, Bernard F. *American Dramatists, 1918–1945.* New York: Grove Press, 1984.

Dulles, Foster Rhea. *America Learns to Play: A History of Popular Recreation.* New York: D. Appleton-Century, 1940.

Durham, Frank. *Elmer Rice.* New York: Twayne, 1970.

Durham, Weldon B. "The Revival and Decline of the Stock Company Mode of Organization, 1886–1930." *Theatre History Studies* 6 (1986): 165–88.

Durham, Weldon B., ed. *American Theatre Companies, 1749–1887.* Westport, Conn.: Greenwood Press, 1986.
   American Theatre Companies, 1888–1930. Westport, Conn.: Greenwood Press, 1987.
   American Theatre Companies, 1931–1986. Westport, Conn.: Greenwood Press, 1989.

Dyer, Richard. *Stars.* London: British Film Institute, 1979.

Easto, Patrick C., and Marcello Truzzi. "Towards an Ethnography of the Carnival Social System." *Journal of Popular Culture* 6 (Winter 1972): 550–66.

Eaton, Walter Prichard. *Plays and Players.* Cincinnati, Oh.: Stewart and Kidd, 1916.
   The Theatre Guild: The First Ten Years. New York: Brentano's, 1929.

Eckley, Wilton. *The American Circus.* Boston: Twayne, 1984.

Eddleman, Floyd, ed. *American Drama Criticism: Interpretations, 1890–1977.* 2nd ed. and Supplements I, II, and III. Hamden, Conn.: Shoe String, 1979, 1984, 1989, 1992.

Edwards, Ann. *The DeMilles, An American Family.* New York: Abrams, 1988.

Edwards, Christine. *The Stanislavsky Heritage: Its Contribution to the Russian and American Theatre.* New York: New York University Press, 1965.

Egan, Leona Rust. *Provincetown as a Stage: Provincetown, The Provincetown Players, and the Discovery of Eugene O'Neill.* Orleans, Mass.: Parnassus Imprints, 1994.

Ehrenberg, Lewis. *Stepping Out: Nightlife and the Transformation of American Culture, 1890–1930.* Westport, Conn.: Greenwood Press, 1981.

Eisen, Kurt. *The Inner Strength of Opposites: O'Neill's Novelistic Drama and the Melodramatic Imagination.* Athens: University of Georgia Press, 1994.

Ellison, Ralph. *Invisible Man.* New York: Random House, 1952.
   Going into the Territory. New York: Random House, 1986.

Ely, Melvin Patrick. *The Adventures of Amos 'n' Andy: A Social History of an American Phenomenon.* New York: Free Press, 1991.

Emanuel, James A. *Langston Hughes.* New York: Twayne, 1967.

Emerson, Ken. *Doo-dah! Stephen Foster and the Rise of American Popular Culture.* New York: Simon and Schuster, 1997.

Emerson, Ralph Waldo. "Nature." In *The Selected Writings of Ralph Waldo Emerson.* Ed. Brooks Atkinson. New York: Random House, 1940.

Engel, Edwin A. *The Haunted Heroes of Eugene O'Neill.* Cambridge, Mass.: Harvard University Press, 1953.

Engel, Lehman. *Words with Music: The Broadway Musical Libretto.* New York: Macmillan, 1972.

Engle, Ron, and Tice L. Miller, eds. *The American Stage: Social and Economic Issues from the Colonial Period to the Present.* Cambridge and New York: Cambridge University Press, 1993.

Erenberg, Lewis A. *Steppin' Out: New York Nightlife and the Transformation of American Culture, 1890–1930.* Westport, Conn.: Greenwood Press, 1981.

Ernst, Alice H. *Trouping in the Oregon Country: A History of Frontier Theatre.* 1961. Rpt. Westport, Conn.: Greenwood Press, 1974.

Estrin, Mark W., ed. *Conversations with Eugene O'Neill.* Jackson: University Press of Mississippi, 1990.

Ethington, Philip. *The Public City: The Political Construction of Urban Life in San Francisco, 1850–1900.* New York: Cambridge University Press, 1994.

Eustis, Morton. *Broadway, Inc.: The Theatre as a Business.* New York: Dodd, Mead, 1934.

Evans, Sara M. *Born for Liberty: A History of Women in America.* New York: Free Press, 1989.

Falk, Doris V. *Eugene O'Neill and the Tragic Tension: An Interpretive Study of the Plays.* Rev. ed. New York: Gordian, 1982.

Fawkes, Richard. *Dion Boucicault.* London: Quartet Books, 1979.

Fearnow, Mark. *Clare Boothe Luce: A Research and Production Sourcebook.* Westport, Conn.: Greenwood Press, 1995.

The American Stage and the Great Depression: A Cultural History of the Grotesque. New York and Cambridge: Cambridge University Press, 1997.

The Federal Theatre Project: A Catalog-Calendar of Productions. Compiled by the staff of the Fenwick Library, George Mason University. Westport, Conn.: Greenwood Press, 1986.

Felheim, Marvin. *The Theater of Augustin Daly: An Account of the Late Nineteenth-Century American Stage.* Cambridge, Mass.: Harvard University Press, 1956.

Fell, John, ed. *Film Before Griffith.* Berkeley: University of California Press, 1983.

Fiedler, Leslie. *Freaks: Myths and Images of the Secret Self.* New York: Simon and Schuster, 1978.

Fields, Armond, and L. Marc Fields. *From Bowery to Broadway: Lew Fields and the Roots of American Popular Theater.* New York: Oxford University Press, 1993.

Fisher, Judith L., and Stephen Watt, eds. *When They Weren't Doing Shakespeare.* Athens: University of Georgia Press, 1989.

Flanagan, Hallie. "Introduction." *Federal Theatre Plays: Triple-A Plowed Under, Power, Spirochete.* New York: Random House, 1938.

Arena: The Story of the Federal Theatre. New York: Duell, Sloan, and Pearce, 1940.

Flexner, Eleanor. *American Playwrights: 1918–1938.* New York: Simon and Schuster, 1939.

Flink, James J. *The Automobile Age.* Cambridge, Mass.: MIT Press, 1988.

Floan, Howard Russell. *William Saroyan.* New York: Twayne, 1966.

Floyd, Virginia. *The Plays of Eugene O'Neill: A New Assessment.* New York: Ungar, 1985.

Floyd, Virginia, ed. *Eugene O'Neill at Work: Newly Released Ideas for Plays.* New York: Ungar, 1981.

Eugene O'Neill: The Unfinished Plays. New York: Ungar, 1988.

Foner, Eric. *Reconstruction: America's Unfinished Revolution.* New York: Harper and Row, 1988.

Foner, Eric, ed. *The New American History.* Revised and expanded edition. Philadelphia: Temple University Press, 1997.

Foner, Eric, and John A. Garraty, eds. *The Reader's Companion to American History.* Boston: Houghton Mifflin, 1991.

Fort, Tim. "The Introduction of Electrical Incandescence into American Theatres." *Theatre Design & Technology* 29 (Spring 1993): 21–28.

Fox, Charles (C. P. "Chappie"). *Circus Baggage Stock.* Boulder, Colo.: Pruett, 1983.

America's Great Circus Parade. Greendale, Wis.: Country Books, 1993.

Fox, Charles, and Tom Parkinson. *Biller, Banners and Bombast: The Story of Circus Advertising.* Boulder, Colo.: Pruett, 1985.

Fox, Robin W., and T. J. Jackson Lears, eds. *The Culture of Consumption: Critical Essays in American History, 1880–1980.* New York: Pantheon, 1983.

Fraden, Rena. *Blueprints for a Black Federal Theatre 1935–1939.* Cambridge and New York: Cambridge University Press, 1994.

Fraley, Tobin. *The Great American Carousel: A Century of Master Craftsmen.* San Francisco: Chronicle Books, 1994.

France, Richard. *The Theatre of Orson Welles.* Lewisburg, Pa.: Bucknell University Press, 1977.

France, Richard, ed. *Orson Welles on Shakespeare.* Westport, Conn.: Greenwood Press, 1990.

Franklin, John Hope, and Alfred A. Moss, Jr. *From Slavery to Freedom: A History of Negro Americans.* 6th ed. New York: Alfred A. Knopf, 1988.

Freedberg, David. *The Power of Images: Studies in the History and Theory of Response.* Chicago: University of Chicago Press, 1989.

Frick, John W. *New York's First Theatrical Center: The Rialto at Union Square.* Ann Arbor, Mich.: UMI Research Press, 1985.

"From Uncle Tom's Cabin to A Chorus Line: The Long Run on the American Stage." *Southern Theater* (Spring 1990): 10–16.

Frick, John W., and Stephen M. Vallillo. *Theatrical Directors: A Biographical Dictionary.* Westport, Conn.: Greenwood Press, 1994.

Fried, Fred, and Mary Fried. *America's Forgotten Folk Arts.* New York: Pantheon Books, 1978.

Fuchs, Theodore. *Stage Lighting.* Boston: Little, Brown, 1929.

Funnell, Charles E. *By the Beautiful Sea: The Rise and High Times of That Great American Resort, Atlantic City.* New York: Alfred A. Knopf, 1975.

Furnas, J. C. *The Americans: A Social History of the United States 1587–1914.* New York: Putnam, 1969.

Gallup, Donald, ed. *Eugene O'Neill: Work Diary 1924–1943.* 2 vols. New Haven, Conn.: Yale University Press, 1981.

Gänzl, Kurt. *The Encyclopedia of the Musical Theatre.* New York: Schirmer Books, 1994.

Garfield, David. *A Player's Place: The Story of the Actors Studio.* New York: Macmillan, 1980.

Gassner John. *Best Plays of the Modern American Theatre.* 2nd series. New York: Crown, 1947.

Best Plays of the Early American Theatre, From the Beginning to 1916. New York: Crown, 1967.

Gelb, Arthur, and Barbara Gelb. *O'Neill.* Rev. ed. New York: Perennial, 1987.

Gellert, Lawrence, ed. *Lost Plays of Eugene O'Neill.* New York: Citadel, 1963.

Giedion, Siegfried. *Mechanization Takes Command: A Contribution to Anonymous History.* New York: Oxford University Press, 1948; Norton, 1969.

Gifford, Denis. *Books and Plays in Films, 1896–1915.* Jefferson, N.C.: McFarland, 1991.

Gilbert, Anne. *The Stage Reminiscences of Mrs. Gilbert.* Ed. Charlotte M. Martin. New York: Scribner's, 1901.

Gilbert, Douglas. *American Vaudeville: Its Life and Times.* New York: Whittlesey House, 1940.

Gilder, Rosamond, ed. *Theatre Arts Anthology.* New York: Theatre Arts Books, 1948.

Gill, Brendan. *Cole: A Biographical Essay.* Ed. Robert Kimball. New York: Holt, Rinehart and Winston, 1971.

Glaab, Charles N., and A. Theodore Brown. *A History of Urban America.* 2nd ed. New York: McMillan, 1976.

Glaspell, Susan. *The Road to the Temple.* New York: Frederick A. Stokes, 1927.

Glassberg, David. *American Historical Pageantry: The Uses of Tradition in the Early Twentieth Century.* Chapel Hill: University of North Carolina Press, 1990.

Glasstone, Victor. *Victorian and Edwardian Theatre.* Cambridge, Mass.: Harvard University Press, 1975.

Golden, John. *Stage Struck.* New York: Samuel French, 1930.

Golden, Joseph. *The Death of Tinker Bell: The American Theatre in the 20th Century.* Syracuse, N.Y.: Syracuse University Press, 1967.

Goldman, Herbert G. *Jolson: The Legend Comes to Life.* New York: Oxford University Press, 1988.

Goldsack, Bob. *Work of Mirth Shows: A Remembrance. The Largest Midway on Earth.* Rudolph Center, Vt.: Greenhills Books, 1984.

Carnival Trains. Nashua, N.H.: Midway Museum Press, 1991.

Goldstein, Malcolm. *The Art of Thornton Wilder.* Lincoln: University of Nebraska Press, 1965.

The Political Stage: American Drama and Theatre of the Great Depression. New York: Oxford University Press, 1974.

George S. Kaufman: His Life, His Theater. New York: Oxford University Press, 1979.

Goodale, Katharine. *Behind the Scenes with Edwin Booth.* Boston: Houghton Mifflin, 1931.

Gossett, Thomas F. *Uncle Tom's Cabin and American Culture.* Dallas, Tex.: Southern Methodist University Press, 1985.

Gottlieb, Lois. *Rachel Crothers.* Boston: Twayne, 1979.

"Looking to Women: Rachel Crothers and the Feminist Heroine." In Helen K. Chinoy and Linda Jenkins, eds., *Women in American Theatre.* New York: Crown, 1981.

Graham, Philip. *Showboats. The History of an American Institution.* Austin: University of Texas, 1951.

Gray, Paul. "Stanislavski and America: A Critical Chronology." *Tulane Drama Review* 9, No. 2 (Winter 1964): 21–60.

Green, Abel, and Joe Laurie, Jr. *Show Biz: From Vaude to Video.* New York: Holt, 1951.

Green, Paul. *The Field God and In Abraham's Bosom.* New York: McBride, 1927.

Green, Stanley. *Ring Bells! Sing Songs! Broadway Musicals of the 1930s.* New York: Galahad Books, 1971.

Encyclopedia of the Musical. New York: Dodd, Mead, 1976.

The World of Musical Comedy. 4th ed. San Diego: Barnes, 1980.

The Great Clowns of Broadway. New York: Oxford University Press, 1984.

Broadway Musicals: Show by Show. Milwaukee, Wis.: Hal Leonard, 1985.

The Rodgers and Hammerstein Fact Book. New York: Drama Book Specialists, 1988.

Greenfield, Thomas Allen. *Work and the Work Ethic in American Drama, 1920–1970.* Columbia: University of Missouri Press, 1982.

Gross, Robert F. *S. N. Behrman: A Research and Production Sourcebook.* Westport, Conn.: Greenwood Press, 1992.

Gutman, Herbert G. *Work, Culture, and Society in Industrializing America: Essays in American Working-Class and Social History.* New York: Vintage, 1977.

Haberman, Donald. *Our Town: An American Play.* Boston: Twayne, 1989.

Halfmann, Ulrich, ed. *Eugene O'Neill: Comments on the Drama and the Theater.* Tubingen: Gunter Narr Verlag, 1987.

Hall, Stuart. "Notes on Deconstructing 'The Popular.'" In Raphael Samuel, ed., *People's History and Socialist Theory.* London: Routledge and Kegan Paul, 1981.

Halline, Allan G., ed. *American Plays.* New York: American Book Company, 1935.

Hamm, Charles. Y*esterdays: Popular Song in America.* New York: Norton, 1979.

Hammarstrom, David Lewis. *Big Top Boss: John Ringling North and the Circus.* Urbana: University of Illinois Press, 1992.

Harding, Alfred. *The Revolt of the Actors.* New York: William Morrow, 1929.

Harner, James L. *Literary Research Guide: A Guide to Reference Sources for the Study of Literatures in English and Related Topics.* 2nd ed. New York: Modern Language Association, 1993.

Harrigan, Edward. *The Mulligan Guard Ball.* In Richard Moody, ed., *Dramas from the American Theatre, 1762–1909.* Cleveland, Oh.: World, 1966.

Harris, Neil. *Humbug: The Art of P. T. Barnum.* Boston: Little, Brown, 1973.

Cultural Excursions: Marketing Appetites and Cultural Tastes in Modern America. Chicago: University of Chicago, 1990.

Harris, Neil, ed. *The Land of Contrasts, 1880–1901.* New York: George Braziller, 1970.

Harris, Neil, Wim deWit, James Gilbert, and Robert W. Rydell. *Grand Illusions: Chicago's World's Fair of 1893.* Chicago: Chicago Historical Society, 1993.

Harris, Jed. *Watchman, What of the Night?* New York: Doubleday, 1963.

A Dance on the High Wire. New York: Crown, 1979.

Harrison-Pepper, Sally. *Drawing a Circle in the Square.* Jackson: University Press of Mississippi, 1990.

Harrity, Richard. *The World Famous Harrity Family.* New York: Trident Press, 1968.

Hart, Moss. *Act One, An Autobiography.* New York: Random House, 1959.

Hartman, John Geoffrey. *The Development of American Social Comedy from 1787 to 1936.* New York: Octagon, 1939.

Hartmann, Louis. *Theatre Lighting.* New York: Appleton, 1930.

Hay, Samuel A. *African American Theatre: An Historical and Critical Analysis.* New York and Cambridge: Cambridge University Press, 1994.

Hays, Samuel P. *The Response to Industrialism, 1885–1914.* Chicago: University of Chicago Press, 1961.

Hazelton, Nancy J. Doran, and Kenneth Krauss. *Maxwell Anderson and the New York Stage.* Monroe, N.Y.: Library Research Associates, 1991.

Hearn, Charles R. *The American Dream in the Great Depression.* Westport, Conn.: Greenwood Press, 1977.

Helburn, Theresa. *A Wayward Quest.* Boston: Little, Brown, 1960.

Hemenway, Robert E. *Zora Neale Hurston: A Literary Biography.* Urbana: University of Illinois Press, 1977.

Henderson, Mary C. *The City and the Theatre: New York Playhouses from Bowling Green to Times Square.* Clifton, N.J.: James T. White, 1973.

    Theater in America. New, updated edition. New York: Abrams, 1996.

Herne, James A. *Shore Acres and Other Plays.* Rev. ed. by Mrs. James A. Herne. New York: Samuel French, 1928.

    See also Arthur Hobson Quinn.

Hertzberg, Arthur. *The Jews in America: Four Centuries of an Uneasy Encounter, A History.* New York: Simon and Schuster, 1989.

Heuvel, Michael Vanden. *Elmer Rice: A Research and Production Sourcebook.* Westport, Conn.: Greenwood Press, 1996.

Hewitt, Barnard. *Theatre U.S.A., 1668–1957.* New York: McGraw-Hill, 1959.

    "King Stephen of the Park and Drury Lane." In *The Theatrical Manager in England and America.* Ed. Joseph Donohue. Princeton, N.J.: Princeton University Press, 1971.

Higgs, Robert. *The Transformation of the American Economy, 1865–1914: An Essay in Interpretation.* New York: John Wiley, 1971.

Higham, John. "The Reorientation of American Culture in the 1890s." In *The Origins of Modern Conciousness.* Ed. John Weiss. Detroit: Wayne State University Press, 1965.

    Strangers in the Land: Patterns of American Nativism, 1860–1925. New York: Atheneum, 1966.

    Send These to Me: Immigrants in Urban America. Rev. ed. Baltimore: Johns Hopkins University Press, 1984.

Highfill, Philip H. Jr., Kalman A. Burnim, and Edward A. Langhans. *A Biographical Dictionary of Actors, Actresses . . . and Other Stage Personnel in London, 1660–1800.* 16 vols. Carbondale: Southern Illinois University Press, 1973–93.

Hill, Erroll. *Shakespeare in Sable: A History of Black Shakespearean Actors.* Amherst: University of Massachusetts Press, 1984.

Himelstein, Morgan Y. *Drama Was a Weapon: The Left-Wing Theatre in New York, 1929–1941.* New Brunswick, N.J.: Rutgers University Press, 1963.

Hinden, Michael. *Long Day's Journey into Night: Native Eloquence.* Boston: Twayne, 1990.

Hirsch, Foster. *A Method to Their Madness: The History of the Actors Studio.* New York: Norton, 1984.

    George Kelly. Boston: Twayne, 1975.

Hixon, Don L., and Don A. Hennessee. *Nineteenth-Century American Drama: A Finding Guide.* Metuchen, N.J.: Scarecrow Press, 1977.

Hofstadter, Richard. *The Age of Reform.* New York: Vintage, 1955.

Hogan, Robert. *Dion Boucicault.* New York: Twayne, 1969.

Hoh, LaVahn G., and William H. Rough. *Step Right Up! The Adventure of Circus in America.* White Hall, Va.: Betterway Publications, 1990.

Hopkins, Arthur. *How's Your Second Act?* New York: Philip Goodman, 1918; Samuel French, 1931.

Horn, Barbara Lee. *Maxwell Anderson: A Research and Production Sourcebook.* Westport, Conn.: Greenwood Press, 1996.

Hornblow, Arthur. *Training for the Stage: Some Hints for Those about to Choose the Player's Career.* Philadelphia: Lippincott, 1916.

A History of the Theatre in America from Its Beginnings to the Present Time. 2 vols. Philadelphia: Lippincott, 1919.

Horowitz, Joseph. *Wagner Nights, An American History*. Berkeley: University of California Press, 1994.

Houseman, John. *Run-through: A Memoir*. New York: Simon and Schuster, 1972.

Unfinished Business. New York: Applause Books, 1989.

Howard, Bronson. *Autobiography of a Play*. 1886. Rpt. New York: Dramatic Museum of Columbia University, 1914.

Howard, Lillie P. *Zora Neale Hurston*. Boston: Twayne, 1980.

Howard, Sidney. *The Silver Cord*. In S. Marion Tucker, ed., *Modern British and American Plays*. New York: Harper, 1931.

Howe, Irving. *World of Our Fathers: The Journey of East European Jews to America and the Life They Found and Made*. New York: Harcourt Brace Jovanovich, 1976.

Hoyt, Charles, and Percy Gaunt. "The Bowery, 1892." In Robert Freemount, ed., *Favorite Songs of the Nineties*. New York: Dover, 1973.

Hoyt, Harlowe R. *Town Hall Tonight: Intimate Memories of the Grassroots Days of the American Theatre*. New York: Bramhall House, 1955.

Hughes, Glenn. *A History of the American Theatre, 1700–1950*. New York: Samuel French, 1951.

Hughes, Glenn, and George Savage, eds. *The Heart of Maryland and Other Plays by David Belasco*. Vol. 18 of *America's Lost Plays*, ed. Barrett H. Clark. Princeton, N.J.: Princeton University Press, 1941.

Hughes, Langston. *Five Plays by Langston Hughes*. Ed. Webster Smalley. Bloomington: Indiana University Press, 1968.

Hutton, Laurence. *Plays and Players*. New York: Hurd and Houghton, 1875.

Inge, M. Thomas, ed. *Handbook of American Popular Culture*. 2nd ed. 3 vols. Westport, Conn.: Greenwood Press, 1989.

Irwin, John T. *American Hieroglyphics: The Symbol of the Egyptian Hieroglyphics in the American Renaissance*. New Haven, Conn.: Yale University Press, 1980.

Isaacs, Edith, J R., ed. *Theatre: Essays on the Arts of the Theatre*. Boston: Little, Brown, 1927.

Architecture for the New Theatre. New York: Theatre Arts Books, 1935.

Izenour, George C. *Theater Design*. New York: McGraw-Hill, 1977.

Theater Design and Modern Architecture. Pittsburgh, Penn.: Carnegie-Mellon University, 1978.

Theater Technology. New York: McGraw-Hill, 1988.

Jablonski, Edward. *Gershwin*. New York: Doubleday, 1987.

Jackson, Esther M. "Dramatic Form in Eugene O'Neill's *The Calms of Capricorn*." *Eugene O'Neill Newsletter* 13 (Winter 1988): 35–42.

Jackson, John Brinckerhoff. *American Space: The Centennial Years, 1865–1876*. New York: Norton, 1972.

Jackson, Kenneth T., ed. *Encyclopedia of New York City*. New Haven, Conn.: Yale University Press and New York: New-York Historical Society, 1995.

Jay, Ricky. *Learned Pigs & Fireproof Women*. New York: Villard Books, 1987.

Jefferson, Joseph. *The Autobiography of Joseph Jefferson*. New York: Century, 1890.

Jenner, C. Lee. "The Duchess of Arch Street." In Warren Kliewer, ed., *The Drews and the Barrymores: A Dynasty of Actors, Vol. 13: Performing Arts Resources*. New York: Theatre Library Association, 1988.

Jennings, John. "A History of the New Theatre, New York, 1910–1911." Diss., Stanford University, 1952.

Johnson, Claudia D. *American Actress: Perspective on the Nineteenth Century.* Chicago: Nelson-Hall, 1984.

Johnson, James Weldon. *Black Manhattan.* New York: Atheneum, 1972.

Johnson, Stephen Burge. *The Roof Gardens of Broadway Theatre, 1883–1942.* Ann Arbor: UMI Research Press, 1985.

Jones, Eugene H. *Native Americans as Shown on the Stage, 1753–1916.* Metuchen, N.J.: Scarecrow Press, 1988.

Jones, Howard Mumford. *The Age of Energy: Varieties of American Experience, 1865–1915.* New York: Viking, 1971.

Jones, Robert Edmond. *The Dramatic Imagination.* New York: Theatre Arts Books, 1941.

    The Theatre of Robert Edmond Jones. Ed. Ralph Pendleton. Middletown, Conn.: Wesleyan University Press, 1958.

Jones, Robert Edmond, and Kenneth Macgowan. *Continental Stagecraft.* New York: Harcourt, Brace, 1922.

Josephson, Matthew. *The Robber Barons: The Great American Capitalists, 1861–1901.* Norwalk, Conn.: Easton, 1987 [1934].

Jussim, Estelle. *Visual Communication and the Graphic Arts: Photographic Technologies in the Nineteenth Century.* New York: Bower, 1974.

Kahn, Otto. *Of Many Things, Being Reflections and Impressions on International Affairs, Domestic Topics, and the Arts.* New York: Boni and Liveright, 1926.

Kammen, Michael. *The Lively Arts: Gilbert Seldes and the Transformation of Cultural Criticism in the United States.* New York: Oxford University Press, 1996.

Kanellos, Nicolas. *A History of Hispanic Theatre in the United States, Origins to 1940.* Austin: University of Texas Press, 1990.

Kaplan, Justin. *Walt Whitman, A Life.* New York: Simon and Schuster, 1980.

Kasson, John F. *Civilizing the Machine: Technology and Republican Values in America, 1776–1900.* New York: Grossman, 1976.

    Amusing the Million: Coney Island at the Turn of the Century. New York: Hill and Wang, 1978.

    Rudeness and Civility: Manners in Nineteenth-Century Urban America. New York: Hill and Wang, 1990.

Kaufman, George S., and Marc Connelly. *Dulcy.* In Arthur Hobson Quinn, ed., *Representative American Plays.* 7th ed. New York: Appleton-Century-Crofts, 1953.

Kazan, Elia. *A Life.* New York: Alfred A. Knopf, 1988.

Kelly, George. *Craig's Wife.* In Kathryn Coe and William Cordell, eds., *The Pulitzer Prize Plays.* New York: Random House, 1935.

Kemp, Harry. "Out of Provincetown: A Memoir of Eugene O'Neill." *Theatre Magazine* 51 (April 1930): 22–23.

Kenny, Vincent. *Paul Green.* New York: Twayne, 1971.

Kern, Stephen. *The Culture of Time and Space, 1880–1920.* Cambridge, Mass.: Harvard University Press, 1983.

Keyssar, Helene. *The Curtain and the Veil.* New York: Burt Franklin, 1981.

Kift, Dagmar. *The Victorian music hall: culture, class and conflict.* Cambridge and New York: Cambridge University Press, 1996.

Kimmel, Stanley. *The Mad Booths of Maryland.* Rev. ed. New York: Dover, 1969.

Kiralfy, Bolossy. *Bolossy Kiralfy, Creator of Great Musical Spectacles, An Autobiography.* Ed. Barbara M. Barker. Ann Arbor: UMI Research Press, 1988.

Kiralfy, Imre. *Imre Kiralfy's Grand Historical Spectacle America in Four Acts and 17 Scenes.* 1893.

Kirkland, Jack. *Tobacco Road.* New York: Duell, Sloan and Pearce, 1941.

Klaw, Marc. "The Theatrical Syndicate: The Other Side." *Cosmopolitan* 38 (December 1904): 199–201.

Kline, Herbert, ed. *New Theatre and Film, 1934 to 1937: An Anthology.* New York: Harcourt Brace Jovanovich, 1985.

Klink, William. *Maxwell Anderson and S. N. Behrman: A Reference Guide.* Boston: G. K. Hall, 1977.

Knepler, Henry. *The Gilded Stage: The Years of the Great International Actresses.* New York: William Morrow, 1968.

Koch, Frederick. "Introduction." *American Folk Plays.* New York: Appleton-Century, 1939.

Koszarski, Richard. *An Evening's Entertainment. The Age of the Silent Feature Picture, 1915–1928.* New York: Scribner, 1990.

Kotsilibas-Davis, James. *Great Times, Good Times: The Odyssey of Maurice Barrymore.* Garden City, N.Y.: Doubleday, 1977.

Kouwenhoven, John. *Made in America: The Arts in Modern Civilization.* Garden City, N.Y.: Doubleday, 1948.

Krasner, David. *Resistance, Parody, and Double Consciousness in African American Theatre, 1895–1910.* New York: St. Martin's Press, 1997.

Kreuger, Miles. *Show Boat: The Story of a Classic American Musical.* New York: Oxford University Press, 1977.

Kritzer, Amelia Howe, ed. *Plays by Early American Women, 1775–1850.* Ann Arbor: University of Michigan Press, 1995.

Krows, Arthur Edwin. *Play Production in America.* New York: Henry Holt, 1916.

Krutch, Joseph Wood. *The American Drama Since 1918: An Informal History.* New York: Random House, 1939; George Braziller, 1957.

"Introduction" to Alice Lewisohn Crowley. *The Neighborhood Playhouse: Leaves from a Theatrical Scrapbook.* New York: Theatre Arts Books, 1959.

Kunhardt, Philip B. Jr., Philip B. Kunhardt III, and Peter W. Kunhardt. *P.T. Barnum: America's Greatest Showman.* New York: Alfred A. Knopf, 1995.

Kyriazi, Gary. *The Great American Amusement Parks.* Secaucus, N.J.: Citadel Press, 1976.

Lagner, Lawrence. *The Magic Curtain.* New York: Dutton, 1951.

Larsen, Orville K. *Scene Design in the American Theatre from 1915 to 1960.* Fayetteville: University of Arkansas Press, 1989.

Laurie, Joe Jr. *Vaudeville: From the Honky-Tonks to the Palace.* New York: Henry Holt, 1953.

Lawrence, Elizabeth Atwood. *Rodeo: An Anthropologist Looks at the Wild and the Tame.* Knoxville: University of Tennessee Press, 1982.

Lawson, John Howard. *Theory and Technique of Playwriting.* New York: Putnam, 1936.

Leach, William. *Land of Desire: Merchants, Power, and the Rise of a New American Culture.* New York: Pantheon, 1993.

Leacroft, Richard, and Helen Leacroft. *Theatre and Playhouse.* London and New York: Methuen, 1984.

Lears, T. J. Jackson. *No Place of Grace: Antimodernism and the Transformation of American Culture, 1880–1920.* New York: Pantheon, 1981.

Fables of Abundance: A Cultural History of Advertising in America. New York: Basic Books, 1994.

Lee, Lawrence, and Barry Gifford. *Saroyan: A Biography.* New York: Harper and Row, 1984.

Le Gallienne, Eva. *At 33.* New York: Longmans, Green, 1934.

With a Quiet Heart. New York: Viking Press, 1953.

Leiter, Samuel L. *The Great Stage Directors: 100 Distinguished Careers of the Theater.* New York: Facts on File, 1994.

Leiter, Samuel, L., ed. *The Encyclopedia of the New York Stage 1920–1930.* Westport, Conn.: Greenwood Press, 1985.

The Encyclopedia of the New York Stage 1930–1940. Westport, Conn.: Greenwood Press, 1989.

The Encyclopedia of the New York Stage 1940–1950. Westport, Conn.: Greenwood Press, 1992.

Lemann, Nicholas. *The Promised Land: The Great Black Migration and How It Changed America.* New York: Alfred A. Knopf, 1991.

Levine, Ira A. *Left-wing Dramatic Theory in the American Theatre.* Ann Arbor: UMI Research Press, 1985.

Levine, Lawrence. *Highbrow/Lowbrow: The Emergence of Cultural Hierarchy in America.* Cambridge, Mass.: Harvard University Press, 1988.

The Unpredictable Past: Explorations in American Cultural History. New York: Oxford University Press, 1993.

Lewis, Arthur H. *Carnival.* New York: Trident Press, 1970.

Lewis, Philip C. *Trouping: How the Show Came to Town.* New York: Harper and Row, 1973.

Lewis, Robert. *Slings and Arrows: Theater in My Life.* New York: Stein and Day, 1984.

Lewisohn, Ludwig. "An American Tragedy." *Nation* 110 (February 1920): 241–42.

Leverich, Lyle. *Tom: The Unknown Tennessee Williams.* New York: Crown, 1995.

Leyda, Jay, and Charles Musser. *Before Hollywood.* New York: American Federation of Arts, 1986.

Lhamon, W. T. Jr. *Raising Cain: Blackface Performance from Jim Crown to Hip Hop.* Cambridge, Mass.: Harvard University Press, 1998.

Licht, Walter. *Industrializing America: Nineteenth Century.* Baltimore, Md.: The Johns Hopkins University Press, 1995.

Lifson, David F. *The Yiddish Theatre in America.* New York: Thomas Yoseloff, 1965.

Lindroth, Colette. *Zona Gale.* New York: Twayne, 1962.

Rachel Crothers: A Research and Production Sourcebook. Westport, Conn.: Greenwood Press, 1995.

Lindsay, Vachel. *The Art of the Moving Picture.* New York: Macmillan, 1915.

Lippman, Monroe. "The History of the Theatrical Syndicate: Its Effect Upon the Theatre in America." Diss., University of Michigan, 1937.

"The Effect of the Theatrical Syndicate on the Theatrical Art in America." *Quarterly Journal of Speech* 26 (April 1941): 275–82.

Locke, Alain. "The Drama of Negro Life." In *Plays of Negro Life: A Source Book of Native American Drama.* Eds. Alain Locke and Montgomery Gregory. New York: Harper, 1927.

Lockridge, Richard. *Darling of Misfortune. Edwin Booth, 1833–1893.* 1932. Rpt. New York: Benjamin Blom, 1971.

Logan, Joshua. [Interview]. *SSDC Journal,* No. 9 (1983): 5–23.

Logan, Olive. *Apropos of Women and Theatre.* New York: Carleton, 1870.

Londré, Felicia Hardison. "Money without Glory: Turn-of-the-Century America's Women

Playwrights." In Ron Engle and Tice L. Miller, eds., *The American Stage.* Cambridge and New York: Cambridge University Press, 1993.

Lott, Eric. *Love & Theft: Blackface Minstrelsy and the American Working Class.* New York: Oxford University Press, 1933.

Lounsbury, Warren C. *Theatre Backstage from A to Z.* Rev. ed. Seattle: University of Washington Press, 1972

Lynd, Robert S., and Helen M. Lynd. *Middletown: A Study in Contemporary American Culture.* New York: Harcourt, Brace, 1929.

Lynes, Russell. *The Lively Audience: A Social History of the Visual and Performing Arts in American, 1890–1950.* New York: Harper and Row, 1985.

McArthur, Benjamin. *Actors and American Culture, 1880–1920.* Philadelphia: Temple University Press, 1984.

McCabe, James Jr. *New York by Gaslight.* 1882. Facsimile ed. New York: Arlington House, 1984.

McCandless, Stanley. *A Method of Lighting the Stage.* New York: Theatre Arts Books, 1958.

McClintic, Guthrie. *Me and Kit.* Boston: Little, Brown, 1955.

McConachie, Bruce. *Melodramatic Formations: American Theatre and Society, 1820–1870.* Iowa City: University of Iowa Press, 1992.

McCullough, Edo. *World's Fair Midway: An Affectionate Account of American Amusement Areas from the Crystal Palace to the Crystal Ball.* 1966. Reprint. New York: Arno Press, 1976.

McDermott, Douglas. "The Theatre and Its Audience: Changing Modes of Social Organization in the American Theatre." In Ron Engle and Tice L. Miller, eds., *The American Stage: Social and Economic Issues from the Colonial Period to the Present.* Cambridge and New York: Cambridge University Press, 1993.

McDonald, Arthur. "The Neighborhood Playhouse." In Weldon B. Durham, ed., *American Theatre Companies, 1888–1930.* Westport, Conn.: Greenwood Press, 1987.

McDonald, William F. *Federal Relief Administration and the Arts.* Columbus: Ohio State University Press, 1969.

Macintosh, Iain. *Architecture, Actor and Audience.* London and New York: Routledge, 1993.

Mackay, Constance D'Arcy. *The Little Theatre in the United States.* New York: Henry Holt, 1917.

McKay, Frederic Edward, and Charles E. L. Wingate, eds. *Famous American Actors of Today.* 2 vols. New York: Thomas Y. Crowell, 1896.

MacKaye, Percy. *The Civic Theatre in Relation to the Redemption of Leisure.* New York: Kennerley, 1912.

   Community Drama: Its Motive and Method Neighborliness. Boston: Houghton Mifflin, 1917.

   Epoch: The Life of Steele MacKaye, Genius of the Theatre. 2 vols. New York: Liveright, 1927.

   Introduction to *An Arrant Knave and Other Plays.* Vol. XI of *America's Lost Plays,* Barrett M. Clark, ed. Princeton, N.J.: Princeton University Press, 1940–41; rpt. Bloomington: Indiana University Press, 1963–65.

McKechnie, Samuel. *Popular Entertainment through the Ages.* London: Sampson Low, Marston, 1931.

McKennon, Joe. *A Pictorial History of the American Carnival.* 3 vols. Sarasota, Fla.: Carnival Publishers, 1972–81.

McLaughlin, Robert. *Broadway and Hollywood: A History of Economic Interaction.* New York: Arno Press, 1974.

McLean, Albert F. *American Vaudeville as Ritual.* Lexington: University of Kentucky Press, 1965.

Macmillan's Encyclopedia of Architects. New York: Free Press, 1982.

McNamara, Brooks. "The Scenography of Popular Entertainment." *Drama Review* 18 (March 1974): 16–25.

———. "'Scavengers of the Amusement World': Popular Entertainment and the Birth of the Movies." In *American Pastimes.* Brockton, Mass.: Brockton Art Center, 1976.

———. "Come On Over: The Rise and Fall of the American Amusement Park." *Theatre Crafts* 11 (September 1977): 33, 84–86.

———. *The Shuberts of Broadway.* New York: Oxford University Press, 1990.

———. "The Entertainment District at the End of the 1930s." In William Taylor, ed., *Inventing Times Square.* New York: Russell Sage Foundation, 1991.

———. "A Canvas City . . . Half as Old as Time." In *The County Fair Carnival:* Catalogue of an Exhibition by the Chemung County Historical Society, New York, 1992.

———. *Step Right Up: An Illustrated History of the American Medicine Show.* Rev. ed. Jackson: University Press of Mississippi, 1995.

McNamara, Brooks, ed. *American Popular Entertainments.* New York: PAJ Publications, 1983.

McTeague, James H. *Before Stanislavsky: American Professional Acting Schools and Acting Theory, 1875–1925.* Metuchen, N.J.: Scarecrow Press, 1993.

Magnuson, Landis K. *Circle Stock Theatre: Touring American Small Towns, 1900–1960.* Jefferson, N.C.: McFarland, 1995.

Mamoulian, Rouben. [Interview]. *SSDC Journal* (1986).

Mangels, William F. *The Outdoor Entertainment Business.* New York: Vantage Press, 1952.

Manheim, Michael. *Eugene O'Neill's New Language of Kinship.* Syracuse, N.Y.: Syracuse University Press, 1982.

Mantle, Burns. *The Best Plays of 1933–34.* New York: Dodd, Mead, 1934.

Marcosson, Isaac F., and Daniel Frohman. *Charles Frohman: Manager and Man.* New York: Harper and Brothers, 1916.

Marker, Lise-Lone. *David Belasco: Naturalism in the American Theatre.* Princeton, N.J.: Princeton University Press, 1975.

Mason, Jeffrey D. *Wisecracks: The Farces of George S. Kaufman.* Ann Arbor: UMI Research Press, 1988.

———. *Melodrama and the Myth of America.* Bloomington: Indiana University Press, 1993.

Mast, Gerald. *A Short History of the Movies.* 4th ed. New York: Macmillan, 1986.

———. *Can't Help Singin': The American Musical Comedy on Stage and Screen.* Woodstock, N.Y.: Overlook Press, 1987.

Mast, Gerald, and Marshall Cohen, eds. *Film Theory and Criticism: Introductory Readings.* 3rd ed. New York: Oxford University Press, 1985.

Mates, Julian. *America's Musical Stage: Two Hundred Years of Musical Theatre.* Westport, Conn.: Greenwood Press, 1985.

Matlaw, Myron, ed. *The Black Crook and Other Nineteenth-Century American Plays.* New York: Dutton, 1967.

———. *American Popular Entertainment.* Westport, Conn.: Greenwood Press, 1977.

Matz, Mary Jane. *The Many Lives of Otto Kahn.* New York: Macmillan, 1963.

Matthews, Brander, and Laurence Hutton. *Actors and Actresses of Great Britain and the United States.* 5 vols. New York: Cassell, 1886.

Matthews, Jane DeHart. *The Federal Theatre, 1935–1939: Plays, Relief, and Politics.* Princeton, N.J.: Princeton University Press, 1967.

May, Lary. *Screening Out the Past: The Birth of Mass Culture and the Motion Picture Industry.* Chicago: University of Chicago Press, 1983.

Medovoy, George. "ARTEF." In Weldon B. Durham, ed., *American Theatre Companies, 1888–1930.* Westport, Conn.: Greenwood Press, 1987.

Meinig, D. W. *The Shaping of America: A Geographical Perspective on 500 Years of History.* 4 vols. (projected). New Haven, Conn.: Yale University Press, 1986, 1993.

Meisel, Martin. *Realizations: Narrative, Pictorial, and Theatrical Arts in Nineteenth-Century England.* Princeton, N.J.: Princeton University Press, 1983.

Menefee, Larry T. "A New Hypothesis for Dating the Decline of the 'Road.'" *Educational Theatre Journal* 30 (October 1978): 343–56.

Mersand, Joseph. *The American Drama, 1930–1940.* 1941. Rpt. New York: Kennikat, 1968.

Merk, Frederick. *History of the Westward Movement.* New York: Alfred A. Knopf, 1978.

Meserve, Walter J. *American Drama to 1900: A Guide to Information Sources.* Detroit: Gale Research, 1980.

——. "The American West of the 1870s and 1880s as Viewed from the Stage." *Journal of American Drama and Theatre* 3 (Winter 1991): 48–63.

——. *An Outline History of American Drama.* 2nd ed. New York: Feedback, 1994.

Middleton, George. "David Belasco: The Last of His Line." Interlude in *These Things Are Mine.* New York: Macmillan, 1947.

Mielziner, Jo. *The Shapes of Our Theatre.* Ed. C. Roy Smith. New York: Potter, 1970.

Mikolzyk, Thomas A. *Langston Hughes: A Bio-Bibliography.* Westport, Conn.: Greenwood Press, 1990.

Miller, Arthur. *Timebends.* New York: Grove Press, 1987.

Miller, Jordan Y. *Eugene O'Neill and the American Critic: A Bibliographical Checklist.* 1962; rev. ed. New York: Archon, 1973.

Miller, Jordan Y., ed. *Playwright's Progress: Eugene O'Neill and the Critics.* Chicago: Scott Foresman, 1965.

Miller, Jordan Y., and Winifred L. Frazer. *American Drama between the Wars: A Critical History.* Boston: Twayne, 1991.

Miller, Kerby, and Paul Wagner. *Out of Ireland: The Story of Irish Emigration to America.* Washington, D.C.: Elliott and Clark, 1994.

Miller, Tice L. *Bohemians and Critics, American Theatre Criticism in the Nineteenth Century.* Metuchen, N.J.: Scarecrow Press, 1981.

——. "The Image of Fashionable Society: 1840–1870." In Judith L. Fisher and Stephen Watt, eds., *When They Weren't Doing Shakespeare.* Athens: University of Georgia Press, 1989.

Moderwell, Hiram. *The Theater of To-Day.* New York: John Lane, 1914.

Mohl, Raymond A. *The New City: Urban America in the Industrial Age, 1860–1920.* Arlington Heights, Ill.: Harlan Davidson, 1985.

Monkkonen, Eric H. *America Becomes Urban: The Development of U.S. Cities and Towns, 1780–1980.* Berkeley: University of California Press, 1988.

Monroy, Douglas. *Thrown among Strangers: The Making of Mexican Culture in Frontier California.* Berkeley: University of California Press, 1990.

Moody, Richard. *America Takes the Stage.* Bloomington: Indiana University Press, 1955.

——. *Ned Harrigan, From Corlear's Hook to Herald Square.* Chicago: Nelson-Hall, 1980.

Moody, Richard, ed. *Dramas from the American Theatre, 1762–1909.* Cleveland: World, 1966.

Moore, Abbot H. "Individualism in Architecture: The Works of Herts and Tallant." *Architectural Record* 15 (January 1904): 55–91.

Mordden, Ethan. *The American Theatre.* New York: Oxford University Press, 1981.
  Make Believe: The Broadway Musical in the 1920s. New York: Oxford University Press, 1997.
Morin, Roi L. "Design and Construction of Theaters." *American Architect* 122 (1922): 393–402, 443–50, 453–56, 492–96, 507–10, 537–42, 553–56; 123 (1923): 56–58, 66–71, 101–104, 117–19.
Morison, Samuel Eliot. *The Oxford History of the American People.* New York: Oxford University Press, 1965.
Morison, Samuel Eliot, and Henry Steele Commager. *The Growth of the American Republic.* 4th ed. 2 vols. New York: Oxford University Press, 1950.
Morris, Clara. *Life on the Stage.* New York: McClure, Phillips, 1901.
Morris, Lloyd. *Curtain Time: The Story of the American Theatre.* New York: Random House, 1953.
Morris, Richard B., and Jeffrey B. Morris. *The Encyclopedia of American History.* 7th ed. New York: HarperCollins, 1996.
Morris, Sylvia Jukes. *Rage for Fame: The Ascent of Clare Boothe Luce.* New York: Random House, 1997.
Morrison, Bill. "The Theatre of Herts and Tallant." *Marquee* 22 (Fourth Quarter 1990): 3–22.
  [Herbert J. Krapp]. *Broadside* 16 (Spring 1993): 2–23.
Morrison, Michael A. *John Barrymore, Shakespearean Actor.* Cambridge and New York: Cambridge University Press, 1997.
Morrison, Theodore. *Chautauqua: A Center for Education, Religion, and the Arts in America.* Chicago: University of Chicago Press, 1974.
Morrison, Toni. *Playing in the Dark: Whiteness and the Literary Imagination.* Cambridge, Mass.: Harvard University Press, 1992.
Mosel, Tad (with Gertrude Macy). *Leading Lady: The World and Theatre of Katharine Cornell.* Boston: Little, Brown, 1978.
Moses, L. G. *Wild West Shows and the Images of American Indians, 1883–1933.* Albuquerque: University of New Mexico Press, 1996.
Moses, Montrose. *Famous Actor-Families in America.* New York: Thomas Y. Crowell, 1906.
  The American Dramatist. 2nd ed. Boston: Little, Brown, 1917.
Moses, Montrose J., ed. *Plays by Clyde Fitch.* Boston: Little, Brown, 1915.
  Representative Plays by American Dramatists. New York: Dutton, 1918–21.
Moses, Montrose J., and John Mason Brown, eds. *The American Theatre as Seen by Its Critics 1752–1934.* New York: Norton, 1934.
Mott, Frank Luther. *A History of American Magazines.* 5 vols. Cambridge, Mass.: Harvard University Press, 1957.
Moy, James. *Marginal Sights: Staging the Chinese in America.* Iowa City: University of Iowa Press, 1993.
Mullin, Donald C. *The Development of the Stage.* Berkeley: University of California Press, 1970.
  Victorian Actors and Actresses in Review: A Dictionary of Contemporary Views of Representative British and American Actors and Actresses, 1837–1901. Westport, Conn.: Greenwood Press, 1983.
Mumford, Lewis. *The Brown Decades: A Study of the Arts of America, 1865–1895.* New York: Beacon Press, 1931.
Murphy, Brenda. *American Realism and American Drama, 1880–1940.* Cambridge: Cambridge University Press, 1987.

Musser, Charles. *The Emergence of Cinema: The American Screen to 1907.* New York: Scribner's, 1990.

Before the Nickelodeon: Edwin S. Porter and the Edison Manufacturing Company. Berkeley: University of California Press, 1991.

Nasaw, David. *Going Out: The Rise and Fall of Public Amusements.* New York: Basic Books, 1993.

Nathan, George Jean. *The Popular Theatre.* New York: Alfred A. Knopf, 1918.

The Theatre of the Moment. New York: Alfred A. Knopf, 1936.

Nelson, Stephen. *"Only a Paper Moon": The Theatre of Billy Rose.* Ann Arbor: UMI Research Press, 1985.

Newson, Adele S. *Zora Neale Hurston: A Reference Guide.* Boston: G. K. Hall, 1987.

Newton, Harry. "A Burlesque on Uncle Tom's Cabin." In Brooks McNamara, ed., *American Popular Entertainments.* New York: PAJ Publications, 1983.

Noble, David F. *The Progressive Mind, 1890–1917.* Rev. ed. Minneapolis: University of Minnesota Press, 1981.

North, Joseph H. *The Early Development of the Motion Picture, 1887–1909.* New York: Arno Press, 1973.

Norton, Elliot. *Boston Post,* 13 October 1946. Reprinted in Stephen A. Black, ed., *File on O'Neill.* London: Methuen, 1993.

Norton, Mary Beth, ed. *The American Historical Association's Guide to Historical Literature.* 3rd ed. 2 vols. New York: Oxford University Press, 1995.

Nugent, Walter T. K. *Crossings: The Great Transatlantic Migrations, 1870–1914.* Bloomington: Indiana University Press, 1992.

Nye, Russel. *The Unembarrassed Muse: The Popular Arts in America.* New York: Dial Press, 1970.

Odell, George C. D. *Annals of the New York Stage.* 15 vols. New York: Columbia University Press, 1927–49.

Odets, Clifford. *The Time Is Ripe: The 1940 Journal of Clifford Odets.* New York: Atheneum, 1988.

Oenslager, Donald. *Stage Design: Four Centuries of Scenic Invention.* New York: Viking Press, 1975.

The Theatre of Donald Oenslager. Middletown, Conn.: Wesleyan University Press, 1978.

Oettermann, Stephen. *The Panorama: History of a Mass Medium.* Trans. Deborah Lucas Schneider. New York: Zone Books, 1997.

Oggel, L. Terry. *Edwin Booth: A Bio-Bibliography.* Westport, Conn.: Greenwood Press, 1992.

O'Hara, Frank. *Today in American Drama.* Chicago: University of Chicago Press, 1939; rpt. New York: Greenwood Press, 1969.

O'Neill, Eugene. "A Letter from O'Neill." *New York Times,* 11 April 1920, section VI, p. 2.

"Letter." *New York Times,* 18 December 1921, section VI, p. 1.

"The Playwright Explains." *New York Times,* 14 February 1926, section VIII, p. 2.

Complete Plays of Eugene O'Neill. 3 vols. New York: Library of America, 1988.

Orlandello, John. *O'Neill on Film.* Rutherford, N.J.: Fairleigh Dickinson University Press, 1982.

Orvell, Miles. *The Real Thing: Imitation and Authenticity in American Culture, 1880–1940.* Chapel Hill: University of North Carolina Press, 1989.

Palmieri, Anthony F. R. *Elmer Rice: A Playwright's Vision of America.* Rutherford, N.J.: Fairleigh Dickinson University Press, 1980.

Parkinson, Tom, and Charles Philip Fox. *The Circus Moves by Rail.* Boulder, Colo.: Pruett, 1978.

Patterson, Ada. *Maude Adams, A Biography.* New York: Meyer Bros., 1908.

Peiss, Kathy. *Cheap Amusements: Working Women and Leisure in Turn-of-the-Century New York.* Philadelphia: Temple University Press, 1986.

Perry, John. *James A. Herne, The American Ibsen.* Chicago: Nelson-Hall, 1978.

Peters, Margot. *The House of Barrymore.* New York: Alfred A. Knopf, 1991.

Peterson, Bernard L. *Early Black American Playwrights and Dramatic Writers.* Westport, Conn.: Greenwood Press, 1990.

   A Century of Musicals in Black and White: An Encyclopedia of Musical Stage Works By, About or Involving African-Americans. Westport, Conn.: Greenwood Press, 1993.

Pfister, Joel. *Staging Death: Eugene O'Neill and the Politics of Psychological Discourse.* Chapel Hill: University of North Carolina Press, 1995.

Phillips, Levi Damon. "Arthur McKee Rankin's The Danites 1877–1881: Prime Example of the American Touring Process." *Theatre Survey* 25 (November 1984): 225–47.

Pilat, Oliver and Jo Ranson. *Sodom by the Sea: An Affectionate History of Coney Island.* Garden City, N.Y.: Doubleday, Doran and Co., 1941.

Pitt, Leonard. *The Decline of the Californios: A Social History of the Spanish-Speaking Californians, 1846–1890.* Berkeley: University of California Press, 1970.

Pochmann, Henry A. "The Mingling of Tongues." *Literary History of the United States.* Ed. Robert E. Spiller et al. Rev. ed. New York: Macmillan, 1955 (see also 4th ed., 1974).

Poggi, Jack. *Theater in America: The Impact of Economic Forces, 1870–1967.* Ithaca, N.Y.: Cornell University Press, 1968.

Pollack, Rhoda-Gale. *George S. Kaufman.* Boston: Twayne, 1988.

Porter, Laurin. *The Banished Prince: Time, Memory, and Ritual in the Late Plays of Eugene O'Neill.* Ann Arbor: UMI Research Press, 1988.

Porter, Thomas E. *Myth and Modern American Drama.* Detroit: Wayne State, University Press, 1969.

Postlewait, Thomas. "Simultaneity in Modern Stage Design and Drama." *Journal of Dramatic Theory and Criticism* 3 (Fall 1988): 5–28.

   "Sojourning in Never Never Land: The Idea of Hollywood in Recent Theatre Autobiographies." In Ron Engle and Tice L. Miller, eds., *The American Stage.* Cambridge and New York: Cambridge University Press, 1993.

   "Spatial Order and Meaning in the Theatre: The Case of Tennessee Williams." *Assaph* 10 (1994): 45–73.

   "From Melodrama to Realism: The Suspect History of American Drama." In Michael Hays and Anastasia Nikolopopulou, eds., *Melodrama: The Cultural Emergence of a Genre.* New York: St. Martin's Press, 1996.

Prevots, Naima. *American Pageantry.* Ann Arbor: UMI Research Press, 1990.

Prucha, Francis P. *Handbook for Research in American History: A Guide to Bibliographies and Other Reference Works.* Lincoln: University of Nebraska, 1987.

Quinn, Arthur Hobson. *A History of the American Drama from the Civil War to the Present Day.* Rev. ed. 2 vols. New York: Appleton-Century-Crofts, 1936. (1st ed., New York: Harper, 1927).

Quinn, Arthur Hobson, ed. *Representative American Plays.* New York: Century, 1917. (Also cited in text: 3rd ed., New York: Century, 1925, and 7th ed., New York: Appleton-Century-Crofts, 1953.)

   The Early Plays of James A. Herne, Vol. VII: America's Lost Plays. Ed. Barrett H. Clark. Princeton, N.J.: Princeton University Press, 1940.

Rabkin, Gerald. *Drama and Commitment: Politics in the American Theatre of the Thirties.* Bloomington: Indiana University Press, 1964.

Raleigh, John H. *The Plays of Eugene O'Neill.* Carbondale: Southern Illinois University Press, 1964.

Rampersad, Arnold. *The Life of Langston Hughes, Vol. I: 1902–1941.* New York: Oxford University Press, 1986; *Vol. II: 1941–1967.* Oxford University Press, 1988.

Ranald, Margaret Loftus. *The Eugene O'Neill Companion.* Westport, Conn.: Greenwood Press, 1985.

Raymond, Jack. *Show Music on Record: The First 100 Years* [1890–1990]. New York: Ungar, 1982.

Reardon, William R., and Eugene K. Bristow. "The American Theatre, 1864–1870: An Economic Portrait." *Speech Monographs* 33 (November 1966): 438–43.

Reaves, Joseph Russell. *An O'Neill Concordance.* 3 vols. Detroit: Gale, 1969.

Reed, Kenneth T. *S. N. Behrman.* Boston: Twayne, 1975.

Reynolds, David S. *Walt Whitman's America: A Cultural Biography.* 2 vols. New York: Alfred A. Knopf, 1995.

Reynolds, R. C. *Stage Left: The Development of the American Social Drama of the Thirties.* Troy, N.Y.: Whitson, 1986.

Rice, Elmer. *Minority Report: An Autobiography.* New York: Simon and Schuster, 1963.

Richardson, Gary A. *American Drama, From the Colonial Period Through World War I: A Critical History.* New York: Twayne, 1993.

Riis, Thomas L. *Just before Jazz: Black Musical Theater in New York, 1890–1915.* Washington, D.C.: Smithsonian Institution Press, 1989.

Robbins, Phyllis. *Maude Adams, An Intimate Biography.* New York: Putnam, 1956.

Roberts, J. W. *Richard Boleslavsky: His Life and Work in the Theatre.* Ann Arbor: UMI Research Press, 1981.

Roberts, Nancy L., and Arthur W. Roberts, eds. *"As Ever, Gene": The Letters of Eugene O'Neill to George Jean Nathan.* Rutherford, N.J.: Fairleigh Dickinson University Press, 1987.

Robinson, Alice M., Vera Mowry Roberts, and Milly S. Barranger, eds. *Notable Women in the American Theatre: A Biographical Dictionary.* Westport, Conn.: Greenwood Press, 1989.

Robinson, David. *World Cinema, A Short History.* London: Methuen, 1973.

Robinson, James A. *Eugene O'Neill and Oriental Thought: A Divided Vision.* Carbondale: Southern Illinois University Press, 1982.

Rogers, Lynn. "The Actors' Revolt." *American Heritage* 47 (September 1996): 92–99.

Rogers, Will. *The Autobiography of Will Rogers.* Ed. Donald Day. Boston: Houghton Mifflin, 1949.

Rogin, Michael. *Blackface, White Noise: Jewish Immigrants in the Hollywood Melting Pot.* Berkeley: University of California Press, 1996.

Root, Deane. *American Popular Stage Music 1860–1880.* Ann Arbor: UMI Research Press, 1981.

Root, Deane, ed. *Nineteenth-Century American Musical Theater.* New York: Garland Press, 1994.

Roppolo, Joseph Patrick. *Philip Barry.* New York: Twayne, 1965.

Rosen, Philip, ed. *Narrative, Apparatus, Ideology: A Film Theory Reader.* New York: Columbia University Press, 1986.

Rosenberg, Bernard, and Ernest Harburg. *The Broadway Musical: Collaboration in Commerce and Art.* New York: New York University Press, 1993.

Rosenberg, Emily S. *Spreading the American Dream: American Economic and Cultural Expansion, 1890–1945.* New York: Hill & Wang, 1982.

Rosenfeld, Lulla. *Bright Star of Exile: Jacob Adler and the Yiddish Theatre.* New York: Crowell, 1977.

Rosenthal, Jean, and Lael Wertenbaker. *The Magic of Light.* Boston: Little, Brown, 1972.

Rourke, Constance. *American Humor: A Study of the National Character.* New York: Harcourt, Brace, 1931.

Rubin, Joan Shelley. *Constance Rourke and American Culture.* Chapel Hill: University of North Carolina Press, 1980.

Ruggles, Eleanor. *The Prince of Players: Edwin Booth.* New York: Norton, 1953.

Russell, Don. *The Wild West or, A History of the Wild West Shows.* Fort Worth, Tex.: Amon Carter Museum of Western Art, 1970.

Ryan, Pat M. "A. M. Palmer, Producer: A Study of Management, Dramaturgy, and Stagecraft in the American Theatre, 1872–96." Diss., Yale University, 1959.

Rybezynski, Witold. *City Life: Urban Expectations in a New World.* New York: Scribner's, 1995.

Rydell, Robert W. *All the World's a Fair: Visions of Empire at American International Expositions, 1876–1916.* Chicago: University of Chicago Press, 1984.

World of Fairs: The Century of Progress Expositions. Chicago: University of Chicago Press, 1993.

Salem, James M. *A Guide to Critical Reviews, pt. 1. American Drama, 1909–1982.* 3rd ed. Metuchen, N.J.: Scarecrow Press, 1984.

Salzman, Jack, ed. *American Studies: An Annotated Bibliography,* and *Supplement, 1984–1988.* 3 vols. Cambridge: Cambridge University Press, 1986–90.

Sampson, Henry T. *Blacks in Blackface: A Source Book on Early Black Musical Shows.* Metuchen, N.J.: Scarecrow Press, 1980.

The Ghost Walks: A Chronology of Blacks in Show Business, 1865–1910. Metuchen, N.J.: Scarecrow Press, 1988.

Sanders, Leslie Catherine. *The Development of Black Theater in America.* Baton Rouge: Louisiana State University Press, 1988.

Sandrow, Nahma. *Vagabond Stars: A World History of Yiddish Theater.* New York: Harper and Row, 1977.

Sarlós, Robert K. *Jig Cook and the Provincetown Players.* Amherst: University of Massachusetts Press, 1982.

Saroyan, Aram. *William Saroyan.* San Diego: Harcourt Brace Jovanovich, 1983.

Saxon, A. H. *Enter Foot and Horse: A History of Hippodrama in England and France.* New Haven, Conn.: Yale University Press, 1968.

P. T. Barnum: The Legend and the Man. New York: Columbia University Press, 1989.

Sayler, Oliver M. *Our American Theatre.* New York: Brentano's, 1923.

Revolt in the Arts: A Survey of the Creation, Distribution and Appreciation of Art in America. New York: Brentano's, 1930.

Schanke, Robert. *Eve Le Gallienne: A Bio-Bibliography.* Westport, Conn.: Greenwood Press, 1989.

Shattered Applause: The Lives of Eve Le Gallienne. Carbondale: Southern Illinois University Press, 1992.

Scharine, Richard G. *From Class to Caste in American Drama: Political and Social Themes Since the 1930s.* Westport, Conn.: Greenwood Press, 1991.

Schivelbusch, Wolfgang. *The Railway Journey: Trains and Travel in the Nineteenth Century.* Trans. A. Hollo. Oxford: Blackwell, 1980.

Disenchanted Night: The Industrialization of Light in the Nineteenth Century. Berkeley: University of California Press, 1988.

Schlereth, Thomas J. *Victorian America: Transformations in Everyday Life, 1876–1915.* New York: HarperCollins, 1991.

Schlueter, June, ed. *Modern American Drama: The Female Canon.* Rutherford, N.J.: Fairleigh Dickinson University Press, 1990.

Schroeder, Patricia R. *The Presence of the Past in Modern American Drama.* Rutherford, N.J.: Fairleigh Dickinson University Press, 1989.

The Feminist Possibilities of Dramatic Realism. Rutherford, N.J.: Fairleigh Dickinson University Press, 1996.

Seldes, Gilbert. *The Seven Lively Arts.* New York: Harper, 1924.

Sellers, Maxine Schwarz, ed. *Ethnic Theatre in the United States.* Westport, Conn.: Greenwood Press, 1983.

Senelick, Laurence. *The Age and Stage of George L. Fox, 1825–1877.* Hanover and London: University Press of New England (Tufts University), 1988.

Senelick, Laurence, ed. *Wandering Stars: Russian Emigré Theatre, 1905–1940.* Iowa City: University of Iowa Press, 1992.

Sexton, R. W., and B. F. Betts. *American Theatres of Today.* New York: Architectural Book Publishing, 1927.

Shadegg, Stephen. *Clare Boothe Luce: A Biography.* New York: Simon and Schuster, 1970.

Shafer, Yvonne. *American Women Playwrights, 1900–1950.* New York: Peter Lang, 1995.

Shattuck, Charles H. *The Hamlet of Edwin Booth.* Urbana-Champaign: University of Illinois Press, 1969.

Shakespeare on the American Stage, Vol. 2: From Booth and Barrett to Sothern and Marlowe. Washington, D.C. Folger Shakespeare Library, 1987.

Sheaffer, Louis. *O'Neill: Son and Playwright.* Boston: Little, Brown, 1968.

O'Neill: Son and Artist. Boston: Little, Brown, 1973.

Sheed, Wilfrid. *Clare Boothe Luce.* New York: Dutton, 1982.

Sheehy, Helen. *Eva Le Gallienne.* New York: Alfred A. Knopf, 1996.

Sheldon, Edward. *The Nigger.* New York: Macmillan, 1910.

Shelton, Lewis E. "Mr. Ben Teal." *Journal of American Drama and Theatre* 2 (Spring 1990): 55–80.

Shivers, Alfred S. *The Life of Maxwell Anderson.* New York: Stein and Day, 1983.

Maxwell Anderson: An Annotated Bibliography of Primary and Secondary Works. Metuchen, N.J.: Scarecrow Press, 1985.

Shnayerson, Michael. *Irwin Shaw: A Biography.* New York: Putnam, 1989.

Shubert, Lee. "The Theatrical Syndicate and How It Operated." Ed. Maryann Chach. *The Passing Show* (Fall 1990/Spring 1991): 16–21.

Shuman, R. Baird. *Robert. E. Sherwood.* New York: Twayne, 1964.

Sievers, W. David. *Freud on Broadway: A History of Psychoanalysis and the American Drama.* New York: Hermitage House, 1955.

Silverman, Kenneth. *Houdini!!! The Career of Ehrich Weiss.* New York: HarperCollins, 1996.

Silvester, Robert. *United States Theatre: A Bibliography.* Romsey, England: Motley Press, 1993.

Simon, Linda. *Thornton Wilder: His World.* Garden City, N.Y.: Doubleday, 1979.

Simonson, Harold P., and Lois Gottlieb. *Rachel Crothers.* Boston: Twayne, 1979.

Simonson, Lee. "Basic Theater Planning." *Architectural Forum* 57 (September 1932): 185–93.

Part of a Lifetime. New York: Duell, Sloan and Pearce, 1943.

The Stage Is Set. New York: Theatre Arts Books, 1963.

Skinner, Otis. *Footlights and Spotlights: Recollections of My Life on the Stage.* Indianapolis, Ind.: Bobbs-Merrill, 1923.

Sklar, Robert. *Movie-Made America: A Social History of the American Movies.* New York: Random House, 1975.

Slotkin, Richard. *The Fatal Environment: The Myth of the Frontier in the Age of Industrialization, 1800–1890.* New York: Atheneum, 1985.

Slout, William L. *Theatre in a Tent: The Development of a Provincial Entertainment.* Bowling Green, Oh.: Bowling Green University Popular Press, 1972.

Smiley, Sam. *The Drama of Attack: Didactic Plays of the American Depression.* Columbia: University of Missouri Press, 1972.

Smith, Cecil. *Musical Comedy in America.* New York: Theatre Arts Books, 1950; 2nd ed., with Glenn Litton. New York: Theatre Arts Books, 1981.

Smith, Eric Ledell. *Bert Williams: A Biography of the Pioneer Black Comedian.* Jefferson, N.C.: McFarland, 1992.

Smith, Henry Nash. *The Virgin Land: The American West as Symbol and Myth.* Cambridge, Mass.: Harvard University Press, 1958.

Smith, Madeline, and Richard Eaton. *Eugene O'Neill: An Annotated Bibliography.* New York: Garland Press, 1988.

Smith, Milo L. "The Klaw-Erlanger Bogyman Myth." *Players* 44 (Dec.–Jan. 1969): 70–75.

Smith, Susan Harris. *American Drama: The Bastard Art.* New York and Cambridge: Cambridge University Press, 1997.

Smith, Wendy. *Real Life Drama: The Group Theatre and America, 1931–1940.* New York: Alfred A. Knopf, 1990.

Smith-Rosenberg, Carroll. *Disorderly Conduct: Visions of Gender in Victorian America.* New York: Alfred A. Knopf, 1985.

Snyder, Robert W. *The Voice of the City: Vaudeville and Popular Culture in New York.* New York: Oxford University Press, 1989.

Sothern, Edward H. *The Melancholy Tale of "Me": My Remembrances.* New York: Scribner's, 1916.

Southern, Richard. *Changeable Scenery: Its Origin and Development in the British Theatre.* London: Faber and Faber, 1951.

Speaight, George. *The History of the English Puppet Theatre.* 2nd ed. Carbondale: Southern Illinois University Press, 1990.

Spiller, Robert E., et al., eds. *The Literary History of the United States.* 4th ed. New York: Macmillan, 1974.

Stagg, Jerry. *The Brothers Shubert.* New York: Ballantine Books, 1968.

Steele, James. *Theatre Builders.* Berlin: Academy Editions, 1996 (distributed in the United States by St. Martin's Press).

Stein, Charles W., ed. *American Vaudeville as Seen by Its Contemporaries.* New York: Alfred A. Knopf, 1984.

Steiner, George. *The Death of Tragedy.* New York: Alfred A. Knopf, 1961; London: Faber and Faber, 1961.

Stoddard, Richard. *Stage Scenery, Machinery, and Lighting: A Guide to Information Sources.* Detroit: Gale Research, 1977.

Theatre and Cinema Architecture: A Guide to Information Sources. Detroit: Gale Research, 1978.

Stover, John F. *American Railroads.* Chicago: University of Chicago Press, 1978.

Stowell, Sheila. *A Stage of Their Own: Feminist Playwrights of the Suffrage Era.* Ann Arbor: University of Michigan Press, 1992.

Strang, Lewis C. *Famous Actresses of the Day.* 2 vols. Boston: L. C. Page, 1899–1902.

Famous Actors of the Day. 2 vols. Boston: L. C. Page, 1899–1902.

Players and Plays of the Last Quarter Century. 2 vols. Boston: L. C. Page, 1903.

Strasser, Susan. *Never Done: A History of American Housework.* New York: Pantheon, 1982.

Sturtevant, Catherine, ed. *Man and Wife & Other Plays by Augustin Daly.* Vol. 20 of *America's Lost Plays,* ed. Barrett H. Clark. Princeton. N.J.: Princeton University Press, 1942.

Suskin, Steven. *Show Tunes 1905–1985: The Songs, Shows, and Careers of Broadway's Major Composers.* New York: Dodd, Mead, 1986.

Susman, Warren I. *Culture as History: The Transformation of American Society in the Twentieth Century.* New York: Pantheon Books, 1984.

Swain, Joseph. *The Broadway Musical: A Critical and Musical Survey.* New York: Oxford University Press, 1990.

Swasey, William Albert. "A Few Essentials in Theatre Construction." *American Architecture* 103 (22 January 1913): 53–62.

Taft, Robert. *Photography and the American Scene: A Social History, 1839–1889.* New York: Dover, 1964 [1938].

Takaki, Ronald. *Strangers from a Different Shore: A History of Asian Americans.* Boston: Little, Brown, 1989.

A Different Mirror: A History of Multicultural America. Boston: Little, Brown, 1993.

Tallack, Douglas. *Twentieth-Century America: The Intellectual and Cultural Context.* London: Longman, 1991.

Tallant, Hugh. "The American Theater: Its Antecedents and Characteristics." *Brickbuilder* 23 (December 1914): 285–90; 24 (January 1915): 17–22.

Taussig, F. W., and C. S. Josllyn. *American Business Leaders: A Study in Social Origins and Social Stratification.* New York: Macmillan, 1932.

Taylor, Karen Malpede, ed. *People's Theatre in Amerika: Documents by the People Who Do It.* New York: Drama Book Specialists, 1972.

Taylor, William R., ed. *Inventing Times Square: Commerce and Culture at the Crossroads of the World.* New York: Russell Sage Foundation, 1991.

Teichmann, Howard. *George S. Kaufman: An Intimate Portrait.* New York: Atheneum, 1972.

Thernstrom, Stephen, ed. *Harvard Encyclopedia of American Ethnic Groups.* Cambridge, Mass.: Harvard University Press, 1980.

Thomas, Augustus. *Arizona.* Chicago: Dramatic Publishing Company, 1899.

Alabama. Chicago: Dramatic Publishing Company, 1905.

Thompson, Denman. *The Old Homestead.* Boston: Walter H. Baker, 1927.

Thomson, Rosemarie Garland, ed. *Freakery: Cultural Spectacles of the Extraordinary Body.* New York: New York University Press, 1996.

Thomson, Peter, ed. *Plays by Dion Boucicault.* Cambridge and New York: Cambridge University Press, 1984.

Tidworth, Simon. *Theatres: An Architectural and Cultural History.* New York: Praeger, 1973.

Tiusanen, Timo. *O'Neill's Scenic Images.* Princeton, N.J.: Princeton University Press, 1968.

Toll, Robert C. *Blacking Up: The Minstrel Show in Nineteenth-Century America.* New York: Oxford University Press, 1974.

On with the Show: The First Century of Show Business in America. New York: Oxford University Press, 1976.

The Entertainment Machine: American Show Business in the Twentieth Century. New York: Oxford University Press, 1982.

Toohey, John L. *A History of the Pulitzer Prize Plays.* New York: Citadel, 1967.

Tornqvist, Egil. "To Speak the Unspoken: Audible Thinking in O'Neill's Plays." *Eugene O'Neill Review* 16 (Spring 1992): 55–70.

Tornqvist, Egil, and Kurt Eisen. "Novelization and the Drama of Consciousness in Strange Interlude." *Eugene O'Neill Review* 14 (1990): 39–51.

Towsen, John H. *Clowns.* New York: Hawthorn Books, 1976.

Trachtenberg, Alan. *The Incorporation of America: Culture and Society in the Gilded Age.* New York: Hill and Wang, 1982.

Reading American Photographs: Images as History, Mathew Brady to Walker Evans. New York: Hill and Wang, 1989.

Truzzi, Marcello, ed. "Circuses, Carnivals and Fairs in America." *Journal of Popular Culture* 6 (Winter 1972): 531–619.

Tucker, Sophie, with Dorothy Giles. *Some of These Days; The Autobiography of Sophie Tucker.* Garden City, N.Y.: Doubleday, Doran, 1945.

Turner, Frederick Jackson. "The Significance of the Frontier in American History." *Proceedings of the State Historical Society of Wisconsin* 41 (1893): 79–112; reprinted in *The Frontier in American History,* New York: Henry Holt, 1920.

Turner, Mary M. *Forgotten Leading Ladies of the American Theatre.* Jefferson, N.C.: McFarland, 1990.

Valgemae, Mardi. *Accelerated Grimace: Expressionism in the American Drama of the 1920s.* Carbondale: Southern Illinois University Press, 1972.

Van Hoogstraten, Nicholas. *Lost Broadway Theatres.* Princeton, N.J.: Princeton Architectural Press, 1991.

Vardac, A. Nicholas. *Stage to Screen: Theatrical Method from Garrick to Griffith.* Cambridge, Mass.: Harvard University Press, 1949.

Vena, Gary. *O'Neill's The Iceman Cometh: Reconstructing the Premiere.* Ann Arbor: UMI Research Press, 1988.

Wainscott, Ronald H. *Staging O'Neill: The Experimental Years, 1920–1934.* New Haven, Conn.: Yale University Press, 1988.

The Emergence of the Modern American Theater, 1914–1929. New Haven, Conn.: Yale University Press, 1997.

Waldau, Roy S. *Vintage Years of the Theatre Guild: 1928–1939.* Cleveland, Oh.: Case Western Reserve University Press, 1972.

Walker, Ethel Pitts. "Krigwa: A Theatre By, For, and About Black People." *Theatre Journal* 40 (October 1988): 347–56.

Wallack, Lester. *Memories of Fifty Years.* New York: Scribner's, 1889.

Ward, Carlton, comp. *National List of Historic Theatre Buildings.* Washington, D.C.: League of Historic American Theatres, 1983.

Warde, Frederick. *Washington Square Plays.* New York: Doubleday and Page, 1916 and 1918.

Fifty Years of Make Believe. New York: International Press Syndicate, 1920.

Watermeier, Daniel J., ed. *Between Actor and Critic: Selected Letters of Edwin Booth and William Winter.* Princeton, N.J.: Princeton University Press, 1971.

Edwin Booth's Performances: The Mary Isabella Stone Commentaries. Ann Arbor: UMI Research Press, 1990.

Waters, Ethel, with Charles Samuels. *His Eye Is on the Sparrow.* Garden City, N.Y.: Doubleday, 1951.

Watson, Steven. *The Harlem Renaissance: Hub of African American Culture, 1920–1930.* New York: Random House, 1995.

Watt, Stephen, and Gary A. Richardson, eds. *American Drama, Colonial to Contemporary.* New York: Harcourt Brace, 1995.

Weales, Gerald. *Odets, the Playwright.* New York: Pegasus, 1971.

Weaver, William. *Duse. A Biography.* San Diego/New York: Harcourt Brace Jovanovich, 1984.

Webster, Margaret. *Shakespeare without Tears.* Rev. ed. New York: McGraw-Hill, 1957.
    Don't Put Your Daughter on the Stage. New York: Alfred A. Knopf, 1972.

Wecter, Dixon. "The Education of Everyman." In Robert E. Spiller et al., eds., *The Literary History of the United States,* 4th ed. New York: Macmillan, 1974.

Weedon, Geoff, and Richard Ward. *Fairground Art.* New York: Abbeville, 1981.

Weiss, John, ed. *The Origins of Modern Consciousness.* Detroit: Wayne State University Press, 1965.

Wertheim, Arthur Frank. *The New York Little Renaissance: Iconoclasm, Modernism, and Nationalism in American Culture, 1908–1917.* New York: New York University Press, 1976.

Wharton, Edith. *The Age of Innocence.* New York: Appleton, 1920.

Wharton, John F. *Life among the Playwrights.* New York: Quadrangle, 1974.

White, Sidney Howard. *Sidney Howard.* Boston: Twayne, 1977.

Whitman, Walt. *Complete Poetry and Collected Prose.* New York: Library of America, 1982.

Whitman, Willson. *Bread and Circuses: A Study of Federal Theatre.* New York: Oxford University Press, 1937.

Whitmore, Richard Alan. "The Emerging Ensemble: The Vieux Colombier and the Group Theatre." *Theatre Survey* 24 (May 1993): 60–70.

Wiebe, Robert. *The Search for Order, 1877–1920.* New York: Hill and Wang, 1967.
    The Segmented Society. An Introduction to the Meaning of America. New York: Oxford University Press, 1975.

Wilder, Alec. *American Popular Song: The Great Innovators, 1900–1950.* New York: Oxford University Press, 1972.

Wilder, Thornton. *Three Plays by Thornton Wilder.* New York: Bantam, 1966.

Williams, Gary Jay. "Turned Down in Provincetown: O'Neill's Debut Re-Examined." *Eugene O'Neill Newsletter* 12 (Spring 1988): 17–27.

Williams, Henry B., ed. *The American Theatre: A Sum of Its Parts.* New York: Samuel French, 1971.

Williams, Jay. *Stage Left.* New York: Scribner's, 1974.

Williams, Jesse Lynch. *Why Marry?* In Arthur Hobson Quinn, ed., *Contemporary American Plays.* New York: Scribner's, 1932.

Williams, John Hoyt. *A Great and Shining Road.* New York: New York Times Books, 1988.

Williams, Raymond. *Culture and Society: 1780–1950.* New York: Columbia University Press, 1983.

Willis, Ronald. "The American Laboratory Theatre, 1923–1930." Diss., University of Iowa, 1968.

Wilmeth, Don B. *The American Stage to World War I: A Guide to Information Sources.* Detroit: Gale Research, 1978.

American and English Popular Entertainment: A Guide to Information Sources. Detroit: Gale Research, 1980.

The Language of American Popular Entertainment: A Glossary of Argot, Slang, and Terminology. Westport, Conn.: Greenwood Press, 1981.

Variety Entertainment and Outdoor Amusements. Westport, Conn.: Greenwood Press, 1982.

"Noble or Ruthless Savage?: The American Indian on Stage and in the Drama." *Journal of American Drama and Theatre* 1 (Spring 1989): 37–78.

"Tentative Checklist of Indian Plays." *Journal of American Drama and Theatre* 1 (Fall 1989): 34–54.

Wilmeth, Don B., ed., *Staging the Nation: Plays from the American Theater, 1787–1909.* Boston: Bedford Books, 1998.

Wilmeth, Don B., and Christopher Bigsby, eds., *The Cambridge History of American Theatre, Vol. I: Beginnings to 1870.* New York: Cambridge University Press, 1998.

Wilmeth, Don B., and Rosemary Cullen, eds. *Plays by Augustin Daly.* Cambridge and New York: Cambridge University Press, 1984.

Wilmeth, Don B., and Tice Miller, eds. *Cambridge Guide to American Theatre.* New York and Cambridge: Cambridge University Press, 1993.

Wilson, Edmund. *The Shores of Light: A Literary Chronicle of the Twenties and Thirties.* New York: Farrar, Straus, and Young, 1952.

Wilson, Francis. *Francis Wilson's Life of Himself.* Boston: Houghton Mifflin, 1924.

Wilson, Garff B. *A History of American Acting.* Bloomington: Indiana University Press, 1966; rpt. Westport, Conn.: Greenwood Press, 1980.

Ye Bare and Ye Cubb: Three Hundred Years of American Drama and Theatre. Englewood Cliffs, N.J.: Prentice-Hall, 1973.

Wilstach, Paul. *Richard Mansfield: The Man and the Actor.* New York: Scribner's, 1909.

Wilt, Napier, ed. *My Partner, The White Slave & Other Plays by Bartley Campbell.* Vol. 19 of *America's Lost Plays,* ed. Barrett H. Clark. Princeton, N.J.: Princeton University Press, 1941.

Winokur, Mark. *American Laughter: Immigrants, Ethnicity, and 1930s Film Comedy.* New York: Macmillan, 1997.

Winter, William. *Brief Chronicles.* New York: Dunlap Society, 1889; rpt. Burt Franklin, 1970.

Ada Rehan: A Study. New York: Privately printed for Augustin Daly, 1891; rpt. Benjamin Blom, 1969.

Shadows of the Stage. New York: Macmillan, 1892.

Life and Art of Edwin Booth. New York: Macmillan, 1893.

Other Days: Being Chronicles and Memories of the Stage. New York: Moffat, Yard, 1908.

Shakespeare on the Stage. 3 vols. New York: Macmillan, 1911–16.

Life and Art of Joseph Jefferson. New York: Macmillan, 1913.

Life and Art of Richard Mansfield. 2 vols. New York: Moffat, Yard, 1913.

Tyrone Power. New York: Moffat, Yard, 1913.

The Wallet of Time. 2 vols. 1913; rpt. Benjamin Blom, 1969.

Vagrant Memories. New York: George H. Doran, 1915.

Winther, Sophus K. *Eugene O'Neill: A Critical Study.* Rev. ed. New York: Russell and Russell, 1961.

Witham, Barry B., ed. *Theatre in the United States: A Documentary History, Vol. I: 1750–1915.* Contributors: Martha Mahard, David Rinear, Don B. Wilmeth. Cambridge and New York: Cambridge University Press, 1996.

Woll, Allen. *Black Musical Theatre from Coontown to Dreamgirls.* Baton Rouge: Louisiana State University Press, 1989.

Wolter, Jürgen C., ed. *The Dawning of American Drama: American Dramatic Criticism, 1746–1915.* Westport, Conn.: Greenwood Press, 1993.

Woodward, C. Vann. *The Future of the Past.* New York: Oxford University Press, 1989.

The Strange Career of Jim Crow. 3rd ed. New York: Oxford University Press, 1974.

Woollcott, Alexander. *Mrs. Fiske: Her Views on Actors, Acting, and the Problems of Production.* New York: Century, 1917.

"The Coming of Eugene O'Neill." *New York Times* 8 February 1920, section VIII, p. 2.

"Preface." In George S. Kaufman and Marc Connelly, *Beggar on Horseback.* New York: Boni and Liveright, 1924.

Going to Pieces. New York: Putnam, 1928.

Wyatt, Mark. *White Knuckle Ride. The Illustrated Guide to the World's Biggest and Best Roller Coaster and Thrill Rides.* London: Salamander Books, 1996.

Yagoda, Ben. *Will Rogers, A Biography.* New York: Alfred A. Knopf, 1993.

Young, James Harvey. *The Toadstool Millionaires: A Social History of Patent Medicines in America before Federal Regulations.* Princeton, N.J.: Princeton University Press, 1961.

Young, William C. *Famous American Playhouses: Documents of American Theatre History.* 2 vols. Chicago: American Library Association, 1973.

Famous Actors and Actresses on the American Stage: Documents of American Theatre History. 2 vols. New York: Bowker, 1975.

Ziegfeld, Richard, and Paulette Ziegfeld. *The Ziegfeld Touch: The Life and Times of Florenz Ziegfeld, Jr.* New York: Abrams, 1993.

Zim, Larry, Mel Lerner, and Herbert Rolfes. *The World of Tomorrow: The 1939 New York World's Fair.* New York: Harper and Row, 1988.

Index